NEUROBEHAVIORAL DISORDERS:
A Clinical Approach

NEUROBEHAVIORAL DISORDERS:
A Clinical Approach

RICHARD L. STRUB, M.D.
Staff Neurologist
Ochsner Foundation Medical Center
New Orleans, Louisiana

F. WILLIAM BLACK, Ph.D.
Professor of Psychiatry and Neurology
Tulane University Medical Center
New Orleans, Louisiana

Foreword by D. Frank Benson

F. A. Davis Company • Philadelphia

NOTE: As new scientific information becomes available through basic and clinical research, recommended treatments and drug therapies undergo changes. The author(s) and publisher have done everything possible to make this book accurate, up-to-date, and in accord with accepted standards at the time of publication. However, the reader is advised always to check product information (package inserts) for changes and new information regarding dose and contraindications before administering any drug. Caution is especially urged when using new or infrequently ordered drugs.

Library of Congress Cataloging-in-Publication Data

Strub, Richard L., 1939–
    Neurobehavioral disorders.

    Rev. ed. of: Organic brain syndromes.
c1981.
    Includes bibliographies and index.
    1. Brain—Diseases.   2. Neuropsychiatry.
I. Black, F. William.   II. Strub, Richard L.,
1939–   .   Organic Mental Disorders,
Psychotic.   WM 220 S927o]
RC386.S77   1988   616.8   88-1191
ISBN 0-8036-8213-1

FOREWORD

While this is an introduction to a second edition, the name of the book, *Organic Brain Syndromes,* has been altered, a state that accurately reflects the rapidity and depth of changes in the field since the original volume was published in 1981. As the first edition was being published, interest in problems of behavior based on brain abnormality was heightening and in the succeeding years has burgeoned. For instance, from an almost negligible number in the 1960s, the number of papers now submitted for presentation at the annual meeting of the American Academy of Neurology that deal with behavior runs into the hundreds (almost 20 percent of the total). Alzheimer's disease and related dementing states (well covered in the first issue) and many other problems (e.g., memory disorders, traumatic brain injuries, confusional states, movement disorders and their related mental impairments, psychiatric aspects of epilepsy, the organic basis of psychiatric disorders, and many others) are currently the subject of intense investigations. An explosive expansion of material published on the subject of organic behavioral disturbances has occurred.

Far too much material is being presented for any individual to adequately monitor. However, the organic mental disorders are common, present in a broad variety of guises, and are seen regularly by almost all practitioners of medicine. The need for clear and precise but relatively abridged portrayals of the major neurobehavioral disorders remains great.

Richard Strub and William Black foresaw this need and directed their 1981 volume toward the medical student and house officer level. Rather than attempting to encompass the latest controversies and "breakthroughs," the material was presented in a precise, dogmatic fashion for use by individuals simultaneously attempting to cover other fields of medicine. As such, the original volume proved valuable for the busy practicing physician.

In the more accurately titled second edition, the authors have main-

042107   v

tained their successful format. Much of the information available in the earlier edition is retained but augmented and updated to a considerable degree. This volume contains almost 50 percent more references than the original, and most of the additions are current (since 1980). The format has proved useful and in this reincarnation remains valuable for all who are interested in problems of behavior.

D. Frank Benson, M.D.

PREFACE

This volume presents a clinical discussion of the major behavioral syndromes associated with brain disease or dysfunction. These syndromes —the conditions of dementia, delirium, aphasia, and so forth—fall within the borderland between neurology and psychiatry. They have neurologic etiologies yet primarily behavioral signs and symptoms. Since the publication of the first edition of this book, there has been a significant expansion of the scientific literature in this area. We have tried to include for your reference many of the most important contributions in the appropriate sections of this volume.

Our purpose in writing this basic text is to acquaint physicians, psychologists, speech pathologists, occupational and physical therapists, nurses, social workers, and other interested professionals with the clinical features, diagnostic approaches, and management plans for this interesting group of patients. Where possible, we also discuss newer concepts of pathogenesis and provide the reader with anatomic correlations.

We would like to thank Virginia Howard and the staff of the LSUMC Editorial Office for their continued assistance in the preparation of this manuscript.

R.L.S.
F.W.B.

CONTENTS

SECTION I

ANATOMY AND CLINICAL EVALUATION

Chapter 1

Introduction

TERMINOLOGY
CLASSIFICATION
ORGANIZATION OF THIS TEXT
NEUROBEHAVIORAL DISORDERS IN MEDICAL PRACTICE

The neurobehavioral disorders, sometimes known as the organic brain syndromes, are a commonly encountered group of diseases in which either damage or dysfunction of the brain is manifested for the most part by an alteration in behavior. The behavioral change may be confined primarily to social or emotional behavior, as in the remarkable personality change displayed by the patient with a frontal lobe tumor, or the change can be predominantly manifested in intellectual behavior, as in the complex cognitive deterioration seen in the patient with dementia. Within the category of intellectual change, we include the selective defects of cognition such as aphasia, amnesia, and alexia, in which a focal lesion of the brain impairs a specific cognitive function.

The neurobehavioral disorders are acquired syndromes that can occur at any age but are most commonly seen in adults. In this volume we will not discuss the behavioral syndromes that are developmental or congenital, such as mental retardation, learning disabilities, or minimal brain

3

dysfunction. In our opinion, most of these conditions result from a basic organic cause that manifests as an alteration in the developmental process as opposed to being the result of an acquired brain lesion. These developmental disorders are very important because of their frequency and social impact but are beyond the scope of this book.

We will also, by intention, exclude from our primary discussion the major psychiatric diseases of schizophrenia and manic depressive illness. Although recent advances in genetics, pharmacology, and neurochemistry have begun to provide strong evidence that these classic functional psychiatric disorders have, at least in part, an organic basis, we do not yet consider them to fall within the category of the neurobehavioral disorders.

TERMINOLOGY

In the second edition of this book we have chosen to denote the syndromes of behavioral change secondary to brain disease by the term *neurobehavioral disorders* rather than by the previously used older term *organic brain syndromes*. Neurobehavioral disorders and the field of behavior neurology are rapidly becoming widely recognized, not only among neurologists but also by psychiatrists, general practitioners, and psychologists. Because of this, it seems prudent to help our readers accept this new and more accurate nomenclature. The American Psychiatric Association has also begun to embrace a change in terminology. In its revised edition of the *Diagnostic and Statistical Manual of Mental Disorders*, Third Edition, Revised (DSM-III-R), the term "organic brain syndromes" has been replaced with "organic mental syndromes," a much more logical term.

CLASSIFICATION

After defining the general field of the neurobehavioral disorders and finding a suitable and acceptable term with which to label it, the next problem has traditionally been and still is to classify the different syndromes that constitute these organic behavioral disorders. In the past, the American Psychiatric Association has tried to divide these conditions into two major categories. In 1952[1] the APA used the terms *acute* and *chronic*, and in 1968,[2] *psychotic* and *nonpsychotic organic brain syndromes*. Each individual disease (e.g., cerebral infection) became a subheading within the classification schema (i.e., organic brain syndrome with psychosis associated with cerebral infection). We have found these earlier classifications to be unworkable and to bear little relationship to the clinical syndromes themselves. We are very pleased that the revision of the organic classification within the DSM III[3] and DSM-III-R, largely through the influence and writings of Lipowski,[13,14] has adopted a much more phenomenologic approach and has divided the syndromes by their clinical psychologic features rather than by one isolated and often vague feature such as chronicity or psychosis. Because this is the manner in which we have traditionally taught the symptoms, diagnosis, and management of these conditions to medical students and residents, we welcome this general trend and believe that the organization of this book will be in concert with the recent thinking of the psychiatric as well as neurologic community.

The primary point that must be made regarding the classification of these disorders is that there is no single *neurobehavioral disorder*, but rather a group of disorders, many of which have their own distinctive behavioral and pathologic features. There are, however, certain symptom clusters or syndromes that correspond to rather specific disease entities, and therefore the disorders within each group can be approached similarly from the standpoint of both diagnosis and management. The main categories of disorders in the classification system are as follows:

1. *The acute confusional states* (delirium). These are, in general, the acute, reversible, rather generalized behavioral disruptions that occur with temporary metabolic or toxic brain dysfunction.
2. *The dementias.* These are syndromes of slowly progressive deterioration in intellectual and adaptive social processes. Dementia is usually associated with irreversible brain atrophy or damage; however, this is not invariably true, as will be discussed in Chapters 6 and 7. The DSM III combined delirium and dementia into a unifying category of "disorders of global cognitive impairment," but we believe that this represents an unnecessary lumping, because the two general conditions are so distinct in regard to pathophysiology, clinical picture, differential diagnosis, evaluation, management, and prognosis. The DSM-III-R remedied this by splitting these syndromes into two distinct categories.[4]
3. *Focal brain syndromes.* Because of the complex, yet rather localized, anatomic substrate of intellectual, emotional, and social functions, lesions in disparate areas of the cortex and subcortex will produce distinct clinical behavioral syndromes. There are many such syndromes, which are discussed in detail in Chapter 8.

A fourth category of neurobehavioral disorders, the "symptomatic functional syndromes," has been proposed.[3,4,14] Symptomatic functional syndromes are organically based syndromes that clinically resemble functional psychiatric disease. For example, the schizophrenic behavior seen in some patients with chronic temporal lobe epilepsy, systemic lupus erythematosus, or chronic LSD use would be considered a schizophreniform syndrome or organic delusional syndrome within this classification. Other entities within this category are organic affective disorder for organically based depression or mania, the organic personality syndrome for characterologic disorders of probable organic cause, and organic anxiety disorder.

ORGANIZATION OF THIS TEXT

This book is intended to serve as a clinical guide to the diagnosis, evaluation, and management of neurobehavioral disorders. We have organized it following the classification system discussed above, with the material being divided into four main sections. The first section serves as an introduction to the relevant terminology and includes an overview of the neuroanatomic substrate involved in the production of human behavior. The third and fourth chapters in this section cover the clinical and neuropsychologic evaluation of these patients.

The second, and clinically most important, section discusses in detail the major clinical neurobehavioral disorders: confusional states, dementia, and focal syndromes. The typical clinical picture, the behavioral and medical evaluation, differential diagnosis, laboratory evaluation, management, and pathology of each syndrome are given. Wherever possible within each general syndrome, we have attempted to outline methods of making specific diagnoses on the basis of behavioral and other clinical grounds alone. This is generally impossible for most confusional patients but is very valuable in the careful study of the clinical presentation of both patients with dementias and patients with focal lesions.

The third section discusses the various neurobehavioral disorders seen in patients with specific categories of disease, such as head trauma, cerebrovascular disease, or alcoholism. This second method of classification is presented for several reasons. First, a large number of neurobehavioral syndromes do not fall conveniently within the major clinical categories described in Section II and yet are of great practical importance in the day-to-day practice of medicine. An example is the patient who is having difficulty concentrating on work after a relatively minor head injury. The patient's alteration in behavior is subtle, possibly the result of a focal brainstem dysfunction, but is so typically a transient sequela of head injury that we believe it is best discussed in a special chapter dealing with the problems resulting from trauma (Chapter 9). Second, most textbooks and medical courses are organized around a disease or organ system approach; accordingly, the physician is accustomed to thinking in terms of the features and evaluation of specific types of disease (e.g., tumor, vascular disease). By discussing the behavioral disorders that occur with specific diseases, we hope to alert the physician to possible behavioral sequelae that might develop in the patient with alcoholism, cerebrovascular disease, or epilepsy during the course of a lifetime.

Using two classification systems within a single book will obviously cause considerable overlap, but we have attempted to minimize redundancy. In those instances in which a specific disease (e.g., cerebrovascular accident) results in a specific neurobehavioral syndrome (e.g., Broca's aphasia), the behavioral disorder will be discussed in the relevant chapter of Section II, whereas the specific disease will be mentioned in the relevant chapter of Section III. At this point in the evolution of our thinking about these diseases, we view this as the most satisfactory method of presenting these conditions. In reality, patients present in two principal ways: either with a specific clinical syndrome such as dementia or with a specific disease process such as head trauma or toxic poisoning. The physician must be equipped to deal with the behavioral component associated with each mode of presentation; therefore, we feel justified in discussing the disorders using this double classification. The fourth and final section of this volume is a short discussion of some of the less distinctly organic syndromes (e.g., Gilles de la Tourette's syndrome, narcolepsy) and an overview of the clinical interactions of the fields of neurology and psychiatry.

NEUROBEHAVIORAL DISORDERS IN MEDICAL PRACTICE

As a final point, we must stress the very real importance of these neurobehavioral disorders. They are extremely common in medical practice and constitute, in many instances, not only difficult medical diagnostic and management problems but also very complicated social problems. Over one third of all beds in chronic psychiatric hospitals are occupied by patients with organic brain diseases. As the population of elderly persons increases, this statistic will climb. Stroke, with its attendant behavioral sequelae such as aphasia, is the third most frequent cause of death in this country and certainly one of the greatest causes of chronic disability. Brain damage secondary to head trauma, alcohol abuse, toxic exposure, and epilepsy produces large populations of patients with organically based behavioral disorders requiring appropriate medical care.

Despite the high incidence of such problems, neurobehavioral disorders receive little or no attention in many medical school and residency curricula. As a consequence, practicing physicians frequently fail to recognize the presence of atypical organic brain disease and even more frequently misdiagnose the symptoms as being purely functional. For example, we have seen many patients with infarcts, hemorrhages, and tumors of the dominant temporoparietal area who were initially misdiagnosed as functionally psychotic because of the clinician's failure to recognize the patient's abnormal speech as being aphasic rather than psychotic.

Since publication of the first edition of the book, however, there has been a considerable increase in interest, research, and publication of information about these diseases. Entire books are currently devoted to delirium,[15] dementia,[6,16] and focal syndromes.[9,10,12,19,20] Several general texts have also been written as well as a spate of multi-authored books on behavioral neurology and neuropsychology.[5,7,8,11] The recent interest in Alzheimer's disease has spawned a large number of symposium proceedings and other multi-authored texts.[18] Because of the explosion of information, the average clinician is far more sophisticated in diagnosing these conditions than he was 10 years ago.

Beyond the clinical importance of recognizing such conditions, these diseases have a significant social impact that must concern all clinicians. Organic brain diseases frequently follow a long and complicated course. For instance, the patient with dementia may experience many years of declining intellectual capacity during which the family and eventually society become increasingly involved in providing medical and institutional care. The financial as well as emotional strain on such families is considerable, and in many cases, society must eventually assume total responsibility for the patient's care.

Caring for the patient with a neurobehavioral disorder is a multidisciplinary team effort. The physician must learn to enlist the assistance of family, nurses, physical and occupational therapists, speech pathologists, social service workers, psychologists, family support groups, and other specialists within the medical profession. Only with the assistance of all these varied individuals can the patient with a neurobehavioral disorder receive the best possible evaluation and management. This volume should serve as a significant aid to the clinician in understanding and dealing with the patient with a behavioral change secondary to organic brain dysfunction.

REFERENCES

1. American Psychiatric Association: Diagnostic and Statistical Manual of Mental Disorders DSM-I. Washington, DC, 1952.
2. American Psychiatric Association: Diagnostic and Statistical Manual of Mental Disorders DSM-II. Washington, DC, 1968.
3. American Psychiatric Association: Diagnostic and Statistical Manual of Mental Disorders DSM-III. Washington, DC, 1980.
4. American Psychiatric Association: Diagnostic and Statistical Manual of Mental Disorders DSM-III-R. Washington, DC, 1987.
5. Cummings, JL: Clinical Neuropsychiatry. Grune & Stratton, New York, 1985.
6. Cummings, JL and Benson, DF: Dementia: A Clinical Approach. Butterworths, London, 1983.
7. Frederiks, JAM (ed): Handbook of Clinical Neurology. vol 1 (45), Clinical Psychology. Elsevier, Amsterdam, 1985.

8. Frederiks, JAM (ed): Handbook of Clinical Neurology. vol 2 (46), Neurobehavioral Disorders. Elsevier, Amsterdam, 1985.
9. Geschwind, N and Galaburda, AM: Cerebral Dominance: The Biological Foundations. Harvard University Press, Boston, 1984.
10. Goodglass, H and Kaplan, E: The Assessment of Aphasia and Related Disorders, ed 2. Lea & Febiger, Philadelphia, 1983.
11. Heilman, KM and Valenstein E: Clinical Neuropsychology, ed 2. Oxford University Press, New York, 1985.
12. Kertesz, A (ed): Localization in Neuropsychology. Academic Press, New York, 1983.
13. Lipowski, ZJ: Organic brain syndromes: Overview and classification. In Benson, DF and Blumer, D (eds): Psychiatric Aspects of Neurologic Disease. Grune & Stratton, New York, 1975, pp 11–35.
14. Lipowski, ZJ: Organic brain syndromes: A reformulation. Compr Psychiatry 19:309, 1978.
15. Lipowski, ZJ: Delirium. Charles C Thomas, Springfield, Ill, 1980.
16. Mayeux, R and Rosen, WG (eds): The dementias. Advances in Neurology, vol 38. Raven Press, New York, 1983.
17. Mesulam, M-M (ed): Principles of Behavioral Neurology. FA Davis, Philadelphia, 1985.
18. Reisberg, B (ed): Alzheimer's Disease. Free Press, New York, 1983.
19. Squire, LR and Butters, N (eds): Neuropsychology of Memory. Guilford Press, New York, 1984.
20. Stuss, DT and Benson, DF: The Frontal Lobes. Raven Press, New York, 1986.

Chapter 2

The Anatomy of Behavior

To understand the changes in behavior that occur in patients with brain disease, it is important to have a working knowledge of the anatomy and physiology of those parts of the brain involved in the production and maintenance of normal behavior. Human behavior and its neurologic substrate are extremely complex and far from completely understood. Over the past 100 years, however, sufficient clinical and experimental material has been amassed to support a working hypothesis concerning the correlation between brain function and many aspects of behavior. The schema presented here is simplified for clarity, but it does provide a model that will aid the student in understanding the neuroanatomic substrates of normal behavior and the alterations in behavior seen subsequent to brain damage and disease.

Human behavior is multifaceted; there are, however, several distinct, yet interrelated, general categories or levels of behavior. The first is consciousness and basic arousal. Simply defined, consciousness is one's state of awareness of both the environment and internal thought processes. Humans must be able to maintain a wakeful and alert condition in order to receive environmental stimulation and to initiate any meaningful mental or physical activity. Without such capacity, only sleep can occur. This rudimentary function is governed by the ascending activating system, which consists of the brain stem reticular formation and its widespread projections to the thalamus, limbic system, and cortex. A corollary of consciousness is selective attention, a function relying not only on the ascending activating system but also on the modulating effect of reciprocal descending input from cortex, limbic system, and thalamus, which focuses and controls attention.

The second level of behavior consists of basic drives and survival instincts. Largely unlearned, this basic force leads one to eat when hungry, sleep when tired, fight when attacked, flee when appropriate, and procreate to preserve the species. These functions are largely the province of the hypothalamus and other related structures in the limbic system. Emotion, an internal state in which the person responds with conscious feelings to events within the environment or within the person's own mind or body, is closely associated with instinctual behavior. Emotional experiences are also primarily limbic functions. A final and critical function under limbic control is the ability to facilitate the storage and retrieval of experiences, a function known as new learning, recent memory, or simply "memorization."

The third major category of human behavior is intellectual behavior, a complex, highly human quality that includes the high-level processes of verbal reasoning, calculating, and abstract thought, as well as their building blocks: language and perception. The cerebral cortex is the principal structure responsible for these high-level functions, and a knowledge of cortical structure and functional organization is an important step in understanding normal behavior and in comprehending the behavioral syndromes seen with focal brain lesions such as stroke, tumor, or abscess.

The fourth category of behavior is social behavior and personality, an extremely complex level of behavior involving the interaction of all levels of behavior and integration of all systems of the brain. Developing an individual lifestyle, planning a career, or establishing a family are all examples of this level of behavior. A substantial portion of these functions is the result of an interaction between the limbic system and the neocortex, an interaction that primarily takes place in the frontal lobes.

As previously stated, the anatomic outline presented below is a simplification; each aspect of behavior requires the contribution of many diverse systems within the brain. Although certain functions are localized to an extent, the reader must think of individual behaviors as complex neuropsychologic phenomena rather than as simple unidimensional functions.

ASCENDING RETICULAR SYSTEMS

Ascending Activating System

The ascending activating system is an arousal system whose activity maintains wakefulness and alertness and thereby allows the person to interact with the environment. The ascending activating system originates in the reticular cells of the brain stem. These cells lie in nuclear groupings in the perimedian areas of the medulla, pons, and midbrain (mesencephalon) (Figs. 2–1 to 2–4).

The medial group is gigantocellular and is the actual origin of the ascending and descending tracts. This effector zone receives its input from the lateral, small-celled zone (parvicellular), which in turn receives its input from the ascending sensory pathways. Taken together, these cell groups are designated as the *brain stem reticular formation* or *reticular core*.

The most important fibers concerned with arousal are the ascending axons that originate in the gigantocellular zone of the pontine and mesencephalic reticular formation.[42] Fibers arising from the pontine neurons project to nonspecific nuclei of the thalamus (interlaminar nucleus, reticular nucleus, and midline nuclei such as the centrum medianum); these nonspecific nuclei then have diffuse projections to wide areas of brain. From these thalamic nuclei, there is also extensive interconnection with other thalamic nuclei, projection back to the pontine reticular cells, and a major outflow to the ventral anterior thalamic nucleus. This anterior nucleus sends diffuse projections to the cortex. These efferents from the thalamus are known as the *diffuse thalamic projection system*.

The mesencephalic reticular formation sends a significant number of ascending fibers to structures within the limbic system, principally the

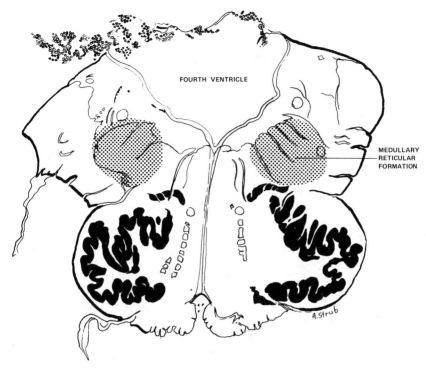

FOURTH VENTRICLE

MEDULLARY
RETICULAR
FORMATION

A. Strub

Figure 2-1. Cross section of medulla. Stippled area represents the reticular formation.

hypothalamus and the septal nuclei. Other reticular-limbic interaction occurs throughout the entire upper brain stem. In this area, reticular cells send a rich network of short collateral fibers to the central gray area of the pons and mesencephalon. This central gray substance represents the caudal extension of the limbic system into the brain stem[8] and, in essence, serves as a secondary arousal system.

In recent years much has been learned about the neurochemistry of these ascending systems of the reticular core. The fibers from the locus ceruleus (see Fig. 2-2) (just lateral to the pontine reticular formation) are noradrenergic (norepinephrine) and project first to the frontal pole, then spread laterally and caudally over the entire cortex. This system plays a critical role in arousal and attention. A dopaminergic system arises from the pons and projects to the limbic areas of the angular gyrus, frontal lobe, and septum (nucleus accumbens). This system affects limbic function, but its precise role is as yet unknown.

The input to the reticular formation comes primarily from the ascending sensory tracts. Incoming noxious stimuli traveling through the brain stem in the spinothalamic tract are transferred to the lateral (small cell)

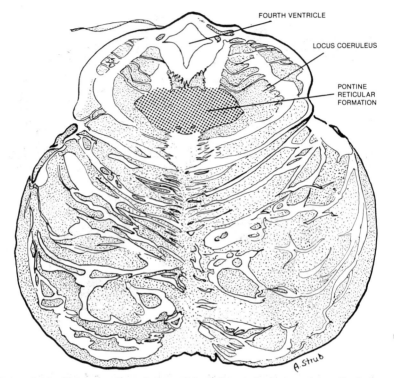

Figure 2-2. Cross section of pons. Stippled area is the pontine reticular area.

zone of the reticular formation. Stimuli carried by the paleospinal portion of the spinothalamic tract are transferred to the reticular formation through short collateral branches throughout the brain stem. Stimuli traveling by way of the primitive archispinal (spinoreticular) portion of the system terminate in the pontine and medullary (parvicellular) reticular formation. In this way, a stimulus to the skin (e.g., a bee sting) will immediately arouse the activating system at all levels. Through the ascending pathways described above, arousal and basic alerting take place throughout the thalamus, limbic system, and cortex. This arousal occurs at the same time the stimulus arrives at the sensory cortex via the ventral posterolateral thalamus. The final level of arousal produced by the painful stimulus is the combined effect of these inputs. Of course, not all sensory input is as intense as a bee sting; rather a constant flow of incoming environmental stimuli maintains arousal and alertness. Arousal is not totally reliant on external stimulation, however; it can also be a self-generated phenomenon (e.g., the student "forcing" himself to stay awake while studying in a warm, quiet room). In most instances, arousal and the level of alertness result from a combination of environmental stimulation, the person's need or desire to remain alert, and the reticular system's own intrinsic activity.

The arousal system can be adversely affected by a variety of disease processes. In cases of metabolic imbalance, as with liver failure or diabetic acidosis, the entire system becomes depressed, and the patient becomes lethargic or stuporous. A specific destructive lesion (such as an infarction, hemorrhage, or traumatic contusion) involving the pontine or mesencephalic portion of the system (Fig. 2–5) will render the patient comatose, a state in which the patient is totally unresponsive to even the most vigorous stimulation. If, on the other hand, damage occurs in the projection system in the thalamus and subthalamus, there is a marked reduction in ascending activation; and the patient, although appearing alert, can respond only minimally to stimulation. Such patients can initiate eye opening, mumble a few words, and occasionally move but otherwise remain akinetic and mute.

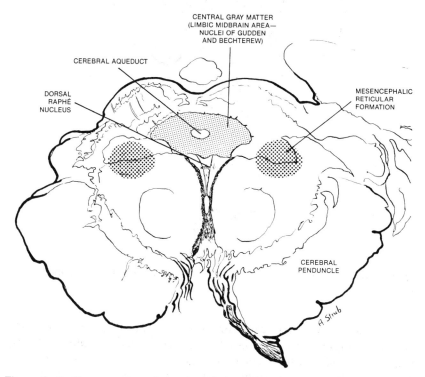

Figure 2–3. Cross section of mesencephalon (midbrain). The lightly stippled area surrounding the cerebral aqueduct (periaqueductal grey) is the caudal extension of the limbic system and has very extensive interconnection with the ascending activating system. The darkly stippled areas lateral to the periaqueductal grey represent the mesencephalic reticular formation.

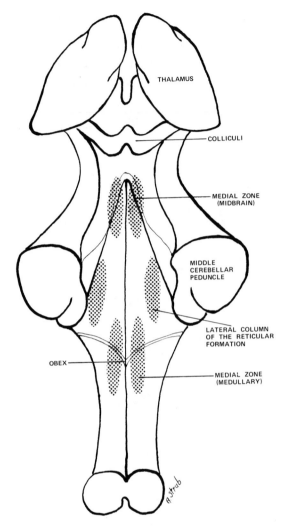

Figure 2–4. Longitudinal view of brain stem. Stippled areas represent the reticular nuclei.

The activation system can also respond with overactivity, and a state of hyperalertness can be observed. This is seen in anxiety states or during fright; under such conditions the person is acutely sensitive to any environmental stimulus. Such a heightened state of arousal may be beneficial (e.g., a soldier on patrol) or detrimental (e.g., an anxious student trying to study in a noisy dormitory). Increased alertness can also occur after use of such benign pharmacologic agents as coffee, tea, or cola. By use of such agents, the human has learned to manipulate his level of arousal to suit his immediate needs.

Ascending Inhibiting System

The ascending activating system operates in concert with the ascending inhibitory system. It was previously thought that sleep, for example, occurred when there was a simple decrease in activation. Recent studies, however, have demonstrated that stimulation of the parallel inhibitory system can produce sleep rather than activation.[52] Accordingly, it appears that the clinical level of alertness is determined by a dynamic balance of activity in both ascending systems. The main transmitter of this inhibitory system is serotonin. These serotoninergic pathways primarily project from the dorsal raphe nuclei in the upper pontine reticular formation, slightly ventral to the aqueduct and periaqueductal gray.

In some conditions, damage can occur primarily to the ascending inhibitory system. As a result of the epidemic of influenzal encephalitis in 1918–1921, a number of patients developed a syndrome of hyperactivity that was called "organic driveness."[28] These patients had extensive lesions in the reticular formation, although the damage apparently affected primarily the inhibitory centers. This selective damage unbalanced the system and allowed an unbridled release of arousal activity.

In recent years, there has been considerable interest in young children who display hyperactive and/or distractible behavior. It is tempting to

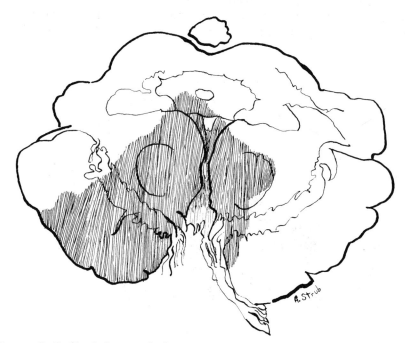

Figure 2–5. Shaded area indicates a typical coma producing lesion of mesencephalon.

postulate that these hyperactive children may have some type of imbalance in the operation of these brain stem systems, but with our current clinico-pathologic knowledge, there is no evidence to support such a hypothesis.

These ascending brain stem systems are the anatomic substrate for the most basic levels of behavior: consciousness and alertness. Their primary function is to provide the level of arousal energy necessary to maintain normal functioning of higher centers in the limbic system and the cortex.

LIMBIC SYSTEM

The limbic system is composed of a ring of phylogenetically old cortex and a group of subcortical structures that serve as the anatomic substrate for survival instincts, emotions, and memory. Stimulation or destruction of specific nuclei or areas within the system can markedly alter such basic behaviors as eating, sleeping, or emotional response. The system is newer phylogenetically than the basic arousal system, but is older than the neocortex. It is well developed in the rat, cat, and monkey, and these animals have been used in much of the experimental study of limbic functions. In humans, limbic activity is constantly modified by higher centers in the neocortex, and basic instinctual behaviors are rarely seen in a pure form.

The limbic system is so named because its structures form a limbus or ring around the inner aspect of the cerebral hemispheres. This limbus consists of the cingulate and hippocampal gyri (Fig. 2–6). As knowledge of

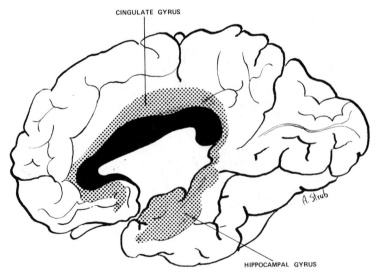

Figure 2–6. Sagittal cut of cerebrum showing limbic cortex.

the physiology and functional significance of the limbic system has increased, the concept of the system has been expanded to include a large number of structures and fiber systems that are involved in the elaboration of instinctual and emotional behavior. Its limits are somewhat vague; however, the limbic system is conceptually sound, and most investigators are in agreement as to its basic structures and functions. In this chapter we discuss the major structures and connections usually included in the system and show how each structure contributes to basic behavioral functioning.

Anatomy

MAJOR STRUCTURES

The anatomy of the limbic system is complex with rich reciprocal interconnections among its principal structures. The central point of most limbic activity is the hypothalamus. The *hypothalamus* is that portion of the diencephalon lying anterior to the thalamus. It forms the floor and the ventrolateral walls of the anterior third ventricle and is directly superior to and intimately associated with the pituitary gland (Figs. 2–7 and 2–8). The hypothalamus has many nuclei, but the main areas of importance in regard to behavior are the ventromedial nuclear complex, the lateral hypothalamus, and the mamillary bodies.

A limbic structure closely related to the hypothalamus is the *amygdala*, a large nuclear mass situated in the anterior and medial portions of the temporal lobe. Dorsomedial to the amygdala and ventral to the globus pallidus lies a randomly organized, poorly defined group of cells called the substantia innominata, or basilar nucleus of Meynert (Fig. 2–8). This nucleus is the origin of the primary cholinergic system of the basilar forebrain. Its neurons and the neurons of the nucleus of the diagonal band of Broca, located medial and anterior to it, supply cholinergic input to the hippocampus, amygdala, and other areas of the cortex. These areas are important in memory function, particularly in the memory loss experienced by Alzheimer patients.[62] Immediately posterior to the amygdala and in the medial temporal lobe itself is the *hippocampal formation*; this structure runs along the medial surface of the temporal horn of the lateral ventricle. The hippocampus is not seen on the medial surface of the hemisphere but is demonstrated after dissection into the temporal lobe (Fig. 2–9). The hippocampus is a two-layered allocortex and consists of several important structures: dentate gyrus, Ammon's horn (cornu ammonus CA_1–CA_4), and subiculum (Fig. 2–10). Other nuclear structures intimately associated with limbic function are the *septal nuclei in the posteromedial frontal lobe* (Fig. 2–7), the *dorsomedial and anterior nuclei*

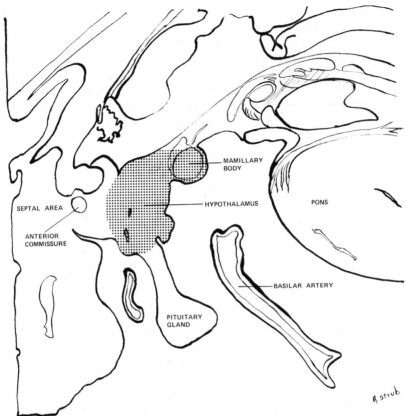

Figure 2-7. Sagittal cut of brain, close-up of upper brain stem, diencephalon, and environs. Stippled area represents the hypothalamus.

of the thalamus, and the *limbic midbrain area.* The midbrain area is composed primarily of the *periaqueductal gray substance* and the *nuclei of Gudden and Bechterew,* which lie in the midline ventral to it (see Fig. 2-3).

The *hippocampal (parahippocampal) gyrus* and *cingulate gyrus* are the cortical aspects of the limbic system and form the limbus or paralimbic belt of cortex on the medial surface of the hemisphere (see Fig. 2-6). Portions of the orbital and medial cortex of the frontal lobe are often considered to be a part of the limbic system, not only because of their rich anatomic connections with other limbic structures but also because of the characteristic emotional changes that occur if they are damaged or destroyed. A significant amount of medial temporal cortex (piriform and entorhinal) is also limbic. This cortex is associated with the olfactory system and is part of the old rhinencephalon. The rhinencephalon is of great importance in lower animals and remains an integral part of the limbic system in humans. All the cortex associated with the limbic system is three-layered mesocortex.

FIBROUS PATHWAYS

In association with the limbic system are many fibrous pathways, serving both as interconnections within the system and as connections between the limbic structures and other areas of the brain. As with many fiber systems in the brain, limbic pathways have fibers that go in both directions between any two structures. The rich reciprocating systems of the limbic system make constant feedback possible and allow continuous adjustment of the system.

The first limbic fiber bundle described, and certainly the largest, is the *fornix*. The fibers of the fornix originate in the cells of the hippocampus (dentate gyrus) and are the major outflow from that structure. The fornix arches forward along the medial surface of the hippocampus, then curves to join the contralateral fornix beneath the corpus callosum. The columns of the fornix proceed ventrally in the septum pellucidum, then divide to terminate both in the mamillary bodies of the hypothalamus and in the septal nuclei of the frontal lobe (Fig. 2-11).

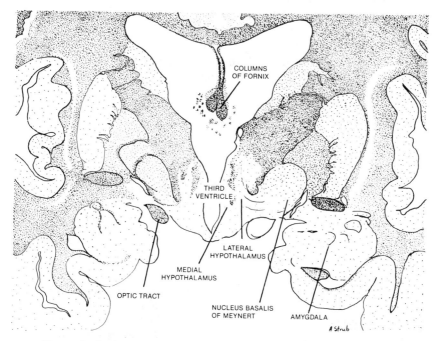

Figure 2-8. Coronal section of the brain showing limbic structures.

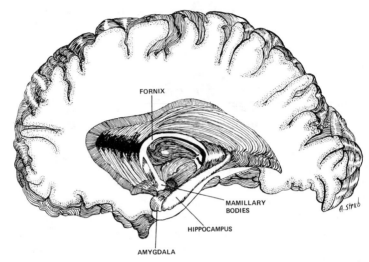

Figure 2 – 9. Dissection of cerebral hemisphere showing hippocampus and amygdala within temporal lobe.

A second major pathway originates in the mamillary bodies and terminates in the anterior nucleus of the thalamus; this is the *mamilothalamic tract of Vicq d'Azyr.* Fibers then project from the anterior thalamus to the cingulate gyrus (see Fig. 2 – 11). This circuit from the hippocampus to the mamillary bodies via the fornix and then to the anterior thalami and cingulate gyri is known as the Papez circuit.[45] Historically, this was the first

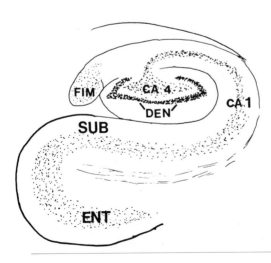

Figure 2 – 10. Coronal cut of the medial temporal lobe at the level of the hippocampus. ENT, entorhinal area (hippocampal gyrus); SUB, subiculum; CA, cornuammonus (or ammons horn) 1 through 4; DEN, dentate gyrus; FIM, fimbria of fornix. Hippocampal formation is made up of the dentate gyrus and ammons horn.

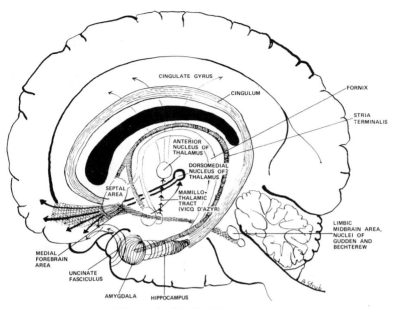

Figure 2-11. Limbic structures.

pathway hypothesized as a possible mechanism for the appreciation and expression of emotion in humans.

A third important limbic pathway is the *stria terminalis*, which runs almost parallel to the fornix in the lateral wall of the lateral ventricle. Its fibers originate in the amygdala and project to the ventromedial hypothalamus and the septal region (see Fig. 2-11).

The fourth major fiber pathway is the *medial forebrain bundle*. The bundle originates in the inferior frontal cortex and septal nuclei. It passes through the lateral hypothalamus and continues to the limbic midbrain area. Throughout its course, it provides rich collaterals to the regions it traverses.

In addition to these four major fiber systems, there are important connections from the hypothalamus and amygdala to the orbitofrontal cortex via the dorsomedial thalamus. The amygdala itself has three additional fiber connections: (1) the *ansa peduncularis*, which connects the amygdala directly with the hypothalamus; (2) the *uncinate fasciculus*, which runs to the orbitofrontal cortex; and (3) the *stria medullaris*, a pathway connecting the amygdala, habenula, and septum. Diffuse interconnections also exist between the brain stem reticular formation and the limbic midbrain area. More extensive anatomic information is available, and the interested student is referred to Isaacson,[25] Crosby and coworkers,[12] and Mesulam.[37]

Function

Through stimulation and ablation studies in animals and the clinical study of humans with lesions in the limbic structures, evidence has accumulated to support the hypothesis that the limbic system does serve as the substrate for innate drives, emotional behavior, and memory. The following pages provide a basic outline of the functional anatomy of the system and give specific examples of the relationships between the limbic system and these behaviors.

Basic to all behavior is a set of innate behavioral patterns that are instinctual. These instincts, including eating, fighting, fear, and sexual desire, are found in all animals and are vital to self-preservation and perpetuation of the species. The exact neuroanatomic substrate of such instincts is elusive, yet most can be identified as being predominantly functions of specific limbic structures. Limbic activity does not, however, operate in isolation; close interaction with the ascending arousal system, basal ganglia, and neocortex is critical. In humans, the basic instincts are not expressed in pure form but are dramatically modified by learned behavior patterns.

BASIC INSTINCTS

Feeding instincts seem to be controlled primarily by the hypothalamus.[7] Excessive feeding, for instance, can be initiated in animals by stimulation of the lateral hypothalamus or destruction of the ventromedial hypothalamic nuclei.[25] This relationship of feeding behavior to hypothalamic function has also been verified in humans with tumors destroying the ventromedial or lateral hypothalamus. Patients with lesions in the ventromedial zone show a marked hyperphagia as the primary symptom, whereas patients with lateral damage demonstrate anorexia and emaciation.[18,50,61]

Experimental evidence from animal (monkey) studies suggests that damage to the ventromedial hypothalamus does not produce *insatiable* hyperphagia but will increase food intake to the point of establishing a much heavier baseline weight.[35] The hypothalamus modulates the drive considerably but does not have absolute control of feeding function. Both excessive eating and starvation have also been produced in animals by means of stereotactic lesions in the amygdala,[17] although no comparable cases in humans have yet been reported. Some of the lip smacking and chewing movements seen during temporal lobe seizures could possibly represent feeding behavior of purely amygdalar origin, although this has not yet been supported by clinical evidence.

The *olfactory apparatus* is another part of the limbic system that is intimately associated with feeding activity. The olfactory system is sensory, and its stimulation does not directly result in feeding behavior; however, olfactory inputs to the amygdala and hypothalamus will trigger an orienting response and a host of autonomic functions including salivation and changes in gastrointestinal motility. Occasionally, experimental amygdalar lesions in animals cause a very complex alteration in feeding behavior in which the animals actually display a violent attack behavior toward food.[47] This type of aggressive feeding behavior demonstrates the rather close association in the nervous system of such disparate functions as feeding and aggression. Among humans, eating is usually a calm and civilized activity, but in many carnivorous animals, a close alliance between aggressive and feeding instincts is required to ensure survival.

Feeding, however, is more complicated than the expression of simple drive. Hunger is a physiologic state controlled by a complex interaction between gastrointestinal and neural structures. The presence of hunger initiates the drive to eat. Food search then begins. The individual then orients toward potential edible items. The particular item is analyzed by the various senses and compared with stored memories concerning the edibility of the item; then actual feeding behavior is begun. If the individual is not hungry and is confronted with the edible item, usually the feeding response is not elicited (unless, of course, the item is so inviting as to be irresistible).

Aggressiveness (fighting) and knowing when to escape from danger (fleeing) are extremely important instincts in all animals. Humans, through an elaborate civilizing process, have modified these instincts considerably, but they nevertheless remain, usually in cryptic form. In general, *fighting* and *fleeing behaviors* are controlled by the limbic structures in the temporal lobe, the amygdala, and hippocampus, although the hypothalamus is also an important modulator. The relationship between aggressiveness and temporal-limbic structures was first recognized with the discovery that vicious monkeys were made calm and tractable by removal of the temporal lobes bilaterally. This observation, by Klüver and Bucy,[30] was one of the milestones in elucidating the relationship of instincts and emotions to specific brain structures. Destruction of the temporal lobes can produce docility in some animals, whereas stimulation of the amygdala or hippocampus often causes violent attack behavior. The literature contains several clinical reports of violent or aggressive behavior in patients with epileptogenic lesions in the temporal lobes. (These cases will be discussed in detail in Chapter 12, Epilepsy). Aggressive behavior has also been reported in patients with destructive lesions in the ventromedial hypothalamus,[50] which again points out the close interrelationship of the temporal and hypothalamic limbic structures in producing and modulating instinctual behaviors.

The neurophysiologic mechanisms by which an animal attacks and kills another animal for food are speculative; however, the following model hypothesizes a relationship between limbic structures and feeding behavior. Assuming that a hungry animal first detects the prey by its scent, an olfactory stimulus would travel along the olfactory tracts to the amygdala and septal nuclei. These structures then cause an orienting response toward the stimulus and an arousal of aggressive gustatory feelings. The stimulus is then carried from the amygdala via the stria terminalis and ventrofugal fibers (ansa peduncularis) to the hypothalamus, caudate nucleus, and septum. From the hypothalamus and septum, stimulation passes via the medial forebrain bundle to the limbic midbrain area, where interdigitation with the ascending arousal system occurs. At this point, arousal level is high, aggressiveness and feeding instincts are acute, and attack behavior is then integrated through basal ganglia, motor cortex, and other subcortical motor systems. This simplified model can also be applied to an animal's response to a food stimulus received through any sensory modality (e.g., the sight of food). Feeding and aggressive instincts in humans are usually well controlled by learned cortical inhibitions, but these instincts do remain and may emerge in extreme situations, such as war and famine.

The final major instinct under limbic control is *mating*. Ostensibly present to ensure that each species will procreate and thereby avoid extinction, sexual drives often surpass this basic need.

Mating, like eating or fighting, is a very complex behavior that is guided by an internal need state or drive—in this case, the libido. The anatomic substrate for the libido is not known, but certain evidence suggests that midline limbic structures (cingulate gyrus, septal nuclei, hypothalamus, limbic midbrain structures, and possibly anterior thalamus) are involved. Some evidence is indirect. For example, removal of the temporal lobes (Klüver-Bucy syndrome) releases both inappropriate and exaggerated sexual activity. Conversely, chronic subclinical stimulation of temporal lobe structures in temporal lobe epileptics often results in global hyposexuality.[5] These observations indicate that the basic sexual drive emanates from medial limbic structures rather than temporal ones. Prefrontal lobotomy is also well known to uninhibit sexual interest and behavior, suggesting that the deep or midline structures control the actual drive. Hypersexuality has also been observed in a patient with scattered lesions in the mesodiencephalic region secondary to encephalitis, but no precise statement concerning the specific lesions responsible for the release of the hypersexuality could be made.[46] An additional case of hypersexuality was described by Erickson.[16] The patient had a tumor in the cingulate gyrus that was causing focal seizures characterized by sensory experiences (pleasurable) in her genital region as well as by heightened libido. This case is problematic because one cannot say whether the stimulation of the cingulate caused the increase in libido or whether the genital sensations evoked the sexual desire.

From available data, the mating drive appears to originate in the deep frontal lobe structures of the anterior cingulate gyrus and the septal nuclei but is significantly modified by the inhibitory input from the temporal lobe limbic structures. In humans, of course, the learned social behavioral patterns that develop in the cortex form yet another strong controlling influence on sexual behavior.

EMOTIONAL BEHAVIOR

The innate limbic instincts discussed above form the basis of the survival drives that allow animals to satisfy their basic needs. In some animals, but particularly in humans, the limbic system also serves as a substrate for emotional behavior. Emotional reactions, by definition, are not neutral experiences. They involve the appreciation and expression of positive feelings such as desire, joy, or love or the negative emotions of sadness, hate, or anger. Emotions have two distinct aspects: they are felt internally and expressed externally. The conscious appreciation of an emotion is a cortical phenomenon probably subsumed by the cingulate and phylogenetically older limbic cortex of the temporal and frontal lobes. It seems justifiable to surmise that the temporal lobe cortex associated with the structures of the amygdala and hippocampus is concerned with the initial appreciation of negative emotions, whereas the frontal cortex in association with the septal nuclei and cingulate gyrus is concerned with positive emotions. Ultimately, however, the entire cortex will participate in the full emotional experience.

Underlying the more gentle emotions of happiness and sadness are the more basic and intense feelings of pleasure and fear. These subjective experiences stand somewhere between drives and emotions. They reinforce the drives by rewarding the behavior that satisfies the drive, and they color the emotion, also as a way of rewarding and promoting certain feelings and the behavior that has evoked them. Through animal and human experimentation, stimulation to various points in the limbic system, especially the median forebrain bundle, septal area, parts of hypothalamus, olfactory system, periacqueductal gray, amygdala and certain areas of hippocampus, has been found to produce very pleasurable feelings.[23,26,44] Animals implanted with electrodes in the septal and median forebrain bundle areas will perform tasks to receive electrical stimulation to these areas to the exclusion of eating or drinking.[49] These areas have been called by some the pleasure or reward centers. Because pleasure-producing neuronal populations are more widespread than these restricted areas, it is best not to call them "centers." It is important to know, however, that there are specific populations of neurons whose stimulation will produce feelings of pleasure and thereby reward and reinforce learning. Recent neuropharmacologic studies have shown that many of the pleasure-producing neurons are involved in endogenous opiate (endorphin) production, a discovery that ties together behavior, anatomy, and chemistry in a most rewarding fashion.[31]

The negative feelings of horror, fear, and anguish can also be evoked by stimulating electrodes placed in various locations in the limbic system, the amygdala, and hippocampus, as well as areas in the posteromedial hypothalamus.[29,36] Selective stereotactic lesions in these areas have been used, with some success, to control negative behaviors such as violence and aggressiveness.

The outward expression of emotion is a rudimentary and basic process that seems to involve two levels of action. First, and concomitant with the appreciation of the emotion, the autonomic nervous system is stimulated, primarily by the hypothalamus, to change heart rate, respiration pattern, peripheral vascular tone, and a host of other endocrine and autonomic functions. Along with these changes in homeostasis, motor patterns are stimulated in the basal ganglia by the other limbic structures, which initiate changes in such factors as facial expression (smile, frown, or fear) and body attitude (attack or flight postures).

A mechanism by which the appreciation and expression of emotions are integrated by the limbic system was first proposed by Papez,[45] and his hypothesis can still be used as a framework for understanding the function of the system. He suggested that the emotional information from the environment spreads to the hippocampus from the various cortical receiving areas. The fornix, being the major outflow of the hippocampus, carries the stimulus to mamillary bodies. From the mamillary bodies (the posterior nuclear group of the hypothalamus), the stimulus spreads within the hypothalamus to initiate emotional expression. At the same time, the stimulus spreads to the anterior nucleus of the thalamus via the mamillothalamic tract (Vicq d'Azyr tract) and then through a diffuse projection in the internal capsule to the cingulate gyrus, where the emotion is consciously appreciated. The stimulus then returns to the hippocampus via the cingulum, thus completing the circuit. This model, known as the Papez circuit, has served as a foundation for theorizing about the functional properties of the limbic system.

To synthesize all the anatomic and clinical information thus far presented into a coherent functional concept, let us postulate what happens within the limbic system when a person encounters an emotionally charged situation, such as watching his parked car being smashed by a reckless driver. The visual and auditory perceptions of the crash enter the primary visual cortex in the occipital lobes and the auditory cortex in the temporal lobes. This input travels in two directions: first to the association areas within the neocortex, where the event is perceived in a largely objective fashion ("A red car driven at a high rate of speed just demolished my car and is now leaving the scene"). Because there is limbic input to the association cortex, there is some emotional coloring of the pure sensory experience in the parietal association areas.[37] In conjunction with this spread of the stimulus within the neocortex, impulses are sent to the hippocampus and thence to the amygdala.[33] At this point, negative feelings and aggression are added to the input and sent along the Papez circuit via the fornix to the mamillary bodies, septum, anterior thalamus, and then to the cingulate cortex for the conscious appreciation of the associated affect (anger and aggression). Other pathways from the hippocampus/amygdala reach the hypothalamus via the stria terminalis and the direct amygdalo-hypothalamic pathway. The hypothalamus, with the septal and frontal lobe inputs, then initiates a discharge down the medial forebrain bundle into the limbic midbrain area, where interaction occurs with the reticular system, thus adding a tremendous arousal and alerting to the entire brain. Rage is now truly beginning. Simultaneously, the hypothalamus initiates a massive autonomic response of hyperventilation, increased heart rate, and pupillary dilation. Motor patterns of rage are expressed through various interactions within the cortical and subcortical motor systems, and now the person looks angry as well as feels angry. How each person deals with this anger and aggression is a separate issue and results from a combination of the person's basic temperament and the way he has been taught to react to such situations (social learning). These learned behavioral patterns, which constitute so much of our personality, are discussed later in this chapter.

TEMPERAMENT

Before leaving the topic of the limbic system, it seems justified to introduce briefly the concept of temperament, and to postulate a possible substrate for individual temperamental differences. Temperament refers to that underlying basic and characteristic way in which a person reacts in his environment, the activity level expressed, the tempo of action, the degree of satisfaction or dissatisfaction that is felt in each situation, and the person's general mood or emotional tone. Each person is born with a basic temperamental pattern that remains relatively constant throughout his lifetime.[10,57,58]

This lifelong consistency in temperamental traits has been described in various populations: retarded persons, different social and ethnic classes,[58] and more recently, adults who had been hyperactive as children.[60] In the latter case, the hyperactive child appears to be much more likely than his nonhyperactive schoolmate to become an impulsive, unsettled adult with an above-average likelihood of becoming involved in substance abuse or developing antisocial behavior. This temperament determines to a great extent the fashion in which the person reacts to inner drives, environmental stimulation, and stress. A child's temperament may be very different from that of the parents, and these differences in temperament within a family (a poor fit) can cause considerable stress even before formation of learned personality patterns. For instance, an infant who is very difficult to satisfy, who cries unless fed or held, and who has a high activity level may well be born to a calm, passive, somewhat sensitive and timid couple. The tension in that family will be much higher than if those parents had an easy, calm child who spent much of his time cooing, eating, and sleeping. This basic temperament is presumed to be constitutional and strongly influences the environment's responses and interactions with the developing personality. If we assume that each person is born with a specific temperament, we must postulate that temperament is the product of the person's individual brain structure and physiology. Accordingly, everyone must have a slightly different arousal system that gives each a different basic activity level, capacity for sustained attention, and sleep needs. At the extreme end of this spectrum are some children who are readily recognized as being extremely overactive, hyperreactive, and distractible. In many such cases there is no primary emotional problem, and the hyperactivity and distractability appear to be caused by an organic imbalance between the arousal system and the inhibitory activities of the brain stem and cortex. This activity can often be controlled by medications (amphetamines and methylphenidate) and exacerbated by others (barbiturates). These responses are paradoxical to those expected in normal persons, which further suggests a physiologic basis for these temperamental differences.

Temperament implies more than activity level alone. It also refers to drive level, need for attention, degree of satisfaction gained from rewards, and mood. These functions are in the province of the limbic system. Thus, it could be postulated that basic temperament is the product of each person's limbic and arousal systems as he interacts with the learning process and socialization.

MEMORY

The limbic system has one additional critical function that serves as a transition between innate and learned behavior. This function is memory, the basis of all learning. Experimental and clinical evidence has shown that many structures within the limbic system are essential for learning. The anatomy underlying the memory process is reviewed here; the clinical memory syndromes and case studies are discussed in Chapter 8, Neurobehavioral Syndromes Associated with Focal Brain Lesions. Removal of, or damage to, the hippocampi bilaterally has been shown to significantly disrupt a person's ability to learn.[54] Sensory information (e.g., a person's name, a word, a face, or the street locations in a new city) apparently must traverse the hippocampus for the data to be stored in recent memory. The mamillary bodies and dorsal medial thalami are also critical structures for the process of memory retrieval. Combined damage to these structures will also block the memory process.[59] It is possible that areas in the limbic midbrain, and orbital frontal lobe[2] are also vital links in the complicated chain of limbic structures necessary to establish permanent memory storage.[34]

Memory traces are probably complex patterns that are consolidated and stored within the neocortex and not the limbic system.[27] Exactly why the cortex is dependent on these subcortical systems for memory storage and retrieval is uncertain. Because learning requires reinforcement or reward, the limbic system, through its role in the generation and satisfaction of both basic and socially learned needs, logically serves as the essential link in learning (storage of memories). The limbic system very possibly assesses the reward values of each incoming stimulus. For example, there is a positive emotional reward for learning particular facts (e.g., an important person at a meeting). Conversely, negative emotional responses can also stimulate learning (e.g., the fear of not remembering an important lecture or neuroanatomic structure when a test is imminent). The limbic system serves to give all environmental inputs a relative value in terms of survival; factors with high survival value will be remembered, whereas factors with no personal relevance will not be learned efficiently.

This discussion of limbic functions is based primarily on an anatomic model. In recent years, neurochemical research has shown that many of the limbic circuits are composed of neurons that produce a single transmitter substance. Some neuronal systems are dopaminergic, others either serotoninergic, cholinergic, or adrenergic. Someday it may be possible to further break down emotional, motivational, and learning functions to specific chemical subsystems rather than relying on an anatomic model alone. Research into the relationship of cholinergic systems and learning has been the most rewarding to date.[14,62]

THE CORTEX

The neocortex is the most recently and highly developed portion of the central nervous system. In this area, intellectual processes are carried out, and refinements in personality and social behavior are developed. Our knowledge of higher cortical functions comes primarily from the study of the human brain, because the human's use of language permits both clinical and experimental study. The cortex has been extensively studied anatomically and has been divided into many separate areas based on cytoarchitecture. Because the divisions described by Brodmann[9] have been widely accepted, we will use that numbering system in our discussion (Fig. 2-12).

Inherent in the cortex is the capacity for intellectual development; however, the actual functions of language, perception, abstract thought, and social interaction must be learned through the person's day-to-day

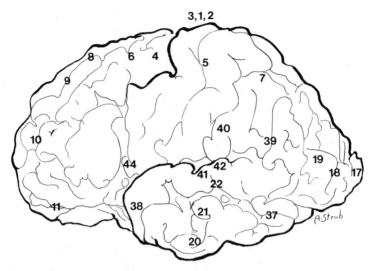

Figure 2-12. Cortex with Brodmann's anatomic divisions.

interaction with his environment. The raw material for this learning process comes to the cortex through the various sensory systems both from
extrapersonal space via sight, sound, touch, and smell and from the internal milieu. The sensory input is constantly augmented by motor activity;
this activity allows the person to manipulate objects and move effectively
through the environment.[15]

The basic sensory and motor systems have well-established cortical
representation, called the primary motor areas (area 4 and part of 6) and
the primary sensory receiving areas (area 17—visual area; areas 3, 1, and
2—tactile; and areas 41 and 42—auditory). Our discussion of intellectual
functions, although assuming the presence of intact basic sensory and
motor areas, is primarily concerned with the association areas. Within
these areas, the raw sensory and motor data are elaborated, compared with
existing memory patterns, and then manipulated to meet environmental
demands.

The visual system receives information through the primary visual
cortex (area 17); these stimuli then spread to the primary and secondary
association areas (areas 18, 19, 20, 21, and 37). In these association areas
(unimodal visual association areas), the basic visual sensations of light,
dark, line, and position are transformed into forms or objects that can be
compared with previous experience.[32] This sophisticated ability to discriminate between different shapes and to compare the present sensory pattern
with past impressions is the basis of the visual perceptual process. The
same type of process occurs in auditory perception. Sounds are first received in the primary auditory cortex (areas 41 and 42), then transferred to

the primary auditory association area (area 22), and finally to the secondary association area (area 21). In the auditory association areas, sounds are appreciated as being specific types (e.g., boat whistles, cars starting, human voices). As the stimulus spreads, human voice input can then be recognized as language.

Tactile perception is analogous. Tactile stimuli spread from the primary receiving cortex (areas 3, 1, and 2) to the association area (area 5). The ability to discern objects placed in the hand (stereognosis) is localized in both the primary receiving areas and in the association area. Accordingly, the primary tactile receiving cortex is somewhat more highly developed than the primary visual and auditory cortex.[51] Areas 5 and 7 interdigitate with the visual system and are involved more in visually guiding the limbs in space than in elaborating tactile perception.

In humans, a large, phylogenetically recent area of cortex called the inferior parietal lobule serves as a tertiary association area (supramarginal gyrus—area 40; and angular gyrus—area 39). This third-level association of cortex receives the spreading sensory stimuli (of all visual, auditory, and tactile input) from the secondary association areas. Because it receives input from several sensory modalities, it is often called heteromodal cortex. By virtue of this confluence of all inputs, this area is capable of forming sensory associations (cross-modal association), allowing humans to link visual, auditory, and tactile inputs in such a way that they are able to apply words to visual stimuli and describe what they see or touch. This high-level capacity to associate all inputs is the basis of most higher cognitive functions. These areas also receive input from limbic and arousal systems and are thus an important part of the selective attention system, a system that allows the mind to focus and concentrate, not only on relevant objects in the environment but also on one's own thoughts and feelings.

Localization of Function

This section hypothesizes that intellectual functions develop through interactions among sensory inputs and their concurrent impact on motor learning. Each of these interactions occurs in a different area of the cortex and, accordingly, lesions in different parts of the brain will produce different clinical syndromes. A knowledge of the cortical localization of cognitive function is important because an examiner can then determine the location of a lesion such as a tumor or stroke by systematically testing a series of intellectual functions.

The following discussion of cortical localization has been simplified and should serve as an introduction to the concept of cortical functioning. Specific cortical functions are complex and involve the interaction of many cortical and subcortical systems. For example, a simple auditory comprehension task such as listening to a weather report on the radio involves more than merely decoding the key elements of temperature, likelihood of rain, and wind velocity. The attentional system must constantly screen out environmental noise. The received information is interpreted in terms of inner feelings of hot, cold, and so forth. The system has been preset to expect certain general information (e.g., January temperatures should be cold), and any information that does not fit (e.g., "It will be 86 degrees the 15th of January in Toronto") will be difficult to properly "comprehend." In addition, the information is constantly being interpreted in light of plans for the future (e.g., if the first words from the announcer are "heavy thunderstorms," temperature readings that follow may not be comprehended because of the impact of the first bits of information). Normal comprehension, therefore, requires much more than an intact left superior temporal gyrus (area 22). Destruction of area 22, however, in the left hemisphere of a right-handed person usually does severely impair auditory comprehension. This section on the localization of normal brain function is based primarily on the findings in patients with focal brain lesions. Using such lesion data, neurobehaviorists have hypothesized the localization of normal function based on the loss of function that occurs with damage to a specific area.

Localization of function within the human cortex is made considerably easier by the fact that in many instances the two hemispheres subserve very different functions. The left hemisphere, in almost all right-handed persons, is dominant for the learning of skilled fine-motor movements. This left hemispheric superiority for motor learning apparently is the neuroanatomic substrate for right-handedness. Interestingly enough, the left hemisphere of the right-handed person is also dominant for the development of both the comprehension and expression of language. This remarkable lateralization of language is very probably a genetic trait based on a structural asymmetry of the language cortex. The homologous cortex of the opposite hemisphere is capable of developing language, however, as damage to the dominant hemisphere early in life can cause a transfer dominance.[53] It has been demonstrated anatomically that the auditory cortex of the left hemisphere is larger and more developed in the right-handed adult.[20] This asymmetry does not appear to be an effect of language exposure because it has also been observed in the brains of newborns.[63]

This strong left-hemispheric dominance for language is not as pronounced in the left-handed person; in fact only 60 percent of left-handed persons are strongly left-brain dominant.[3,19] Lateralization for language in general is not as strongly established in the left-handed person; 80 percent of the left-handed population have some degree of language capacity in both hemispheres.[21] Because of this bilateral language representation, or anomalous dominance, lateralization of a lesion in the left-handed patient should be made on grounds other than the presence of a language deficit alone.

LANGUAGE

Because the left hemisphere is dominant for language in most of the population, we will use left-hemispheric function as the model for the discussion of the anatomy of language. Language and the ability to communicate our needs and thoughts are the bases for many of our intellectual processes. The complete use of language requires the following five basic processes: (1) comprehension of spoken language, (2) verbal reasoning, (3) production of speech, (4) deciphering written language, and (5) writing. Through the study of brain-damaged patients with language disturbances (aphasia), many of these processes have been localized to general areas within the left hemisphere. The comprehension of spoken language occurs in the posterior area of the temporal lobe and adjoining parietal cortex (Fig. 2–13, area 1). The superior temporal gyrus (area 22) subsumes the most basic level of comprehension, whereas the association cortex (areas 21, 39, and 40) is more involved in higher level complex comprehension and verbal reasoning. The higher the level of the mental process (e.g., verbal abstract reasoning), the more widespread the cortical representation necessary for carrying out that process.

The actual production of speech is a motor act and, by virtue of this fact, is intimately associated with the area of the motor cortex responsible for the movement of the buccofacial apparatus. The actual cortical area

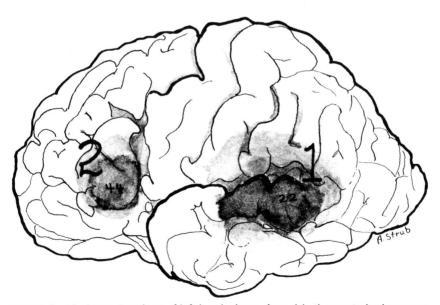

Figure 2–13. Lateral surface of left hemisphere. Area 1 is the posterior language area. Area 2 is the anterior language area.

necessary for producing speech is a sizable region of the frontal lobe surrounding and including Broca's area (area 44) (Fig. 2–13, area 2).[41] The comprehension and production of spoken language, although not as discretely localized as some texts might suggest, does rely on the posterior portions of the hemisphere surrounding the sylvian fissure for comprehension and the anterior portions for speech production.

For a person to comprehend and discuss events occurring in the environment, a further step in language processing is required. This step is the integration of visual or tactile stimuli with the language system. Because there is an extensive overlap within the association cortex, verbal labels or names can be attached to visually presented objects or written symbols. In this way, language can be used to describe ongoing events within the environment. The same process pertains to the decoding of specific written symbols (reading). This overlap of vision and language occurs in the tertiary association areas of the left inferior parietal lobule (areas 39 and 40). This cortical localization of reading has been well established; there have been reports[4] on many patients who lost the ability to read and write with the destruction of areas 39 and 40.

VISUAL PERCEPTION

Visual perception is a very important function that allows exploration of the environment and learning of relationships between various objects in space. In humans, basic perceptual functions develop before the acquisition of verbal skills. The infant learns about his environment—the constancy of objects, certain laws of cause and effect, and the geography of his life space—long before he utters his first intelligible word. As language develops, these visual perceptual processes become less apparent but remain critically important to the child learning to write or to the architect who must be able to translate visual ideas to paper and then into structure. These basic perceptual skills are vital for our functioning but become so automatic that we are seldom aware of them. Visual perception and appreciation of spatial orientation in the environment are carried out within the association areas of occipital lobes (areas 18 and 19), in the visual association areas in the inferior temporal lobe/temporoccipital area (areas 20, 21, and 37), and in the inferior parietal lobule (areas 39 and 40). Here, visual input is manipulated within the visual association areas and compared with previous visual experiences. These visual skills are somewhat better developed in the right nondominant hemisphere. Accordingly, it is possible to say that the right posterior hemisphere is somewhat dominant for visual spatial tasks in the same manner that the left is more specifically specialized for verbal tasks. Language dominance, however, is much more strongly lateralized than is perceptual spatial dominance.

TACTILE PERCEPTION

Tactile perception develops in conjunction with the kinesthetic sensory system in much the same way as does visual perception. Basic tactile information concerning texture, weight, shape, and size of an object is processed in the sensory cortex (areas 3, 1, and 2) and to an extent, in adjacent association cortex (area 5). This tactile information can then be compared with kinesthetic memories so that one can identify objects by touch alone. This comparison occurs over a wide area of the parietal lobe. Because of the rich overlap among tactile, visual, and language association areas, the person is able both to use language to identify and name objects perceived tactilely and also to evoke visual memories from tactile stimulation (e.g., recognition of eye glasses when touched in the dark or identification of a coin's denomination when felt in the pocket). Tactile-auditory associations are probably most highly developed in the blind because they rely so heavily on tactile input. Use of the Braille system demonstrates the high level to which this skill can be developed. Basic tactile skills are developed in both hemispheres and are primarily controlled by the cortex contralateral to the hand stimulated. When Braille is read with the left hand, the tactile images must be transferred from the right parietal lobe (tactile input) to the left inferior parietal lobe (association area) to be comprehended as language.

HIGHER INTELLECTUAL PROCESSES

The basic building blocks of human's intellect are language, perception (visual and tactile), and the motor skills that develop under the guidance of the basic sensory systems. Higher intellectual processes such as verbal reasoning or complex visual-spatial problem solving (e.g., replacement of a heart valve by a surgeon) require the interaction and mental manipulation of stored language, visual memories, and tactile images. The ability of the human to actively manipulate his store of information and to form different and novel combinations is the essence of thought and the creative process. This higher-order mental activity is possible because of the rich association areas in the postrolandic cortex. Much of our nonemotional intellectual processes are carried out in this posterior region of the brain. Removal of both frontal lobes, although causing distinct changes especially in personality, leaves many basic cognitive processes relatively intact.[22,38]

THE FRONTAL LOBES

Whereas the parietal lobes and contiguous temporal and occipital lobes are the loci of intellectual processes, and the limbic system is the substrate for instincts and emotions, the frontal lobes serve to mediate between the intellect and the emotions. These premotor or prefrontal cortical structures (areas 9, 10, 11, 12, 45, 46, and 47) are both the most recent phylogenetic addition to the central nervous system and also the last areas of the brain to mature in the child. Their architecture is distinctly granular, a feature that relates them more closely anatomically with the sensory than with the motor cortex. This association with the sensory cortex can be better understood after a discussion of the fiber pathways connecting the frontal lobe with the posterior sensory association areas.

The afferent and efferent connections of the frontal lobe are largely reciprocal. Afferents to the frontal lobes originate from two principal sources: The first is the sensory association cortex in the posterior hemisphere (inferior parietal lobule) via several pathways: (1) long chains of corticocortical neurons, (2) long association fibers (inferior and superior occipitofrontal fasciculi), and (3) the uncinate fasciculus from the temporal cortex. Most of the frontal input comes from heteromodal cortex (60 percent), whereas only about 25 percent comes from unimodal association areas.[37] These pathways carry information concerning the external environment as well as data about thought processes being carried out within the parietal association cortex. These pathways project for the most part to the lateral convexity of the frontal cortex. The second major input comes from the limbic structures via several pathways: (1) the uncinate fasciculus from the amygdala, (2) the hypothalamus and amygdala via the internal capsule from the thalamic nuclei, (3) the limbic midbrain area and the hypothalamus via the medial forebrain bundle, (4) the cingulum, and (5) direct communications from the septal nuclei. This extensive limbic input is projected primarily to the orbitomedial or inferior surface of the frontal lobes (area 12). By virtue of this direct limbic connection, the prefrontal cortex receives continuous information concerning the person's feeling and the state of internal needs.

Fears, threats, and desires for food, sleep, and sex are constantly communicated to the frontal granular cortex. All sensory and intellectual processing from the posterior cortex is also projected onto the frontal lobes.[43] This area of the cortex thus serves as the brain's final or quaternary association area. Within the frontal lobes, the interactions of inputs from the posterior centers and the limbic system allow basic emotional and intellectual behaviors to be synthesized and elaborated.

The prefrontal region does not have a major motor efferent pathway; rather, the output of this region is reciprocal. The principal reciprocal paths to the limbic system are to the cingulate gyrus, hippocampus, septum, hypothalamus (via the medial forebrain bundle), and the amygdala (via the uncinate fasciculus and a pathway through the dorsal medial thalamus). The efferents to neocortical structures are to the temporal cortex (via uncinate fasciculus) and to the inferior parietal lobule (via fronto-occipital bundles). This reciprocal innervation of the frontal connections suggests that the frontal lobe acts to modulate the activities of the intellectual and emotional systems through the synthesis of both types of input. The function of reciprocal circuitry has been postulated to explain some of the subtle intellectual defects seen in patients with frontal lesions. For example, the frontal cortex has been shown to emit a preparatory discharge to the visual system before the movement of the eyes. This preparation stimulus ensures that the person will be prepared perceptually for the movement and not feel that the environment is moving when it is only the eyeball itself that is moving.[56] This preparatory process by the frontal lobes has been postulated to act as an active guidance system to control those environmental stimuli that will receive attention, those mental processes that shall be continued, and the time when change in any mental direction should be started.[48]

It has been amply demonstrated clinically that patients with frontal damage have great difficulty shifting mental processes from one concept to another. For instance, if a patient with damage to the frontal lobes is told to sort playing cards into piles and is rewarded when he places all hearts and diamonds in one pile and all clubs and spades in another, he will soon learn this task. If the examiner suddenly (without a change in instructions to the patient) begins to reward him only when he places odd-numbered cards in one pile and even-numbered cards in the other, he will be unable to make this shift efficiently.[40] This tendency to perseverate and the inability to shift mental set efficiently are typical of the difficulties experienced by patients with frontal lobe injury. The card-sorting task relies heavily on the patient's desire to continue to be rewarded for his correct answers. The ability to learn from reward is a main function of the limbic system, and in the patient with frontal damage, the reward value from the limbic system has been disconnected from the sensory input from the parietal lobes and can no longer adequately interact with the now meaningless task of sorting cards. Accordingly, the patient has no incentive or drive to alter his behavior on the task. Although subtle, this ability to actively shift mental sets and to adjust to changes in the environment is a very important aspect of higher cognitive processing.

Another cognitive activity directed by the frontal lobes is the ability to appreciate the temporal order of a series of events and the capacity to compare relative merit in importance of each event.[39] To compare specific alternatives and to keep all possibilities in mind, the person must be able to actively shift attention from one alternative to another.

The basic functions of changing mental set, appreciating temporal order, controlling attention, and being able to compare various alternatives are all components of the more sophisticated and critical role that the frontal lobes play in making decisions[24] such as the selection of a career, a spouse, or a school. Making these decisions utilizes the ability of the frontal lobes to consider both the practical (parietal) and the emotional (limbic) aspects of the situation. In addition, the cortex draws on its capacity to evaluate the probable outcomes of all possible alternatives to each decision. It then chooses the course of action that appears to best suit the person's true needs. The frontal lobes allow the practical aspects of a situation to be projected against the emotional input from the limbic system, permitting the positive and negative emotional and practical aspects of each alternative to be sampled. Internal emotional reactions are critical to reasoning applied to human situations. Without input from the frontal lobes, decisions are made without the advantage of emotional reflection (e.g., the patient who acts in a coldly intellectual fashion without any concern for how his actions will affect others). Similarly, the disconnection of limbic from cortical structures secondary to frontal lobe lesions may result in impulsive emotional behavior untempered by rational consideration.

The frontal lobes have another important role in behavior: using the learned behavior of the intellect to modulate and control the forceful drives that emanate from the limbic system. In the absence of the frontal lobes, emotions and instincts may become dysinhibited. Patients with damage to the frontal lobes can have complete reversals in personality (e.g., ambitious, productive persons can become apathetic and desultory, whereas proper, reserved persons can become euphoric and loud, acting completely inappropriately in social situations). Although it is not possible to accurately localize specific emotional functions within the frontal lobes, some evidence indicates that damage to the lateral convexity results in an apathetic state, whereas damage to the orbital/medial portion causes the more animated or manic type of disturbance.

Because frontal damage releases abnormal behavior, it has been assumed that in the intact person the frontal lobes control and guide social behavior. Viewed developmentally, the child is born with many simple needs and instincts to ensure survival. These needs are initially met by the environment. As the child grows, however, he must learn that needs are neither always met immediately nor satisfied completely. This learning represents the process of socialization. This inculcation of social behavior is an example of the modification of basic instinctual behavior. It is within the frontal lobes that environmental experiences interact with the limbic drive system to produce the final and appropriate course of action in a given situation. Without this limbic/frontal interaction, a person cannot properly learn from experience. Clinical experience with patients with frontal damage supports the postulate that frontal lobes are the place where temperament, drive, and experience interact.

SUMMARY

Human behavior is the product of many cortical and subcortical systems. Each person's unique behavior and personality are the totality of his basic instincts, his constitutional temperament, and the sum of his learned experiences. Behavior relies on an arousal system that allows the maintenance of alertness and on the widespread inhibitory system in the cortex, limbic system, and brain stem that allows the person to focus and sustain mental energy on an individual task or problem. The vast and complicated limbic system works in concert with the arousal system and the basal ganglia to provide an anatomic substrate for survival instincts, emotional expression and appreciation, and temperament. The limbic system adds reinforcement to learning and accordingly is vital to the acquisition and retrieval of memories. The cortex is the repository for the memories of all life experiences. The association cortex in the inferior parietal area has the capacity to actively manipulate in both familiar and novel ways the information stored therein. This active manipulation represents the basic physiologic process of thought and is the groundwork of the intellect.

The intellect and instincts must be guided for activities to be productive and survival to be ensured, while actions and behavior remain socially appropriate. These last elements are the responsibility of the frontal lobes and are the final product of the brain's activity—human behavior.

REFERENCES

1. Ackerly, SS and Benton, AL: Report of case of bilateral frontal lobe defect in the frontal lobes. Assoc Res Nerv Ment Dis 27:479, 1947.
2. Alexander, MP and Freedman, M: Amnesia after anterior communicating artery aneurysm rupture. Neurology 34:752, 1984.
3. Benson, DF and Geschwind, N: Cerebral dominance and its disturbances. Pediatr Clin North Am 15:759, 1968.
4. Benson, DF and Geschwind, N: The aphasias and related disturbances. In Baker, AB (ed): Baker's Clinical Neurology, vol 1, chap 8. Harper & Row, New York, 1975.
5. Blumer, D: Changes in sexual behavior related to temporal lobe disorder in man. J Sex Res 6:173, 1970.
6. Blumer, D and Benson, DF: Personality changes with frontal and temporal lobe lesions. In Benson, DF and Blumer, D (eds): Psychiatric Aspects of Neurologic Disease. Grune & Stratton, New York, 1975, pp 151–170.
7. Bray, GA and Gallagher, TF Jr: Manifestations of hypothalamic obesity in man: A comprehensive investigation of eight patients and a review of the literature. Medicine 54:301, 1975.
8. Brodal, A: Anatomical points of view on the alleged morphological basis of consciousness. Acta Neurochir 12:166, 1965.

9. Brodmann, K: Vergleichende Lokalisationslehre der Grosshirnrinde in thren Prinzipien dargestellt auf Grund des Zellenbaues. JA Barth, Leipzig, 1909.
10. Chess, S and Thomas, A: Temperament in Clinical Practice. Guilford Press, New York, 1986.
11. Coyle, JT: Aminergic projections from the reticular core. In Asbury, AK, McKhann, GM and McDonald, WI (eds): Diseases of the Nervous System: Clinical Neurobiology. WB Saunders, Philadelphia, 1986, pp 880–889.
12. Crosby, EC, Humphrey, T, and Lauer, EW: Correlative Anatomy of the Nervous System. MacMillan, New York, 1962.
13. Damasio, AR, et al: Amnesia following basal forebrain lesions. Arch Neurol 42:263, 1985.
14. Drachman, DA: Memory and the cholinergic system. In Fields, WS (ed): Neurotransmitter Function—Basic and Clinical Aspects. Symposia Specialists, 1977.
15. Duffy, CJ: The legacy of association cortex. Neurology 34:192, 1984.
16. Erickson, TC: Erotomania (nymphomania) as expression of cortical epileptiform discharge. Arch Neurol Psychiat 53:226, 1945.
17. Fonberg, E: The normalizing effect of lateral amygdalar lesions upon the dorsomedial amygdala syndrome in dogs. Acta Neurobiol Exp 33:449, 1973.
18. Fulton, JF and Bailey, P: Tumors in the region of the third ventricle: Their diagnosis and relation to pathological sleep. J Nerv Ment Dis 69:1, 1929.
19. Geschwind, N and Galaburda, AM: Cerebral Dominance: The Biological Foundations. Harvard University Press, Cambridge, 1984.
20. Geschwind, N and Levitsky, W: Human brain: Left-right asymmetries in temporal speech region. Science 161:186, 1968.
21. Gloning, I, et al: Comparison of verbal behavior in right-handed and non-right-handed patients with anatomically verified lesions of one hemisphere. Cortex 5:43, 1969.
22. Hamlin, RM: Intellectual function 14 years after frontal lobe surgery. Cortex 6:299, 1970.
23. Heath, RG: Brain function and behavior. I. Emotion and sensory phenomena in psychiatric patients and in experimental animals. J Nerv Ment Dis 160:159, 1975.
24. Hecaen, H and Albert, ML: Disorders of mental functioning related to frontal lobe pathology. In Benson, DF and Blumer, D (eds): Psychiatric Aspects of Neurologic Disease. Grune & Stratton, New York, 1975, pp 137–149.
25. Isaacson, RL: The Limbic System. Plenum Press, New York, 1974.
26. Jacques, S: Brain stimulation and reward: "Pleasure centers" after twenty-five years. Neurosurgery 5:277, 1979.
27. John, ER, et al: Double-labelled metabolic maps of memory. Science 233:1167, 1986.
28. Kahn, E and Cohen, LH: Organic driveness: A brainstem syndrome and an experience. N Engl J Med 210:748, 1934.
29. Kelly, D: Neurosurgical treatment of psychiatric disorders. In Glenville-Grossman, K (ed): Recent Advances in Clinical Psychiatry. Churchill Livingston, London, 1976, pp 227–261.
30. Klüver, H and Bucy, PC: Preliminary analysis of the temporal lobes in monkeys. Arch Neurol Psychiat 42:979, 1939.

31. Krieger, DT: Brain peptides: What, where and why? Science 222:975, 1983.
32. Luria, A: Higher Cortical Functions in Man. Basic Books, New York, 1966.
33. MacLean, PD and Creswell, G: Anatomical connections of visual system with limbic cortex of monkey. J Comp Neurol 138:265, 1970.
34. McEntee, WJ, et al: Diencephalic amnesia: A reappraisal. J Neurol Neurosurg Psychiatry 39:436, 1976.
35. McHugh, PR, et al: Inhibitions on feeding examined in rhesus monkeys with hypothalamic disconnexions. Brain 98:441, 1975.
36. Mark, VH and Ervin, FR: Violence and the Brain. Harper & Row, New York, 1970.
37. Mesulam, M-M: Patterns in behavioral neuroanatomy: Association areas, the limbic systems and hemispheric specialization. In Mesulam, M-M (ed): Principles of Behavioral Neurology. FA Davis, Philadelphia, 1985, pp 1-70.
38. Mettler, FA (ed): Selective Partial Ablation of the Frontal Cortex. Hoeber, New York, 1949.
39. Milner, B: Interhemispheric differences and psychological processes. Br Med Bull 27:272, 1971.
40. Milner, B and Teuber, HL: Alteration of perception and memory in man. In Weiskrantz, L (ed): Analysis of Behavioral Change. Harper & Row, New York, 1968, pp 268-375.
41. Mohr, JP: Broca's area and Broca's aphasia. In Whitaker, H and Whitaker, HA (eds): Studies in Neurolinguistics. Academic Press, New York, 1976, pp 201-235.
42. Moruzzi, G and Magoun, HW: Brainstem reticular formation and activation of the EEG. Electroencephalogr Clin Neurophysiol 1:455, 1949.
43. Nauta, WJH: The problem of the frontal lobe: A reinterpretation. J Psychiatr Res 8:167, 1971.
44. Olds, J and Milner, P: Positive reinforcement produced by electrical stimulation of septal area and other regions of rat brain. J Comp Physiol Psychol 47:417, 1954.
45. Papez, JW: A proposed mechanism of emotion. Arch Neurol Psychiat 38:725, 1937.
46. Poeck, K and Pilleri, G: Release of hypersexual behaviour due to lesion in the limbic system. Acta Neurol Scand 41:233, 1965.
47. Pribram, KH: Languages of the Brain. Experimental Paradoxes of Principles in Neuropsychology. Prentice-Hall, Englewood Cliffs, NJ, 1971.
48. Pribram, KH and Melges, FT: Psychophysiological basis of emotions. In Vinken, PJ and Bruyn, GW (eds): Handbook of Clinical Neurology, vol 3. Elsevier-North Holland, New York, 1969, pp 316-342.
49. Redgrave, P and Dean, P: Intracranial self-stimulation. Br Med Bull 37:141, 1981.
50. Reeves, AG and Plum, F: Hyperphagia, rage and dementia accompanying a ventromedial hypothalamic neoplasm. Arch Neurol 20:616, 1969.
51. Roland, PE: Astereognosis. Arch Neurol 33:543, 1976.
52. Rossi, GF: Brainstem facilitating influences on EEG synchronization. Experimental findings and observations in man. Acta Neurochir 13:257, 1965.
53. Satz, P: Pathological left-handedness: An explanatory model. Cortex 8:121, 1972.

54. Scoville, WB and Milner, B: Loss of recent memory after bilateral hippocampal lesions. J Neurol Neurosurg Psychiatry 20:11, 1957.

55. Stuss, DT and Benson, DF: The Frontal Lobes. Raven Press, New York, 1986.

56. Teuber, HL: The riddle of frontal lobe function in man. In Warren, JM and Akert, K (eds): The Frontal Granular Cortex and Behavior. McGraw-Hill, New York, 1964, pp 410–444.

57. Thomas, A and Chess, S: Temperament and Development. Brunner/Mazel, New York, 1977.

58. Thomas, A, Chess, S, and Birch, HG: Temperament and Behavior Disorders in Children. New York University Press, New York, 1968.

59. Victor, M, Adams, RD, and Collins, GH: The Wernicke-Korsakoff Syndrome. FA Davis, Philadelphia, 1971.

60. Weiss, G and Hechtman, LT: Hyperactive Children Grown Up. Guilford Press, New York, 1986.

61. White, LE and Hain, RF: Anorexia in association with a destructive lesion of the hypothalamus. Arch Pathol 68:275, 1959.

62. Whitehouse, PJ, et al: Alzheimer's disease and senile dementia: Loss of neurons in the basal forebrain. Science 215:1237, 1982.

63. Witelson, SF and Pallie, W: Left hemisphere specialization for language in the newborn: Neuroanatomical evidence of asymmetry. Brain 96:641, 1973.

Chapter 3

Mental Status Evaluation

New Learning
Visual Memory (Hidden Objects)
Remote Memory
Constructional Ability
Reproduction Drawing
Drawing to Command
Higher Cognitive Processes

The neurobehavioral disorders are complex processes to evaluate clinically and often present a confusing picture to the inexperienced examiner. The symptoms can be easily overlooked or minimized, such as often happens with the vague anxiety and subjective complaints of memory difficulty in the patient with early dementia. Organic behavioral symptoms can also be misinterpreted as manifestations of functional psychiatric disorder (e.g., the paranoid aggressive behavior, impaired comprehension, and inappropriate speech of Wernicke's aphasia). And, at times, the symptoms may be unrecognized when associated with more striking physical findings (e.g., an apraxia in a patient with hemiparesis). It is an unfortunate fact that even in patients with documented neurologic injury or disease many cognitive and emotional organic sequelae are not fully appreciated during the initial hospital evaluation. We have seen patients with mild aphasia, memory deficits, or constructional impairment after neurosurgical procedures; impaired attention and heightened irritability after head trauma; or mood fluctuations and emotional lability following central nervous system infection who have been discharged from the hospital after physical recovery from the acute stage of the injury or illness without recognition of these neurobehavioral changes. Such patients often have appreciable difficulty in readjusting socially and vocationally because of their deficits; they become frustrated, anxious, and depressed both because of their basic neurobehavioral deficits and because of the physician's failure to recognize and adequately explain the difficulties. The families also experience frustration and confusion when they do not understand the patient's inability to resume normal activities or his subtle change in personality.

An early evaluation of neurobehavioral status in such patients will document any cognitive and emotional residua. Such documentation helps to delineate any subtle disability more fully and will serve as the basis for counseling both the patient and his family. This precludes the development of misunderstanding and promotes appropriate posthospitalization management. The data gained from a complete mental status examination are also valuable for planning subsequent social and vocational rehabilitation, if indicated. All patients with known brain disease or injury should receive a definitive mental status examination as outlined in the pages to follow. Those patients who demonstrate abnormal findings on the screening mental status exam should then be referred for more comprehensive evaluation by a consultant specializing in the area of the detected deficit (e.g., speech pathologist for the aphasic patient, psychiatrist for the individual with associated or reactive emotional disorder, neuropsychologist for the patient requiring a more comprehensive evaluation and rehabilitation planning).

In our clinical practice, it has become increasingly apparent that there are many demonstrable neurobehavioral problems within the population of patients having apparently functional complaints. Organic brain disease frequently presents initially in the guise of either subtle or not-so-subtle behavioral and emotional changes. This is particularly true of frontal and temporal lobe tumors, undetected temporal lobe seizures, hydrocephalus, and cortical atrophy. We have also seen patients with acute focal left hemisphere strokes or subdural hematomas whose resulting receptive aphasia and associated agitation and paranoia were initially diagnosed in the emergency room as "acute schizophrenic reaction." Some patients with acute confusional states secondary to metabolic imbalance or drug toxicity are also prime candidates for misdiagnosis because they frequently show psychoticlike symptoms. Only a thorough review of medical records and a careful examination will reveal the organic nature of the disorder. Because neurologic disease so frequently masquerades as functional illness, we feel that all patients with a major psychiatric diagnosis should be screened with a complete mental status examination. This is particularly true in those cases in which the psychiatric symptomatology is acute in onset or is superimposed upon a life history of relatively stable normal emotional functioning. It is far more efficacious in terms of time and money to spend 15 to 30 min additional time with the patient, administering a complete mental status examination in search of possible organic etiology, than to embark upon an expensive and lengthy regimen of psychiatric treatment. We have seen a number of patients who have undergone long periods of outpatient psychotherapy, psychotropic medication, electroshock, and psychiatric hospitalization, who have shown clear evidence of primary central nervous system disease that was later verified by neurodiagnostic procedures.

Another group in whom a complete mental status evaluation may prove invaluable comprises patients with no previous history of brain disease who have vague and subjective complaints such as anxiety, a lack of concentration, memory deficits, or a loss of interest in family or work. Any such complaint should alert the clinician to the possibility of organic disease, even in the absence of clear-cut physical findings. A number of neurobehavioral disorders, notably the early stages of dementia or confusional state, initially present with primarily behavioral and cognitive symptoms. In such cases, the clinician must be prepared to make an often difficult differential diagnosis between functional and organic etiologies. The results of the mental status examination in such patients are often as valuable in making the correct diagnosis as are most other neurodiagnostic procedures including the CT scan, MRI scan, or EEG. Because the behavioral and cognitive findings often appear before overt physical symptoms, the mental status examination will often reveal diagnostic abnormalities prior to any indication of pathology on the standard neurologic examination.

In general, we believe that the following broad categories of patients should receive at least a screening mental status examination:

1. Patients with documented central nervous system disease or injury of any type and degree.
2. Patients with primary major psychiatric diagnoses.
3. Patients with suspected neurologic disease, even (or especially) if the diagnosis cannot be made on the basis of a standard physical and neurologic examination.
4. Patients presenting with vague subjective behavioral, cognitive, or physical complaints that cannot be substantiated from physical and neurologic examination.
5. Any patient noted to have an unexplained change in physical behavior, emotional status, or cognitive behavior.

Although the examination as outlined in the following pages may seem to be lengthy and time-consuming, with familiarity and experience one can administer a full exam in 30 to 60 min. The experienced examiner will find that the exam can be tailored to the individual patient and usually performed in 10 to 15 min. The value of the information it provides far exceeds the cost of the time expended in its administration.

The following pages provide a broad, yet relatively concise, outline of a medical history and mental status examination designed for use with patients having known or suspected organic brain syndromes. We believe that all neurologists, psychiatrists, psychologists, and well-trained primary care physicians should be familiar with the administration and interpretation of these important techniques.

MEDICAL AND SOCIAL HISTORY

As in any area of medicine, the history is extremely important in the evaluation of patients with organic brain syndromes. This aspect of the evaluation process should never be minimized in favor of the physical or laboratory examinations. It is often only from details in the history that organic disease may be accurately differentiated from functional disorders or from atypical lifelong patterns of behavior. As an example of the latter differential, we have not infrequently seen inexperienced residents make an initial misdiagnosis of dementia based on abnormalities noted during a cursory mental status examination, only to find after a careful social history that the patient had completed only 4 years of formal education.

If the patient is able to provide a history, even if memory problems and confabulation make the examiner suspicious of the obtained data's validity, an initial medical and social history should be obtained directly. This provides an opportunity to observe the patient's thinking and behavior under a situation of minimal stress and may offer historical information unavailable elsewhere (e.g., the family being unaware that the patient had contracted syphilis during an overseas military assignment and had been inadequately treated because of the pressures of combat necessities). In addition, this period of observation allows the careful observer to make a subjective assessment of the patient's interaction, attention, memory, language, and general behavior. Many patients are unable to provide a coherent and useful history; in these situations, the history must also be taken from a reliable family member or friend. This is generally possible; however, in many large public hospitals there may be a dearth of family or visitors for some patients. Unfortunately, these are often the patients with apparent chronic alcoholism, progressive dementia, or acute confusional states who find their way to public clinics and wards. It is virtually impossible to obtain valid histories from such persons. In such cases, obtaining medical records from previous hospitalizations and telephoning the patient's family to determine the necessary medical and social information are required. Despite the apparent aversion of some young physicians to do this type of "medical social work," the value of the obtained information to the patient's evaluation and management far outweighs the minor inconveniences involved. If available, social workers may be utilized to aid in the compilation of data from geographically scattered hospitals and family members.

There are specific aspects of the medical and social history that are especially important in the evaluation of patients with organic brain syndromes. The outline below contains the essential framework for a comprehensive evaluation.

 I. Medical history
  A. Description of present illness
   1. Nature of onset
   2. Duration of illness
   3. Characterization of the course of the illness
   4. Description of behavioral changes associated with illness

    B. Other relevant neurobehavioral data
       1. Unusual or bizarre behavior (e.g., nocturnal wanderings, paranoia, hallucinations)
       2. Attention and concentration problems
       3. Recent onset of speech or language problems
       4. Memory difficulty
       5. Evidence of poor social judgment (obtained from someone other than the patient)
       6. Difficulty with geographic orientation (i.e., getting lost or inability to find items)
       7. Recent onset of reading, writing, calculating difficulties
       8. Apathy, neglect, and lack of interest or motivation
    C. Psychiatric symptoms
       1. Depression
       2. Paranoia
       3. Hallucinations
       4. Delusions
       5. Anxiety and agitation
    D. Past medical history
       1. Previous neurologic or psychiatric disease
       2. Significant head trauma
       3. Seizures
       4. Other medical diseases requiring hospitalization
    E. Birth and developmental history
       1. Prenatal, perinatal, or postnatal brain damage
       2. Delays in normal development
         a. Motor
         b. Language
         c. Intellectual
         d. Academic
    F. Family history
       1. Presence of neurologic or psychiatric disease in another family member. Obtain diagnosis and nature of the disease
       2. Familial neurologic disease (e.g., Huntington's chorea)
       3. Family predilection for a particular disease process that may involve the central nervous system (e.g., hypertension and cerebrovascular disease)
       4. Cause of and age at death of parents and siblings
II. Social history
    A. Social development
       1. Abnormalities in behavior
       2. Family and peer interaction
       3. Intellectual development
    B. Educational history

1. Highest educational level attained
2. Nature of any training following high school
3. Specific or general school problems (e.g., "slow learner," dyslexic)
4. Reason for terminating education
C. Vocational history
  1. Present occupation
    a. Length of current job
    b. Nature of job responsibilities
  2. Types of previous jobs. Note upward or downward mobility
  3. Frequency of job changes. Note reasons for leaving
  4. Any recent difficulties with work
    a. Type
    b. Severity
  5. Toxic exposure
D. Other relevant data
  1. Adequacy of social adjustment
  2. Nature of specific social, behavioral, or emotional problems
  3. Use (duration, frequency, and quantity) of
    a. Alcohol
    b. Tobacco
    c. Licit and illicit drugs
  4. Family's description of the current problem

MENTAL STATUS EXAMINATION

After completing the history and the routine physical or neurologic examination, the physician should next administer the mental status examination. In some cases, a rapid screening evaluation will suffice, whereas with other patients a more comprehensive assessment of a wider range of functions is necessary. The material presented in the following pages can be readily adapted to either the brief screening or a more comprehensive evaluation. Those items marked with an asterisk are considered necessary and should be administered to all patients. The remaining items provide a means of more thoroughly evaluating a wider range of functioning.

The physician must recognize that the mental status examination is organized in a systematic and hierarchical fashion. The higher cognitive functions (e.g., verbal abstraction or calculating ability) rely on the integrity of more basic functions (e.g., attention or language). Thus, impairment of these basic functions will interfere with the ability to validly assess higher functions. For example, the patient with disturbed attention and vigilance secondary to an acute confusional state will be unable to perform validly on most parts of the mental status exam because of his inability to concentrate and assimilate details. Similarly, verbal memory or other functions relying on language cannot be objectively evaluated in the patient with aphasia. Accordingly, the examiner must not haphazardly sample various aspects of neurobehavioral functioning as this will result both in confusing results and in potentially erroneous conclusions. The mental status outline that follows has been placed in the hierarchical order that both neurobehavioral theory and clinical use suggest is most efficacious. Those readers desiring a more complete review of the administration, interpretation, and clinical implications of the mental status exam are referred to Strub and Black.[4]

Behavior

During the examination, the physician should make a systematic observation of the patient's appearance, behavior, and mood. This is important because (1) some behavioral syndromes are associated with particular neurologic lesions (e.g., the denial and neglect syndrome associated with right hemispheric lesion); (2) behavioral observations are extremely helpful in making the differential diagnosis between functional and organic processes; (3) findings on the formal structured aspects of the mental status exam (e.g., memory or abstract reasoning) must be interpreted in light of the patient's behavior, including mood and cooperation; and (4) a significant behavioral disturbance will adversely affect formal testing (e.g., a floridly schizophrenic patient will perform poorly on structured memory testing because of inattention, tangential thinking, and intrusions).

The purpose of this aspect of the evaluation is to provide an objective framework to aid the examiner in systematically observing behavior. Our primary concern here is with the identification and description of organically based behavioral changes; readers desiring a more extensive psychiatric orientation are referred to the many excellent texts in that field.

Physical Appearance

Patients with either functional or organic disorders may demonstrate characteristic patterns of appearance. Classic examples range from that of the patient with unilateral neglect who neglects or denies one side of the body (failing to shave, wash, dress, or even recognize the presence of that side of the body) to the bizarre clothing styles affected by some chronic schizophrenics.

Assessment of the following aspects of physical appearance is important and should be systematically reviewed and recorded:

I. General appearance
   A. Appropriateness of appearance for age

    B. Posture
    C. Facial expression
    D. Eye contact
  II. Personal cleanliness
    A. Skin
    B. Hair
    C. Nails
    D. Teeth
    E. Beard
    F. Indications of unilateral neglect
  III. Habits of dress
    A. Type of clothing
    B. Cleanliness of clothing
    C. Care in dressing
    D. Evidence of unilateral neglect
  IV. Motor activity
    A. General activity level
    B. Abnormal posturing (tics, grimaces, bizarre gestures, and other involuntary movements)

Mood and General Emotional Status

The term mood in this context refers to the prevailing emotional feeling expressed by the patient during the course of the mental status examination. Moods tend to be more persistent and are usually less intense than are the more specific emotional responses to particular situations. Emotional status is a term that encompasses the totality of the patient's emotional response and behavior. Both organic (e.g., frontal lobe disease) and functional (e.g., reactive depression) disorders may be manifested as a disturbance of mood and emotional status and can often be differentiated by their rather characteristic patterns. Accordingly, a careful and systematic review of these behavior areas is important for the interpretation of mental status exam findings, for the identification of organically based behavioral change, and for assistance in the differential diagnosis of functional and organic disease.

The following outline provides a framework for a brief evaluation of emotional status.

  I. Mood
    A. Mood normal to the situation
    B. Feeling of sadness or depression (hopelessness, grief, loss)
    C. Feeling of elation (inappropriate optimism or boastfulness)
    D. Apathy or lack of appropriate concern
    E. Stability or fluctuations of mood

  F. Mood inappropriate to the situation, or mood expressed is not consistent with the patient's thought content

II. Emotional status

 A. Degree of cooperation with the examiner

 B. Anxiety

 C. Suspiciousness

 D. Depression

 E. Anger

 F. Insight

 G. Emotional responses inappropriate to specific situations

 H. Reality testing

  1. Delusions (false beliefs)

  2. Illusions (misperceptions of real stimuli)

  3. Hallucinations (subjective sensory experiences without actual environmental stimuli)

  4. Paranoid thinking

 I. Indications of specific neurotic symptomatology

  1. Phobias

  2. Chronic anxiety (object and degree)

  3. Obsessive-compulsive thinking or behavior

 J. Abnormalities in language or speech

  1. Neologisms (personal formation and use of a new word without meaning except to patient)

  2. Flight of ideas in thinking and speaking

  3. Loose (tangential) associations in thinking and speaking

Levels of Consciousness*

  Before embarking on any formal mental status testing, the physician must initially assess the patient's basic level of consciousness. This will determine the patient's capability of relating to the examiner and the external environment. Anyone with an altered level of consciousness will inevitably demonstrate depressed functioning of some degree on various parts of the mental status examination.

TERMINOLOGY

  Although many terms have been used to describe the basic states or levels of consciousness, we have found the following terms to be most appropriate descriptive labels:

  Alertness. This state implies that the patient is awake and normally

---

*Administer to all patients.

aware of both internal and external stimuli. He is able to respond to such stimuli except in cases of paralysis.

Lethargy or Somnolence. In this state the patient fails to maintain normal alertness and will drift into sleep unless specifically stimulated. Both awareness of the external environment and purposeful spontaneous movements are considerably reduced. When aroused, the lethargic patient is generally unable to sustain a state of alertness, often fails to attend closely to the examiner, and will lose the train of thought in conversation. This impairment in the normal level of alertness will hinder performance on the formal mental status tasks of memory, comprehension, calculations, and abstract reasoning. Accordingly, if the complete mental status exam is carried out with the lethargic patient, the results of specific findings must be interpreted with considerable caution and only in light of the patient's altered level of consciousness.

Obtundation. Obtundation denotes the stage between lethargy and stupor. The obtunded patient is difficult to arouse and usually confused. Repeated stimulation is necessary to maintain any level of cooperation. Valid mental status testing is usually impossible.

Stupor or Semicoma. This term is used to describe patients who are not self-alerting and respond only to rather persistent and vigorous external stimulation. The stuporous patient does not rouse spontaneously and when aroused by the examiner is incapable of normal alertness or interaction.

Coma. The term coma has traditionally been reserved to describe the state of those patients who cannot be aroused. Coma may be defined as a state in which there is a total absence of behavioral response to stimulation; in this sense it is an absolute end point on the continuum of consciousness or arousability. The reader interested in a more detailed discussion of the clinical, pathologic, and theoretical aspects of altered states of consciousness is referred to Fisher[1] and Plum and Posner.[2]

These five terms are general and qualitative, encompassing a wide range of possible points on the spectrum of consciousness. The use of such terms in isolation (e.g., "The patient was lethargic") lacks the objectivity and reliability that can be achieved with a more complete assessment and rating scheme. We suggest that any qualitative term such as "stupor" be amended with a series of short, behaviorally related statements that more accurately document the patient's actual response.

EVALUATION

First, determine the intensity and type of stimulation needed to arouse the patient by (1) calling the patient by name in a normal conversational tone, (2) calling in a loud voice, (3) lightly touching the arm, (4) vigorously shaking the patient's shoulder, and (5) using painful stimulation. Second, describe the patient's behavioral response, including (1) degree and quality of movement, (2) content and coherence of speech, (3) comprehension, (4) presence of eye opening and eye contact with the examiner, and (5) quality of alertness and interaction. Finally, describe what the patient does on cessation of stimulation. This qualitative and quantitative description provides much more usable data on the patient's level of consciousness, arousability, and capacity for interaction than the simple terms "lethargy" or "stupor." Charting the level of consciousness in the progress notes allows both the medical and the nursing staff to assess and monitor rapid fluctuations in consciousness. These changes may often be of considerable clinical significance, as in the patient with a progressive subdural hematoma, with a stroke in evolution, or in recovery from neurosurgery.

Attention

Having documented the patient's basic level of consciousness, the examiner must next carefully assess the patient's ability to sustain attention over time. This ability must be determined before evaluating the more complex functions of memory, new learning, and problem solving because it is frustrating to both patient and examiner, as well as a waste of time, to attempt to assess higher cognitive functions in a patient who is continually distracted by cars in the street, the play of light and shadow on the office wall, or other irrelevant stimuli.

Attention refers to the ability to focus on a specific stimulus without being distracted by extraneous stimuli. Attention differs from alertness, which is a more basic arousal state in which the patient is awake and responsive to *any* environmental stimulus. The patient who is alert but inattentive will tend to be attracted by a novel sound or movement in the room, but will be incapable of selectively *sustaining* attention to the appropriate stimulus. Thus, attention presupposes alertness, whereas alertness does not necessarily imply attentiveness. Vigilance (or concentration) refers to the patient's ability to sustain attention for long periods. The ability to concentrate is important in carrying out intellectual tasks, in learning, and especially for functioning in academic situations. For the purpose of the mental status examination, testing vigilance for a period of 30 sec is sufficient. Information regarding the environmental aspects of vigilance (e.g., ability to concentrate for extended periods on a demanding job) may be determined from the history.

OBSERVATION*

Basic alertness has been evaluated during that part of the examination concerning levels of consciousness. A careful observation of the patient's

---

*Administer to all patients.

general behavior, interaction with the examiner, and ability to maintain a logical conversation will provide valuable information regarding general attentiveness. Specifically note any evidence of distractability, difficulty in attending to the examiner, and inability to sustain attention for an extended period.

HISTORY*

Information regarding problems in concentrating on the job or on routine tasks can generally be obtained from the patient or his family. In fact, this is often a presenting complaint, as will be discussed in the clinical chapters. Simple questioning of the patient regarding difficulties in attending (attention) or concentrating (vigilance) often reveals evidence of problems even when the information is not given spontaneously.

DIGIT REPETITION*

A quantifiable measure of the patient's basic level of attention can be readily made by utilizing the digit repetition test. The use of this test, of course, presumes that the patient is alert, has sufficient comprehension to understand the task, and has language that is sufficiently intact to say the numbers. Adequate performance on this test indicates that the patient is able to attend to verbal stimuli and to sustain attention for the time necessary to comprehend and repeat the digits.

Directions. Tell the patient, "I am going to say some simple numbers. Listen carefully, and when I am finished, say the same numbers after me." State the digits in a normal tone of voice at a rate of one digit per second. Take care not to group digits either in pairs (e.g., 2 – 4, 6 – 9) or in sequences that could serve as an aid to repetition (e.g., as in the telephone number format, 376 – 8439). Numbers should be presented randomly without natural sequence (i.e., not 2 – 4 – 6 – 8). Begin with a two-number sequence and continue until the patient fails.

Test Content
3 – 7
7 – 4 – 9
8 – 5 – 2 – 7
2 – 9 – 6 – 8 – 3
5 – 7 – 2 – 9 – 4 – 6
8 – 1 – 5 – 9 – 3 – 6 – 2
3 – 9 – 8 – 2 – 5 – 1 – 4 – 7
7 – 2 – 8 – 5 – 4 – 6 – 7 – 3 – 9

---

*Administer to all patients.

Interpretation. The typical patient of average intelligence can repeat five to seven digits without difficulty. The inability to repeat less than five digits by a nonretarded patient without obvious aphasia is strongly suggestive of defective attention.

"A" TEST FOR VIGILANCE

The random letter test is a simple test of vigilance that can be readily administered in the office or at the bedside. This test consists of a series of random letters among which a target letter appears with greater than random frequency. The patient is required to indicate whenever the target letter is spoken by the examiner.

Directions. Tell the patient, "I am going to read you a long series of letters; whenever you hear the letter A, indicate by tapping the desk with this pencil." Read the following list of letters in a normal tone of voice at a rate of one letter per second.

Test Content
L T P E A O A I C T D A L A A
AN I A B F S A M R Z E O A D
P A K L A U C J T O E A B A A
Z Y F M U S A H E V A A R A T

Interpretation. Normals should complete the task without errors. Less than perfect performance raises the suspicion of impaired vigilance. Typical organic errors include (1) failure to indicate when the target letter has been presented (error of omission), (2) indication made when a nontarget letter has been presented (error of commission), and (3) failure to discontinue tapping with the presentation of subsequent nontarget letters (perseveration).

Language*

Language is the basic tool of human communication; as such it is crucial both to the patient's general functioning and in assessing most areas of cognitive functioning. Accordingly, the integrity of language functions must be evaluated early in the course of the mental status examination. Acquired language disturbances (aphasia) have been well studied, as they are common sequelae of both focal and diffuse brain disease. The characteristic patterns of specific aphasic disturbances and their distinct neuroanatomic correlations are covered in Chapter 8, Neurobehavioral Syndromes Associated with Focal Brain Lesions.

---

*Administer to all patients.

This section deals with a systematic approach to the evaluation of language disorders. During this part of the examination, particular attention must be paid to spontaneous speech, language comprehension, ability to repeat, and facility in naming. Reading and writing are additional important areas of language functioning that may be assessed clinically after completion of the verbal language evaluation. The aphasic patient is almost always agraphic (has lost the ability to write) and is commonly alexic (has lost the ability to read); accordingly, in the aphasic patient, the reading and writing assessment may be abbreviated.

HANDEDNESS*

As handedness and cerebral dominance for language are closely related, the patient's handedness should be determined before language testing. Initially ask the patient whether he is right- or left-handed and whether he has been forced to change hands because of family or school pressure. Also, ask whether he has any tendency to use the opposite hand for any skilled activity. Observe the patient using a paper and pencil, fork, stirring coffee, or carrying out other unilateral activities. A family history of left-handedness or ambidexterity is important, as dominance is strongly affected by hereditary factors. There appears to be a spectrum of handedness ranging from strong right-handedness to moderately strong left-handedness, with weakly lateralized dominance, mixed dominance, and ambidexterity occupying central positions. (See Chapter 8 for an extended discussion of this topic.)

SPONTANEOUS SPEECH

The first step in formal language testing is to carefully listen to the patient's spontaneous speech. If he offers no spontaneous speech, ask relatively uncomplicated open-ended questions that require more than a single world or phrase in response. Requests such as "Tell me why you are in the hospital," or "Tell me something about your work," are appropriate. Care must be taken to avoid questions that can be answered with a "yes," "no," or shake of the head.

The examiner should note the following aspects:

1. Is speech output present?
2. Is the speech dysarthric?
3. Is there evidence of aphasia?

---

*Administer to all patients.

Aphasic language is characterized by some or all of the following errors: errors of grammatical structure, difficulty in finding and using the appropriate word (anomia), word substitutions (paraphasia), and impaired comprehension.

COMPREHENSION*

The patient's ability to comprehend language must be assessed in a structured fashion without reliance on his ability to produce speech. A frequent error made by inexperienced examiners is to evaluate language comprehension by asking complex or open-ended questions. This type of evaluation taxes the entire language system and is not a measure of verbal comprehension in isolation. The two most efficacious ways of testing comprehension are to require the patient to follow pointing commands and to respond to questions that can be answered with yes or no.

Asking the patient to point to single named objects in the room, body parts, or objects is an excellent way to quantify single-word comprehension. If the patient is capable of performing on the single-word level, the task may be increased in complexity by gradually adding to the number of items in the sequence until the patient fails. The mildly aphasic patient may be capable of responding at the one- or two-word level with consistent accuracy but fail without exception at the three-word level. As both the quality and nature of performance will vary among patients and between examinations, for clarity the patient's responses should be reported as follows: "Patient consistently pointed to two items in series but failed all trials at three items."

Next, a series of questions requiring a simple yes or no response that gradually increase in difficulty should be asked. "Is it raining today?" or "Will a stone float on water?" are examples of the general type of question we suggest. Before beginning this task, ensure that the patient is capable of expressing both yes and no, either verbally or by gesture (or by any other nonverbal means). The items should initially be simple, to gain a baseline of comprehension; the task can then be made as complex as necessary to obtain a ceiling or consistent failure level. Several questions should be used. The correct answers to the questions should alternate randomly from yes to no, as perseveration is common in patients with brain dysfunction, and it is not infrequent for a patient to respond "yes" to multiple questions without any conception of the correct answers.

---

*Administer to all patients.

REPETITION*

The ability to repeat spoken language is linguistically and, to an extent, anatomically distinct from other language functions. Because this function may be impaired or spared in isolation, it is important to test repetition specifically. Dysfunction of any of the steps of auditory processing, verbal retention, disturbed speech production, or disconnection between the receptive and expressive language areas will disrupt the ability to repeat verbal material. Therefore, impaired repetition performance is clinically significant but not pathognomonic of a specific language disturbance.

Testing should be carried out with verbal material of increasing difficulty. Begin with single-syllable words and proceed to complex sentences. We recommend the following items, which provide an appropriate range of difficulty. Merely tell the patient to repeat the word or sentence after you say it.

1. Ball
2. Help
3. Airplane
4. Hospital
5. Mississippi River
6. The little boy went home.
7. We all went over there together.
8. The old car wouldn't start on Tuesday morning.
9. The short fat boy dropped the china vase.
10. Each fight readied the boxer for the championship bout.

Record the level of complexity at which the patient failed to repeat accurately. In addition, the examiner should listen and note any paraphasia, grammatical errors, omissions, and added material.

OBJECT NAMING*

The ability to name objects to visual confrontation is a very basic language function that is almost always impaired in most types of aphasia. Problems in word finding may be detected by listening to the patient's spontaneous speech, asking the patient to describe a picture, or asking an open-ended question. Anomia (loss of the ability to accurately name objects) is best tested by asking the patient to name specific items. If time

---

*Administer to all patients.

allows, several categories of objects should be used because some aphasic patients show an interesting disparity between the ability to name items in various categories (e.g., colors, shapes). The ability to name items is closely related to their frequency in language usage (e.g., *car* is far easier to name than *philodendron*), so it is important to employ both common (high frequency) and uncommon (low frequency) items in the confrontational naming test. Many aphasics will name common items with relative facility, only to have considerable difficulty with less frequently used items, demonstrating hesitancy, paraphasic errors, and circumlocutions. The examiner should record both correct and incorrect responses as well as the nature of specific errors (e.g., refusal, paraphasic response, or circumlocution). A list of specific items for naming in order of frequency by object category is available in Strub and Black.[4]

Paraphasias are errors in word usage that are common in aphasia. They may be substitutions for the correct word (e.g., "I drove home in my *pen*") or contain substituted syllables (e.g., "I drove home in my *lar*"). A third type of paraphasia is the neologistic (new word) paraphasia, which is the substitution of a totally non-English word (e.g., "I drove home in my *burts*"). Paraphasic speech is easily recognized by the careful listener and can be evaluated during all aspects of the mental status examination. The examiner should note the frequency and type of paraphasic errors made by the patient.

READING AND WRITING

After the evaluation of verbal language, a brief clinical assessment should be made of the patient's ability to read and write. The initial reading evaluation should be made with single simple words, progressing to phrases and then sentences. Similarly, writing can be easily tested by having the patient write first words and then sentences on command. Assessment of these areas, of course, presumes that the patient has sufficiently intact language skills to understand the nature of the task.

Memory*

Because disturbances in memory are frequently the initial complaint of early organic brain disease and because they often have the most significantly disabling impact on the patient's ability to function effectively in society, careful attention should be paid to memory testing. Memory is not a unitary process, and each of its various aspects must be assessed in some detail. From this evaluation, the examiner will be able to determine the

---

*Administer to all patients.

type of memory disturbance (if any), the cause of the disturbance (organic or functional), the degree of memory loss, and the probable impact of the deficit on the patient's ability to function in a social or vocational role. Patients with language disorders cannot be validly tested with memory tests using verbal material but must be tested using nonverbal material. The valid assessment of the patient's recent memory requires that any question asked by the examiner be verifiable from a source other than the patient. There is no use asking a patient what he ate for lunch, where he attended high school, or to name the mayor of his hometown if the examiner is unable to ascertain the accuracy of the patient's responses. Many patients with organic disease will deny their memory disorders and produce confabulated responses that superficially appear perfectly appropriate to the naive examiner.

ORIENTATION*

The patient's ability to orient himself with respect to person (who he is), time (including day of week, date), and place (where he is) is important preliminary information. Orientation to time and place is actually an example of recent memory or the ability of the patient to learn and retain these ongoing events in his life. If a patient is not fully oriented, this finding strongly suggests a significant recent memory deficit. The examiner should note and record in a quantified way the integrity of the patient's orientation in each of these three major areas.

IMMEDIATE RECALL (SHORT-TERM MEMORY)

Immediate recall is traditionally tested by the digit repetition task, which was covered in the section on Attention.

RECENT INCIDENTAL MEMORY

Recent incidental memory refers to the patient's ability to recall, on request, events that have occurred during the hours or days before the evaluation. Personal events or recent news events that the patient might reasonably be expected to know are appropriate.

NEW LEARNING*

This section evaluates the patient's ability to actively learn new material, a process that requires establishing new memories. Normal perform-

---

*Administer to all patients.

ance requires the integrity of the total memory system: recognition and registration of the initial verbal or visual input, retention and storage of the information, and recall or retrieval of that stimulus at a later time. An interruption of any one of these interrelated processes will impair new learning performance.

Four Unrelated Words*

Tell the patient, "I am going to tell you four words that I want you to remember. In a few minutes, I will ask you to recall the words." The four words we have used clinically because of their semantic, phonemic, and categorical diversity are:

1. Brown
2. Honesty
3. Tulip
4. Eyedropper

Ensure that the patient has understood and initially retained the four words by having him repeat them after presentation. Correct any initial errors made during this repetition. To eliminate the possibility of mental rehearsal (e.g., repeating the words to oneself mentally), provide verbal interference between presentation and requested recall. The examiner may wish to present the four words, conduct another verbal section of the examination, and then go back to this task and ask the patient to recall the four words. It is best to use either general conversation or recent incidental memory testing as a distractor rather than presenting another new learning task. Five minutes should elapse between the initial presentation and the request for recall. If the patient is unable to recall any of the four words, it is often possible to obtain an indication of some memory storage by the use of either semantic cues (e.g., "One word is a color"), phonemic cues utilizing syllabic components of the target word (e.g., "Hon . . ., hones . . ., honest. . . ."), or contextual cues (e.g., "A common flower in Holland is the _____ ?"). If this degree of cueing does not result in recall, the examiner may resort to asking the patient if he recognizes the target word within a series (e.g., "Was the color red, green, *brown*, or yellow?"). The average normal patient should have no difficulty remembering all four words.[3]

---

*Administer to all patients.

Verbal Story for Immediate or Delayed Recall

Tell the patient, "I am going to read you a short paragraph. Listen carefully, because when I finish reading, I want you to tell me everything that I told you." After reading the story, say, "Now tell me everything that you can remember of the story. Start at the beginning of the story and tell me all that happened." In the example below, the separate items in the story are indicated by slash (/) marks. As the patient retells the story, indicate the ideas recalled, errors, and confabulations.

It was July/and the Rogers/had packed/their four children/in the station wagon/and were off/on vacation./
They were taking/their yearly trip/to the beach/at Gulf Shores./
That year/they were making/a special/two-day stop/at the ill-fated/World's Fair/in New Orleans./
After a long day's drive/they arrived/at the motel/only to discover/that in their excitement/they had left/the twin boys/and their suitcases/in the front yard./

The story contains 27 relatively separate items of information. In our experience, the average patient should produce approximately 10 of these items (or paraphrases of the items) on immediate recall. This story can also be used to assess delayed recall by asking the patient to repeat the story and noting the amount of recall after 30 min.

VISUAL MEMORY (HIDDEN OBJECTS)

Nonverbal memory testing is especially useful in evaluating the memory of aphasics. The examiner may utilize any four or five small, easily recognizable objects that can be readily hidden in the patient's vicinity. The use of four or five objects provides a reasonable span for most patients. Hide the items while the patient is watching, naming each object as it is hidden. This ensures that the patient is attentive to the task and is aware of which object was hidden in a given place. After hiding the objects, the examiner should provide interfering stimulation by asking the patient routine questions or engaging him in general conversation. After 10 min, ask the patient to find each of the hidden objects. If he is unable to recall the location of any object, ask him to name the hidden objects. If he is unable to do so, ask him to find the objects by name or location.

The average patient should find each of the hidden objects after a 10-min delay without difficulty.

---

*Administer to all patients.

REMOTE MEMORY*

Tests in this section evaluate the patient's ability to recall personal and social events from his store of remote memories. As has been previously emphasized, the answer to any question asked regarding personal events must be verified by a reliable source to ensure validity. This area of memory functioning relates closely to both premorbid intelligence and educational level. The following categories of questions are provided as representative samples; each clinician should assemble his own battery of questions appropriate to his patient.

    I. Personal information
    II. Historical facts
        A. Name the last four Presidents.
        B. What was the last major war the United States fought?
        C. Famous people (e.g., who is Geraldine Ferraro?)

Constructional Ability*

Constructional tasks are frequently not included in the routine mental status examination despite their importance and proven clinical utility. Because problems in constructional performance are often present in the early stages of brain dysfunction and may appreciably aid in the differential diagnosis between organic and functional disorders, we strongly recommend their inclusion in the mental status examination of every patient with suspected organic brain disease.

Drawing to command and reproducing drawings from examples are the most easily administered and interpreted tests of constructional ability.

REPRODUCTION DRAWING*

We suggest that reproduction drawings be administered first when assessing constructional ability because of their apparent simplicity and familiarity. The drawings presented in Figure 3–1 are organized in order of increasing difficulty. Both two- and three-dimensional drawings are included because of the frequent discrepancies in the quality of performance on these two somewhat different tasks. Each design may be drawn carefully on a blank sheet of white paper. Under no circumstances should lined progress note paper, consultation forms, and other readily available but visually confusing paper be used. The patient should be told to draw a design (or picture) that looks just like the one drawn by the examiner. The

---

*Administer to all patients.

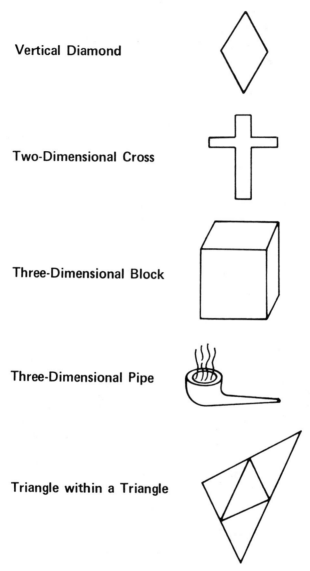

Figure 3-1. Test items for Reproduction Drawings Test.

five designs that we have found to be most useful clinically are shown in Figure 3-1.

A formal scoring system for assessing the quality of the patient's constructional performance is available in Strub and Black.[4] The examiner should rate the quality of each design, preferably on a four-point scale ranging from 0 (poor) to 3 (excellent).

Particular attention should be paid to any evidence of perseveration, rotations of more than 90 degrees, or "closing-in" (i.e., a tendency to either overlap parts of the stimulus design or to assimilate a part of the stimulus design into the reproduction).

DRAWING TO COMMAND*

Provide the patient with a blank sheet of paper and a pencil (or more ideally a felt-tip pen) and ask him to draw a picture of a clock with the numbers and hands on it, a daisy in a flower pot, and a house in perspective so that you can see two sides and the roof.

In general, any patient with evidence of perseveration, rotation, or rating scores of 0 or 1 on any of the reproduction drawings or drawings done to command should be considered as demonstrating constructional impairment.

Higher Cognitive Processes

Basic attention, language, and memory are the primary processes on which the higher intellectual abilities are developed. These basic functions are necessary, but are not in and of themselves sufficient, for the execution of more complex cognitive functions and the ability to function effectively within the environment. We include within the testable higher cognitive functions the following: abstract reasoning, problem solving, and arithmetic calculations. These complex functions represent the highest levels of intellectual functioning, and their evaluation often demonstrates evidence of the early effects of cortical damage before the more basic processes are impaired. Important information regarding the patient's ability to function within his social and vocational environment can often be extrapolated from a careful examination of these higher processes.

The following tests are recommended to evaluate a spectrum of relevant higher cognitive processes:

1. Proverb interpretation. The patient is required to interpret well-known proverbs (e.g., Rome wasn't built in a day).
2. Similarities. The patient is required to explain the essential similarity between two overtly different objects (e.g., fly and tree).
3. Calculations. All basic arithmetic processes (i.e., addition, subtraction, multiplication, and division) should be tested in both the verbal and graphic modalities.

---

*Administer to all patients.

SUMMARY

Following the mental status outline presented in this chapter enables the clinician to systematically evaluate those behavioral and cognitive functions that accurately differentiate patients with organic brain disease from those with functional disorders. In the organically affected patient it is often possible to elucidate the type, locus, and degree of disease. The mental status examination provides an excellent, albeit brief, description of the person's performance over a broad range of functions. Repeated examinations allow efficient comparisons for documenting improvement or deterioration. In some cases, the results of the mental status examination may be indicative of, or even pathognomonic for, a specific neurobehavioral disorder (e.g., Wernicke's aphasia or Alzheimer's disease). In this way the mental status examination can be as efficacious as any other neurodiagnostic procedure.

We have emphasized throughout this section the need to record both how a function was evaluated (i.e., the question asked or the command given) and what the patient's response was to each item. A composite mental status recording form is included in Strub and Black[4] to aid in this data recording. The use of such forms allows more efficient documentation of changes in patient's status over time and communication of findings to other professionals.

After completion of the mental status examination, the primary physician must determine whether further specialized evaluation is necessary, and, if so, which area should be emphasized.

REFERENCES

1. Fisher, CM: The neurological examination of the comatose patient. Acta Neurol Scand (Suppl) 36:1, 1969.
2. Plum, F and Posner, JB: The Diagnosis of Stupor and Coma, ed 3. FA Davis, Philadelphia, 1980.
3. Simpson, N, Black, FW, and Strub, RL: Memory assessment using the Strub-Black mental status examination and the Wechsler Memory Scale. J Clin Psychol 42:147, 1986.
4. Strub, RL, and Black, FW: Mental Status Examination in Neurology, ed 2. FA Davis, Philadelphia, 1985.

Chapter 4

Neuropsychology and Other Consultations

Trail Making Test
Category Test
Wisconsin Card Sorting Test
Proverbs Test
Finger Tapping Test
Wide Range Achievement Test (WRAT-R)
Minnesota Multiphasic Personality Inventory (MMPI)
ORGANIC "SOFT SIGNS"
COGNITIVE REMEDIATION
OTHER CONSULTATIONS
  Neurology
  Psychiatry
    Referral
    Evaluation
    Treatment
  Social Work
  Speech Pathology
    Referral
    Speech and Language Evaluation
    Treatment
  Physical and Occupational Therapy
  Other Related Professions

NEUROPSYCHOLOGIC EVALUATION

The following section is intended primarily as an introduction for physicians; however, clinical psychologists and others involved in the evaluation and management of patients with neurobehavioral problems may find it useful as a brief overview. Clinical neuropsychologists will find the information to be abbreviated. All readers interested in a more comprehensive review of this field and its applicability are referred to the several excellent texts mentioned throughout the chapter.

The field of clinical neuropsychology and its attendant literature have expanded greatly during the past 10 years, particularly since publication of the first edition of this text in 1981. Several consequences of this development have relevance for the practicing physician and the study of neurobehavioral disorders: (1) there are now more and better trained neuropsychologists who have a good understanding both of neuropsychological assessment and of its applications to the spectrum of neurologic syndromes; (2) neuropsychologists are increasingly available in settings where they can be used efficiently; (3) the field and its practitioners are becoming increasingly experienced and knowledgeable in dealing with a variety of neurologic conditions and in working in collaboration with physicians and other rehabilitation specialists; and (4) the neuropsychologic literature is both more abundant and more sophisticated. Because of the increasing impact of the neuropsychologist and neuropsychologic literature, this chapter is a brief overview of the potential contributions of such specialists for those physicians and others concerned with the management and study of patients having central nervous system disorders.

The clinical neuropsychologist uses a wide variety of standard psychometric tests and specialized neuropsychologic assessment procedures to provide both an intensive and a comprehensive evaluation of patients having known or suspected organic brain disease (organic mental disorders). Although not medically trained, neuropsychologists do have an academic background in neuroanatomy, physiology, and basic clinical neurology in addition to more traditional clinical psychology. The clinical neuropsychologist is primarily concerned with the identification, quantification, and description of those changes in cognition and emotion that are associated with brain dysfunction. Because of this specialized training, the neuropsychologist's main areas of interest and expertise are the relationships between disturbed human behavior and abnormal brain function. Accordingly, the neuropsychologist's activities can contribute to answering a variety of important neurologic questions, including differential diagnosis, localization of lesions (now of more theoretical than practical interest), objective assessments of level of disability or residual ability in a variety of relatively discrete cognitive areas, and the establishment of baseline measurements of behavior from which improvement or deterioration can be accurately gauged. The neuropsychologist has assumed an increasing role in the determination of mental and legal competence, as well as the determination of the degree of cognitive/social/vocational disability for purposes of civil court proceedings. An area of increasing interest within the field of neuropsychology is the provision of behavioral management recommendations and the development of specific remedial methods for the rehabilitation of the individual brain-damaged patient.[37,56]

The neuropsychologic evaluation, briefly defined, is an objective comprehensive assessment of a wide range of cognitive, adaptive, and emotional behaviors that reflect the adequacy (or inadequacy) of cerebral functioning. In essence, the neuropsychologic evaluation is a greatly expanded and objectified mental status examination. Whereas the mental status examination is designed to briefly (within 15 to 60 min) screen a variety of critical areas, the neuropsychologic evaluation assesses a wider variety of performance, in more depth, and over a longer time (2 to 6 hours). It differs from the mental status examination in that it generally uses tests and evaluation procedures that have been standardized using samples of either normal persons (e.g., Wechsler series of intelligence scales) or brain-damaged patients (e.g., Memory for Designs Test or the Trail Making Test). By means of these standardized measures, the individual patient's performance can be readily compared with that of normative groups. In addition the adequacy of the same patient's performance in a variety of different cognitive functions and modalities can be assessed. The objective and highly quantified nature of the most neuropsychologic tests aids in the detection of subtle changes in performances over time (e.g., the slow deterioration in dementia or improvements in specific cognitive functions after neurosurgery). Because of the wide range of performance assessed and the depth in which it is evaluated, the neuropsychologic evaluation may detect, early in the course of a disease, subtle deficits that are not apparent on the mental status examination.

The neuropsychologic evaluation has a number of advantages not shared by most standard neurodiagnostic techniques. It is a noninvasive procedure and has no risk of mortality or morbidity, making the evaluation useful in cases in which any risk is too great or when the probability of abnormal findings is so low that an invasive procedure is unwarranted (e.g., learning disability). The tests are inherently interesting to most patients and do not produce the possible adverse complications of anxiety and pain that result from some invasive procedures. The evaluation also provides important descriptive and prognostic information that other techniques cannot. This is especially true in the description of the effects of neurologic disease on the patient as a person and its probable impact on the patient's academic, social, and vocational adjustment.

The physician without ready access to a trained neuropsychologist can benefit from an evaluation made by a clinical psychologist who has had some experience in evaluating patients with brain disease. Such basic training is now included in many graduate programs and clinical internships.[11] It is especially helpful if the referring physician is familiar with the types of psychologic tests that are used, understands the nature and limitations of the data that can be provided by the psychologist, and knows how to interpret both the objective and subjective aspects of the reports. A review of the information below should greatly aid in this familiarization and interpretation.

Criteria for Referral

A. Patients for whom the physician requires further information concerning (1) diagnosis, (2) the effects of a well-verified lesion on behavior and social/vocational competence, and (3) prognosis and management should be referred for neuropsychologic evaluation.

B. Mild cognitive and behavioral disturbances frequently occur in the absence of any clear-cut physical signs of cerebral disease on the standard clinical neurologic exam; this is particularly true in cases of early dementia and in some cases of resolving head injury. A patient with dementia typically presents with vague behavioral complaints such as mental dullness, concentration problems, increasing apathy, loss of interest in job or family, chronic fatigue without apparent organic cause, depression, and subjective memory problems. Neuropsychologic evaluation of such patients can often contribute to an early diagnosis of dementia, help differentiate between dementia and depression, or determine the relative effects of organic and functional factors in a mixed disorder. The neuropsychologic evaluation can provide strong supporting data for the presumptive diagnosis of brain disease and thus serve as a basis for ordering more extensive and specific neurodiagnostic procedures.

C. Any patient with a known brain lesion should have a neuropsychologic evaluation as part of planning their rehabilitation program. Such lesions include head trauma, particularly significant closed head injury, a focal brain lesion, and lesions of neurosurgery (e.g., postaneurysm rupture). The comprehensive nature of the evaluation provides valuable information regarding the effect of the lesion on cognitive functioning, emotional status, behavior, and social adjustment. Both specific areas of impairment and residual abilities will be identified. This delineation of the patient's strengths and weaknesses is valuable in describing the effects of specific neurologic lesions on the individual and provides information critical for vocational and social rehabilitation.

D. Serial testing can provide reliable objective information regarding the speed and degree of recovery. Repeated evaluations can also be used to document deterioration in cases of progressive disease or to rule out such progression in equivocal cases. Neuropsychologic evaluations conducted before and after neurosurgery document the effects of the surgery on the patient's total functioning. The effects of any medical treatment (e.g., levodopa in parkinsonism or anticonvulsants in epilepsy) may also be readily demonstrated by neuropsychologic evaluations conducted before and after treatment is initiated. These changes over time are difficult to assess and impossible to quantify without adequate initial baseline data.

E. In any case of trauma or suspected brain damage involving litigation or compensation, the objective data obtained from the neuropsychologic evaluation are obviously of great value in documenting and describing the presence, absence, or degree of disability and vocational incapacity. There is considerable and increasing legal precedent for admission of the testimony of psychologists as expert witnesses in such cases.

The Neuropsychologic Report

The clinical information provided in the report by the neuropsychologist is summarized below.

DESCRIPTION

The report should contain a comprehensive description of the patient's current level of functioning in a wide range of cognitive, adaptive, personality, and behavioral areas. From the academic and social history and an analysis of the variation of performance on various tests, an estimate of the patient's premorbid level of functioning is made. By comparing the estimated premorbid level of function with current performance on standard tests, an accurate indication of deterioration in any of the areas assessed by the battery may be made. Comparison of the patient's performance in the major cognitive areas assessed reveals areas of deficient and residual ability. An overview of performance in each cognitive and emotional area is made. This describes current functioning, explains present behavior, determines the relative effects of organic and functional factors, and provides a baseline of data from which to judge future change. Statements should be made to document the effect of the patient's current neurologic disease and its associated deficits on his subsequent academic, vocational, and social adjustment. Assessments of mental competency and social independence are made in this section of the report

CATEGORIZATION

The section of the report regarding categorization provides information as to the presence or absence of brain dysfunction as well as the presence or absence of significant emotional disturbance. The differential diagnosis between a primary organic or a primary functional disorder is made. If significant effects of both organic and functional components are present, the relative importance and impact of each are discussed.

LOCALIZATION

Typically, performance on the neuropsychologic test battery can be analyzed to determine whether the brain dysfunction is diffuse or focal. Further analysis enables determination of the lateralization of the lesion to the right or left hemisphere and the localization of the lesion in the anterior or posterior regions of the hemisphere.

IMPRESSIONS AND PROGNOSIS

This section of the report is a synthesis of all data obtained during the evaluation. It should include a brief diagnostic statement, degree and nature of impairment, residual strengths, and hypothesized localization of the lesion when unknown (or corroboration of the locus of a known lesion with test findings). The social/vocational significance of the patient's deficits should be addressed. Based on the nature of the neurologic disease, the pattern and degree of cognitive and behavioral deficits documented during the neuropsychologic evaluation, and the type of treatment proposed, the probability and degree of expected recovery or course of deterioration is determined. As previously mentioned, serial evaluations some months apart greatly aid the ability to make valid prognostic statements in cases of either deterioration or recovery.

RECOMMENDATIONS

On the basis of all available data, recommendations for further ancillary evaluations, including those of psychiatry, speech pathology and audiology, occupational and physical therapy, social service, and specialized cognitive remediation professionals are made when warranted.

Components of the Neuropsychologic Evaluation

Russell[72] stated that there are two primary approaches to neuropsychologic assessment: the neurologic and the psychologic. The neurologic is modeled on the traditional symptom-oriented medical examination (as exemplified by Luria and Majovski[55]), whereas the psychologic is more strongly founded on an objective psychometric base (e.g., the Halstead-Reitan battery[70]). At present most neuropsychologic assessment combines some aspects of each approach in formulating a comprehensive battery. Three general methods of assessment can be identified at this time, each of which is to some degree a synthesis of the two primary philosophic approaches. These methods are (1) a standard battery such as the Halstead-Reitan or to a lesser degree the more controversial Luria-Nebraska;[30] (2) an eclectic, but standard, comprehensive battery selected from the range of available objective tests of cognitive function, with variations designed to meet the needs of the invidual cases;[53] and (3) an individualized battery designed to assess the deficits posed by each patient (e.g., an analytic or process approach).[84] We have found the eclectic approach to be the most useful for an objective, cost-effective, comprehensive evaluation of the range of cognitive and emotional problems demonstrated by brain-damaged patients. Such an approach retains the value of standard batteries, with the additional advantage of supplementing the battery with other well-standardized tests of cognitive and emotional functioning. See Lezak,[53] Grant and Adams,[36] and Russell[73] for more comprehensive reviews of this topic.

Specific tests used in the neuropsychologic evaluation will vary with the age of the patient, the nature of the medical problem and its symptoms, specific referral questions, and the particular approach of the psychologist. Virtually all such test batteries, however, will include objective tests of the following functions:

1. Behavior, attention, and mood
2. Intelligence, including general intelligence, verbal intelligence, and nonverbal intelligence
3. Language, including single word and sentence comprehension, auditory discrimination, repetition, visual confrontation naming, verbal fluency, and sentence construction
4. Memory, including verbal and nonverbal memory, short- and long-term memory, and new learning ability
5. Abstract ability, including verbal and nonverbal abstract reasoning, the ability to make conceptual shifts, and the ability to learn (including the ability to plan ahead and shift concepts rapidly and visual sequency)
6. Constructional ability, including paper-and-pencil reproduction, reproduction from memory, and other constructive tasks
7. Geographic orientation
8. Achievement, including reading, spelling, and arithmetic
9. Perceptual motor speed
10. Motor strength and coordination
11. Personality
12. Social functioning

Some specific tests that are commonly used in neuropsychologic evaluations and reported in standard reports are discussed below. This listing is by no means comprehensive and does not include many tests currently in use.

HALSTEAD-REITAN BATTERY

This comprehensive neuropsychologic battery includes tests of general intelligence, concept formation, expressive and receptive language, auditory perception, time perception, verbal and nonverbal memory, perceptual-motor speed, tactile performance, spatial relations, finger gnosis, double simultaneous stimulation, and personality.

The basic elements of the extended battery are (1) Wechsler Adult Intelligence Scale-Revised (see p. 79), (2) Category Test (conceptual learning via trial and error, see p. 87), (3) Trail Making Test (see p. 86), (4) Aphasia Screening Examination (naming, spelling, expressive and receptive language, reading, arithmetic, drawing, and left-right orientation), (5)

Rhythm Perception Test (perception of same or different tonal rhythms), (6) Speech Sound Perception Test (discrimination of similar sounding words), (7) Finger Tapping Test (see p. 88), (8) Tactile Performance Test (form-board requiring performance by the dominant and nondominant hand, both hands, and drawing of the stimulus from memory), and (9) Perceptual Examination (including evaluation of double simultaneous stimulation, finger agnosia, discrimination of fingertip number writing and tactile form recognition). In many cases, the Minnesota Multiphasic Personality Inventory (see p. 89) is administered as well.

The battery is a complex and quite expensive set of tests and apparatus. Testing demands considerable effort from both the examiner and examinee and requires from 5 to 10 hours of trained examiner time. The test results are typically interpreted by a supervising, highly trained clinical neuropsychologist.

An Impairment Index is derived from the patient's overall performance; this score has been demonstrated to accurately differentiate most organic from nonorganic conditions. In the hands of a well-trained examiner, the battery can also provide valuable information regarding the locus and nature of the lesion (e.g., intrinsic neoplasm vs. atrophy) and the effect of the neuropsychologic deficit on the patient's social and adaptive functioning.

Initially devised by Halstead,[38] the battery has been subsequently revised and refined for many years by Reitan and coworkers[65-69] and has been statistically analyzed by Russell and associates.[74] Swiercinsky[81] provides a relatively comprehensive manual for administration, scoring, and interpretation of most tests in the battery as well as other neuropsychologic tests. A standard manual for administration, scoring, and interpretation of the complete battery is now available.[70] Golden[28,29] has written critical evaluations of the advantages and disadvantages of the Halstead-Reitan Battery and of other tests used to evaluate patients with suspected brain dysfunction, whereas Anthony and associates,[1] Hevern,[44] and Lenzer[52] have dealt with the Halstead-Reitan Battery's validity.

This battery is probably the best standardized and certainly the most widely reported neuropsychologic research battery in use in the United States at this time. The primary obstacles to its routine use are time and expense.

LURIA-NEBRASKA NEUROPSYCHOLOGIC BATTERY

The Luria-Nebraska Battery[30] has been controversial since its introduction,[76,79] but has become one of the more popular test instruments used, especially by psychologists not specifically trained as neuropsychologists, to test patients having suspected brain damage. Essentially, it represents an attempt to apply modern objective psychometric and statistical methods to some of the examination procedures developed by Luria and made available in useable form by Christensen.[15] Its advantages are its brevity (1.5 to 2 hours), its ability to differentiate between brain-damaged and normal adults, the relative simplicity of administration and basic interpretation, and a reporting format that resembles the popular Minnesota Multiphasic Personality Inventory and gives the impression of an objective comprehensive assessment of patient performance in a wide variety of areas. Major objections have been raised regarding the content of individual test items, the limited number of test items within certain cognitive and motor scales, the statistical validity and reliability of the test in its current form, and its utility in the valid assessment of many common neurobehavioral problems. See Lezak[53] for a review of this controversy. At present, despite its popularity and the possibility that it does represent a beginning step in the process of synthesizing the neurologic and psychometric approaches to neuropsychologic assessment, use of the Luria-Nebraska as the sole measure of neuropsychologic functioning cannot be recommended.

WECHSLER ADULT INTELLIGENCE SCALE–REVISED (WAIS-R)

The 1981 revision and restandardization of the original Wechsler Bellevue Scale, known as the Wechsler Adult Intelligence Scale-Revised, is one of the most commonly used psychometric tests and is probably the test of cognitive functioning that is most familiar to all practicing clinicians. It is a well-constructed and standardized test that is recognized as the standard measure of intelligence when time (1 to 1.5 hours) allows its use. Although standardized for use with the normal adult population, it has proved especially useful in the evaluation of patients with dementia and a wide variety of neurologic conditions. The WAIS-R provides a Full Scale IQ (mean of 100 at any age) and both Verbal and Performance (nonverbal) Scale IQs. The results of six subtests make up the Verbal Scale: (1) Information (general stored knowledge: e.g., What is the capital of Italy?), (2) Digit Span (repetition both forward and backward), (3) Vocabulary (verbal definition: e.g., What does *reluctant* mean?), (4) Arithmetic (achievement in verbal arithmetic problems: e.g., A man with $18.00 spends $7.50, how much money does he have left?), (5) Comprehension (social awareness and the ability to deal with hypothetical situations: e.g., Why should people pay taxes?), and (6) Similarities (verbal conceptualization: e.g., In what way are air and water alike?). The five primarily nonverbal subtests are (1) Picture Completion (recognition of omitted details from pictured objects), (2) Picture Arrangement (visual sequencing of a series of pictures to complete a logical story, (3) Block Design (reproduction of pictorially presented designs with two multicolored blocks), (4) Object Assembly (construction of simple picture puzzles), and (5) Digit Symbol (a perceptual motor sequencing writing task involving symbol coding). Each subtest has a mean of score of 10 at any age, allowing comparisons of the patient's performance discrepancy from the expected score for the normal population and assessment of the variations in performance among the various subtests. As a specific example, the WAIS-R performance of a patient with Alzheimer's dementia appears in Figure 4–1.

The Verbal and Performance Scale IQs and the scaled scores for the specific subtests do not vary appreciably in normal persons. This is not as true for a patient with brain dysfunction. Discrepancies between the Verbal and Performance Scale IQs ranging from 10 to 30 or more points are not infrequent in such patients.[10] Similarly, considerable variation in subtest performance may be seen in patients with organic disease (note the performance of the patient in Fig. 4–1).

IQs within the range of 90 to 110 are classified as Average, between 80 and 89 as Low Average, between 70 and 79 as Borderline, and below 70 as Mentally Retarded. Because there is a strong positive correlation between intelligence and educational level, historical information regarding achievement, as well as general social background and vocation, must be considered when interpreting measured intelligence. An IQ within the Average Range may reflect the effects of a progressive dementing process in a patient with probable superior premorbid functioning. For example, we evaluated a 67-year-old physician whose performance on the WAIS-R resulted in a Full Scale IQ of 80. Although this score was Low Average for his age, our patient's academic history, profession, and well-documented previous success as a surgeon strongly suggested a significant deterioration in intellectual functioning. His dementia was further indicated by impaired performance on more demanding neuropsychologic tests and was subsequently confirmed by CT scan and the progressive course of his deterioration.

In general, the existence of organic disease would be suspected in a patient when the WAIS-R results show:

1. A discrepancy between the current Full Scale IQ and that which would be predicted on the basis of premorbid historical information
2. A Verbal-Performance discrepancy that is greater than expected (+15 points)
3. An appreciable degree of intersubtest scatter
4. Significantly impaired performance on areas of the test considered sensitive to the effects of organicity (i.e., Similarities, Digit Symbol, Block Design)

The discrepancy between Verbal and Performance Scale IQs and the variations among subtest scores may be used to determine the patient's

WAIS-R RECORD FORM

WECHSLER ADULT
INTELLIGENCE SCALE—
REVISED

NAME J.W., MD

ADDRESS

SEX Male AGE 67 RACE Cauc. MARITAL STATUS M

OCCUPATION Physician - Surgeon EDUCATION Medical School plus residency

PLACE OF TESTING N/P Lab LSUMC TESTED BY FWB

TABLE OF SCALED SCORE EQUIVALENTS*

Scaled Score	Information	Digit Span	Vocabulary	Arithmetic	Comprehension	Similarities	Picture Completion	Picture Arrangement	Block Design	Object Assembly	Digit Symbol	Scaled Score
19	—	28	70	—	32	—	—	—	51	—	93	19
18	29	27	69	—	31	28	—	—	—	41	91-92	18
17	—	26	68	19	—	—	20	20	—	—	89-90	17
16	28	25	66-67	—	30	27	—	—	49	40	84-88	16
15	27	24	65	18	29	26	—	19	47-48	39	79-83	15
14	26	22-23	63-64	17	27-28	25	19	—	44-46	38	75-78	14
13	25	20-21	60-62	16	26	24	—	18	42-43	37	70-74	13
12	23-24	18-19	55-59	15	25	23	18	17	38-41	35-36	66-69	12
11	22	17	52-54	13-14	23-24	22	17	15-16	35-37	34	62-65	11
10	19-21	15-16	47-51	12	21-22	20-21	16	14	31-34	32-33	57-61	10
9	17-18	14	43-46	11	19-20	18-19	15	13	27-30	30-31	53-56	9
8	15-16	12-13	37-42	10	17-18	16-17	14	11-12	23-26	28-29	48-52	8
7	13-14	11	29-36	8-9	14-16	14-15	13	10	20-22	24-27	44-47	7
6	9-12	9-10	20-28	6-7	11-13	11-13	11-12	5-7	14-19	21-23	37-43	6
5	6-8	8	14-19	5	8-10	7-10	8-10	3-4	8-13	16-20	30-36	5
4	5	7	11-13	4	6-7	5-6	5-7	—	3-7	13-15	23-29	4
3	4	6	9-10	3	4-5	2-4	3-4	—	—	9-12	16-22	3
2	3	3-5	6-8	1-2	2-3	1	2	1	1	6-8	8-15	2
1	0-2	0-2	0-5	0	0-1	0	0-1	0	0	0-5	0-7	1

*Clinicians who wish to draw a profile may do so by locating the subject's raw scores on the table above and drawing a line to connect them. See Chapter 4 in the Manual for a discussion of the significance of differences between scores on the tests.

	Year	Month	Day
Date Tested	87	3	22
Date of Birth	20	2	18
Age	67	1	

SUMMARY

VERBAL TESTS	Raw Score	Scaled Score	Age
Information	15	8	(9)
Digit Span	14	9	(11)
Vocabulary	39	8	(9)
Arithmetic	8	7	(8)
Comprehension	3	2	(2)
Similarities	1	2	(4)
Verbal Score	36		

PERFORMANCE TESTS			
Picture Completion	9	5	(8)
Picture Arrangement	2	4	(7)
Block Design	2	3	(5)
Object Assembly	14	4	(6)
Digit Symbol	6	1	(3)
Performance Score 17			

	Sum of Scaled Scores	IQ
VERBAL	36	84
PERFORMANCE	17	75
FULL SCALE	53	80

Figure 4-1. Performance on the Wechsler Adult Intelligence Scale of a male patient with Alzheimer's dementia.

specific areas of intellectual strength and weakness and, with some caution, to aid in cerebral localization.

PEABODY PICTURE VOCABULARY TEST-REVISED

The PPVT-R[22] is a briefly administered test of single-word receptive vocabulary comprehension, with current standardization and normative data. Two alternate sets of stimuli plates contain four pictures per plate. The stimulus words are arranged in increasing order of difficulty and reduced frequency in general speech use. The patient is asked to indicate which of the four pictures represents the word spoken by the examiner. Norms are provided for age groups between 2½ and 41 years. The test is useful to obtain an early (in the evaluation process) and brief estimate of the patient's level of functioning because of the relatively high correlation between the PPVT-R and standard tests of intelligence (0.65 to 0.75). It also provides an objective assessment of the patient's ability to understand spoken language at the single-word level, while not requiring a verbal response. The Peabody is not a test of intelligence and should not be misconstrued as such; however, it is a useful tool in the objective evaluation of language problems.

BOSTON NAMING TEST

The Boston Naming Test,[48] a test of visual-confrontation naming or word-finding ability, requires the patient to name a 60-item series of pictured objects ordered in increasing difficulty from "bed" to "abacus." When the patient is unable to spontaneously name the item, categorical (e.g., "to sleep on") and then phonemic (e.g., beginning sound of the target word) cues are provided. Provisional norms are currently available for children, normal adults, and aphasic adults.

VERBAL FLUENCY TEST

Several variations of standardized tests of verbal fluency are available. The two that have proved most effective in our setting are the Controlled Oral Word Association Test (F-A-S), adopted from the Multilingual Aphasia Examination,[3] and the Animal Naming Test, adopted from the Boston Diagnostic Aphasia Examination.[33] Both are tests of the patient's ability to produce single words under the restrictions of a limited category (e.g., "F" or "animals") and time (60 sec). Normative data allowing an objective assessment of word finding ability are available. Analogs of this verbal task have been designed for written language and reading.

REPETITION

The two most widely used tests of sentence repetition are the Revised NCCEA Sentence Repetition Test (Spreen, personal communication, 1986) and the Multilingual Aphasia Examination Sentence Repetition subtest.[3] Both tests evaluate the patient's ability to repeat verbally presented sentences of increasing length and semantic complexity. Norms are available for both normal and neurologically impaired adults.

COMPREHENSIVE APHASIA BATTERIES

When a patient has an obvious organic language deficit (aphasia), a more comprehensive assessment of language functioning is necessary. The most widely used tests for this purpose include: (1) The Boston Diagnostic Aphasia Examination,[34] (2) The Multilingual Aphasia Examination,[3] (3) The Neurosensory Center Comprehensive Examination for Aphasia,[77] (4) The Porch Index of Communicative Ability,[58] and (5) The Western Aphasia Battery.[49] See Lezak[53] for descriptions of these batteries.

WECHSLER MEMORY SCALE (WMS)

The Wechsler Memory Scale is a relatively brief (30 min) objective memory test for clinical use. The WMS assesses a number of aspects of memory functioning including Personal and Current Information (e.g., In what year were you born? Who is the governor of your state?), Orientation to Time and Place (e.g., What is the month? What is the name of this place?), Mental Control (tested by counting backward from 20 to 1, reciting the alphabet, and counting by serial 3s), Logical Memory (the immediate recall of paragraph-length material read aloud by the examiner), Digit Repetition (both forward and backward), Visual Memory (paper-and-pencil reproduction from memory of simple line designs), and Paired Associate Learning (using three-trial learning pairs, having both strong natural associations ["north" and "south"] and no logical association ["dig" and "guilty"]).

The test was standardized so that a Memory Quotient (MQ) is derived that is analogous to the WAIS IQ. Accordingly, an MQ of 100 is about equivalent to the same WAIS-R IQ. The WMS for many years was the only objective memory test that provided a global assessment index, although there is research evidence that the test results should not be evaluated in this fashion.[29,72] Unfortunately, performance on the various components of the test cannot be easily compared by inspection (e.g., verbal vs. visual or new learning vs. long-term memory) as is possible on the WAIS-R. A degree of familiarity with the test and clinical ingenuity, however, does allow such comparisons to be made by interpolation or the use of clinically constructed charts.[45] Despite the continuing research and clinical controversies regarding the construction and basic factors implicit in this test,[21,23] the WMS remains a widely used objective measure of memory functioning. Performance on the test can be compared with scores on standard intelligence tests (e.g., the discrepancy between a WAIS IQ of 94 and WMS IQ of 69 may be very significant clinically). The WMS is often useful in providing a quantified measure of memory and in providing information to aid in differentiating between organic and functional memory disorders. Its use in neuropsychologic assessment is gradually being replaced by more recent and more sophisticated memory tests.

The Wechsler Memory Scale is now being replaced by a revised version of the test that was not available for either review or clinical use at the time this book was written. From the limited information currently available, the Wechsler Memory Scale-Revised appears to be a vastly improved measure of memory functioning. It will assess an additional three areas of nonverbal memory and includes a 30-min delayed-recall phase. The revised test has been completely restandardized on clinical samples from subjects ranging in age from 16 to 74 years.

RUSSELL ADAPTATION OF THE WECHSLER MEMORY SCALE

Russell[72] selected the logical memory paragraph and visual reproduction subtests from the WMS and devised new administration and scoring procedures. After standard administration and scoring of each subtest, a delayed recall trial is given 30 min later. This technique results in (1) a short-term memory score, (2) a 30-min delayed-recall score, and (3) a retained-memory score obtained by the formula:

$$\frac{\text{Delayed Recall}}{\text{Immediate Recall}} \times 100$$

This revision has proved effective in discriminating between normals and patients having various types of cognitive dysfunction. It is also useful for comparing verbal with visual memory and delayed recall with immediate recall.

RANDT MEMORY TEST

Randt and his associates[13,59,60] designed and standardized a brief (30 min) test to assess memory acquisition, storage, and both short-term (minutes) and delayed (24 hours) retrieval. The test is based on a more up-to-date, coherent theory of memory functioning, uses a distractor variable between stimulus presentation and retrieval, and is psychometrically superior to other clinical memory tests. It was originally designed with five alternate forms to assess memory deterioration in aged patients but has been shown to be clinically useful with a variety of populations. The test includes subtests of general populations. The test includes subtests of general information, recall of five items, digit repetition, paired associate learning, verbal memory for paragraph-length material, visual recognition of pictured items, and incidental memory (recall of material not specifically identified for recall, e.g., the names of the subtests used). The inclusion of a 24-hour delayed recall by telephone is a significant advantage. The Randt shares the WMS's verbal emphasis, with disproportionately fewer sensitive measures of visual memory. This limits its utility with patients having language impairment, a limitation shared by almost all available "memory batteries." It is psychometrically vastly superior, however, to the now outdated Wechsler Memory Scale. Full standardization of the Randt is still in progress, although currently available clinical and experimental work suggests that it will become a useful component of the neuropsychologic evaluation when an objective measure of global memory functioning is needed.

DENMAN NEUROPSYCHOLOGY MEMORY SCALE

The Denman[19] represents the most current attempt to devise a reasonably comprehensive objective test of memory. The test includes both a short form (20 to 25 min) and long form (45 to 55 min) battery that assesses immediate recall, short-term memory, and long-term memory in verbal and nonverbal spheres. Its primary advantage is a reasonably balanced independent evaluation of both verbal and visual memory. The Denman is an adaptation and synthesis of several traditional approaches to memory testing in one objective test that presently is normed on a relatively small (246) sample of normals aged 10 to 69 years. Standardization of the test with both normals and clinical samples continues to this date. It may well prove to be an important part of the repertoire of tests available to the clinical neuropsychologist.

BENDER GESTALT TEST

The Bender Gestalt is a venerable test that is commonly used to assess constructional ability. It consists of nine geometric line designs that the patient is asked to copy with paper and pencil. A memory component may be introduced after completion of the standard administration by requiring the patient to draw the designs again from memory. Errors in reproduction may be objectively scored,[50] with the primary pathologic features being (1) distortion or simplification of the gestalt, (2) failures in the integration of parts, (3) rotation of the reproduced design, and (4) perseveration. The stimulus designs are sufficiently simple that perfect reproduction is expected by age 12. Any errors by an adult that are unexplained by physical or sensory limitations, mental retardation, or lack of exposure to graphic tasks are assumed to reflect organic dysfunction. Lacks[51] recently introduced a promising method of objectively scoring Bender Gestalt protocols. This scoring system has been standardized on brain-damaged adults and is used to differentiate them from normals.

BENTON VISUAL RETENTION TEST

In the Benton Visual Retention Test, a series of increasingly complex line drawings is presented to the patient's view for periods of varying duration. The patient must then reproduce the design after different delay periods (direct copy, immediate reproduction from memory, and reproduction after a delay of 15 sec). The patient's reproductions are scored for errors of omission, addition, distortion, rotation, perseveration, size, and misplacement. A relatively well-standardized normative system allows a quantified comparison of the patient's performance with that expected for age. This test was designed to assess visual perception, visuoconstructive ability, and visual memory. Its advantages are the objective scoring system and normative cutoff points for normal and brain-damaged subjects, whereas its primary drawback in routine clinical use is the time required for administration, scoring, and interpretation (up to 30 min when all forms are used).

RAVEN'S PROGRESSIVE MATRICES

Raven's Matrices[61-63] are tests of visuospatial analysis, spatial conceptualization, and nonverbal numerical reasoning. The test is available in three levels of difficulty, ranging from the Colored Matrices for children and impaired adults to the Advanced Matrices for highly functioning adults. It is easily administered and scored, taking from 15 to 45 min depending on the age and degree of impairment of the patient. The test requires the patient to select, from various different pictured patterns, one design that correctly completes a stimulus pattern containing an omitted portion. The matrices are clinically useful for assessing visual pattern matching, nonverbal reasoning, unilateral neglect, and cognitive style.

When used with patients with known perceptual motor constructional deficits, the test can be used to differentiate between the visuospatial analysis and motor-integration components of the problem. In cortically damaged patients, the degree of impairment tends to be directly related to the degree of damage, with a tendency for patients with right-hemisphere damage to perform less adequately than patients with similar left-hemisphere damage, especially on the colored version of the test.

TRAIL MAKING TEST

The Trail Making Test, which is part of the Halstead-Reitan battery, involves two somewhat different tasks. In Form A, 25 small circles are randomly printed on a sheet of paper and numbered from 1 to 25. The patient is required to connect the numbered circles in sequence as rapidly as possible. In Form B, 25 randomly printed circles (the mirror image of Form A) are numbered from 1 to 13 and lettered from A to L. The patient draws a connecting line, alternating between numbers and letters (i.e., 1-A-2-B-3). Form A is assumed to be a right-hemisphere task, primarily requiring perceptual-motor speed, whereas Form B is considered a left-hemisphere task involving efficiency in conceptual shifting, verbal mediation, and perceptual-motor speed. The brief (5 min) test is reputedly sensitive to both diffuse and lateralized brain damage and is frequently useful as a test of frontal lobe function. Normative data are available.[66,78]

CATEGORY TEST

The Category is a subtest of the Halstad-Reitan Battery and is frequently used independently. It is generally considered to be a test of concept formation and abstract problem-solving behavior. From a series of visually presented stimuli, the patient is required to abstract basic principles of similarity and difference and to learn sorting behavior based on variables such as size, shape, number, brightness, color, and position. The Category Test is a very complex method of assessing abstract reasoning and learning under reinforcement conditions. Although patients with brain damage tend, as a group, to demonstrate deficient performance,[68] factors such as intelligence, memory, and comprehension all impair performance and may be the crucial components in explaining discrepant scores.[29,81]

WISCONSIN CARD SORTING TEST

The Wisconsin Card Sorting Test,[5] originally designed to assess abstract ability, conceptual shifting, and "learning to learn," has recently been restandardized in terms of administration and scoring directions and has been subjected to a more refined normative study.[40] The test requires the patient to sort a set of 128 cards according to the categories of color, form, and number, with the category shifting without notice after a criterion of 10 consecutive correct responses is reached. The patient is told whether a response is correct or incorrect, but is not told what the categories are or that the required category will change. This test has proved valuable in neuropsychologic assessment because it (1) provides an objective measure of abstract ability, (2) is sensitive to the effects of frontal-lobe lesions, and (3) gives information as to the particular reasons for difficulty on the test (e.g., impaired conceptualization, failure to maintain the correct set, perseveration, or difficulties in learning across several trials). It is sensitive to the effects of brain damage, but may also reflect lowered intelligence, impaired attention, frustration, attempts to "beat the test" by searching for methods of matching stimulus cards to an incidental category, and problems in motivation. In the context of a complete test battery, this test is especially useful.

PROVERBS TESTS

There are probably as many forms of the proverbs test as there are examiners; each of us has a repertoire of familiar sayings that are used during the mental status exam. All proverbs tests are tests of verbal abstract ability, educational knowledge, and the ability to apply previously learned knowledge to novel situations. The patient either explains the meaning of proverbs or chooses the best explanation from among a series of choices. Because of the relationship between proverb interpretation and education, poor performance must be interpreted in the total context of the patient's background. Gorham[35] devised a multiple-choice proverb interpretation test with interpretations of each proverb ranging between the extremes of abstraction and concreteness. Proverbs of increasing levels of difficulty are also provided. Examples of responses of varying quality provided in the test manual facilitate an objective scoring of the degree of abstraction versus concreteness of the individual patient's performance. The use of this standardized test eliminates the need to rely on observation and the examiner's subjective impressions of the quality of the patient's responses. This allows a quantification of the individual patient's performance and a more systematic comparison with expected performance.

FINGER TAPPING TEST

The Finger Tapping Test is commonly used in various forms in standard clinical neurologic exams and has been well standardized by Reitan[68] among others. The form of the test most commonly used by neuropsychologists requires the patient to tap a mechanical counter with the index finger of each hand. Three to five trials of 10 sec each are used, alternating between hands. An averaged score is obtained for each hand; these scores are then compared with norms for age, sex, and hand dominance. Assuming that the patient has no peripheral neuromusculoskeletal abnormalities, significant discrepancies between expected norms and actual performance by either hand or discrepancies exceeding 10 percent between hands are considered diagnostic of organic brain disease.[67] The most commonly used expected mean scores for normal adults are 50 taps with the dominant hand and 45 taps with the nondominant hand. Somewhat slower performance is expected with older subjects, although standardized data regarding the quantification of the relationship between age and finger tapping speed are not yet available. Age-related norms are also available for children.[78]

WIDE RANGE ACHIEVEMENT TEST (WRAT-R)

The Wide Range Achievement Test is a briefly administered (15 to 20 min) clinical test of reading (word recognition), spelling to dictation, and written arithmetic. The items in the WRAT-R are steeply graded in difficulty, allowing its use on all levels from kindergarten to college. It is a useful test when a standardized and objective assessment of academic deficits is needed.[46]

MINNESOTA MULTIPHASIC PERSONALITY INVENTORY (MMPI)

The most commonly used standardized test of personality, the Minnesota Multiphasic Personality Inventory consists of 566 statements (e.g., I seldom worry about my health) to which the patient responds true or false as they apply to him. The test is then objectively scored, with the resultant profile graphically representing performance in the clinical areas of hypochondriasis, depression, hysteria, psychopathic deviancy, masculinity-femininity of interests, paranoia, psychasthenia (obessive-compulsive thinking), schizophrenia, hypomania, and social introversion. Validity scales L (lie), F (attempts to "fake bad"), and K (a suppressor variable reflecting attempts to "fake good") are also obtained. A number of guidebooks to aid the examiner in interpretation of the significance of individual MMPI configural profiles are available. There are some suggestions that the test may be useful in differentiating organic from functional states and as a lateralizing index for patients with organic brain disease,[9,12,32,39] although others question these uses.[20] The MMPI can be used to document the emotional changes seen in some cases of brain dysfunction.

This brief review covers only some of the tests commonly used in neuropsychologic evaluations. See Lezak[53] for a more comprehensive treatment of this entire area.

ORGANIC "SOFT SIGNS"

A common feature of the psychologic reports of many clinical psychologists and even some neuropsychologists is the frequent reporting of so-called organic signs. This can be difficult for the physician to interpret without some knowledge of the term. Such "organic signs" typically include the following:

Verbal-Performance Discrepancies. These discrepancies are appreciable differences between the Verbal and Performance Scale IQs on the Wechsler series of intelligence tests. Differences exceeding 25 points have consistently been shown to be statistically significant,[24] whereas differences of 15 points have been shown to be of clinical value in identifying neurologic dysfunction.[8] Verbal-Performance discrepancies must be cautiously interpreted in the light of the overall psychologic test profile, the patient's social and educational background, emotional factors, and the presence of any primary sensory or motor deficit (e.g., a visual impairment or cerebral palsy).

Scattering of Performance Levels. A scattering of performance levels on the various subtests of the Wechsler tests or among any of the scores obtained on the full psychologic test battery (e.g., a subtest score of 12 on the WAIS-R Vocabulary subtest and 6 on the Similarities subtest or a

WAIS-R IQ of 105 and a Wechsler Memory Scale Quotient of 67) indicates discrepant cognitive functioning that must be explained. The physician should recognize, however, that a number of factors (social, psychologic, and educational) as well as brain dysfunction may result in such subtest "scatter." Accordingly, this organic indicator should not be interpreted in isolation as an unequivocal sign of brain damage or dysfunction.

Visual Motor Dysfunction. An indication of visual motor dysfunction may be detected by any measure of constructional ability, including the nonverbal WAIS-R subtests, the Bender Gestalt, and Drawings to Command. The best predictors of brain dysfunction on constructional tests are the specific errors of rotation and perseveration. Errors related to the overall integration of separate parts or the distortion of the design gestalt often tend to be maturational rather than pathologic, although they may certainly suggest organic cognitive dysfunction. Constructional ability and its impairment are covered in more depth in the section on the mental status examination in this chapter and in Chapter 8, Neurobehavioral Syndromes Associated with Focal Brain Lesions. A wide variety of social, maturational, motor, and sensory factors as well as brain damage may affect constructional ability. Therefore, information regarding performance in this area must be evaluated within the context of the total neurologic and neuropsychologic evaluations and the patient's social and educational history.

Behavioral Findings. Behavioral findings including hyperactivity, distractibility, mixed laterality, motor incoordination, clumsiness, and so forth are all regarded as signs of organic disease. It is well established that the incidence of such findings is higher in brain-damaged persons than in normals, especially among children. Because of the variability of maturation, the use of such behavioral indicators in isolation as diagnostic of brain damage is definitely unwarranted.

In sum, the information provided by the clinical psychologist may be of significant value to the physician in describing the abilities and disabilities of the patient and in helping to make a diagnosis of brain dysfunction. The referring physician must, however, utilize the services of a well-trained and experienced psychologist, understand something of the nature of the commonly used psychologic tests, and be able to interpret both the utility and especially the limitations of the so-called brain-damage indicators or "organic signs."

Those readers desiring more detailed information regarding the specific tests and procedures included in the neuropsychologic evaluation are referred to the excellent reviews of Lezak,[53] Reitan and Davidson,[69] Golden,[28,29] Reitan and Wolfson,[70] Bigler,[7] and Swiercinsky.[81] In addition, the publications of Hecaen and Albert,[41] Heilman and Valenstein,[43] and Walsh[83] provide very valuable overviews of the field of clinical neuropsychology and of specific topics within the field.

Clinical neuropsychology is a rapidly expanding field with many of its practioners located in universities or medical centers. The availability of well-trained specialists, however, is increasing rapidly, with some now in group or private practice.

COGNITIVE REMEDIATION

The rehabilitation of patients with organic brain dysfunction is an area that has received increasing attention by neuropsychologists and related professionals. Publications in the lay and professional literature have burgeoned in the past 10 years. See Grimm and Bleiberg[37] for a review of this trend and its current status. Traditional neuropsychologic assessment has amply documented the cognitive, emotional, and social deficits that result from brain damage or disease. The obvious next theoretical step in the management of such cases is to provide techniques and specialized environments that will (1) augment the natural process of recovery in some cases, and (2) attempt to remediate specific cognitive deficits after spontaneous recovery has plateaued in others. The major premise appears to be that neuropsychologic principles and specific remedial or "retraining" techniques will facilitate improvement and may actually help the patient to circumvent or better manage certain cognitive impairments. Ben Yisha,[4] Trexler,[82] and Goldstein and Ruthven[31] have produced texts dealing with the philosophy, format, and logistics of such training programs. In addition, journal articles regarding specific approaches with individual patients and limited patient samples are currently available in voluminous quantity. The attempt to provide such services has considerable "face validity" and certainly appeals to the social conscience of professionals attempting to help patients with brain damage function more effectively in their environments. Programs that attempt to help patients to deal with their deficits by teaching compensatory methods (e.g., memory management by use of a written schedule or structured time management) appear to be reasonably useful. Critical reviews of currently available procedures and programs generally have concluded that the practical results of the field of cognitive remediation have failed to meet its premises and goals.[6,75] Remediation of cognitive deficits is a field in search of well-established research and documentation of its efficacy. The void in, and need for, such services is unquestioned; however, at this time the void still exists.[6] One hopes for an optimistic future, for the development of programs that can empirically demonstrate improvements in patients undergoing such treatment and that will legitimize the often faddish nature of the field to date. Certainly the need is present and can only increase in our population, which is both aging and suffering cerebral trauma at a rate that is reaching epidemic proportions.

OTHER CONSULTATIONS

Neurology

Because the neurobehavioral disorders are neurologic diseases, the neurologist is an extremely helpful consultant when the physician is evaluating a patient with altered mental function. The neurologist usually spends from 30 to 60 min taking an initial history and doing an extensive neurologic examination. With these standard data, he can make a specific neurologic diagnosis or plan a full neurodiagnostic evaluation.

Most neurologists are also willing and able to manage the short- and long-term care of the patient with organic disease in conjunction with the patient's own physician. It is best to consult the neurologist early in the evaluation process before ordering a large and expensive battery of laboratory tests. We have seen far too many patients with a simple postoperative delirium who have been dragged screaming through a series of laboratories. After hundreds of dollars of diagnostic procedures, many of which are of questionable reliability because of movement artifact and other factors, the neurologist is finally asked to see the patient. In such cases the EEG, MRI, CT scan, and so forth are unnecessary to make the clinical diagnosis. Confusional behavior (delirium) in the postoperative period is usually due to a medication or metabolic disturbance and not to structural brain disease. Valuable time and money may be unnecessarily spent if the physician attempts to "get all the tests done" before calling the consultant. The neurologic consultation is often the cheapest, most efficacious neurologic test and should yield the most pertinent information to the primary physician. See Strub and Black[80] for a thorough review of the neurologist's role.

Psychiatry

Many patients with neurobehavioral disorders have a concomitant emotional disturbance that requires psychiatric consultation for inpatient and long-term management. Patients referred for psychiatric evaluation include (1) those with psychiatric disorders predating their neurologic problem, (2) those with emotional reactions to brain disease (e.g., reactive depression), (3) those in whom an emotional reaction complicates dementia, or other organic conditions, (4) those with functional disorders presenting as neurologic conditions (e.g., hysterical paralysis), and (5) those with emotional change secondary to brain lesions (e.g., frontal lobe syndrome as a result of communicating anterior artery aneurysm rupture).

Emotional factors may be significant obstacles to the rehabilitation and social reintegration of any patient with organic disease. The psychiatrist should be consulted to aid in the management of the patient with an emotional disturbance sufficiently severe as to interfere with rehabilitative efforts or home adjustment.

Some psychiatrists have a great interest in organic mental disorders and can be very valuable consultants for diagnosis and management in all such cases.

REFERRAL

Because of the relatively high incidence of both mental illness and brain disease, many patients have coexisting psychiatric and neurologic conditions (e.g., a brain tumor in a schizophrenic patient or a seizure patient with a manic depressive disorder). For example, we recently saw a 37-year-old woman with a 7-year history of schizophrenia. The patient was also an alcoholic and over the years had sustained several significant head injuries. After alcohol withdrawal, she had several grand mal seizures and was admitted to the neurology ward. As her postictal confusion cleared, she demonstrated gross delusional and aggressive behavior. After a complete history and medical evaluation, we determined that the patient had an acute neurologic condition that was superimposed on a pre-existing chronic schizophrenia. Because of the significant functional psychosis, a psychiatrist was consulted for treatment and long-term management. In general, psychiatrists should be consulted on patients with pre-existing psychiatric disease regardless of the nature of the coexisting medical disorder.

It is not uncommon for emotionally stable persons to develop a significant emotional reaction to a recent neurologic or neurobehavioral disorder such as aphasia. Depressive reactions, anxiety, paranoia, and aggressiveness may all develop in response to brain damage. Such emotional reactions may significantly interfere with any rehabilitation efforts. For example, a 62-year-old woman developed right hemiplegia and anomic aphasia secondary to a left middle cerebral artery thrombosis. After the acute stage, she became increasingly depressed to a point of apathy, self-depreciation, and constant crying. She would no longer actively participate in physical therapy and appeared to abandon any hope of improvement. When a serious emotional reaction such as this is superimposed on an organic deficit, the emotional component must be specifically treated in conjunction with the medical treatment. Psychiatric referral in the course of such cases will significantly aid the total rehabilitation program.

Demented patients present a particular challenge because they have both intellectual and emotional changes as a part of their disease. These changes produce a variety of difficult management problems that are often best handled with the aid of a psychiatrist. During the early stages of dementia, many patients retain considerable insight; this capacity to realize the seriousness of their condition often results in a profound reactive depression. Other patients with dementia become unaware of their deteriorating intellectual ability and often push themselves beyond their capability and develop frustration and severe anxiety. This situation is aptly illustrated by the following case: A 58-year-old businessman was referred because of failing memory. Examination revealed a genuine memory deficit and other evidence of an early dementia. Severe anxiety was prominent and interfered with both specific test performance and his social and vocational life. This anxiety was greatly reduced by restructuring his lifestyle (e.g., his wife helped him with his business and he discontinued many civic duties) and the use of a mild tranquilizer to aid in sleeping. After several months, retesting showed improvement in many cognitive areas, and he was better able to carry out his home and job responsibilities. Any degree of anxiety or depression can greatly exacerbate the mental and social disability experienced by the demented patient. The psychiatrist can provide great assistance through the use of psychotrophic drugs, family counseling, and general procedures of patient management.

The diagnostic problem of differentiating among dementia, depression, and dementia with depression is both common and often difficult in clinical practice. Because this differential diagnosis is critical in terms of patient management and treatment, the psychiatrist should be involved early in the evaluation process. Misdiagnosis of depression as dementia will deprive the patient of appropriate treatment and leave the family with the erroneous impression that the disease is progressive and irreversible. Conversely, the misdiagnosis of dementia as depression may lead to ineffective and costly psychotherapy, leaves the patient subject to social and vocational problems resulting from intellectual deterioration, and misleads the family as to the prognosis of the disease.

Psychiatric referral is also indicated for patients who develop depression in response to a chronic neurologic disease such as myasthenia gravis, epilepsy, multiple sclerosis, or parkinsonism. These patients can frequently live long and productive lives if they are able to accept and deal with their disability in a realistic fashion.

Other patients often requiring psychiatric referral are those who suffer emotional and behavioral changes directly attributable to the locus of their brain lesion. The causal relationship between brain damage and emotional sequelae is well known (see Benson and Blumer;[2] Heilman, Bowers, and Valenstein;[42] and Ruckdeschel-Hibbard, Gordon, and Diller[71] for reviews of this topic).

Many patients with chronic neurobehavioral disorders such as aphasia, dementia, traumatic encephalopathy, or Korsakoff's disease become management problems and eventually require long-term care in a psychiatric hospital. Early referral to the psychiatrist or psychiatric social worker can help the family and the physician with the administrative and legal details involved in institutionalization.

A final group of patients who may initially be seen by the neurologist but who will require referral to the psychiatrist are those with hysterical conversion reactions. Many patients will present with symptoms that mimic neurologic disease (e.g., limb paralysis, loss of speech, or sensory loss), but that demonstrate no organic etiology. The treatment of choice for such functional disorders is psychotherapy.

EVALUATION

The standard psychiatric evaluation is amply discussed in most texts and will not be covered here. When dealing with brain-damaged patients, it is necessary to differentiate among pre-existing conditions, exacerbations of previous traits, changes directly attributable to the brain lesion, secondary reactive behavior changes, and emotional conditions that are disproportionate to the degree and nature of the neurologic disorder.

TREATMENT

Even though specific treatment is frequently unavailable for the primary brain disease, behavioral and pharmacologic treatment can improve the lives of many of these patients. Medication is particularly useful in patients with pre-existing psychiatric disease; the underlying psychiatric disorder will respond to a standard regimen of psychotrophic medication. Antianxiety or mood-elevating drugs are effective in treating the anxiety or depression frequently seen as a reaction to organic brain disease. Major tranquilizers are often required to control the agitation and nocturnal wanderings of the deteriorated patient with organic brain disease.

Standard psychotherapeutic methods can be used in some patients with organic disease who retain sufficient comprehension, memory, and insight. On the other hand, insight therapy is less than useful in many organically affected patients (e.g., severe amnesics, demented patients, those with significant frontal lobe behavioral changes, and Wernicke's aphasics). In this latter group of patients, behavior modification techniques in an effort to change specific behaviors are more appropriate.

Family counseling is often the most useful form of patient management. Through discussion, the psychiatrist is able to help the family understand the patient's problem and to offer suggestions on management. With the psychiatrist's help, the family can then restructure the patient's routine in an effort to minimize environmental stress and confusion.

The medicolegal aspects of organic brain disease are also very important and must be part of any long-term management program. The patient's competence to make a will, to conduct personal financial affairs, and to enter into contracts such as marriage should be established in each case.

Finally, every treatment plan should include a consideration of possible eventual full-time supervision if the patient becomes unmanageable in the home. The details of nursing home or institutional placement should be worked out with the help of the psychiatrist, social workers, and the patient's family. Such plans should be considered early in the course of the disease to allow time to assess family financial and personal resources; to determine the availability of home nursing services, nursing homes, and institutions; and to preclude the necessity of unsatisfactory and hasty decisions made at a time of crisis.

Social Work

Clinical social workers can provide invaluable assistance in cases that require family education and counseling, social planning, and placement. The social worker usually has more familiarity with resources available to patients and families than any other professional. In some situations, the social worker will prove to be the most effective case manager, coordinating the various aspects of evaluation and treatment/management. This is particularly true in those cases in which the neurobehavioral disorder is longstanding (e.g., Alzheimer's dementia). Their participation in patient management in conjunction with the neurologist or psychiatrist is frequently necessary.

Speech Pathology

Patients with significant difficulty in communicating should be evaluated by a trained speech pathologist. Not all such patients will be treatment candidates, but by means of a thorough language evaluation, the speech pathologist will be able to determine appropriate candidates for rehabilitation and provide other services to those patients and their families who are not selected for treatment. Patients with primary neurologic disease (e.g., aphasia, apraxia of speech, or dysarthria) should routinely be referred. The speech pathologist is an important member of a comprehensive rehabilitation team; this is particularly true when the unit deals with a large number of stroke patients. Functional speech and language disorders such as elective mutism and hysterical aphonia are also ideal problems for speech evaluation and treatment. An evaluation by the speech pathologist provides a description of the patient's overall level of communication, the possible benefits of therapeutic intervention, and a plan for family counseling to facilitate alternate methods of communicating with the patient.

Virtually every physician has access to a speech pathologist, either in private practice or in hospital, university, or community clinics. Most speech pathologists will have specialized knowledge and experience in treating patients with delayed speech acquisition, articulation disorders, stuttering, and some acquired communication problems. The evaluation and treatment of aphasia and other acquired communication disorders is a very specialized field; the physician should determine the speech pathologist's competence in dealing with the specific disorder before referring his aphasic patients.

REFERRAL

The major reasons for referring patients to the speech pathologist are (1) the mental status examination indicates the presence of a communication disorder that requires a more thorough evaluation; (2) obvious communication disorders exist that require a detailed screening evaluation to determine the appropriateness of speech therapy; and (3) a significant communication disorder requires family counseling to inform the family members as to the patient's problem and to assist in maximizing communication within the home.

The physician will see the following general types of speech and language problems that will require more comprehensive evaluation than can be provided in his office:

1. Articulation disturbances such as the dysarthrias seen in pseudo-bulbar palsy, bulbar paralysis, neuromuscular disease such as myasthenia gravis, cerebellar disorders including cerebral palsy, and basal ganglia disease such as parkinsonism.
2. Functional (hysterical) aphonias, especially in patients with a history of minor trauma or surgery to the throat or vocal cords.
3. Elective mutism.
4. Dysfluency (stuttering), seen in both children and adults. If untreated, it may pose a significant obstacle to successful social and vocational adjustment.
5. Patients with acquired language disorders (aphasia, alexia, agraphia). Such patients deserve an initial speech and language evaluation, both to determine the potential for benefit from speech therapy and to aid the patient's family in understanding and dealing with the communication disorder. Because of the rapid changes in language that occur during the first 2 to 4 weeks after an acute cerebral lesion, speech evaluations will be most valid and prognostically useful if done after this initial period.
6. Patients with buccofacial apraxia in the presence or absence of aphasia. These patients may benefit from speech evaluation and therapy directed toward articulation and the intelligibility of speech, as well as other buccofacial activities such as drinking and swallowing.

SPEECH AND LANGUAGE EVALUATION

Features of the Evaluation

The comprehensive speech and language evaluation can be expected to provide the following information:

Diagnosis. A definition of the primary language diagnosis (e.g., nonfluent aphasia, dysarthria, buccofacial apraxia) will be included.

Description. The evaluation will contain a comprehensive description of the type of language disorder, including all areas of deficit (e.g., word-finding problems, alexia, or auditory comprehension problems) and residual language abilities. The description should contain some qualitative index of the degree of problem in each area assessed to allow comparison with subsequent evaluations. Some statement should be made about the effect of the language deficit on the patient's communicative ability in formal (test or interview) and informal (social) areas.

Recommendations. Recommendations should answer such specific questions as: Is speech therapy indicated and if so, what will be the emphasis of the therapy? What will be the frequency of therapy visits, what is the projected duration of therapy, and what are the specific plans for home therapy by family members and for family counseling?

Goals of Therapy and Prognosis. The establishment of goals will answer the following questions: What are the primary goals of speech and language therapy? What is the prognosis for language recovery? What will be the long-term social impact of the language disorder?

Evaluation Components

The systems and methods of speech and language evaluation are numerous. The system and specific tests used are determined in part by the problems presented by the particular patient and partly by the individual speech pathologist's training and experience. As the enumeration of all of these methods is beyond the scope of this book, the interested reader is referred to the writings of Costello,[16] Darley,[17] Davis and Wilcox,[18] and Johns.[47]

A comprehensive evaluation should include the following elements:

1. An examination of the oral physiology, including evaluation of the strength and alacrity of the muscles of articulation.
2. A description of the characteristics of speech articulation: dysarthria, dysfluency, and dysprosody.
3. A description of apraxias if present, both verbal (speech) and nonverbal (nonspeech facial movements).
4. An evaluation for aphasia, specifically including a description of

spontaneous speech and an assessment of verbal comprehension, repetition, and word-finding ability.

5. An assessment of reading and writing.
6. An evaluation of the adequacy of nonverbal communication, including an assessment of the ability to communicate by utilization of gestures or other methods.
7. A description of the patient's general behavior and specific behavioral responses to the stress of language testing.

TREATMENT

Treatment is not universally efficacious in all speech and language disorders. The following is a general breakdown of the expected results with a number of patient types based on our clinical experience.

Excellent results can often be produced in rehabilitating patients with (1) functional voice disorders, exclusive of elective mutism (which is more resistant to traditional forms of speech therapy), (2) mild to moderate articulation problems, and (3) delayed speech in nonretarded children.

Good results can be expected in patients with (1) anomic aphasia, (2) oral apraxia, (3) moderate articulation problems, and (d) developmental reading and learning disorders.

Fair results are generally obtained in patients with (1) Broca's aphasia, (2) moderate to severe articulation problems, (3) aphasia with mild to moderate comprehension defects, (4) developmental aphasia, and (5) elective mutism (unless intensive behaviorally oriented therapy is used, in which case the prognosis is improved).

Poor results typically result from therapeutic efforts with patients with (1) global aphasia, (2) Wernicke's aphasia, (3) severe dysarthria and oral apraxia, and (4) language disturbances secondary to dementia.

We emphasize that these are only general rules of thumb; the individual patient with a particular language disorder will not always respond to therapy as projected. Accordingly, a complete speech and language evaluation of the patient with any developmental or acquired communication disorder is important to provide at least the consideration of therapy for those patients who may benefit from it.

Physical and Occupational Therapy

The physical therapist (PT), the occupational therapist (OT), or both are often integral participants in the comprehensive treatment of the brain-damaged patient. Although the traditional primary role of the PT was in the remediation of gross muscle and motor deficits, and that of the OT was in the rehabilitation of fine motor, self-help, and associated cognitive problems, there have been progressive overlap and complement of the roles of these specialists. Commonly, the PT and OT assist each other as well as other therapists in facilitating optimal therapeutic opportunities for the patient. For example, a physical therapist may assist the speech therapist in establishing a comfortable sitting position for the patient, thus allowing better attention and sustained strength during the session. For patients having motor or functional deficits as the result of brain damage or disease, the role of the physical or occupational therapist in rehabilitation may be as important as that of the speech therapist with a patient having an acquired language deficit. The numbers of trained practitioners in both fields are sizable, and the related literature is massive; see Carr and Shepherd[14] and Reed[64] for introductions to these important areas.

Other Related Professionals

A number of other professionals deal in the rehabilitation of patients having neurobehavioral disorders. Within the context of this book, their duties cannot be described in detail; however, the reader should be aware that the physiatrist or physical medicine and rehabilitation specialist, the rehabilitation nurse, the rehabilitation counselor, and the vocational rehabilitation specialist may all have significant roles in the management of those patients discussed in this book. In many settings, it is the physiatrist who coordinates the management and care of the brain-damaged patient after he has been medically stabilized and has received initial evaluations. There are an increasing number of hospital-based and freestanding rehabilitation centers that deal with brain-damaged patients, offering comprehensive rehabilitation programs.

For purposes of rehabilition prognosis, patients with neurobehavioral disorders can be subdivided into four primary categories: (1) those who recover with minimal sequelae after medical treatment and short-term (1 to 3 months) rehabilitation, (2) those who require short- to intermediate-term rehabilitation (2 to 12 months) after discharge from the primary treating hospital, (3) those who require chronic care for extended periods (years), and (4) those who deteriorate over time (e.g., Alzheimer's dementia). Treatment and management programs are currently being developed for each of these categories. Only with time and empirical studies of specific intervention strategies will we know the the true value of current rehabilitation techniques.

SUMMARY

The management of patients with neurobehavioral disorders is a multidisciplinary effort. Physicians are strongly encouraged to acquaint themselves with the services offered by their colleagues in related specialized fields. By using their resources, the physician will be better able to understand his patients and to provide them more comprehensive and effective care.

REFERENCES

1. Anthony, WZ, Heaton, RK, and Lehman, RAW: An attempt to cross-validate two actuarial systems for neuropsychological test interpretation. J Consult Clin Psychol 48:317, 1980.
2. Benson, DF and Blumer, D (eds): Psychiatric Aspects of Neurologic Disease, vol 2. Grune & Stratton, New York, 1982.
3. Benton, AL and Hamsher, K: Multilingual Aphasia Examination. University of Iowa Press, Iowa City, 1978.
4. Ben Yishay, Y (ed): Working approaches to remediation of cognitive deficits in brain-damaged persons. Rehabilitation Monograph No. 62. New York University Medical Center, Institute of Rehabilitation Medicine, New York, 1981.
5. Berg, EA: A simple objective technique for measuring flexibility in thinking. J Gen Psychol 39:15, 1948.
6. Bielianskas, LA: The void still exists. J Clin Exp Neuropsychol 8:465, 1986.
7. Bigler, ED: Diagnostic Clinical Neuropsychology. University of Texas Press, Austin, 1984.
8. Black, FW: WISC verbal performance discrepancies or indications of neurological dysfunction in pediatric patients. J Clin Psychol 30:165, 1974.
9. Black, FW: Unilateral lesions and MMPI performance: A preliminary study. Percept Mot Skills 40:87, 1975.
10. Black, FW: WAIS verbal-performance discrepancies as predictors of lateralization in patients with discrete missile wounds. Percept Mot Skills, 51:213, 1980.
11. Black, FW: Internship training in clinical neuropsychology: One model. Prof Psychol Res Pract 17:308, 1986.
12. Black, FW and Black, IL: Anterior-posterior locus of lesion and personality: Support for the caudality hypothesis. J Clin Psychol 38:468, 1982.
13. Brown, ER, Randt, CT, and Osborne, DP: Assessment of memory disturbances in aging. In Agnoli, A et al (eds): Aging Brain and Ergot Alkaloids. Raven Press, New York, 1983.
14. Carr, JH and Shepherd, RB: Physiotherapy in Disorders of the Brain: A Clinical Guide. William Heineman Medical Books, London, 1980.
15. Christensen, AL: Luria's Neuropsychological Investigations. Spectrum, New York, 1975.
16. Costello, JM (ed): Speech Disorders in Adults: Recent Advances. College Hill Press, San Diego, 1985.
17. Darley, FL: Aphasia. WB Saunders, Philadelphia, 1984.
18. Davis, GA and Wilcox, MJ (eds): Adult Aphasia Rehabilitation: Applied Pragmatics. College Hill Press, San Diego, 1985.

19. Denman, SB: Denman Neuropsychology Memory Scale. SB Denman, Charleston, NC, 1984.

20. Dikmen, S and Reitan, R: MMPI correlates of adaptive ability deficits in patients with brain lesions. J Nerv Ment Dis 165:247, 1977.

21. Dujoune, BE and Levy, BI: The psychometric structure of the Wechsler Memory Scale. J Clin Psychol 27:251, 1971.

22. Dunn, LM and Dunn, LM: Peabody picture vocabulary text–Revised. American Guidance Service, Circle Pines, MN, 1981.

23. Erickson, RC and Scott, ML: Clinical memory testing: A review. Psychol Bull 84:1130, 1977.

24. Field, J: Two types of tables for use with Wechsler's Intelligence Scales. J Clin Psychol 16:3, 1960.

25. Filskov, SB and Boll, TJ: Handbook of Clinical Neuropsychology. Wiley-Interscience, New York, 1981.

26. Filskov, SB and Boll, TJ: Handbook of Clinical Neuropsychology, vol 2. Wiley-Interscience, New York, 1986.

27. Fisher, C: The neurological examination of the comatose patient. Acta Neurol Scand (Suppl) 36:1, 1969.

28. Golden, CJ: Diagnosis and Rehabilitation in Clinical Neuropsychology. Charles C Thomas, Springfield, IL, 1978.

29. Golden, CJ: Clinical Interpretation of Objective Psychological Tests. Grune & Stratton, New York, 1979.

30. Golden, CJ, Hammeke, TA, and Purisch, AD: Manual for the Luria-Nebraska Neuropsychological Battery. Western Psychological Services, Los Angeles, 1980.

31. Goldstein, G and Ruthven, L: Rehabilitation of the Brain-Damaged Adult. New York, Plenum Press, 1983.

32. Good, P and Banter, J: The Physician's Guide to the MMPI. University of Minnesota Press, Minneapolis, 1961.

33. Goodglass, H and Kaplan, E: The Assessment of Aphasia and Related Disorders. Lea & Febiger, Philadelphia, 1972.

34. Goodglass, H and Kaplan, E: The Assessment of Aphasia and Related Disorders, ed 2. Lea & Febinger, Philadelphia, 1983.

35. Gorham, D: The Proverbs Test. Psychological Test Specialists, Missoula, MT, 1956.

36. Grant, I and Adams, KM: Neuropsychological Assessment of Neuropsychiatric Disorders. Oxford University Press, New York, 1986.

37. Grimm, BH and Bleiberg, J: Psychological rehabilitation in traumatic brain injury. In Filskov, SB and Boll, TJ: Handbook of Clinical Neuropsychology, vol 2. Wiley-Interscience, New York, 1986, pp 495–560.

38. Halstead, W: Brain and Intelligence: A Quantitative Study of the Frontal Lobes. University of Chicago Press, Chicago, 1947.

39. Hathaway, S and McKinley, J: Minnesota Multiphasic Personality Inventory. Psychological Corporation, New York, 1951.

40. Heaton, RK: Wisconsin Card Sorting Text Manual. Psychological Assessment Resources, Odessa, FL, 1981.

41. Hecaen, H and Albert, ML: Human Neuropsychology. John Wiley & Sons, New York, 1978.

42. Heilman, KM, Bowers, D, and Valenstein, E: Emotional disorders associated with neurological diseases. In Heilman, KM and Valenstein, E (eds): Clinical Neuropsychology, ed 2. Oxford University Press, New York, 1985, pp 377–402.

43. Heilman, KM and Valenstein, E: Clinical Neuropsychology, ed 2. Oxford University Press, New York, 1985.

44. Hevern, VW: Recent validity studies of the Halstead-Reitan approach to clinical neuropsychological assessment: A critical review. Clin Neuropsychol 107:135, 1966.

45. Hullicka, IM: Age differences in Wechsler Memory Scale Scores. J Genet Psychol 107:135, 1966.

46. Jastak, S and Wilkison, GS: The Wide Range Achievement Test, rev. Jastak Associates, Wilmington, DE, 1984.

47. Johns, DF (ed): Clinical Management of Neurogenic Communicative Disorders, ed 2. Little, Brown & Co, Boston, 1985.

48. Kaplan, E, Goodglass, H, and Weintraub, S: Boston Naming Test. Lea & Febiger, Philadelphia, 1983.

49. Kertez, A: The Western Aphasia Battery. Grune & Stratton, New York, 1982.

50. Koppitz, EM: The Bender Gestalt Test for Young Children. Grune & Stratton, New York, 1964.

51. Lacks, P: Bender Gestalt: Screening for Brain Dysfunction. Wiley-Interscience, New York, 1984.

52. Lenzer, II: Halstead-Reitan test battery: A problem of differential diagnosis. Percept Mot Skills 50:611, 1980.

53. Lezak, MD: Neuropsychological Assessment. Oxford University Press, New York, 1983.

54. Luria, AR: Higher Cortical Functions in Man. Basic Books, New York, 1980.

55. Luria, AR and Majovski, LV: Basic approaches used in American and Soviet clinical neuropsychology. Am Psychol 32:959, 1977.

56. Parsons, O: Clinical Neuropsychology. In Speilberger, C (ed): Current Topics in Clinical and Community Psychology, vol 2. Academic Press, New York, 1970, pp 1–60.

57. Plum, F and Posner, J: Diagnosis of Stupor and Coma, ed. 3. FA Davis, Philadelphia, 1980.

58. Porch, B: Porch Index of Communicative Ability. Consulting Psychologists Press, Palo Alto, 1971.

59. Randt, CT and Brown, ER: Administration Manual: Randt Memory Test. Life Science Associates, Bayport, NY, 1983.

60. Randt, CT, Brown, ER, and Osborne, DP: A memory test for longitudinal measurement of mild to moderate memory deficits. Clin Neuropsychol 2:184, 1980.

61. Raven, JC: Guide to Using the Coloured Progressive Matrices. HK Lewis Psychological Corporation, London, 1977.

62. Raven, JC: Guide to the Standard Progressive Matrices. HK Lewis Psychological Corporation, London, 1977.

63. Raven, JC: The Advanced Progressive Matrices. HK Lewis Psychological Corporation, London, 1977.

64. Reed, KL: Models of Practice in Occupational Therapy. Williams & Wilkins, Baltimore, 1984.

65. Reitan, R: Investigation of the validity of Halstead's measures of biological intelligence. Arch Neurol Psychiatry 48:474, 1955.

66. Reitan, R: Validity of the trail making test as an indicator of organic brain damage. Percept Mot Skills 8:271, 1958.

67. Reitan, R: The effects of brain lesions on adaptive abilities in human beings (mimeo). Indiana University Medical Center, Indianapolis, 1959.

68. Reitan, R: A research program on the psychological effects of brain lesions in human beings. In Ellis, N (ed): International Review of Research in Mental Retardation, Vol. 1. Academic Press, New York, 1966, pp 153–218.

69. Reitan, R and Davidson, L (eds): Clinical Neuropsychology: Current Status and Applications. John Wiley & Sons, New York, 1974.

70. Reitan, RM and Wolfson, D: The Halstead-Reitan Neuropsychological Test Battery. Arizona Neuropsychology Press, Tucson, 1985.

71. Ruckdeschel-Hibbard, M, Gordon, WA, and Diller, L: Affective disturbances associated with brain damage. In Filskov, SB and Boll, TJ: Handbook of Clinical Neuropsychology, Vol 2. Wiley-Interscience, New York, 1986, pp 305–337.

72. Russell, EW: A multiple scoring method for the assessment of complex memory functions. J Consult Clin Psychol 43:800, 1975.

73. Russell, EW: The psychometric foundation of clinical neuropsychology. In Filskov, SB and Boll, TJ: Handbook of Clinical Neuropsychology. Vol 2. Wiley-Interscience, New York, 1986, pp 45–80.

74. Russell, EW, Neuringer, C, and Goldstein, G: Assessment of Brain Damage. Wiley-Interscience, New York, 1970.

75. Shore, DL: The rush to fill the void. J Clin Neuropsych 6:345, 1984.

76. Spiers, PA: Have they come to praise Luria or bury him? The Luria-Nebraska Battery controversy. J Consult Clin Psychol 49:331, 1981.

77. Spreen, O and Benton, AL: Neurosensory Center Comprehensive Examination for Aphasia. University of Victoria Neuropsychology Laboratory, Victoria, BC, 1969.

78. Spreen, O and Gaddes, WH: Developmental norms for 15 neuropsychological tests, age 6 to 15. Cortex 5:170, 1969.

79. Stambrook, M: The Luria-Nebraska Neuropsychological Battery: A promise that may be partly fulfilled. J Clin Neuropsychol 5:247–269.

80. Strub, RL and Black, FW: The Mental Status Examination in Neurology, ed 2. FA Davis, Philadelphia, 1985.

81. Swiercinsky, D: Manual for the Adult Neuropsychological Evaluation. Charles C Thomas, Springfield, IL, 1978.

82. Trexler, LC (ed): Cognitive Rehabilitation: Conceptualization and Intervention. Plenum Press, New York, 1982.

83. Walsh, KW: Neuropsychology: A Clinical Approach. Churchill Livingston, London, 1978.

84. Weintraub, S and Mesulam, M-M: Mental state assessment of young and elderly adults in behavioral neurology. In Mesulam, M-M (ed): Principles of Behavioral Neurology. FA Davis, Philadelphia, 1985, pp 71–123.

MAJOR CLINICAL NEUROBEHAVIORAL SYNDROMES

Chapter 5

Acute Confusional States (Delirium)

LABORATORY EVALUATION
General Testing Procedures
Special Neurodiagnostic Tests
Electroencephalogram (EEG)
Computerized Axial Tomography (CT) or Magnetic Resonance Imaging (MRI)
Spinal Fluid Examination
Invasive Neuroradiologic Procedures
CONSULTATIONS
PATIENT MANAGEMENT
Environmental Structuring
Medication
Recovery
PATHOLOGY AND DISCUSSION

A 72-year-old man was referred for evaluation of a recent "change in mental status." The patient had a long history of heart disease and was taking a variety of antihypertensive and antiarrhythmia medications. In the year before this referral, we had evaluated him for a 2- to 3-year history of failing memory. At that time we had made a clinical diagnosis of early Alzheimer's disease. In the year since our initial examination, the patient had had several episodes of mild congestive heart failure and had become despondent about his health problems and was not sleeping well.

Five days before his most recent referral, he had started taking amitriptyline 25 mg at bedtime. For the first 2 days his wife noticed that he slept well at night but was sleepy the following day. By the third day, he was having trouble paying attention to the television news (a hobby of his), and his speech began to be rambling and incoherent. The day before we saw him, he had begun to "see" people who were not there and was visibly agitated and disoriented.

On examination he was awake but inattentive and mildly lethargic. His speech was incoherent at times, and he seemed nervous and restless. Physically he had pedal edema and basilar rales in both lungs. Findings on neurologic examination were normal with the exception of his blatantly abnormal mental status.

A diagnosis of an acute confusional state secondary to amitriptyline use and early congestive heart failure was made. Discontinuation of the medication and an increase in the dosage of his diuretic for 2 days resulted in a prompt reversal of the confusional behavior.

The above case is an example of a typical acute confusional state. This condition is encountered frequently in the routine practice of medicine and surgery, and its features should be familiar to all physicians.[30] The confusional state is usually of medical origin, caused most frequently by a metabolic imbalance, adverse drug reaction, alcohol or drug withdrawal, organ failure, or, as in the case above, a combination of these factors. The abrupt change in behavior can be most upsetting to family and physician alike, but with prompt evaluation and therapy, the condition is usually completely reversible. If the physician fails to appreciate that this acute behavior change is caused by a primary medical problem and is not a functional psychiatric disorder, the patient's condition will worsen. Ultimately, the untreated patient can slip into a coma and die. It is because of the frequency, seriousness, and reversibility of this problem that the confusional state is the most important of the neurobehavioral syndromes for the primary-care physician to recognize. Because physicians in general are more familiar with the management of coma than of a confusional state, it is clinically useful to think of acute confusional behavior as a coma seen in its incipient phase.

Not all patients present with the same clinical picture and that is why the plural, confusional *states*, rather than the singular confusional *state,* is used. The behavior of some confusional patients is very bizarre, with agitation, shouting, and active hallucinations dominating the clinical picture. Other patients present primarily with lethargy and incoherent speech. Because of this diversity of clinical presentation, no single term has been universally adopted in the literature to indicate these conditions. The neurologic literature most commonly uses the terms *acute confusional states, delirium,* or *metabolic encephalopathy*; whereas psychiatrists at various times have used the terms *toxic psychosis, acute brain syndrome* (Diagnostic and Statistical Manual of Mental Disorders I), *psychosis associated with organic brain syndrome* (Diagnostic and Statistical Manual of Mental Disorders II), and *delirium* (Diagnostic and Statistical Manual of Mental Disorders III and III-R).[6] Each of the above terms emphasizes a specific aspect of the syndrome, and all have been used interchangeably to denote cases such as the one presented at the beginning of the chapter. The history and clinical implications of this condition have been extensively reviewed by Lipowski; the interested reader is referred specifically to his writings.[29,31]

We prefer the term *acute confusional states* because it stresses both the acuteness of the process and the principal mental change seen. Simply defined, an acute confusional state is a rapidly developing, yet fluctuating, reversible change in behavior that is characterized by a clouding of consciousness, incoherence in the train of thought, and difficulty with attention and concentration.

DESCRIPTION OF THE CLINICAL SYNDROME

The major diagnostic feature of the confusional states is a clouding of consciousness, a term that has not gained full scientific recognition because of the difficulty in establishing a solid operational definition. The concept has great descriptive value, however, and implies that the patient has "reduced clarity of awareness of the environment" (DSM III,[6] p. 107) or, in Adams and Victor's[4] words, confusion is the "incapacity of the patient to think with customary speed and clarity." In most patients the level of alertness and arousability are affected as well as the content and coherence of thought processes. These alterations of consciousness may be subtle and present only during a portion of the day; such intermittent clouding is typical early in the course of the illness. If, however, this sign is not fully appreciated and the underlying condition progresses, the more dramatic behavioral changes of lethargy, disorientation, or agitation will develop. These alterations in consciousness and the tendency to fluctuate during the day are critical in identifying this condition as organic rather than primarily psychogenic. The schizophrenic patient may present with incoherent thought processes and the outward appearance of confusion, but his level of consciousness is normal and does not vary over time.

Inattention is also a major diagnostic feature in confusional states and to some investigators is the cardinal behavioral feature of the condition.[34] Most patients do have great difficulty maintaining concentration and are easily distracted.

In the early stages, patients are frequently restless, particularly at night. Sleep is disturbed, and mild behavioral changes such as anxiety or depressive feelings may appear. These patients experience difficulty concentrating, and their conversation tends to drift from the subject. As the condition progresses, they become unable to think clearly and efficiently and their thoughts lack coherence. Patients often lose track of the temporal sequence of recent events and will describe events as having happened that day that actually occurred in the recent past. All these symptoms fluctuate but are usually accentuated at night.

In later stages, inattention and distractibility become prominent, speech is less coherent, and the patients appear confused and bewildered. They are unsure of the date and gradually show disorientation for place as well as time. Activity level changes. In some patients restlessness may be accentuated to the point of agitation and hyperactivity, whereas in most patients the level of consciousness decreases and psychomotor retardation and lethargy are evident. The agitated patient may show swings from hyperactivity to lethargy during each 24-hour period. In this more severe stage, abnormalities in perception can occur, and patients may misperceive unfamiliar people in their environment as being familiar. It is not uncommon for a patient in the incipient phase of delirium tremens to steadfastly hold to the belief that the doctor is a close relative. This is a vastly different situation from that seen in schizophrenic patients. To them, the familiar figure is often thought to be a stranger and in some way threatening.[15,44] Such delusions and illusions may be accompanied by frank visual or tactile hallucinations.

Eventually, confusional patients lose touch with reality; they are grossly disoriented, incoherent, and hallucinatory. Fluctuations in level of awareness are more dramatic, and the patients are totally unable to sustain attention. At this point the behavioral disorder can be classified as psychotic in degree. If the disease process is not reversed, the patients will rapidly become stuporous. Patients who have been grossly agitated may present with a muttering stupor (i.e., requiring vigorous stimulation to arouse, yet emitting constant muttering noises).

The total clinical picture of most patients in the acute confusional state falls into two main categories: lethargic or agitated. In some patients the picture is consistent throughout the course of the acute episode, whereas in others, it varies from lethargy to agitation during the same day. Often the lethargic patient can become very anxious and agitated when the lights are turned off in the room at night and he is left alone with reduced sensory stimulation. The following case exemplifies this point:

A 72-year-old woman suffered an episode of confusion during a transient global amnesic episode. The next morning the patient was clear mentally, but somewhat lethargic. Her daughter stayed with her throughout the day and reported that the patient had only several short periods when she was unsure of why she was in the hospital. Early in the evening the patient was sleeping; the daughter turned out the room light and went home to clean up and have supper. The daughter returned 3 hours later to find the nurses greatly disturbed because the patient had pulled out her intravenous infusion, had tried to climb over the side rails of the bed, and was shouting violently that everyone was trying to kill her.

When a patient becomes agitated and hyperactive as did this woman, we consider her confusional behavior as delirious. The agitated confusional state or classic delirium, in addition to having the behavioral changes seen with any confusional state, also has the added feature of autonomic overactivity with pupillary dilatation, flushed facies, tachycardia, and tachypnea. Delirium can be a phase of any confusional state or can be the predominant behavioral pattern, as in cases of delirium tremens from alcohol withdrawal. Regardless of the mode of presentation and activity level, the basic features of the acute confusional syndrome are common to all such patients.

One additional feature of these states that is often useful in differentiating them from the dementias or the schizophrenias is their rapidity of onset. Confusional behavior develops over a period of hours to days rather than over months or years. In taking the history from the family of a demented or schizophrenic patient, many clues of disordered behavior slowly developing over a long time are usually found. The family of the confusional patient is frequently very upset and distraught because of the sudden appearance of bizarre and uncharacteristic behavior in a previously normal person.

Some patients are predisposed to developing confusional states, and the physician must be aware of them and keep a watchful eye for the development of rapid changes in mental status. By far the most susceptible population of patients is demented or senile persons. Mild metabolic imbalances, sleep loss, or minor head trauma is often all that is necessary to produce a florid delirium in such patients. Patients who have become confusional during a previous hospitalization, particularly after surgery, are very likely to replay their delirium in similar circumstances. A third group of vulnerable patients is those with brain damage, regardless of cause.

THE NEUROBEHAVIORAL EVALUATION

The acute confusional state is a purely behavioral syndrome that can readily be diagnosed at the bedside by recognizing its specific behavioral features.

Acuteness of Onset

The acuteness of onset can be readily evaluated by clinical observation of the patient by the nursing staff if the confusional state developed in the hospital or by the history obtained from family members if the condition arose at home. The evolution of abnormal behavior over a course of hours to days is strongly suggestive of an acute confusional state, whereas a history of months to years of progressively confused behavior raises the question of a progressive dementia. In some cases the confusion comes on gradually and can become chronic, lasting for months.

Clouding of Consciousness

Evaluation of the clouding of consciousness involves the assessment of both the level of alertness and the content of thought processes. The level of alertness is determined by the quality of the patient's response to environmental stimulation. When evaluating the patient, the examiner should use graded levels of stimulation to quantify the patient's responsiveness.

The initial stimulation should consist of calling the patient's name in a conversational tone. If the patient fails to respond at this level, a louder and more persistent tone of voice should be used. Next, gentle shaking of the patient's arm should accompany the vocal stimulation. Finally, more vigorous stimulation (auditory and tactile) should be applied. Patients who respond only to vigorous stimulation or who fail to respond at all are classified as stuporous or comatose and do not fall within the category of the acute confusional state. The confusional patient is typically lethargic and responds to a loud spoken voice and minimal tactile stimulation. The agitiated confusional (delirious) patient, on the other hand, is hyperresponsive to environmental stimuli and, because of this, responds readily to any attempt at stimulation. Despite their alertness, these agitated patients are distractible and fail to sustain attention to the examiner.

The level of alertness of the acutely confusional patient fluctuates during the course of the day and night. Such patients are often lethargic and sleepy during the day and become agitated at night. In the early stages of the confusional state, the patient may appear normally alert and respond appropriately much of the time. Because of these fluctuations, the physician must carefully evaluate the level of alertness on a number of occasions during the day and question nurses and visitors concerning variations in the patient's responsiveness.

Recognition of the clouding or impairment of thought processes requires careful observation of the patient's behavior and conversation. It is important for the physician to actually converse with the patient several times a day to determine whether he is thinking clearly and coherently. It is surprising how many doctors enter the patient's room after a review of the chart and say, "How are you today? Things seem to be going well; the heart test was normal, and you will be having some x-rays today." The patient is frequently given time only to say "Hello, I'm fine," and then nod in agreement with the day's plan before the busy physician, with a stack of charts in hand, is off to the next room. From this cursory glance, things seem to be all right, but the patient has not been allowed to demonstrate if he can think and talk coherently. It is useful to ask the patient about what he has been doing in the hospital and particularly to have him review the tests that he has had and laboratories to which he has been taken. This information is known to the doctors, and it is easy to verify whether the patient is fully aware of what is transpiring.

If the nurse or family has reported an episode of confusion, ask the patient about it. One of our patients, questioned after being missing from the ward for 2 hours, reported that he "got up to see a friend in the lobby and could not see what all the fuss was about," failing to see the inappropriateness of wandering about the hospital lobby at 2:00 a.m. in an open hospital gown. Such inconsistencies in the patient's logic and the abnormal behavior are important bits of evidence in diagnosing an early confusional state. When listening to the patient, it is important to look for signs of slow and imprecise thinking. This is very easy to recognize if the physician has known the patient for some time but is more difficult for the consultant seeing the patient for the first time. It is therefore very important for the primary physician to listen carefully to the patient's conversation. Any sign of incoherent thinking should alert the examiner to the fact that mentation is becoming confused. It is useful to ask basic questions concerning orientation (e.g., date, time, place, and person). Many hospitalized patients have difficulty with exact dates, but the confusional patient demonstrates more flagrant disorientation.

Attention

The next step in the mental status evaluation is the assessment of attention. Throughout their course, confusional patients have difficulty with attention and concentration. This problem may not be obvious to the casual observer, although the patient himself may complain of difficulty in concentrating. During the examination the physician should look for signs of inattention or distractibility. If it is not obvious that the patient is inattentive, specific tests of attention and concentration should be administered. The best and most commonly used is the digit repetition test. The average nonaphasic person should be able to repeat 6 to 7 digits forward, and any difficulty with this task suggests inattention. A more complicated yet better test of vigilance or concentration is the "A" test (see Chapter 3). The serial subtraction test (the patient is asked to subtract 7s serially beginning with 100 (i.e., 100–93–86–79) is a complex yet commonly used test of concentration. This test can be failed for numerous reasons other than inattention and concentration (e.g., aphasia or calculation problems), so we prefer to use the digit repetition and "A" tests as measures of attention.

Perception

Disorders of perception (illusions, delusions, and hallucinations) are evaluated by carefully observing the patient's behavior, questioning him about any strange or unusual feelings or sensory experiences, and asking the nursing staff and visitors if they have observed any indications of these misperceptions or hallucinations. The patient may not overtly display this behavior and often will not report such events spontaneously. We saw an elderly patient with parkinsonism who was apparently doing well on levodopa. During one office visit, the patient's wife asked us if her husband had told us about the animals that he reported seeing. He had not told us about this experience, but when asked, he described "nice little rabbits and other furry animals climbing over the bed and TV set at night." When asked why he had not reported these before, he replied simply, "I kind of liked them and didn't think that it was important to tell you." Other confusional patients, particularly those in acute delirium tremens, actively hallucinate and frequently become paranoid, shouting at the object of their hallucination (e.g., blue spiders crawling on the skin or snakes infesting their bed).

Disorientation, Memory Loss, and Other Cognitive and Emotional Changes

Disorientation is another typical feature of the more floridly confusional patient and may readily be assessed by asking the patient the date, where he is, who he is, and what he is doing here. Frequently such patients will insist that they are at home or in some other familiar place and that the medical staff are all personal acquaintances. Disorientation to person is relatively infrequent and is indicative of the most severe stage of confusion.

If careful mental status testing is carried out (an all-too-often futile and unrewarding exercise), most will demonstrate recent memory loss, difficulty writing, poor calculating ability, and global problems with high-level abstract reasoning. With these cognitive changes, emotional abnormalities can also be observed: anxiety, fear, depression, paranoia, and delusions.

Fluctuations in Behavior

As previously mentioned, it is important for the physician to note any fluctuations in the patient's mental status during the course of the day and night. Because of the great diurnal variation of behavior in the confusional state, it is not unusual for the night nurse to report that a patient is agitated, confused, and wandering, yet on morning rounds, the patient is alert, bright, and capable of carrying on a normal conversation. Nocturnal peregrinations and confusion are frequently the first signs of an impending confusional state and must be recognized as such by the physician. Although confusional behavior is more typical at night, fluctuations may also occur at any time during the day. With this behavioral fluctuation, the sleep/wake cycle is also frequently reversed; the patient sleeps all day only to awaken at dark and be up all night.

In summary, the evaluation of the acute confusional state relies heavily on the examiner's ability to observe and elicit the various behavioral abnormalities that compose the syndrome. No simple physical or neurologic signs can establish the diagnosis; the diagnosis must be made on behavioral grounds alone.

DIFFERENTIAL DIAGNOSIS

Several vastly different conditions can be present with rapidly evolving disordered behavior. Some are organic in cause, whereas others are purely psychiatric. It is important for the clinician to consider these various possible diagnoses, especially when the cause of the abnormal behavior is not readily apparent.

In their most florid stages, acute schizophrenic episodes, acute mania[11] (manic-depressive illness, manic-type), severe psychotic depressive reactions with marked psychomotor retardation, and the severe adjustment reaction of adulthood (acute panic state) may demonstrate some of the behavioral features of acute confusional states. Of the organic conditions, fluent aphasia and dementia are the conditions most commonly misdiagnosed as acute confusional states. All of the above conditions have an acute onset, an alternation of activity level that may be either restlessness and hyperactivity or lethargy and hypoactivity, disordered thinking, and inattention and distractibility.

Despite these similarities, the organic and functional conditions can usually be readily differentiated by careful observation and examination. The findings that allow the examiner to make the differential diagnosis include those that follow.

Clouding of Consciousness

The most important differential feature is the presence or absence of alterations in the level of consciousness. Confusional patients typically have a decreased but fluctuating level of awareness. The patients with an acute fluent aphasia secondary to stroke may have superimposed confusion initially, but the language disturbance is out of proportion to the confusion and should make the diagnosis easy. In contrast, demented patients and patients with a functional illness maintain a constant and normal level of consciousness. The use of major sedating medication in the psychiatric patient will, of course, result in a decreased level of awareness, thereby making the differential diagnosis more difficult.

Cognitive Impairment

The organically brain-damaged patient demonstrates an impairment of cognitive functions. The aphasic shows primarily language disturbances, whereas both demented and confusional patients will show global cognitive loss. History and level of alertness are the critical factors in differentiating these conditions. It must be remembered that demented persons are prone to develop a superimposed confusional state, so it is not uncommon to encounter the two conditions in the same patient. Psychiatric patients, conversely, show little evidence of true cognitive deficit, although their inattention and disordered thought processes cause them to make errors on mental status testing, particularly on measures of memory, calculation, and complex reasoning.

Nature of Incoherent Thought Processes

The thought processes of the patient with organic brain damage tend to be fragmented, slow, and disordered. Their language is often circumlocutory, and sometimes aphasic. Paranoid ideation and delusions may be present in both patients with organic and those with functional conditions; however, symbolic and systematized delusions are more typical of the functional psychotic disorders. Manic and acutely anxious (panic) patients have a press of thought, flight of ideas, and a very rapid production of speech; these features are not seen in the typical organic confusional state. In psychotic depression, the thought processes are slowed but only infrequently are they incoherent. The speech production in such patients tends to be laconic and measured, a feature not found in acute confusional patients.

Quality of Disordered Perception

Although both patients with organic brain disease and those with functional brain disorders may have delusions and/or hallucinations, the nature of the perceptual disturbance is usually different. The organically brain-damaged patient experiences primarily visual and tactile hallucinations, whereas the functionally psychotic patient more commonly has auditory hallucinations. The delusions of the organically damaged patient are characterized by the misperception of the unfamiliar as familiar, whereas the reverse is true in the patient with a functional disorder (i.e., the familiar as unfamiliar).

MEDICAL EVALUATION

The diagnostic challenge presented by the confusional patient is similar to, and equally as critical as, that presented by the patient in coma. A systematic and deliberate evaluation is imperative. The first step, as in any diagnostic problem, is to obtain the available historical data from family, friends, or the nursing staff in cases in which the patient's confusional behavior has developed while the patient was in the hospital. The best place to start when evaluating an inpatient is the patient's chart. Carefully read the nurses' notes, particularly the night nurses'; check the medication sheet and graphic chart for evidence of fever, hypotension, and bradycardia. After the history, careful physical and neurologic examinations are necessary. Table 5–1 shows a convenient assessment form for confusional

Table 5-1 Assessment for Confusional Behavior

1. Level of Arousal
   Day: Mild lethargy   1 point
          Significant lethargy   2 points
   Night: Asleep   0 point
          Awake   1 point
          Agitated   2 points   _____

2. Disorientation
   Time   1 point
   Place   2 points
   Person   3 points   _____

3. Inattention
   Mild   1 point
   Moderate   2 points
   Severe   3 points   _____

4. Incoherence in Conversation
   Mild   2 points
   Moderate   3 points
   Marked   4 points   _____

5. Misperceptions
   Misidentifies individuals   3 points
   Illusions   4 points
   Halucinations   5 points   _____

6. Behavior Change
   Restlessness   1 point
   Agitation   3 points
   Paranoia   4 points   _____

7. Inappropriate Behavior
   Mild, such as walking out in
     open gown asking to go
     home   3 points   _____
   Significant agitated behavior
     with yelling and
     attempting to pull out
     catheters, climb over bed
     rails, etc.   5 points   _____

   Date_____Time_____   Total   _____

behavior. Point scores roughly correspond to the pathological significance of each item.[40] Evaluation can be done at frequent intervals (every 2 hours) to document fluctuation or to plot daily (same time each day) change in baseline functioning. Table 5-2 lists the most important factors to con-

Table 5-2 Medical Evaluation of the Confusional Patient

History
1. Medications: Particularly psychotropic, antiparkinsonism, diuretic, anorexic, or sedative
2. Illicit drug use
3. Medical illness:
   Heart disease
   Diabetes
   Liver or kidney disease
   Hypertensive or arteriosclerotic vascular disease
   Thyroid disease or previous thyroid surgery
   Other endocrine disturbances
   AIDS
4. Alcohol use
5. Neurologic disease:
   Epilepsy,
   Evidence of early dementia (e.g., memory failure, difficulty doing job)
   Recent onset of neurologic symptoms (e.g., visual disturbance, gait difficulty)
6. Psychiatric illness (e.g., anxiety, depression, psychosis)
7. Recent trauma
8. Recent surgery

Physical Examination

Parameter	Finding	Clinical Implication
1. Pulse	Bradycardia	Hypothyroidism
		Stokes-Adams syndrome
		Increased intracranial pressure
	Tachycardia	Hyperthyroidism
		Infection
		Heart failure
2. Temperature	Fever	Sepsis
		Thyroid storm
		Vasculitis
3. Blood Pressure	Hypotension	Shock
		Hypothyroidism
		Addison's disease
	Hypertension	Encephalopathy
		Intracranial mass
4. Respiration	Tachypnea	Diabetes
		Pneumonia
		Cardiac failure
		Fever
		Acidosis (metabolic)
	Shallow	Drug or alcohol intoxication
5. Carotid vessels	Bruits or decreased pulse	Transient cerebral ischemia

Table 5-2 Continued—**Physical Examination**

Parameter	Finding	Clinical Implication
6. Scalp and face	Evidence of trauma	
7. Neck	Evidence of nuchal rigidity	Meningitis Subarachnoid hemorrhage
8. Eyes	Papilledema	Tumor Hypertensive encephalopathy
	Pupillary dilatation	Anxiety Autonomic overactivity (e.g., delirium tremens)
9. Mouth	Tongue or cheek lacerations	Evidence of generalized tonic-clonic seizures
10. Thyroid	Enlarged	Hyperthyroidism
11. Heart	Arrhythmia	Inadequate cardiac output, possibility of emboli
	Cardiomegaly	Heart failure Hypertensive disease
12. Lungs	Congestion	Primary pulmonary failure Pulmonary edema Pneumonia
13. Breath	Alcohol Ketones	Diabetes
14. Liver	Enlargement	Cirrhosis Liver failure
15. Nervous system		
a. Reflexes-muscle stretch	Asymmetry with Babinski's signs	Mass lesion Stroke Pre-existing dementia
	Snout	Frontal mass Bilateral posterior cerebral artery occlusion
b. Abducens nerve (6th cranial nerve)	Weakness in lateral gaze	Increased intracranial pressure
c. Limb strength	Asymmetrical	Mass lesion Stroke
d. Autonomic	Hyperactivity	Anxiety Delirium

sider in taking the history, performing the examination, and choosing the appropriate laboratory tests.

Differential Diagnosis

Myriad medical illnesses can present with acute confusional behavior. It is impossible to discuss each in detail; however, we will try to cover those conditions that are most frequently encountered in clinical practice, to enable the physician to develop a systematic approach to the investigation of an individual case.

Before considering specific causes, it is important to re-emphasize that several significant factors predispose patients to develop confusional behavior. Advancing age or existing brain disease are by far the most prominent. The elderly and particularly those patients showing evidence of early senility (dementia) are unusually susceptible to any physiologic or environmental disruption. The mentally retarded also have a greater probability of developing a confusional state.[30] A history of alcohol or drug abuse or of recent sleep or sensory deprivation can all contribute. In fact, sleep or sensory deprivation alone can cause concentration difficulties, perceptual distortions, and decreased reasoning ability.[37,42] In any confusional patient, sleep loss can be a major factor in perpetuating the confusional state even though the medical problem has been ameliorated.

Another factor about which there has been considerable disagreement is the role of premorbid personality.[25] It is generally agreed that anyone can develop a full-blown confusional state if the brain's physiology is sufficiently disturbed.[29] It is also true that each person has his own threshold for the development of confusional behavior. Major psychiatric disease, either in the patient or his family, however, does not appear to be the factor establishing that threshold.[10] Stress and the anxiety generated by a serious illness do seem to have a significant disrupting effect on some patients and may precipitate confusional behavior.

Awareness of all these predisposing factors not only helps the physician understand the confusional behavior in a specific patient but also alerts him to watch the confusion-prone patient very carefully when he has a minor illness, has surgery, or uses a new medication.

When confronted with a patient in a confusional state, the physician must be able to logically determine its cause. Occasionally the offending agent is obvious, for instance, the confusion that occurs after a grand mal seizure, but frequently the cause must be carefully sought. The following factors should be considered in the differential diagnosis.

MEDICATIONS

Barbiturates; tranquilizers such as diazepam and chlordiazepoxide; antiparkinsonism drugs, particularly levodopa preparations, bromocriptine, trihexyphenidyl HCl, benztropine mesylate, and amantadine; and digitalis preparations, cimetidine, steroids, and a host of other medicines routinely used in medical practice are known to precipitate confusional behavior in some patients. Atropine and scopalamine are other common offenders and need not be given in large doses to cause a toxic response, as the following case history demonstrates.

A 42-year-old oil-field worker was given a premedication of 0.6 mg of atropine sulfate before a cardiac catheterization. The procedure went smoothly with no suggestion of arrhythmia or anoxia. As the premedication sedative wore off, however, the patient became extremely agitated. He pulled out his intravenous needle, started climbing over the side rails of the bed, and began talking in a loud voice about a recent sexual escapade. He was bewildered, disoriented, and inattentive. The patient was then sedated with chlorpromazine for 12 hours, and the delirium passed without recurrence.

Atropine ophthalmic solution contains 0.75 mg of atropine sulfate per drop and sufficient absorption can occasionally occur to cause toxicity.[27]

Although toxic reactions can occur at therapeutic dosages of these medications, many patients in whom confusional behavior develops have either misused prescribed medication or have been prescribed multiple medications whose combined effect is adverse. Some patients increase dosages in an effort to gain additional effect; this is most frequently seen with analgesics, psychotropic drugs, and anorexics (diet pills). This polypharmacy is often the cause of confusional behavior and can be corrected by tailoring and monitoring the patient's drug regimen. The elderly patient with memory difficulty is particularly at risk because of tendency to forget prescribed dosages or times of administration.

The abrupt withdrawal of certain medications can also precipitate a confusional state. Barbiturates, alcohol, opiates, and psychotropic drugs are the most frequent offenders, but others have been known to demonstrate this effect.

NONMEDICINAL SUBSTANCES

Acute alcoholic intoxications and acute alcohol withdrawal in the heavy drinker are classic and well-recognized causes of confusional behavior. Cases of confusion have also been reported with excessive coffee intake in otherwise normal young adults.[6,18]

One of the most frequent causes of acute confusional behavior in young patients is the use of illicit drugs. Opiates, cannabis, amphetamines, phencyclidine (PCP), cocaine, and hallucinogens are commonly implicated. Exposure to the hallucinogenic drugs in particular can cause an acute psychotic delirium that is not unlike an acute schizophrenic state. Usually the patients have bizarre hallucinations (e.g., hearing colors), vivid visual illusions, and distortions of perception rather than the auditory hallucinations typically seen in schizophrenia. The schizophrenic is usually more withdrawn and autistic in his behavior and thinking than is the drug user.[1,45] PCP is an unusually dangerous drug; in high doses, it can produce violent behavior as well as catatonic states.

ELECTROLYTE IMBALANCE

Electrolyte imbalance can develop in any patient and particularly in those using diuretics. Any medical condition in which gastrointestinal function is abnormal (e.g., vomiting, diarrhea, fistulae, or obstruction) can lead to marked shifts in electrolytes and subsequent dysfunction of the brain. Patients taking intravenous fluids are an obvious group at risk for developing electrolyte problems. Water intoxication, although rare, can occur and will cause an acute confusional episode until corrected.

METABOLIC DISEASE

Several metabolic diseases cause sufficient disruption in cerebral metabolism to produce confusional behavior. Diabetes is by far the most common. Hyperglycemia with or without acidosis (nonketotic hyperosmolar state) or hypoglycemia, primarily in the treated diabetic, can all cause a clouding of consciousness and confusion.

Thyroid disease with either hyperthyroidism or myxedema is another common cause of confusional behavior. In thyrotoxicosis, the patient becomes very agitated and hyperactive, but beneath this agitation may be elements of mood depression. We saw a 58-year-old man who had been admitted to the psychiatric unit with a diagnosis of agitated depression and unexplained recent weight loss. On examination, the patient was agitated, inattentive, and showed varying degrees of clouded consciousness. His T_3 and T_4 were found to be extremely elevated. With prompt treatment of his hyperthyroidism, his mental confusion, depression, and agitation all cleared within 2 weeks.

Hypothyroidism or myxedema can present in various ways, the most common being characterized by slowness, apathy, and poor performance on intellectual tasks. Other patients, however, do present with a full-blown psychotic confusional state known as myxedema madness.[8]

Deficiencies as well as overactivity of the parathyroid or adrenal glands have also been implicated as causes of confusion and must be considered in the differential diagnosis.[15]

Vitamin deficiencies have long been known to cause various mental syndromes including the confusional states. Acute thiamine deficiency produces a confusional state known as Wernicke's encephalopathy (discussed more fully in Chapter 10). Nicotinic acid deficiency leading to pellagra, although not common, does occur in alcoholics and people with abnormal dietary habits. Pellagra can present with an acute confusional state even in the absence of the other clinical features of the disease (rash and diarrhea). B_{12} or folic acid deficiency can also be associated with mental confusion.[14,21] These patients often have a previous history of gastric surgery, although the condition can appear in isolation.

We have recently seen several patients who developed chronic confusional behavior after having had gastric plication procedures done for weight control. The presumed cause was malnutrition and vitamin deficiency.

Abnormalities in copper metabolism are rare but of particular interest to the neurologist. Wilson's disease is a recessive genetic disease that has changes in mental function as one of its major symptoms. Although psychiatric or chronic mental deterioration are more typical presentations in this disease, acute episodes of confusional behavior can occur.

Another rare disease that frequently presents as acute confusion is acute intermittent porphyria. When patients develop a syndrome of confusion, inappropriate antidiuretic hormone secretion, repeated seizures, and a history of abdominal pain, this diagnosis should be considered.

ORGAN FAILURE

The decompensation of any major vital organ can often be accompanied by confusional behavior. Cardiac or pulmonary failure produces a relative anoxia that is poorly tolerated by the brain. Arrhythmias can also result in a significant decrease in cardiac output, thereby reducing cerebral oxygenation. Hepatic and renal failure cause a build-up of metabolic products that eventually act as toxins and cause cerebral dysfunction.

INFECTION

Any infectious disease, if sufficiently severe, can lead to an acute confusional state. Infections produce confusional behavior through several mechanisms. In encephalitis, the brain cells themselves are infected with viral particles. In meningitis, there is an inflammation of the cortical surface and edema, as well as a secondary vasculitis that develops in the vessels on the cortical surface, causing ischemia of patches of cortex. The most common infectious cause of a confusional state is the indirect effect on the brain seen in systemic sepsis. Although at one time each specific agent was thought to produce a distinct type of confusional state, it is now recognized that the clinical picture of abnormal behavior is the same for any infective agent.[9]

OTHER NEUROLOGIC DISEASE

In several neurologic diseases, confusional behavior can be the only clinical manifestation. One such condition is increased intracranial pressure, which may be secondary to a tumor, infection, obstruction of cerebrospinal fluid flow, hypertensive crises, or benign intracranial hypertension (pseudotumor cerebri).

Seizure disorders of various types can produce an acute confusional state.[28,43] In grand mal epilepsy (generalized tonic-clinic seizures), the confusional behavior is most often seen after the seizure (postictal), although the prodrome or aura can also be characterized by a clouding of consciousness. In psychomotor or temporal lobe epilepsy (partial seizure complex symptomatology) the seizure itself can simulate a confusional state. These patients often walk around aimlessly muttering to themselves for as long as an hour during a series of seizures.[32] The following case is an example of a patient in petit mal (absence) status epilepticus who presented in a confusional state.

A 55-year-old woman was brought to the office by the police. An officer stated that he had found the woman wandering around a bus stop mumbling incoherently. On neurologic examination she appeared to be completely out of contact with reality. She would try to talk but could produce only four or five slurred words and would then stop and begin to blink her eyes. She was agitated and restlessly pulled at her clothes and hair. Because many of her restless movements looked like psychomotor automatisms, she was taken to the electroencephalographic laboratory. Her EEG tracing showed almost continuous 3-cycle-per-second spike-and-wave bursts, compatible with petit mal (absence) status epilepticus. The patient was promptly treated with intravenous diazepam and within 15 min was conversing normally. The patient is now 68 years old and still has occasional periods of confusion related to absence seizures despite therapeutic anticonvulsant drug levels.

Head trauma, particularly in the child and elderly adult, can lead to a behavioral change in the postconcussive period. Often the confusional state is present immediately after the injury, as is seen in football players or boxers after a severe blow to the head. On some occasions, the onset is delayed by several days.

A 78-year-old man had been beaten up. Immediately after injury, he was clear mentally and required only stitching of his wounds and a cast on a broken arm. He returned home the same day. That night he did not sleep well because of pain and was given stronger analgesic medication. The second night he became quite restless and began to have rather florid paranoid ideation. On the following day, he was agitated and had great difficulty thinking and talking clearly. Neurologic evaluation did not reveal any focal findings, and results on the brain scan and skull films were negative, but the EEG showed diffuse moderate slowing. The patient was treated conservatively with reassurance, thioridazine, and chloral hydrate for sleep. He made an uneventful recovery within several days and has not had any further difficulty.

This is the typical course of a post-traumatic confusional state, but occasionally the behavioral change is the first sign of a more serious condition.

A 76-year-old woman was admitted to the hospital in a confusional state after head trauma. Her neurologic examination was normal, but her level of consciousness steadily decreased over a 24-hour period. Evaluation including EEG, CT scan, and angiography revealed a large subdural hematoma. Surgery was immediately performed but unfortunately she died postoperatively.

This case demonstrates the great importance of an aggressive evaluation and close observation of the patient with behavioral change after head trauma.

VASCULAR DISEASE

Vascular disease is well known for its ability to cause focal brain lesions with specific behavioral syndromes. There are, however, several vascular conditions that can produce an acute confusional state. The first results from subarachnoid hemorrhage. The mechanism by which the subarachnoid blood causes generalized disruption of brain function is uncertain, but several explanations are possible: (1) irritation of the cortex by blood or blood breakdown products, (2) vascular spasm, or (3) development of hydrocephalus from interference with cerebrospinal fluid circulation. The second vascular condition associated with confusional behavior is hypertensive encephalopathy. These patients are usually somewhat lethargic and complain of headache, but the outstanding features are occasionally incoherent thought, clouding of consciousness, and bizarre behavior. The third condition is cerebral vasculitis, particularly systemic lupus erythematosus. Although seizures are the most common cerebral manifestation of vasculitis, mental disorders occur in about one third of the cases.[24] The confusional state of delirious type is one of the most common of these mental disorders, whereas the remainder mimic psychiatric disorders. The fourth vascular cause is occlusive cerebrovascular disease. It is common for patients to show a degree of confusion after any acute cerebral infarct. This confusion may be somewhat overshadowed by the more obvious neurologic deficits of hemiplegia and aphasia. Nevertheless, these patients frequently act inappropriately, display agitation, and have the typical clouding of consciousness seen in a confusional state. Usually this acute postinfarct confusion clears within 24 to 48 hours unless brain swelling is significant and intracranial pressure greatly increased.

Some patients with focal infarcts, however, do develop prolonged, significant confusional states. These cases are interesting because they raise the possibility that confusional behavior may be due in part to damage or dysfunction of specific brain areas. The first group of such patients described in the literature had occlusions of the anterior cerebral arteries or rupture of anterior communicating artery aneurysms.[38] These lesions resulted in infarction or destruction of the anterior cingulate gyri, orbital frontal cortex, and septal nuclei.[7] These patients usually had motor and reflex changes in their legs, but often the outstanding feature of their illness was the acute onset of confusion with lethargy or agitation. An "agitated delirium" has also been reported with occlusion of the posterior cerebral arteries and infarction of the occipital lobes plus the fusiform, lingual, and hippocampal gyri. In the most dramatic cases, the patients had bilateral lesions, but the syndrome can be produced by a unilateral lesion.[22,33]

Some patients develop a transient confusional state with a very prominent memory disturbance. This state has been called a transient global amnesia and is believed to be secondary to vascular insufficiency in the distribution of the posterior cerebral arteries. This condition is more fully discussed in Chapter 8.

Recently there has been a series of reports of cases in which patients with right middle cerebral artery occlusions presented with the features of a classic confusional state.[35,41] The lesions were confined to the inferior frontal or inferior parietal lobes, and the patients did not have abnormalities on routine neurologic examination. They were initially diagnosed as having "confusional state secondary to metabolic imbalance." Only after a brain scan revealed the cortical lesion was it realized that these confusional states were secondary to focal lesions. The principal feature of the confusional state in these patients was inattention. Reticulocortical and limbic-cortical input is substantial in these areas and, in the normal person, these regions are very important substrates for selective attention.[34]

A final type of occlusive vascular lesion that can produce confusional behavior is that seen with severe bilateral extracranial carotid artery disease. In these patients, marked stenosis or occlusion of the carotid arteries significantly reduces the blood flow to the cerebral hemispheres. Any sudden change in hemodynamics can cause transient cerebral ischemia and confusion. Usually there are other transient neurologic symptoms and signs that suggest a vascular cause, but on occasion confusional behavior is the only clinical manifestation.

SURGERY

The postoperative period is a common clinical setting for confusional behavior. As with all causes, the elderly are the most vulnerable. The abnormal behavior pattern frequently appears on the third or fourth postoperative night, but it can arise any time during the first 2 weeks. Many factors contribute to the development of confusional behavior in the patient after surgery, and the surgeon must carefully review the entire history, operative period, and postoperative course to determine the cause of the confusion. Table 5-3 lists causative factors.

Anoxia during the operative procedure is a major factor, and a review of the anesthesia record can help to uncover prolonged periods of hypotension, difficulty with adequate air exchange, or significant cardiac arrhythmia. The anesthetic agents themselves do not seem to be a problem, but premedication, particularly atropine, can be a factor. An inadequate oxygen supply to brain tissue, however, can cause cerebral dysfunction. If significant anoxia has been present during surgery, the patient will show confusion on awaking from anesthesia. This is quite different from the patient who develops confusional behavior in the third or fourth postoperative day as a result of electrolyte imbalances that have arisen subsequent to surgery.

Cardiac surgery is one type of surgery in which postoperative confusion and delirium have been common and significant problems. Patients undergoing valve replacement frequently develop not only a confusional state but also scattered abnormal neurologic signs in the postoperative period.[46] Pathologic study of fatal cases has revealed multiple microemboli and evidence of anoxic damage to neurons in the hippocampus. It had been postulated that the microemboli came from the bypass pump and caused both microinfarcts and decreased cerebral oxygenation.[12] The in-

Table 5-3 Factors Leading to the Postoperative
Development of an Acute Confusional State

1. Anoxia during surgery
2. Sepsis
3. Electrolyte imbalance
4. Abnormal reaction to sedatives and analgesics
5. Atelectasis with decreased oxygen pressure
6. Loss of sleep
7. Pain
8. Fear and stress
9. Cerebral emboli, particularly microemboli in cardiac surgery
10. Drug or alcohol withdrawal
11. Any combination of the above

troduction of a small-pore filter into the pump-oxygenator has considerably decreased the incidence of postoperative brain damage and dysfunction.[20] Confusional behavior, however, continues to be a problem. In a study reported in 1979, postoperative delirium developed in 38 percent of 48 patients receiving single valve replacements. In this series, cardiac output was carefully monitored, and it was apparent that a significant drop in output was a major factor in the production of the delirium. Patients undergoing valve replacement surgery have a higher incidence of confusional behavior than those having coronary bypass operations. Accordingly, intracardiac surgery appears to involve higher risk.

The actual surgery, however, is not the only factor, because cardiac patients, like most other postoperative patients, tend to develop confusional states 2 to 5 days after surgery. The cardiac surgery patient has a somewhat different postoperative course because he remains in a special intensive care unit for several days before being returned to his regular hospital room. Nursing routines and general activity in such units give the patients virtually no sustained periods of sleep.[23] One study showed that the patients were disturbed an average of 47 times during each of the first three nights after surgery.[47] Such units are very sterile-appearing and, in general, the environment is monotonous, nonstimulating, and disrupting. This sleep and sensory deprivation coupled with pain, uncertainty about prognosis, and the general stress of the illness combine to produce what has become known as "the intensive care unit psychosis" or "I.C.U. psychosis." That this is the origin of the psychosis is supported by the fact that patients usually have a rapid clearing of their confusion on return to their own rooms.[26] Although first appreciated in postsurgery patients, this syndrome is also common in other patients restricted to coronary or medical intensive care units.

The physician must also be very attentive to the problems of electrolyte imbalance, adverse effect of analgesics, and fever. Electrolyte balance is particularly important in those patients requiring intravenous infusion for an extended period. One surgical procedure that is known to cause an immediate electrolyte imbalance and confusional behavior is the transurethral prostatectomy. During this surgery, copious amounts of water are used to irrigate the operative field and some patients absorb large quantities of pure water and develop a dramatic water intoxication syndrome. This is easily recognized by the urologist, and the patient's water intake is restricted. The use of hypertonic saline is dangerous because the patients are usually elderly and are already hypervolemic. The addition of salt will exacerbate the hypervolemia and often cause cardiac decompensation.

The postsurgical confusional state is an excellent sample of how a combination of factors can produce a confusional syndrome. Advancing age with the additional possibility of early dementia; the adverse effects of strong analgesics, pain, fear, loss of sleep, and relative sensory deprivation;

and the effects of sepsis and metabolic imbalance all may be present to some degree in the same patient. Although each may seem insignificant in isolation, their combined presence may exceed the patient's individual threshold and confusional behavior can ensue.

LABORATORY EVALUATION

After completing the history and physical examination, and considering the differential diagnosis, the medical basis of the patient's problem may be obvious and the laboratory need only be consulted for confirmatory evidence. As is all too frequently the case, however, the cause may be elusive. At this point the following series of tests should be used to screen for the major causes of the confusional state.

General Testing Procedures

1. White blood count and differential
2. Sedimentation rate
3. Urine examination
    Sugar and acetone
    Leukocytes
    Albumin
    Porphyria screen
4. Serum tests
    Blood urea nitrogen and creatinine
    Sugar
    HTLV-LTV-III virus titer (selected patients)
    T_3, T_4 TSH
    Electrolytes
    Mg^{++}, Br^+
    Alcohol
    Specific drug levels
5. X-rays, routine
    Chest

Special Neurodiagnostic Tests

ELECTROENCEPHALOGRAM (EEG)

The EEG can be very useful in evaluating patients diagnosed as or suspected of having an acute organic confusional state. Most patients who have clouding of consciousness and are confusional will have a diffusely slow EEG.[17] This fact can be very useful in separating the organic from a functional, purely psychiatric psychosis. Schizophrenics, although having occasional EEG slowing, will show neither the degree nor magnitude of slowing seen in the confusional patient. In patients with delirium tremens the EEG usually shows slowing.[3] The EEG is also useful in determining whether the confusional state represents an ictal (seizure) or postictal phenomenon. If the patient is actually in status epilepticus (a seizure state in which repeated seizures do not allow mental clearing between seizures), the EEG is highly diagnostic. If the patient is postictal, epileptiform activity may have been suppressed and replaced by slow activity. Accordingly, the absence of epileptiform discharges does not rule out seizures as the cause of the confusional state.

COMPUTERIZED AXIAL TOMOGRAPHY (CT) OR MAGNETIC RESONANCE IMAGING (MRI)

In cases in which the diagnosis is uncertain, brain scanning can help to rule out the presence of a brain tumor, subdural hematoma, hemorrhage, or hydrocephalus. Ventricular size will be normal in most patients with confusional states of metabolic or toxic cause unless the patient has pre-existing dementia. Increased ventricular size without cortical atrophy is indicative of obstructed cerebrospinal fluid flow, a condition (hydrocephalus) that can present with increased pressure and confusional behavior.

SPINAL FLUID EXAMINATION

A spinal puncture is frequently advised, particularly when the cause is uncertain. Viral meningoencephalitis, unsuspected subarachnoid hemorrhage, and the chronic meningitides (tuberculosis, cryptococcal, and fungal infections) are not rare and are readily diagnosed with examination of the cerebrospinal fluid. Pressure measurements, cell count, protein, sugar, and extensive culture and staining procedures should be carried out.

INVASIVE NEURORADIOLOGIC PROCEDURES

Cerebral angiography should be done only in special cases in which a tumor or specific vascular lesion is suspected.

CONSULTATIONS

If a specific brain lesion such as tumor or stroke is suspected, it is wise to consult the neurologist or neurosurgeon to assist in the evaluation. This is particularly important before undertaking any invasive neurodiagnostic procedures (e.g., angiography).

Both neurologists and psychiatrists can be of assistance in the diagnostic evaluation, and psychiatrists can also often be especially helpful in the management of these cases.

PATIENT MANAGEMENT

Two important avenues of treatment must be followed in the management of an acute confusional state: (1) the identification and correction of the underlying medical problem and (2) the control of the abnormal and often disruptive behavior. Optimistically, the primary physician can recognize the behavioral pattern as being an acute organically based behavioral change and will initiate medical management. If, however, he is unsure of the diagnosis, he should consult a psychiatrist or neurologist. It is the primary physician's responsibility to review the patient's medical status and take steps to reverse any physiologic imbalance. With specific medical treatment, the behavior will eventually revert to the premorbid level. Unfortunately, this can sometimes take several days or even weeks. Accordingly, control of behavior must be an integral part of the overall treatment plan. If the physician is uncomfortable with this aspect of the treatment, he should consult a colleague in psychiatry to assist him. The psychiatrist is accustomed to managing psychotic behavior, and he can also serve as a valuable resource in supporting and reassuring the family and nursing staff.

Environmental Structuring

Effective control of the psychotic behavior is best achieved by a combination of the judicious use of tranquilizing medications and the rearrangement of the patient's immediate environment. If possible, the patient should be moved to a private room so that he can get adequate sleep and will not disturb other patients. Private duty nurses or family members should be with the patient at all times, particularly at night. This is very important for a number of reasons. The delirious patient may climb out of bed or pull out intravenous needles if not carefully watched. Regular nursing personnel cannot possibly be in the room constantly to prevent falls and other accidents; therefore, an attendant in the room both protects the patient and reassures him that someone is there and that he is being taken care of properly. This reassurance is especially helpful at night when the effects of sensory deprivation are the greatest. The nurse or family member can also greatly reduce disorientation by talking frequently to the patient and actively trying to reorient him. Whenever the patient awakens or becomes agitated, a simple statement like, "John, it's me, Mary. Remember you are in the Memorial Hospital. It's Sunday and the doctor says that you are doing very well," can be very effective in calming and reorienting the patient. This type of environmental input is extremely helpful in both treating the confusional patient and preventing confusion in patients at risk. The incidence of confusional behavior after surgery can be greatly reduced if the nurses or family members will reorient patients at frequent intervals during the day.[13] We cannot stress too much the value of a constant attendant (which may be a family member) in handling the confusional patient.

The use of restraints is a question that frequently arises when dealing with the delirious patient and must always be discussed with the nursing staff. In general, restraints tend to agitate patients; they should be used only when absolutely necessary to prevent accidents or disruption of life support apparatus. With most patients, restraints can be used intermittently and should be removed promptly during periods of relative calm.

The room should be well lighted, but without bright lights aimed at the patient's face. At night, a light should be left on so that the patient can reorient himself quickly to his environment if he should awaken. It is good to have a clock, calendar, pictures, and perhaps a television in the room to ensure adequate sensory stimulation. Night-time interruptions should be kept to an absolute minimum so that the patient can get adequate sleep. If the patient can be moved from the bed, it is often helpful to let him sit up during part of the day. Warm tub baths or merely wiping the patient's face and hands with a warm cloth during the day can have a definite calming effect and is a useful adjunct in dealing with the agitated patient.

Medication

Environmental manipulations create an atmosphere that maximizes the effects of medical management. Usually, however, there is a need for sedation and tranquilization. We prefer the use of the major tranquilizers, chlorpromazine, haloperidol, and thioridazine; haloperidol is the drug of first choice. The choice of dosage and route of administration will depend on the degree of the patient's agitation. A dosage of 50 mg of chlorpromazine, 25 mg of thioridazine, or 0.5 mg of haloperidol three to four times daily is usually effective in ameliorating the agitation and other abnormal behavior. Haloperidol has the advantage of being administrable intramuscularly in severe cases. The initial intramuscular dose of haloperidol should be 0.5 to 5 mg t.i.d. or q.i.d., although doses as high as 5 mg per hour have been suggested.[36] In elderly patients it is advisable to start with 0.5 or 1.0 mg. The dose can be repeated every 30 min until a calming effect is achieved. Intravenous administration has been advocated by many psychiatrists who deal with a large number of highly agitated patients; however, the FDA has yet to approve the drug's use in this fashion.[2] The oral form should supplant the injectable as soon as is practical. Chlorpromazine given intravenously will cause a severe drop in blood pressure and should not be used. Paraldehyde is probably the safest drug to use (5 to 15 ml orally, rectally, or intramuscularly four or five times daily), but the odor is often offensive to those caring for the patient. Other minor tranquilizers such as chlordiazepoxide and diazepam can be used, but these can sometime excite the elderly patient and increase the agitation. Chlordiazepoxide, however, is very effective and the drug of choice in treating delirium tremens, with doses of 100 to 400 mg per day required. Barbiturates such as sodium butabarbital can also be used, but the same caveat as with benzodiazepines obtains.

Patients whose confusional state is secondary to anticholinergic medication (e.g., atropine) can be managed by the careful use of cholinesterase inhibitors. Physostigmine salicylate in small doses (0.5 mg to 1.0 mg) given intramuscularly or intravenously (check Physician's Desk Reference for method of administration) can promptly reverse this drug-induced delirium.

Because sleep deprivation and disruption are major contributory factors in production of the acute confusional states, it is best to sedate the patient at night until the confusion clears. Often all that is needed is an extra measure of tranquilizer at the hour of sleep, but at times the addition of a soporific is necessary. Chloral hydrate, 500 mg to 1 gm, is usually sufficient. Barbiturates should be a last choice in the elderly because of their occasional paradoxical effect. The benzodiazepines have the same problem but are often effective.

Recovery

When the above steps of primary medical management, environmental structuring, and sedation/tranquilization are followed, the uncomplicated confusional state should gradually reverse, and the patient's behavior return to its premorbid level. The period of recovery is highly variable. In some cases, confusion can clear in a matter of hours; this is most dramatically seen in patients who become confusional after cataract surgery. This confusion clears almost immediately after the removal of the eye patches. In such cases, the confusional state was caused primarily by sensory deprivation; reinstatement of normal sensory input reorients the patients. In other cases of acute confusional state, the confusion will take several days to clear. Frequently there is a lag between the return to normal of serum chemistry levels and the re-establishment of normal cellular function. The return of normal synaptic membrane function may also be slow, and in some cases the total recovery process may take 3 to 4 weeks.

The degree of recovery varies and is predicated to a great extent on the type and severity of the underlying cause and the patient's age and general medical condition. Patients who experience a confusional state secondary to a drug reaction or postoperative electrolyte imbalance can usually expect a full recovery, whereas the patient who has sustained a period of anoxia with microembolism during cardiac surgery may suffer residual neurologic and cognitive impairment.

Statistically the long-term prognosis is not good. It has been shown that 35 percent of the patients who develop a delirium die within 1 year of their confusional event.[39] Although much of this ominous statistic comes from patients in the terminal stages of metabolic disease or organ failure, it is nevertheless impressive.

In many patients, the early signs of dementia or senility go unrecognized until they develop a confusional state secondary to a superimposed minor illness or after elective surgery. On initial examination it is usually impossible to discern whether a pre-existing dementia has been present. This determination must await either an accurate history from the family or evaluation after the acute confusion has completely cleared. The superimposition of an acute organic behavioral change on a chronic organic deterioration of mental function has been called "beclouded dementia," a convenient term that accurately describes this common clinical situation.[3] Although some families steadfastly claim that the patient's mental functioning was flawless before the illness, often careful questioning of the family elicits a history of failing memory or difficulty with work predating the acute illness or surgery by a number of months or even years. It is uncertain whether the physiologic disruption experienced during a confusional episode can actually exacerbate an early dementia or whether the family, patient, and physician are now able to see more clearly the early cognitive impairment. The following case history exemplifies this problem.

A 62-year-old marble cutter was working in his shop late one evening when he was hit on the head from behind by a prowler. The blow was not sufficient to render the man unconscious but merely frightened him. When the assailant left the building, the patient called a family member to take him to the hospital. On arrival at the hospital, he was anxious, somewhat lethargic, and restless. His conversation was somewhat disjointed and contained paranoid ideation. After admission, he was inattentive, and his level of consciousness fluctuated throughout the next day. This initial confusional period cleared in several days, and his neurodiagnostic evaluation revealed only a slightly slow EEG. The patient was discharged and returned to work. He then found that he was unable to concentrate and that he could not keep the accustomed work details in proper order. He complained of memory difficulties and had become extremely anxious. He insisted that his mental functioning had been completely normal before the trauma, but mental status testing showed severe memory disturbance, retrograde amnesia for a period of several years, impaired abstract ability, and constructional impairment.

It was obvious on this examination and subsequent psychologic testing that this man had a substantial cognitive deficit that was consistent with a diagnosis of a degenerative dementia (Alzheimer's disease). At this point we questioned his wife more closely, and she admitted reluctantly that his memory had, in fact, been getting worse over the last 1 to 2 years and that the head injury had only seemed to exacerbate it. A CT scan showed enlarged cerebral ventricles and generalized cortical atrophy.

This case could have been considered a posttraumatic encephalopathy had not additional investigation been undertaken. Although no pathology is available, we are positive that the trauma with its attendant confusional state served only to unmask a significant pre-existing organic disorder.

PATHOLOGY AND DISCUSSION

Acute confusional behavior is characteristically the result of a physiologic disruption of the brain's entire neuronal population. Arousal, emotion, and intellectual processes are all disturbed. Although it is not possible to localize this behavioral pattern to involvement of any specific region of the brain, it is of theoretical interest to point out the possible contributions made by dysfunction of various anatomic structures.

Clouding of consciousness, the central symptom of the confusional states, implies an alteration both in the level of alertness and in the content of conscious processes. The level of alertness is largely determined by a balance between the ascending activating and inhibiting systems. Therefore, these systems are probably dysfunctional in the confusional state. Patients with quiet or lethargic manifestations can be postulated to have suppression of the activating portion of the system and/or stimulation or release of the inhibiting portion. Conversely, the agitated or delirious type of patient may have the activating component stimulated and the inhibitory one suppressed. Damage to the cerebral cortex can also cause a decrease in the level of consciousness.[5] Accordingly, cortical as well as subcortical systems are probably involved in the regulation of alertness. The clouding of mental processes reflected in incoherent thinking, disorientation, misperception, and the disruption of specific cognitive functions is the result of widespread cortical dysfunction.

The alterations in mood and emotions such as anxiety, paranoia, depression, and irritability do not seem to be primary personality reactions to illness but rather are the direct effect of organic limbic dysfunction or release.

Inattention and distractibility are often other characteristic features of the confusional syndrome and may reflect dysfunction of specific anatomic structures. Attention requires cortical and limbic input to focus the basic arousal energy. In the confusional patient, alterations in function are present at all three levels: ascending activation system, limbic system, and cortex. Not surprisingly, the ability to selectively attend to some stimuli in the environment and to exclude other irrelevant stimulation is impaired in these patients. Although in most cases inattention is the result of widespread dysfunction, some cases of confusional behavior with gross alterations in attention have been described in patients with focal brain infarcts.[22,35] These infarctions have involved the right inferior frontal lobe, or the right inferior parietal lobule and the inferomedial temporal lobes, or the medial and deep frontal lobes. These areas are the convergence points for environmental stimuli and are necessary for continual monitoring of all incoming environmental input. The inattention and confusional behavior produced by damage to these areas seem to result from the person's inability to maintain a coherent sampling of ongoing thoughts or events.[35]

One aspect of the confusional state that cannot be well explained on anatomic grounds is the curious fact that some persons develop a delirium from the same basic metabolic disturbance that produces lethargy in another. It is possible that individual differences in anatomy and membrane function result in these different reactions, but it is equally possible that each type of clinical presentation is determined by a unique combination of factors, with the most obvious cause of the illness being only one.

Although the anatomy and pathophysiology of the acute confusional state is not yet established, the clinical picture is well defined and may be readily recognized. The patient having an acute confusional state should be considered to have a serious medical problem; a prompt and extensive evaluation is mandatory. With appropriate treatment, most patients will respond favorably with little, if any, residual. Without efficient evaluation and treatment, these patients may become comatose or even die.

REFERENCES

1. Abruzzi, W: Drug induced psychosis . . . or schizophrenia? Am J Psychoanal 35:329, 1975.
2. Adams, F: Neuropsychiatric evaluation and treatment of delirium in the critically ill cancer patient. The Cancer Bulletin 36:156, 1984.
3. Adams, RD, and Victor, M: Delirium and other confusional states. In Wintrobe, MM, et al (eds): Principles of Internal Medicine. McGraw-Hill, New York, 1974, pp 149–156.
4. Adams, RD, and Victor, M: Delirium and other confusional states. In Harrison's Principles of Internal Medicine. McGraw-Hill, New York, 1980, p 131.

5. Albert, ML, et al: Cerebral dominance for consciousness. Arch Neurol 33:453, 1976.
6. American Psychiatric Association: Diagnostic and Statistical Manual of Mental Disorders (I, II, III, and III-R). American Psychiatric Association, Washington, 1952, 1968, 1980, 1987.
7. Amyes, EW, and Nielsen, JM: Clinicopathologic study of vascular lesions of the anterior cingulate region. Bull LA Neurol Soc 20:112, 1955.
8. Asher, R: Myxoedematous madness. Br Med J 2:555, 1949.
9. Bleuler, M: Acute mental concomitants of physical disease. In Benson, DF, and Blumer, D (eds): Psychiatric Aspects of Neurologic Disease. Grune & Stratton, New York, 1975, pp 37–61.
10. Bleuler, M, Willi, J, and Buehler, HR: Akute psychische Begleiter-scheinungen Koerperlicher Krankheitan. Thieme, Stuttgart, 1966.
11. Bond, TC: Recognition of acute delirious mania. Arch Gen Psychiatry 37:553, 1980.
12. Brennan, RW, Patterson, RH, and Kessler, J: Cerebral blood flow and metabolism during cardiopulmonary bypass: Evidence of microembolic encephalopathy. Neurology 21:665, 1971.
13. Budd, S, and Brown, W: Effect of a reorientation technique on postcardiotomy delirium. Nurs Res 23:341, 1974.
14. Camp, CD: Pernicious anemia causing spinal cord changes and a mental state resembling paresis. Med Rec (New York) 81:156, 1912.
15. Cohen, S: The toxic psychoses and allied states. Am J Med 15:813, 1953.
16. Ebaugh, FG, Barnacle, CH, and Ewalt, JP: Delirious episodes associated with artificial fever: A study of 200 cases. Am J Psychiatry 24:191, 1936.
17. Engel, AI and Romano, J: Delirium: A syndrome of cerebral insufficiency. J Chronic Dis 9:260, 1959.
18. Furlong, FW: Possible psychiatric significance of excessive coffee consumption. Can Psychiatr Assoc J 20:577, 1975.
19. Heller, SS, et al: Postcardiotomy delirium and cardiac output. Am J Psychiatry 136:337, 1979.
20. Hill, JD, et al: Experience using a new Dacron wool filter during extracorporeal circulation. Arch Surg 101:649, 1970.
21. Holmes, JM: Cerebral manifestations of vitamin B_{12} deficiency. Br Med J 2:1394, 1956.
22. Horenstein, S, Chamberlain, W, and Conomy, J: Infarction of the fusiform and calcerine regions: Agitated delirium and hemianopia. Trans Am Neurol Assoc 92:85, 1967.
23. Johns, MW, et al: Sleep and delirium after open heart surgery. Br J Surg 61:377, 1974.
24. Johnson, RT, and Richardson, EP: The neurological manifestations of systemic lupus erythematosus. Medicine 47:337, 1968.
25. Knox, SJ: Severe psychiatric distrubances in the postoperative period—a five-year survey of Belfast hospitals. J Ment Sci 107:1078, 1961.
26. Kornfeld, DS, Zimberg, S, and Malm, JR: Psychiatric complications of open-heart surgery. N Engl J Med 273:287, 1965.
27. Kounis, NC: Atropine eye-drops delirium. Can Med Assoc J 110:750, 1974.
28. Lee, SI: Nonconvulsive status epilepticus: Ictal confusion in later life. Arch Neurol 42:778, 1985.

29. Lipowski, ZJ: Delirium, clouding of consciousness and confusion. J Nerv Ment Dis 145:227, 1967.
30. Lipowski, ZJ: Delirium: Acute Brain Failure in Man. Charles C Thomas, Springfield, IL, 1979.
31. Lipowski, ZJ: Transient cognitive disorders (delirium, acute confusional states) in the elderly. Am J Psychiatry 140:1426, 1983.
32. Mayeux, R, et al: Poriomania. Neurology 29:1616, 1979.
33. Medina, JL, Rubino, FA, and Ross, A: Agitated delirium caused by infarction of the hippocampal formation and fusiform and lingual gyri: A case report. Neurology 24:1181, 1974.
34. Mesulam, M-M: Attention, confusional states, and neglect. In Mesulam, M-M (ed): Principles of Behavioral Neurology. FA Davis, Philadelphia, 1985, pp 125–168.
35. Mesulam, M-M, et al: Acute confusional states with right middle cerebral artery infarctions. J Neurol Neurosurg Psychiatry 39:84, 1976.
36. Moore, DP: Rapid treatment of delirium in critically ill patients. Am J Psychiatry 134:1431, 1977.
37. Morris, GO, and Singer, MT: Sleep deprivation: The context of consciousness. J Nerv Ment Dis 143:291, 1966.
38. Okawa, M, et al: Psychiatric symptoms in ruptured anterior communicating aneurysms: Social prognosis. Acta Psychiatr Scand 61:306, 1980.
39. Rabins, PV, and Folstein, MF: Delirium and dementia. Br J Psychiatr 140:149, 1982.
40. Sadler, PD: Nursing assessment of postcardiotomy delirium. Heart Lung 8:745, 1979.
41. Schmidley, JW, and Messing, RO: Agitated confusional states in patients with right hemisphere infarctions. Stroke 15:883, 1984.
42. Solomon, P, et al (eds): Sensory deprivation: A symposium held at Harvard Medical School. Harvard University Press, Cambridge, 1961.
43. Somerville, ER, and Bruni, J: Tonic status epilepticus presenting as confusional state. Ann Neurol 13:549, 1983.
44. Stengel, E: The organic confusional state and the organic dementias. Br J Hosp Med 2:719, 1969.
45. Stone, MH: Drug related schizophrenic syndrome. Int J Psychiatry 11:391, 1973.
46. Tufo, HM, Ostfeld, AM, and Shyekelle, R: Central nervous system dysfunction following open-heart surgery. JAMA 212:1333, 1970.
47. Woods, NF: Patterns of sleep in postcardiotomy patients. Nurs Res 21:347, 1972.

Chapter 6

Alzheimer's/Senile Dementia Alzheimer Type

Confusional State
Chronic Drug Use
LABORATORY EVALUATION
   Electroencephalogram
   Studies for Visualization of Cerebral Ventricles and Cortical Sulci (CT or MRI)
   Positron Emission Tomography (PET)
   Cerebrospinal Fluid Examination
CONSULTATIONS
   Neurologist
   Neuropsychologist
   Psychiatrist
PATIENT MANAGEMENT
   Medical Management
   Treatment
ETIOLOGY AND PATHOLOGY

Mrs. R.B. was a 55-year-old poetess when her family initially brought her to the neurology clinic in 1975. Her husband gave the history that the patient had been experiencing a gradual loss of memory and mental capacity for about 1 year. Six months previously, she had been fired from a job as a real estate agent because of frequent errors and personality clashes with other employees. Her ability to keep her personal calendar of upcoming events had declined, and thus she frequently missed scheduled commitments. She forgot household details as well and seemed oblivious to the date and season. She had always been a very verbal person who spoke frequently in metaphor, but in the few months preceding her hospitalization her family noted that her speech had become rambling, tangential, and often empty of meaning. Although her personality had not changed substantially, her eccentric traits had become more dramatic. In retrospect the family reported that she had developed these eccentricities some years before the onset of her memory disturbance. These behavioral changes could possibly have been the initial symptoms of her disease. At the time we first saw her, she had also become irritable, argumentative, and often paranoid.

On initial medical and neurologic examination, the abnormalities were confined to the mental status examination. She was awake, hyperalert (any stray stimulus in the environment attracted her attention), and very inattentive to the examiner's specific questions. She denied any illness and staunchly held to the belief that she was in the hospital to see about a shoulder that had been bruised during a minor bus accident some months before. She demonstrated a remarkable press of speech, and her conversation was loosely organized, perservative, and almost completely tangential. Although extremely agitated and occasionally paranoid, she seemed very content to remain in the hospital and to be examined for short sessions.

She demonstrated no aphasia in running speech. Comprehension was impaired for complex material but not for routine conversation. She had some difficulty in naming objects and occasionally produced frank paraphasic errors. Her orientations and ability to learn were markedly impaired as was her recall of recent events. Her remote memory, however, was quite intact. Her drawings were relatively good, but block construction was impaired. Her thinking was very concrete and despite many years of using metaphorical language in her speech and poetry, she was unable to give an abstract interpretation to even the simplest of proverbs.

Neuropsychologic testing showed a Verbal IQ (WAIS) of 90, with very low scores on Comprehension and Similarities, and a Performance IQ of 76. Full Scale IQ was 83, a remarkable group for a college graduate with additional graduate-level work in journalism. Her Memory Quotient was only 52, considerably less adequate than her depressed IQ scores.

The only abnormal laboratory test results were an EEG that showed mild generalized slowing and a computerized tomography scan that demonstrated generalized cerebral atrophy (Fig. 6–1). A tentative diagnosis of Alzheimer's disease was made.

In 1977, because of failing mental capacity and the inability of her family to care for her at home, she was placed in the geriatric section of a state psychiatric hospital for custodial care. Her condition progressed slowly; she became mute, bedridden, and ultimately developed the typical paraplegia in flexion. She died in the spring of 1984, 9 years after the diagnosis was made. Unfortunately an autopsy was not performed.

This case history exemplifies one of today's major mental health problems—dementia. This problem affects those under 65 years of age as well as the elderly. Alzheimer's disease alone has a prevalence of about 2,000,000 cases in the United States; of that number 3 to 5 percent of those affected are severely impaired and have significant care demands.[78,104] In a Finnish study of 2000 consecutive hospital admissions to a medical service, it was found that 9.1 percent of all patients over the age of 55 years had moderate to severe dementia. Prevalence ranged from 0.8 percent in the 55- to 64-year-old group to 31.2 percent in the patients over 85 years of age.[41] The dementias alone have been estimated to account for a staggering 70,000 to 110,000 deaths in the United States each year.[80] As life expectancy increases, the percentage of elderly in our society will increase disproportionally. With age, unfortunately, comes the increasing probability of

I. PATIENT IDENTIFICATION
 Name: Last ＿＿＿＿＿＿ First ＿＿＿＿＿＿ Middle initial ＿＿＿
 Patient #: ＿＿＿ Social Security #: ＿＿＿ Medicare #: ＿＿＿＿＿
 Address: Street & #: ＿＿＿＿ City: ＿＿＿＿ State & Zip: ＿＿＿＿.
 Telephone: ＿＿＿＿＿＿＿＿
II. PRIMARY CONTACT
 Name: Last ＿＿＿＿＿＿ First ＿＿＿＿＿＿ Middle initial ＿＿＿
 Address: Street & #: ＿＿＿＿ City: ＿＿＿＿ State & Zip ＿＿＿＿
 Telephone: (DAY) ＿＿＿＿＿＿ (NIGHT) ＿＿＿＿＿＿
 Relationship to Alzheimer patient: ＿＿＿＿＿＿＿＿＿
III. PATIENT INFORMATION
 Date of birth: ＿＿＿＿＿＿＿＿ Age: ＿＿＿ Sex: ＿＿＿
 Marital status: ＿＿＿＿＿＿ Number of brothers: ＿＿＿ sisters: ＿＿＿
 Do any siblings have Alzheimer's disease? ＿＿＿＿＿＿＿＿
 Parents:
 Father living? ＿＿＿＿ Age: ＿＿＿
 If deceased, age at death and cause of death: ＿＿＿＿＿＿＿
 Mother living? ＿＿＿＿ Age: ＿＿＿
 If deceased, age at death and cause of death: ＿＿＿＿＿＿＿
 Any family member with Down's syndrome (Mongolism)? ＿＿＿＿
 Any family member with other neurologic or psychiatric illness? ＿＿＿ If so,
 explain: ＿＿＿＿＿＿＿＿＿＿＿＿＿＿＿
 ＿＿＿＿＿＿＿＿＿＿＿＿＿＿＿＿＿＿＿
 ＿＿＿＿＿＿＿＿＿＿＿＿＿＿＿＿＿＿＿

IV. DIAGNOSIS
 Has a diagnosis been made? ＿＿＿＿ Date of diagnosis: ＿＿＿＿＿
 If yes, by whom and what hospital? ＿＿＿＿＿＿＿＿＿
 ＿＿＿＿＿＿＿＿＿＿＿＿＿＿＿＿＿＿＿
 Which of the following tests have been done? Where?
 ＿＿＿＿ MRI scan of brain ＿＿＿＿＿＿＿＿＿＿＿
 ＿＿＿＿ CAT (CT) scan of brain＿＿＿＿＿＿＿＿＿＿
 ＿＿＿＿ Spinal tap ＿＿＿＿＿＿＿＿＿＿
 ＿＿＿＿ EEG (brainwave) ＿＿＿＿＿＿＿＿＿＿
 When was the first symptom noticed? ＿＿＿＿＿＿＿＿＿
 What was the first symptom? ＿＿＿＿＿＿＿＿＿
 Has there been any specific treatment? ＿＿＿＿ What was it and was it
 effective? ＿＿＿＿＿＿＿＿＿＿＿＿＿＿＿
 ＿＿＿＿＿＿＿＿＿＿＿＿＿＿＿＿＿＿＿

V. CURRENT PROBLEMS
 A. Does the patient have problems with:
  1. ＿＿＿＿ Attention and concentration: ＿＿＿＿＿＿＿
   ＿＿＿＿＿＿＿＿＿＿＿＿＿＿＿＿＿
   ＿＿＿＿＿＿＿＿＿＿＿＿＿＿＿＿＿
  2. ＿＿＿＿ Personality change: ＿＿＿＿＿＿＿＿
   ＿＿＿＿＿＿＿＿＿＿＿＿＿＿＿＿＿
   ＿＿＿＿＿＿＿＿＿＿＿＿＿＿＿＿＿

Figure 6–1. Alzheimer patient history form.

3. _____ Abnormal behaviors (e.g., depression, paranoia, hallucinations):

_____

_____

4. _____ Social withdrawal: _____

_____

5. _____ Speech and language (talking or understanding): _____

_____

6. _____ Memory: _____

_____

7. _____ Intellectual functioning: _____

_____

8. _____ Getting lost: _____

_____

9. _____ Episodes of confusion: _____

_____

10. _____ Incontinence: _____

_____

11. _____ Judgment: _____

_____

B. Is the patient better or worse at certain times of the day? _____ Describe: _____

_____

VI. EDUCATIONAL AND VOCATIONAL BACKGROUND
  A. Education
    1. Highest grade completed: _____
    2. Where (city and state): _____
    3. General quality of academic performance:
       a. _____ Poor _____ Below average _____ Average _____ Above average _____ Superior
       b. Any grade failures? _____ If so, what grade? _____
    4. Reason for leaving school and age at that time: _____

_____

    5. Any specific school problems or learning disabilities? _____

_____

    6. Schools attended
       a. Grade school _____
       b. High school _____
       c. College (degree?) _____

Figure 6-1. Continued.

       d. Vocational _____

       e. Other _____

  B. Vocation

    1. Age of beginning full-time employment: _____

    2. First job: _____

    3. Primary job in life: _____

    4. Exposure to toxins or hazardous substances:

       _____

       _____

    5. Age of retirement and reason for retirement:

       _____

       _____

VII. MEDICAL HISTORY

  A. Does the patient have or has the patient had:

    1. _____ High blood pressure

       a. When diagnosed: _____

       b. How treated: _____

    2. _____ Diabetes

       a. When diagnosed: _____

       b. How treated: _____

    3. _____ Heart disease

       a. What type: _____

    4. _____ Stroke: _____

    5. _____ Cancer: _____

       a. When diagnosed: _____

       b. How treated: _____

    6. _____ Significant head trauma (knocked unconscious): _____

    7. _____ Exposure to toxic substance: _____

    8. _____ Alcohol use (how much): _____

    9. _____ Other medical disease: _____

    10. _____ Psychiatric disorder: _____

  B. Medication use:

    1. Prescribed medications (please list): _____

       _____

       _____

    2. Over-the-counter medications (e.g., antacids, aspirin): _____

       _____

       _____

Figure 6–1. Continued.

some type of dementing illness developing. In a sample of 80-year-olds, for instance, a clinical picture of significant dementia is present in about 20 percent.[81] Organic brain syndromes in general account for 75 percent of all first admissions to mental hospitals in the 65- to 74-year-old age group. This percentage reaches 90 for those over the age of 75.[81] These figures are impressive and will certainly not reverse in the foreseeable future.

    Dementia is a descriptive term that is usually used to denote a group of brain diseases in which the patients have a slowly progressive deterioration in intellectual and adaptive functions. The process is not necessarily irreversible, nor is there usually a uniform or generalized decline of *all* cognitive and social functions. The actual clinical picture of dementia can develop acutely after head injury, encephalitis, anoxia, and other conditions. We prefer to call these conditions by the pathologic label of *encephalopathy*, but in regard to the clinical feature of reduced mental capacity, they are often included under the rubric of dementia. In their Diagnostic and Statistical Manual III-R (DSM-III-R), the American Psychiatric Association defines a dementia by the mental status features seen at one point in time and not as a progressive disease process. They diagnose the mental changes seen after head trauma, anoxia, or encephalitis as posttraumatic, postanoxia, or postinfectious dementia;[2] we prefer to call such mental changes that occur after a single neurologic insult by the pathologic term, *encephalopathy*. We reserve the term *dementia* for diseases with slowly progressive mental changes. The diagnosis of dementia requires that the patient meet certain clinical criteria.

1. Slowly progressive changes in cognitive and social coping abilities.
2. Absence of clouding of consciousness (this factor clearly differentiates dementia from delirium or confusional states).
3. Evidence on formal mental status testing of deficits in several areas of cognitive functioning. Memory is usually, but not always, one of the deficits. This is one area in which we differ with the DSM-III-R; it requires memory loss as a major criterion. Many dementias have spared memory function, particularly in the early stages.

In a given patient, a dementia must be distinguished from a primary amentia or mental retardation, a situation in which mental development was defective from birth or early life.

Dementia is a common clinical syndrome that has both varied causes and clinical presentation. Although the dementias known as Alzheimer's disease, Pick's disease, and multi-infarct dementia have fairly characteristic modes of presentation, there is considerable variation within each group. In this first chapter on the dementias, we describe the general clinical features, the neurologic and laboratory evaluations, and the general principles of patient management. Because of its frequency, we have chosen to use Alzheimer's disease as the prototype for our discussion. Although at one time Alzheimer's disease and senile dementia had been considered distinct entities, they are now considered to be the same disorder. Their clinical picture and pathologic findings are identical, and the only substantial difference seems to lie in the arbitrary assignment of one label to those patients under 65 years of age (i.e., Alzheimer's presenile dementia) and another to those in the senium (i.e., senile dementia).[52,77]

Presenile Alzheimer's disease was thought to be a devastating dementia with extensive neuropathologic abnormalities, whereas the senile form was more indolent, less dramatic, and had similar, yet less intense, pathologic changes. Some investigators have found that presenile patients have more extensive language problems and, on neuropsychologic testing, demonstrate lower performance on items requiring concentration and mental tracking than do the older Alzheimer patients.[43,91] Whether there are, in fact, two different conditions has not yet been proven. The suggestion has been made that the disease itself is the same in both conditions, yet the neuropathologic and clinical response differs at different ages.[149] As immunologic systems and host responses change with age, diseases often also change in their clinical expression; this is certainly true of lymphomas, hepatitis, and tuberculosis. Accordingly, a similar variation in host response may be responsible for the differences within the Alzheimer spectrum.[8] Because the concept of separating this condition into two groups has not withstood close scrutiny, we feel justified in discussing all patients with this type of degenerative dementia under the term *Alzheimer's disease.*

Specific research criteria have been developed for the diagnosis of Alzheimer's disease.[99] Although it is true that a definitive diagnosis cannot be made without biopsy or autopsy examination of brain tissue, a clinical diagnosis can be made in about 90 percent of the cases using stringent clinical criteria.[78] Table 6-1 below is the summary of the work-group report[99] concerning diagnosis.

Table 6-1. Criteria for Clinical Diagnosis of
Alzheimer's Disease

I. The criteria for the clinical diagnosis of PROBABLE Alzheimer's disease include

Dementia established by clinical examination and documented by the Mini-Mental Test,[11] Blessed Dementia Scale,[15] or some similar examination, and confirmed by neuropsychologic tests

Deficits in two or more areas of cognition

Progressive worsening of memory and other cognitive functions

No disturbance of consciousness

Onset between ages 40 and 90; most often after age 65

Absence of systemic disorders or other brain diseases that by themselves could account for the progressive deficits in memory and cognition

II. The diagnosis of PROBABLE Alzheimer's disease is supported by

Progressive deterioration of specific cognitive functions such as language (aphasia), motor skills (apraxia), and perception (agnosia)

Impaired activities of daily living and altered patterns of behavior

Family history of similar disorders, particularly if confirmed neuropathologically

(continued)

Table 6-1. Criteria for Clinical Diagnosis of
Alzheimer's Disease—*continued*

Laboratory results of:
Normal lumbar puncture as evaluated by standard techniques
Normal pattern or nonspecific changes in EEG, such as increased
slow-wave activity
Evidence of cerebral atrophy on CT with progression documented by
serial observation

III. Other clinical features consistent with the diagnosis of PROBABLE
Alzheimer's disease, after exclusion of causes of dementia other than
Alzheimer's disease, include
Plateaus in the course of progression of the illness
Associated symptoms of depression; insomnia; incontinence; delusions;
illusions; hallucinations; catastrophic verbal, emotional, or physical
outburst; sexual disorders; weight loss; other neurologic abnormalities
in some patients, especially with more advanced disease and including
motor signs such as increased muscle tone, myoclonus, or gait disorders
Seizures in advanced disease
CT normal for age

IV. Features that make the diagnosis of PROBABLE Alzheimer's disease
uncertain or unlikely include
Sudden, apoplectic onset
Focal neurologic findings such as hemiparesis, sensory loss, visual field
deficits, and incoordination early in the course of the illness
Seizures or gait disturbances at the onset or very early in the course of
the illness

V. Clinical diagnosis of POSSIBLE Alzheimer's disease:
May be made on the basis of the dementia syndrome, in the absence of
other neurologic, psychiatric, or systemic disorders sufficient to cause
dementia, and in the presence of variations in the onset, in the
presentation, or in the clinical course
May be made in the presence of a second systemic or brain disorder
sufficient to produce dementia, which is not considered to be the
cause of the dementia
Should be used in research studies when a single, gradually progressive
severe cognitive deficit is identified in the absence of other identifiable
cause

VI. Criteria for diagnosis of DEFINITE Alzheimer's disease are
The clinical criteria for probable Alzheimer's disease
Histopathologic evidence obtained from a biopsy or autopsy

VII. Classification of Alzheimer's disease for research purposes should specify
features that may differentiate subtypes of the disorder, such as
Familial occurrence
Onset before age of 65
Presence of trisomy-21
Coexistence of other relevant conditions such as Parkinson's disease

DESCRIPTION OF THE CLINICAL SYNDROME

Alzheimer's disease can occur at almost any age, the youngest recorded case being that of a child only 6 years old,[21] but 96 percent of the cases present after the age of 40.[129] There is a preponderance of cases in the female, with a female/male ratio of 2:1 at all ages of onset.[129] The incidence of the disease increases with age, as does the prevalence; about 10 percent of the population over the age of 65 are estimated to be affected to some degree.[77,79] There is a genetic factor in the disease, with a dominance pattern seen in some families and a less certain, polygenic pattern suggested in others.[21,129] The genetic data are reviewed at the end of this chapter in the section on cause and pathology.

Initial Stage

Clinically the initial symptoms and signs of Alzheimer's disease fall into several categories: emotional, social, or intellectual (cognitive). In most cases the symptoms gradually become apparent, but in some instances the dementia can be abruptly unmasked during a period of stress caused either by an upheaval in the patient's environment (e.g., the death of a spouse) or by an intercurrent illness or injury. As we mentioned in the previous chapter, a superimposed confusional state often evinces a latent, unsuspected dementia. Although the disease is usually slowly progressive, several cases have been reported in which it ran a highly malignant course, with death occurring within 6 weeks from the time of onset of symptoms.[40]

The full-blown dementia, whether of Alzheimer type or another, is usually not difficult to recognize; rather it is the subtle early signs that the clinician must train himself to recognize if he is to help his patients avoid the social disaster of trying to "keep up the pace" of life when they cannot. Emotional changes can often be the first clue. These include a loss of interest in work, family, and vocation or increased irritability. A recent patient described himself by saying, "I just don't find work interesting anymore. I go and do my work, but it isn't any fun. Little things get on my nerves." Many patients try to find a physical explanation for their feeling that "something is wrong." They come to the physician's office with increasing frequency, complaining of minor aches and pains that do not seem to have a physical basis. This hypochondriasis in a previously healthy middle-age or elderly patient should always raise the suspicion of dementia. Other patients, however, steadfastly deny any problem at all with their health and euphorically state that they have never felt better when, in fact, they are showing definite signs of intellectual deterioration.

Depression and anxiety can also constitute early features of the illness; this may represent not only the primary effects of neuronal degeneration in the frontal lobes and limbic system but also the patient's emotional reactions to his declining mental acuity.[119] Although depression can be an early sign of dementia[90,94] (see pseudodementia sections later in this chapter), it is not significantly more common in Alzheimer patients than in age-matched controls.[85] Restlessness, feelings of fatigue, and lack of initiative are frequent, subtle emotional changes experienced by the Alzheimer patient in the first stage of his illness. Activity level tends to be high, and the patient often wanders incessantly.[132] These behavioral symptoms are usually better appreciated by the patient's family and coworkers than by the physician; it is therefore important to listen carefully and ask the appropriate questions of relatives if these early symptoms are to be recognized.

The social behavior and personality of the patient during the initial phases of his illness most often show an accentuation of previous personality traits superimposed on a background of apathy or euphoria.[122] R.B.'s son-in-law remarked on one occasion, "My mother-in-law always acted a little strange, but now she seems really crazy." Some patients, in whom the degeneration of the frontal lobe is extensive (particularly in Pick's disease, Huntington's chorea, and general paresis), develop a full-blown frontal lobe syndrome with inappropriate behavior that is totally uncharacteristic of their previous personalities. This is less likely in the patient with early Alzheimer's but can occur.

Cognitive changes occur early and are frequently the presenting complaint of the patient or his family. Memory disturbance is by far the most common and is manifested by a significant difficulty in forming new memories (i.e., new learning ability or recent memory). For example, an inspector at a local shipbuilding yard described his problem graphically, "When I go out on an inspection tour in the morning, there are a lot of different places that I have to check because the work is in different phases in various parts of the yard. I find now that I get out to the first station all right, but after that I can't remember where I am supposed to go next. I have to carry a schedule around with me to make sure I don't miss any stops on my rounds." This problem with details at work plus misplacing things around the house and forgetting names are usually the most common complaints. Remote, well-established memories, on the other hand, are usually quite well retained. It is not uncommon for a sympathetic relative to remark, "Now, his memory is better than all of ours. He can remember things about our childhood that I had long forgotten."

Although it is common, memory difficulty is not the only intellectual dysfunction noticed by the patient with Alzheimer's disease. General problem-solving ability wanes; this problem is particularly evident when the patient attempts to solve complex, novel problems in which he cannot rely on well-established, routinized skills and strategies. We saw a real-estate accountant who was showing signs of personality change but could still do the routine bookkeeping for his firm. The company tolerated his gradually progressing, inappropriate social behavior because the books always balanced. One day, however, the company took over the establishment and management of a very different type of business, and the patient was asked to carry out a financial prospectus on the venture; he did so with great effort, frustration, and error. The business failed, and the firm finally realized that the patient was totally incompetent outside of the most routine bookkeeping matters. When we tested the man, he was not even able to accurately carry out written compound multiplication problems. He rejoined that he "always used a calculator and I've become rusty with arithmetic."

Comprehension and expression of complex ideas, thinking in an abstract fashion, and making critical judgments are all dulled in the patient with early Alzheimer's disease. Along with these higher level cognitive deficits, there can be a loss of basic visual-motor integrative ability (constructional ability). Most patients will not complain of this problem unless they are architects or engineers, but it can be demonstrated on mental status testing by having the patients draw pictures to command or reproduce block designs.

During this first stage of memory difficulty and subtle high-level intellectual failing, results of the routine neurologic examination remain normal. The diagnosis, therefore, depends entirely on the clinician's ability to carry out a careful mental status examination and recognize these early behavioral signs.

Although frequently appearing as described above, the presentation and course of the disease vary considerably; in some cases the emotional change is more dramatic than the intellectual, whereas in others the reverse is true. In most patients, memory failure will be the first complaint, although we saw one patient whose initial symptom was a disturbance in writing and calculating.[135] The most important clinical point is that these patients are experiencing a change in behavior, and it is this change that the clinician must learn to search for and recognize.

Second Stage

As the disease progresses to the second stage, the emotional, social, and cognitive changes discussed above are accentuated. Patients are less able to manage their personal and business affairs because of failing memory, increasing lack of initiative, and decreased ability to meet the challenges of any demand.

Language, which earlier had been normal, now becomes very concrete, tangential, circumlocutory, and perservative. R.B., for instance, when asked why she was in the hospital would start by saying that she had some trouble with her arm, which she needed for writing, and did we know that she was putting together a group of her poems for a new publication. Within moments we had been told about her name appearing in *Who's*

Who in American Poetry and then about her graduate school experience at Cornell. This general string of conversation was produced with clockwork regularity after almost every inquiry. These changes in language are primarily a reflection of a dissolution of intellectual processing, although true aphasic errors can appear. Speech remains fluent at first but can contain paraphasias, word-finding pauses, circumlocution, and a surprising lack of substantive words (nouns and action verbs). For instance, a hospitalized patient, on being asked what kind of place she was in, answered, "Oh, it's a sort of place where people are, and it is a resting area, a sort of clinic but not really for sick people."

During the first two stages of the dementing process, the patients often retain sufficient insight into their condition to develop secondary anxiety and depression. It is very important to recognize these reactive emotional states because they cause the dementia to appear more severe than it is. Specific treatment of these emotional states can produce a remarkable improvement in the patient's overall functioning.

Third Stage

With further progression, patients enter a more distinctly aphasic, apractic, and agnosic stage. Not only have their general intellectual capacities deteriorated, but they begin producing unmistakably aphasic speech. Spontaneous speech decreases. They tend to echo what is said to them (echolalia), their comprehension is greatly reduced, and they have significant anomia (inability to name objects to confrontation or to come up with the names of people or things in running speech). They often, however, have remarkably preserved repetition.

Their anomia is interesting because the difficulty with naming objects is more than a simple linguistic problem in which the word is unavailable. They actually seem not to recognize previously familiar objects. For instance, one patient was shown a pen and asked what it was. He picked it up as though he had never seen such an implement before, toyed with it for a moment, and then handed it back without verbal response. This type of failure of recognition is called an *object agnosia* and is one of the typical features of advancing Alzheimer's disease.

Difficulty in the execution of previously learned skilled movements (apraxia) also becomes prominent during this stage. The apraxia becomes more than mere difficulty with individual limb movements, such as hammering a nail, flipping a coin, or combing the hair (ideomotor praxis). These patients experience disruption in the ability to carry out a serial act such as taking a match from a box and lighting a cigarette (ideational praxis). We watched one woman carefully unwrap a lump of sugar for her coffee only to be completely baffled about what to do thereafter. She had the sugar in one hand, wrapper in the other, and after painful deliberation, she put the paper in the coffee and threw away the sugar. Another woman, age 53, who was moderately demented, found it almost impossible to turn down the sheets and get into the hospital bed. We watched her as she regarded the bed, put her hand on it, turned around, touched it again, then finally looked at us sheepishly and said, "I just can't get in." This combined apraxia agnosia (occasionally called apractagnosia) is a prominent feature of moderately advanced Alzheimer's disease in many patients. The patient's ability to carry out routine activities are also adversely affected by their memory loss and poor judgment. R.B.'s husband called frantically one day to say that she had almost set the house on fire. She was working in the kitchen when one of the dish towels became very wet, and she decided to dry it in the oven. She then forgot about the towel, only to be led back to the kitchen some minutes later by the smell and billows of smoke. Such disasters are the fate of patients at this point in their disease and frequently precipitate admission to the hospital.

Inattention and distractibility also become very common at this stage. Personality changes are accentuated, and insight becomes very tenuous. At times patients seem painfully aware of what is happening, and at other times they seem totally oblivious of their plight. They have crying spells, which at times appear related to the patients' realization of the loss they are suffering, whereas at other times the emotions seem involuntary and manifestations of a developing pseudobulbar state. In this third stage, the primitive or infantile reflexes such as the snout, root, grasp, and palmomental begin to show themselves. Individual patients rarely show all these reflexes but rather demonstrate one or two.[113,114] The snout reflex is the most common, seen in our experience occurring in about 25 percent of demented patients. The grasp reflex is the least frequent, appearing in less than 20 percent.[113] The palmomental reflex is seen in over 50 percent of all people over the age of 65, thus it cannot be used alone to suggest the presence of dementia.[71,112] In our series, it was present in only 10 percent of stage 2 and 3 Alzheimer patients.[134] The limbs begin to resist passive motion (gagenhalten or paratonia), and the naive examiner often thinks that the patient either has parkinsonism or is intentionally uncooperative. In fact, this inability to relax the limbs to passive motion is the result of both a loss of the patient's ability to inhibit his natural reflexes (a cortical, probably frontal, phenomenon) and actual cell loss in the basal ganglia producing a genuine cogwheel rigidity.[129] This resistance to movement is less consistent than is seen in the parkinson patient. Eye tracking movements become abnormal as a result of atrophy of the frontal eye fields,[66] another example of the subtle breakdown in higher-level motor integration.

Patients in this stage may become extremely upset at night and tend to wander about the house and neighborhood. They become excessively restless, and their hands are frequently found to be picking at imaginary bits of lint on their clothes (carphologia) or constantly manipulating objects in their hands. A napkin or handkerchief is commonly folded and refolded as the patient sits in a chair.

Carphologia is quite prominent and frequently accompanied by chewing movements. Urinary and fecal incontinence also begin during this stage. Occasional emotional outbursts coupled with periods of agitation and shouting also may occur. One additional curious behavioral aberration that has been described in these advanced Alzheimer patients is that of sitting in front of a mirror ("mirror sign") and talking to themselves.[129,132] When the demented person begins to display this and other bizarre behavior and is obviously becoming completely out of touch with reality, his dementia has reached the point of organic psychosis. At times fixed delusions occur; this feature has been found more frequently in patients with previous psychiatric problems.[9]

Muscle stretch reflexes may be somewhat increased, and scattered other pathologic reflexes occasionally appear (e.g., Babinski toe signs), but in other respects, the results of routine neurologic examination remain remarkably normal. Another feature that is typical of Alzheimer's disease is that during the early stages, the patients appear very alert. Although often disinterested in carrying out any sustained activity, their ability to shift attention quickly to any novel stimulus in the environment characteristically makes them appear much brighter than they actually are.[96] An outstanding example of this was a 53-year-old violinist who had become extremely demented intellectually but retained a pleasant, yet formal, demeanor. He still enjoyed music and frequently went with his wife to the symphony. One of us (R.L.S.) saw him there one night and introduced him and his wife to my wife. The patient nodded formally, then walked on. This apparent aloofness prompted my wife to comment, "Is that one of your snooty professors from the medical school?"

Final Stages

In the final stages of the disease, the patients become very noncommunicative, uttering only short phrases or undirected babbling. They often show evidence of pseudobulbar effect (i.e., involuntary emotional expression, either crying or laughing), aimless wandering, and little meaningful social interaction. They become peevish if bothered, delusional, and finally completely apathetic, withdrawn, and mute. The patients develop a masked facies (facial diparesis), and 22 percent will have generalized seizures during their last year of life.[58] At this point they often take on the features of the Klüver-Bucy syndrome with its attendant memory loss, constant mouthing, sexual inappropriateness, and emotional outbursts. If patients remain in bed for any length of time, either because of apathy or intercurrent illness, they begin to experience flexion of the lower extremities. At first they are noted to sleep in a fetal position, but with time their legs draw up during the waking hours as well, and pelvicrural contractures develop (paraplegia in flexion).[159] Once this process starts, it is almost impossible to reverse, and the patient remains in this fetal position, muttering and taking only small amounts of food. Seizures and myoclonus develop in approximately 10 percent of all patients.[58,97] Myoclonus is usually a late manifestation but can occur at any stage. Death usually results from pneumonia, aspiration, or urinary infection and sepsis. In this final stage of virtual decortication, Alzheimer's disease is clinically indistinguishable from any other dementia. In the earlier stages, however, Alzheimer's disease has some specific features that help differentiate it clinically.

Atypical Alzheimer's Disease

Katzman[78] estimated that about 20 percent of all Alzheimer patients present with clinical symptoms that are atypical compared with the pattern described above. A broad spectrum of clinical syndromes has been reported. Some patients have early symptoms suggesting focal cortical disturbance, whereas others have significant motor abnormalities. In a small group of cases, the onset may be unusually abrupt. In our series of patients, we noted a poverty of motor signs and primitive frontal release signs, yet a remarkable degree of variation in cognitive features. Forty percent of our stage 2 and 3 patients had very good language and constructional ability yet severely affected memory and abstract reasoning ability. Twenty-three percent (almost all men) of the patients had spared language function and poor performance in all other areas of the mental status examination. Five percent showed excellent constructional ability but impaired performance on other tasks.[134]

Other investigators have reported patients who presented initially with aphasia,[19,28,127] progressive visual agnosia,[35] Gerstman syndrome,[135] a right parietal syndrome,[26] unilateral neglect, frontal syndrome, Balint's syndrome, and many others. Studies of these patients by means of PET scanning techniques have demonstrated focal areas of decreased glucose and oxygen utilization that correspond to the localization predicted by the clinical findings.[28,46]

Some patients with typical Alzheimer changes seen at autopsy had presented with dramatic ataxia and spasticity accompanying their mental changes.[1] A small percentage of patients with the younger-onset presenile form of the disorder have myoclonus, extrapyramidal signs early in their disease. The prognosis in this situation is poor because the disease progresses rapidly and profound mental changes occur early.[97]

An additional, interesting variant is a small group of patients who present with hyperactivity and uninhibited, almost manic behavior. Called *presbyphrenia* by some, these patients show a remarkable atrophy of the locus ceruleus at autopsy. Why this noradrenergic deficit should produce these specific behavioral symptoms is open to speculation.

Why Alzheimer's disease can present with so many clinical variations is not known. Like so many diseases, the clinical spectrum widens, and the edges blur as the conditions are more widely and intensively studied. There may be more than one genetic type, or there may be various environmental factors that may produce these variations; perhaps continued study will answer these questions.

Course

The course of the illness is variable; the average life span from time of diagnosis to death is slightly over 7 years.[129] Although usually slowly progressive, some patients' symptoms plateau for periods of up to 2 years before continuation of their deterioration.[78] Late in the course of the illness, symptom severity often appears to accelerate, which precipitates the need for custodial care either in a hospital or in a nursing home. Twenty-five to 30 percent of the patients, however, live over 10 years, and some live for as long as 20 years.[22] The longevity ranges from a few months to 25 years; accordingly, it is very difficult to advise a family concerning the prognosis until a period of observation indicates the rate of progression. Several factors, however, have been found to have predictive value in respect to mortality and merit special mention. In general, the degree of functional impairment of the patient is of more value in predicting longevity than is structural change (atrophy) demonstrated on the CT scan.[76] Patients with poor memory scores and decreased expressive language function appear to have the least favorable prognosis irrespective of the degree of cortical atrophy.[76] When the disease has progressed to the point where hospitalization is required, life expectancy is severely limited. Eighty-two percent of patients will die within 2 years of their hospitalization.[118] The fact remains that Alzheimer's disease is a long and emotionally painful illness for both the patient and his family. The diagnosis should not be made lightly, for a false-positive diagnosis of Alzheimer's disease may take years to correct and cause considerable unnecessary anguish.

HISTORY AND EVALUATION

The diagnosis of dementia relies on a comprehensive history and appropriate physical examination. Before seeing a patient we routinely ask the family to complete a history form that provides information regarding the patient's current problems and overall medical history (see Fig. 6-1). This information greatly expedites the evaluation. Below we have provided an outline of the essential elements in the routine history and examination that will help the physician to identify patients with a dementing illness. We have emphasized both the specific symptoms that should alert the physician that his patient may be developing a dementia and also, once suspicion has arisen, those additional symptoms and signs that will verify or negate the initial diagnostic impression.

The diagnosis of dementia in general can often be made on historical information alone, but, unlike most patients with medical conditions, patients with dementia are all too frequently unable to provide accurate information concerning the evolution of their illness. For this reason, it is extremely important for the physician to verify and augment the patient's history by consulting family members, friends, or co-workers. This second history is best taken in the patient's absence, so that the informant will feel free to discuss the problem openly without fear of upsetting or embarrassing the patient. In our setting, we use the information obtained on the history form as a guide for the family interview.

First and most important, the sequence of events that resulted in the patient's presenting problem (i.e., a history of the present illness) must be established. Most dementing illnesses have a slow and relentless course, and it is important to inquire at what time the patient was thought to be completely normal and how long the problem has been noticeable. With a typical dementia, particularly Alzheimer's disease, the history spans months to years rather than the days to weeks seen in confusional states. When taking the history, the interviewer should conscientiously explore many specific symptoms. Many of these will be spontaneously offered by the patient as specific complaints, whereas others may have to be specifically elicited. The important areas of symptomatology are outlined below:

1. Change in behavior: In general, is the patient's present behavior different than his previous behavior? If so, how?
2. Was the change gradual and steady, or have there been sudden stepwise alterations? This latter pattern is typical of the vascular dementia that develops after multiple small cerebral infarctions. Gradual diminution in function is characteristic of degenerative diseases such as Alzheimer's disease.
3. Changes in emotion: Significant emotional illness can produce behavioral symptoms that may lead the less experienced clinician to make an erroneous diagnosis of dementia. Such cases have been labeled "pseudodementia." Demented patients may also, however, have superimposed emotional symptoms. The interplay of cognitive and emotional symptoms can be complex and requires careful mental status testing to sort out the various components of the clinical picture.
   a. Is there evidence of depression?

b. Are anxiety and agitation developing?

c. Does the patient sense that things are not right? Is there insight that something is amiss?

d. Is there a general lack of interest in work, family, and hobbies or avocations?

e. Is paranoia, grandiosity, or confabulation present?

f. Does it seem that previous personality traits have been exaggerated?

g. Has the patient developed multiple physical complaints that do not have an organic basis?

4. Social behavioral change: Patients with dementia primarily involving the frontal lobes, such as Pick's disease, frequently display very inappropriate social behavior early in their illness, whereas these exaggerated changes are less typical of Alzheimer's disease.

a. Has the patient become embarrassingly loud and jocular?

b. Has sexual interest and action changed? Has it escaped the bounds of social propriety?

c. Has the patient become short-tempered, irritable, or aggressive?

d. Is social judgment impaired?

5. Changes in intellectual behavior.

a. Is memory affected? Memory disturbance is both the most frequent and earliest symptom in many dementias but particularly in Alzheimer's disease. Ask about the patient's ability to remember recent events. The maintenance of old, remote memories is generally spared in the early stages of Alzheimer's disease, whereas the ability to learn new facts is impaired. It is therefore important to stress recent memory or new learning ability in questioning the patient and family.

b. Is the patient having difficulty doing his or her work? Is the ability to solve difficult or unfamiliar problems and keep track of complicated work details intact? Because abstract reasoning and conceptualization are often affected early, patients with demanding occupations will notice difficulty earlier than those with menial jobs.

c. Does the patient become disoriented in new environments or become lost when driving and walking to other-than-routine places? Does the patient actually get lost even in familiar places? Spatial and geographic disorientation are frequently seen in Alzheimer's disease, although rarely are they the only initial symptoms.

d. Does the patient have difficulty and make mistakes when carrying out complex skilled motor tasks (apraxia)?

e. Is the patient's language normal? Does his speech ramble and wander from the point (tangential)? Does he talk around a point without ever clearly stating what he means (circumlocution)? Does he have difficulty comprehending complex or extensive amounts of material? Does he have trouble remembering names of people and objects (anomia)? Difficulty in writing (agraphia) often is manifest early in dementia and is an important sign when elicited.

6. Is there a fluctuation in the patient's level of consciousness? Such fluctuations are not characteristic of Alzheimer's disease, and their presence should suggest either a different disease or a superimposed confusional state.

The above areas of inquiry were specifically chosen because they represent specific symptoms of dementia and are not usually included in the routine medical history. Taking a complete medical history is well covered in standard physical diagnosis texts and will not be covered here. Because the differential diagnosis of dementia is extensive, the following specific medical and neurologic conditions must be considered when taking the history of an apparently demented patient:

1. Cerebral vascular disease: Transient ischemic attacks, hypertension, diabetes, previous strokes.
2. Seizures: Can be the symptom of brain tumors, old cerebral infarctions, late events in the course of the degenerative dementias, particularly Alzheimer's disease, or central nervous system infection.
3. Unilateral weakness: Could be due to vascular or neoplastic disease.
4. Headaches: Can be associated with tumors, infections of central nervous system, hydrocephalus, depression.
5. Abnormal movements: Choreiform movements look like restlessness and often go unnoticed; therefore, careful observation of the patient at rest is important. Huntington's chorea is a common disorder and must be considered in the differential diagnosis of dementia.
6. Imbalance: Parkinsonism and progressive supranuclear palsy result in both dementia and balance problems. A curious imbalance of gait is also seen in hydrocephalus.
7. Thyroid surgery or symptoms of hypothyroidism: Myxedema can present as dementia.
8. Stomach surgery: Vitamin B_{12} deficiency can develop after gastrectomy, and this may produce dementia.
9. Old subarachnoid hemorrhage: Can lead to hydrocephalus.
10. Old or recent head trauma: Brain damage or subdural hematoma may produce a dementia.

11. History of venereal disease: Syphilis is often unrecognized and undertreated in patients with gonorrhea or other venereal infection.
12. Cancer, particularly reticuloendothelial: The remote effects as well as direct metastases can mimic dementia.
13. Medication use or abuse: Chronic overuse of barbiturates, antidepressant medications, and combinations of psychotropic drugs can cause mental changes.
14. Use of illicit drugs.
15. Heavy use of alcohol.
16. History of AIDS or other autoimmune deficiency syndrome.

This review of current symptoms and past medical history provides most of the historical data necessary in the differential diagnosis of dementia.

MENTAL STATUS EXAMINATION

The neurobehavioral or mental status examination is most easily done directly after taking the history because the patient is usually seated in a chair or on the edge of the bed, as yet unruffled by the process of physical and neurologic examination. When dementia is suspected from the history, the mental examination provides the definitive data for the diagnosis.[135] Throughout the history, the clinician should be making mental note of the patient's behavior and mental functioning. He should also assess the patient's ability to give an accurate history, remember details, and comprehend complicated or lengthy questions. His ability to communicate at a level commensurate with his education should also be evaluated. Below is summarized a complete examination with brief discussion of the abnormalities noted in our study of patients with Alzheimer's disease.[134]

Level of Consciousness

The patient with Alzheimer's disease is usually bright and alert early in the course of his illness. Several exceptions to this bear mentioning:

1. Superimposed confusional state.
2. Concomitant depression: Although not actually decreasing the level of consciousness, per se, depression causes the patient to become sleepy, withdrawn, and adynamic.
3. Extensive frontal lobe atrophy: This is not the usual pattern in Alzheimer's disease, but some patients will have marked frontal

lobe involvement that results in apathy and lack of spontaneity disproportionate to the intellectual changes.

In the late stages of the disease, demented patients do become very apathetic, unable to interact, and seem to have a true decreased level of arousal.

Behavioral Observations

APPEARANCE

The patient with Alzheimer's disease usually shows no changes in his dress and appearance in the early stages of his illness. The exceptions are those patients with marked frontal atrophy who, early in their course, will be slovenly in personal hygiene. As the disease progresses, most patients lose interest in their physical appearance and must be coaxed to bathe, cut their nails, and comb their hair.

ORGANIC BEHAVIORAL CHANGES

Apathy, euphoria, lack of insight, irritability, fatuousness, and inappropriate social interactions are often seen. These changes are not as prominent in the early stages of Alzheimer's disease as they are in Pick's disease. Restlessness and overactivity are, however, typical behavioral patterns in patients with Alzheimer's disease.

SECONDARY DEPRESSION OR AGITATION

Personality reactions to the primary organic condition, such as depression or agitation, should be noted because they can often be successfully treated psychotropically.

Attention

In the very early stage, the demented patient is usually attentive, but with time, concentration powers fail. In the late stages the patient can no longer understand the nature of the "A" test. Digit repetition usually remains fairly intact until very late in the course of the disease. Clinically, the patients exhibit two rather interesting alterations in attention: (1) they can be easily distracted by any extraneous stimulus in the environment, and (2) they will sometimes rivet their attention on one thing in the environment and be unable to shift to other stimuli. This can be well demonstrated by asking a patient to follow your finger when testing extraocular eye movements. Frequently, the patient stares only into the examiner's face and will not follow the moving finger.

Language

The patient with Alzheimer's disease should have careful language testing because this function begins to show changes early in the disease and shows a rather typical pattern of deterioration. Initially the amount of language output decreases; this can best be demonstrated by having the patient produce lists of words under the pressure of time. The patient with Alzheimer's disease produces significantly fewer animal names, words beginning with a specific letter, and so forth, under time limits than do normal persons. This deficiency in generating word lists precedes other language changes and is one of the earlier cognitive changes noted. As the disease progresses, spontaneous speech tends to become circumlocutory, repetitive, concrete, and tangential, and exhibits word-finding pauses, yet remains fluent.[27,84,95,103] Comprehension of complex material decreases, and naming begins to show errors, but repetition ability is usually spared until quite late. In the later stages, aphasia becomes more obvious, with increased comprehension difficulty, word-finding pauses, anomia, echolalia, and a general emptiness of discourse. Spontaneous speech may eventually deteriorate to the point of stereotyped utterances. Writing skills decrease along with spoken language but at a more rapid rate. It is often helpful to ask the patient to write a short paragraph about his job or the weather in hopes of demonstrating language errors if none are apparent in spoken language.

Memory

Memory testing is the most important aspect of the mental status examination in dementia. Memory problems develop in many of the dementias, but failure of recent memory is the outstanding early feature in Alzheimer's disease. Remote memories are relatively resistant until the disease is far advanced. It is especially common for a patient with Alzheimer's disease to carry on endlessly about events in the past but be unable to keep track of the date and what he is supposed to do that day.

Memory testing should include orientation, recent historic events, ability to remember four unrelated words, and visual memory. The dementing patient typically will remember only one word or hidden object when in stage 2 and none in stage 3. He will know a recent President (often not the current one), but will not remember the date. Patients with memory trouble tend to confabulate or try to lead the examiner away from memory questions, so the examiner must often be persistent. One patient, when asked the date, looked with disgust at the examiner and said, "What, do you think I'm crazy? What do you mean asking me a silly question like that?" Undaunted, the examiner finally coaxed the patient to divulge the fact that he thought it was 1962 (it was actually 1986).

Most patients in stages 2 and 3 are oriented to name, age, and home address, but have considerable difficulty with time orientation. Memory for verbal stories (paragraphs) and paired associate learning are also impaired at the level of other tests of new learning.

Constructional Ability

Because of their relative sensitivity in producing objective documentation of brain disease in some patients, drawings can be a very useful part of the examination. Every patient should be asked to draw and copy a series of line drawings. Abnormalities in these constructional tasks are seen in many patients with Alzheimer's disease. We have found that drawings to command are far more sensitive than reproduction drawings in the earlier stages. Sixty-four percent of our stage 2 and 21 percent of our stage 3 patients demonstrated relative sparing on reproduction drawings while showing significant impairment on drawings to command. As the disease progresses, drawing ability deteriorates dramatically.[129,134] Figure 6-2, B, shows examples of drawings executed by patients with Alzheimer's disease. Compare these with the ones made by a patient with hydrocephalus (Fig. 6-2, A) in which the cortex is distorted but not severely damaged.

Higher Cortical Function

ARITHMETIC

Arithmetic errors are common early in the course of Alzheimer's disease, particularly when the task is complicated and requires carrying, borrowing, and multiple steps as in complex multiplication. Errors may occur in basic arithmetic concepts, memory of rote tables, and number alignment in compound written problems.

PROVERB INTERPRETATION

Interpretation of proverbs or maxims, such as, "People in glass houses shouldn't throw stones," is an exercise in abstract verbal reasoning that is frequently disturbed in the early stages of Alzheimer's disease. Patients become very concrete in their approach to such sayings and often answer glibly, "Well, if you throw stones you will break the glass. That's clear enough." Despite attempts to cajole these patients into adopting a metaphorical stance, they steadfastly hold to their concrete interpretations.

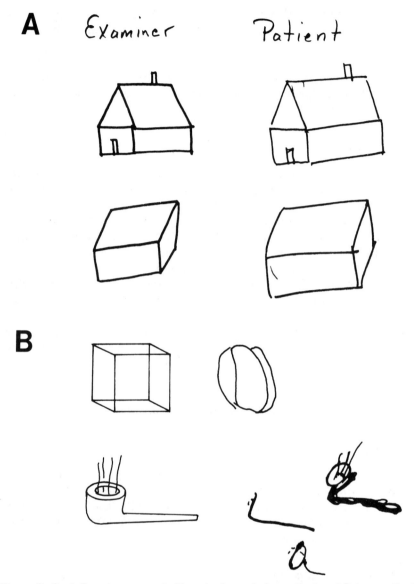

Figure 6–2. *A*, Drawings executed by a hydrocephalus patient and *B*, by a patient with Alzheimer's disease.

SIMILARITIES

Recognition of similarities is an abstract verbal reasoning task that, like proverb interpretation, is often taken literally by the demented patient. The question, "What is the similarity between an apple and a banana?" often brings the concrete response, "Why, they aren't alike at all. One is round and one is long." We find that, in Alzheimer patients, the recognition of similarities is of equal sensitivity to the interpretation of proverbs.

With a complete history, physical, and neurologic examination, and a mental status evaluation, a positive diagnosis of dementia can be established in most cases. In many instances, it is also possible to make a presumptive diagnosis of Alzheimer's disease, but as confident as we may feel at times about the diagnosis, it is essential to consider a wide range of possibilities in the differential diagnosis in any patient with a picture of dementia.

MEDICAL EVALUATION

The physical examination should be complete and concentrate on the factors suggested by the outline provided in the history: hypertension, cerebral vascular disease, hypothroidism, infections, systemic cancer, chronic alcoholism, and vitamin B_{12} deficiency (pernicious anemia). In patients in the early stages of Alzheimer's disease, the examination result is usually normal.

The neurologic examination should be complete, with particular emphasis on the following features:

1. Cranial nerves
   a. Optic fundus examination: Evidence of acute or chronic increased intracranial pressure and vascular changes should be looked for.
   b. Pupils: Irregular pupils that react to accommodation but not light (Argyll Robertson pupil) are seen in central nervous system syphilis.
   c. Extraocular rotations: Weakness of outward gaze (abduction) with diplopia may indicate increased intracranial pressure.
   d. Downward gaze: Parkinson patients often have gaze paralysis, whereas specific downward gaze difficulty is a typical sign in progressive supranuclear palsy.
2. Nuchal rigidity: Chronic meningitis, particularly cryptococcal
3. Motor examination.
   a. Strength: Unilateral weakness suggests a lateralized cerebral lesion.
   b. Gait: Imbalance is seen in hydrocephalus, parkinsonism, and progressive supranuclear palsy (PSP) (retropulsion is especially typical of PSP and parkinsonism). "Stickiness" of gait (small steps with feet seemingly stuck to the floor) is seen in patients with frontal lesions as well as those with hydrocephalus.
   c. Reflexes (muscle stretch): Asymmetries suggest unilateral central

nervous system lesions. Increased leg reflexes (bilateral) can be seen in frontal or parasagittal tumors and hydrocephalus.

d. Primitive reflexes (snout, grasp, root, and palmomental): These are extremely uncommon but are usually the only abnormal neurologic findings in Alzheimer's disease until the later stages. These signs are also present in patients with other frontal lesions.

4. Sensory examination (particularly the integrative functions of stereognosis and graphesthesia): Abnormalities of these cortical sensations occur on the side opposite a parietal lesion. In the later stages of Alzheimer's disease, patients fail to recognize shapes or numbers traced on the hand.

As mentioned, in the early stages of Alzheimer's disease, findings on the routine neurologic examination are usually normal except for the occasional presence of primitive reflexes. If prominent abnormalities are found in cranial nerve function, motor control, or elementary sensation, it is important to carry out an extremely comprehensive neurodiagnostic evaluation in search of a cause for the dementia other than Alzheimer's disease.

DIFFERENTIAL DIAGNOSIS

There are many causes of the clinical syndrome of dementia. Because some are treatable, it is important to undertake a comprehensive evaluation to determine the exact cause of the dementia. Some of these conditions mimic Alzheimer's disease in its gradual onset of subtle emotional changes, memory difficulty, drawing problems, and slowness in abstract reasoning, but many others have somewhat distinctive clinical features that should alert the clinician to suspect an alternate diagnosis. Chapter 7 is devoted to an extensive discussion of dementias other than those caused by Alzheimer's disease. Some patients have changes in behavior that can be confused with dementia. Those conditions are discussed in the following section.

Aging

A number of elderly patients complain of symptoms that superficially resemble Alzheimer's disease, yet they do not show the typical history of progressive deterioration. They continue to be able to care for themselves and live an independent life until their death from unrelated causes. For the various reasons discussed below, this group of patients, who represent a part of the normal aging population, give a superficial appearance of senility but never actually become demented. The clinician must determine which of these patients with complaints of apathy, failing memory, and difficulty at work actually have Alzheimer's disease and which are part of the normal aging population.

Before discussing this differential process, it is important to review the present knowledge on aging as it applies to mental functioning. Although it had been traditionally believed that the intellect begins to fade rather perceptibly after age 60[145] in the normal person, recent studies have not supported this view.[10,83]

The Wechsler Adult Intelligence Scale-Revised (WAIS-R), for instance, awards an IQ of 92 to a 30-year-old patient who earns a total scaled score of 100 points, whereas the 74-year-old patient receives an IQ of 113 for the same total score.[144] The difference is not great, but built into this "age credit" is the implication that a loss of intellectual abilities is the natural course of aging. More careful analysis of the older population reveals many unsuspected reasons that the overall population of elderly citizens performs less adequately on standard tests than do their younger counterparts: (1) Many older persons have medical diseases such as hypertension, atherosclerotic disease, or diabetes, which may not cause a major stroke but often cause intellectual decline through the occurrence of multiple small areas of cortical infarction. (2) Emotional problems, such as depression, are common in the elderly, particularly in those persons who are retired, live alone, or have medical illnesses that limit their activities. (3) Physical illness alone often reduces the patient's ability or motivation to perform at his level of competence either in daily living or in formal testing situations. (4) Educational level and life experience are very different for the general population of 70- to 80-year-olds (born at the turn of the century) and the 25- to 35-year-olds who have had all their education in the post-World War II era. All these factors affect performance but are not an effect of aging brain cells. The questions then arise: Is there any actual alteration in the functioning of the brains of those elderly who have escaped the effects of the problems mentioned above? Is there such a thing as "normal" or expected changes in behavior that result from the aging process itself? The answer is probably yes, but the changes are more subtle than previously appreciated. For instance, complex problem-solving tasks that do not rely on familiar routine strategies (fluid intelligence) are more difficult for the older person. Many factors, such as the older person's lack of competitiveness or motivation, can certainly be important in reducing performance, but, beyond this, there seems to be a genuine decline in the ability to carry out high-level abstract thinking.[83] In contrast, tests that assess vocabulary, general information, and comprehension (crystallized intelligence) do not show this decline with age.[73] Beginning in the seventh decade, there is a subtle decline in nonverbal memory, problem solving, digit supraspan learning, and facial recognition. These functions are principally nonverbal and may indicate that the right hemisphere "shows its age" before the left.[64] The elderly also have difficulty integrating parts into the whole and sustaining attention, and they tend to be distractible. On memory tasks, the older person tends to be less efficient in learning in general. All these features tend to worsen very slowly until the ninth decade, when changes become more prominent.

Some elderly persons complain primarily of forgetting specific dates and people's names, yet unlike the patient with Alzheimer's disease, accurately keep track of ongoing events. The memory deficit is inconsistent, and names forgotten one day may be recalled with ease the next. An additional feature of interest is that the information forgotten is frequently from remote rather than from recent memory stores. This type of memory disturbance is exactly the opposite of that found in Alzheimer's disease. This condition, often called *benign senescent forgetfulness*, shows only mild deficits on formal memory testing. Whereas the memory problem may progress slightly with the passing years, other cognitive deterioration does not occur in these patients, and they live a normal life span.[86] Patients with complaints of intellectual decline who show minor abnormalities on mental status testing must be carefully followed up. A substantial percentage of these patients will prove to have Alzheimer's disease when tested 1 to 3 years later. In retrospect, these patients were in the first stage of the disease when initially tested, despite mental status testing results that were within the normal range.[78,119]

It would be most surprising not to find some changes in behavior accompanying aging, because nerve cell changes are seen on pathologic study of the brains of elderly people. The changes are similar to those seen in Alzheimer's disease, but they are much less numerous and widespread.[22,139,140] These observations suggest that Alzheimer's disease may represent an acceleration of the aging process, although this position remains unproved at present. These normal changes of aging do not interfere with the social adaptive skills of most persons; so, in the absence of any complicating factors, it does not appear that aging per se compromises intelligence to a significant degree.

If the clinician accepts this view of aging and understands the factors that complicate a valid assessment of the elderly patient with memory loss or other similar complaints, he should be able to separate most normal patients from those with Alzheimer's disease. The following steps must be taken in the differential diagnosis:

1. Assess the patient's social situation, previous education, and personality to see whether there is any obvious reason for the problem.
2. Examine the patient closely for evidence of depression and anxiety.
3. Do a careful mental status examination; the normal patient will not have genuine new learning problems, will not show evidence of aphasia, and will be able to interpret proverbs satisfactorily. The

dementing patient, on the other hand, will usually show evidence of errors in several areas of mental status testing.

Pseudodementia

There are some patients who are referred or refer themselves with complaints of progressive memory loss and other cognitive changes whose symptoms are eventually shown to have been secondary to an emotional or mood disturbance rather than true dementia. The term *pseudodementia* has been applied to these cases.[82,109,118] Depression is the most common of the emotional disorders that can masquerade as dementia, a situation that is not surprising because the two conditions share many common symptoms: memory problems, lack of motivation, poor concentration, and a loss of interest in work and hobbies. To misdiagnose a depressed patient as being demented is an unfortunate diagnostic error; however, with careful evaluation, this can usually be avoided.

The memory, concentration, and problem-solving complaints are very much related to the depressed patient's lack of motivation rather than to a true cognitive deficit. To learn new material or to keep track of ongoing work details, dates, or plans requires effort. Some memories are stored in a rather passive fashion, such as remembering whether one had breakfast, but most memory storage is an active process that requires continual rehearsal and concentration on the details (the truth of this should be obvious to any student who has had to prepare for an examination).[108] The depressed patient simply cannot muster the mental energy for this type of sustained mental work.

Folstein and McHugh[45] believe that the chemical and physiologic changes in the brain that produce the depression and the subsequent cognitive changes should be considered organic and that the syndrome should be labeled a dementia syndrome of depression rather than a pseudodementia. Irrespective of the label applied to this condition, a genuine reduction in cognitive ability has been shown in various populations of depressed patients. Young depressed patients demonstrate deficits on all intellectual subjects except for vocabulary and similarities;[120] their performance was particularly poor on visual tasks requiring the identification of figures embedded on a distracting background. It is clinically significant that patients with focal cortical lesions also experience a reversible decline in the focal cognitive function when they have a superimposed depression.[44]

It is the difficult differential diagnosis between depression and dementia in the elderly that poses the greatest clinical challenge. Not only do the two conditions share many similar symptoms, but depression in the elderly is a much less dramatic and obvious condition than it is in the younger patient. The elderly person with depression is less likely to verbally express guilt, self-deprecation, or dysphoria.[72] Vegetative signs are prominent. Behavior is characterized by social withdrawal, psychomotor retardation, and incapability.[87,119] There is a masked depression, with a tendancy to be critical and irritable. They are acutely aware of their loss of esteem and control and show envy of those younger and more vital than themselves.[147] Because of this sense of loss of mental and physical control, the older depressed patient often complains of failing memory and intellectual ability.

Many features of the patient with depressive pseudodementia are distinctly different from those of the truly demented patient, as summarized in Table 6-2. In our experience, despite the patient's complaints of memory and cognitive problems, the sympathetic yet persistent examiner is usually able to elicit nearly normal performance from the depressed patient when care is taken. The cognitive problems that are found on mental status evaluation are usually mild,[16,24] but to diagnose a condition as a pseudodementia with absolute certainty, all cognitive deficits elicited during the depressive episode must completely reverse when the depression clears.

The dexamethasone suppression test (DST) has been used with variable results to aid in the differential diagnosis of "depressive pseudodementia" from true dementia. Widely disparate rates of DST suppression have been reported, ranging from 50 percent in demented/depressed patients to 100 percent in nondepressed, demented patients with concomitant chronic medical illness.[51] An additional series of studies has suggested a higher rate of *nonsuppression* in patients with moderate to severe dementia than in patients with mild to moderate dementia.[74] Greenwald and associates[51] attempted to further determine whether DST is useful in identifying covert depression in diagnosed demented patients, which by extension would be potentially useful in differentiating pseudodementia from true dementia. In a study of 22 nondepressed patients with Alzheimer's disease, 50 percent were nonsuppressor. The nonsuppressors were older than the suppressors, but neither their ratings of depression nor their degree of dementia differed.[51] The most severely demented subjects had the greatest number of endogenous, but not exogenous, depressive symptoms. Despite the great deal of research focused on this test, considerable doubt remains regarding the utility of the DST as a laboratory measure for distinguishing depressive pseudodementia from true dementia.

By definition, the short-term prognosis of a pseudodementia is excellent, because the cognitive symptoms must reverse when the depression clears. The long-term prognosis is less encouraging. Results of several follow-up studies have clearly demonstrated that a progressive dementia later develops in a high percentage of these patients.[87,119] Whether the depression is the first symptom of the dementia or is merely a coincidental event is not known.

Table 6-2. Differences Between Pseudodementia and Dementia*

	Pseudodementia	Dementia
Clinical course and history	1. Onset fairly well demarcated	1. Onset indistinct
	2. History short	2. History quite long before consultation
	3. Rapidly progressive	3. Early deficits often go unnoticed
	4. History of previous psychiatric difficulty or recent life crisis	4. Previous psychiatric problems or emotional crisis uncommon
Clinical behavior	1. Detailed, elaborate complaints of cognitive dysfunction	1. Little complaint of cognitive loss
	2. Little effort expended on examination items	2. Struggle with cognitive tasks
	3. Affective change often present	3. Usually apathetic with shallow emotions
	4. Behavior does not reflect cognitive loss	4. Behavior compatible with cognitive loss
	5. Rarely has exacerbation at night	5. Nocturnal accentuation of dysfunction common
Examination findings	1. Frequently answers "I don't know" before even trying	1. Usually will try on items
	2. Inconsistent memory loss for both recent and remote items	2. Memory loss for recent events worse than remote
	3. May have particular memory gaps	3. No specific memory gaps
	4. In general, performance is inconsistent	4. Rather consistently impaired performance

*Table adapted from Wells.[148]

Patients with character disorders such as hysterical personality disorder, hysterical neurosis with conversion reactions, and more serious psychiatric conditions are also known to present with a spurious dementia.[148] In contrast to the depressive patient, the hysterical person, when asked a specific question concerning his life, will often emphatically state, "I don't remember. You see, doc, that's the kind of thing that happens all the time. Things that I used to know I just can't remember." These nondepressive pseudodementia patients, like the depressive patients, frequently have a previous psychiatric history and at the time of examination have many current emotional symptoms such as anxiety, depressive mood, and psychophysiologic symptoms (e.g., headaches, gait abnormalities).

Confusional State

Although most confusional states are not mistaken for dementia, on occasion confusional behavior can be present for weeks or months and initially be misdiagnosed as dementia. Usually the alteration and fluctuation in the level of consciousness and the other features of the confusional state are sufficiently obvious to allow the differentiation from early Alzheimer's disease. If the patient with Alzheimer's disease, however, has a superimposed physiologic disturbance, the features of both illnesses will be present, and the clinical picture will be that of a beclouded dementia.

Chronic Drug Use

Most patients with alterations in mental and adaptive capacities from the excessive intake of sedatives or combinations of psychotropic medications display alterations in consciousness and intermittent confusional behavior, although some patients have a clinical picture more typical of a dementia than a confusional state. This is particularly true for chronic barbiturate use[49] and possibly with tricyclic antidepressant use.

LABORATORY EVALUATION

Because the differential diagnosis of Alzheimer's disease in particular and dementia in general includes some potentially reversible conditions, it behooves the physician to carry out an extensive evaluation when the initial diagnosis is made or suspected. To diagnose Alzheimer's disease in a patient is tantamount to saying, "You have ahead of you 5 to 10 years of progressive enfeeblement. Go forth and put your affairs in order." Such a pronouncement should be made (in more gentle terms) only after the diagnosis has been firmly established. The few hundred dollars spent on the initial evaluation is nothing compared with the years of unnecessary mental anguish suffered by the family and patient in whom later (optimistically, not too late) the diagnosis of myxedema or benign brain tumor is made.

With the idea of doing a complete screening evaluation, we recommend the standard laboratory tests listed in Table 6–3, all of which are readily available.

Table 6-3. Blood Tests

Tests	Results	Implication in Relation to Dementia
Hemoglobin and hematocrit	High	Polycythemia
	Low	Pernicious anemia
White blood cell count	High	Chronic infection
	Low	Systemic lupus erythematosus
VDRL	High	Syphilis
Erythrocyte sedimentation	High	Collagen disease
		Metastatic cancer to brain
		Chronic infection
Calcium (phosphate)	High	Hyperparathyroidism
	Low	Hypoparathyroidism
Liver function studies	Abnormal	Hepatocerebral degenerations
Bromide, barbiturate	High	Chronic toxicity
Cholesterol	High	Myxedema
T_3, T_4, TSH	High	Thyrotoxicosis
	Low	Hypothyroidism/myxedema
Lipid profile	High	Cerebral vascular disease
		Rare hyperlipidemic dementia[40]
Vitamin B_{12}, folate	Low	Pernicious anemia

Electroencephalogram

The electroencephalogram (EEG) is more helpful in ruling out other causes of dementia such as tumor, metabolic disturbance, subdural hematoma, or the rare case of Creutzfeldt-Jakob disease, than it is in making the positive diagnosis of Alzheimer's disease.

One of the problems in using the EEG to diagnose Alzheimer's disease is that not only is the EEG normal in many early cases, but subtle abnormalities in the EEG occur with increasing frequency in the normal elderly population.[15,88] In many older patients, the EEG shows a decrease in the percentage and frequency of the background alpha as well as the appearance of scattered slowing (unilateral temporal or bilateral frontoparietal).[110] Unfortunately, the identical changes can also be seen in early Alzheimer's disease.[56] Patients with Alzheimer's disease will have a greater percentage of EEG abnormalities than will normal patients, but the EEG alone can never be the deciding factor in an individual case.

Despite this, there is a direct relationship between the degree of dementia and the slowness of the EEG.[146] Therefore, as the dementia progresses, more consistent and extensive slowing usually emerges. In normal elderly, the alpha slows slightly to 8 to 9 Hz but in Alzheimer's disease the background falls to the theta range of 7 Hz.[115] The slowing is usually diffuse or scattered and can contain both theta and delta activity.[126] Bursts of high-voltage frontotemporal delta are also commonly seen.[115] Low-voltage fast records, which are common in the normal elderly, are uncommon in patients with Alzheimer's disease.[126]

Studies for Visualization of Cerebral Ventricles and Cortical Sulci (CT or MRI)

To evaluate any demented patient properly, the physician *must* obtain a test that can demonstrate whether the patient has enlargement of the cerebral ventricles and/or cortical atrophy. In Alzheimer's disease, there is often widespread atrophy of the cerebral cortex, which is reflected pathologically and radiologically as narrowing of cortical gyri and widening of the intergyral sulci (Fig. 6–3). The cerebral ventricles are also enlarged, principally as a result of the loss of the fiber tracts from degenerated cortical neurons. This hydrocephalus ex vacuo is mild to moderate and is usually not as extensive as the hydrocephalus seen in obstructive conditions.

The tests of choice for the evaluation of cortical atrophy and ventricular enlargement are the computerized axial tomography (CT) scan[65] and the magnetic resonance imaging (MRI) scan. These procedures not only allow the evaluation of the ventricles and subarachnoid spaces but also can

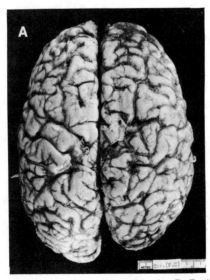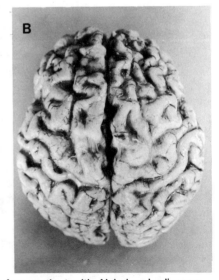

Figure 6–3. *A*, Normal brain. *B*, Brain from patient with Alzheimer's disease.

identify the presence of tumor, abscess, infarction, or hemorrhage. The evaluation for dementia is rarely, if ever, an emergency, and the patient can usually have the scan done electively as an outpatient.

Any laboratory test has limitations that must be fully appreciated and incorporated into the diagnostic evaluation of each individual case. The correlation of dementia with cortical atrophy is high, although not 100 percent. Several investigators have noted that 15 to 30 percent of normal elderly persons have mild cerebral atrophy.[38,93,139] This atrophy is seen on scanning and has been verified by autopsy studies of patients with normal mental status who died of unrelated medical illnesses.[139] Thus, the demonstration of atrophy on a scan in a patient with migraine headaches, for example, is not adequate justification for suggesting that a patient is also becoming demented. Conversely, some patients who died of Alzheimer's dementia have shown all the microscopic features of the disease but no evidence of gross atrophy.[140] The degree of dementia, therefore, correlates more strongly with the microscopic evidence of senile plaques and neurofibrillary tangles than it does with cortical atrophy. These exceptions to the rule that Alzheimer's disease has atrophy and that atrophy indicates dementia serve to caution the physician to use these radiologic tests as an aid to diagnosis and not as the absolute arbiter.

Positron Emission Tomography (PET)

In recent years selected patients with Alzheimer's disease have been studied with PET scanning, a technique that records the glucose metabolism, oxygen utilization, and cerebral blood flow in the brain. In most cases, the values of all measurements generally decrease, with posterior parietal regions showing the greatest defect, followed by posterior temporal regions. The decrease in metabolic activity in the frontal areas was relatively less. Asymmetries (right/left) are noted, and regional areas of hypometabolism correlate well with clinical findings.[29,37,47]

Cerebrospinal Fluid Examination

Several diseases that produce dementia can be diagnosed only by examination of the cerebrospinal fluid. These conditions—late syphilis and chronic meningitis such as cryptococcosis, tuberculosis, sarcoidosis, or fungal infection—are rare, occurring in less than 1 percent of patients. In several studies of a large series of patients who were being evaluated for dementia, the spinal puncture never yielded an unexpected diagnosis. All cases with chronic meningitis had fever, nuchal rigidity, and subacute mental change.[7,54]

CONSULTATIONS

Neurologist

In conjunction with the laboratory investigation, the physician will often wish to ask the assistance of a consultant in evaluating and managing an individual patient. Because many of the treatable conditions are primary neurologic disease (e.g., tumors, hydrocephalus, or chronic meningitis), a neurologist should see the patient and supervise the evaluation whenever possible. If necessary, the neurologist will order more extensive neuroradiologic studies and consult a neurosurgeon.

Neuropsychologist

Whenever possible, a neuropsychologist should also evaluate the patient. The neuropsychologist's value is greatest in the early stages of the condition when the diagnosis may be in doubt or emotional factors may have clouded the clinical picture. When a patient is severely demented with aphasia, amnesia, apraxia, and gross atrophy on the scan, the neuropsychologist's services are not usually necessary for diagnosis but may be needed for management or placement suggestions. In the early phase of Alzheimer's disease, psychologic testing can supply a tremendous amount of important information: (1) Testing can determine whether dementia is actually present. (2) The extent of cognitive deficits and residual strengths can be objectively assessed; this information can help to determine the patient's capability of meeting his vocational demands and also his general mental and legal competence. (3) A complete test battery can also evaluate whether the patient has significant concomitant emotional difficulty that is influencing his overall adaptive and cognitive functioning.

The patient with Alzheimer's disease often shows a rather characteristic neuropsychologic test profile in the early stage:

1. Performance on objective tests of memory is less adequate than overall intellectual performance, with the lowest scores typically found on the logical memory paragraphs, paired associate words, and visual memory subtests.
2. Performance Scale IQ is usually but not always lower than the Verbal Scale IQ as a result of impairments of speed and accuracy.
3. Verbal IQ is more resistant to deterioration, with the exception of performance on the Comprehension and Similarities subtests, which require higher-level abstract interpretation and judgment (fluid intelligence). Subtests such as Vocabulary, Digit Repetition, and Information rely primarily on previously well-learned material, and results usually remain relatively good (crystallized intelligence).

4. Overall IQ declines, and there is usually an appreciable variation (scatter) of subtest scores.
5. Drawing is more defective than expected from intellectual level.
6. Abstract reasoning tests (e.g., Categories test, Wisconsin Card Sorting, proverbs) show extreme impairment.
7. Trail-Making Test performance is within the organic range, particularly on Form B (alternating number and letter sequences). Other problem-solving and judgment tests are similarly impaired.

Comparison of the psychological test profile with the history and estimates of premorbid intellectual functioning usually establishes the presence or absence of organic dementia and may suggest the diagnosis of Alzheimer's disease.[111]

Psychiatrist

A third consultant who is helpful in the evaluation but especially with the management of these patients is the psychiatrist. The psychiatrist can evaluate the possible emotional components of the patient's condition and is familiar with the psychotropic medications used for controlling the behavioral aberrations. Psychiatrists are also familiar with and have access to inpatient psychiatric units and institutions. This type of in-hospital care is usually not necessary in the early stages of the illness, but because the patient is often brought to the physician in a crisis situation, temporary hospitalization in a psychiatric facility may be necessary.

PATIENT MANAGEMENT

A diagnosis of Alzheimer's disease or any of the other irreversible dementias, at least currently, requires that the management of the case shift from specific disease treatment to minimizing the adverse effects of the condition and planning for the social future of the patient and his family. The physician can be of invaluable continuing assistance and should not feel that his job is complete after the diagnosis of an untreatable disease has been made. A sympathetic physician who understands the many problems of dementia can help the patient to avoid personal and social disaster while giving the family much needed support and direction.

There are two major areas of difficulty for the demented patient: (1) the insidious intellectual decline and (2) the significant organic and reactive emotional changes that accompany the disease. The demented patient reacts negatively both to the basic realization of his failing mental ability and to the stress in general. Whenever demands are made that cannot be met or the environment changes so that familiarity is lost, the patient responds with exaggerated anxiety that sometimes completely overwhelms him and produces agitated confusional behavior. At the extreme, such responses are termed "catastrophic reactions."

The physician must be prepared to deal effectively with all these psychologic and psychosocial problems. The precise details of management depend on the stage of the patient's disease. Accordingly, the problems arising at each stage and their appropriate management are outlined below.

The initial step must be to discuss as fully as possible with the patient and his family the nature of the patient's problem. Point out that the initial complaints, such as of memory trouble, are in fact real and that the patient is having genuine difficulty with tasks that had previously been easy for him. We usually suggest that "he is having the type of problems that many older persons have." Such comments are much less offensive than allusions to a "shrinking brain" or "early senility." Many patients and families are familiar with the term Alzheimer's disease and frankly ask if that is the suspected diagnosis. In such cases it is best to be honest and then help them deal with this information. We find that most families are anxious to know the diagnosis so that they can make concrete plans for the future. Advising them that the condition probably will not improve but is usually very slowly progressive with a longevity of many years is not overly comforting but at least allows everyone involved to realize that plans can be formulated and the family's emotional adjustments to the situation arrived at gradually. The need for logical planning and the physician's willingness to help cannot be overemphasized; families caring for a dementing patient need a great deal of emotional support for extended periods.

Referring the family to the local chapter of the Alzheimer's Disease and Related Disorder Association (ADRDA) is especially important. This organization (National Headquarters, 70 East Lake Street, Chicago, IL 60601) is made up of families and local resource personnel who can help by providing information, emotional support, and practical advice. We also suggest recommendation of the fine book, *The 36-Hour Day*,[92] which helps families answer their many questions concerning the disease and its management.

In terms of practical management, the first consideration should be to determine the extent of the patient's intellectual loss and how this loss affects his work and social life. The following decisions must be made: (1) Is the patient able to continue his work? (2) Is he competent to carry on his personal business (i.e., pay bills and manage his own money)? (3) Is he legally competent to enter into legal contracts and to make a will (testamentary capacity)? (4) Does he need supervision for such activities as cooking or smoking? (5) Can the patient continue to drive a motor vehicle safely? None of these questions can be easily answered during the early stages of the illness. For instance, we have one patient who owns and runs a dry goods store who, when his memory began to fail, carried a notebook with him and constantly wrote down various things that he had to re-member. As his memory worsened, his wife worked with him so that she could attend to many of the details that he could not. This patient could continue working without any great liability to either himself or his busi-ness. The same degree of memory failure in a judge, physician, accountant, or a building engineer would probably be sufficiently serious to prevent adequate performance of duties. If we think that a patient's disease is sufficiently severe, we encourage early retirement. Although it is impossi-ble to force a patient to stop working, we feel justified in trying to convince the patient and his family that he should not continue to work in his present state. This issue of fitness for work among older persons is a difficult problem. Unfortunately, no satisfactory mechanism exists for evaluating independent citizens with highly responsible positions such as government officials, lawyers, accountants, and physicians in the hope of avoiding embarrassing and possibly very serious errors.

The question of when a dementing patient should turn over his mon-etary affairs to a responsible relative or agent is too often asked too late. The following vignette illustrates this point.

A 65-year-old widow was referred because she was extremely agi-tated and according to the family had become very suspicious and "scat-terbrained." On examination, the patient was obviously paranoid, anxious, and almost frantic. Her memory, drawings, object naming, and proverb interpretation were all faulty, and it was obvious that she was in fact demented. After we gained her confidence, she told us that the precipitat-ing event for all her problems was that she had made many errors in paying her rent and that she was threatened with immediate eviction. When she tried to correct her errors, they only increased, and she sank into a veritable financial morass. She became anxious and paranoid, and when her well-meaning lawyer son-in-law said that he would manage her affairs, she believed that he was only after her money.

In this case, the situation had deteriorated to such a point that legal interdiction was necessary, and a conservator was appointed. It is far better for the patient and family to realize the seriousness of the situation early and to have a lawyer help them with the responsibility of everyday finan-cial affairs than to wait until the issue is forced and ill will created within the family. In patients in whom the disease is in the early stage and mental competency is adequate, a power of attorney can be executed. In this way an appointed person can act in the patient's stead. In some states this power of attorney is durable (will continue regardless of the eventual decline in the patient's mental capacity); in others, formal interdiction is necessary if the patient becomes incompetent.

Early in the course of the illness, a will should be written; this must be done at a time when the patient understands what is contained within his estate and clearly knows what relatives should share this estate. If the patient's memory is poor and he does not remember what he owns or is irrational concerning financial affairs, it is best to have legal declaration that the patient is incompetent to make a will.[53] In such cases, the court appoints a conservator and approves the will.

Supervision at home is usually not a major problem during the early stages of Alzheimer's disease. Most of these patients can fairly well attend to their personal affairs and function within a familiar environment. As the disease progresses, however, patients tend to wander and become lost, their memory for the details of cooking is faulty, and apraxia can develop to the point that simply preparing a cup of coffee or lighting a cigarette becomes impossible. Obviously the patient at this point needs constant supervision.

Driving is another difficult situation in which there are no absolute guidelines. We, quite frankly, are not too enthusiastic about having our demented patients drive! Their spatial orientation is not good, judgment is failing, and they tend to become very upset whenever anything out of the ordinary occurs. These factors plus their poor memory make us think it prudent to gently urge them to give up driving for their own safety and protection as well as for the protection of others.

Most of the above suggestions are aimed at manipulating the patient's environment so that stressful situations are avoided. Stress leads to anxiety, feelings of failure, depression, and occasionally confusional behavior. These are best avoided by simplifying the patient's environment and life. Make life as routine as possible. Nothing is more upsetting to a dementing patient than moving him from place to place. That trip to Europe or across the country might sound like "just what grandpa needs to relax," but by the fifth day, in the fourth hotel, and the third country, grandpa is so confused and agitated that he has to be sent home under heavy sedation. The need for order and structure is not as acute in the beginning of the disease process but becomes increasingly important as adaptive capacities dwindle.

At some point in the progression of the disease the patient becomes largely dependent on others to meet all his daily needs. This is a crisis point for many families; they simply do not have anyone in the family who has the amount of time necessary to care for the patient. The crisis is frequently precipitated by an episode of incontinence, a nocturnal wander about the neighborhood, or a particularly boisterous series of verbal or social outbursts during a trip to the grocery store. At this time a sensible long-term care plan must be made. A social worker will now be the physician's best ally. We encourage our patients' families to establish contact with the social worker before the crisis arises, but this suggestion is often not very enthusiastically received until the obvious need is at hand. Regardless of the timing, the social worker can help assess the patient's and the family's needs and is then able to advise the family of the resources available in the community to meet those needs. Visiting nurses, aides, or sitters are one solution. Day-care centers for the elderly will occasionally accommodate some demented patients in the earlier stages of their illness. At times nursing home or institutional placement may be required. Unfortunately, all these services are expensive. For the wealthy patient, the easiest and most satisfactory solution is to have help in the house constantly. In this way the patient does not undergo the upsetting experience of being moved; he is in his own home, and family members can help when they are available. Expensive, elaborate nursing or residential facilities are also available to give very comfortable care to those who can afford it. In recent years, nursing homes have become increasingly sensitive to the problems of the patient with Alzheimer's disease, and the quality of care has improved. Unfortunately some homes are not set up to handle the idiosyncratic behavior of some of these patients and psychiatric facilities are the only alternative. Some centers have adopted the hospice approach to the terminal care of the Alzheimer patient,[143] and others have established Alzheimer family centers for comprehensive care.[50] The poor often have a variety of services available through welfare programs, although these services are usually not as satisfactory as those for patients with financial means. Middle-class, fixed-income families who own their own homes are the most hard-pressed to provide the necessary care because they do not have the available finances to buy adequate help and do not qualify for public assistance programs. This is a genuine social problem in our country. Many of our patients' families have had to make considerable personal and financial sacrifices to care for their loved ones as they slowly become more and more incapacitated.

Medical Management

In addition to social and environmental aspects of management, there are avenues of medical management the physician must follow in treating the patient with dementia. Some of these are similar to those discussed in Chapter 5, on the confusional states. Good, conscientious medical care will prevent confusional behavior and greatly simplify the patient's overall care. Judicious use of nonbarbiturate sleeping medication (e.g., diphenhydramine hydrochloride 25 mg, chloral hydrate 500 mg, or a mild tranquilizing medication) when sleep has been interrupted on several consecutive nights is advisable.

A major area in which the physician may be of assistance is in the treatment of concomitant depression or anxiety. As mentioned earlier, these emotional manifestations or reactions in patients with dementia can adversely affect the intellectual and adaptive functioning of the patient; it is thus important to treat these problems promptly. Antidepressants can be safely used in patients with dementia; however, the doses should be small, and medications with high anticholinergic activity should be avoided. Because of the acetylcholine deficit present in Alzheimer's disease, any drug that further decreases the availability of this transmitter is detrimental and can produce a confusional state. We find trazodone 50 mg b.i.d., nortriptyline 25 mg at bedtime or 10 mg t.i.d., or desipramine 25 mg at bedtime or 10 mg t.i.d. to be the most satisfactory. To control anxiety and agitation in the earlier stages of the illness, we use lorazepam 0.5 mg, chlordiazepoxide 5 to 10 mg, alprazolam 0.25 mg, and occasionally meprobamate. We avoided diazepam because of its long half-life. In the later stages when agitation is more of a problem than minor anxiety, a major tranquilizer is more appropriate (e.g., chlorpromazine 25 mg, haloperidol 0.5 to 1.0 mg, or thioridazine 25 mg). Some physicians successfully treat agitation with barbiturates, but we find the risk of additional agitation plus the frequent rather substantial sedative effect undesirable. It is advisable initially to use small doses of any medication because the demented patient is often very sensitive to these psychotropic drugs. When used, antidepressant medications must be taken daily, but we believe that tranquilizing drugs should be used only when necessary and not on a regular basis except when absolutely required. The physician may wish to consult a psychiatrist before prescribing any psychotropic medication.

The use of medications that are advertised as improving the patient's mental status by increasing blood flow or cerebral oxygen uptake (e.g., Deapril or Hydergine) is controversial. Alzheimer's is a disease of degenerating nerve cells, and the metabolic error that causes this to occur has not yet been discovered. It is generally believed that these medications have not been shown to significantly help the patient with Alzheimer's disease; therefore, we do not prescribe them.[36,161]

The most recent medical treatment has been the use of choline or its precursor lecithin. The rationale for this treatment is that the cholinergic neurons are the first and primary neurons to deteriorate in Alzheimer's disease. Using the same reasoning as that of treating parkinsonism with dopamine, many investigators are attempting to reduce the memory and intellectual deficits of Alzheimer's disease by supplying exogenous acetylcholine precursors[42,128,131] or inhibiting cholinesterase activity.[33,117,130]

The use of the precursors alone has not produced successful results; however, by using parenteral physostigmine with or without oral lecithin, significant, albeit transient, memory improvement has been reported.[33,117]

Treatment

In all the studies, some patients have responded positively. In a recent lecithin study, the study group as a whole did not improve, but individual patients showed considerable change. It will be interesting to study those individuals who responded; they may represent a different type or sub-type of the disease.[89] Some modestly encouraging results have also been reported from the use of oral acetylcholinesterase inhibitors—tetra-hydroanoacridine (THA) and physostigmine—certainly a far preferable method of administration of these drugs.[104,136]

Several new treatment modalities are largely experimental at this time but may prove to be efficacious in the future. The first, and one that has already been used in patients with Alzheimer's, is the constant delivery of bethanechol chloride (a choline-like compound) into the lateral ventricles. The first few patients were reported to have positive responses in both social and cognitive functioning.[55]

The second treatment, intracerebral transplantation of cholinergic neurons, is still in the animal experimentation stage. In this procedure, embryonal tissue from cholinergic neurons in the nucleus basalis is trans-planted into the cortex. This procedure has been done on aged rats; the tissue not only survived but neuronal connections were established and memory improved.[4]

The third treatment possibility is based on the discovery that nerve growth factor (NGF) is a neurotropic factor for cholinergic neurons in the basal forebrain.[59] Observations in rats indicate the NGF acts to prevent degeneration of cholinergic neurons. If this observation proves to be true, such treatment in Alzheimer patients, or in the normal elderly, might enhance the survival of the brain's cholinergic system.

A final issue in treatment is the ethical and humane problem of when to support life by extreme means when patients become bedridden and totally unable to care for themselves. The questions of (1) resuscitation, (2) feeding tubes, (3) antibiotic treatment for infection, and (4) urinary cath-eter use are all important. At this writing, no firm guidelines have been established. The legal system has become involved, and at this point, its involvement has caused confusion in the minds of both physicians and patients' families.[143]

ETIOLOGY AND PATHOLOGY

The gross and microscopic features of Alzheimer's disease have been well known since their initial description in 1906 by Alois Alzheimer.[100] Only very recently, however, have researchers begun to understand the pathophysiology of this curious condition. Unfortunately, its cause still eludes investigators.

In the past 10 years, there has been a tremendous emphasis on re-search on Alzheimer's disease. Its pathology and neurochemistry have been exhaustively studied, and our knowledge of its pathophysiology greatly expanded. Any reported description is outdated virtually as soon as it is written, but the following general discussion introduces many of the presently known features of the pathophysiology. Implicit in the discussion are two basic lines of inquiry: the cause of the disease and the pathologic process itself.

The only strong evidence concerning cause centers around genetic issues. Certain families have a very strong dominant inheritance pattern,[107] constituting a small percentage of cases (about 5 percent) but nevertheless establishing a genetic factor. In these families, the disease usually starts in younger patients (<65 years), a fact that makes it easier to see the full genetic expression because of the relative longevity of siblings. A second well-established fact is that the risk is much greater for anyone in a family in which Alzheimer's disease has developed in a family member under the age of 70 years.[20,57,61,62,129]

If the disease developed after age 70, the risk to other family members is no greater than in the general population. Some investigators believe that all families that have a member in whom the disease developed under age 70 have a dominant pattern; however, they exhibit an age-dependent variable penetrance. If all family members live into their 90s, 50 percent will have clinical and pathologic evidence of Alzheimer's disease.[12,13]

In his studies in Switzerland, Constantinidis[20] found that the presenile patients followed a dominant pattern, but he thought that the senile-onset patients followed a recessive pattern wherein siblings were more at risk but not future generations. Opinions obviously vary from a strict dominance pattern to polygenic theories.[149,157]

Another major discovery that has placed new emphasis on the genetic theory is that after age 40 virtually all patients with Down's syndrome develop Alzheimer's disease.[30,138,150,153,156] Although this observation was first made in 1948, its significance was not fully appreciated until recently.[75] This discovery has turned interest to the possible role of chromosome 21 as the location of the gene responsible for the pathologic process seen in Alzheimer's disease.

Some investigators, particularly Wisniewski and associates,[154] believe that genetics are not the entire answer to the disease but prefer to view certain families as having a genetic susceptibility rather than a genetic certainty. The question then is, susceptibility to what? Various theories have been proposed. Because of the presence of neuritic plaques in both Alzheimer's disease and dementias caused by unconventional viruses (Creutzfeldt-Jakob disease), Wisniewski and his associates[154] hypothesized that a slow infectious agent (prion or protienaceous infectious particle) can invade the neurons and microglia in the brains of susceptible persons.[23]

A second theory of cause evolved from the observation that the brains of Alzheimer patients contained a high concentration of aluminum in the areas of maximum pathologic change.[17,25] Whether this accumulation of aluminum acts as a primary toxic agent or is merely an element that is picked up by the diseased nerve cells is not known.

A third factor is the possible contribution to the pathologic process of head trauma. Head trauma could possibly be a factor in damaging either brain cells themselves or the blood-brain barrier.[50] Repeated head trauma is known to produce a dementia (dementia pugilistica) in boxers, and the brains of boxers have shown evidence of the neurofibrillary change seen in Alzheimer's disease (see Chapters 7 and 9). Further epidemiologic study of this issue has shown that a significantly greater number of Alzheimer patients report a history of previous concussive head injury than do normal age-matched controls.[63,105]

The contribution of these various hypothesized causes is not fully understood; however, a great deal is now known about the pathologic changes.

Pathologic change first occurs in the hippocampus and the association cortex of the parietal lobes.[39] Regional blood flow studies[69] as well as PET scanning have corroborated this finding.[29] Damage in this area correlates well with the clinical findings of decreased memory (hippocampi) and abstract reasoning (parietal lobes) seen in early Alzheimer's disease. Cellular atrophy and degeneration are also found in certain subcortical regions, particularly the basilar nucleus,[152] but also in substantia nigra and cerebellum.[124,129]

The gross brain usually shows rather significant atrophy, with increased sulcal width and ventricular dilation. As was mentioned previously, the degree of dementia often correlates more directly with the intensity of the microscopic change than with gross atrophy. This observation does not, however, negate the fact that extensive cortical atrophy is the usual gross pathologic picture of this condition (Fig. 6-3).

The brain of the patient with Alzheimer's disease also frequently has areas of cerebral softening from small infarctions. In some cases there can be enough of these areas to contribute to production of the dementia, whereas in others the number is small and clinically unimportant.[140] Patches of white matter degeneration (leukoencephalopathy) secondary to areas of hypoperfusion are also often demonstrated.[14]

The gross and basic microscopic features were known to Alzheimer. In 1976, however, Davies and Maloney[32] made the observation that there was a selective loss of cholinergic neurons in the brains of patients with Alzheimer's disease.[11,116,151] It was not until several years later that investigators discovered that the major source of acetylcholine in the brain was the basilar nucleus of Meynert and other associated nuclei in the basal forebrain.[18,102,152] Pathologic studies confirmed that these cells were some of the earliest to be affected in Alzheimer's disease.[31] This anomaly was initially thought to be the sole defect in the disease, but continued neurochemical and pathologic investigation have shown other defects. There is cell loss in the locus ceruleus and a concomitant decrease in the brain noradrenergic system;[141] cell loss and neurofibrillary change in the dorsal raphe nucleus also increase,[160] causing a decrease in serotonin in the brain;

and finally there is a widespread decrease in somatostatin in cortex (maximum temporally but also in frontal and occipital lobes) and hypothalamus.[5,6,34] With these advances in our neurochemical knowledge of the disease has come a more detailed understanding of the pathology of the changes in the temporal lobes. The degenerative process primarily affects the cells in the entorhinal areas and in the dentate gyrus; however, there is also some cell loss in the subiculum and the CA_1 segment of the hippocampus. This devastating loss of neurons in these vital parts of the temporal lobe literally disconnects all input from the unimodal and heteromodal cortex to the limbic/memory system.[67,68] These neurochemical and pathologic studies have indicated that certain groups of neurons in the brain are specifically affected; why it is these cells and not others is unknown.

The final area of research on this disease has centered on the pathophysiology of the production of the major pathologic features: the neurofibrillary tangle (Fig. 6–4); the Marinesco plaque (Fig 6–5); and the granulovacuolar inclusions (Fig. 6–6). The pathologic link among these three features is not known. The plaque is the most specific for Alzheimer's disease; it is seen only in normal aging, dementia from slow unconventional virus, and Alzheimer's disease. The neurofibrillary tangle is seen in dementia pugilistica, viral dementia, postencephalitic parkinsonism, the

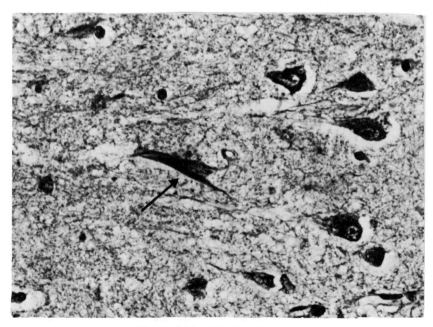

Figure 6–4. Alzheimer tangle.

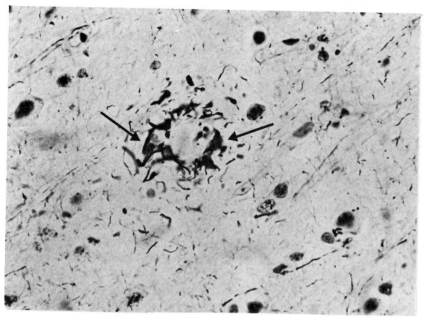

Figure 6-5. Senile plaque of Marinesco.

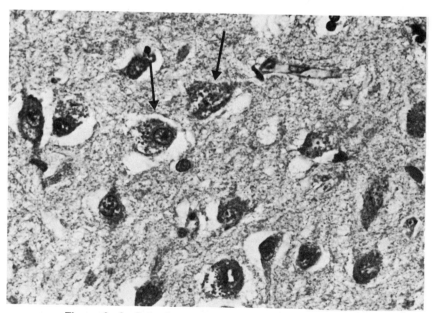

Figure 6-6. Cells demonstrating granulovacuolar change.

parkinsonism ALS/dementia complex seen in Guam, and in Down's syndrome.

The first pathologic changes seem to be the degeneration of the neurites (both axon and dendrite) of the cholinergic processes in the temporal lobes. At the same time, microglial cells in the region of these degenerating neuronal processes begin to produce amyloid. One theory holds that the precursor amyloid proteins are neurotoxic and precipitate the neurite degeneration, but this theory is yet unproved.[155] The amyloid and neuritic processes form the plaque. With time, the amyloid increases and produces a solid "burned out" amyloid plaque.[81,101,124,137] Amyloid also deposits in the walls of cerebral blood vessels in patients with Alzheimer's, a condition termed *amyloid angiopathy*.

The neurofibrillary tangle has also been the subject of intense study. At the heart of the pathophysiology of the tangle is a posttranscriptional error in the protein production mechanism in the degenerating cells.[123] Because of this, the neurons produce abnormal proteins (tau proteins).[70,158] These abnormal proteins polymerize and form pathologic neurotubules that eventually form the very durable paired-helical filaments with extensive crosslinking that are visible microscopically as the neurofibrillary tangle.[3,155] These tangles prohibit axonal transport and eventually kill the cell.[48]

The uncanny pathologic similarity of this disease to the normal aging process raises an unanswered question. All the pathologic features described above are noted in the brains of so-called normal old persons. The intensity and extent of the changes are not as great, but the process appears to be identical.[139] Senile plaques can be quite widespread in the normal old brain and tangles are also seen in the elderly, albeit restricted to the hippocampi. The question as to whether Alzheimer's disease is merely an accelerated aging process or a discrete disease entity awaits future investigation. Aging has been characterized by Wisniewski and colleagues[155] as a stage of pathology without clinical expression.

REFERENCES

1. Aikawa, H et al: Atypical Alzheimer's disease with spastic paresis and ataxia. Ann Neurol 17:297, 1985.
2. American Psychiatric Association: Diagnostic and Statistical Manual of Mental Disorders, III Revised. American Psychiatric Association, Washington, DC, 1987.
3. Anderton, BH et al: The nature of neurofibrillary tangles. In Traber, J and Gispen, WH (eds): Senile Dementia of the Alzheimer Type. Springer-Verlag, Berlin, pp 205–216, 1985.
4. Arendash, GW, Strong, PN, and Mouton, PR: Intracerebral transplantation of cholinergic neurons in a new animal model for Alzheimer's disease. In

Hutton, JT, and Kenny, AD (eds): Senile Dementia of the Alzheimer Type. Alan R Liss, New York, 1985, pp 351–376.

5. Beal, MF et al: Widespread reduction of somatostatin-like immunoreactivity in the cerebral cortex in Alzheimer's disease. Ann Neurol 20:489, 1986.

6. Beal, MF et al: Reduced numbers of somatostatin receptors in cerebral cortex in Alzheimer's disease. Science 229:289, 1985.

7. Becker, PM et al: The role of lumbar puncture in the evaluation of dementia: The Durham Veterans Adminstration/Duke University Study. J Am Geriatr Soc 33:392, 1985.

8. Berg, L: Does Alzheimer's disease represent an exaggeration of normal aging? Arch Neurol 42:737, 1985,

9. Berrios, GE and Brook, P: Delusions and the psychopathology of the elderly with dementia. Acta Psychiatr Scand 72:296, 1985.

10. Black, FW and Paddison, RM: Neurobehavioral changes in the elderly. In Rothschild, H (ed): Risk Factors for Senility. Oxford University Press, New York, 1984, pp 30–43.

11. Bowen, DM and Davison, AN: Changes in brain lysosomal activity, neurotransmitter related enzymes, and other proteins in senile dementia. In Katzman, R, Terry, RD, and Bick, KL: Aging. Vol 7. Alzheimer's Disease: Senile Dementia and Related Disorders. Raven Press, New York, 1978, pp 421–426.

12. Breitner, JCS and Folstein, MF: Familial nature of Alzheimer's disease. N Engl J Med 311:192, 1984.

13. Breitner, JCS and Folstein, MF: Familial Alzheimer dementia: A prevalent disorder with specific clinical features. Psychol Med 14:63, 1984.

14. Brun, A and Englund, E: A white matter disorder in dementia of the Alzheimer type: A pathoanatomical study. Ann Neurol 19:253, 1986.

15. Busse, EW et al: Psychological functioning of aged individuals with normal and abnormal electroencephalograms. I. A study of non-hospitalized community volunteers. J Nerv Ment Dis 124:135, 1956.

16. Caine, ED: Pseudodementia: Current concepts and future directions. Arch Gen Psychiatry 38:1359, 1981.

17. Candy, JM et al: Co-localization of aluminium and silicon in senile plaques: Implications for the neurochemical pathology of Alzheimer's disease. In Traber, J and Gispen, WH (eds): Senile Dementia of the Alzheimer Type. Springer-Verlag, Berlin, 1985, pp 183–204.

18. Candy, JM et al: Pathological changes in the nucleus of Meynert in Alzheimer's and Parkinson's diseases. J Neurol Sci 54:277, 1983.

19. Chui, HC et al: Clinical subtypes of dementia of the Alzheimer type. Neurology 35:1544, 1985.

20. Constantinidis, J: Genetic of vascular and degenerative dementias: The Geneva studies. Interdiscipl Topics Geront 19:1, 1985.

21. Cook, RH, Ward, BE, and Austin, JH: Studies in aging of the brain: IV. Familial Alzheimer disease: Relation to transmissible dementia, a aneuploidy, and microtubular defects. Neurology (Minneap) 29:1402, 1979.

22. Corsellis, JAN: Aging and dementia. In Blackwood, W and Corsellis, JAN (eds): Greenfield's Neuropathology. Arnold, London, 1976, pp 796–848.

23. Corsellis, JAN: On the transmission of dementia. Br J Psychiatry 134:553, 1979.

24. Coughlan, AK and Hollows, SE: Use of memory tests in differentiating organic disorder from depression. Br J Psychiatry 145:164, 1984.
25. Crapper, DR, Krishnan, SS, and Quittkan, S: Aluminum neurofibrillary degeneration and Alzheimer's disease. Brain 99:67, 1976.
26. Crystal, HA et al: Biopsy-proved Alzheimer's disease presenting as a right parietal lobe syndrome. Ann Neurol 12:186, 1982.
27. Cummings, JL et al: Aphasia in dementia of the Alzheimer type. Neurology 35:394, 1985.
28. Cutler, NR: Brain imaging: Aging and dementia. Ann Intern Med 101:355, 1984.
29. Cutler, NR et al: Clinical history, brain metabolism, and neuropsychological function in Alzheimer's disease. Ann Neurol 18:298, 1985.
30. Cutler, NR et al: NIH Conference, Alzheimer's disease and Down's syndrome: New insights. Ann Intern Med 103:566, 1985.
31. Davies, P: An update on the neurochemistry of Alzheimer's disease. In Mayeux, R and Rosen, WG (eds): Advances in Neurology, Vol 38. Raven Press, New York, 1983, pp 75–86.
32. Davies, P and Maloney, AJF: Selective loss of central cholinergic neurons in Alzheimer's disease. Lancet 2:1403, 1976.
33. Davis, KL, Mohs, RC, and Tinklenberg, JR: Enhancement of memory by physostigmine. Lancet 2:946, 1979.
34. Delfs, JR: Somatostatin and Alzheimer's disease: Possible pathological associations. In Hutton, JT and Kenney, AD (eds): Senile Dementia of the Alzheimer Type. Alan R Liss, New York, 1985, pp 243–261.
35. DeRenzi, E: Slowly progressive visual agnosia or apraxia without dementia. Cortex 22:171, 1986.
36. Drugs for dementia. Drug Ther Bull 13:25, 1975.
37. Duara, R et al: Positron emission tomography in Alzheimer's disease. Neurology 36:879, 1986.
38. Earnest, MP et al: Cortical atrophy, ventricular enlargement, and intellectual impairment in the aged. Neurology 29:1138, 1979.
39. Cholinergic involvement in senile dementia. Editorial. Lancet 1:408, 1977.
40. Ehle, AL and Johnson, PC: Rapidly evolving EEG changes in a case of Alzheimer's disease. Ann Neurol 1:593, 1977.
41. Erkinjuntti, T et al: Dementia among inpatients: Evaluation of 2000 consecutive admissions. Arch Intern Med 146:1923, 1986.
42. Etienne, P et al: Clinical effects of choline in Alzheimer's disease. Lancet 1:508, 1978.
43. Filley, CM, Kelly, J, and Heaton, RK: Neurolpsychological features of early —and late—onset of Alzheimer's disease. Arch Neurol 43:574, 1986.
44. Fogel, BS and Sparadea, FR: Focal cognitive deficits accentuated by depression. J Nerv Ment Dis 173:120, 1985.
45. Folstein, MF and McHugh, PP: Dementia syndrome of depression. In Katzman, R, Terry, RD, and Bick, KG (eds): Aging. Vol 7. Alzheimer's Disease: Senile Dementia and Related Disorders. Raven Press, New York, 1978, pp 87–93.
46. Foster, NL et al: Alzheimer's disease: Focal cortical changes shown by positron emission tomography. Neurology 33:961, 1983.

47. Foster, NL et al: Cortical abnormalities in Alzheimer's disease. Ann Neurol 16:649, 1984.
48. Gajdusek, DC: Sounding board hypothesis: Interference with axonal transport of neurofilament as a common pathogenetic mechanism in certain disease of the central nervous system. N Engl J Med, 312:714, 1985.
49. Geschwind, N: Personal communication, 1977.
50. Glenner, GG: Alzheimer's disease: The pathology, the patient, and the family. In Hutton, JT and Kenny, AD (eds): Senile Dementia of the Alzheimer Type. Alan R Liss, New York, 1985, pp 275–291.
51. Greenwald, BS et al: Cortisol and Alzheimer's disease. II. Dexamethasone suppression, dementia severity, and affective symptoms. Am J Psychiatry 143:442, 1986.
52. Grufferman, S: Alzheimer's disease and senile dementia: One disease or two? In Katzman, R, Terry, RD, and Bick, KL (eds): Aging. Vol 7. Alzheimer's Disease: Senile Dementia and Related Disorders. Raven Press, New York, 1978, pp 35–41.
53. Gunn, AE: Mental impairment in the elderly: Medical-legal asessment. J Am Geriatr Soc 25:193, 1977.
54. Hammerstrom, DC and Zimmer, B: The role of lumbar puncture in the evaluation of dementia: The University of Pittsburgh Study. J Am Geriatr Soc 33:397, 1985.
55. Harbaugh, RE et al: Preliminary Report: Intracranial cholinergic drug infusion in patients with Alzheimer's disease. Neurosurgery 15:514, 1984.
56. Harner, RN: EEG evaluation of the patient with dementia. In Benson, DF and Blumer, D (eds): Psychiatric Aspects of Neurological Disease. Grune & Stratton, New York, 1975, pp 63–82.
57. Harris, R: Genetics of Alzheimer's disease. Editorial. Br Med J 284:1065, 1982.
58. Hauser, WA et al: Seizures and myoclonus in patients with Alzheimer's disease. Neurology 36:1226, 1986.
59. Hefti, F and Weiner, W: Nerve growth factor and Alzheimer's disease. Ann Neurol 20:275, 1986.
60. Heilman, KM and Fisher, WR: Hyperlipidemic dementia. Arch Neurol 31:67, 1974.
61. Heston, LL: Clinical genetics of Alzheimer's disease. In Hutton, JT and Kenny, AD (eds): Senile Dementia of the Alzheimer Type. Alan R Liss, New York, 1985, pp 197–203.
62. Heston, LL et al: Dementia of the Alzheimer type, clinical genetics, natural history, and associated conditions. Arch Gen Psychiatry 38:1085, 1981.
63. Heyman, A et al: Alzheimer's disease: A study of epidemiological aspects. Ann Neurol 15:335, 1984.
64. Hochanadel, G and Kaplan, E: Neuropsychology of normal aging. In Albert, ML (ed): Clinical Neurology of Aging. Oxford University Press, New York, 1984, pp 231–244.
65. Huckman, MS, Fox, J, and Topel, J: The validity of criteria for the evaluation of cerebral atrophy by computerized tomography. Radiology 116:85, 1975.

66. Hutton, JT, Nagel, JA, and Loewenson, RB: Eye-tracking dysfunction in Alzheimer-type dementia. Neurology 34:99, 1984.

67. Hyman, BT et al: Alzheimer's disease: Cell-specific pathology isolates the hippocampal formation. Science 225:1168, 1984.

68. Hyman, BT et al: Perforant pathway changes and the memory impairment of Alzheimer's disease. Ann Neurol 20:472, 1986.

69. Ingvar, DH, Risberg, J, and Schwartz, MS: Evidence of subnormal function of association cortex in presenile dementia. Neurology 25:964, 1975.

70. Iqbal, K et al: Defective brain microtubule assembly in Alzheimer's disease. Lancet 2:421, 1986.

71. Jacobs, L and Grossman, MD: Three primitive reflexes in normal adults. Neurology 30:184, 1980.

72. Janowsky, DS: Pseudodementia in the elderly: Differential diagnosis and treatment. J Clin Psychiatry 43:19, 1982.

73. Jarvick, LF, Eisdorfer, C, and Blum, JE (eds): Intellectual Functioning in Adults. Springer-Verlag, New York, 1973.

74. Jenike, MA and Albert, MS: The dexamethasone suppression test in patients with presenile and senile dementia of the Alzheimer type. J Am Geriatr Soc 32:441, 1984.

75. Jervis, GA: Early senile dementia in mongoloid idiocy. Am J Psychiatry 105:102, 1948.

76. Kasniak, AW et al: Predictors of mortality in presenile and senile dementia. Ann Neurol 3:246, 1978.

77. Katzman, R: The prevalence and malignancy of Alzheimer's disease. Arch Neurol 33:217, 1976.

78. Katzman, R: Clinical presentation of the course of Alzheimer's disease: The atypical patient. Interdiscipl Topics Geront 20:12, 1985.

79. Katzman, R: Alzheimer's disease. N Engl J Med 314:964, 1986.

80. Katzman, R and Karasu, TB: Differential diagnosis of dementia. In Fields, WS (ed): Neurological and Sensory Disorders in the Elderly. Stratton Intercontinental Medical Book, New York, 1974, pp 103–134.

81. Kay, DWK: Epidemiological aspects of organic brain disease in the aged. In Gaitz, CM (ed): Aging and the Brain. Plenum, New York, 1972, pp 15–27.

82. Kiloh, LG: Pseudodementia. Acta Psychiatr Scand 37:336, 1961.

83. Kinsbourne, M: Cognitive decline with advancing age: An interpretation. In Smith, WL and Kinsbourne, M (eds): Aging and Dementia. Spectrum, New York, 1977, pp 217–235.

84. Kirshner, HS, Webb, WG, and Kelly, MP: The naming disorder of dementia. Neuropsychologia 22:23, 1984.

85. Knesevich, JW et al: Preliminary report on affective symptoms in the early stages of senile dementia of the Alzheimer type. Am J Psychiatry 140:233, 1983.

86. Kral, VA: Benign senescent forgetfulness. In Katzmann, R, Terry, RD, and Bick, KL (eds): Aging. Vol 7. Alzheimer's Disease: Senile Dementia and Related Disorders. Raven Press, New York, 1978, pp 47–52.

87. Kral, VA: The relationship between senile dementia (Alzheimer type) and depression. Can J Psychiatry 28:304, 1983.

88. Levy, R: The neurophysiology of dementia. Br J Psychiatry, Special No 9, 1975, pp 119–123.

89. Levy, R et al: The effects of long-term administration of lecithin on the course of Alzheimer senile dementia. Interdiscipl Topics Geront 20:153, 1985.

90. Liston, EH: Occult presenile dementia. J Nerv Ment Dis 164:263, 1977.

91. Loring, DW and Largen, JW: Neuropsychological patterns of presenile and senile dementia of the Alzheimer type. Neuropsychologia 23:351, 1985.

92. Mace, NL and Rabins, PV: The 36-Hour Day. Johns Hopkins, Baltimore, 1981.

93. Mann, AH: Cortical atrophy and air encephalography: A clinical and radiological study. Psychol Med 3:374, 1973.

94. Marsden, CD and Harrison, MJG: Outcome of investigation of patients with presenile dementia. Br Med J 2:249, 1972.

95. Martin, A and Fedio, P: Word production and comprehension in Alzheimer's disease: The breakdown of semantic knowledge. Brain Lang 19:124, 1983.

96. Mayer-Gross, W: Discussion on the presenile dementias: Symptomatology, pathology and differential diagnosis. Proc R Soc Med 31:1443, 1938.

97. Mayeux, R, Stern, Y, and Spanton, S: Heterogeneity in dementia of the Alzheimer type: Evidence of subgroups. Neurology 35:453, 1985.

98. McDermott, JR et al: Brain aluminum in aging and Alzheimer disease. Neurology 29:809, 1979.

99. McKhann, G et al: Clinical diagnosis of Alzheimer's disease: Report of the NINCDS-ADRDA Work Group under the auspices of Department of Health and Human Services Task Force on Alzheimer's Disease. Neurology 34:939, 1984.

100. McMenemey, WH: Alois Alzheimer and his disease. In Wolstenholme, GEW and O'Connor, M (eds): Alzheimer's Disease and Related Conditions. Churchill, London, 1970, pp 5–10.

101. Mehraein, P, Yamada, M, and Tarnowska-Dzidusko, E: Quantitative study on dendrites and dendritic spines in Alzheimer's disease and senile dementia. In Kreutzberg, GW (ed): Advances in Neurology, Vol 12. Raven Press, New York, 1975, pp 453–458.

102. Mesulam, M-M et al: Cholinergic innervation of cortex by the basal forebrain: Cytochemistry and cortical connections of the septal area, diagonal band nuclei, nucleus basalis (substantia innominata), and hypothalamus in the rhesus monkey. J Comp Neurol 214:170, 1983.

103. Miller, E and Hague, F: Some characteristics of verbal behavior in presenile dementia. Psychol Med 5:255, 1975.

104. Mohs, RC et al: Intravenous and oral physostigmine in Alzheimer's disease. Interdiscipl Topics Geront 20:140, 1985.

105. Mortimer, JA et al: Head injury as a risk factor for Alzheimer's disease. Neurology 35:264, 1985.

106. Mortimer, JA and Hutton, JT: Epidemiology of Alzheimer's disease. In Hutton, JT and Kenny, AD (eds): Senile Dementia of the Alzheimer Type. Alan R Liss, New York, 1985, pp 177–196.

107. Nee, LE et al: A family with histologically confirmed Alzheimer's disease. Arch Neurol 40:203, 1983.

108. Neisser, U: Cognitive Psychology. Appleton-Century-Crofts, New York, 1967, pp 219–242.
109. Nott, PN and Fleminger, JJ: Presenile dementia: The difficulties of early diagnosis. Acta Psychiatr Scand 51:210, 1975.
110. Obrist, WD: The electroencephalogram in normal aged adults. Electroencephalogr Clin Neurophysiol 6:235, 1954.
111. Orme, JE: Non-verbal and verbal performance in normal old age, senile dementia, and elderly depression. J Gerontol 12:408, 1957.
112. Otomo, E: The palmomental reflex in the aged. Geriatrics 20:901, 1965.
113. Paulson, G: The neurological examination in dementia. In Wells, CE (ed): Dementia. FA Davis, Philadelphia, 1971, pp 169–188.
114. Paulson, G and Gottlieb, G: Development reflexes: The reappearance of foetal and neonatal reflexes in aged patients. Brain 91:37, 1968.
115. Pedley, TA and Miller, JA: Clinical neurophysiology of aging and dementia. In Mayeux, R and Rosen, WC (eds): Advances in Neurology, Vol 38. Raven Press, New York, 1983, pp 31–49.
116. Perry, EK et al: Necropsy evidence of central cholinergic deficit in senile dementia. Lancet 1:189, 1977.
117. Peters, BH and Levin, HS: Effects of physostigmine and lecithin on memory in Alzheimer's disease. Ann Neurol 6:219, 1979.
118. Post, F: Dementia, depression and pseudodementia. In Benson, DF and Blumer, D (eds): Psychiatric Aspects of Neurologic Disease. Grune & Stratton, New York, 1975, pp 99–120.
119. Reding, M, Haycox, J, and Blass, J: Depression in patients referred to a dementia clinic, a three-year prospective study. Arch Neurol 42:894, 1985.
120. Robertson, G and Taylor, PJ: Some cognitive correlates of affective disorders. Psychol Med 15:297, 1985.
121. Roth, M: The natural history of mental disorder in old age. J Ment Sci 101:281, 1955.
122. Roth, M and Myers, DH: The diagnosis of dementia. Br J Psychiatry. Special No 9, 1975, pp 87–99.
123. Sajdel-Sulkowska, EM and Marotta, CA: Alzheimer's disease brain: Alterations in RNA levels and in ribonuclease-inhibitor complex. Science 225:947, 1984.
124. Scheibel, AB: Structural aspects of the aging brain: Spine systems and dendritic arbor. In Katzman, R, Terry, R D, and Bick, KL (eds): Aging. Vol 7. Alzheimer's Disease: Senile Dementia and Related Disorders. Raven Press, New York, 1978, pp 353–373.
125. Scheibel, ME et al: Progressive dendritic changes in the aging human limbic system. Exp Neurol 53:420, 1976.
126. Short, MJ and Wilson, WP: The electroencephalogram in dementia. In Wells, CE (ed): Dementia. FA Davis, Philadelphia, 1971, pp 81–97.
127. Shuttleworth, EC: Atypical presentation of dementia of the Alzheimer type. J Am Geriatr Soc, 32:485, 1984.
128. Signoret, JL, Whiteley, A, and Lhermitte, F: Influence of choline on amnesia in early Alzheimer's disease. Lancet 2:837, 1978.
129. Sjogren, T, Sjogren, H, and Lindgren, AGH: Morbus Alzheimer and Morbus

Pick: Genetic, clinical and pathoanatomic study. Acta Psychiatr Scand (Suppl) 82:1, 1952.

130. Smith, CM and Swash, M: Physostigmine in Alzheimer's disease. Lancet 1:42, 1979.

131. Smith, CM et al: Choline therapy in Alzheimer's disease. Lancet 2:318, 1978.

132. Stengle, E: A study on the symptomology and differential diagnosis of Alzheimer's disease and Pick's disease. J Ment Sci 89:1, 1943.

133. Strub, RL and Black, FW: The Mental Status Examination in Neurology, ed 2. FA Davis, Philadelphia, 1985.

134. Strub, RL and Black, FW: The clinical diagnosis of Alzheimer's disease: Relative sensitivity of various mental status and neurological examination test items. Ann Neurol 20:129, 1986.

135. Strub, RL, and Geschwind, N: Gerstmann syndrome without aphasia. Cortex 10:378, 1974.

136. Summers, WK et al: Oral tetrahydroaminoacridine in long-term treatment of senile dementia, Alzheimer type. N Engl J Med 315:1241, 1986.

137. Terry, RD and Wisniewski, HM: Ultrastructure of senile dementia and experimental analogs. In Gaitz, CM (ed): Aging and the Brain. Plenum Press, New York, 1972, pp 89–116.

138. Thase, ME et al: Clinical evaluation of dementia in Down's syndrome: A preliminary report. J Ment Defic Res 26:239, 1982.

139. Tomlinson, BE, Blessed, G, and Roth, M: Observations on the brains of non-demented old people. J Neurol Sci 7:331, 1968.

140. Tomlinson, BE, Blessed, G, and Roth, M: Observations on the brains of demented old people. J Neurol Sci 11:205, 1970.

141. Tomlinson, BE, Irving, D, and Blessed, G: Cell loss in the locus coeruleus in senile dementia of Alzheimer type. J Neurol Sci 49:419, 1981.

142. Van Doorm, JM and Hemker, HC: Aluminum and Alzheimer's disease. Lancet 2:708, 1977.

143. Volicer, L et al: Hospice approach to the treatment of patients with advanced dementia of the Alzheimer type. JAMA 256:2210, 1986.

144. Wechsler, D: Manual for the Weschler Adult Intelligence Scale. Revised. The Psychological Corporation, New York, 1981.

145. Weschler, D: The Measurement and Appraisal of Adult Intelligence. Williams & Wilkins, Baltimore, 1958.

146. Weiner, H and Schuster, DB: The electroencephalogram in dementia—some preliminary observations and correlations. Electroencephalogr Clin Neurolphysiol 8:479, 1956.

147. Weiss, IK, Nagel, CL, and Aronson, MK: Applicability of depression scales to the old old person. J Am Geriatr Soc 34:185, 1986.

148. Wells, CE: Pseudodementia. Am J Psychiatry 136:895, 1979.

149. Whalley, LJ et al: A study of familial factors in Alzheimer's disease. Br J Psychiatry 140:249, 1982.

150. Whalley, LJ, Wright, AF, and Clair, DM St: Genetic factors in Down's syndrome and their possible role in the pathogenesis of Alzheimer's disease. Interdiscipl Topics Geront 19:18, 1985.

151. White, P et al: Neocortical cholinergic neurons in elderly people. Lancet 1:668, 1977.

152. Whitehouse, PJ et al: Alzheimer's disease and senile dementia—loss of neurons in the basal forebrain. Science 215:1237, 1982.
153. Wisniewski, KE et al: Alzheimer's disease in Down's syndrome: Clinicopathologic studies. Neurology 35:957, 1985.
154. Wisniewski, HM, Merz, GS, and Carp, RI: Current hypothesis of the etiology and pathogenesis of senile dementia of the Alzheimer type. Interdiscipl Topics Geront 19:45, 1985.
155. Wisniewski, HM et al: Morphology and biochemistry of Alzheimer's disease. In Hutton, JT and Kenny, AD (eds): Senile Dementia of the Alzheimer Type. Alan R Liss, New York, 1985, pp 263–274.
156. Wisniewski, KE, Wieniewski, HM, and Wen, GY: Occurrence of neuropathological changes and dementia of Alzheimer's disease in Down's syndrome. Ann Neurol 17:278, 1985.
157. Wright, AF and Whalley, LJ: Genetics, aging and dementia. Br J Psychiatry 145:20, 1984.
158. Wolozin, BL et al: A neuronal antigen in the brains of Alzheimer patients. Science 232:648, 1986.
159. Yakovlev, PI: Paraplegia in flexion of cerebral origin. J Neuropathol Exp Neurol 13:267, 1954.
160. Yamamoto, T and Hirano, A: Nucleus raphe dorsalis in Alzheimer's disease: Neurofibrillary tangles and loss of large neurons. Ann Neurol 17:573, 1985.
161. Yesavage, JA et al: Vasodilators in senile dementia. Arch Gen Psychiatry 36:220, 1979.

Other Dementias

A 57-year-old businessman was referred for neurologic evaluation because of a 6-year history of increasing forgetfulness. The patient dated the onset of his difficulty from a bout of supposed encephalitis. At the time we saw him, the patient required assistance in remembering the everyday details of his work. Fortunately, he supervised a family business, and relatives were willing to assist him. As a memory aid, he also carried a little book in which to jot down important details and appointments. His only other complaint was an occasional feeling of gait unsteadiness. According to his wife, his geographic orientation was failing, and he had great difficulty orienting himself in new environments. In addition, his wife reported a general increase in irritability and diminished ability to cope with normal day-to-day stress.

On examination he appeared very anxious but was alert and cooperative. Mental status testing showed good attention, with a digit span (forward) of 7. His language was intact, as was his constructional ability (Fig. 7–1) and proverb interpretation, but his memory was definitely faulty. He could recall only one of four words after a 5-minute delay, and his knowledge of recent political events was extremely sketchy. Routine neurologic examination demonstrated brisk reflexes bilaterally but no abnormalities of gait or motor control.

Intelligence testing showed a Verbal IQ of 137 and a Performance IQ of 116 (Full Scale IQ of 129). His Memory Quotient, however, was only 94. Verbal abstraction, using a test of complex verbal reasoning (Shipley-Hartford), was compromised (Conceptual Quotient only 80).

Findings on brain scan, skull x-rays, EEG, and routine serum studies were negative. Pneumoencephalography was attempted, but ventricular filling was not attained. Questionable cortical atrophy was noted in the

Examiner

Patient

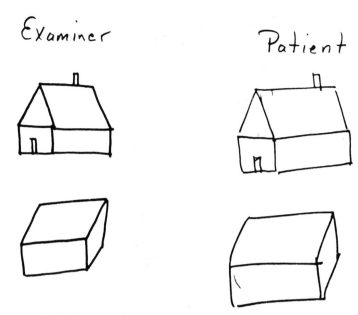

Figure 7-1. Construction ability of patient with mild hydrocephalus.

sylvian cisterns. After the test, the patient had a severe headache and refused a repeat study. A presumptive diagnosis of Alzheimer's disease was made; however, the history of mild gait difficulty and the absence of constructional impairment were worrisome features.

Over the next 2 years, the patient did quite well. His memory actually improved with the use of mild tranquilizers to ameliorate his marked anxiety, but his gait had become exceptionally broad-based and unstable. He also had experienced several confusional episodes and began to notice urinary urgency. At neuropsychologic reevaluation, his measured IQ remained at previous levels, and his Memory Quotient had actually increased to 122. Because a CT scanner had recently been installed in the city, it was suggested that this test would be a much better alternative than a repeated attempt at pneumoencephalography. The study showed obstructive hydrocephalus (Fig. 7-2). At this point the patient was hospitalized, a pneumoencephalogram revealed aqueductal stenosis, and a ventriculoperitoneal shunt was placed in the right lateral ventricle.

Since surgery the patient has done very well. The lateral ventricles have decreased in size (Fig. 7-3), his Memory Quotient is now 130, and general activities have returned almost completely to normal. The only significant residual of the hydrocephalus is a Conceptual Quotient that remains impaired relative to his other cognitive performance (CQ = 93).

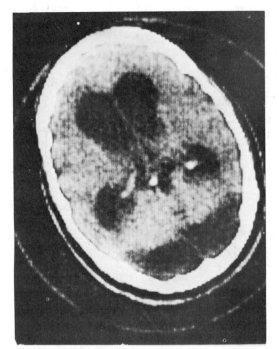

Figure 7–2. Preoperative CT scan.

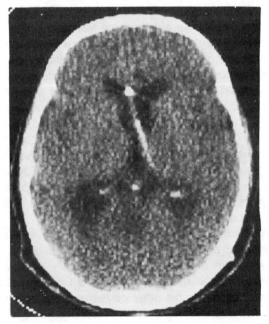

Figure 7–3. Postoperative CT scan.

The above case exemplifies the vagaries of dementia. Other than the disturbing lack of constructional impairment, this patient's initial history of memory difficulty and anxiety certainly was compatible with a diagnosis of Alzheimer's disease. One year later, however, after his memory had actually improved and his gait had become more impaired, his clinical picture was more typical of a patient with hydrocephalus. Such cases emphasize the necessity of carrying out a full evaluation, including visualization of the cerebral ventricles and cortical sulci in all cases of suspected dementia. This patient could have been correctly diagnosed a year earlier if a CT scanner had been available in the community.

In this chapter, we discuss many of the different diseases in which dementia is the principal or at least a prominent symptom. It is obviously impossible to discuss all the rare and obscure conditions in which an associated dementia has been described. Extensive lists of these less common conditions are found in Wells,[242] Pearce and Miller,[176] Slaby and Wyatt,[216] and Cummings and Benson.[51]

In many of the dementias, other neurologic or systemic features of the illness typically manifest before mental deterioration. In such cases the differential diagnosis is not difficult, but it is important that the clinician appreciate the fact that dementia can be a part of that particular illness and be prepared to cope with that eventuality should it arise. This is true for parkinsonism, pernicious anemia, pituitary disease, and many other conditions.

We stress two primary clinical points in this chapter: (1) some of the dementias are treatable, and (2) the clinical presentations in the various dementias often have subtle differences that allow the clinician to make the specific diagnosis from physical and mental status findings alone. Dementia was once considered to be a nonreversible condition regardless of its type; several recent studies, however, have shown this to be untrue. In an investigation of 106 patients with a presumptive diagnosis of dementia, 22 actually had psychiatric or other diagnoses, and 13 of the remaining 84 patients had treatable, albeit not always curable, lesions.[143]

Table 7–1 is a compilation of data from several investigations of the etiology of dementia in different samples. It is apparent from this table that most patients with dementia have untreatable diseases such as Alzheimer's disease. As clinicians have gained sophistication in recognizing the mental and neurologic changes in the diseases producing dementia, fewer patients are referred to dementia centers for diagnosis. Because of this, the percentage of patients with Alzheimer's disease and vascular dementia seen in these settings is even higher today. The reversible dementias, such as those seen with myxedema and pernicious anemia, are decidedly rare, but are extremely important to diagnose because of their reversibility. Hydrocephalus, which is certainly potentially reversible in many cases, represents between 5 to 10 percent of all cases of dementia reported in these series and

Table 7–1. Etiology of Dementia Expressed in Percentages

Diagnosis	Marsden and Harrison[143]	Harrison and Marsden[95]	Freeman[74]	Pearce and Miller[176]	Sourander and Sjogren[218]	Tomilson, Blessed, and Roth[233]	Malamud[140]	Todorov et al[232]	Seltzer and Sherwin[212]
Atrophy									
Alzheimer's disease	57	39	44	92	51	50	42	40	48
Pick's disease							3		
Arteriosclerotic dementia	10	10	8		28	18	29	29	2
Mixed atrophy/arteriosclerotic dementia						18	23	24	
Mass lesion	9	4	3	3					
Hydrocephalus	6	6	12						
Alcoholic dementia	7	8	7			2			23
Huntington's dementia	3.5		7						
Creutzfeldt-Jakob disease	3.5						3		
Chronic drug toxicity		4	8						
Post-trauma	1.5					2			7
Post-subarachnoid hemorrhage	1								
Encephalitis	1.5								4
Syphilis			2	1					
Subclinical hematoma				1					
Hypothyroidism			1	1					
Other		29	7	2	21	10		7	16
Total number of patients	84	49	59	63	258	50	1225	675	44

further points out the need for careful evaluation of the demented patient. The outlook for the demented patient is still not overly hopeful in general; but, compared with the futile view of the past, the diagnostic and treatment possibilities available today offer hope to some patients.

TREATABLE DEMENTIAS THAT ARE REVERSIBLE OR POTENTIALLY REVERSIBLE

Hydrocephalus

Hydrocephalus is a general term denoting an enlargement of the cerebral ventricles. In Alzheimer's disease or other degenerative dementias, the ventricles expand as the underlying brain tissue atrophies. This process is called *hydrocephalus ex vacuo* and is a secondary rather than a primary hydrocephalus. The type of hydrocephalus discussed in this section is that which occurs with obstruction to cerebrospinal fluid (CSF) flow or absorption. The obstruction can be at the cerebral aqueduct (most common in children), at the outlets of the fourth ventricle, around the base of the brain, over the convexities of the hemispheres from arachnoid adhesions, or in the arachnoid granulations themselves. Hydrocephalus secondary to aqueductal stenosis is called *noncommunicating hydrocephalus*, whereas ventricular dilation resulting from circulation obstruction or absorptive failure in the subarachnoid spaces is called *communicating hydrocephalus*.

Although communicating hydrocephalus has been recognized for many years, interest in this condition has been renewed following reports of an idiopathic variety of communicating hydrocephalus with normal CSF pressure.[3,91,154] The reasons for the tremendous attention given these reports were: (1) the lumbar CSF pressure was within normal limits, (2) the patients were demented, and (3) the dementia reversed after a ventricular shunt procedure was carried out. Considerable controversy has surrounded the evaluation and management of patients with normal pressure (noncommunicating) hydrocephalus. Several review articles[43,60,119] have appeared, and current thinking is summarized below.

CLINICAL PICTURE

The clinical picture of communicating and noncommunicating hydrocephalus is similar. The patients usually initially develop a gait disturbance that can have various features, with imbalance being the most characteristic. The most common behavioral changes seen are those usually associated with frontal lobe disease: apathy, euphoria, irritability, and disinhibited social behavior.[33,171,237,246] Intermittent episodes of lethargy and confusion are also frequently present. Increased reflexes, particularly in the legs, are seen in 40 percent of patients, with Babinski's signs found in only 12 percent.[246] Urinary urgency or frequency is also commonly seen. Cognitive changes are usually minimal during the early stage of the hydrocephalus. Mild forgetfulness, dullness in thinking, and some slowness in carrying out work assignments may be the patient's only behavioral complaints. Occasionally, severe memory deficits are seen, but this is the exception. Vigilance, attention, and general arousal are often impaired. On formal testing, many patients also have some problems on visual spatial tasks. In general, the cognitive and emotional changes seen in early hydrocephalus are much less dramatic than the gait and reflex abnormalities. This is an important feature in differentiating between hydrocephalus and Alzheimer's disease. In the latter, cognitive and emotional changes are usually pronounced before there is any suggestion of primary motor difficulty.

The clinical picture in hydrocephalus can remain stable or fluctuate over long periods but usually progresses over a period of weeks to months. Balance becomes worse, and patients have increasing difficulty in initiating gait. They take small steps and appear almost rooted to the floor. Active toe grasping is often seen, and patients will easily fall if lightly pushed. This type of prehensile gait with marked imbalance is the typical finding of a severe frontal gait disturbance, called by some a gait apraxia.[55] Emotionally, the patients become progressively abulic (without animation) and eventually are totally mute. Some cases of dramatic psychiatric problems including paranoia, depression, and attempted suicide have been described, but these are unusual.[184,190] During these later stages, the dementia continues to progress, incontinence becomes pronounced, and primitive reflexes (e.g., snout, grasp) appear.

The clinical signs are usually the result of the expansion of the anterior horns of the lateral ventricles. The behavioral changes are typical of frontal lobe damage, and the gait, reflex, and bladder changes are also secondary to expansion of the frontal horns. As the frontal horns expand, fiber tracts from the frontal vertex (e.g., motor fibers to legs and autonomic fibers) are stretched and rendered nonfunctional. This produces the leg spasticity, imbalance, and incontinence so characteristic of the syndrome.[253] The paucity of early cognitive signs is due to the gradual distortion of the cortex rather than to its destruction.

LABORATORY EVALUATION

The laboratory evaluation of these patients has included many studies: EEG, CT scan, MRI scan, RISA cisternography (injection of radioactive iodinated serum albumin into the subarachnoid space), subarachnoid saline infusion, and intracranial pressure monitoring. The EEG has not been a particularly useful tool in diagnosing hydrocephalus because it is normal in as many as 50 percent of all cases.[22] When considering the diagnosis of hydrocephalus, the most efficacious initial test is the CT or MRI brain scan. This safe, rapid test will correctly diagnose the presence or absence of hydrocephalus, often demonstrate whether the hydrocephalus is communicating, and will also show cortical atrophy if present.[113] Transependymal leakage of CSF around the frontal horns of the lateral ventricles can be seen on CT but is particularly well visualized on weighted images on MRI. This is a typical feature of hydrocephalus. Demonstration of significant cortical atrophy usually rules out the possibility of shunting, even though occasionally a patient with significant hydrocephalus plus atrophy has been shown to improve with shunting.[113] Some patients with atrophy in the Sylvian cisterns but not over the hemispheres do respond well to shunting.[201]

In cases of noncommunicating hydrocephalus, the patients are referred for neurosurgical evaluation and shunting. Cases of communicating hydrocephalus require additional evaluation to determine which patients will benefit from shunting. Because the CT and MRI scans give only a static picture of the ventricular system, additional studies to measure spinal fluid pressure, CSF flow dynamics, and saline absorption have been advocated.[70,76,86,119,157] We have not had sufficient experience with the saline infusion technique; however, many investigators find it a very useful procedure in determining suitability of surgery.[231] Our procedure includes a measurement of spinal fluid pressure and RISA cisternography, with brain scans taken at 6, 24, and 48 hours to assess cerebrospinal fluid circulation and absorption. An abnormal cisternogram is one in which RISA (1) fills the ventricles within 6 hours, (2) fails to circulate out of the ventricle in 24 hours, and (3) is still in the cisterns and over the convexity at 48 hours.[14,148,157]

A final procedure that can be carried out if other tests strongly favor the diagnosis is the monitoring of intracranial pressure for at least 48 hours.[37,50] Patients with communicating hydrocephalus often have waves of sustained increased intracranial pressure (B waves). The presence of such waves for at least 2 hours during the 2-day period of monitoring suggests that the patient's hydrocephalus has not stabilized and that shunting may reverse the neurologic picture.

CRITERIA FOR SHUNTING

One of the great problems in evaluating these patients has been to determine what findings on which tests will not only diagnose the disease but also predict those patients who will benefit from a shunt procedure. Many tests and factors have been considered, but there is still no infallible formula for making these important decisions.[14] The currently accepted criteria for shunting include many factors. The first and most important is the clinical picture. Patients with significant gait difficulty yet little or mild dementia are unequivocally the best candidates for surgery.[70,84,112,213] In one study of 30 cases involving surgery, 12 of 16 patients having successful outcomes initially had gait symptoms with little dementia, whereas 9 of the 11 patients in whom the treatment failed had appreciable dementia as the initial and most prominent feature.[70] In the remaining 3 cases, the patients could not maintain a functional shunt. Patients with dementia and no motor signs typically do not respond favorably.[112] A second important prognostic factor is etiology. If the patient has a well-documented history of an antecedent neurologic illness, particularly subarachnoid hemorrhage, meningitis, or head trauma, he has a 65 percent chance of improvement with surgery. Patients with idiopathic hydrocephalus have a less certain success rate.[119] Some centers report a 75 percent rate of initial improvement but with only 42 percent showing sustained benefit.[178] Others are less enthusiastic.

Laboratory criteria for the selection of patients for shunt surgery are less certain. The CT or MRI scan should not show cortical atrophy and actually should not show sulcal markings at all. In the typical case of hydrocephalus, the sulci have been obliterated completely. On CT scan, there is frequently evidence of low-density areas capping the anterior horns of the lateral ventricles as a result of the transependymal absorption of spinal fluid. The width across the frontal horns of the lateral ventricles should be greater than 53 mm.[71,245,246] In many cases that are destined to improve with shunting, a temporary improvement can often be seen. Such improvement has been reported to last up to 4 months in some cases and leads some clinicians to treat their patients with periodic lumbar punctures rather than shunting.[71] It is difficult to understand why this treatment might work because the small amount of CSF removed would ordinarily be replaced in a few hours, but the period of lowered pressure after the tap may possibly alter some critical membrane function and allow normal absorption to be re-established during the period of clinical improvement.

If patients are carefully selected (as they should be because shunt complications such as subdural hematoma and infection are common), at least 50 percent of patients undergoing shunting should improve significantly. Dramatic improvement sometimes is seen in the first few days after surgery, but usually a course of gradual amelioration is experienced during the first postoperative month. The degree of improvement, however, is inversely proportional to the total duration of the patient's symptoms. This fact makes early detection and intervention essential.[112]

ETIOLOGY AND PATHOPHYSIOLOGY

The etiology and pathophysiology of communicating hydrocephalus, especially that with normal CSF pressure, has been actively discussed since

1964. The basic mechanism involves some interference of CSF flow or absorption. In many cases, the history of subarachnoid hemorrhage, meningeal inflammation, trauma, or tumor easily leads to the conclusion that subarachnoid adhesions have been formed, blocking CSF flow. In some cases, fibrosis of the arachnoid granulations has been demonstrated at autopsy.[54] In many cases even detailed microscopic examination has not revealed the cause of the obstruction. Some patients with either Alzheimer's disease or multi-infarct disease develop an associated meningeal thickening and hydrocephalus; these patients have the combined features of the two diseases but seldom benefit from shunting.[37,43,59,119,126]

One puzzling feature of the cases in which normal CSF pressure has been recorded is the mechanism of ventricular expansion in the presence of normal pressure. One situation must obtain if the ventricles are to expand: the pressure in the ventricles must be sufficient to overcome the tensile strength of the ventricular walls and surrounding brain parenchyma. In some cases of Alzheimer's disease or multi-infarct disease, the tensile strength of the ventricle may weaken and allow normal intraventricular pressure to stretch the walls.[79] In other cases, the basal obstruction may create low pressure in the subarachnoid spaces over the convexity because of the negative hydrostatic pressure in the dural sinus. Such a pressure differential between ventricle and subarachnoid space could allow the ventricles to expand while maintaining essentially normal intraventricular pressure.[158]

Although there may be many mechanisms at work, it seems most probable that the subarachnoid or arachnoid granulation block initially causes increased pressure that expands the ventricles. As the ventricles expand, the ependymal lining stretches, and CSF enters the surrounding parenchyma. Over time the ependyma and brain tissue absorb the CSF, and a new production-absorption balance is established. On many occasions, the CSF pressure is in the normal range, but from intracranial pressure monitoring, we know that the pressure frequently is increased for short periods.[37,50,97] These intermittent pressure waves seem to be the dynamic feature causing progression of the hydrocephalus.

Brain Tumors

The behavioral manifestations associated with brain tumors are usually either those of a confusional state secondary to increased intracranial pressure or specific behavioral deficits secondary to focal pathology.[128,224] Tumors involving the temporal and frontal lobes, however, are well known for their propensity to produce a variety of mental changes, of which dementia is only one.[88] This is particularly true of tumors arising in the frontal lobes, in which the earliest and most characteristic clinical signs are mental dullness, amnesia, and confusion.[102] Often personality changes such as apathy, euphoria, irritability, and inappropriate social intrusiveness are common. In one large series of patients with temporal lobe tumors, 8 percent of patients experienced memory difficulty and 20 percent intellectual decline as the initial symptoms.[122] Eighty percent of these patients, however, developed sensorial changes by the time of definitive diagnosis. In general, it is unlikely that a brain tumor would produce a dementia simulating Alzheimer's disease without producing either concomitant neurologic abnormalities or a clouding of consciousness. A careful neurologic examination will identify many of the tumor cases, but a CT or MRI scan should always be obtained on all patients suspected of having a brain tumor. Tumors of the posterior fossa or those obstructing spinal fluid flow will create hydrocephalus and demonstrate the findings outlined in the previous section.

Subdural Hematoma

Chronic subdural hematoma can occur at any age but is particularly common in older patients. The elderly person's brain has often undergone slight atrophy, a process that stretches the fine subdural veins. These delicate bridging veins are thus highly susceptible to tearing from minor head trauma—trauma often so insignificant that it is unappreciated by the patient and not reported. At least 50 percent of all elderly patients with verified subdural hematomas do not recall a specific incident of head trauma. As the hematoma enlarges from blood leaking into the subdural space, focal neurologic findings or alterations in level of consciousness are usually present. Occasionally, however, a picture of dementia is all that is evident clinically. In one series of 75 elderly patients who were treated for subdural hematoma, the vast majority (94 percent) had altered levels of consciousness or other neurologic findings, whereas 12 (16 percent) were hospitalized because of mental or personality changes alone.[225] In our experience, we have seen several patients with dominant hemisphere subdural hematomas who presented with subtle aphasia that was initially unrecognized and misdiagnosed as a toxic delirium. Although the patient with a subdural hematoma does not typically present with a clinical picture of dementia, subdural hematoma must be ruled out in the differential diagnosis of any patient presenting with significant cognitive or behavioral changes.

If the CT or MRI scan is not definitive, but the history and clinical picture strongly suggests a subdural clot, cerebral arteriography should be done. We saw a 53-year-old woman with a large subdural hematoma in which the CT scan was negative, and only our persistence in obtaining an arteriogram allowed us to make the diagnosis.

Surgery for removal of the hematoma is, of course, the treatment of choice, and prompt restitution of mental function usually occurs if the dementia has been of short duration. Conversely, if the dementia has been present for many months or years, a less favorable response to surgery is to be expected.

Vasculitis (Systemic Lupus Erythematosus)

Systemic lupus erythematosus (SLE) is probably the most common of the collagen vascular diseases and is certainly the one with the most prominent central nervous system manifestations. A variety of neurologic symptoms has been reported, with mental symptoms being among the most frequently recorded findings.[115] From 10 to 50 percent of patients with SLE display some mental change during the course of their illness.[41,169] The most common mental symptoms are psychiatric or emotional (usually acute confusional behavior or rapid psychiatric change[12]), and they are discussed more fully in Chapter 13, Cerebrovascular Disease.

Cognitive impairment, often subtle, has been demonstrated in 66 percent of documented SLE patients.[35] Such problems were more common in SLE patients who also had emotional symptoms (80 percent of that group) but were also present in 40 percent of the patients with no history of SLE-induced psychiatric problems. Cases have been described in which symptoms of dementia, including difficulty in work performance, failing memory, and problems with concentration, were the patient's initial symptoms of SLE[40,136]; however, in most cases, the diagnosis of SLE has been firmly established from the other systemic signs and symptoms before the appearance of dementia.[204] Therefore, the dementia seen in SLE rarely presents as a differential diagnostic problem.

An important point in differentiating SLE from Alzheimer's dementia is that lupus is characteristically a disease of young women. The average age of onset is the mid-thirties, at least two decades before the usual onset of Alzheimer's disease.[100] This age differential, the difference in quality of the mental symptoms, and the presence of other systemic signs should greatly increase the suspicion of systemic lupus in any woman under the age of 40 who presents with a picture of apparent dementia.

Lupus can now be readily diagnosed with the aid of standard laboratory tests, particularly of the erythrocyte sedimentation rate, antinuclear factor, serum electrophoresis, and complement fractionation. Prompt diagnosis and treatment with steroids have been known to reverse many of the acute mental symptoms and on occasion can also improve a long-standing dementia.[40] The degree of improvement depends on the extent of the pathologic changes in each case. The neuropathologic change seen in lupus consists of multiple areas of cerebral infarction. Because the SLE patient with longstanding dementia does have infarcted brain tissue, improvement will be limited to reversal of those mental changes caused by the superimposed acute immune or inflammatory encephalopathy and/or vasculitis.[66,169]

Metabolic Disorders and Deficiency States

Most metabolic imbalances or vitamin deficiencies will eventually result in a form of dementia if they are unrecognized and allowed to run their natural course. In most of these conditions, however, characteristic systemic signs allow identification of the disease before the cognitive features become prominent. In the exceptional case, the mental changes of dementia may precede the other manifestations of the disease. Thus, the physician should include these metabolic and deficiency states in a comprehensive differential diagnosis of dementia.

In most of these conditions, emotional or psychiatric mental changes are more frequent than primary cognitive changes. Depression, agitation, and paranoid feelings with delusions of grandeur are especially typical of the early mental symptoms. The cognitive changes, when they do occur early, are characteristically a dullness of intellect, slow thinking, memory problems, and occasional difficulty with abstract thinking. Whether the memory problem is a genuine memory deficit or merely a reflection of depression and lethargy has never been adequately established.

If these conditions remain untreated, a clinically significant dementia will almost invariably develop. The longer that the dementia is present, the less likely it is that the intellectual changes can be reversed by treating the primary disease.

In general, these dementias are not difficult to separate clinically from Alzheimer's disease. The patients are usually younger, have the appearance of lethargy and dullness, typically show other signs of the primary disease, and most frequently present with confusional behavior or psychiatric symptoms. Some of the more common of these conditions are described below.

THYROID DISEASE

Hyperthyroidism can have associated behavioral abnormalities that are usually characterized by either confusional behavior or psychiatric symptoms (more specifically, anxiety or agitated depression). Hypothyroidism or myxedema, to the contrary, can present with the symptoms of gradual intellectual failure typical of dementia.[202]

The mental changes of myxedema were well recognized in the 19th century.[45] These observations fell into relative obscurity, however, until 1949 when Asher drew attention to the condition he called myxoedematous madness.[10]

As is true with all the diseases discussed in this section, the other clinical features of the primary metabolic disease usually precede or accompany the mental changes. Well-documented cases of a pure dementia syndrome as the initial manifestation of myxedema are distinctly uncommon.[131]

It has been reported that approximately one third of all patients with myxedema have psychiatric changes and that 30 percent will also show memory changes.[114,168] Many of the patients who have mental changes caused by hypothyroidism display emotional symptoms of psychotic proportions. Paranoia and depression are the most common features, but hypomania, agitation, explosiveness, and schizophreniform psychosis have been described.[10] Of the dementia symptoms, mental dullness, slow thinking, decreased memory, and difficulty in abstract reasoning are the most common. Full-blown confusional states are also seen at times, with active hallucinations reported in 50 percent of these cases.[45]

We have seen one patient in whom the T_3,T_4 levels were normal, and the patient was referred for evaluation of mild myotonia and forgetfulness. On examination, she had a typical myotonic response on percussion of the thenar eminence but no other neurologic signs. On mental status testing, she was dull and slow in thinking and speaking, with impaired recent memory and concentration. Emotionally she was apathetic but otherwise normal. Her TSH level was over 100 units per ml. Prompt treatment of her hypothyroidism reversed the mental symptoms and myotonia within 2 months. She stated that she "hadn't felt better in years."

Although the clinical diagnosis is usually not difficult to make because of the overall clinical picture of myxedema (e.g., weight gain, husky voice, thin dry hair, loss of lateral eye brow hair, facial puffiness, cold intolerance, and hearing difficulty), we routinely screen all dementia patients for thyroid disease by means of a serum T_3,T_4 and TSH.

Treatment can dramatically reverse all symptoms, but permanent intellectual change has been noted in about 10 percent of cases.[10,88,114,141] Infrequently, these patients' mental changes can actually worsen when they are given thyroid medications. In our experience, confusional and psychotic behavior, rather than worsening dementia, are more common adverse effects of treatment.

PITUITARY/ADRENAL DISEASE

As with thyroid disease, mental changes, including dementia, can be seen with either hyperfunction or hypofunction of the pituitary or adrenal gland. The hyperfunction that produces adrenal hyperplasia and Cushing's syndrome also commonly causes a mental state that can mimic the early signs of dementia. Easy fatigability, irritability, depression, mental dullness, and memory impairment are the most common symptoms. These symptoms are seen in moderate or greater degree in 40 percent of patients with Cushing's syndrome and to a milder degree in an additional 30 percent of the cases.[219,236] Anxiety, hypomania, and mania can also occur but are less common. Interestingly, however, it is this "pepped-up" feeling that is most common when exogenous steroids are given. Depression with or without lethargy is by far the most common of the behavioral features of the disease. The depression is present in 62 percent to 86 percent of Cushing's disease patients who were specifically examined for affective disorder; the depression is rarely severe and, in a high percentage of cases, resolves with treatment.[44,61,98,121,200] Patients are typically young (25 to 50 years of age) and have weight gain and other physical signs of excessive steroid production by the time that mental changes are noticed. Because of the characteristic features, this condition can usually be easily differentiated from the more common degenerative dementia described by Alzheimer. Diagnosis can readily be confirmed by a dexamethasone suppression test and urinary and serum 17-hydroxysteroid levels. Treatment of the primary disease will reverse the mental symptoms unless they are longstanding.

Hypopituitarism, although uncommon, can also present with slowly evolving mental changes that must be differentiated from degenerative disease. As with other metabolic conditions, mental slowness, memory loss, depression, and other emotional changes dominate the clinical behavioral syndrome. The disease usually occurs in young patients, with many cases occurring in the postpartal period secondary to hemorrhage into the pituitary gland (Sheehan's syndrome). Again, prompt treatment with replacement steroids will usually reverse the mental symptoms. Hypoadrenalism (Addison's disease) will result in a similar behavioral syndrome but has the classic symptoms of hyperpigmentation, weight loss, hypotension, and nausea.[42]

PARATHYROID DISEASE

Mental symptoms occur with both the elevation (hyperparathyroidism) and depression (hypoparathyroidism) of serum calcium levels seen in parathyroid disease. In hypercalcemia, the picture is more characteristic of a confusional state than of a dementia, although the chronic nature of the behavioral change can sometimes lead to diagnostic uncertainty. Two thirds of the patients primarily have personality or emotional changes, whereas less than 20 percent demonstrate memory difficulty or other organic cognitive changes.[177] Loss of spontaneity and initiative are also common subjective complaints. The most common cause of hypercalcemia is a parathyroid adenoma. This lesion must be assiduously sought in every case. Removal of the tumor and restoration of normal serum calcium levels have been reported to rapidly reverse the mental changes in most cases, even when they had been of longstanding duration.[177]

Low serum calcium, caused by either hypoparathyroidism or pseudohypoparathyroidism, will induce mental changes that can present as a dementia even in the absence of tetany.[64,194] More commonly, the patient demonstrates a confusional state accompanied by tetany.[214,226] The type of

mental picture is somewhat related to the rapidity of the fall of serum
calcium. A gradual drop in calcium will result in less dramatic personality
and memory changes, whereas a precipitous lowering will produce an
acute agitated confusional state (delirium).

The condition is usually seen in middle-aged patients (40 to 50 years
of age), but cases of idiopathic hypoparathyroidism have been reported in
patients up to the age of 80.[64] Most cases are secondary to inadvertent
removal of all parathyroid tissue during total thyroidectomy. Accordingly,
any patient with a progressive mental syndrome who has had recent thyroid surgery must be screened for parathyroid dysfunction. Cataracts,
features of parkinsonism, seizures, and increased intracranial pressure are
also seen in patients with hypoparathyroidism, and their presence can aid
in establishing the diagnosis clinically. Laboratory investigation typically
demonstrates a depressed serum calcium level and elevated phosphate level
in the presence of normal renal function. Treatment with calcium has been
known to reverse the mental picture quite dramatically, but frequently
permanent intellectual loss is seen.

HEPATOCEREBRAL DEGENERATION

Wilson's Disease (Hepatolenticular Degeneration)

Wilson's disease is a somewhat rare, recessively inherited condition in
which an abnormality in copper metabolism causes deposition of the
copper ion in the liver, various structures in the nervous system (primarily
the putamen and globus pallidus), and other tissues.[249] The usual onset of
the disease in its adult form is during the patient's 20s, although cases have
been reported in patients whose first symptoms were not noted until the
middle and late 40s.[83,240]

In most cases, the patient first presents with neurologic symptoms
(tremor, involuntary grimacing, dystonic posturing, choreoathetosis, dysarthria, and rigidity), although at least 25 percent of the patients present
initially with only behavioral abnormalities.[206,239,240,248] Patients with a
behavioral manifestation as the initial sign of their disease tend to be those
with late onset, making Wilson's disease one of the diseases that should be
considered in the differential diagnosis of mental changes occurring in
middle age. The patients tend to be explosive, immature, silly, impulsive,
sexually promiscuous, unkempt, and emotionally labile. Many patients
become delusional and despondent, and some attempt suicide.[110] In conjunction with these psychiatric or behavioral changes, some patients demonstrate cognitive difficulties including memory failure, decreased judgment and academic performance, and lack of concentration. If the disease
remains untreated, a progressive, severe dementia develops. By the time

that a full picture of dementia is seen, the other neurologic manifestations of the disease are also present.

The diagnosis of Wilson's disease can be made in most cases by laboratory studies showing low serum ceruloplasmin, low serum copper, and high urinary copper. A liver biopsy for copper content is more definitive but somewhat more risky than collecting a 24-hour urine sample. Demonstration of a greenish-brown ring in the limbus of the cornea (Kayser-Fleicsher ring) on slitlamp examination can also verify the presence of abnormal tissue deposits of copper. Treatment with penicillamine can effect a remarkable improvement in behavioral as well as neurologic symptoms. In one group of 17 patients who had psychologic testing before and after treatment, the authors reported a significant improvement on the WAIS Verbal IQ and the memory score of the Wechsler Memory Test.[83] In a larger series of 49 patients in which 61 percent had significant psychiatric abnormalities, over half experienced demonstrable improvement in both their moods and their antisocial behavioral problems with treatment.[206] Although Wilson's disease is uncommon, the encouraging response to treatment in many cases makes us feel justified in mentioning Wilson's disease in this discussion of the mental changes occurring in middle life.

Acquired Hepatocerebral Degeneration

A small percentage of patients with liver disease of any cause will develop a general intellectual deterioration secondary to their hepatic disease. This dementia usually begins as a sequela of hepatic coma, but in 15 percent of the cases, the patient has cognitive symptoms before the diagnosis of liver disease is made.[2] Alcoholic cirrhosis and other liver diseases are sufficiently common that the physician should be aware of the possibility of hepatocerebral degeneration in the differential diagnosis of dementia.

VITAMIN DEFICIENCIES

Pellagra

Niacin deficiency will characteristically produce a mental syndrome of confusion, memory impairment, disorientation, apathy, irritability, and apprehension. This mental picture, which can often look superficially like an early degenerative dementia, is soon followed by the dermatitis, peripheral neuropathy, and diarrhea that constitute the full clinical syndrome of pellagra. The epidemic form of this condition is no longer seen in this country; rather it has become a sporadic disease in alcoholics, food faddists, and others with extremely abnormal eating habits.

Vitamin B$_{12}$ and Folate Deficiency

In the search for treatable causes of psychiatric disease and dementia, vitamins B$_{12}$ and folate have received considerable attention. Depletion of either substance can produce a mental syndrome that can be confused with early Alzheimer's disease.[78,103,196,203,209] Mild depression and anxiety, loss of sexual interest, irritability, memory impairment, and concentration difficulty constitute the typical clinical presentation. All these findings can occur years before the onset of hematologic abnormalities.[191,203] The cause of the symptoms does not seem, therefore, to be directly related to the anemia frequently associated with the vitamin deficiency but rather to the vitamin deficiency itself. There is little doubt that B$_{12}$ deficiency causes a neurologic syndrome with prominent mental changes, but the actual relationship of B$_{12}$ to folate and to mental symptoms is much debated. Some authors allege that there is a close relationship between the two vitamins in the production of dementia.[189] Others question the fact that folate itself is an important factor.[199,209]

Because efficient screening methods for determining B$_{12}$ and folate levels are not available in every laboratory, the physician must be selective in requesting these tests. Certainly, the condition of any patient with a history of gastric surgery, malabsorption, or strict vegetarianism should be investigated.[81] Serum levels of B$_{12}$ and folate should be determined in any case of dementia without cerebral atrophy for which no alternate explanation can be established. Patients with well-documented abnormal levels of B$_{12}$ (<100 pg per ml) and/or folate (<2 ng per ml) who also have dementia and/or mental symptoms should be treated with both B$_{12}$ (100 mg daily for 7 days, then 3 times weekly for 1 month, and then once a week for 1 year) and folate (5 mg daily). In some patients, the serum B$_{12}$ level may be normal even though a deficiency syndrome is present. If vitamin deficiency is strongly suspected, the Schilling test should be done because it is still the most definitive of such tests. If the mental condition is of recent onset, the behavioral changes should reverse. If it is longstanding, however, demyelination will have occurred, and the cognitive as well as psychiatric changes may be permanent.[4,118]

Chronic Meningitis

Tuberculosis, Cryptococcus, Coccidioides, and various rarer fungal agents produce indolent infections that can result in a chronic meningitis, frequently without signs of the illness in other organs.[163] In such cases, mental symptoms are especially prominent features. For example, mental changes have been reported in more than 50 percent of all patients with cryptococcal meningitis.[205]

The typical clinical picture is of a middle-age patient (many such patients have been on therapy with immunosuppressive drugs or steroids, or have lymphomas) who develops a chronic headache (almost 100 percent of patients) with memory difficulty, chronic confusion, clouding of consciousness, fever (almost 100 percent of patients), malaise, and often scattered neurologic signs such as ataxia, visual blurring, or seizures. The headache, fever, and mental confusion dominate the early clinical picture, whereas a decreased level of consciousness, nuchal rigidity, cerebellar dysfunction, and cranial nerve signs develop as the disease progresses.[130,153,198]

In the case of tuberculosis, the progression of symptoms is usually extremely rapid, with death occurring in the undiagnosed patient within 4 to 6 weeks. These cases should not be confused with a degenerative dementia because of their characteristic rapid clinical course. Indolent cases do occur; therefore, tuberculosis stains and cultures must be obtained in all cases of chronic meningitis.

The patient with the more slowly developing infections, as with Cryptococcus or one of the fungi, can have a history ranging from several weeks to as long as 24 months of gradual mental change — not an atypical history for Alzheimer's disease. Dementia caused by these infections is uncommon, but as they are amenable to treatment, they should be considered in the differential diagnosis.

The diagnosis of such infectious processes is made most efficiently on spinal fluid examination. Spinal fluid protein and often pressure are elevated, sugar is depressed, and cells (mostly lymphocytes) are present. The infective agent can frequently be identified on microscopic examination or culture. The aptly named Cryptococcus, however, is often especially difficult to find on a single microscopic examination (even with India ink), and repeated spinal punctures may be necessary. Cryptococcal antibody tests are now available and are extremely helpful in establishing the diagnosis if the initial India ink preparation is negative.

Treatment is effective for all the chronic meningitides, although it is lengthy, and many of the drugs have significant side effects. As with most of the diseases discussed in this section, the reversal of mental symptoms is best achieved with early treatment before the inflammatory reaction in the meninges causes extensive vasculitis in the basal vessels and widespread infarction.

General Paresis (Parenchymatous Neurosyphilis, General Paralysis of the Insane, Dementia Paralytica)

Neurosyphilis has long been known for its ability to produce an extremely wide variety of clinical syndromes. One of the most common of these is a form of dementia usually referred to as general paresis. Since the advent of penicillin, the later stages of syphilis are infrequently seen, but every physician should be acquainted with the clinical picture of this disease to complete his knowledge of dementia. Because the condition is much less common in this country today, one must look to foreign or older literature for comprehensive clinical descriptions.[38,159,248]

Although general paresis has many different behavioral manifestations, the most commonly recognized features are those relating to frontal lobe damage. In the early stage of paresis, the patient shows subtle changes in personality, which are frequently exaggerations of his premorbid personality traits. A lack of attention to personal appearance, poor judgment, aggressiveness, and abnormal or bizarre behavior are also often seen initially. In time, "peculiarities of conduct,"[248] irritability, mood swings, apathy, memory and concentration deficits, geographic disorientation with aimless wandering, and a deterioration in personal habits occur.[38] Delusions are often present; these are very grandiose in 10 to 20 percent of the patients.[159] At least 45 percent of the patients, however, present with a simple dementia alone, with apathy as a major symptom.[38]

The literary picture of the paretic is that of a man with a napoleonic complex, strutting about like a megalomaniac, and claiming to have extraordinary powers, financial resources, or physical prowess. Such cases certainly do occur but are not common. Less spectacular presentations predominate. With progression of the disease, the patients become more severely demented with marked memory failure, aphasia, apraxia, and agnosia.[248] The duration of symptoms before diagnosis varies, with 20 percent of the patients presenting in the first 4 weeks of their illness, 25 percent in 1 to 6 months, and a few after a year of behavioral change.[38]

The behavioral features of paresis can be the initial and, during the early stages of the illness, the only clinical findings in some patients. The physician should look, however, for other neurologic signs because they are frequently seen in conjunction with the behavioral change. Argyll Robertson pupils (irregular, unreactive to light but reactive to accommodation), tremors of tongue and limbs, slurring dysarthria, and increased reflexes in the legs are the signs most commonly seen in the paretic patient.[159,248]

The diagnosis is easily made on spinal fluid examination. Increases in cells and protein are present in many cases, but the most accurate test is the VDRL (Venereal Disease Research Laboratory) test. Treatment with penicillin can have a very favorable influence on prognosis when used early in the course of the disease.[15,88,209] How much penicillin should be used and the necessary duration of treatment are subject to question, but it is consensually considered to be within the range of millions of units daily for several weeks. Intravenous infusion is preferable to intramuscular injection.

The pathology of paresis has been well studied, and there is a good correlation with the clinical features. The frontal lobes have extensive atrophy with associated meningeal thickening. The infection enters the outer layers of cortex and causes neuronal loss and reactive gliosis. Vascular lesions may also be seen; these account for many of the focal neurologic signs seen in patients with advanced neurosyphilis.[159]

TREATABLE, NONREVERSIBLE DEMENTIAS

In several conditions that cause dementia, treatment of the underlying disease can slow or arrest further progression of the dementia, yet cannot reverse the damage already present. The two most important treatable but nonreversible dementias are those associated with arteriosclerotic and/or hypertensive cerebrovascular disease and the chronic abuse of alcohol.

Arteriosclerotic Dementia

Some physicians still loosely apply the term "arteriosclerotic dementia" to any elderly patient who shows signs of senility. Although it is true that "hardening of the arteries" (arteriosclerosis) and hypertension are extremely common in older patients, these diseases, per se, are implicated in the production of a clinical dementia in only a small number of patients. Table 7–1, summarizing the clinical and pathologic studies of demented patients, demonstrates that only 10 percent of the patients in the *clinical* studies had a dementia judged to be secondary to vascular disease, whereas about 20 to 25 percent of the *autopsied* patients were found to have vascular disease judged by the neuropathologist to be sufficient to produce a dementia. In the autopsy series, patients who had had multiple major strokes were often included in the arteriosclerotic dementia category, thereby exaggerating the incidence of dementia attributed to vascular disease. Of the patients whose dementia is secondary to cerebral vascular disease, most have a history of multiple small strokes or transient ischemic episodes and should not be confused clinically with the gradual decline seen in Alzheimer's disease. There are exceptions, and these are the cases in which radiologic studies or autopsy are the only ways of making the final diagnosis. As can be seen from Table 7–1, Alzheimer's disease remains by far the most common cause of dementia in patients over the age of 50.

Within the group of patients in whom dementia is, in fact, due to arteriosclerotic disease, there is a variety of both proved and postulated mechanisms by which vascular disease can produce the progressive mental changes.

MULTIPLE MAJOR STROKES

If a patient has sustained several significant vascular accidents destroying large areas of cortex in both cerebral hemispheres, he will characteristically show intellectual loss in association with his other obvious neurologic impairments. The reason for mentioning this encephalopathy in this section is not because this condition is likely to be confused with a degenerative dementia, but because many such patients are admitted to chronic care facilities with a subdiagnosis of dementia secondary to arteriosclerosis. Because of the subdiagnosis, any statistical or pathologic study of such patients will greatly increase the percentage of cases of dementia attributed to arteriosclerosis in the sample. This leaves the erroneous impression that a high percentage of the progressive dementias are due to arteriosclerosis.

MULTI-INFARCT DEMENTIA

The progressive dementia syndrome that is caused by arteriosclerotic or hypertensive cerebrovascular disease is secondary to multiple small cerebral infarctions.[68,90,96] Clinically, these patients are usually easily differentiated from those with Alzheimer's disease. The important features of the multi-infarct dementia are as follows:

1. Presence of hypertension and/or arteriosclerotic cerebrovascular disease (e.g., transient ischemic attacks, carotid bruits)
2. A history of stepwise decreasing mental and neurologic functions that may or may not be associated with a history of transient ischemic attacks[68,234]
3. Neurologic signs that are more dramatic than the dementia: asymmetric reflexes, abnormal reflexes, sensory abnormalities
4. Presence of a pseudobulbar state (found early in multi-infarct dementia and infrequently and late in Alzheimer's disease)[67]
5. Memory that is much better than other cognitive functions, particularly speech (a feature uncharacteristic of Alzheimer's disease)[69]

These clinical features, combined with a history of a previous stroke that cleared completely, should result in a relatively sound diagnosis of multi-infarct dementia.

There has been some difference of opinion concerning the classification, terminology, and the pathophysiologic mechanisms involved in vascular dementia. Hachinski,[89] who originally used the term *multi-infarct dementia*,[90] restricts the use of the diagnosis for patients who have multiple *cortical* infarcts secondary to emboli from the heart and extracranial vessels. This seems unnecessarily restrictive for two main reasons: one, emboli do not restrict their path to the cortex alone, and many patients will have both cortical and subcortical infarcts; and two, hypertensive patients with arteriolar disease certainly have multiple infarcts that can cause a dementia.

Lacunar State

The lacunar state represents one of the end stages of hypertensive cerebrovascular disease in which multiple small infarctions have occurred primarily in the subcortical regions of the brain, leaving small lacunae.[68] Clinically these patients frequently demonstrate the pseudobulbar state, with emotional lability. Behaviorally they often have symptoms of apathy, lack of motivation, and akinetic mutism, yet preservation of insight and personality.[109] Memory is faulty, intellectual processes slowed, and complex cognitive abilities diminished.

Subcortical Arteriosclerotic Encephalopathy of Binswanger

Binswanger's disease is fairly uncommon in its fulminant form, but the multiple white matter lesions that are its hallmark are frequently seen in the brains of hypertensive patients. Clinically the disease is a fairly typical multi-infarct dementia, except that it usually is seen in a slightly younger age group, with an onset between 50 and 60 years of age.[34,172] Most patients present with accompanying motor and sensory signs and a stuttering onset, but some patients give a history of slowly progressive mental deterioration with no abnormal neurologic signs.[123,132] The patients usually are hypertensive and may have extensive atheromatous change in their cerebral vessels.[29] The brain lesions consist of a combination of perivascular infarctions in the cerebral white matter and an unexplained secondary, often massive, demyelination of all but the corticocortical (μ) fibers in the cerebral hemispheres (leuko-araiosis). See Figure 7–4.[106]

Granular Atrophy

Granular atrophy consists of an extensive C-shaped band of multiple microinfarctions in the border zones between anterior and middle cerebral arteries and middle and posterior cerebral arteries (Fig. 7–5). This border zone infarction occurs primarily because of significant carotid artery disease that decreases the overall blood flow in the entire carotid system. Under such conditions, the border zones suffer the most extensive ischemia and subsequent infarction.[68,195]

DEMENTIA SECONDARY TO CAROTID STENOSIS AND ANOXIA WITHOUT INFARCTION

A great controversy surrounds the very appealing concept that carotid stenosis decreases blood flow to the brain and therefore can, if chronically present, cause gradual atrophy of cortical neurons and an attendant de-

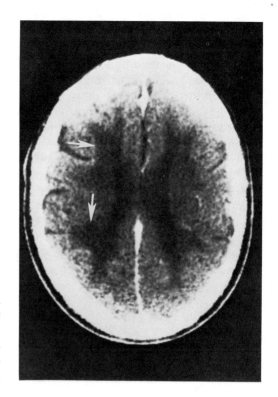

Figure 7–4. CT scan of patient with vascular dementia of presumed Binswanger type. Note irregular patches of demylination (*arrows*); these appear as areas of radiolucency.

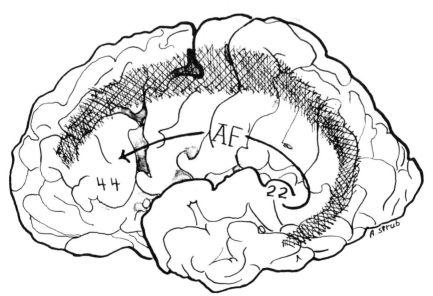

Figure 7–5. Border zone infarction.

mentia. Although this concept is seemingly logical,[67,175] evidence to support this contention is lacking.[68]

Carotid stenosis can produce transient cerebral ischemia; when it is localized, specific neurologic symptoms are produced, but when it is generalized, a confusional state results. What may occur is that some patients suffer repeated episodes of transient ischemia without actual infarction, but physiologic function fails to return to full capacity between attacks. Clinically such patients would present a picture of chronic, fluctuating confusion or focal neuropsychologic dysfunction, findings that could be called a dementia if they persisted over a period of months.

In this group of patients, carotid artery surgery, which increases blood flow, can increase overall mental functioning and to an extent reverse the dementia-like symptoms. This situation is extremely rare, and in most of the cases reported, the patients have had some evidence of residual cerebral infarction and a clear history of focal transient cerebral ischemia.[57,65] Some patients will develop cognitive loss and memory failure secondary to the cerebral anoxia associated with cardiac arrest of myocardial infarction, but this condition is more properly termed a post-anoxic encephalopathy rather than a dementia.[238]

MIXED DEGENERATIVE AND ARTERIOSCLEROTIC DEMENTIA

When evaluating demented patients and attempting to classify the cause in the individual patient, one must remember that some demented patients have both atrophic brain disease and significant numbers of small cerebral infarctions (see Table 7–1). This mixed group is very confusing diagnostically because (1) the dementia seems too great for the paucity of neurologic signs necessary to diagnose a multi-infarct dementia, and (2) the presence of focal neurologic findings is inconsistent with the diagnosis of a typical Alzheimer's disease.

Evaluation of the patient suspected of having a vascular dementia should include evaluation of blood pressure, heart rhythm, evidence of old myocardial infarction, and a full evaluation of the cerebral vasculature, particularly the extracranial vessels. Treatment cannot reverse cerebral infarction but is guided toward preventing additional strokes. Hypertension, cardiac arrhythmia, and other cardiovascular disease should be treated. The patients should discontinue smoking and reassess their dietary and exercise habits. Anticoagulation therapy, carotid surgery, and other treatment of cerebrovascular disease should be undertaken where indicted. As mentioned in the previous chapter, we have not found the use of vasodilators to be clinically efficacious. Unfortunately, the overall prognosis is not good in vascular disease of the brain; nevertheless, some cases can be helped, thereby justifying the effort expended.

Alcoholic Dementia

Several chronic neurobehavioral syndromes are associated with long-term alcohol abuse. The first is a true dementia, most commonly seen in the middle-aged alcoholic who has been drinking excessively for 15 to 20 years. The initial signs are a progressive lack of interest and concern for events in the environment, carelessness about personal appearance, impairment of judgment, defective attention, and a general slowness in all thought processes.[58,99,105] Most of these abnormalities are those usually associated with frontal lobe disease and are similar to the changes seen in general paresis. The similarity was so striking to many of the earlier investigators that they called the condition an alcoholic pseudoparesis. The marked personality lability and grandiosity of the true paretic, however, are not found in such prominence in alcoholic pseudoparesis.[99]

Intellectually, such patients show difficulty with abstract reasoning, problems with new learning (recent memory), some mild aphasic symptoms, and perseveration.[105] In one study, 95 percent had some difficulty with recent memory, whereas a smaller percentage (61 percent) suffered disorientation in their environment. Only 10 percent of the patients, however, had difficulty with drawings or constructional tasks.[105] Constructional impairment is more frequently seen in Alzheimer's disease and can be a helpful differential point when present. On formal neuropsychologic testing, the patients show deficits in the Full Scale IQ, memory testing, complex perceptual motor tasks (particularly those requiring rapid performance), and frontal lobe tests such as the card-sorting test that requires shifting from one scheme of sorting to another (e.g., first by shape, then by color or size).[21,124,228]

If the patients continue to drink, these symptoms and signs of dementia will continue; exacerbations are often brought on by bouts of delirium tremens. Improvement is slight and infrequent even if temperance is achieved. CT or MRI scanning shows ventricular dilation in as many as 70 percent of chronic alcoholics, even though the dementia is not obvious. These findings support the contention that alcohol can and often does produce irreversible brain damage.[21,73]

The pathophysiology of alcoholic dementia is still not completely understood and in many patients seems to be a combination of factors. First, alcohol itself appears to be toxic to brain cells, and actually causes pigmentary degeneration of cortical neurons. On the other hand, a significant percentage of alcoholics are known to experience episodes of delirium tremens, seizures, repeated head trauma, and the effects of chronic liver disease. The actual part played by each of these factors is not known and certainly differs in each case.

Pathologically, the findings are characteristic. There is macroscopic cortical atrophy frontally, a finding that correlates well with the clinical picture; thinning of the cerebral cortex; and enlargement of the ventricular system. Microscopically, pigmentary atrophy and loss of cortical neurons, maximally in the frontal areas and primarily in the middle layers of the cortex, are obvious. There is some glial proliferation (astrocytic), and occasionally a patient is found to have an actual laminar necrosis of the third cortical layer.[49,162,166,241]

The other chronic mental syndromes associated with alcoholism are Marchiafava-Bignami disease and Korsakoff's syndrome. Marchiafava-Bignami's disease is a dementing illness, but sufficiently rare that we do not think it merits specific discussion here. Korsakoff's syndrome is not a dementia as we define it, but it is rather a disease with a discretely localized pathology and a restricted type of cognitive impairment. We discuss this syndrome in the next chapter in the section on the organic amnesias.

UNTREATABLE DEMENTIAS

Degenerative Diseases

Many of the degenerative diseases have intellectual and social deterioration as either the primary or an associated manifestation of the illness. The most common of these is Alzheimer's disease, a condition that traditionally was considered synonymous with presenile dementia. Another of the classic degenerative dementias that should be differentiated from Alzheimer's disease is Pick's disease. Other conditions such as Huntington's chorea, parkinsonism, progressive supranuclear palsy, and the spinocerebellar degenerations usually have dementia as a late or associated component of the illness. In these cases, the dementia is an additional manifestation to be taken into account in managing the patient and his illness. Such cases do not typically present a diagnostic problem.

PICK'S DISEASE

Many textbooks disagree on the clinical separability of Pick's from Alzheimer's disease. Although it should be acknowledged that each condition has a clinical spectrum that makes differentiation in every case impossible, particularly during the later stages, the initial symptoms of the two conditions are usually distinct and recognizable.[117,120,142,193,215,216,222]

The clinical picture varies and correlates with the pathology.[46] Some patients have primarily frontal lobe atrophy and therefore present with a change in personality and social behavior rather than a primary memory loss and cognitive deterioration. These patients usually become disinhibited in social situations and are often known for their transgressions beyond the line of propriety. In concert with this loss of social inhibition, such patients develop a pervasive lack of interest in their responsibilities and surroundings. Soon the lack of interest supersedes the inappropriate social behavior, and aspontaneity and apathy pervade the clinical picture. Almost all patients lack insight into their problem. This is frequently not the case in Alzheimer's disease, where failing mental prowess is all too often tragically felt in the early stages.

Cognitive functions are relatively spared during the early stage of marked behavioral change. Memory, constructional ability, geographic sense, and language are far better preserved than in the patient with Alzheimer's disease at the same stage of his illness. During the second stage, however, general cognitive changes do develop. Scant speech production is noted in a high percentage of this group of patients with Pick's disease, whereas excessive rambling speech (logorrhea) by contrast is rare.[142] The patients develop an anomic aphasia (difficulty in naming objects) but do not produce paraphasias (word or letter substitutions) as do patients with Alzheimer's disease. The typical patient with Alzheimer's disease seems to suffer a much more complete disruption of language than the patient with Pick's disease, the latter producing little, yet better organized, speech. With a progression, the patients gradually lose their comprehension for language, but many retain the ability to repeat accurately. About a third of the patients actually develop an echolalia in which they tend to repeat, almost reflexively, all that they hear.[142] Perseveration is common in their speech, and stereotyped language is also frequent.

A second group of Pick's patients have temporal or frontotemporal atrophy. These patients present initially with memory loss, mood disturbances, and childish behavior.[46]

Patients with Pick's disease have much less apraxia than do patients with Alzheimer's disease and, in general, parietal lobe functions are spared. Patients in this second stage often demonstrate a marked lack of facial expression (amimia). Some also develop an astoundingly ravenous appetite. As the disease progresses to its third stage, clear distinctions from Alzheimer's disease blur and terminal mutism, profound dementia, and paraplegia in flexion are characteristically seen.[253]

The diagnosis of Pick's disease should usually not be difficult to make, with chance strongly favoring Alzheimer's disease because of its comparative frequency. In most parts of the world, both the clinician and pathologist will see 50 to 100 cases of Alzheimer's disease to every case of Pick's disease.[176,230] Exceptions to this rule exist in Malaya, where Alzheimer's disease has not yet been reported,[254] and in Stockholm, Sweden, where there is a genetic pool of Pick's dementia.[215] Incidence of the disease among men and women is about equal, unlike the 2:1 female predominance seen in Alzheimer's disease. There is a somewhat stronger genetic tendency in Pick's disease, with a suggested autosomal dominant pattern.

Pathologically, the disease has a very distinctive appearance. In the gross specimen, marked frontal and temporal atrophies are seen (Figs. 7–6 and 7–7). This pattern of atrophy correlates well with the clinical features

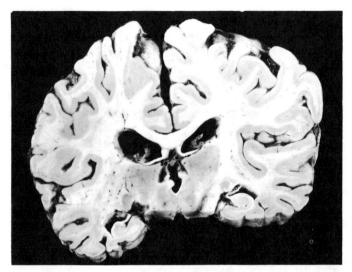

Figure 7-6. Brain of patient with Pick's lobar sclerosis. Note marked temporal atrophy.

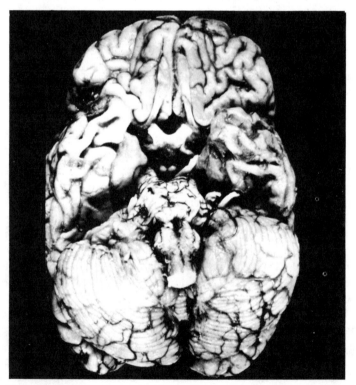

Figure 7-7. Brain of a patient with Pick's disease showing focal atrophy of both temporal lobes, more pronounced on the left.

of personality change (frontal atrophy) and speech abnormality and memory loss (temporal atrophy). It allows the clinical diagnosis to be reinforced by CT or MRI scan. This classic pattern of atrophy gave the disease its original name, lobar sclerosis. The pattern of atrophy, however, is frequently not uniform. Pure temporal atrophy is seen in 17 percent of the cases, pure frontal atrophy in 25 percent, mixed frontotemporal atrophy in 54 percent, and atypical atrophy including occipital or parietal lobes in the remaining 4 percent.[47,254] Only one third of the cases have symmetrical atrophy in both hemispheres, whereas atrophy on the left is greater in over 40 percent and on the right in less than 20 percent.[254] In all cases, the primary projection areas (post central gyrus, superior temporal gyrus, and the visual cortex in the occipital lobe) are consistently spared, with the atrophy involving primarily the association areas.

Microscopically, the cortex shows cell loss, astrocytic gliosis, and many enlarged balloon-shaped cells (Pick's cells) that contain argyrophilic (silver staining) intranuclear inclusions (Fig. 7–8). The outer layers of the cortex seem to be more severely involved.[251] As with Alzheimer's disease, no cause is known. Patients with frontal atrophy have the ballooned neurons, but no argyrophilic inclusions, whereas patients with temporal atrophy have both the Pick cells and inclusions on pathologic examination.[46] Neurochemical studies have shown that dopamine, acetylcholine, and GABA levels are normal; however, acetycholine muscarinic receptors are greatly decreased. Zinc levels have also been noted to be high in the

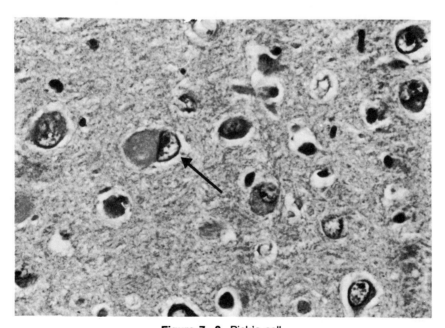

Figure 7–8. Pick's cell.

hippocampus, a finding that has prompted some investigators to use chelating agents in Pick's patients to remove this substance.[46]

DEMENTIAS WITH A STRONG SUBCORTICAL COMPONENT

In several degenerative diseases with associated dementia, the most prominent pathologic features are in the subcortical structures — more precisely, the substantia nigra in parkinsonism, the caudate nucleus in Huntington's chorea, the subcortical white matter in progressive subcortical gliosis,[167] the thalamus in thalamic degeneration and subacute diencephalic angioencephalopathy[53,210,223] (not a degenerative disease, but mentioned here because of the association between subcortical lesions and dementia), and subcortical and cerebellar structures in progressive supranuclear palsy. In Huntington's disease and parkinsonism, there are also cortical lesions, but the degree of dementia seen in these patients appears more extensive than can be accounted for by the degree of cortical pathology alone.[9] Therefore, the degeneration of the subcortical structures seems to be, at least in part, producing or accentuating the symptoms of intellectual and adaptive deterioration. Neurosurgeons have also noted psychologic changes in their patients after stereotactic thalamotomy, providing additional data to support the contention that subcortical structures are intimately involved in the workings of the mind.[116,170,211] The fact that subcortical lesions can produce clinical symptoms that were once thought to be produced exclusively by cortical lesions is a fascinating new chapter in the assessment and localization of cognitive processes. Unfortunately this issue has been somewhat overshadowed by a dispute about the clinical and pathologic separability of subcortical from cortical dementia.[151,243]

The primary clinical features of these subcortical dementias are mental slowness or sluggishness, forgetfulness, difficulty performing complex verbal abstractions, failure of high-level concept formation and mental flexibility (being able to quickly switch from one way of doing something to another), and a personality change reminiscent of patients with frontal lobe damage (e.g., apathy, indifference, and irritability).[5,6] In many of these conditions, it is easy to see why a certain behavioral change would be associated with a given lesion; for instance, extensive lesions in the thalamus interrupt many important input pathways to the frontal lobes and may produce many of the behaviors exhibited by patients who have undergone frontal leukotomies. Involvement of the ascending activating system above the level of the brain stem can cause impaired arousal and inefficiency in maintaining attention and concentration. Although as yet unproved, reticular and other subcortical inputs may in fact play a role in directing and coordinating cortical activity. In recent PET scan studies of patients with aphasia secondary to thalamic hemorrhage, cortical hypometabolism was clearly demonstrated in the temporal and parietal lobes on the side of the thalamic lesion.[161] CT scans did not reveal damage or atrophy in the cortex. These findings suggest that the subcortical lesions have actually caused the overlying cortex (by some yet unexplained mechanism) to become hypofunctional. The role of such subcortical structures as the dorsal medial thalamus and the mamillary bodies in the memory process is less speculative. Damage to these structures, particularly when associated with an interruption of frontal projections, can also result in apathy.

The problem has centered around the comparison between Alzheimer's disease (a cortical dementia that has pathologic evidence of subcortical degeneration) and Parkinson's disease/Huntington's disease (two diseases that have a dementia from primarily subcortical lesions yet have evidence of cortical cell loss as well). The contention is made that these diseases are not pure examples of either subcortical or cortical degeneration. Furthermore, Whitehouse[243] pointed out that no adequate systematic neuropsychologic studies have shown that there are two distinct clinical syndromes of dementia associated with cortical or subcortical disease.

Although agreeing that the concept of subcortical dementia may have somewhat indistinct scientific margins at this point, we continue to believe that the clinical picture of cortical dementia differs both qualitatively and quantitatively from subcortical dementia.[107]

Each of the diseases in this group of subcortical dementias has its own specific clinical features. The most common types will be discussed below; others are referenced.

Huntington's Chorea

Huntington's chorea is a familial disease with an autosomal dominant inheritance pattern. The disease has two major clinical features by which it can be readily recognized: mental deterioration and chorea. One third of the patients present initially with a history of mental change without chorea; therefore, Huntington's chorea is an important condition to consider in the differential diagnosis of dementia appearing in the presenile period.[173] The disease is usually manifest between the ages 45 and 55; an onset after age 60 is distinctly uncommon and after 70 is very rare.[173]

Clinically, the early mental picture has many of the features seen in Pick's disease. Changes in emotional status and social behavior are characteristic. Apathy is especially common; however, emotional instability, impulsiveness, irritability, and explosive behavior are frequently seen. Patients with Huntington's disease are usually moody, quick-tempered, aggressive, and even physically abusive. On occasion, they can develop the psychiatric picture of manic-depressive illness or a delusional hallucinatory state resembling an acute schizophrenic episode.[32,156] Patients suffer a general loss of interest in work and are unmotivated to complete an assigned job.[28] They often become sloppy in their physical appearance and their living quarters. Insight is often retained early in the disease; the resultant despair coupled with poor impulse control leads to a high rate of suicide in these patients.

Despite this rather significant deterioration of emotional and social behavior, their cognitive processes typically show less dramatic alteration. The IQ, although lower than that of matched controls, may remain within the normal range.[16,31] On extensive neuropsychologic testing, performance on problem-solving tasks, the trail making test, block designs, and puzzle assembly are all significantly depressed. Controlled studies have shown that these impairments represent a degradation of performance that is greater than could be explained solely by any motor problems.[16,229]

As the disease progresses, chorea develops in all cases and mental deterioration continues. The aphasia, agnosia, apraxia, and severe amnesia, however, that are so characteristic of Alzheimer's and Pick's diseases do not appear. Muscle stretch reflexes increase in more than two thirds of the patients, and frank pathologic reflexes or clonus are present in one third.[173] Speech becomes dysarthric, abnormal movements are more constant, and eventually the patients become bedridden, cachectic, and grossly demented. Death usually occurs within 15 years after the onset of the disease.[88]

Laboratory evaluation is not specific for making the diagnosis of Huntington's chorea. The EEG is frequently abnormal, and the CT or MRI scan often shows a rounding of the lateral wall of the lateral ventricle secondary to the atrophy of the caudate nucleus. The diagnosis of Huntington's chorea is basically a clinical diagnosis based on family history and neurologic findings.

Pathologically, the gross brain usually shows mild to moderate cerebral atrophy, with frontal atrophy being most prominent. This frontal atrophy correlates well with the clinical picture of a predominantly emotional change. The caudate nucleus is markedly atrophic, and the putamen and globus pallidus also show atrophy.[47] Microscopically, cell loss is prominent in the areas of atrophy, with some reactive astrocytic proliferation, but there are no specific cellular changes such as those seen in Alzheimer's or Pick's disease.

Huntington's disease, like parkinsonism and Alzheimer's disease, has been shown neurochemically to involve rather specific transmitter systems. Glutamic acid decarboxylase (GAD), which is critical to the synthesis of the neurotransmitter gamma aminobutyric acid (GABA), and choline are reduced 85 and 50 percent respectively in the caudate nuclei of patients with Huntington's chorea. Receptor-binding sites for serotonin and muscarinic acetylcholine are also reduced 50 percent in the Huntington patient's caudate nucleus. Binding sites in the frontal cortex, however, are normal.[62] Cholecystokinin is decreased in the globus pallidus and substantia nigra, but somatostatin levels are greatly increased.[144] These findings suggest that a specific metabolic defect in the production and maintenance of certain neurotransmitters or transmitter systems is responsible for the eventual death of specific cells, thus producing the clinical syndrome.

Genetic studies in recent years have identified a genetic marker on chromosome 4 in the families studied to this point. Perhaps, in the future, the actual gene can be found and the biochemical defect discovered; if this can be done, the possibility of treatment can be addressed.[144]

Parkinson's Disease

Parkinsonism is a relatively common neurologic disorder in which patients slowly develop rigidity, tremor, slowness of movement, and difficulty maintaining balance. Early studies of this disease paid little attention to any associated mental changes, but recently a number of studies have convincingly demonstrated a true dementia in many patients with parkinsonism.[11,19,27,104,107,127,145,146,150,183,188] Because the dementia occurs only in patients with well-established disease and is not a presenting symptom, parkinsonism need not be considered in the differential diagnosis of a patient with the initial presentation of a progressive dementia. Some patients develop a combined Alzheimer's/Parkinson's degeneration,[17,91] and other patients with Alzheimer's, Pick's, or other dementing diseases develop rigidity, tremor, and other parkinsonian features late in the progression of their disease. These disorders should be recognized as combined syndromes and not considered as parkinsonism alone.

Because the motor and other disabling features of parkinsonism are present before the appearance of mental changes, it has been difficult to determine whether the patient's mental changes represent a true dementia or merely result from a combination of physical and emotional symptoms that limit full performance on mental status and psychologic tests. Performance is slow and fraught with motor problems; speech is often inaudible or very difficult to understand; and the chronic physical disability often leads to a depressive reaction and reluctance to cooperate. All these factors must be considered when attempting to assess the intellectual functioning of the patient with parkinsonism. Despite these obstacles, it is becoming obvious that a large percentage of patients with parkinsonism (25 to 80 percent) develop true intellectual deterioration as the disease progresses.[145,146,227] If the atypical cases (pyramidal and/or cerebellar signs) are excluded, the prevalence is closer to 20 percent.[27] Atypical cases show upward of 70 percent prevalence of dementia.[220] In at least 50 percent of the patients having dementia, the dementia is mild and not a significant problem in the patient's overall disability. If careful neuropsychologic testing is done, most patients (over 90 percent) will show some subtle cognitive deficits. Most of these deficits are not clinically significant in terms of day-to-day functioning.[181] In general, the severity of the dementia correlates well with the severity of other parkinsonian features; patients with severe neurologic signs, particularly bradykinesia, tend to have the greatest degree of dementia, whereas those with only tremor have less.[134,145,146,164]

The mechanisms underlying the bradykinesia and the cognitive loss seem to be different; treatment of the motor symptoms does not correct the cognitive problems.[185] In addition, patients with idiopathic parkinsonism alone, either Lewy body type or Alzheimer tangle variety, have a lower incidence of dementia than those patients with parkinsonism who have a history of concomitant cerebral arteriosclerosis.[146,183]

The actual behavioral features of the Parkinson dementia have been consistent. Most investigators believe that a general lack of activation or arousal pervades all behavior and impedes normal cognitive and social functioning.[5,19,192] This general slowness and inefficiency in cognitive processes has often been aptly named *bradyphrenia*.[107,185,250] Patients have difficulty with complex problem solving and concept formation, they often exhibit a lack of insight and poor judgment, and many have features of a frontal lobe syndrome with indifference and social impropriety.[11,19] On specific psychologic testing, the patient with parkinsonism often exhibits difficulty with constructional tasks, nonverbal reasoning tests such as Raven's Matrices, and a general decrease in Performance IQ.[5,104,135] Memory deficits, problems with verbal fluency, and speech perception problems have also been stressed by some investigators.[5,87] The patient with parkinsonism is also especially prone to episodes of confusional behavior. This behavior is often related to medication but can occur in unmedicated patients.

In addition to the cognitive changes discussed above, Parkinson patients have been shown to have a much higher incidence of depression than other physically disabled patients of the same age.[87,104] Depression is seen in both demented and nondemented Parkinson patients, with slightly higher incidence in the demented patients.[150] Depression seems more common in the pure-Parkinson patients who have primarily a subcortical dementia than in the patients with the global dementia seen in the combined Alzheimer/Parkinson picture.[151] Recent theories concerning the pathophysiology of endogenous depression postulate a decrease in neurotransmitters, particularly dopamine. Because parkinsonism is primarily a disease of dopaminergic neurons, a similar mechanism may be operating to produce the depression in these patients. Clinically, mood swings are noted with fluctuations in motor performance in patients with significant "on-off" phenomenon.[80] The highly positive clinical response of these patients to the standard antidepressant medications also strengthens the neurotransmitter hypothesis.

The prognosis of the dementia seen in parkinsonism is unfortunately little better than that of the other degenerative diseases. With the introduction of L-dopa therapy, it was hoped that mental symptoms would reverse as steadily as the physical; however, this has not proved to be true. At times there is temporary improvement, but within 2 years the dementia typically has continued its inexorable march.[18,93,133,135,192] In some patients with a Parkinson-like syndrome including moderate dementia and mild extrapyramidal findings, a fairly dramatic improvement in mental state has been reported with L-dopa therapy.[56] Although these patients did not have classic parkinsonism, their response was so positive that we think they deserve mention.

There was some early concern that L-dopa itself caused the dementia in patients with parkinsonism, but this position has not withstood careful scrutiny.[227] Possibly the increased longevity and lessened disability that have resulted from the use of L-dopa have allowed dementia, when present, to become more apparent.

A behavioral side effect of L-dopa, discussed in Chapter 6, is the frequent precipitation of confusional behavior. In some studies, as many as 60 percent of the patients with parkinsonism developed this problem,[227] and in at least one case, a patient on L-dopa therapy developed a significant, irreversible encephalopathy after a severe confusional episode.[252] Permanent sequelae after confusional episodes can have various causes; the actual mechanisms are not well understood.

There is some indication that drug-related confusional episodes are much more likely to occur in the patient with parkinsonism who has evidence of dementia and slowing on his EEG.[227] The clinician should exercise caution in his use of L-dopa in such patients. When confusion occurs, we find that the only way to treat it is to decrease the dose of L-dopa.

The pathophysiology of the dementia in parkinsonism is not clear. Although some authors mention that frontal atrophy is seen in these patients, little pathologic study of the cortex has been done in this disease.[9] The demented patient with parkinsonism does have greater cortical atrophy than age-matched normals, as demonstrated on CT scan,[220] but the degree of atrophy does not seem sufficient to explain the degree of dementia, suggesting that many features of the dementia may relate to the subcortical lesions, not to cortical disease.

Pathologically, most patients with subcortical type dementia have classic Lewy body changes subcortically. In general, Parkinson patients have more tangles and plaques than normals; however, these do not correlate with the degree of dementia.[39] Some demented patients have no tangles, whereas others have tangles without dementia. In patients with severe dementia and aphasia, the pathology is most likely to show significant neuronal tangles in subcortical structures (not hippocampus or cortex).[39] Most demented Parkinson patients also demonstrate a loss of cells in the basilar nucleus of Meynert, which suggests another common factor between the dementias of Alzheimer's disease and parkinsonism.[244] Another similarity is the observation that cortical somatostatin is reduced in the cortex of demented Parkinson patients.[63]

In some patients with a rather significant degree of dementia, the clinical picture suggests that a combined degenerative process with features of both parkinsonism and Alzheimer's disease is present.[129] Clinical pathologic studies verifying a complex degenerative process are few.[17,72,91] Because such patients have a defect in both the dopamine and acetylcholine systems, treatment of the parkinsonian symptoms with anticholinergic medications may cause deterioration in memory function. It is therefore important to be extremely careful in the selection of medication for the patient with both parkinsonism and significant dementia. Dopamine precursors seem to be both the safest and most effective.

Progressive Supranuclear Palsy

Progressive supranuclear palsy (PSP) is a relatively uncommon Parkinson-like syndrome that was first fully described in 1964.[221] The disease usually begins when patients are in their 50s with vague emotional problems, imbalance, and difficulty with downward gaze. As the condition progresses, the patients develop a total external ophthalmoplegia, with vertical gaze involved first and most severely; rigidity, with nuchal rigidity being a very prominent feature; retropulsion with a marked tendency to fall backward; and a dementia characterized by slowness, memory loss, apathy, and difficulty with abstract reasoning, but with sparing of language and constructional ability.[6,160,221] Unfortunately, insight remains reasonably intact until the final stages of the disease, and the patients are often painfully aware of the situation. Formal neuropsychologic evaluation of PSP patients has revealed evidence of cognitive deficits in the majority. The pattern of abnormalities suggests bifrontal dysfunction.[138] The disease has been most commonly reported in men (60 percent), although some studies have reported a more equal male/female incidence ratio.[111,137] PSP runs a slow course, with death occurring most frequently in 5 to 7 years (mean time from onset to death = 5.9 years).[137]

Neuropathologic examination demonstrates extensive subcortical cell loss, gliosis, and neurofibrillary changes. The most heavily involved areas include the subthalamus, the inner aspect of the pallidum, substantia nigra and the red nuclei, the superior colliculi and mesencephalic periaqueductal grey matter, locus ceruleus, and the dentate nuclei. Other subcortical lesions are seen less frequently and less prominently.[174] The lateral and third ventricles are often slightly dilated, although marked atrophy is rare. The cerebral cortex and white matter are unremarkable.[221] To date, treatment efforts have been ineffective in reversing the relentless downward course, although the use of dopamine agonists such as bromocriptine and pergolide have shown some short-term positive effects.[111,174]

Rare Degenerative Diseases

Dementia is associated with a large group of rare degenerative diseases of the central nervous system. Most are hereditary and are found in population pockets where consanguinity is common and population mobility minimal. Several forms of spinocerebellar or olivopontocerebellar degeneration fall into this category and are often associated with a dementia. Of these, Friedreich's ataxia is probably the best known. The course of these classic abiotrophies is slow, with the dementia usually appearing late in the illness.

Familial myoclonic epilepsy is another rare condition in which dementia is a prominent symptom in most cases. The seizure state, however, is usually well established before the onset of the dementia, and the diagnosis is not difficult to make.

CREUTZFELDT-JAKOB DISEASE

Creutzfeldt-Jakob disease is an uncommon (1 in 1 million) dementia, yet it is extremely important because of its scientific implications. The disease is caused by an unconventional (often transmissible) virus that has a very long incubation period (2 years). The disease has a relatively long clinical course (average: 9 months; extremes: 1 month and 16 years).[52,77,149] In a review of 357 histologically proved cases, about 10 percent of the patients survived longer than 2 years. These patients tended to be younger at onset and had a higher familial prevalence, less myoclonus, and less EEG abnormality.[26] The onset and symptomatology of the disease vary considerably, with mental symptoms predominating in two thirds of cases, whereas neurologic signs are most prominent in the others.[23] The disease most frequently presents with nervousness, an increased startle response, anxiety, or other vague mental symptoms. Memory loss, confusional behavior, and frank psychosis are also seen.[88,149]

Neurologic signs of motor neuron involvement, cerebellar, basal ganglian, or pyramidal tract damage can all be seen either in combination or alone. Signs may be asymmetric and may undergo short periods of remission.[88] Myoclonic jerking is especially common as the disease progresses. Myoclonus is seen in over 90 percent of cases at some time during the course, and is one of the primary distinguishing features. Severe dementia usually occurs within 6 months and progressive rigidity and mutism lead to death within 9 months in most cases.[197] In the patients who live more than 2 years, the initial phase is slow, but the terminal phase is rapid.[26]

The classic diagnostic triad of dementia, myoclonus, and periodic EEG is present in 75 percent of cases; however, a variety of atypical cases do occur. The electroencephalogram is frequently of great assistance in making the diagnosis; it is abnormal and characteristic in 90 percent of the cases.[88] Initially, the EEG shows diffuse, often asymmetric slowing; however, the typical pattern of high-voltage bursts of biphasic and triphasic slow waves soon appears (Fig. 7–9).

Diagnosis can be made on tissue from brain biopsy by identification of a marker protein.[24] A similar, very specific protein has also been identified in the spinal fluid of these patients.[94]

The disease is caused by a virus, yet 10 percent of cases have a strong dominant inheritance pattern. Transmission has been reported via surgical instruments, depth electrodes, corneal transplantation, and to surgeons and pathologists conducting surgery and autopsy, presumably through breaks in the skin.[77,235] Recently a disturbing number of cases have occurred when the virus was inoculated from a batch of human growth hormone.[25]

Pathologically, the virus first causes vacuolation in the dendrite and axonal processes and the cell bodies of the neurons. Astroglia and oligodendroglia are less extensively affected. With progression, extensive gliosis occurs, and finally a spongy degeneration. Unlike conventional viruses, no inflammatory response occurs, no cells are found in the spinal fluid, and the protein in the CSF is normal.[77]

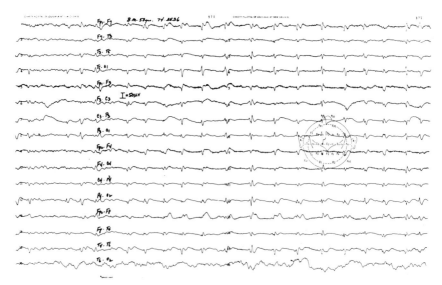

Figure 7–9. EEG of patient with Creutzfeldt-Jacob disease.

DIALYSIS DEMENTIA

With the increase in the use of hemodialysis for chronic renal failure, a variety of neurologic syndromes has appeared. An unusual syndrome of mental change, speech disorder, and myoclonus has been reported in some patients who have received dialysis for several years.[7,8,30,139] The disease, at first thought rare, was the leading cause of death in the chronic dialysis patient in some centers. Usually the condition is first noticed during the last hour or two of dialysis and is characterized primarily by a subtle personality change often associated with hesitancy in speech production and stuttering. These changes clear during the first 12 hours after dialysis. With successive dialysis periods, however, the changes progress: The speech disorder becomes more dramatic, and eventually the patients are mute by the end of the dialysis period; asterixis, facial grimacing, and myoclonus appear; confusional behavior occurs; general cognitive functioning decreases; seizures often occur; and the patients become almost immobile. This progression usually evolves over 4 to 6 months. During this time the patient's symptoms are slower and slower to clear between dialysis sessions, and eventually a chronic unremitting dementia develops. Focal neurologic findings are seen in 40 percent of cases, with facial and limb weakness being the most common features.[247]

The electroencephalogram is always abnormal, with background slowing and superimposed paroxysmal high voltage, very slow waves (delta), triphasic waves, and often frank spikes.[139,165,186] In some patients, the EEG changes have been noted 6 months before the development of the dementia syndrome.[30] Treatment could logically be started during this early stage, and development of the entire syndrome prevented.

The condition is not part of the disequilibrium syndrome, and most evidence points toward an accumulation of aluminum in the brain as the cause. Some autopsy material has shown a clear increase in brain aluminum in patients dying with the syndrome,[154] and increased serum aluminum levels in some demented patients have been clinically documented.[147,182] Clear reversal of the dementia has also been demonstrated in these patients when the aluminum level was reduced.[147,182] Elevated tin or calcium or decreased rubidium or phosphate have also been considered as the cause, but toxicity from aluminum seems by far the most likely.[8,180] The source of the aluminum is varied, but in most cases it is either from exogenous aluminum gels taken by the patients,[7,146,182] or from the water or purifying apparatus used during dialysis.[75,154]

Treatment has varied; renal transplantation shows only marginal success[30] but control of exogenous aluminum is more encouraging. Nadel and Wilson[165] were struck by the abnormal EEG findings in their patients and used diazepam (Valium) to suppress the epileptiform activity, rationalizing that the behavior change might actually be merely an epileptic state. The four patients in their report did improve. Their experience is certainly encouraging, compared with the bleak prognosis experienced in most centers. An anticonvulsant regimen of diphenylhydantoin (Dilantin) and phenobarbital had been tried in earlier studies without effect.[8]

The pathology of this condition is nonspecific. The gross brain is not abnormal, but microscopically the cortex shows widespread nerve cell damage, suggesting slow cell death from some adverse metabolic or toxic substance. The neurons appear shrunken and hyperpigmented with pyknotic hyperchromatic nuclei. Mild gliosis is present, and occasionally spongiform changes occur.[30]

MULTIPLE SCLEROSIS

Multiple sclerosis is a relatively common neurologic disease in which widespread destruction of myelin results in a remarkable array of neurologic signs and symptoms. Usually seen only in advanced cases, dementia may be the initial and predominant symptom in a few patients. In such cases, the disease is typically of later onset (41 to 72 years) and mimics other dementia except that the onset is especially rapid and includes memory loss, personality change, and confusional behavior as the primary symptoms.[125] Most patients show mild neurologic symptoms suggestive of myelopathy.

In one case, a 20-year-old man was left with a significant recent memory defect after his initial attack. On examination, even after overheating in a hot bath, no positive neurologic signs were present. Examination during the acute phase and on subsequent followup[13] showed clear-cut brain stem and other findings.

Cases in which cognitive findings predominate are distinctly uncommon. In a series of 389 cases, Adams found only 7 patients in whom the initial symptoms of the patient's demyelinating disease were organic mental symptoms.[1] Cognitive losses are often unrecognized in early cases; however, comprehensive neuropsychologic testing will frequently demonstrate subtle problems with recent memory as well as scattered abnormalities on a wide variety of cognitive tests.[85,187] The degree of cognitive loss correlates well with the chronicity of the disease. Conversely, emotional or personality changes are often harbingers of the disease. Emotional lability, euphoria, and irritability are all rather common findings, and the multiple sclerosis patient is often diagnosed initially as being hysteric. Although clinically obvious intellectual decline is not a prominent feature of the disease, a recent study using a full battery of psychologic tests clearly demonstrated subtle, yet significant, cognitive impairment in a substantial number of patients with multiple sclerosis.[179]

Pathologically, the major cerebral lesions are frequently in the frontal white matter closely surrounding the anterior horns of the lateral ventricles. This type of lesion disconnects many of the limbic fibers from the cingulate to the frontal lobes and has an effect similar to that of a cingulu-motomy or frontal leukotomy. No pathologic studies are available on the patients with the dementia syndrome reported by Koenig,[125] and a clinical pathologic correlation cannot be made on these cases.

DEMENTIA AS A REMOTE EFFECT OF CARCINOMA

The remote effect of carcinoma on the nervous system is a fascinating chapter in the study of cancer and its relation to the host. Many neurologic symptoms are seen in cancer patients; however, dementia is quite common. In one series of 42 patients with nervous system involvement, 14 (33 percent) were affected.[20] The dementia is described as "simple, with progressive intellectual impairment and memory failure."[20] The dementia is frequently associated with other central nervous system symptoms, particularly cerebellar findings.

A second type of dementia seen in carcinoma has been called *limbic encephalitis*[36,48,101]; in it, rapidly developing memory and cognitive loss is accompanied by seizures and neurologic signs. Many cases present as an encephalomyelitis, whereas others have prominent cerebellar or brain stem signs. Seen mostly with small-cell carcinoma of the lung, the pathologic findings suggest an inflammatory process, but no infectious agent has yet been identified.

Another syndrome, progressive multifocal leukoencephalopathy, produces an interesting group of neurologic symptoms but not a true dementia. This condition, caused by a viral invasion of the brain is discussed in Chapter 11.

DESTRUCTIVE ENCEPHALOPATHIES

Within the symptom complex of dementia are a number of conditions more properly called encephalopathies caused by specific causes. These conditions do not follow the usual gradual progression seen in dementia, but rather, their onset is abrupt and due to a specific widespread insult to the brain parenchyma. Serious head trauma, encephalitis, meningitis, and severe anoxia are the most common varieties. The clinical picture is usually one of mental status changes and neurologic findings that differ in each case. These conditions will be discussed in subsequent chapters because they are not involved in the differential diagnosis of dementia in the traditional sense.

EVALUATION AND MANAGEMENT

Other than specific treatment of the underlying cause of diseases such as myxedema, the general principles of evaluation and management of dementia are the same as were outlined in the previous chapter. It is obvious that the prognosis, genetic aspects, and associated systemic and neurologic problems vary tremendously.

REFERENCES

1. Adams, DK, Sutherland, JM, and Fletcher, WB: Early clinical manifestations of disseminated sclerosis. Br Med J 2:431, 1950.
2. Adams, RD: Acquired hepatocerebral degeneration. In Vinken, PJ and Bruyn, GW (eds): Handbook of Clinical Neurology, Vol 6. Elsevier, New York, 1968, pp 279–297.
3. Adams, RD et al: Symptomatic occult hydrocephalus with "normal" cerebrospinal fluid pressure. N Engl J Med 273:117, 1965.
4. Adams, RD and Kubik, CS: Subacute combined degeneration of the brain in pernicious anemia. N Engl J Med 231:1, 1944.
5. Albert, ML: Subcortical dementia in Alzheimer's disease. In Katzman, R, Terry, RD, Bick, KL (eds): Senile Dementia and Related Disorders. New York, Raven Press, 1978, pp 173–180.
6. Albert, ML, Feldman, RG, and Willis, AL: The subcortical dementia of progressive supranuclear palsy. J Neurol Neurosurg Psychiatry 37:121, 1974.
7. Alfrey, AC, LeGendre, GR, and Kaehny, WD: The dialysis encephalopathy syndrome. N Engl J Med 294:184, 1976.
8. Alfrey, AC et al: Syndrome of dyspraxia and multifocal seizures associated with chronic dialysis. Trans Am Soc Artif Intern Organs 18:257, 1972.
9. Alvord, EC, Jr: Pathology of Parkinsonism: Part II. An interpretation with special reference to other changes in the aging brain. In McDowell, FH and Markham, CH (eds): Recent Advances in Parkinson's Disease. FA Davis, Philadelphia, 1971, pp 131–161.
10. Asher, R: Myxoedematous madness. Br Med J 2:555, 1949.
11. Barbeau, A: Long-term appraisal of levodopa therapy. Neurology (May suppl) 22:22 , 1972.
12. Bennett, R et al: Neuropsychiatric problems in systemic lupus erythematosus. Br Med J 4:342, 1972.
13. Benson, DF: Personal communication. August, 1978.
14. Benson, DF et al: Diagnosis of normal-pressure hydrocephalus. N Engl J Med 283:609, 1970.
15. Bockner, S and Cultart, N: New cases of general paralysis of the insane. Br Med J 1:18, 1961.
16. Boll, TJ, Heaton, R, and Reitan, RM: Neuropsychological and emotional correlates of Huntington's chorea. J Nerv Ment Dis 158:61, 1974.
17. Boller, F et al: Parkinson's disease, dementia, and Alzheimer's disease: Clinicopathological correlations. Ann Neurol 7:329, 1980.
18. Botez, MI and Barbeau, A: Long-term mental changes in levodopa-treated patients. Lancet 2:1028, 1973.
19. Bowen, FP et al: Parkinsonism: Effects of levodopa treatment on concept formation. Neurology 25:701, 1975.

20. Brain, R and Henson, RA: Neurological syndromes associated with carcinoma. Lancet 2:971, 1958.
21. Brewer, C and Perrett, L: Brain damage due to alcohol consumption: An air-encephalographic, psychometric, and electroencephalographic study. Br J Addict 66:170, 1971.
22. Brown, DG and Goldensohn, ES: The electroencephalogram in normal pressure hydrocephalus. Arch Neurol 29:70, 1973.
23. Brown, P et al: Creutzfeldt-Jakob disease: Clinical analysis of a consecutive series of 230 neuropathologically verified cases. Ann Neurol 20:597, 1986.
24. Brown, P et al: Diagnosis of Creutzfeldt-Jakob disease by Western blot identification of marker protein in human brain tissue. N Engl J Med 314:547, 1986.
25. Brown, P et al: Potential epidemic of Creutzfeldt-Jakob disease from human growth hormone therapy. N Engl J Med 313:728, 1985.
26. Brown, P et al: Creutzfeldt-Jakob disease of long duration: Clinicopathological characteristics, transmissibility, and differential diagnosis. Ann Neurol 16:295, 1984.
27. Brown, RG and Marsden, CD: How common is dementia in Parkinson's disease? Lancet 2:1262, 1984.
28. Bruyn, GW: Huntington's chorea—history, clinical and laboratory synopsis. In Vinken, PJ and Bruyn, AW (eds): Handbook of Clinical Neurology, Vol 6. Elsevier, New York, 1968, pp 298–378.
29. Burger, PC, Burch, JG, and Kunze, U: Subcortical arteriosclerotic encephalopathy (Binswanger disease). Stroke 7:626, 1976.
30. Burks, JS et al: A fatal encephalopathy in chronic haemodialysis patients. Lancet 1:764, 1976.
31. Caine, ED et al: Huntington's dementia. Arch Gen Psychiatry 35:377, 1978.
32. Caine, ED and Shoulson, I: Psychiatric syndromes in Huntington's disease. Am J Psychiatry 140:728, 1983.
33. Caltagirone, C et al: Neurophysiological study of normal pressure hydrocephalus. Acta Psychiat Scand 65:93, 1982.
34. Caplan, LR and Schoene, WC: Clinical features of subclinical arteriosclerotic encephalopathy (Binswanger disease). Neurology 28:1206, 1978.
35. Carbotte, RM, Denburg, SD, and Denburg, JA: Prevalence of cognitive impairment in systemic lupus erythematosus. J Nerv Mental Dis 174: 357, 1986.
36. Case Records of the Massachusetts General Hospital: Case 30–1985, N Engl J Med 313:249, 1985.
37. Chawla, JC, Hulme, A, and Cooper, R: Intracranial pressure in patients with dementia and communicating hydrocephalus, J. Neurosurg 40:376, 1974.
38. Chia, BH and Tsoi, WF: A study of 136 cases of general paralysis of the insane (dementia paralytica) in a mental hospital. Singapore Med J 12:264, 1971.
39. Chui, HC et al: Pathologic correlates of dementia in Parkinson's disease. Arch Neurol 43:991, 1986.
40. Chynoweth, R and Foley, J: Pre-senile dementia responding to steroid therapy. Br J Psychiatry 115:703, 1969.

41. Clark, EC and Yoss, RE: Nervous system findings associated with systemic lupus erythematosus. Minn Med 39:517, 1956.

42. Cleghorn, RA: Adrenal cortical insufficiency: Psychological and neurological observations. Can Med Assoc J 65:449, 1951.

43. Coblentz, JM et al: Presenile dementia. Arch Neurol 29:299, 1973.

44. Cohen, SI: Cushing's syndrome: A psychiatric study of 29 patients. Br J Psychiatry 136:120, 1980.

45. Committee of Clinical Society of London: Report on myxedema. Clinical Society's Transactions 21(Suppl):1, 1888, Gongman's Green and Company, London.

46. Constantinidis, J: Pick dementia: Anatomoclinical correlations and pathophysiological considerations. Interdiscipl Topics Geront 19:72, 1985.

47. Corsellis, JAN: Aging and the dementias. In Blackwood, W and Corsellis, JAN (eds): Greenfield's Neuropathology. Arnold, London, 1976, pp 796–848.

48. Corsellis, JAN, Goldberg, GJ, and Norton, AR: Limbic encephalitis and its association with carcinoma. Brain 91:481, 1968.

49. Courville, CB and Myers, RO: Effects of extraneous poisons on the nervous system. II: The alcohols. Bull Los Angeles Neurol Soc 19:66, 1957.

50. Crockard, HA et al: Hydrocephalus as a cause of dementia; evaluation by computerized tomography and intracranial pressure monitoring. J Neurol Neurosurg Psychiatry 40:736, 1977.

51. Cummings, JL and Benson, DF: Dementia: A Clinical Approach. Butterworths, Boston, 1983.

52. Cutler, NR et al: Creutzfeldt-Jakob disease: A case of 16 years duration. Ann Neurol 15:107, 1984.

53. DeGirolami, U, Haas, ML, and Richardson, EP, Jr: Subacute diencephalic angioencephalopathy. J Neurol Sci 22:197, 1974.

54. Deland, FH et al: Normal pressure hydrocephalus: A histologic study. Am J Clin Pathol 58:58, 1972.

55. Denny-Brown, DD: Nature of apraxia. J Nerv Ment Dis 126:9, 1958.

56. Drachman, DA and Stahl, S: Extrapyramidal dementia and levodopa. Lancet 1:809, 1975.

57. Drake, EW, Jr, et al: The quality and duration of survival in bilateral carotid occlusive disease: A preliminary survey of the effect of thromboendarterectomy. In Toole, JF, Siekert, RG, and Whisnant, JP (eds): Cerebral Vascular Disease: Sixth Conference. Grune & Stratton, New York, 1968, pp 242–259.

58. Dreyfus, PM: Amblyopia and other neurological disorders associated with chronic alcoholism. In Vinkin, PJ and Bruyn, GW (eds): Handbook of Clinical Neurology, Vol 28. Elsevier, New York, 1976, pp 331–347.

59. Earnest, MP et al: Normal pressure hydrocephalus and hypertensive cerebrovascular disease. Arch Neurol 31:262, 1974.

60. Editorial: Communicating hydrocephalus. Lancet 2:1011, 1977.

61. Editorial: Depression and Cushing's syndrome. Lancet 2:550, 1986.

62. Enna, SJ et al: Huntington's chorea. N Engl J Med 294:1305, 1976.

63. Epelbaum, J et al: Somatostatin and dementia in Parkinson's disease. Brain Res 278:376, 1983.

64. Eraut, D: Idiopathic hypoparathyroidism presenting as dementia. Br Med J 1:429, 1974.

65. Ferguson, GG and Peerless, SJ: Extracranial-intracranial arterial bypass in the treatment of dementia and multiple extracranial arterial occlusion. Presented at the Congress of Neurological Surgeons, New Orleans, October 25–29, 1976.

66. Fessel, WJ and Solomon, GF: Psychosis and systemic lupus erythematosus: A review of the literature and case reports. Calif Med 92:266, 1960.

67. Fisher, CM: Senile dementia: A new explanation of its causation. Can Med Assoc J 65:1, 1951.

68. Fisher, CM: Dementia in cerebrovascular disease. In Toole, JF, Siekert, RG, and Whisnant, JP (eds): Cerebral Vascular Disease: Sixth Conference. Grune & Stratton, New York, 1968, pp 232–236.

69. Fisher, CM: Case records of the Massachusetts General Hospital. N Engl Med J 291:966, 1974.

70. Fisher, CM: The clinical picture in occult hydrocephalus. Clin Neurosurg 24:270, 1977.

71. Fisher, CM: Communicating hydrocephalus. Lancet 1:37, 1978.

72. Forno, LS, Barbour, PJ, and Norville, RL: Presenile dementia with Lewy bodies and neurofibrillary tangles. Arch Neurol 35:818, 1978.

73. Fox, JH et al: Cerebral ventricular enlargement. JAMA 236:365, 1976.

74. Freeman, FR: Evaluation of patients with progressive intellectual deterioration. Arch Neurol 33:658, 1976.

75. Flendrig, JA, Kruis, H, and Das, HA: Aluminum and dialysis dementia. Lancet 1:764, 1976.

76. Gado, MH et al: Correlation between computerized transaxial tomography and radionuclide cisternography in dementia. Neurology 26:555, 1976.

77. Gajdusek, DC: Unconventional viruses and the origin and disappearance of kuru. Science 197:943, 1977.

78. Geagea, K and Ananth, J: Response of a psychiatric patient to vitamin B_{12} therapy. Dis Nerv Syst 36:343, 1975.

79. Geschwind, N: The mechanism of normal pressure hydrocephalus. J Neurol Sci 7:481, 1968.

80. Girotti, F et al: Motor and cognitive performances of Parkinsonian patients in the on and off phases of the disease. J Neurol Neurosurg Psychiatry 49:657, 1986.

81. Godt, P and Kochen, M: Vitamin B_{12} deficiency due to psychotic-induced malnutrition. Lancet 2:1087, 1976.

82. Gold, AP and Yahr, MD: Childhood lupus erythematosus. Trans Am Neurol Assoc 85:96, 1960.

83. Goldstein, NP et al: Psychiatric aspects of Wilson's disease: Results of psychometric tests during long-term therapy. Birth Defects 4:77, 1968.

84. Graff-Radford, N and Godersky, J: Normal-pressure hydrocephalus: Onset of gait abnormality before dementia predicts good surgical outcome. Arch Neurol 43:940, 1986.

85. Grant, I et al: Deficient learning and memory in early and middle phases of multiple sclerosis. J Neurol Neurosurg Psychiatry 47:250, 1984.

86. Greitz, T and Grepe, A: Encephalography in the diagnosis of convexity block hydrocephalus. Acta Radiol [Diagn] (Stockh) 11:232, 1971.
87. Haaland, KV and Matthews, G: Cognitive and Motor Performance in Parkinsonism of Increasing Duration. Presented at the International Neuropsychology Society Meeting, Sante Fe, NM, February, 1977.
88. Haase, GR: Diseases presenting as dementia. In Wells, CE (ed): Dementia. FA Davis, Philadelphia, 1977, pp 27–67.
89. Hachinski, V: Multi-infarct dementia. In Barnett, HJM (ed): Neurology Clinics, Symposium on Cerebrovascular Disease, WB Saunders, Philadelphia, 1983, pp 27–36.
90. Hachinski, VC, Lassen, NA, and Marshall, J: Multi-infarct dementia. Lancet 2:207, 1974.
91. Hakim, AM and Mathieson, G: Dementia in Parkinson disease: A neuropathologic study. Neurology 29:1209, 1979.
92. Hakim, S and Adams, RD: The special clinical problem of symptomatic hydrocephalus with normal cerebrospinal fluid pressure. Observations in cerebrospinal fluid dynamics. J Neurol Sci 2:307, 1965.
93. Halgin, R, Riklan, M, and Misiak, H: Levodopa, parkinsonism, and recent memory. J Nerv Ment Dis 164:268, 1977.
94. Harrington, MG et al: Abnormal proteins in the cerebrospinal fluid of patients with Creutzfeldt-Jakob disease. N Engl J Med 315:279, 1986.
95. Harrison, MJG and Marsden, CD: Progressive intellectual deterioration. Arch Neurol 34:199, 1977.
96. Harrison, MJG et al: Multi-infarct dementia. J Neurol Sci 40:97, 1979.
97. Hartmann, A and Alberti, E: Differentiation of communicating hydrocephalus and presenile dementia by continuous recording of cerebrospinal fluid pressure. J Neurol Neurosurg Psychiatry 40:630, 1977.
98. Haskett, RF: Diagnostic categorization of psychiatric disturbance in Cushing's syndrome. Am J Psychiatry 142:911, 1985.
99. Hecaen, H and DeAjuriaguerra, J: Les encephalopathies alcooliques subaigues et chroniques. Rev Neurol (Paris) 94:528, 1956.
100. Heine, BE: Psychiatric aspects of systemic lupus erythematosus. Acta Psychiatr Scand 45:307, 1969.
101. Henson, RA and Urich, H: Cancer and the Nervous System: The Neurological Manifestations of Systemic Malignant Disease. Blackwell, Boston, 1982.
102. Holmes, G: Discussion on the mental symptoms associated with cerebral tumors. Proc R Soc Med 24:65, 1931.
103. Holmes, JM: Cerebral manifestations of vitamin B_{12} deficiency. Br Med J 2:1394, 1956.
104. Horn, S: Some psychological factors in parkinsonism. J Neurol Neurosurg Psychiatry 37:27, 1974.
105. Horvath, TB: Clinical spectrum and epidemiological features of alcoholic dementia. In Rankin, JG and Lambert, SL (eds): International Symposium on Effects of Chronic Use of Alcohol and Other Psychoactive Drugs on Cerebral Function, Toronto, October, 1973. Alcoholism and Drug Addiction Research Foundation of Ontario, 1975, pp 1–16.

106. Huang, K, Wu, L, and Luo, Y: Binswanger's disease: Progressive subcortical encephalopathy of multi-infarct dementia? Can J Neurol Sci 12:88, 1985.
107. Huber, SJ, Shuttleworth, EC, and Paulson, GW: Dementia in Parkinson's disease. Arch Neurol 43:987, 1986.
108. Huber, SJ et al: Cortical vs subcortical dementia: Neuropsychological differences. Arch Neurol 43:392, 1986.
109. Ishii, N, Nishihara, Y, and Imamura, T: Why do frontal lobe symptoms predominate in vascular dementia with lacunes? Neurology 36:340, 1986.
110. Inose, T: Neuropsychiatric manifestations in Wilson's disease: Attacks of disturbance of consciousness. Birth Defects 4:74, 1968.
111. Jackson, JA, Jankovic, J, and Ford, J: Progressive supranuclear palsy: Clinical features and response to treatment in 16 patients. Ann Neurol 13:273, 1983.
112. Jacobs, L et al: Normal pressure hydrocephalus. JAMA 235:510, 1976.
113. Jacobs, L and Kinkel, WR: Computerized axial transverse tomography in normal pressure hydrocephalus. Neurology 26:501, 1976.
114. Jellinek, EH: Fits, faints, coma, and dementia in myxoedema. Lancet 2:1010, 1962.
115. Johnson, RT and Richardson, EP: The neurologic manifestations of systemic lupus erythematosus. Medicine 47:337, 1968.
116. Jurko, MF and Andy, OJ: Psychological changes associated with thalamotomy site. J Neurol Neurosurg Psychiatry 36:846, 1973.
117. Kahn, E and Thompson, JJ: Concerning Pick's disease. Am J Psychiatry 90:935, 1934.
118. Kass, L: Pernicious anemia. In Smith, LH (ed): Major Problems in Internal Medicine, Vol 7. WB Saunders, Philadelphia, 1976, pp 116-122.
119. Katzman, R: Normal pressure hydrocephalus. In Wells, CE (ed): Dementia. FA Davis, Philadelphia, 1977, pp 69-92.
120. Katzman, R and Karasu, TB: Differential diagnosis of dementia. In Fields, WS (ed): Neurological and Sensory Disorders in the Elderly. Stratton, New York, 1974.
121. Kelly, W et al: Cushing's syndrome and depression: A prospective study of 26 patients. Br J Psychiatry 142:16, 1983.
122. Keschner, M, Bender, MB, and Strauss, T: Mental symptoms in cases of tumor of the temporal lobe. Arch Neurol Psychiatry 35:572, 1936.
123. Kinkel, WR et al: Subcortical arteriosclerotic encephalopathy (Binswanger's disease) computed tomographic, nuclear magnetic resonance, and clinical correlations. Arch Neurol 42:951, 1985.
124. Kleinknecht, RA and Goldstein, SC: Neuropsychological deficits associated with alcoholism: A review and discussion. Quart J Stud Alcohol 33:999, 1972.
125. Koenig, H: Dementia associated with the benign form of multiple sclerosis. Trans Am Neurol Assoc 93:227, 1968.
126. Koto, A et al: Syndrome of normal pressure hydrocephalus: Possible relation to hypertensive and arteriosclerotic vasculopathy. J Neurol Neurosurg Psychiatry 40:73, 1977.

127. Lees, AJ: Cognitive deficits in Parkinson's disease. In Traber, J and Gispen, WH (eds): Senile Dementia of the Alzheimer Type. Springer-Verlag, Berlin, 1985, pp 60–71.

128. Levin, S: Brain tumors in mental hospital patients. Am J Psychiatry 195:897, 1949.

129. Lieberman, A et al: Dementia in Parkinson disease. Ann Neurol 6:355, 1979.

130. Littman, ML and Zimmerman, LE: Cryptococcus. Grune & Stratton, New York, 1956.

131. Logothetis, J: Psychotic behavior as the initial indicator of adult myxedema. J Nerv Ment Dis 136:561, 1963.

132. Loizen, LA, Kendall, BE, and Marshall, J: Subcortical arteriosclerotic encephalopathy: A clinical and radiological investigation. J Neurol Neurosurg Psychiatry 44:294–304, 1981.

133. Loranger, AW et al: Levodopa treatment of parkinsonism syndrome. Arch Gen Psychiatry 26:163, 1972.

134. Loranger, AW et al: Intellectual impairment in Parkinson's syndrome. Brain 95:405, 1972.

135. Loranger, AW et al: Parkinsonism, L-dopa, and intelligence. Am J Psychiatry 130:1386, 1973.

136. MacNeill, A et al: Psychiatric problems in systemic lupus erythematosus. Br J Psychiatry 128:442, 1976.

137. Maher, ER and Lees, AJ: The clinical features and natural history of the Steele-Richardson-Olszewski syndrome (progressive supranuclear palsy). Neurology 36:1005, 1986.

138. Maher, ER, et al: Cognitive deficits in the Steele-Richardson-Olszewski syndrome (progressive supranuclear palsy). J Neurol Neurosurg Psychiatry 48:1234, 1985.

139. Mahurkar, SD et al: Dialysis dementia. Lancet 1:1412, 1973.

140. Malamud, N: Neuropathology of organic brain syndromes associated with aging. In Gaitz, CM (ed): Aging and the Brain, Vol 3. Advances in Behavioral Biology. Plenum, New York, 1972, pp 63–87.

141. Malmquist, CP and Kincannon, JC: Psychiatric and psychological aspects of myxedema. Dis Nerv Syst 21:529, 1960.

142. Mansvelt, JV: Pick's Disease. NV Voorheen Firma JJVD Loeff Enschede, Netherlands, 1954.

143. Marsden, DD and Harrison, MJG: Outcome of investigation of patients with presenile dementia. Br Med J 2:249, 1972.

144. Martin, JB and Gusella, JF: Huntington's disease: Pathogenesis and management. N Engl J Med 1267, 1986.

145. Martin, WE et al: Parkinson's disease. Clinical analysis of 100 patients. Neurology 23:783, 1973.

146. Marttila, RJ and Rinne, VK: Dementia in Parkinson's disease. Acta Neurol Scand 54:431, 1976.

147. Masselot, JP et al: Reversible dialysis encephalopathy: Role for aluminium-containing gels. Lancet 2:1386, 1978.

148. Mathew, NT et al: Abnormal cerebrospinal fluid-blood flow dynamics. Arch Neurol 32:657, 1975.

149. May, W: Creutzfeldt-Jakob disease. Acta Neurol Scand 44:1, 1968.

150. Mayeux, R and Stern, Y: Intellectual dysfunction and dementia in Parkinson's disease. In Mayeux, R and Rosen, WG: The Dementias, Raven Press, New York, 1983, pp 211–227.

151. Mayeux, R, Stern, Y, and Rosen, J: Is "subcortical dementia" a recognizable clinical entity? Ann Neurol 14:278, 1983.

152. Mayeux, R et al: Depression, intellectual impairment, and Parkinson disease. Neurology 31:645, 1981.

153. McCullough, NB et al: Cryptococcus. Clinical staff conference at the National Institutes of Health. Ann Intern Med 49:642, 1958.

154. McDermott, JR et al: Brain-aluminium concentration in dialysis encephalopathy. Lancet 1:901, 1978.

155. McHugh, PR: Occult hydrocephalus. Q J Med 33:297, 1964.

156. McHugh, PR and Folstein, MF: Psychiatric syndromes of Huntington's chorea: A clinical and phenomenologic study. In Benson, DF and Blumer, D (eds): Psychiatric Aspects of Neurological Disease. Grune & Stratton, New York, 1975, pp 267–286.

157. Meacham, WF and Young, AB: Radiological procedures in the diagnosis of dementia. In Wells, CE (ed): Dementia. FA Davis, Philadelphia, 1971, pp 100–110.

158. Meadows, JC: Normal pressure hydrocephalus. Lancet 1:618, 1973.

159. Merritt, HH, Adams, RD, and Solomon, HC: Neurosyphilis. Oxford University Press, New York, 1946.

160. Messert, B and Van Nuis, C: A syndrome of paralysis of downward gaze, dysarthria, pseudobulbar palsy, axial rigidity of neck and trunk and dementia. J Nerv Ment Dis 143:47, 1966.

161. Metter, EJ et al: Left hemisphere intracerebral hemorrhages studied by (F-18)-fluorodeoxyglucose PET. Neurology 36:1155, 1986.

162. Morel, F: Une forme anatomo-clinique particuliere de l'alcoolisme chronique: Sclerose cortical laminaire alcoolique. Rev Neurol (Paris) 71:280, 1939.

163. Mosberg, WH and Arnold, JG: Torulosis of the central system: Review of literature and report of five cases. Ann Intern Med 32:1153, 1950.

164. Mortimer, JA et al: Relationship of motor symptoms to intellectual deficits in Parkinson disease. Neurology 32:133, 1982.

165. Nadel, AM and Wilson, WP: Dialysis encephalopathy: A possible seizure disorder. Neurology 26:1130, 1976.

166. Neubuerger, KT: The changing neuropathologic picture of chronic alcoholism. Arch Path 63:1, 1957.

167. Neumann, MA and Cohen, R: Progressive subcortical gliosis: A rare form of presenile dementia. Brain 90:405, 1967.

168. Nickel, SN and Frame, B: Neurological manifestations of myxedema. Neurology 8:511, 1958.

169. O'Conner, JF and Musher, DM: Central nervous system involvement in systemic lupus erythematosus. Arch Neurol 14:157, 1966.

170. Ojemann, GA (ed): The thalamus and language. Brain Lang (Special issue) 2:1, 1975.

171. Ojemann, RG et al: Further experience with the syndrome of "normal" pressure hydrocephalus. J Neurosurg 31:279, 1969.

172. Olszewski, J: Subcortical arteriosclerotic encephalopathy: Review of the literature on the so-called Binswanger's disease and presentation of two cases. World Neurology 3:359, 1962.

173. Oltman, JE and Friedman, S: Comments on Huntington's chorea. Dis Nerv System 22:313, 1961.

174. Ostergaard, KM: Progressive supranuclear palsy: 20 years later. Acta Neurol Scand 71:177, 1985.

175. Paulson, GW, Kapp, J, and Cook, W: Dementia associated with bilateral carotid artery disease. Geriatrics 21:159, 1966.

176. Pearce, J and Miller, E: Clinical Aspects of Dementia. Bailliere-Tindall, London, 1973.

177. Petersen, P: Psychiatric disorders in primary hyperparathyroidism. J Clin Endocrin 28:1491, 1968.

178. Petersen, RC, Mokri, B, and Laws, ER, Jr: Surgical treatment of idiopathic hydrocephalus in elderly patients. Neurology 35:307, 1985.

179. Peyser, JM et al: Cognitive function in patients with multiple sclerosis. Arch Neurol 37:577, 1980.

180. Pieridas, AM, Ward, MK, and Kerr, DNS: Haemodialysis encephalopathy: Possible role of phosphate depletion. Lancet 1:1234, 1976.

181. Pirozzolo, FJ et al: Dementia in Parkinson disease: A neuropsychological analysis. Brain 1:71, 1982.

182. Poisson, M, Mashaly, R, and Lebkiri, B: Dialysis encephalopathy: Recovery after interruption of aluminium intake. Br Med J 2:1610, 1978.

183. Pollock, M and Hornabrook, RW: The prevalence, natural history and dementia of Parkinson's disease. Brain 89:429, 1966.

184. Price, TRP and Tucker, GJ: Psychiatric and behavioral manifestations of normal pressure hydrocephalus. J Nerv Ment Dis 164:51, 1977.

185. Rafal, RD et al: Cognition and the basal ganglia, separating mental and motor components of performance in Parkinson's disease. Brain 107:1083, 1984.

186. Raskin, NH and Fishman, RA: Neurologic disorders in renal failure. N Engl J Med 294:204, 1976.

187. Rao, SM et al: Memory disturbance in chronic progressive multiple sclerosis. Arch Neurol 41:625, 1984.

188. Reitan, RM and Boll, TJ: Intellectual and cognitive functions in Parkinson's disease. J Consult Clin Psychol 37:364, 1971.

189. Reynolds, RH: The neurology of vitamin B_{12} deficiency. Lancet 2:832, 1976.

190. Rice, E and Gendelman, S: Psychiatric aspects of normal pressure hydrocephalus. JAMA 223:409, 1973.

191. Riggs, CE: Some nervous system symptoms of pernicious anemia. JAMA 61:481, 1913.

192. Riklan, M, Whelihan, W, and Cullinan, T: Levodopa and psychometric tests performance in parkinsonism: 5 years later. Neurology 26:173, 1976.

193. Robertson, EE, le Roux, A, and Brown, JH: The clinical presentation of Pick's disease. J Ment Sci 104:1000, 1958.

194. Robinson, KC, Kallberg, MH, and Crowley, WF: Idiopathic hypoparathyroidism presenting as dementia. Br Med J 2:1203, 1954.

195. Romanul, FC and Abramowicz, A: Changes in the brain and pial vessels in the arterial border zones. Arch Neurol 11:40, 1964.

196. Roos, D and Willanger, R: Various degrees of dementia in a selected group of gastrectomized patients with low serum B_{12}. Acta Neurol Scand 55:363, 1977.

197. Roos, RP and Johnson, RT: Viruses and dementia. In Wells, CE (ed): Dementia. FA Davis, Philadelphia, 1977, pp 93–112.

198. Rose, FC, Grant, HC, and Jeanes, AL: Torulosis of the central nervous system in Britain. Brain 8:542, 1958.

199. Rose, M: Why assess vitamin B_{12} deficiency due to psychotic-induced malnutrition? Lancet 2:1087, 1976.

200. Ross, EJ and Linch, DC: Cushing's syndrome—killing disease: Discriminatory value of signs and symptoms aiding early diagnosis. Lancet 2:646, 1982.

201. Salibi, N, Lourie, GL, and Lourie, H: A variant of normal-pressure hydrocephalus simulating Pick's disease on computerized tomography. J Neurosurg 59:902, 1983.

202. Sanders, V: Neurologic manifestations of myxedema. N Engl J Med 266:547, 1962.

203. Sapira, JD, Tullis, S, and Mullaly, R: Reversible dementia due to folate deficiency. South Med J 68:776, 1975.

204. Sargent, JS et al: Central nervous system disease in systemic lupus erythematosus. Am J Med 58:644, 1975.

205. Sarosi, GA et al: Amphotericin B in cryptococcal meningitis. Ann Intern Med 71:1079, 1969.

206. Scheinberg, IH, Sternlieb, I, and Richman, J: Psychiatric manifestations in patients with Wilson's disease. Birth Defects 4:85, 1968.

207. Schmidt, RP and Gonyea, EF: Neurosyphilis. In Baker, AB and Baker, LH (eds): Clinical Neurology. Harper & Row, New York, 1976.

208. Schulman, R: Vitamin B_{12} deficiency and psychiatric illness. Br J Psychiatry 113:252, 1967.

209. Schulman, R: The present status of vitamin B_{12} and folic acid deficiency in psychiatric disease. Can Psychiatr Assoc J 17:205, 1972.

210. Schulman, S: Bilateral symmetrical degeneration of the thalamus. J Neuropathol Exp Neurol 16:446, 1957.

211. Schulman, S: Impaired tool-using behavior in monkeys from bilateral destruction of the dorsomedial nuclei of the thalamus. Trans Am Neurol Assoc 97:138, 1973.

212. Seltzer, B and Sherwin, I: Organic brain syndromes: An empirical study and critical review. Am J Psychiatry 13:21, 1978.

213. Shenkin, HA et al: Ventricular shunting for relief of senile symptoms. JAMA 225:1486, 1973.

214. Simpson, JA: The neurological manifestations of idiopathic hypoparathyroidism. Brain 75:76, 1952.

215. Sjogren, T, Sjogren, H, and Lindgren, AGH: Morbus Alzheimer and Morbus Pick: Genetic, clinical and pathoanatomic study. Acta Psychiatr Neurol Scand Suppl 82, 1952.

216. Slaby, AE and Wyatt, RJ: Dementia in the Presenium. Charles C Thomas, Springfield, IL, 1974.

217. Sohn, RS et al: Alzheimer's disease with abnormal cerebrospinal fluid flow. Neurology 23:1058, 1973.

218. Sourander, P and Sjogren, H: The concept of Alzheimer's disease and its clinical implications. In Walstenholme, GEW and O'Connor, M (eds): Alzheimer's Disease and Related Conditions. Churchill, London, 1970, pp 11–32.

219. Spillane, JD: Nervous and mental disorders in Cushing's syndrome. Brain 74:72, 1951.

220. Sroka, H et al: Organic mental syndrome and confusional states in Parkinson's disease: Relationship to computerized tomographic signs of cerebral atrophy. Arch Neurol 38:339, 1981.

221. Steele, JC, Richardson, JC, and Olszewski, J: Progressive supranuclear palsy. Arch Neurol 10:333, 1964.

222. Stengle, E: A study on the symptomatology and differential diagnosis of Alzheimer's disease and Pick's disease. J Ment Sci 89:1, 1943.

223. Stern, K: Severe dementia associated with bilateral symmetrical degeneration of the thalamus. Brain 62:157, 1939.

224. Strauss, I and Keschner, M: Mental symptoms in cases of tumor of frontal lobe. Arch Neurol Psychiatry 33:986, 1935.

225. Stuteville, P and Welch, K: Subdural hematoma in the elderly person. JAMA 168:1445, 1958.

226. Sugar, O: Central neurological complications of hypoparathyroidism. Arch Neurol Psychiatry 70:86, 1953.

227. Sweet, RR et al: Mental symptoms in Parkinson's disease during chronic treatment with levodopa. Neurology 26:305, 1976.

228. Tarter, RE: An analysis of cognitive deficits in chronic alcoholics. J Nerv Ment Dis 157:138, 1973

229. Taylor, GH and Hansotia, P: Neuropsychological testing of Huntington's patients: Clues to progression. J Nerv Ment Dis 8:492, 1983.

230. Terry, RD: Dementia. Arch Neurol 33:1, 1976.

231. Thomsen, AM et al: Prognosis of dementia in normal-pressure hydrocephalus after a shunt operation. Ann Neurol 20:304, 1986.

232. Todorov, AB et al: Specificity of the clinical diagnosis of dementia. J Neurol Sci 26:81, 1975.

233. Tomilson, BE, Blessed, G, and Roth, M: Observations on the brains of demented old people. J Neurol Sci 11:205, 1970.

234. Torvik, A: Aspects of the pathology of presenile dementia. Acta Neurol Scand (Suppl) 43, 46:19, 1970.

235. Traub, R, Gajdusek, DC, and Gibbs, CJ, Jr: Transmissible virus dementia: The relation of transmissible spongiform encephalopathy to Cruetzfeldt-Jakob disease. In Smith, WL and Kinsbourne, M (eds): Aging and Dementia. Spectrum Publications, New York, 1977, pp 91–168.

236. Trethowan, WH and Cobb, S: Neuropsychiatric aspects of Cushing's syndrome. Arch Neurol Psychiatry 67:283, 1952.

237. Vassilouthis, J: The syndrome of normal-pressure hydrocephalus. J Neurosurg 61:501, 1984.

238. Volpe, BT and Petito, CK: Dementia with bilateral medial temporal lobe ischemia. Neurology 35:1793, 1985.

239. Walker, S: The psychiatric presentation of Wilson's disease (hepatolenticular degeneration) with an etiologic explanation. Behav Neuropsychiatry 1:38, 1969.

240. Walshe, JM: Wilson's disease. In Vinken, PV and Bruyn, GW (eds): Handbook of Clinical Neurology, Vol 27. Elsevier, New York, 1976, pp 379–414.

241. Warner, FJ: The brain changes in chronic alcoholism and Korsakov's psychosis. J Nerv Ment Dis 80:629, 1934.

242. Wells, CE: Dementia. FA Davis, Philadelphia, 1977.

243. Whitehouse, PJ: The concept of subcortical and cortical dementia: Another look. Ann Neurol 19:1, 1986.

244. Whitehouse, PJ et al: Basal forebrain neurons in the dementia of Parkinson disease. Ann Neurol 13:243, 1983.

245. Wikkelso, C et al: The clinical effect of lumbar puncture in normal pressure hydrocephalus. J Neurol Neurosurg Psychiatry 45:64, 1982.

246. Wikkelso, C et al: Normal pressure hydrocephalus: Predictive value of the cerebrospinal fluid tap-test. Acta Neurol Scand 73:566, 1986.

247. Willis, MR and Savory, J: Aluminium poisoning: Dialysis encephalopathy, osteomalacia, and anaemia. Lancet 2:29–33, 1983.

248. Wilson, SAK: Neurology. Williams & Wilkins, Baltimore, 1940.

249. Wilson, SAK: Progressive lenticular degeneration: A familial nervous disease associated with cirrhosis of the liver. Brain 34:296, 1912.

250. Wilson, RS et al: High speed memory scanning in parkinsonism. Cortex 16:67, 1980.

251. Wisniewski, NM, Coblentz, JM, and Terry, RD: Pick's disease. Arch Neurol 26:97, 1972.

252. Wolf, SM and Davis, RL: Permanent dementia in idiopathic parkinsonism treated with levodopa. Arch Neurol 29:276, 1973.

253. Yakovlev, PI: Paraplegias of hydrocephalics: A clinical note and interpretation. J Ment Defic 51:561, 1947.

254. Yakovlev, PI: Pick's disease. Special Lecture given at the Boston Veterans Administration Hospital, February, 1973.

Chapter 8

Neurobehavioral Syndromes Associated with Focal Brain Lesions

A 29-year-old man was brought to the Charity Hospital in New Orleans with a 2-day history of abnormal behavior. The young man had been out with a group of friends the night previous to the onset of his strange behavior. The friends did not admit to the use of any drugs and said only that the patient had gone home early complaining of being tired. The following morning, he was very slow to awaken. His family reported that he was talking very strangely and did not seem to answer their questions appropriately. This abnormal behavior persisted throughout the day, and the family brought him to the hospital that evening.

The patient appeared to be a normal, well-developed male who demonstrated no abnormalities on routine physical and neurologic examination. In the emergency room, he was awake, alert, and attentive but seemed somewhat withdrawn and uneasy. The psychiatric consultant stated that the patient was "grossly psychotic; he answers all questions totally inappropriately." Because of his inappropriate responses, withdrawal, and rather flat affect, he was admitted to the psychiatric ward with an initial diagnosis of an acute schizophrenic reaction, possibly drug-related.

During the subsequent several days, the patient's condition did not improve, and a neurologic consultation was sought to rule out any organic cause for the bizarre behavior. Standard neurologic examination was again normal, but the mental status examination demonstrated striking abnormalities. The patient was alert and appeared attentive but could not repeat digits or comprehend the nature of the "A" test. Spontaneous speech was fluent, yet laconic, was always off the point of the question, and contained occasional paraphasic substitutions. Comprehension was nil; he could not point to any objects on command and performed at only chance level when asked to point to one of three common objects placed in front of him. He could not answer questions requiring yes or no answers and could not follow simple verbal commands. He could not repeat words or sentences. He was able to name only a few simple objects and even then showed considerable word-searching and paraphasia.

With the demonstration of a significant aphasic disturbance, the neurologist quickly realized that the patient most likely had a left temporal-lobe lesion. A neurodiagnostic evaluation was then undertaken. Arteriography demonstrated a large posterior temporal-lobe mass. At surgery a large intracerebral hematoma with evidence of contusion and subdural blood was found in the left posterior temporal area. Postoperatively the patient's language and behavior gradually returned to normal. Soon thereafter he was able to tell us that he had been in a dispute in a bar room and had been struck on the left side of the head with a pool cue.

This case demonstrates how a knowledge of cerebral localization and an appreciation of the clinical syndromes associated with focal brain damage, in this case aphasia, are of clinical importance in the management of many patients with acute behavioral change. Because many of the behavioral syndromes seen with focal brain damage show little, if any, evidence of abnormality on the standard neurologic testing of motor, sensory, and reflex function, it is imperative that a complete mental status examination be done in all patients exhibiting recent behavioral change.

Focal syndromes are the manifestation of an entirely different type of lesion than those seen in the confusional states or the dementias. The focal syndrome is usually caused by a localized pathologic process such as a vascular lesion (stroke), brain tumor, abscess, or traumatic hematoma. Many of these lesions can be removed by surgery; therefore, such cases require an extensive neurodiagnostic evaluation. Focal lesions within the brain, particularly those affecting the cortex, can often be localized accurately by careful mental status testing. This is possible because of the relatively high degree of localization of certain cognitive functions, for example, memory in the limbic structures, language in the perisylvian area of the left hemisphere, and constructional abilities in the parietal lobes.

Rather characteristic clusters of neurobehavioral abnormalities have been described; the identification of these specific syndromes allows the clinician to recognize the presence and localization of focal brain disease.

HANDEDNESS, HEMISPHERIC SPECIALIZATION, AND DOMINANCE

One of the most helpful factors in functional localization is the high degree of hemispheric specialization for language. Almost all right-handed persons are left-hemisphere dominant for language; thus, an aphasic disturbance in a right-handed patient almost always indicates damage in the left side of the brain. Language function in the left-handed person is less strongly lateralized, and we will discuss this problem further in this chapter.

Although dominance for language is the most strongly lateralized of the cognitive functions, it is not the only one. Constructional abilities, visual-spatial orientation, and geographic orientation all tend to be lateralized to the right parietal lobe. The degree of dominance for these abilities, however, is far less than for language. Musical abilities, particularly the appreciation and production of tones and tone patterns, are dominant in the right hemisphere, principally in the temporal lobe, and the learning of skilled hand movements seems to be the province of the sensory-motor cortex opposite the preferred hand.

The degree of hemispheric specialization is similar for all right-handed persons who are from a right-handed family. The situation is vastly different, however, for the person who is not right-handed or for the right-handed person with non–right-handed members in his immediate family. Handedness, hemispheric specialization, and dominance are all related and must be appreciated if functional localization is to be fully understood.

The situation is made less complicated by the fact that about 90 to 95 percent of the population is rather firmly right-handed.[92,126,148,169] There is a spectrum of handedness, however, from exclusive right-handedness to strong left-handedness. Opinions vary as to the percentage of the population having standard left-hemisphere-dominant right-handedness. Geschwind and Galaburda[80] postulated that as many as 30 to 35 percent of people have some degree of mixed or anomalous dominance. The actual percentages of left-handedness or anomalous dominance can vary considerably and are based solely on the strictness of the criteria and extent of testing of lateralized functions. In general, the left-handed person is not as firmly left-handed as the right-handed person is right-handed; in fact, very few people seem to be purely or exclusively left-handed.[169] The average left-handed person carries out some skilled movements with the right hand or at least can demonstrate significant agility with both hands. Testing of left-handed people with a series of motor tests reveals that about 15 percent actually show superior performance with their right hand, despite their claim of left-handedness.[20,22,92] Why this should be true is unclear; it is doubtful that these persons chose to write and throw a baseball with their left hand because it was more difficult. The point is that left-handedness is less well established than right-handedness and that many left-handed persons have a strong tendency toward ambidexterity.

Several factors determine handedness and have direct bearing on the hemispheric specialization of the person. Genetic influence is a major factor. A right-handed couple, for example, has only a 2 percent chance of having a left-handed child, whereas a left-handed couple (both parents being left-handed) has a 46 percent chance of producing left-handed off-spring, and a mixed couple (one left-handed, one right-handed) has a slightly greater than 17 percent chance of having a left-handed child.[41] The family history is interesting also in that persons who are left-handed and have a family history of left-handedness (parents or siblings) tend to have less strongly established left-handedness than the sporadically left-handed person. Having left-handed family members also weakens the strength of handedness in the right-hander, a factor that may be important in explaining some of the mild aphasias seen in right handers with right-hemispheric lesions.[126]

A second influence on handedness is early brain damage to the dominant hemisphere. If the left hemisphere is damaged in a child who was genetically destined to be right-handed, he will often, but not always, switch dominance and become left-handed. This is called *pathologic* or *symptomatic left-handedness.* Statistically there are probably also pathologic right-handed persons, although their number is small.[159,160] A third factor involved in determination of handedness is social pressure or identification with parents and peers. This factor has been used to help explain the high percentage of left-handed children in families in which both parents are left-handed. A fourth factor that has been recently postulated as having a major influence on the establishment of cerebral dominance is the effect of testosterone and other hormones on the developing fetal brain.[80]

The specific cause for each person's handedness is often elusive and may be a combination of familial, pathologic, hormonal, and social influences. A strong correlation exists between hand dominance and foot dominance and a positive, yet less impressive, correlation with eye preference.[169] The significance of eye dominance is somewhat suspect because of both the high incidence of refraction errors and the fact that vision from each eye is projected to both cerebral hemispheres.

The major clinical importance of handedness is its close relationship with cerebral dominance for language. In all but a few rare instances, right-handed persons from right-handed families are completely left-hemisphere dominant for language. This strong dominance is somewhat weaker if the right-handed person has a family history of left-handedness (usually two left-handed close family members); in such cases (about 16 percent of the population), there is a slight tendency toward bilateral language representation.[126] The left-handed person presents a somewhat less consistent pattern: 60 to 70 percent are primarily left-hemisphere dominant for language, but the incidence of some degree of bilateral language representation is 80 percent.[85] Strongly left-handed persons with no family history of left-handedness tend to have the strongest left-hemisphere dominance for language of all left-handers. With a family history of left-handedness or a tendency toward ambidexterity, unilateral language dominance weakens, and bilateral speech representation is expected.[92,126] Conversely, patients with maximum right-hemisphere language dominance are usually the left-handers who have had early brain damage, although 20 percent of left-handed persons without brain damage have right-hemisphere dominance.[35]

Although somewhat complicated and a problem in only the 5 to 10 percent of the population that is left-handed, it is especially important to understand these issues of cerebral dominance when evaluating and managing the condition of a left-handed patient who has a focal cerebral lesion. Exposing an aneurysm by a generous surgical resection that leaves the left-handed patient unexpectedly severely aphasic is tragic. Similarly, the failure to adequately resect a tumor in the left hemisphere of a left-handed person with a family history of left-handedness (such a patient has strong bilateral speech and can recover well) is equally unfortunate. With a knowledge of the intricacies of cerebral dominance in the left-handed person and the use of intracarotid sodium amytal testing to determine dominance before surgery, neurosurgical procedures can be much more satisfactorily carried out in the left-handed population.

DESCRIPTION OF THE FOCAL BRAIN SYNDROMES

The Aphasias

Aphasia is a language disturbance caused by damage to the language areas of the brain. The term *aphasia* does not refer to errors in pronunciation or articulation but rather to true linguistic errors in word choice, comprehension, or syntax. The brain damage resulting in aphasia is usually in the left hemisphere, but in left-handed persons and in a few right-handed persons lesions in the right hemisphere can also produce a language disorder. Although language disturbances can be seen in demented or confusional patients, the syndromes discussed below are restricted to those seen with focal lesions.

The degree and characterization of an aphasic disturbance are largely determined by the size and location of the lesion, but also, in part, by the nature of the underlying pathologic process and how long after the onset of the aphasia the patient is examined. Patients with brain tumors and acute lesions such as caused by trauma and stroke often have associated confusional behavior in which the aphasia may be overshadowed by the general incoherence of mental processes. In the case of a large cerebral infarction, language function is often greatly reduced for the first few hours or days but improves rapidly thereafter. Occasionally, the acute aphasia is sufficiently distinct to permit determination of the exact location of the lesion within the hemisphere, but frequently definitive localization must wait. Usually within 3 weeks of onset, the aphasia has stabilized, and detailed language testing can be carried out. Language recovery is often a slow and somewhat erratic process that can continue for months and even years. It is best to be cautious about prognosis in aphasia and not to give a final determination of linguistic competence until a clear-cut plateau of function is reached (often months after onset).

In assessing a patient's language, the clinician should conduct a full language evaluation as outlined in Chapter 3. If the patient produces language with errors of grammar or abnormal word usage (paraphasia), or fails on tests of comprehension, repetition, or naming, he should be considered aphasic, and a left-hemisphere lesion should be assiduously sought. The following case clearly demonstrates this point.

A 53-year-old woman was referred because of recent "confusion." Her physician thought she had probably developed a confusional state from overuse of analgesics for back pain. On examination, the patient was fully alert but had occasional word-finding pauses in spontaneous speech. Her comprehension of long or complex sentences was faulty, and she had great difficulty in correctly naming objects. Other neurologic testing was unremarkable. Because her behavioral change strongly suggested an isolated aphasia and not a confusional state, a brain scan was obtained immediately. The scan showed, overlying the left hemisphere, a questionable crescentic uptake that was suggestive of a subdural hematoma. Arteriography verified the presence of a subdural clot, and surgery was done. After surgery, her language improved but unfortunately never returned to its premorbid level of adequacy.

Language testing is designed both to establish the presence of aphasia, as in the case above, and to localize the pathology as outlined below. The syndromes described here follow the classic descriptions offered by Broca, Wernicke, and others in the 19th century. They are based on an analysis of very general linguistic features such as auditory comprehension, repetition, naming ability, and fluency of expressive language. This traditional conceptualization of aphasic syndromes and their associated focal brain lesions continues to be a popular clinical and theoretical approach to the study of language. In recent years, neurolinguists have begun to analyze the linguistic breakdown of basic language structure in aphasia, using the same categories of linguistic analysis used to describe the rules of normal language syntax and word choice.[40,155] At some point, a reorganization of aphasic syndromes based on these studies may be possible; however, at the present time, we find the classic system the most useful in understanding aphasia and the correlation of these syndromes to specific focal lesions.

GLOBAL APHASIA

Global aphasia, the most severe of the aphasic disorders, is characterized by a severe comprehension deficit and a virtual absence of speech production. Patients with global aphasia cannot read, write, repeat words, or name objects, and most are hemiplegic. They often produce syllabic fragments or stereotyped utterances but little else. The lesion causing a global aphasia is most commonly large, involves the entire perisylvian area of the frontal, temporal, and parietal lobes[109,176] (Fig. 8 – 1), and is most frequently caused by an occlusion of the internal carotid artery or the middle cerebral artery at its origin. Global aphasia can, however, occur with less extensive lesions. In a group of 37 global aphasics examined by

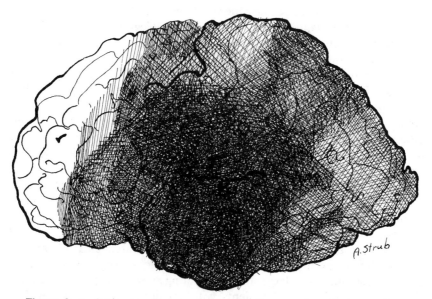

Figure 8–1. Brain showing composite of lesions causing global aphasia.

Vignolo and his associates,[177] large lesions encompassing both anterior and posterior language regions were demonstrated in only 22 of the patients. In 8 patients, all women, the lesion was anterior, completely sparing the superior temporal gyrus (area 22); 3 patients, all men, had posterior lesions sparing Broca's area; and the remaining 4 had deep lesions involving the putamen and insula. Others have reported similar results.[6,145] At present, there is no satisfactory explanation for these findings. Unfortunately, the prognosis for recovery of speech in the global aphasic, regardless of the extent of the lesion, is not good. Despite long-term speech therapy these patients rarely recover usable language function.[122,158]

BROCA'S APHASIA

In Broca's aphasia, comprehension of both spoken and written language is excellent, and there are only mild problems understanding complex syntax involving sequences or relational grammar. Verbal expression, on the other hand, is severely impaired. The term "expressive aphasia" is often used to denote Broca's aphasia, but the term can be confusing because most aphasics, regardless of type, have some abnormalities in expressing themselves. Because of this, the inexperienced examiner tends to classify all aphasics as being "expressive aphasics."

The verbal output of a patient with Broca's aphasia is nonfluent, effortful, and dysarthric, and contains mostly nouns and verbs with a paucity of other grammatical forms.[10] Repetition and reading aloud demonstrate similar deficits. Because the speaking style often has the sound of a sententious telegram, the speech is often called telegraphic or agrammatic. A patient with Broca's aphasia describing several men loading a moving van might produce the following: "Ah . . . chair . . . table . . . truck . . . going away . . . ah, ah, men walking, wolking, welking, oh I don't know." The patients often produce phonemic paraphasias, which they have no difficulty recognizing but have great difficulty correcting. The patient with Broca's aphasia is also impaired in object naming to confrontation, and paraphasic responses are common. Writing ability is severely involved and shows similar but even more severe errors than does spontaneous speech. Most patients are hemiplegic.

The lesion causing Broca's aphasia is usually a fairly large, deep lesion with maximal damage in the inferior frontal lobe, a lesion that usually includes the classic Broca's area 44[10,93,109,126,176] (area 2 in Fig. 8–2). Exceptions to this classic localization exist. In missile-wound patients, 23 percent have been shown to have lesions that spared area 44, but all patients had a lesion involving the precentral gyrus superior to Broca's area.[124] In addition, one large study correlating aphasic type to CT localization demonstrated several patients with classic Broca's aphasia with a lesion restricted to the temporal parietal region.[5] On the other hand, small

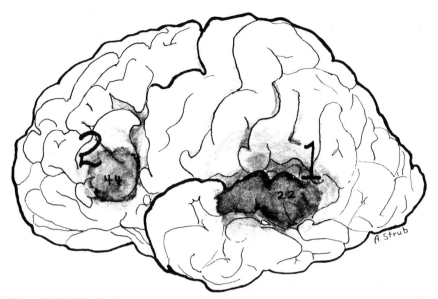

Figure 8-2. The lesion causing Broca's aphasia occurs in area 2 and incorporates the inferior frontal gyrus, 44. The lesion causing Wernicke's aphasia occurs in area 1, the posterior language zone, and usually destroys the superior temporal gyrus, 22.

lesions restricted to area 44 alone produce only transient mild aphasia, with dysarthria and dysprosody being the principal features.[138,191]

In general, prognosis for such patients is good because of their retained comprehension. Specific language recovery, however, is slow. These patients initially recover the ability to name objects, but fluency and grammatical complexity often remain impaired.[87] Emotionally, the patient with Broca's aphasia frequently experiences depression, frustration, and irritability[11]—important factors that must be dealt with in rehabilitation. The precise cause of these emotional changes has not been identified, but a combination of psychologic (awareness of the deficit) and organic (frontal lobe damage) factors is probably involved.

WERNICKE'S APHASIA

Wernicke's aphasia is clinically one of the most important aphasic syndromes because it often presents without evidence of either hemiparesis or a visual field defect. The patient's initial symptoms are typically those of abnormal speech production and abnormal behavior. The case presented at the beginning of this chapter is one example. The person with Wernicke's aphasia produces fluent, effortless, well-articulated speech that is frequently out of context and smattered with paraphasias.[10,76,87] On occasion, the spontaneous speech consists of a string of paraphasias that are completely meaningless (jargon aphasia). The individual with Wernicke's aphasia describing a scene of moving men loading their truck might produce the following: "Well yes, there they are all doing the thing with chegles and laps or those who put it here up and there. Well yes I say how, well, you know over there and well yes I tlable flet omnit well yes."

The most outstanding feature of these patients' aphasia is the severe deficit in auditory comprehension. They are unable to comprehend their own speech or that of others, and for this reason this syndrome has often been called a receptive aphasia. Repetition, reading, and writing are all severely affected, and object-naming is usually grossly paraphasic. The patients often develop unusual behavioral reactions including euphoria, indifference, paranoia, and agitation.[11] At times, this behavior can be severe enough to simulate psychosis. When this occurs, the patient requires sedation and occasionally must be transferred to a psychiatric ward.

Wernicke's aphasia is most frequently caused by a lesion in the posterior language zone (area 1 in Fig. 8–2). The lesion usually destroys the superior temporal gyrus (area 22 in Fig. 8–2), which is the primary auditory association cortex; this area is important in auditory comprehension as well as repetition, because all basic auditory processing is accomplished there. The size and exact location of the lesion vary considerably, but it involves a rather large area of posterolandic temporal and parietal cortex.[10,93,109,126,176] As with global and Broca's aphasia, there are exceptions to the classic localization. Some patients have the clinical features of Wernicke's aphasia, but their lesions on CT are completely anterior to the rolandic fissure.[5] In other cases, damage to the entire left-hemisphere speech area is extensive, and yet clinically the patients have a Wernicke-type aphasia. These exceptions are interesting and demonstrate the individual differences in language localization and dominance.

Because of the abnormal behavior often demonstrated by the Wernicke's aphasic and his bizarre speech, lack of comprehension, and paucity of expected neurologic signs, it is easy to see why these patients are at times confused with those with functional psychotic illness. The correct diagnosis is usually readily made, however, by carrying out a careful language examination. Schizophrenics almost always demonstrate adequate comprehension, repetition, reading, writing, and naming, whereas the aphasic will not. The evaluation of a very disorganized schizophrenic is not always easy, but persistent attempts at testing will generally yield a correct diagnosis. We recently saw a 17-year-old man who was referred because of strange language and inappropriate responses to questioning. On examination, his running speech was bizarre indeed. He had extremely loose associations, mumbled considerably, and would often stop in the middle of a sentence and not continue. His language production alone sounded like a fluent aphasia. Comprehension testing, however, proved to be normal, although very difficult to assess. When asked a question such as "Is it raining today?" the patient would look puzzled, wait for a long time, and then answer, "What do you want to know that for? You can see it's not, look, no rain, no rainwater, water. . . ." When asked to point to his nose, ear, and the floor, he performed accurately, but again with much suspiciousness, blocking, mumbling, and tangential thoughts. A complete language and mental status evaluation was carried out, and the patient performed very well on all items except proverbs, to which he gave concrete interpretations (a typical finding in schizophrenic patients). No aphasia was demonstrated. EEG and brain scan were normal, and the patient was referred to a psychiatrist for further evaluation and care.

The reason for stressing this case is that language production alone can be misleading. Therefore, the examiner is obligated to pursue his initial impressions concerning a patient's language production by taking a complete history and performing a complete neurologic and mental status examination. The severely disorganized language production of schizophrenia (often called word salad) was traditionally described in patients with a long history of the disease and usually after a long period of relative isolation in a mental hospital.[16] As demonstrated by the case above, however, the language of an undiagnosed schizophrenic can initially be remarkably deteriorated and simulate an aphasia.

The patient with Wernicke's aphasia and the patient with schizophrenia have another feature in common that can be difficult to interpret at times — the use of neologistic speech. The fluent aphasic produces frequent neologistic paraphasias in running speech; however, they differ considerably from those of the schizophrenic. The aphasic's neologisms tend to be random, changeable, and frequent, whereas those used by the schizophrenic are very infrequent and are consistent and systematized, and have delusional significance. The aphasic may call a comb a "clom" one time then correct it to a "come" or a "hair thing," whereas the schizophrenic may consider all combs to be "fleebles" that everyone carries around to monitor his thoughts.

A differential point that should be reiterated is that such neologisms are very common in aphasia, yet rare in schizophrenia.[73] Other types of paraphasias (i.e., letter or whole-word substitutions) are strictly aphasic and not heard in the schizophrenic. Another subtle differential feature is that the schizophrenic tends to produce much longer responses to general questions than does the aphasic,[73] and the schizophrenic's discourse is also usually distinctly delusional and systematized.

Although mental status testing will almost always correctly establish the diagnosis, historical information is invaluable. A history of the age and rapidity of onset of the language disorder is important. Obviously, a previous history of schizophrenia weighs heavily on the side of that diagnosis.

A young patient who has gradually developed bizarre language is much more likely to be schizophrenic than aphasic (although a temporal lobe tumor can certainly produce a slowly progressive aphasia). Conversely, the acute onset of rambling, disjointed, neologistic discourse in an elderly person with no history of previous mental problems is not likely to be due to a functional psychosis but is more likely to be the result of a vascular accident in the posterior temporal area. This simple observation is not always made, however; we have seen several elderly patients with Wernicke's aphasia who had been initially admitted to psychiatric units because of the acute onset of bizarre language and behavior.

Another disease in which abnormal language production can be confused with Wernicke's aphasia is advanced dementia. In such patients, the history and mental status examination should be sufficient to make the correct diagnosis, but a full neurodiagnostic evaluation may be necessary. Usually the demented patient's comprehension and repetition are far better than those of the Wernicke's aphasic and his general mental functioning far worse. There are cases in which a demented patient is stricken with a superimposed temporal parietal lobe infarct. In these cases, the problem of sorting out the array of linguistic problems into those caused by the dementia and those secondary to the recent infarct becomes virtually impossible.

The prognosis in Wernicke's aphasia is variable and is almost completely dependent on the degree of damage to the posterior superior temporal and infrasylvian supramarginal regions.[162] Clinically, the language improvement is determined by the degree to which auditory comprehension recovers. In patients with severe comprehension deficits, speech therapy is not useful, so therapeutic intervention must also await improvement in comprehension. If comprehension improves sufficiently, the patient's aphasia typically progresses to a level resembling conduction aphasia or frequently a simple anomic aphasia.[87]

CONDUCTION APHASIA

Conduction aphasia is a less common type of fluent aphasia in which the outstanding linguistic deficit is in the repetition of spoken language. These patients produce fairly adequate spontaneous speech that has only occasional word-finding pauses and paraphasias. Comprehension is very good, as is reading, although there may be errors in object naming and writing.

The importance of the syndrome is less practical than it is theoretical. The lesion causing this type of aphasia is usually in the cortex bordering the superior lip of the sylvian fissure yet extending deep enough to affect the arcuate fasciculus (AF)[19,75,93,109] (Fig. 8–3), which forms a direct connection from the auditory receiving area (22) to the motor speech area (44). A

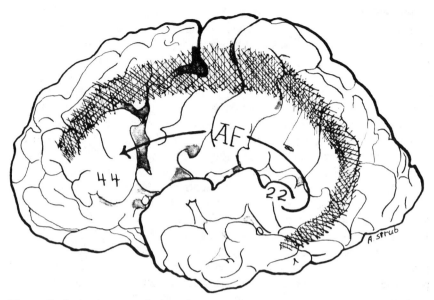

Figure 8-3. Lesions causing conduction aphasia are usually in the parietal area close to the Sylvian fissure. The lesion extends deep enough to affect the arcuate fasciculus (AF) which forms a direct connection from the auditory receiving area (22) to the motor speech area (44).

second, less common, lesion causing conduction aphasia is one involving the insula and the auditory cortex with their underlying white matter.[56] Of considerable theoretical interest is that damage to this fasciculus and its neighboring cortex can disrupt a specific linguistic process (repetition), yet relatively spare other higher-level language processes (i.e., conversational or propositional speech and comprehension). From observation of children during the period of speech acquisition, it is obvious that word repetition frequently precedes association of the sounds with the meaning of the words. With the study of conduction aphasia and the transcortical aphasias to be discussed next, it is now appreciated that there is a rather distinct anatomic separation between the high-level language process of conversational speech, which is used to express thought and describe the environment, and the more rudimentary and mechanical process of repetition.

TRANSCORTICAL APHASIA

The transcortical aphasias are the linguistic opposite of conduction aphasia. In cases of transcortical aphasia, patients are able to repeat perfectly, yet have difficulty with comprehension, speech production, or both.

These conditions, although known clinically for years, were dramatized by a recent case report of a patient with perfect repetition yet absolutely no comprehension of what was said to her and no ability to express her own wants and desires.[84] This remarkable syndrome was caused by a large crescentic infarction that spared the perisylvian tissue while destroying much of the association cortex (see Fig. 8–3). Because of the destruction of the association cortex, the patient could not comprehend what was said to her, and she also had inadequate association cortex for verbal reasoning or thought processes; however, the uninvolved perisylvian temporal, frontal, and parietal cortex with their interconnections, including the arcuate fasciculus, were sufficient to ensure completely normal repetition.

The several varieties of transcortical aphasia depend on the extent and location of the lesion. If the infarct or mass lesion involves only the anterior portion of the crescent, the patients demonstrate what is called transcortical motor aphasia: They repeat perfectly, comprehend well, yet are unable to adequately initiate spontaneous speech. Patients with posterior lesions are much the opposite: They repeat well, produce fluent, albeit paraphasic speech, yet comprehend little. These transcortical sensory aphasics are, of course, much more severely disabled because of their comprehension deficit. Those patients with the complete syndrome (isolation of the speech area) have intact repetition ability with no other language capabilities. The more severe the syndrome, the more the patients tend to echo everything they hear (echolalia). It is not difficult to demonstrate their prowess at repetition even in the face of severe comprehension deficits because of this echoing tendency. Their repetition is so mindless and slavish that they are able to repeat foreign languages they have never heard before, although their facial expressions often indicate that the language is strange and unfamiliar. Interestingly, they also tend to transpose pronouns and other grammatical structures automatically. For instance, if asked, "Is *your* name Mary Smith?" they may respond, "Is *my* name Mary Smith?"

Pathologically, this unusually shaped lesion represents an infarction of the border-zone tissue between the perfusion territories of the major cerebral blood vessels. The anterior area is between the anterior and middle cerebral arteries and the posterior area falls at the border of the middle, posterior, and posterior extent of the anterior cerebral arteries. What causes ischemia to occur in these areas is decreased blood flow from cardiac arrest, arrythmia, or significant carotid stenosis, or anoxia from insufficient blood oxygenation, as with carbon monoxide poisoning.

A clinician who is aware of the transcortical aphasias will be able to explain the pathophysiologic mechanism of many of the aphasias encountered. This ability can be particularly useful in those aphasic syndromes that occur after surgery or arteriography. If a patient displays a transcortical disturbance, a drop in blood pressure or an arrythmia is more likely the cause of the aphasia than an embolus in the middle cerebral territory. Often transient ischemia in the border-zone has a more favorable prognosis than does an embolus with its resultant infarction of brain tissue. Although most transcortical aphasias are caused by ischemia or infarction, tumors of the anterior frontal lobe or the supplementary motor area have been known to cause a transcortical motor aphasia. Whether this is a true aphasia or a form of mutism from frontal damage is not known.[55,151]

ANOMIC APHASIA

Anomic aphasia is another of the fluent aphasias. The primary language deficits in such patients are a difficulty in naming objects to confrontation and word-finding problems in running speech. Comprehension, repetition, reading, and writing are all typically excellent, except when the material contains many nouns with few grammatical fillers. A sentence such as, "Let's go over there when she comes back," for instance, will be easily repeated or read, whereas "The short fat boy dropped the china vase" will not. In all language tasks (e.g., spontaneous speech, repetition, and naming), the patient may produce paraphasic utterances with object names but not as commonly as in Wernicke's aphasia. On confrontation naming tasks, it is more typical for the anomic aphasic to produce circumlocutory responses than paraphasias. When asked to name a comb, an anomic might answer, "Oh you know, the thing that you use to do your hair, to make you look nice when you go out." The patient also typically demonstrates the object's use to emphasize his knowledge of the nature of the object.

Anomic aphasia can result from a wide variety of lesions in the language zone. Frontal as well as parietal and temporal lesions have been shown to produce the same linguistic syndrome of anomia.[93,109] Lesions of the inferior temporal region (area 37) tend to produce the most severe word-finding difficulties without a loss of comprehension of the words or the concept of the object's use.[12] In lesions affecting the parietal language area (primarily area 39), the anomia seems to be more profound in that the patients seem to have lost both the concept of the object *and* its name when it is presented visually. These parietal anomias have been called "semantic aphasias" because of this total loss of concept of the object as well as its associated name.[126] Anomia with phonemic (letter substitutions, e.g., "greel" for *green*) paraphasias is often seen with lesions in the insula-putamen region.[116]

Anomic aphasia is frequently associated with an alexia and agraphia in cases in which the inferior parietal lobule is damaged (areas 39 and 40). This syndrome will be more fully discussed in the section on alexia.

WORD DEAFNESS

Pure word deafness is an uncommon, yet fascinating language disturbance in which patients are able to hear but are unable to understand spoken words. Most patients also demonstrate some degree of auditory agnosia (inability to recognize nonspeech sounds such as a car horn, dog bark, or alarm clock) as well as some impairment of musical abilities.[38] In sharp contrast to patients with Wernicke's aphasia, such patients produce normal conversational speech, read without difficulty, and write normally. This is not a true aphasia because basic language processes are intact, but it is a type of disconnection syndrome in which auditory input from the primary auditory area (Heschl's gyri, areas 41 and 42) is interrupted before reaching Wernicke's area (particularly area 22).[75,102]

Pure word deafness is usually produced by bitemporal cortico-subcortical lesions that disconnect the auditory radiations of the primary auditory cortex (area 41) or the primary auditory association cortex (area 42) from the secondary auditory association cortex (area 22). Because the auditory system projects bilaterally, the lesion must also disconnect the callosal fibers on their course from the right auditory area (area 42) to the corresponding area in the left hemisphere. Because such a lesion, either in the left hemisphere or symmetrically in both hemispheres, is rather unlikely, this syndrome in pure form is rare. There are a number of cases, however, in which associated damage to area 22 causes a syndrome of word deafness with concomitant paraphasic speech.

APHASIA IN THE LEFT-HANDED PERSON

Aphasia in the left-handed patient includes several clinically important and interesting features. First, because 80 percent of left-handed persons have some element of language in both hemispheres, the left-handed person is more prone than the right-handed one to develop some type of language disturbance from a brain lesion. The right-handed person develops an aphasia only with a left-hemisphere lesion, but the left-handed person can have an aphasia resulting from a lesion in either hemisphere.[85] This unfortunate aspect of being left-handed has a positive side, in that aphasia in the left-handed person proves to be much less severe initially, to clear more rapidly, and to have good prognosis for full language recovery.[126] In a study of soldiers sustaining missile wounds to the left hemisphere, Luria reported that 95 percent of the right-handed soldiers developed a severe aphasia acutely and 75 percent showed little improvement on follow-up evaluation. In sharp contrast, the left-handed and ambidextrous patients had a 77 percent incidence of initial severe aphasia but only a 7 percent residual severe aphasia.[126] It can be conjectured from these findings that the linguistic capacity of the right hemisphere of the left-handed patients was quite adequate to compensate for the language loss produced by the left-hemisphere lesion.

The aphasic syndromes seen in left-handed persons are somewhat different from the classic syndromes of the right-handed. At least 35 to 40 percent of such cases are not classifiable, whereas only 15 percent of the aphasias in right-handed persons are unclassifiable according to standard typology.[85] The aphasia itself very rarely involves auditory comprehension, and when it does, the comprehension loss is minimal. A true sensory aphasia is seen in fewer than 10 percent of the cases.[37,96] Expressive difficulties are common (> 50 percent), with frequent decreased verbal fluency and dysarthria, but agrammatism is not usually seen. Repetition is seldom more than mildly involved, but anomia with its attendant word-finding difficulty is common. Anomia is much more frequently seen with left-hemisphere lesions and, in fact, is rarely found with right-sided lesions. Reading disturbances follow the same laterality pattern as anomia.

Anatomic correlation demonstrates that the language areas in the left-handed are the same as those in the right-handed, but it is the degree of bilateral representation that produces the anomalous clinical picture.[37,85] Auditory comprehension, particularly, seems to be especially strongly represented in both hemispheres in the left-handed person.

CROSSED APHASIA

Aphasia is occasionally observed in a right-handed patient with a right-hemisphere lesion. The patients are often agrammatic, commonly have decreased comprehension, demonstrate good naming, and rarely have reading or writing deficits. As case material accumulates, the aphasic syndromes and lesion localization appear to mirror the syndromes in the right-handed person with a left-hemisphere lesion.[103] The syndrome, like that in the left-handed person, is usually transient.[192] Why certain right-handed persons have this variance from the general rule is not clear. This syndrome of crossed aphasia is only described when the patient has no history of early left-hemisphere damage or familial left-handedness.

APHASIA WITH THALAMIC AND
OTHER SUBCORTICAL LESIONS

Some rather consistent language abnormalities have been described in patients with thalamic and putamenal lesions. Initially, the patients are almost mute, with little, if any, spontaneous speech. As they improve slightly, they respond to testing if the examiner makes a great effort to hold their attention. Once communication is established, the patients perform well for a number of seconds, then their peformance deteriorates rapidly into runs of paraphasic, neologistic language.[139,153,156] In many cases, the patient has comprehension difficulty as well, and a diagnosis of a mixed aphasia or moderate global aphasia is made initially.[61,63,104] In most of the patients, repetition has been remarkably spared and an echolalic tendency noted.[44,61,104,139,156] Naming difficulty is also usually present. The language pattern does not follow any of the patterns seen in cortical aphasia. Patients with more anteriorly placed lesions, however, tend to have more dysarthria and fairly good comprehension, whereas the behavior of patients with posterior lesions mimics the behavior of those with Wernicke's aphasia in many ways.[52,140]

The clinical features of the syndrome have been similar in many cases, but the actual mechanism of the disorder has been much debated. Because the cerebral cortex is the basic repository of language, true aphasic disturbances have been assumed to be produced only when the cortex itself is damaged. Because of this assumption, some investigators have found it difficult to consider the speech difficulty experienced by patients with these subcortical lesions to be a true aphasia.[127,139] They believe that these patients have a severe defect in attention and that their thalamic lesions prevent them from focusing on what is being said to them or on what they want to say. Because of this severe inattention and distractibility, the patients produce incoherent and garbled speech when not being strictly forced to pay close attention by the examiner. For this reason, this language disturbance has been likened to a confusional state rather than an aphasia.[54] To us, an aphasia is a clinical finding reflecting a central disturbance in language regardless of the mechanism. We agree that the thalamus and striatum are not an actual repository of language in the brain, but we believe that damage to them can influence cortical functioning of areas with which they interact. Recent studies using PET scan have shown decreased activity in the parietal cortex overlying deep aphasia-producing lesions. This finding suggests that the deep lesions have a distinct physiologic effect on the cortex and lead it to function inefficiently.[134]

SLOWLY PROGRESSIVE APHASIA

Most of the aphasic syndromes are described in patients who have either suffered cerebral infarcts or had surgical resections within the language area. Recently, there have been reports of a few cases of slowly progressive aphasia in patients without generalized dementia.[42,133] Most patients had primarily an anomic aphasia. PET scanning revealed a decrease in glucose metabolism in the left parietal-posterior temporal region.

Dysarthria

Articulation disturbances are commonly seen in brain diseases of diverse cause and varied location. Because they are often misconstrued by the naive examiner as being an aphasia, it is important to point out again the necessity of carrying out a full language examination on any patient with problems in speech production. Several years ago, one of our junior residents presented to us a young hypertensive woman who reportedly had an expressive (Broca's) aphasia but whose writing was entirely normal. She also, however, had difficulty swallowing, could not protrude her tongue on command, and had a snout reflex. This patient had a pseudobulbar palsy from bilateral corticobulbar tract damage; her speech problem was a severe dysarthria because of an interruption of innervation to the muscles of articulation and not an aphasia.

Any lesion disrupting control of the muscles of articulation will result in dysarthria: lesions of the cortical motor area (there is considerable dysarthria in patients with Broca's aphasia), basal ganglia (Parkinson's disease, dystonia, or chorea), corticobulbar tract (pseudobulbar palsy), the motor neurons of the 9th, 10th, and 12th cranial nerves (polio or amyotrophic lateral sclerosis), and in the muscles or muscle endplates themselves (myasthenia gravis or polymyositis). Speech disorders resulting from all these conditions must be differentiated from the aphasias. Treatment of many of these dysarthrias with conventional speech therapy is not usually efficacious, and many patients resort to writing or using flash cards to make their needs known.

Aprosody

Prosody is a term that encompasses the melodic qualities of language. It has been known for years that some patients with brain lesions experience a dramatic change in the intonation patterns in their expressive language. The usual case is of a right-handed person who sustains an insult to the right hemisphere and thereafter speaks with a monotonal delivery. Recently, Ross[150] described a group of patients with right-hemisphere perisylvian lesions and abnormalities in prosody (aprosody). The clinical aprosody correlated well with the type of language disturbance seen with comparable lesions in the left hemisphere. Patients with anterior lesions could not express themselves in a normal melodic fashion but could understand and detect melody in the speech of others. Conversely, the patient with a posterior lesion could express but not comprehend the prosodic qualities of language. These observations provide us with another useful clinical way to localize lesions in the brain.

Alexia

Alexia is a syndrome in which reading ability has been adversely affected by an acquired brain lesion. This condition is in contrast to dyslexia, which is applied to persons who have normal intelligence yet are unable to learn to read effectively despite adequate educational exposure.

A neurolinguistic analysis of reading disorders can be carried out, and the exact psycholinguistic nature of the reading problem can be identified. Some patients have deficits in visual perception that prevent them from understanding written words; others have a more basic problem with associating the visual symbol with the auditory word, a step critical for comprehension. This type of analysis is beyond the scope of this book, but the interested reader is referred to Friedman and Albert[66] for a full discussion. The discussion below considers alexia as a single entity.

Several lesions can produce alexia; the most common occurs in the posterior language zone and is associated with a fluent aphasia. There is also a rather specific type of alexia seen in patients with Broca's aphasia. This alexia is often especially severe, and its major characteristics are difficulty with comprehending complex grammatical constructions, inability in reading individual letters (literal alexia), and problems with maintaining the logical sequence of material read.[13]

In several alexic syndromes, however, reading alone or reading and writing are affected in the absence of an associated aphasia. The classic syndrome of pure alexia without aphasia or writing disturbance (agraphia) is seen with a left posterior cerebral artery occlusion.[75] Other conditions affecting the same region can produce the identical syndrome.[91] Anatomically, the lesion damages the posterior limb of the corpus callosum as well as destroying the left visual cortex (Fig. 8–4) and prevents visual written information from entering the left hemisphere because of the damage to the corpus callosum. The language areas of the left hemisphere do not receive the written words and therefore cannot decode them. Because there is no damage to the language areas of the left hemisphere itself, the patient is neither aphasic nor agraphic. The written message originates in the left posterior language area and is then carried out within the motor cortex in that hemisphere. It is dramatic to see such a patient spontaneously write a letter to a friend and then be totally unable to read what he has just written. Because the area of cortex that processes written language is functional, the patient can understand words spelled aloud to him and can also sometimes read very slowly by spelling words out loud letter by letter. There are several other interesting yet curious aspects to this syndrome: these patients seem to have little difficulty in naming objects or commenting verbally about what is going on in the world as perceived visually. This means that visual information for these tasks is transferred to the language hemisphere via more anterior callosal fibers than is written language. Along with written words, color information seems to cross in the posterior aspect of the callosum; these patients usually lose ability to name colors accurately (they are not color blind, however, as they can match colors well; they merely cannot name them).[81] Although this syndrome of alexia without

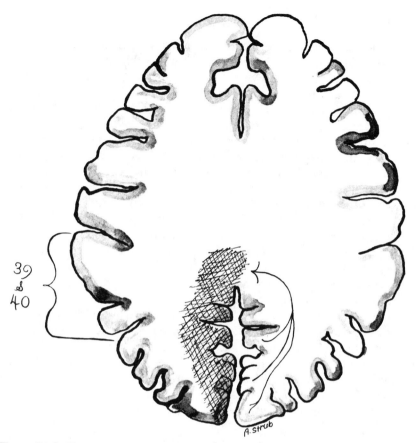

Figure 8–4. The cross-hatched area represents infarction of the left visual cortex and the posterior portion of the corpus callosum. Visual information from the right visual cortex (arrow) is unable to reach the left inferior parietal lobule (39 and 40) because of the callosal lesion. This produces the syndrome of pure alexia without aphasia or agraphia.

agraphia is usually seen with rather large lesions that cause an associated right homonymous hemianopia, cases have been described in which a rather small lesion deep in the occipital lobe prevents all visual information from reaching areas 39 and 40. Such patients are alexic but do not have a visual field defect.[90,91]

The second syndrome of a relatively isolated alexia is that seen with destruction in the inferior parietal lobule (areas 39 and 40) of the dominant hemisphere itself. In these patients, the alexia is accompanied by an equally severe agraphia and, on occasion, an anomia. This lesion, in essence, obliterates the patient's literacy and completely prevents the patient from using literal symbols to communicate thoughts or ideas.

Agraphia

Agraphia is a specific defect in producing written language. The term does not refer to the abnormalities in writing mechanics, which are often seen in parkinsonism, limb weakness, or gross constructional problems, but rather to a deficit in syntax, spelling, and word choice. Agraphia is most commonly seen in conjunction with aphasia or in delirium.[43] In fact, aphasics (except those with pure word deafness), invariably demonstrate some degree of agraphia that is usually in excess of their verbal language deficit. On the other hand, agraphia can rarely be seen in isolation. In the few cases that have been recorded, the lesion has been in the superior parietal area of the left hemisphere[6,154] or a deep parietal tumor.[7] Although it was once postulated that a lesion in the premotor cortex anterior to the motor area for the hand would produce an isolated writing disturbance, such a case has never been described.[60] Currently, investigators believe that writing activity is another function of Broca's area and is not separately located.[118] There is one unusual situation in which a patient can develop a pure agraphia with the left hand only; this condition is seen in lesions of the corpus callosum and will be discussed later in this chapter.

Two syndromes have been described in which agraphia is found in nonaphasic patients, but both these syndromes have other associated cognitive disturbances. The first is the alexia with agraphia described above and the second is Gerstmann's syndrome (a syndrome of finger agnosia, right-left disorientation, acalculia, and agraphia).[167] Both syndromes are caused by lesions in the dominant inferior parietal lobe and are frequently associated with other higher cortical deficits.

Apraxia (Ideomotor)

Apraxia is a disorder in carrying out or learning complex movements that cannot be accounted for by elementary disturbances of strength, coordination, sensation, comprehension, or attention.[77] The type of movement affected is one that requires the patient to select and execute several changes in body position.[112] Examples of such praxic movements are flipping a coin, saluting, brushing teeth, or blowing out a candle.[144] Simple repetitious movements such as tapping the index finger on the table would not be classified as being praxic movements. Apraxia is best seen with the movement elicited by verbal command without a concrete object for the patient to use (e.g., "Show me how you would flip a coin"). It can, however, be demonstrated if the patient is asked to imitate the examiner or to use an actual object to carry out the task. An apraxic movement is one in which the various changes in position or integration of the motor pattern is distorted (e.g., the patient takes the coin in his hand and proceeds to merely toss it in the air or turn the hand over and back, dropping the coin to the floor; in blowing out a candle the patient opens the mouth, cannot pucker, and coughs on the candle with variable success in actually extinguishing the flame).

The control of praxic movements, arm, leg, and mouth, in a right-handed person is usually directed by the language-dominant left hemisphere, and therefore ideomotor apraxia results from left brain lesions. In left-handed persons, praxic movements are more likely controlled by the right hemisphere even when language functions are on the left. The skilled movements are more closely correlated with handedness than with language dominance.[98] The lesion can be localized anywhere from the inferior parietal area (B in Fig. 8–5) posteriorly to the motor association cortex (D in Fig. 8–5) anteriorly. The movement to be executed is indicated to the patient either verbally by command via the auditory cortex (A in Fig. 8–5) or visually by imitation utilizing the visual system. The information concerning the desired movement is transferred to the inferior parietal area where kinesthetic images are evoked (B in Fig. 8–5). This kinesthetic pattern is sent to the motor association cortex (D in Fig. 8–5) via the intrahemispheric association fibers (C in Fig. 8–5). The motor association cortex effects the final motor programming before directing the motor neurons (E in Fig. 8–5) to proceed with the movement. Recent evidence has suggested that the supplementary motor area (SMA) on the medial surface of the superior frontal lobe is also important in the motor program-

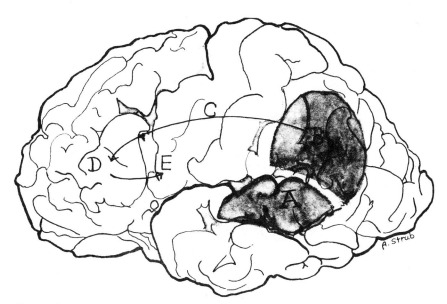

Figure 8–5. The lesion in ideomotor apraxia can be located anywhere from the inferior parietal area (B) to the motor association cortex (D). A, auditory cortex; C, intrahemispheric association fibers; E, motor neurons.

ming of praxic movements of the limbs.[181] Lesions in the SMA produce a bilateral limb apraxia, but without buccofacial apraxia.

Because of its dominant role in movement, lesions in the left hemisphere will cause a bilateral ideomotor apraxia. This is seen dramatically in Broca's aphasia, in which the nonparalyzed left hand frequently has a marked apraxia. Because of the close anatomic relationship between language and praxia, apraxia is frequently an accompanying and compounding factor in cases of aphasia. Many aphasics have difficulty with an apraxia of the buccofacial musculature, and the resultant difficulty in approximating speech sounds, often called verbal apraxia, can greatly exaggerate and on occasion constitute the entirety of the patient's speech production problem. This aspect of the aphasic deficit must be appreciated by the speech pathologist and dealt with specifically during therapy.

Ideomotor apraxia of the limbs can be a complicating factor in physical rehabilitation, in which the patient is frequently attempting to train his left hand to take over the tasks traditionally managed by the right. With a severe apraxia of the left hand, the acquisition of skills for daily living is very difficult. Again, the therapist must appreciate this limitation in brain-damaged patients and work with it as a separate problem.

Agnosia

Agnosia is a specific defect in object recognition in the absence of any disturbance in the primary sensory system. For example, a visual agnosia is diagnosed when a patient is able to see yet cannot recognize objects presented visually. Tactile agnosia and auditory agnosia are operationally defined in a similar fashion. There are also several interesting specific agnosias, prosopagnosia (face recognition), color agnosia, and finger agnosia, which are all occasionally seen with focal brain lesions.

TACTILE AGNOSIA

The most common agnosia is the tactile agnosia that occurs in the hand contralateral to a hemispheric lesion. These patients appreciate primary tactile sensation in their limb, yet cannot integrate sensations sufficiently to identify an object placed in the hand (astereognosis). The lesions causing these defects in sensory integration are in the postrolandic cortex, areas 3, 1, 2, and 5 of the parietal lobes.[149]

AUDITORY AGNOSIA

Auditory agnosia is an uncommon disorder that probably never occurs alone but is associated with other auditory processing difficulties, partial cortical deafness, word deafness, and aphasia. This condition has as its primary feature the patient's inability to distinguish among various nonverbal sounds (e.g., rustling paper, bird songs, car horns, and dog barks) while being able to perceive (hear) the sounds and perform adequately on pure tone audiometry. Brain[34] claimed that all patients with auditory agnosia would, by necessity, be word-deaf; however, this hypothesis has not proved true, because cases of striking auditory agnosia have been reported in patients who have very good comprehension of spoken language.[4] Although it has been postulated that this condition could be seen with a single lesion in the left superior temporal lobe,[34] it seems more likely that bilateral lesions are responsible for most such cases.

VISUAL AGNOSIA

In visual agnosia, the patient has adequate visual acuity yet is unable to visually recognize objects or pictures of objects. In association with their deficit in visual recognition, the patients are also impaired in their ability to describe or revisualize previously stored visual images from memory.[119] This syndrome has been better established clinically than has auditory agnosia but is an equally uncommon disorder. Two major types of visual agnosia have been described: a visual form or aperceptive agnosia and an associative visual agnosia. In the first type, the patient experiences a gross perceptual distortion that prevents identification of the object.[17] If the object is placed in his hand, he is able to immediately identify it kinesthetically. This variety of visual agnosia has been hypothesized to be produced by bilateral lesions of the visual association cortex (areas 18 and 19).[17]

The second variety, associative visual agnosia, is a type of disconnection syndrome in which vision and visual perception have been demonstrated to be normal in visual matching tasks, although this intact visual information area has been disconnected from language areas. In such a case, the patient cannot name an object but clearly recognizes it and can demonstrate its use or match it with other similar objects or pictures of the object.[9,47,152] The lesion causing this type of visual agnosia is similar to the one causing an alexia without agraphia, namely a left posterior cerebral artery occlusion and subsequent infarction of the left occipital lobe plus the posterior corpus callosum.[121] The syndrome has also been described in a patient with bilateral posterior cerebral artery lesions.[3] Because of the similarity of this lesion to that causing pure alexia, it is not surprising that many, but not all, patients with associative visual agnosia also have alexia.[2]

PROSOPAGNOSIA

Prosopagnosia is a very unusual and interesting visual agnosia in which the patient's major complaint is an inability to recognize familiar faces. These patients do not recognize family members until they speak, do not recognize famous faces in newspapers or magazines, and cannot learn to recognize new faces such as those of the doctors and nurses caring for them. Many of the patients also have a color agnosia and an alexia. The mechanism for such a discrete visual agnosia is still in question, and there may be various explanations. In some of the cases, there seems to be a visual perceptual defect that is specific for this one type of visual stimulus, namely faces.[189] In other cases, however, the defect may not be quite that specific. Four cases have been reported in which the patients have also lost their ability to differentiate various makes of cars or individual cows in a herd (a skill developed by some dairymen).[33] These factors suggest that the basic defect in such cases is an inability to perceive subtle discriminating features in objects that are all within the same category (e.g., faces, cars, cows). Yet other possibilities are that some prosopagnosic patients have a specific type of visual memory defect or an inability to match the perception of the face to the stored memory of the face, both of which could explain the agnosia.[23,53] As with many clinical syndromes, a particular finding can be produced by various mechanisms. The lesions responsible for producing prosopagnosia are usually bilateral and symmetric. The lesions are in the lower visual association cortex with involvement of the occipitotemporal fasciculus in the white matter of the occipitotemporal junction.[53,131]

FINGER AGNOSIA

Finger agnosia is an unusual, yet relatively common type of agnosia. It represents a rather isolated type of failure to recognize and localize particular parts of the body. The patients demonstrate an inability to recognize, name, and/or point to individual fingers on themselves or on the examiner.[74] The agnosia is most commonly apparent when testing the middle, index, and ring fingers but can, at times, be sufficiently severe to include the thumb and little fingers.[46] The lesion most commonly causing finger agnosia is in the dominant parietal lobe, although the symptom has also been found in patients with diffuse brain disease and as a developmental finding in some people.[114,141]

Occipital Lobe Syndromes

The occipital lobes are primarily responsible for high-level visual processing, and the syndromes associated with their dysfunction fall within the visual sphere. Gross bilateral destruction causes cortical blindness, but partial and selected damage or stimulation produces a variety of interesting syndromes. Disconnection of visual input from the left parietal lobe results in an alexia as previously outlined. Damage to the visual association areas can produce a variety of visual agnosias including prosopagnosia. The appreciation or perception of color is also a function of the occipital lobes, and lesions damaging both occipital lobes frequently cause an acquired color blindness or color agnosia.[48,59,132] The lesions producing color agnosia are closely associated with those producing prosopagnosia; hence, these two symptoms are often seen concurrently in the same patient.

Many perceptual distortions can occur with occipital lobe disease; such symptoms as monocular polyopia, metamorphopsia (distortion of images), persistent after-images (palinopsia), and loss of depth perception can all occur and are sometimes initially considered to be of hysterical rather than organic origin.[70] It is always best to investigate the visual system very carefully when a patient complains of bizarre visual symptoms rather than to grasp for a psychiatric label too quickly.

Patients with acute cortical blindness, usually secondary to bilateral posterior cerebral artery occlusion, occasionally develop a curious type of behavior syndrome in which they actively deny *any* loss of vision. The syndrome, often called Anton's syndrome, can be so blatant that the examiner may, at first, be completely unaware of the patient's blindness. For example, we saw a patient on rounds with a group of students. We talked to the patient, and then said that we would like to have some of the students examine him. He said, "That would be all right, but please tell me when they are coming so that I can get dressed." The students were surrounding his bed while he spoke. On the following day, one of us went back alone, and the patient greeted the examiner and said, "I see you have your crew here again today." Such patients are quick to confabulate, often charge about the room without regard for furniture and other obstacles in their paths, and if confronted with their problem, often evade the issue by making disclaimers about having misplaced their glasses or "having something in my eyes."

Another visual syndrome of interest is Balint's syndrome. Most likely caused by parietal or parietoccipital lesions, the syndrome primarily involves defective visual scanning. Patients are unable to voluntarily refixate to objects in the periphery of the visual field. Because of this paralysis of fixation, the patients cannot scan a visual scene and properly interpret its meaning. This defect is called simultanagnosia because the patient cannot grasp an entire scene but merely one or two parts that are at the point of fixation. The patient with Balint's syndrome is also not able to visually guide limb movements, a deficit termed "optic apraxia."[50]

A final behavioral manifestation of occipital lobe disease that should be mentioned is the occurrence of visual hallucinations in patients with occipital epileptic foci. The type of hallucination varies depending on the localization of the focus within the occipital lobe. Posterior lesions usually produce formless, colored flashes of light or spots, whereas more anterior lesions will cause the hallucination of fully formed images. We have observed one patient who has an epileptogenic focus in his right occipitotemporal region. His seizures consist solely of the hallucination in his left visual field of driving down a road through a forest. Such hemihallucinations are uncommon and can be seen in the blind field of some patients with damage to the calcarine cortex. In such patients, the visual association areas in the anterior portions of the occipital lobe are preserved.[157]

Temporal Lobe Syndromes

The temporal lobe is a very important area of the human brain. It not only serves as the cortical area for auditory input, but it is also the auditory processor for language reception. We discussed the aphasic disturbances in an earlier section; here we will reinforce only the fact that damage to the left temporal lobe, particularly the superior-posterior portion, causes a marked defect in auditory comprehension and a general disruption in language processing.

The temporal lobes, because of their auditory function, also play a major role in the appreciation and production of music. This role is not yet as well understood, nor is musical function as distinctly lateralized as is language, but many interesting observations have been made concerning this very fascinating function. After a right anterior temporal lobectomy, patients are significantly less able to judge tone quality and remember tones over short intervals than are patients with left temporal lobectomy.[136] On dichotic listening tasks (simultaneous presentation of a different melody to each ear), the right temporal lobe has been shown to be much better than the left in perceiving melodies.[24,88] In addition to these experimental studies, there have been many clinical reports of both musicians and persons with no musical orientation who have lost or retained many of their musical functions after the acquisition of cerebral lesions.[1,21,49,51,68,187] From these many accounts and reviews, the right hemisphere, and particularly the temporal lobe, appears to be very important in the appreciation and production of melody. This degree of lateralization is somewhat stronger in the naive listener who experiences melodies as entire patterns than in the trained musician who uses his left hemispheric language and analytic skills to assist him in appreciating music.[24] Rhythm, conversely, seems to be adequately handled by either temporal lobe. Music is, of course, a multifaceted ability that accordingly can be affected in a myriad of ways. The interested reader is referred to Critchley and Henson's[49] collection of papers on the topic as an excellent review and reference source.

The right temporal lobe is also very intimately associated with high-level visual processing. Removal of the lobe produces defects in visual perception and visual motor integration.[136]

The temporal lobes also contain two critical components of the limbic system: the amygdala and the hippocampus. These structures are often affected by disease and produce several remarkable behavioral syndromes. If destroyed bilaterally, amnesia results; if damaged by tumor, emotional and personality changes can occur. These clinical problems are separate topics and will be discussed later in the chapter.

The final major area of clinical interest is the behavioral changes that are seen in patients with temporal lobe epilepsy. The problem of epilepsy and especially temporal lobe epilepsy is of sufficient importance that we have devoted an entire chapter, Chapter 12, to this subject.

Parietal Lobe Syndromes

The parietal lobes contain the cross modal association areas for integrating visual, tactile, and auditory input. Input from the limbic system adds relevance to the information being processed, and strong reticulocortical input allows the discrete focusing of attention on the mental activity being carried out. The parietal lobes also have the capacity to manipulate this high-level information and are therefore a principal structure in intellectual processing within the human brain. As with the temporal lobes, there is a preferential processing in the left hemisphere for verbal material and in the right hemisphere for visual perceptual material. The left inferior parietal lobule (areas 39 and 40), as we have seen, is the specialized area for the visual/auditory integration necessary for reading, writing, and to a great extent, calculating. In addition, many of the verbally mediated activities involved in intellectual functioning are carried out in this left parietal region: verbal abstract reasoning such as proverb interpretation is but one example. Motor planning or praxis also takes place to a great extent in this left parietal lobe. Some unusual capacities of the left parietal region are more basic than the highly integrative features already mentioned. One is the appreciation of painful stimulation; on occasion, a patient with a left parietal lesion will actually lose complete appreciation for pain, a condition that has been termed an asymbolia for pain. Also in the tactile sensory field, the left parietal lobe has a certain capacity for integrating tactile stereognosis for both sides of the body and not just for the side opposite the lesion, as is true for the right parietal area.

The left parietal lobe has many connections devoted to the integration of visual perception and the guiding of visual-motor integrative processes needed to reproduce drawings, to construct models, or to carry out any such constructional task. The left hemisphere is not, however, as adept at carrying out these high-level visual tasks as is the right. The right parietal area is particularly skilled at perceiving overall visual patterns, whereas the left tends to perceive things more in terms of individual specific details.[108] With damage to both parietal lobes, the disintegration of constructional abilities can be very striking.

The right parietal lobe, because of its superior ability to conceive space and the relationships of things in space, is best able to visualize and guide us in our environment. This geographic sense also carries over to the abstract spatial orientation used in reading maps and blueprints. In addition, the right parietal area seems to be involved with the integration of both visual and tactile perceptions necessary for properly dressing oneself.

Both parietal lobes assist in the appreciation of right-left sense, knowledge of finger localization, and the stereognosis and localization of touch on the respective contralateral sides of the body. Both parietal lobes are also involved in helping focus attention, particularly to the side of the body or environmental field opposite it (the left is somewhat stronger in this respect).

Given this differential functioning of the two parietal lobes, the clinical syndromes associated with damage to either are easily understood. The syndromes are rarely encountered in pure form; a combination of the various symptoms is usually seen.

I. Left parietal syndromes
   A. Alexia plus agraphia
   B. Alexia plus agraphia plus anomia
   C. Gerstmann's syndrome (agraphia, calculation difficulty [acalculia], right-left disorientation, and finger agnosia)
   D. Also seen in varying combinations are
      1. Constructional difficulty
      2. Astereognosis, right hand or sometimes bilateral
      3. Pain asymbolia
      4. Ideomotor apraxia
      5. Various fluent aphasic disorders
II. Right parietal syndromes
   A. Constructional impairment (apraxia)
   B. Dressing apraxia
   C. Geographic disorientation
   D. Astereognosis on the left side
   E. Calculation and writing problems as a result of grossly distorted placement or production of the actual letters and numbers
   F. Denial and neglect of the left side, both of the body and of the environment

This last finding deserves special attention because denial and neglect can be some of the most dramatic behavioral syndromes seen in focal brain disease. In the full-blown denial syndrome, patients steadfastly deny that they have suffered any neurologic disease. The most common situation in clinical practice is the denial of left hemiplegia. Such patients may claim that the arm or leg is perfectly well but is not moving now because it is tired, or at times they will even state that the immobile limb is not theirs at all but belongs to another person who is in bed with them.

In some cases this explicit denial is not seen, but a less dramatic implicit type of denial is expressed. We saw a 50-year-old accountant who had meningitis with a mild left hemiparesis. His mentation had cleared almost completely, but he told his brother-in-law that it was very nice that he was in this small hospital for people who are not too sick and that the hospital was right next door to his house so he would not have too far to go when he was discharged (actually the hospital was miles from the city in which he lived). He went on to say that it was somewhat inconvenient at times because the door to his house and to the hospital were so close together that people often got into his house by mistake! This type of phenomenon was initially called reduplicative paramnesia but more recently has been referred to as a reduplication of place or implicit denial.[14,143,186] Many examples of this type of behavioral phenomenon have been described, and they represent an interesting way in which patients try to minimize their illness without frankly denying it.[186]

The denial syndrome includes a spectrum of disorders ranging from marked frank denial as its most dramatic manifestation to a subtle inattention to stimuli on the contralateral side of the body during sensory testing with bilateral double simultaneous stimulation. Between these extremes is the very interesting phenomenon of unilateral neglect, which can be seen both alone and in conjunction with the more dramatic forms of denial. In unilateral neglect, the patients have a variety of symptoms. They almost exclusively direct their attention toward the same side as the brain lesion, almost totally neglecting visual, tactile, and auditory stimuli to the contralateral side. If the patient is spoken to by someone standing on the neglected side, he will frequently turn toward his intact side and away from the speaker. On occasion, the neglect is so severe that the patients fail to shave or dress the neglected side. Other patients, whose lesion has not caused a hemiparesis, fail to use the contralateral arm. In drawing tasks, it is common for such patients to complete only half of the picture even when hemianopia is not present. There is a certain degree of dissociation between denial and neglect. Some patients will deny that they have, for example, a hemiplegia yet do not neglect their left side or left hemisphere in the environment.[25] Conversely, there are many cases of neglect in which denial is not present.

Many observations and experiments have been carried out over the years in an attempt to understand these curious phenomena, and a number of clinical features and theoretical explanations have been reported. First, these syndromes are much more common in patients with lesions in the right hemisphere than in the left.[46,75,142,185] Second, the full explicit denial syndrome is almost always seen primarily during the acute phase of the illness when the patient may continue to have elements of confusional behavior.[89,113,186] Third, many other neurologic deficits have been noted in a high percentage of the patients with the full syndrome, including a marked reduction in cutaneous sensation at the contralateral limbs,[89,186] gross visual-constructive defects,[142] jargon aphasia in the patients in whom left-hemisphere lesions have caused the syndrome,[186] and diffuse EEG slowing over the entire hemisphere containing the lesion.[180]

This syndrome is usually caused by a vascular lesion in the right parietal lobe that extends deep into the hemisphere, but the syndrome has also been seen clinically with frontal lesions and right thalamic hemorrhage[182] and experimentally in animals with lesions in the cingulate gyrus and the reticular formation of the mesencephalon.[183] The lesion that most frequently produces the neglect/denial syndrome is one that damages the right inferior parietal lobule.[25,173]

The pathophysiology, both of the basic phenomenon and of its association with right-hemisphere damage, has been the object of considerable debate and speculation. Several factors seem to be important: confusional behavior in the most dramatic cases, sensory defects on the neglected side, and gross constructional defects. These elements help, in part, to explain neglect but do not explain why right-hemisphere lesions more commonly produce the syndrome and why there is active neglect of one side rather than merely a recognized sensory loss. Various explanations have been offered: (1) inability to integrate sensory stimuli from the contralateral side, giving those stimuli less importance than those from the ipsilateral side in their rivalry for attention (amorphosynthesis)[58]; (2) a disconnection of visual and tactile information from the right hemisphere to the left-hemisphere language area, in essence rendering the left side of the brain unable to comment on input from the right hemisphere[75]; (3) interruption of basic reticulocortical and limbocortical connections, leaving the hemisphere with insufficient reticular input to concentrate attention on events entering that hemisphere[100,101]; and (4) a basic imbalance in the orienting response. If one assumes that the orienting tendency toward the right is much stronger than to the left, a marked right orientation is seen with lesions on the left.[113] The reader interested in an in-depth discussion of the topic is referred to *Hemi-Inattention and Hemispheric Specialization*, edited by Weinstein and Friedland.[184]

The behavioral deficits seen in parietal lobe disease are very specialized and are not readily elicited on routine neurologic testing. The parietal lobe was traditionally known as one of the "silent areas" of the brain, but during the last several decades, a tremendous amount has been learned about how to communicate with this region.

Frontal Lobe Syndrome

Bilateral damage to the premotor areas of the frontal lobes (areas 9, 10, 11, 12, 45, and 46) causes a behavioral syndrome that has been recognized for more than a century. The patient, so afflicted, displays a marked change in personality and social behavior while maintaining normal or near normal intellectual and neurologic functioning. Because the syndrome is almost purely behavioral, the examiner must be thoroughly acquainted with its specific features to suspect the presence of frontal lobe damage. The symptom complex may vary from patient to patient, but most commonly the patients demonstrate some degree of apathy, irritability, poor judgment, uninhibited social behavior, lack of motivation and goal direction, and euphoria. The patients generally display very shallow affect and, although easily angered, do not sustain their irritation for more than a few minutes. Cognitive capabilities suffer subtle but real impairment; perseveration is present, which prevents the patient from efficiently shifting his thinking or reasoning from one pattern to another when environmental changes signal the necessity for an alteration in behavior; verbal fluency is decreased (particularly when the left frontal lobe has sustained the maximum insult); and the patient with frontal lobe damage also tends to have a disturbance in the ability to efficiently sequence in temporal order.[97,125,137] Attention is also often disturbed, and such patients are not only unable to sustain their attention on a specific task but are also easily distracted by irrelevant environmental stimuli.[125] Some patients with frontal lobe lesions have a significant memory loss, a loss that exceeds that which can be explained by apathy and inattention alone. Cognitive disruptions are not as obvious as those seen with parietal lobe damage; nevertheless, they add to the overall difficulty experienced by these patients. The following case clearly demonstrates the problems encountered by some of these patients.

A 22-year-old soldier sustained a frontal lobe missile wound during his service in Vietnam. He was evacuated to the United States for recuperation and within 5 weeks had essentially recovered. The attending neurosurgeon found no gross residual neurologic abnormalities, and a brief psychologic evaluation showed that his IQ, memory, and constructional abilities were within normal limits. The patient was returned to active duty at a base in the United States. Within a few weeks, complaints began to be made concerning his behavior. His wife reported that he had changed from an easy-going guy to an irritable, easily angered person who would get into a fight every time they went out socially. At work he constantly got into arguments with his supervisors and peers alike. Two months after his return to active duty, he had been jailed twice for disorderly conduct and assault. At this point he was reevaluated with a more extensive neuropsychologic battery and comprehensive neurologic examination. This evaluation brought into focus the true significance of his behavioral change, and it was finally realized that he had a rather classic frontal lobe syndrome directly attributable to his injury. He was granted a medical discharge from the army and returned to civilian life. On follow-up report, this man has not been able to hold a regular job and has maintained himself only on his disability pension from the military.

The actual clinical frontal lobe syndrome varies somewhat from case to case, and the symptoms appear to be somewhat related to the specific location of the lesion. Patients with lesions in the baso-orbital portion of the frontal lobe tend to display the type of behavior illustrated in the case above (uninhibited, aggressive, and pugilistic). Also seen secondary to these orbital lesions is a more pleasant form of the same disinhibition in which the patient is constantly joking, talking loudly, and acting in a generally euphoric fashion. Sexual disinhibition and irritability can be seen in both forms of the orbitofrontal syndrome.[27,125] Patients with primary damage to the convexities of the frontal lobe tend to have more cognitive deficits and also present a more apathetic, nonmotivated, adynamic picture clinically.[27,125,168] Underlying the behavior of all patients with significant frontal lobe damage is an unfortunate lack of motivation, inability to plan ahead, and poor judgment. These factors, in conjunction with any personality disturbance, severely hinder these patients from leading normally productive lives.

Two critical problems in effectively diagnosing this syndrome need further elucidation. The first is the delay in recognizing the syndrome (as in the case above), and the second is the misidentification of the symptoms as being functional and not organic in origin. Failure to recognize the syndrome stems primarily from failure of the clinician to search for the specific symptoms. If the clinician has not known the patient previously, the patient's relatives and friends must be sought out and questioned concerning any change in specific behaviors. Psychologic testing must be expanded to look for evidence of frontal disturbance on alternating sequence testing, trail making, card-sorting facility, and verbal fluency. As with so many areas of medicine, one can diagnose a disease or syndrome only if one considers and specifically tests for it. This is particularly true with the frontal lobe syndrome.

The second problem in diagnosis is the misconstruing of the signs of apathy, disinhibition, and short temper as being a psychiatric reaction. On first impression, apathy can mimic depression, for the depressed patient is certainly often apathetic. But apathy alone without sadness, tears, self-depreciation, and vegetative signs should strongly arouse the examiner's suspicion of organic and particularly frontal lobe disease. The patient with frontal lobe damage who displays gross antisocial behavior and disinhibition can superficially resemble someone with psychopathic behavior unless a careful history and examination are done. In all cases, familiarity with the frontal lobe syndrome will make the diagnosis considerably easier.

The dramatic behavioral changes seen in frontal lobe damage led many neurosurgeons and psychiatrists to the conclusion that removal or disconnection of part or all of the frontal lobes might be useful in controlling the behavior of patients with uncontrollable psychosis or obsessional neurosis.[36,65,135,170] Over the years, these psychosurgical procedures have been refined to the use of stereotaxic lesions in the medial frontal lobe or the cingulate gyrus to disconnect limbic input to the frontal lobe. The procedures are not as widely used today because of the number of psychotropic drugs available to control abnormal behavior, but surgery can still be a useful method of controlling rare cases of severe obsessive-compulsive neurosis, severe anxiety, depression, and the affective disturbance seen in some schizophrenic patients.[36,170] In recent years, Stuss and Benson examined a number of leukotomy patients 25 years postsurgery; a discussion of their findings is contained in their book, *The Frontal Lobes*.[168]

Limbic Syndromes

Damage or irritation to the structures within the limbic system has been shown to alter the basic instinctual, emotional, and memory functions observed by the system. We have already discussed how certain components of the system can be affected in generalized disease such as confusional behavior or dementia, but in this section the discussion centers on the behavioral symptoms resulting from focal lesions.

AMNESIC SYNDROME

The most common and certainly one of the most fascinating limbic syndromes is the amnesic syndrome. Clinically, the syndrome in its most extreme form is characterized by a severe deficit in recent memory in the face of normal remote and immediate memory, and preservation of other intellectual functions. The amnesic patient can carry on a completely normal conversation but is totally unable to learn any new information. The patient can be told the examiner's name 10 times within the space of an hour, yet 5 minutes after the last reminder the patient may say, "I don't believe I caught your name." The amnesic patient is able to register the information initially and repeat it within a few seconds but is unable to retrieve that information after a few minutes. In experimental settings, it has been shown that amnesic patients with lesions in mamillary bodies and thalamus do store information but cannot recall it. On tests that cue the patient's recall or require the patient to recognize previously presented material, amnesic patients perform as well as controls. They do not realize, however, that the information has been stored and the information is, therefore, totally useless to them in day-to-day functioning.[39,179] Patients with temporal lobe damage appear to have deficits in storage as well as retrieval. Old, well-established memories are spared, and their retrieval is normal.[163] The most severe problem encountered by these patients is in new learning (anterograde amnesia), but they also usually experience an associated period of retrograde amnesia. The memory loss causes the patients to lose orientation in time; they do not remember the date and have no way of mentally recording the passage of days and months. They are also frequently disoriented as to place. One man with Korsakoff's syndrome had settled down to the hospital routine until one day he looked out the window and reported to us that something very unusual had happened, a parking lot had been built overnight outside his window. This upset him very much, and he marveled at it every time he looked out the window. What we later found out was that he thought that the hospital was actually another hospital where he had spent several months after the war. The hospital seemed familiar (they were both Veterans Administration Hospitals), but the disappearance of the garden he remembered viewing from his window upset him visibly.

As if to fill in the gap in their memory, many of the amnesic patients confabulate unabashedly when asked a direct question that they cannot answer. One elderly man, when asked at a conference about the location and nature of the building, said that it was a schoolroom from his old high school and that the doctors were teachers and old friends. He went so far as to single out one of the staff as having been out drinking with him the week before (a quick denial from the staff member presumably verified the confabulatory nature of the response). Spontaneous confabulation is less common, and in general these patients remain quiet rather than initiating conversation.

This curious syndrome of isolated memory difficulty is produced by restricted bilateral lesions in various limbic circuits. The case that initially demonstrated the remarkable clinical pathologic relationship between memory and the limbic system was a surgical removal of both temporal lobes in a young epileptic man.[161] This type of procedure has not been repeated because of the obvious side effects, but damage to the hippocampi with resultant amnesia is regularly seen in cases of severe head trauma, anoxia, and herpes simplex encephalitis. Bilateral hippocampal infarction has also been shown to cause extensive memory difficulty.[18,57] In cases of Korsakoff's syndrome, which is the amnesic syndrome seen after Wernicke's encephalopathy associated with acute thiamine deficiency (primarily in alcoholics), the limbic damage is in the mamillary bodies and the dorsomedial thalami.[175] Tumors involving the dorsomedial thalamus, midbrain, and posterior fornix have also been reported to cause amnesia, thus further strengthening the theory that limbic structures and pathways are critical in the storage and retrieval of memory traces.[99,130]

Amnesia is of sudden onset in almost all cases and of varying degrees of severity. Posttraumatic cases usually improve rapidly, and the retrograde amnesia actually shrinks during the recovery phase.[15] Memory of events preceding the accident returns chronologically until usually it is only the few seconds before the accident that are forever lost to the patient's recall. With infectious and vascular lesions, recovery may be only partial and a mild-to-moderate permanent memory problem can persist. In alcoholic patients who have undergone a full Wernicke's phase with subsequent Korsakoff's amnesia, at least one-third will experience a permanent severe amnesia.[174,175] For the others, recovery ranges from full recovery (20 percent) to moderate disability. The possibility of progressive memory difficulty with alcoholism has not been well studied, but examination of brain specimens certainly shows atrophy in the mamillary bodies in many alcoholics. This fact, combined with the obvious alcoholic dementia seen in some patients, strongly supports the contention that alcohol in large quantities over time can serve as a slow poison to the neurons of the central nervous system.

In one type of amnesic syndrome, probably of vascular origin, the memory deficit is transient. This syndrome has been called *transient global amnesia* and is characterized by a short period, usually less than 24 hours, of confusional behavior and amnesia.[8,64,94,129] When examined during the acute episode, the patients repeatedly ask where they are and what they are doing. If told about their whereabouts, they soon forget and ask again. They also have a short period of retrograde amnesia, as is demonstrated in the following case.

The day before her amnesic episode, a 60-year-old housewife had been shopping and bought some shoes. After arriving home, she decided to return them the following day because they were the wrong color and placed them on the kitchen table so as not to forget them in the morning. The next morning she was stirring some pancake batter when she suddenly looked around and called to her husband. She asked him what she was making and whose shoes were those and what were they doing in the kitchen. The husband explained; no sooner had he finished his explanation than the patient repeated the question, seeming to obsess about the shoes. The patient was taken to the hospital where examination revealed only the confusional behavior and the memory problem. These symptoms cleared rapidly in the following 12 hours, and she then could remember having purchased the shoes but did not remember anything about cooking pancakes or other events of that day.

This condition is probably due to a transient ischemia of the posterior cerebral arteries. The temporal branches of these vessels supply the hippocampi, which are the postulated site of the ischemia. Many affected persons do not have recurrences for many years,[164] whereas others actually develop a progressive stepwise dementing syndrome.[129]

In transient global amnesia there is often a question as to whether the episode is of organic or psychologic cause. The differential diagnosis between a transient organic amnesia and the dissociative type of amnesia seen in hysterical neurosis is simple if either the examiner or a reliable observer has seen the patient during the actual episode. In the organic cases, the patients are actively confused, continually ask where they are, and cannot store any memories during the amnesic period. Conversely, the hysterical patient acts perfectly normal during the episode, can learn things during the amnesia, and only reports a period of amnesia after the episode is over. This latter type of amnesia was illustrated in a young Peace Corps volunteer who had gone to a small town in interior Brazil to work when he soon began to "lose track of days." He returned to the capital and reported that on several occasions he had blanked out entire days. He remembered going out to buy a newspaper each morning only to awaken the following day with the paper beside his bed and no recollection of actually buying it or of the events of the previous day. On cautious inquiry of the townspeople he found out that he had, in fact, spent each day making appropriate contacts, talking to people, and doing all the other things expected of a volunteer during his first few months in a country. This was clearly an emotionally based amnesia and has none of the dramatic behavioral features of transient global amnesia.

OTHER LIMBIC SYNDROMES

Although memory problems are among the most common limbic disorders, some other interesting behavioral abnormalities are seen with specific limbic lesions. When tumors arise in limbic structures, they can cause very dramatic changes in basic vegetative as well as emotional behavior. Tumors arising in and destroying the ventromedial hypothalamus produce a slowly progressive syndrome of hyperphagia, aggressiveness, and eventual confusional behavior. In one case, the patient scratched, hit, and even attempted to bite the examiner during examination.[147] In some patients, manic behavior, sloppiness, and paranoia have been reported with tumors exerting pressure on the hypothalamus from beneath.[128] Accompanying these marked behavioral abnormalities is usually a variety of other endocrine and autonomic disturbances including temperature change, menstrual abnormalities, and diabetes insipidus.

On rare occasions, tumors or demyelination have been reported in which the ventral hypothalamus has been spared, and damage to the lateral nuclei has occurred.[107,188] In such instances, the patients develop an anorexia rather than hyperphagia and can easily be misdiagnosed as having anorexia nervosa. This observation is not to suggest that many patients with true anorexia nervosa are harboring cryptic hypothalamic tumors, as these are decidedly rare, but only to encourage the clinician to entertain this possibility, particularly if neurologic or endocrine abnormalities (other than amenorrhea) appear.

Tumors originating deep in the frontal and temporal lobes and involving the limbic structures therein have long been known to cause behavioral changes that can simulate psychiatric disease.[105,110,128,166] It is very difficult in most cases to decide whether these behavioral changes represent a negative phenomenon (i.e., the result of loss of function from destruction of brain tissue), a positive phenomenon (i.e., the result of an active, associated epileptic focus that stimulates the production of behavioral aberration), or the concomitant effect of increased intracranial pressure. Regardless of the specific mechanisms, lesions in the temporal and frontal limbic tissue can clearly lead to a variety of pseudopsychiatric states ranging from depression to schizophreniform psychosis.

Drs. Klüver and Bucy described a number of dramatic behavioral changes in experimental monkeys who had undergone bilateral temporal lobectomies.[115] Whether the resultant syndrome of placidity, hyperorality, amnesia, hypersexuality, and visual agnosia was secondary to removal of limbic structures or of the temporal neocortex is not settled, but the experiment stimulated interest in the relationship of temporal lobe structures to behavior. This syndrome (Klüver-Bucy) does appear in humans in various clinical settings: bilateral temporal lobectomy,[171] head trauma,[106] and encephalitis. The full syndrome is not usually seen and, as can be seen from the nature of the etiology, it is not always restricted to temporal lobe damage. We have seen several such cases; the most recent was an adolescent boy who had suffered herpes simplex encephalitis. During the recovery phase, he developed aggressive behavior towards his siblings, marked exploratory behavior with hyperactivity, memory difficulty, and hyperorality. When the patient entered the office he immediately began to explore every shelf and object in the room. Objects of interest, such as ashtrays and staplers, were immediately placed in his mouth for further investigation.

Another case was a young man who sustained a rather severe head injury during an automobile accident. After his comatose stage, he became aggressive, amnesic, hyperoral, and sexually obsessive. He required restraint in bed because he would attack female staff members sexually, fight with male staff members, and eat anything that he could get his hands on, including his medical chart. Although the central nervous system damage was relatively diffuse in both these cases, much of the abnormal behavior probably stemmed from damage to limbic structures.

The syndromes discussed thus far are largely due to ablative lesions within the limbic system; remaining are a number of interesting limbic syndromes associated with active epileptogenic lesions. Because much of the information on these active limbic foci comes from the study of temporal lobe epilepsy, we discuss the topic of stimulating lesions in Chapter 12, Epilepsy.

Corpus Callosal Syndromes

The corpus callosum is an immense association pathway that is only infrequently involved in pathologic processes. When it is damaged, the defects produced are subtle, yet their elucidation and study have revealed a great deal concerning the functional interrelationships of the two cerebral hemispheres. We have already discussed the significant problem in reading that occurs when the left occipital lobe and posterior callosum are damaged. Visual information then reaches only the right hemisphere and is prevented from crossing to the language-dominant left hemisphere. The resultant alexia clearly demonstrates the need for the callosal transmission of written language to the language area for processing.

When a lesion occurs in the anterior portion of the callosum, a far more subtle problem develops. In such cases, the right frontal and anterior parietal cortex has essentially been disconnected from the language area of the left hemisphere (Fig. 8-6). The resultant syndrome consists of the following three elements: (1) an agraphia in left-handed writing but not in right-handed writing, (2) an apraxia of the left hand, and (3) an inability to name unseen objects placed in the left hand.[82] All these deficits are due to the fact that the right motor and sensory cortex are unable to utilize the language and praxis centers in the dominant hemisphere. Because the right hemisphere is intact, it can coordinate many activities within itself. For example, the left hand is able to copy line drawings very well, better in fact than the right hand, because of the superiority of the right hemisphere in integrating visual perceptual information.[31]

In recent years, a small number of epileptic patients have undergone complete section of the corpus callosum and anterior commissure in an attempt to control the interhemispheric spread of epileptic discharges. The results of this procedure have made it possible to study more precisely the role of the corpus callosum in human behavior.[28,29,71] In essence, there is no clinically significant change in bimanual motor coordination or in most general behaviors. When verbal tasks are demanded of the left hand, of course, failure is experienced. Also, the left hand under the guidance of its right hemisphere is much better at constructional tasks. An extensive series of interesting observations have been made on these surgical patients using a variety of techniques for presenting information solely to one hemisphere. Gazzaniga[71] reported these observations in a book titled *The Bisected Brain*; the interested reader is referred to this volume. What this work has done, more than to elucidate the function of the corpus callosum, is to help in understanding the functions of the individual hemispheres. Because the hemispheres in these patients are virtually independent, information can be presented to either hemisphere alone, tactually through the contralateral hand, or visually with a tachistoscope. Thus, the functioning of each hemisphere can be assessed independently.

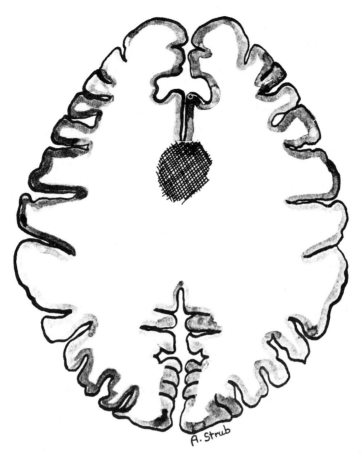

Figure 8-6. The cross-hatched area represents a lesion of the anterior corpus callosum.

The studies mentioned above were all done on patients who had commissurotomies after the acquisition of language and many other skills. In patients born with agenesis of the corpus callosum, the interhemispheric organization is quite different. Reading capacity, for example, has been reported in both hemispheres. Some patients can name objects placed in either hand, whereas transfer of kinesthetic learning is defective, and there is some difficulty with bimanual coordination.[62] Data from these cases seem to indicate that the two hemispheres may develop more independently when there are no callosal connections, leading to the contention that callosal interconnections partly account for the development of cerebral dominance. This idea is conjectural, for agenesis patients have enlarged, intact anterior commissures, and this structure could possibly be performing the full function of an intact corpus callosum.[30] Unfortunately, callosal agenesis is usually not the only cerebral anomaly in these patients, and the presence of seizures and other lesions may produce many of the abnormal findings that have been demonstrated.

General Hemispheric Differences

To superficial inspection, the two cerebral hemispheres appear as mirror images, but as has been demonstrated in studies of patients with lesions in one hemisphere, the initial impression of equality is functionally incorrect. By disconnecting the two hemispheres and through ingenious testing, even greater insights have been gained about their distinct and individual functioning. Encouraged by the obvious functional differences between right and left hemispheres, more detailed anatomic studies were begun. Basic anatomic differences that correlate well with known functional asymmetrics have been discovered, the most notable being the increase in the auditory association areas in the left hemispheres of right-handed persons.[78,83,190] Despite the fact that basic anatomic asymmetrics indicate that the substrate for left-hemisphere language dominance is present at birth, the right hemisphere is capable of completely and efficiently taking over all language functions if the left is damaged early in life.[165] This remarkable plasticity of cortical function is one of the most interesting aspects of the developing nervous system. It is almost complete for higher cortical functions at birth and rapidly decreases as language is acquired and established. By late childhood, the degree of compensation for brain damage is much less, and in the adult, loss of the left hemisphere leaves the patient capable of producing only a few expletives under stress.

In general, the left hemisphere is most efficient in all verbal tasks including verbal memory (although it requires bilateral damage to produce a severe amnesic state, unilateral left–temporal-lobe damage results in a measurable decrement in verbal learning).[136] This verbal or language dominance is by far the most outstanding of all functional hemispheric asymmetries. The right hemisphere, in contrast, is nonverbal or mute, but has its prominence in the realm of visual spatial activities. This left-verbal, right-visual spatial dichotomy is consistent in most of the population, but as we have discussed, it is influenced by genetic and other factors that determine basic handedness and dominance. Although this dichotomy is the same for both male and female, the relative capacities for these functions differ according to sex. The female shows a consistent superiority in verbal skills, whereas the male shows an equally strong overall strength in spatial abilities and high-level mathematical skills.[45] These differences are further dramatized by the much higher incidence of both delayed speech and written language problems (dyslexia) in male children (a 6 to 1 predominance).

Hemispheric differences have been examined in many ways; currently it is popular to discuss the mode of functioning of the individual hemispheres rather than the specific function being carried out. The term "cognitive style" has been adopted to indicate this functional concept. The right hemisphere, because of its superior capacity for appreciating patterns or overall spatial concepts, has a so-called synthetic or holistic style, whereas the left hemisphere has a more analytic and logical style that is attentive to detail but inadequate for rapid synthesis.[120] This style of functioning is well demonstrated in patients with right- or left-hemisphere lesions when they attempt to complete block designs. When the left hemisphere is working alone (right-hemisphere damage) the patient is unable to approximate the overall outline of the design. In the patient with left-hemisphere damage, the outline of the design will be correct, but the details of the internal structure will be faulty.[108] This type of observation has also been made in patients after commissurotomy (corpus callosal section), where each hemisphere can be tested individually.[28,29,31]

The differential role of the hemispheres has been shown to extend beyond pure cognitive capacities and into the field of emotional behavior. Again, both studies of hemisphere damage as well as the observation of commissurotomy patients have elucidated the varying roles of the two hemispheres. One of the earliest observations was made in aphasic patients who, on being asked to perform demanding linguistic tasks such as verbal arithmetic, would suddenly show an intense anxiety reaction.[86] This catastrophic reaction, as it has been called, occurs whenever the patient begins to fail on a task that was previously within his capability. The reaction often develops so rapidly that it appears to be an actual, intrinsic aspect of the inability to carry out the task rather than a secondary emotional reaction of the patient after the realization of his failure. This observation of the emotional reactions of the aphasic patient has led to many systematic studies of patients with unilateral brain lesions, the results of which have verified the initial impression and refined the concept in many ways. Left-hemisphere damage has been repeatedly shown to give a much higher incidence of both the catastrophic anxiety reaction and depression. This observation has been made by clinical observation[67,96] and on psychologic testing using the Minnesota Multiphasic Personality Inventory.[26,123] Within this group of patients with left-hemisphere damage, it is the aphasics and most particularly the Broca's aphasics who have the greatest abnormality.[11,67] Wernicke's aphasics, conversely, demonstrate a very different personality reaction. These patients show indifference rather than anxiety, and paranoia rather than depression.[11,67]

Damage to the right hemisphere causes a considerably different clinical picture than that of similar left-hemisphere damage. Such patients demonstrate a remarkable lack of emotional response and often display the type of apathy seen in patients with frontal damage.[67,95] They are indifferent to their surroundings and, in general, seem to have lost the ability to appreciate and produce appropriate emotional subtleties. Their appreciation of humorous situations is greatly affected, and they tend to respond either with an exaggerated response or none at all.[69] They are largely unable to discriminate and identify the emotional quality or tone of someone's voice and also are reduced in their ability to evoke specific emotional expression.[172] From these observations, it appears that the right hemisphere develops, in addition to its cognitive synthetic abilities, a superior ability to synthesize limbic emotional responsivity to environmental experience.

As knowledge of hemispheric function has become more sophisticated, it is now possible for the neuroscientist to ask philosophical questions concerning the anatomic substrate for such concepts as the self-conscious mind. Is self-consciousness a discrete function that is lateralized to one hemisphere or is it a capacity contained by both hemispheres? In the study of commissurotomy patients, it has been observed that each hemisphere is able to analyze sensory input and guide the behavior of the opposite limb, but it is only the left hemisphere that can actually discuss and verbalize its decisions and actions.[72,117] The right hemisphere is a mute worker whose thoughts and feelings can only be inferred verbally by the left hemisphere's observation of the right's behavior.[72] As is fitting, the workers in this field are split on their interpretation of these observations. Some say that it is only the verbal left hemisphere that is truly self-conscious because of its ability to verbally reflect on its activity,[72] whereas others claim that the mute right hemisphere can make decisions involving judgments and goal setting and therefore is also conscious in its own right.

Popper, the philosopher, and Eccles, the Nobel Laureate in neurophysiology, have queried this same issue in an interesting book titled, *The Self and Its Brain*.[146] These men's opinions are also divided: Eccles believes strongly that the verbal reflectiveness of the left hemisphere is the necessary feature of the human's self-conscious mind; whereas Popper, fully realizing that the self-consciousness of the mute hemisphere is not as developed as the questioning and rhetorical left hemisphere, believes that the right hemisphere has a level of true self-consciousness that may in some ways be similar to the crude self-consciousness experienced by higher animals. The issue is both fascinating and exciting; the study of the brain's activity has now reached a level at which these age-old questions of the philosopher can now be discussed in more than mere abstraction.

NEUROBEHAVIORAL EVALUATION

A complete mental status examination, as outlined in Chapter 3, is particularly useful in diagnosing the focal syndromes. Focal brain disease tends to cause isolated defects in behavior or typical symptom clusters while frequently completely sparing other functions. With a complete examination, the defects stand out sharply against the background of normal functioning and suggest the focal lesion.

Again, it is necessary to evaluate handedness and familial handedness when localizing focal lesions. This is of greatest importance in assessing disorders involving language but should be ascertained in all cases.

MEDICAL EVALUATION

A complete medical and neurologic history and examination are necessary. Specific attention should be paid to the following factors:

I. Onset of symptoms: Acute onset suggests a vascular accident; a slowly progressive onset indicates an expanding mass in most cases
II. History of medical disease (e.g., vascular disease, trauma, cancer)
III. Seizures
IV. Focal neurologic signs

DIFFERENTIAL DIAGNOSIS

Unilateral Hemispheric Lesions

The differential diagnosis of unilateral hemispheric lesions is straightforward and is well discussed in most standard neurologic texts. The primary lesions are:

I. Acute
   A. Cerebral vascular accidents
   B. Migraine: Usually very short lived (<12 hours)
   C. Bleeding into tumor
   D. Trauma
II. Slowly progressive deficit
   A. Tumor: Primary or metastatic
   B. Abscess
   C. Cyst
   D. Subdural lesion

Bilateral Hemispheric Lesions

The differential diagnosis of the bilateral syndromes is somewhat different. The frontal lobe syndrome can be caused by various conditions including frontal tumors (gliomas, metastatic lesions, subfrontal and peri-sagittal meningiomas, and large pituitary tumors), hydrocephalus, general paresis, Huntington's chorea, Pick's disease, alcoholic and Parkinson's dementia, other frontal masses such as abscess or cyst, and head trauma. The amnesic syndrome from bilateral limbic damage is most commonly seen secondary to trauma but can occur with alcoholism, encephalitis, discrete vascular lesions, and rarely, a tumor in the region of the posterior third ventricle and upper midbrain.

LABORATORY EVALUATION

Laboratory tests consist primarily of brain scans and cerebral contrast studies, but certain general screening tests should also be obtained.

1. Complete blood profile
2. Sedimentation rate
3. Coagulation studies
4. Sickle cell preparation or hemoglobin electrophoresis if indicated
5. Serologic test for syphilis
6. Chest and skull x-rays
7. Electrocardiogram

The specific neurodiagnostic test in evaluating focal intracranial lesions is the computerized tomography (CT) scan or magnetic resonance imaging (MRI). The electroencephalogram is sometimes helpful in focal disease, but only in cases in which no clear-cut lateralizing signs are found on other components of the evaluation. When evaluating a left-handed patient or one with a strong family history of left handedness, the physician should do the intracarotid sodium amytal (Wada) test during arteriography to establish language dominance.[178]

CONSULTATIONS

Neurologic or neurosurgical consultation should be obtained in most cases of focal brain disease. Early in the course of the patient's illness, a full neuropsychologic evaluation should be completed. This evaluation serves many purposes: It can further delineate the deficit diagnosed on the mental status examination, it quantifies the extent of the deficit, and it outlines the patient's residual strengths. The neuropsychologist can also be extremely helpful in interpreting the nature and significance of the behavioral deficit to the family.

In the aphasic patient, it is often useful to have the speech pathologist see the patient early in the evaluation, even though therapy may not be initiated at that time. The speech pathologist can assess the language problem and help the patient, his family, and the medical personnel understand the patient's language limitations. This explanation often relieves anxiety and helps establish a sensible communication system.

PATIENT MANAGEMENT

The medical or neurosurgical management of strokes, brain tumors, and other such focal brain lesions is a broad subject and is described in more generalized medical, neurologic, and neurosurgical texts. Here we emphasize the elements of comprehensive rehabilitation rather than the basic medical management. Because many focal lesions are isolated events in the lives of the patients (and do not represent progressive diseases), the prognosis for survival is often good. The direction of long-term management, then, is rehabilitative rather than medical. This rehabilitation is a lengthy process that usually starts with a period of intensive inpatient evaluation and therapy.

Initially, comprehensive evaluations should be done by the rehabilitation physician, the neuropsychologist, the speech pathologist, and the physical and occupational therapists. This evaluation will outline both the physical and cognitive strengths and weaknesses so that a full rehabilitation program can be started. This extensive evaluation and treatment program is usually begun several weeks after the initial hospitalization (physical therapists may be seeing the patient much earlier, but a comprehensive rehabilitative effort usually awaits the passing of the acute medical or surgical period).

In the rehabilitation setting, the physical therapist is involved primarily in gross motor and gait training, whereas the occupational therapist is concerned mostly with fine motor control of the hands and the skills involved in the routine activities of daily living. The speech pathologist can be of assistance in articulation problems, buccofacial apraxia, and certain aphasic disturbances. Global aphasia and severe Wernicke's aphasia do not respond well to standard speech therapy; therefore any speech pathologist working with these patients should concentrate on other communication systems among the family members (e.g., picture cards, sign language).

A number of specific behavioral deficits that may not be obvious at first can significantly interfere with the rehabilitative effort and cause considerable frustration and wasted time if not recognized. The apathy and lack of motivation associated with frontal-lobe damage is one such factor. Trauma, postoperative aneurysm, or tumor patients with frontal lobe damage often do not put an enthusiastic effort into therapy and thus gain little. Frequently, the therapist misinterprets the organically based apathy as a depression, laziness, or lack of cooperation; such a misunderstanding often engenders an unjustifiable hostility and makes an already difficult situation impossible. Unfortunately, rehabilitation, particularly vocational rehabilitation, of patients with damaged frontal lobes is frequently unsuccessful.

Another problem is caused by the neglect or unilateral inattention seen with right-hemisphere lesions. When these patients have a hemiplegia, their unilateral neglect causes them to attempt full use of the affected limb and they fall. Such a patient must be continually cajoled into moving only after he has gotten himself into a secure standing position with his brace on. These patients may take many months to achieve what a patient without unilateral neglect may achieve in only a few weeks. Patients with right-hemisphere lesions may also have some of the features of apathy or euphoria seen in the frontal–lobe-damaged patient; these emotional changes add yet another obstacle to rehabilitation.

Ideomotor apraxia is a behavioral deficit that can be a problem in retraining fine motor control. Because the apraxia can be present in both hands, switching to the nonpreferred hand does not always solve the problem. Fortunately, the use of real objects is the simplest possible level of fine motor control for the apraxic, so many can carry out actual daily living activities although they cannot follow limb movement commands on verbal request or by imitation. In severely apraxic patients, however, fine motor coordination as well as gross movements may be affected and cause a lasting disability in carrying out complex movements.

A significant memory deficit almost precludes success in any type of rehabilitation effort that requires learning. Paralyzed limbs can be worked with and basic exercises can be done, but there will be little if any carry over from session to session. In general, the amnesic patient requires supervised care regardless of the level of his motor functioning. He can rarely be independent because he cannot remember to pay bills, go to a job, find his way home, or keep in order any of the thousands of details necessary for daily living.

A further problem that should not go unnoticed, if an adequate evaluation has been completed, is the presence of an underlying dementia or bilateral hemispheric disease. Bilateral disease greatly increases the general disability and decreases the chances for successful recovery. If the underlying disease is a progressive cerebral atrophy, rehabilitative efforts should be limited to basic self-care activities and not include vocational rehabilitation. Other bilateral disease, such as that after trauma, must be recognized as a possible impediment to recovery, but an effort should be made to maximize all existing capacities.

A final element that frequently impairs full effort and benefit from therapy is the patient's superimposed emotional responses, usually a reactive depression. Although many of the emotional changes seen in brain damage are organic, a significant proportion are undoubtedly due to the patient's emotional reaction to his illness. In such cases, it is best to consult a psychiatric colleague to assist the patient in dealing with his loss. This very important aspect of rehabilitation is all too often left to the therapist to try to cure with mere encouragement and friendly reinforcement.

In any rehabilitation effort, particularly those dealing with young patients, serious attention must be paid to the eventual vocational possibilities of the patient. In some patients, the disability is obviously too great for the patient to return to his previous work, but in many cases careful planning and counseling can lead to gainful employment. Vocational services should become involved with the patients from their entrance into the program and gather background information on premorbid education and training and carefully assess the psychological test scores to help the patient choose a suitable and realistic vocation. It is often impossible to judge in the abstract setting of the hospital how a patient will readjust vocationally. In those cases in which recovery seems to be especially good, we arrange for the patients to return to work or try a new job for a while and have their supervisors report on the adequacy of their performance.

Throughout the rehabilitation period, it is critical to carefully discuss the progress, goals, and future plans for the patient with both the patient and his family. This family counseling is critical and should be a continual dialogue after discharge. If social workers are available, they can be helpful in working with the family and should become involved early in the patient's hospitalization. Social service workers are acquainted with the facilities and other resources in the community and can coordinate care and training after the period of hospitalization.

Rehabilitation after a focal brain lesion is often slow, with improvement seen over many months or years. Periodic reassessment is necessary to determine when a plateau is reached and maximum hospital benefits have been achieved. By this time, an outpatient plan should have been made, and the patient should be discharged to home or to a free-standing rehabilitation facility before the syndrome of chronic overhospitalization sets in and the patient begins to lose ground from sheer boredom.

REFERENCES

1. Alajouanine, T: Aphasia and artistic realizations. Brain 71:229, 1948.
2. Albert, M, Reches, A, and Silverberg, R: Associative visual agnosia without alexia. Neurology 25:322, 1975.
3. Albert, M et al: The anatomic basis of visual agnosia. Neurology 29:876, 1979; 30:109, 1980.
4. Albert, M et al: A case study of auditory agnosia: Linguistic and non-linguistic processing. Cortex 8:427, 1972.

5. Basso, A et al: Anatomoclinical correlations of the aphasias as defined through computerized tomography: Exceptions. Brain Lang 26:201, 1985.
6. Basso, A, Taborelli, A, and Vignolo, A: Dissociated disorder of speaking and writing in aphasia. J Neurol Neurosurg Psychiatry 41:556, 1978.
7. Baxter, DM and Warrington, EK: Ideational agraphia: A single case study. J Neurol Neurosurg Psychiatry 49:369, 1986.
8. Bender, M: Syndrome of isolated episode of confusion with amnesia. J Hillside Hospital 5:212, 1956.
9. Bender, M and Feldman, M: The so-called "visual agnosias." Brain 95:173, 1972.
10. Benson, DF: Fluency in aphasia: Correlation with radioactive scan localizations. Cortex 3:373, 1967.
11. Benson, DF: Psychiatric aspects of aphasia. Br J Psychiatry 123:555, 1973.
12. Benson, DF: Varieties of anomia. Presented at the Academy of Aphasia, Miami, October, 1976.
13. Benson, DF: The third alexia. Arch Neurol 34:327, 1977.
14. Benson, DF, Gardner, H, and Meadows, JC: Reduplicative amnesia. Neurology 26:147, 1976.
15. Benson, DF and Geschwind, N: Shrinking retrograde amnesia. J Neurol Neurosurg Psychiatry 30:539, 1967.
16. Benson, DF and Geschwind, N: Psychiatric conditions associated with focal lesions of the central nervous system, in Arieti, S (ed): American Handbook of Psychiatry, Vol 4. Basic Books, New York, 1975, pp 208–243.
17. Benson, DF and Greenberg, JP: Visual form agnosia. Arch Neurol 20:82, 1969.
18. Benson, DF, Marsden, C, and Meadows, J: The amnesic syndrome of posterior cerebral artery occlusion. Acta Neurol Scand 50:133, 1974.
19. Benson, DF et al: Conduction aphasia. Arch Neurol 28:339, 1973.
20. Benton, AL: Clinical symptomatology in right and left hemisphere lesions. In Mountcastle, VB (ed): Interhemispheric Relations and Cerebral Dominance. The Johns Hopkins Press, Baltimore, 1962, pp 253–264.
21. Benton, AL: The Amusias, in Critchley, M and Henson, RA (eds): Music and the Brain. Heinemann, London, 1977, pp 378–397.
22. Benton, AL, Meyers, R, and Polder, GJ: Some aspects of handedness. Psychiatr Neurol (Basel) 144:321, 1962.
23. Benton, AL and Van Allen, MW: Prosopagnosia and facial discrimination. J Neurol Sci 15:167, 1972.
24. Bever, TG and Chiarello, RJ: Cerebral dominance in musicians and nonmusicians. Science 185:537, 1974.
25. Bisiach, E et al: Unawareness of disease following lesions of the right hemisphere: Anosognosia for hemiplegia and anosognosia for hemianopia. Neuropsychologia 24:471, 1986.
26. Black, FW: Unilateral brain lesions and MMPI performance: A preliminary study. Percept Mot Skills 40:87, 1975.
27. Blumer, D and Benson, DF: Personality changes with frontal and temporal lobe lesions. In Benson, DF and Blumer, D (eds): Psychiatric Aspects of Neurologic Disease. Grune & Stratton, New York, 1975, pp 151–170.

28. Bogan, JE: The other side of the brain I: Dysgraphia and dyscopia following cerebral commissurotomy. Bulletin of the Los Angeles Neurologic Society 34:73, 1969.
29. Bogan, JE: The other side of the brain II: An appositional mind. Bulletin of the Los Angeles Neurologic Society 34:135, 1969.
30. Bogan, JE: The callosal syndromes. In Heilman, KM and Valenstein, F (eds): Clinical Neuropsychology, ed 2. Oxford University Press, New York, 1985.
31. Bogan, JE and Bogan, CM: The other side of the brain III: The corpus callosum and creativity. Bulletin of the Los Angeles Neurologic Society 34:191, 1969.
32. Bogan, JE and Gordon, HW: Musical tests for functional lateralization with intracarotid amobarbital. Nature 230:524, 1971.
33. Bornstein, B, Sroka, H, and Munitz, H: Prosopagnosia with animal face agnosia. Cortex 5:164, 1969.
34. Brain, WR: Speech Disorders. Aphasia, Apraxia, Agnosia, ed 2. Butterworth, London, 1965.
35. Branch, C, Milner, B, and Rasmussen, T: Intracarotid sodium amytal for the lateralization of cerebral speech dominance. J Neurosurg 21:399, 1964.
36. Bridges, PK and Bartlett, JR: Psychosurgery: Yesterday and today. Br J Psychiatry 131:249, 1977.
37. Brown, JW and Hecaen, H: Lateralization and language representation. Neurology 26:183, 1976.
38. Buchman, AS et al: Word deafness: One hundred years later. J Neurol Neurosurg Psychiatry 49:489, 1986.
39. Butters, N and Miliotis, P: Amnesic disorders, in Heilman, KM and Valenstein, E (eds): Clinical Neuropsychology. Oxford University Press, New York, 1985, p 403–452.
40. Caramazza, A: The logic of neuropsychological research and the problem of patient classification in aphasia. Brain Lang 21:9, 1984.
41. Chamberlain, HD: The inheritance of left handedness. J Hered 19:557, 1928.
42. Chawluk, JB et al: Slowly progressive aphasia without generalized dementia: Studies with positron emission tomography. Ann Neurol 19:68, 1986.
43. Chedru, F and Geschwind, N: Writing disturbances in acute confusional states. Neuropsychologia 10:343, 1972.
44. Clemins, VA: Localized thalamic hemorrhage: A cause of aphasia. Neurology 20:776, 1970.
45. Cohen, D, Schaie, KW, and Gribbin, K: The organization of spatial abilities in older men and women. J Gerontol 35:578, 1977.
46. Critchley, M: The Parietal Lobes. Edward Arnold & Co, London, 1953.
47. Critchley, M: The problem of visual agnosia. J Neurol Sci 1:274, 1964.
48. Critchley, M: Acquired anomalies of colour perception of central origin. Brain 88:711, 1965.
49. Critchley, M and Henson, RA: Music and the Brain. Heinemann, London, 1977.
50. Damasio, AR: Disorders of complex visual processing: Agnosia, achromatopsia, Balint's syndrome, and related difficulties of orientation and construction. In Mesulam, M-M (ed): Principles of Behavioral Neurology. FA Davis, Philadelphia, 1985, pp 259–288.

51. Damasio, AR and Damasio, H: Music faculty and cerebral dominance. In Critchley, M and Henson, RA (eds): Music and the Brain. Heinemann, London, 1977, pp 141–155.
52. Damasio, AR et al: Aphasia with nonhemorrhagic lesions in the basal ganglia and internal capsule. Arch Neurol 39:15, 1982.
53. Damasio, AR, Damasio, H, and VanHoesen, GW: Prosopagnosia: Anatomic basis and behavioral mechanisms. Neurology (NY) 32:331, 1982.
54. Damasio, AR, Ferro, J, and Dimasio, H: Language processing and the thalamus. Presented at the Academy of Aphasia, Miami, October, 1976.
55. Damasio, AR and Kessel, NF: Transcortical motor aphasia in relation to lesions of the supplementary motor area. Presented at the American Academy of Neurology, Los Angeles, April, 1978.
56. Damasio, H and Damasio, AR: Localization lesions in conduction aphasia. In Kertesz, A (ed): Localization in Neuropsychology. Academic Press, New York, 1983, p 231.
57. DeJong, R, Itabashi, H, and Olson, J: Memory loss due to hippocampal lesions. Arch Neurol 20:339, 1969.
58. Denny-Brown, D, Meyer, JS, and Horenstein, S: The significance of perceptual rivalry resulting from parietal lesions. Brain 75:433, 1952.
59. DeRenzi, E et al: Impairment in associating colour to form, concomitant with aphasia. Brain 95:293, 1972.
60. Exner, S: Untersuchungen Uber die lokalization in der Grosshirnrinde des menschen. Wien Wilhelm Braumuller, 1881.
61. Fazio, C, Sacco, C, and Bugiani, O: The thalamic hemorrhage. Eur Neurol 9:30, 1973.
62. Ferriss, GS and Dorsen, MM: Agenesis of the corpus callosum. Cortex 11:95, 1975.
63. Fisher, CM: The pathologic and clinical aspects of thalamic hemorrhage. Trans Am Neurol Assoc 84:56, 1959.
64. Fisher, CM and Adams, RD: Transient global amnesia. Trans Am Neurol Assoc 83:143, 1958.
65. Freeman, W and Watts, JW: Psychosurgery. Charles C Thomas, Springfield, IL, 1950.
66. Friedman, RB and Albert, ML: Alexia. In Heilman, KM and Valenstein, E (eds): Clinical Neuropsychology, ed 2. Oxford University Press, New York, 1985, p 49–73.
67. Gainotti, G: Emotional behavior and hemispheric side of lesion. Cortex 8:41, 1972.
68. Gardner, H: The Shattered Mind. Knopf, New York, 1975.
69. Gardner, H et al: Comprehension and appreciation of humorous material following brain damage. Brain 98:399, 1975.
70. Gassel, MM: Occipital lobe syndromes (excluding hemianopia). In Vinken, PJ and Bruyn, GW (eds): Handbook of Clinical Neurology, Vol 2. 1969.
71. Gazzaniga, MS: The Bisected Brain. Appleton-Century-Crofts, New York, 1970.
72. Gazzaniga, MS, LeDoux, JE, and Wilson, DH: Language, praxis, and the right hemisphere: Clues to some mechanisms of consciousness. Neurology 27:1144, 1977.

73. Gerson, SN, Benson, DF, and Frazier, SH: Diagnosis: Schizophrenia versus posterior aphasia. Am J Psychiatry 134:966, 1977.
74. Gerstmann, J: Some notes on the Gerstmann syndrome. Neurology 7:866, 1957.
75. Geschwind, N: Disconnection syndromes in animals and man: Parts I and II. Brain 88:237;585, 1965.
76. Geschwind, N: Current concepts in aphasia. N Engl J Med 284:654, 1971.
77. Geschwind, N: The apraxias: Neural mechanisms of disorders of learned movement. Am Sci 63:188, 1975.
78. Geschwind, N: Implications of the anatomical asymmetry of the brain. Presented at the Academy of Aphasia, Montreal, October, 1977.
79. Geschwind, N and Galaburda, AM: Cerebral lateralization, part I. Arch Neurol 42:428, 1985.
80. Geschwind, N and Galaburda, AM: Cerebral lateralization, part II. Arch Neurol 42:521, 1985.
81. Geschwind, N and Fusillo, M: Color-naming defects in association with alexia. Arch Neurol 15:137, 1966.
82. Geschwind, N and Kaplan, E: A human cerebral disconnection syndrome. Neurology 12:675, 1962.
83. Geschwind, N and Levitsky, W: Human brain: Left-right asymmetries in temporal speech region. Science 161:186, 1968.
84. Geschwind, N, Quadfasel, F, and Segarra, J: Isolation of the speech area. Neuropsychologia 6:327, 1968.
85. Gloning, K: Handedness and aphasia. Neuropsychologia 15:355, 1977.
86. Goldstein, K: Aftereffects of Brain Injuries in War. Grune & Stratton, New York, 1942.
87. Goodglass, H and Kaplan, E: Assessment of Aphasia and Related Disorders. Lea & Febiger, Philadelphia, 1972.
88. Gordon, HW and Bogan, JE: Hemispheric lateralization of singing after intra-carotid amylobarbitone. J Neurol Neurosurg Psychiatry 37:727, 1974.
89. Green, JB and Hamilton, WJ: Anosognosia for hemiplegia: Somatosensory evoked potential studies. Neurology 26:1141, 1976.
90. Greenblatt, SH: Alexia without agraphia or hemianopsia: Anatomical analysis of an autopsied case. Brain 96:307, 1973.
91. Greenblatt, SH: Localization of lesions in alexia. In Kertesz, A (ed): Localization in Neuropsychology. Academic Press, New York, 1983, pp 323–356.
92. Hardyck, C and Petrinovich, LF: Left-handedness. Psychol Bull 84:385, 1977.
93. Hayward, RW, Naeser, MA, and Zatz, LM: Cranial computed tomography in aphasia. Radiology 123:653, 1977.
94. Heathfield, KWG, Croft, PB, and Swash, M: The syndrome of transient global amnesia. Brain 96:729, 1973.
95. Hecaen, H: Clinical symptomatology in right and left hemispheric lesions. In Mountcastle, VB (ed): Interhemispheric relations and cerebral dominance. Johns Hopkins Press, Baltimore, 1962, pp 215–244.
96. Hecaen, H and Ajuriaguerra, Jde: Left Handedness. Grune & Stratton, New York, 1964.

97. Hecaen, H and Albert, ML: Disorders of mental functioning related to frontal lobe pathology. In Benson, DF and Blumer, D (eds): Psychiatric Aspects of Neurologic Disease. Grune & Stratton, New York, 1975, pp 137–149.

98. Heilman, KM et al: Apraxia and agraphia in a left-hander. Brain 1973; 96:21.

99. Heilman, KM and Sypert, GW: Korsakoff's syndrome resulting from bilateral fornix lesions. Neurology 27:490, 1977.

100. Heilman, KM, Valenstein, E, and Watson, RT: The neglect syndrome. In Vinken, PJ, Bruyn, GW, and Klawans, HL (eds): Clinical Handbook of Neurology, Vol 45. Elsevier, Amsterdam, 1985, p 153.

101. Heilman, KM and Watson, RT: Mechanisms underlying the unilateral neglect syndrome. In Weinstein, EA and Friedland, RP (eds): Hemi-Inattention and Hemispheric Specialization. Raven Press, New York, 1977, pp 93–106.

102. Hemphill, RE and Stengle, E: A study on pure word-deafness. J Neurol Psychiatry 3:251, 1940.

103. Henderson, VW: Speech fluency in crossed aphasia. Brain 106:837, 1983.

104. Hier, DB et al: Hypertensive putamenal hemorrhage. Ann Neurol 1:152, 1977.

105. Holmes, G: Discussion on the mental symptoms associated with cerebral tumors. Proc R Soc Med 24:65, 1931.

106. Hooshmand, H, Sepdham, T, and Vries, JK: Klüver-Bucy syndrome: Successful treatment with carbamazepine. JAMA 229:1782, 1974.

107. Kamalian, N, Keesey, RE, and ZuRheim, GM: Lateral hypothalamic demyelinations and cachexia in a case of "malignant" multiple sclerosis. Neurology 25:25, 1975.

108. Kaplan, E: Personal communication, 1972.

109. Kertesz, A, Lesk, D, and McCabe, P: Isotope localization in infarcts in aphasia. Arch Neurol 34:590, 1977.

110. Keschner, M, Bender, MB, and Strauss, I: Mental symptoms in cases of tumor of the temporal lobe. Arch Neurol Psychiatry 35:572, 1936.

111. Kimura, D: Left-right differences in the perception of melodies. Quart J Exp Psychol 16:355, 1964.

112. Kimura, D: Studies in apraxia. Presented at the Academy of Aphasia, Montreal, October, 1977.

113. Kinsbourne, M: Hemi-neglect and hemisphere rivalry. In Weinstein, EA and Friedland, RP (eds): Hemi-Inattention and Hemispheric Specialization. Raven Press, New York, 1977, pp 41–50.

114. Kinsbourne, M and Warrington, E: A study of finger agnosia. Brain 85:47, 1962.

115. Klüver, H and Bucy, PC: "Psychic blindness" and other symptoms following bilateral temporal lobectomy in rhesus monkeys. Am J Physiol 119:352, 1937.

116. Knopman, DS et al: Recovery of naming in aphasia: Relationship to fluency, comprehension and Ct findings. Neurology 34:1461, 1984.

117. LeDoux, JE, Wilson, DH, Gazzaniga, MS: A divided mind: Observations on the conscious properties of the separated hemispheres. Ann Neurol 2:417, 1977.

118. Lesser, R et al: The location of speech and writing functions in the frontal

language area. Results of extraoperative cortical stimulation. Brain 107:275, 1984.

119. Levine, DN, Warach, J, and Farah, M: Two visual systems in mental imagery: Dissociation of "what" and "where" in imagery disorders due to bilateral posterior cerebral lesions. Neurology 35:1010, 1985.

120. Levy-Agresti, J and Sperry, RW: Differential perceptual capacities in major and minor hemispheres. Proc Natl Acad Sci USA 61:1151, 1968.

121. Lhermitte, F and Beauvois, MF: A visual-speech disconnection syndrome. Brain 96:695, 1973.

122. Lomas, J and Kertesz, A: Pattern of spontaneous recovery in aphasic groups: A study of adult stroke patients. Brain Lang 5:388, 1978.

123. Louks, J, Calsyn, D, and Lindsay, F: Personality dysfunction and lateralized deficits in cerebral functions as measured by the MMPI and Reston-Halstead battery. Percept Mot Skills 43:655, 1976.

124. Ludlow, CL et al: Brain lesions associated with nonfluent aphasia fifteen years following penetrating head injury. Brain 109:55, 1986.

125. Luria, AR: Frontal lobe syndromes. In Vinken, PJ and Bruyn, GW (eds): Handbook of Clinical Neurology, Vol 2. Elsevier, New York, 1969, pp 725–757.

126. Luria, AR: Traumatic Aphasia. Mouton, The Hague, Netherlands, 1970.

127. Luria, AR: On quasi-aphasic disturbances in lesions of the deep structures of the brain. Brain Lang 4:432, 1977.

128. Malamud, N: Psychiatric disorders with intracranial tumors of the limbic system. Arch Neurol 17:113, 1967.

129. Mathew, NT and Meyer, JS: Pathogenesis and natural history of transient global amnesia. Stroke 5:303, 1974.

130. McEntee, WJ et al: Diencephalic amnesia: A reappraisal. J Neurol Neurosurg Psychiatry 39:436, 1976.

131. Meadows, JC: The anatomical basis of prosopagnosia. J Neurol Neurosurg Psychiatry 37:489, 1974.

132. Meadows, JC: Disturbed perception of colours associated with localized cerebral lesions. Brain 97:615, 1974.

133. Mesulam, M-M: Slowly progressive aphasia without generalized dementia. Ann Neurol 11:592, 1982.

134. Metter, EJ et al: Left hemisphere intracerebral hemorrhages studied by (F-18)-fluorodeoxyglucose PET. Neurology 36:1155, 1986.

135. Mettler, FA (ed): Selective Partial Ablation of Frontal Cortex. Hoeber, New York, 1949.

136. Milner, B: Laterality effects in audition. In Mountcastle, VB (ed): Interhemispheric Relations and Cerebral Dominance. Johns Hopkins Press, Baltimore, 1962, pp 177–195.

137. Milner, B: Interhemispheric differences psychological processes. Br Med Bull 27:272, 1971.

138. Mohr, JP: Broca's area and Broca's aphasia. In Whitaker, H and Whitaker, HA (eds): Studies in Neurolinguistics, Vol 1. In Perspectives in Neurolinguistics and Psycholinguistics. Academic Press, New York, 1976.

139. Mohr, JP, Watters, WC, and Duncan, GW: Thalamic hemorrhage and aphasia. Brain Lang 2:3, 1975.

140. Naeser, MA et al: Aphasia with predominantly subcortical lesions sites. Description of three capsular/putaminal aphasia syndromes. Arch Neurol 39:2, 1982.

141. Nielsen, J: Gerstmann syndrome: Finger agnosia, agraphia, confusion of right and left, and acalculia. Arch Neurol Psychiatry 39:536, 1938.

142. Oxbury, JM, Campbell, DC, and Oxbury, SM: Unilateral spatial neglect and impairments of spatial analysis and visual perception. Brain 97:551, 1974.

143. Pick, A: On reduplicative paramnesia. Brain 26:242, 1903.

144. Poeck, K: The clinical examination for motor apraxia. Neuropsychologia 24:129, 1986.

145. Poeck, K, deBleser, R, and Keyserlingk, DG: Neurolinguistic status and localization of lesions in aphasic patients with exclusively consonant-vowel recurring utterances. Brain 107:199, 1984.

146. Popper, KR and Eccles, JC: The Self and Its Brain. Springer-Verlag, New York, 1977.

147. Reeves, AG and Plum, F: Hyperphagia, rage, and dementia accompanying a ventromedial hypothalamic neoplasm. Arch Neurol 20:616, 1969.

148. Roberts, L: Aphasia, apraxia, and agnosia in abnormal states of cerebral dominance. In Vinken, PJ and Bruyn, GW (eds): Handbook of Clinical Neurology, Vol 4. Elsevier, New York, 1969, pp 312–326.

149. Roland, PE: Astereognosis. Arch Neurol 33:543, 1976.

150. Ross, ED: The aprosodias: Functional-anatomic organization of the affective components of language in the right hemisphere. Arch Neurol 38:561, 1981.

151. Rubens, AB: Aphasia with infarction in the territory of the anterior cerebral artery. Cortex 11:239, 1975.

152. Rubens, A and Benson, D: Associative visual agnosia. Arch Neurol 24:305, 1971.

153. Rubens, A and Benson, D: Aphasia with thalamic hemorrhage. Presented at the Academy of Aphasia, Miami, October, 1976.

154. Russell, WR and Espir, MLE: Traumatic aphasia. Oxford University Press, London and New York, 1961.

155. Saffran, EM: Neuropsychological approaches to the study of language. Br J Psychol 73:317, 1982.

156. Samarel, A et al: Thalamic hemorrhage with speech disorder. Trans Am Neurol Assoc 101:283, 1976.

157. Sanders, MD et al: "Blindsight:" Vision in a field defect. Lancet 2:707, 1974.

158. Sarno, MT, Silverman, M, and Sands, E: Speech therapy and language recovery in severe aphasia. J Speech Hear Res 13:607, 1970.

159. Satz, P: Pathological left-handedness: An explanatory model. Cortex 8:121, 1972.

160. Satz, P: Left handedness and early brain insult: An explanation. Neuropsychologia 11:115, 1973.

161. Scoville, W and Milner, B: Loss of recent memory after bilateral hippocampal lesions. J Neurol Neurosurg Psychiatry 20:11, 1957.

162. Selnes, OA et al: Computed tomographic scan correlates of auditory compre-

hension deficits in aphasia: A prospective recovery study. Ann Neurol 13:558, 1983.

163. Selzer, B and Benson, DF: The temporal pattern of retrograde amnesia in Korsakoff's disease. Neurology 24:527, 1974.

164. Shuping, JR, Rollinson, RD, and Toole, JF: Transient global amnesia. Ann Neurol 7:281, 1980.

165. Smith, A: Dominant and nondominant hemispherectomy. In Kinsbourne, M and Smith, WL (eds): Hemispheric disconnection and cerebral function. Charles C Thomas, Springfield, IL, 1974, pp 5–33.

166. Strauss, I and Keschner, M: Mental symptoms in cases of tumor of the frontal lobe. Arch Neurol Psychiatry 33:986, 1935.

167. Strub, RL and Geschwind, N: Localization in Gerstmann Syndrome. In Kertesz, A (ed): Localization in Neuropsychology. Academic Press, New York, 1983, pp 295–321.

168. Stuss, DT and Benson, DF: The Frontal Lobes. Raven Press, New York, 1986.

169. Subirana, A: Handedness and cerebral dominance. In Vinken, PJ and Bruyn, GW (eds): Handbook of Clinical Neurology, Vol 4. Elsevier, New York, 1969, pp 248–272.

170. Sweet, WH: Treatment of medically intractable mental disease by limited frontal leucotomy—justifiable? N Engl J Med 289:1117, 1973.

171. Terzian, H and Ore, GD: Syndrome of Klüver and Bucy: Reproduced in man by bilateral removal of the temporal lobes. Neurology 5:373, 1955.

172. Tucker, DM, Watson, RT, and Heilman, KM: Discrimination and evocation of affectively intoned speech in patients with right parietal disease. Neurology 27:947, 1977.

173. Vallar, G and Perani, D: The anatomy of unilateral neglect after right-hemisphere stroke lesions: A clinical/CT-scan correlation study in man. Neuropsychologia 24:609, 1986.

174. Victor, M: The Wernicke-Korsakoff syndrome. In Vinken, PJ and Bruyn, GW (eds): Handbook of Clinical Neurology, Vol 28. Elsevier, New York, 1976, pp 243–270.

175. Victor, M, Adams, R, and Collins, G: The Wernicke-Korsakoff Syndrome. FA Davis, Philadelphia, 1971.

176. Vignolo, L: The localization of aphasia-producing lesions: Clinical-anatomical correlations with computerized axial tomography (EMI scanning). Presented at the Academy of Aphasia, Montreal, October, 1977.

177. Vignolo, LA et al: Unexpected CT-scan findings in global aphasia. Cortex 22:55, 1986.

178. Wada, J and Rasmussen, T: Intracarotid injection of sodium amytal for the lateralization of cerebral speech dominance. Experimental and clinical observation. J Neurosurg 17:266, 1960.

179. Warrington, EK: Neuropsychological evidence for multiple memory systems. Acta Neurol Scand 64 (Suppl 89):13, 1981.

180. Watson, RT, Andriola, M, and Heilman, KM: The electroencephalogram in neglect. J Neurol Sci 34:343, 1977.

181. Watson, RT et al: Apraxia and the supplementary motor area. Arch Neurol 43:787, 1986.
182. Watson, RT and Heilman, KM: Thalamic neglect. Neurology 29:690, 1979.
183. Watson, RT et al: Neglect after mesencephalic reticular formation lesions. Neurology 24:194, 1974.
184. Weinstein, EA and Friedland, RP (eds): Advances in Neurology, Vol 18, Hemi-Inattention and Hemispheric Specialization. Raven Press, New York, 1977.
185. Weinstein, EA and Friedland, RP: Behavioral disorders associated with hemi-inattention. In Weinstein, EA and Friedland, RP (eds): Advances in Neurology, Vol 18, Hemi-Inattention and Hemispheric Specialization. Raven Press, New York, 1977, pp 51–62.
186. Weinstein, EA and Kahn, RL: Denial of illness. Charles C Thomas, Springfield, IL, 1955.
187. Wertheim, N: The amusias. In Vinken, PJ and Bruyn, GW (eds): Handbook of Clinical Neurology, Vol 4. Elsevier, New York, 1969, pp 195–206.
188. White, LE and Hain, RF: Anorexia in association with a destructive lesion of the hypothalamus. Arch Pathol 68:275, 1959.
189. Whiteley, AM and Warrington, EK: Prosopagnosia: A clinical, psychological, and anatomical study of three patients. J Neurol Neurosurg Psychiatry 40:395, 1977.
190. Witelson, SF and Pallie, W: Left hemisphere specialization for language in the newborn: Neuroanatomical evidence of asymmetry. Brain 96:641, 1973.
191. Zangwill, OL: Personal communication, 1977.
192. Zangwill, OL: Aphasia associated with lesions of the right hemisphere. Presented at the Academy of Aphasia, Montreal, October, 1977.

SECTION III

NEUROBEHAVIORAL SYNDROMES OF SPECIFIC ETIOLOGIES

Chapter 9

Closed Head Trauma

A 48-year-old woman was involved in an automobile accident about 7 months before our seeing her. The accident had been relatively mild; she had struck her head on the windshield of the car and was unconscious for only a few minutes. She had a post-traumatic amnesia of less than 15 min and virtually no retrograde amnesia. Her major complaint after the accident was a rather persistent headache of several months' duration. As the headache lessened, however, she stated, "I just don't feel right." She complained of not having the energy that she previously had and described herself as being extremely apathetic about everything since the injury. Before the accident, she was very active in many social activities, but she had given up much of this subsequently. Even though she was generally less concerned about major events, she found herself irritated by minor problems. She said that she "just cannot cope" with certain situations. In addition to this personality change, she complained of mild memory problems and a definite problem with keeping her checkbook up and with shopping calculations. She stated that she always kept the household accounts because she was good at such matters and enjoyed doing it. Now she was not as quick to do the work and had been "messing up the checkbook" regularly. She previously was able to go shopping, write a series of checks, and then return home and record them accurately but was now unable to do this.

Standard neurologic testing revealed no abnormalities, and she reported no complaints other than the previously stated behavioral ones. On mental status testing she was attentive, nonaphasic, and learned new material relatively well, but when asked about recent events in the local, national, and world news, her responses were very sketchy. Although not aphasic, her discourse was somewhat vague. Not having known the woman before the accident, we were not certain that this was a departure from her normal style of conversation. Her calculations were accurate but very slow, as were her drawings. Proverb interpretation and similarities were also within normal limits.

The changes in this patient exemplify the cognitive and behavioral changes that can be seen after mild head trauma. Such subtle behavioral changes frequently are not recognized by physicians, especially when findings on the standard neurologic examination are normal. In cases in which the patient or his family have specific behavioral complaints, it is not uncommon for the physician to ascribe these to an emotional reaction from the accident. The patient with a mild concussion, for instance, may experience difficulty concentrating for several weeks. If such a patient returns to work prematurely, the difficulty he experiences in carrying out his work can easily be very frustrating to him and will often be misinterpreted by his employer as being a deliberate attempt to receive additional compensation or time off from work.

This failure to recognize behavioral sequelae may at times be a problem in major head trauma as well. We received a frantic call one day from an exasperated physical therapist who told us that she was working with a young woman who absolutely would not cooperate or follow any instructions. On examination, the patient had evidence of imbalance and spasticity but in addition had a moderately severe ideomotor apraxia and a substantial problem with auditory comprehension. Not only did the patient fail to understand much of what was requested of her, but what she could understand verbally, she could not execute motorically. In both of these examples, a great deal of frustration and misunderstanding could have been avoided if the behavioral problems had been recognized early in the post-traumatic period.

Head trauma is a medical and social problem of enormous magnitude. It is currently the third leading cause of death in the United States; ironically because of the increased sophistication of medical and surgical treatment, many patients now survive injuries that would previously have proved fatal,[51] only to live a life of significant disability. Recent estimates suggest an annual incidence of more than 500,000 new cases of serious head injury per year.[37] The National Head Injury Foundation estimates that at least 50,000 of these patients are rendered chronically disabled each year.[23] In addition to these figures reflecting hospitalized brain-damaged patients, an unknown, but substantial, number of patients suffer less medically seriously injuries that also place the patient at risk for neurobehavioral changes. McLean and associates[77] indicated that patients with closed head trauma often judged to be "mild" in fact suffer persisting symptoms that serve as deterrents to successful social-vocational adjustment. The social, emotional, and economic consequences are even more apparent given the male-female ratio of incidence figures (about 2:1) and the age distribution, which peaks between 15 to 24 for whites and 25 to 40 for blacks.[37] The available epidemiologic data are unquestionable: head trauma is a public health problem of major significance that results in multiple neurobehavioral problems for many patients, devastating emotional impacts on the patients' families, and serious economic consequences for society.

It is important to define some of the basic terms used in discussing head trauma before describing the details of clinical post-traumatic syndromes. The first, and in many ways the most complicated, is *concussion*. No definition can satisfactorily encompass all variations of concussion, but two central features are constant: (1) concussion results from a mechanical impact to the head or an abrupt acceleration-deceleration impact of the brain within the skull, and (2) neural function is immediately impaired.[1,2,28] The nature of the impairment of neural function, however, has been difficult to define. Loss of consciousness has often been given as the essential feature and, when present, certainly does indicate concussion. Many significant blows to the head, however, merely daze or stun the patient and do not render him unconscious (football games and boxing matches often produce such instances). Immediately after the trauma, these patients experience varying periods of confused thinking, lethargy, or post-traumatic amnesia, but maintain consciousness. Certainly, the blows did disrupt normal neural functioning, and we maintain that these patients did sustain a concussion.

Another aspect of concussion, which has been considered the requisite feature by some, is a period of absolute amnesia.[36,95,97,112] The amnesic period is measured from the last memory before the trauma (retrograde amnesia) to the point of complete return to continuous memory (anterograde amnesia); the term *post-traumatic amnesia* includes both retrograde and anterograde amnesia. Recovery must be to the point of full orientation, not merely a return to consciousness. Almost all patients with concussions have a period of amnesia that extends beyond the period of unconsciousness. Although a period of permanent memory loss, with or without loss of consciousness, is found in most cases of concussion, in some unusual cases neither amnesia nor loss of consciousness is present. The following case illustrates this point.

A 27-year-old woman was driving on the highway at 55 miles per hour when her car hit the middle divider, and she lost control. The car rolled over several times, and her left occiput was struck with sufficient force to give her a traumatic neuropathy of the occipital nerve but not to render her unconscious. She was dazed and very lethargic for at least 12 hours. During this period, she could not remember the accident or what was done at the hospital. She was also somewhat disoriented as to time. The following day, however, the patient was fully alert, oriented, and could clearly remember all details of the accident and the events subsequent to it. She had no period of permanent amnesia, either retrograde or anterograde. In our opinion, although there was neither a loss of consciousness nor a permanent period of amnesia, this patient had suffered a mild concussion.

Another feature of concussion that has been debated is the question of its reversibility. Many standard definitions of concussion require that the patient's neurologic deficit return completely to premorbid levels and that there be no residual brain damage. We, however, agree with Symonds[104] that this is too rigid a definition and feel that persons sustaining simple concussive injuries may have mild resultant neurologic and cognitive impairment.[2] Being cognizant of the limitations discussed above, we define a concussion as an acute impairment of cerebral function secondary to an impact injury to the head or brain in which the following are usually, but not invariably, present: amnesia, loss of consciousness, and complete recovery.

Once concussion is defined, another problem is the establishment of parameters by which to determine the degree of severity. This is very important because prognosis is closely allied to the severity of the injury.[65] Again, considerable dispute is reflected in the literature. In general, both the length of coma (unconsciousness) and post-traumatic amnesia are directly related to the subsequent prognosis. The relationship between post-traumatic amnesia (PTA) and prognosis has received the most attention.[10,53,62,78,95] The correlation between amnesia and prognosis has been found to be much greater in patients over the age of 30[15] but is also a useful clinical indicator with younger patients. We use the following classification system:

Degree of Severity	Duration of PTA
Slight concussion	0 to 15 minutes
Mild concussion	15 minutes to 1 hour
Moderate concussion	1 to 24 hours
Severe concussion	1 to 7 days
Very severe concussion	>7 days

Another term commonly used in describing patients with head trauma is *cerebral contusion*. This diagnostic label is often applied to any patient who has a residual neurologic deficit after closed head trauma. We believe that this is a misapplication of the term for two reasons: (1) contusion is not a clinical term but refers to a pathologic condition in which superficial damage has been done to the crest of the cortical convolutions and on the inferior surfaces of the frontal and temporal lobes secondary to trauma, literally a "brain bruise,"[1,102] and (2) not all patients with contusions have residual neurologic signs, nor do all patients with residual neurologic signs have cortical contusions. Brain damage with contusions tends to be focal, although there may be multiple areas of damage. As will be discussed later, most of the brain damage resulting from severe closed head trauma is primarily located in subcortical structures and white matter.

Diffuse axonal injury in the white matter is now considered to be the most prominent mechanism of traumatic brain damage.[106] It refers to damage characterized by (1) a focal lesion in the corpus callosum, (2) a focal lesion in one or both dorsolateral quadrants of the rostral brain stem, and (3) evidence of diffuse injury to axons.[1] This is seen in severe injuries, usually resulting in death; most patients remain in a vegetative state until death. A less severe, but serious, form of damage results from a shearing injury to neuronal tissue caused by rapid acceleration-deceleration or rotational movements of the brain within the cranial vault. Brain swelling, hypoxia, and vascular disruption may also contribute to this type of injury. Such damage tends to be diffused and to result in a variety of neurobehavioral deficits. Persisting postconcussion symptoms after seemingly mild head injury may be the result of shearing damage.

The final term to be considered is *traumatic encephalopathy*, which is used in cases of residual clinical evidence of brain damage from trauma.

The term is not restricted to closed, uncomplicated head trauma but may be applied to the sequelae of hematomas (extradural, subdural, and intracerebral), brain lacerations, or open head wounds.

It is unfortunate that standard definitions are not consistently applied by each investigator, for the resultant looseness in terminology makes comparing results from one study to the next virtually impossible. Although admittedly all cases cannot neatly fit within any one group of definitions or classification scheme, an effort toward standardization will yield significant clinical and scientific rewards.

DESCRIPTION OF THE CLINICAL SYNDROMES

Minor Head Injury (Without Gross Neurologic Findings)

In less serious concussive injuries, patients experience a fairly standard series of events during the initial and early post-traumatic period. With the initial impact, there is usually a general paralysis of nervous function that is characterized by loss of muscle tone causing the patient to drop to the ground motionless. Consciousness, reflexes, and respiration are lost concomitantly.[30,95]

In most cases of minor injury, the unconscious patient lies motionless for only a few seconds to a few minutes. Respiration quickly returns, and the patient soon thereafter becomes restless and begins to regain consciousness. During this initial period of consciousness, the patient is usually irritable, apathetic, confusional, and occasionally uncontrollable and abusive. Autonomic dysfunction is common, with nausea, vomiting, hypothermia, and alterations of pulse and blood pressure being the principal vegetative phenomena. This unstable confusional period usually lasts less than 24 hours. During this time, patients act somewhat purposefully but will frequently question what has happened and will not recall anything concerning the injury. Behavior is often similar to that displayed by a patient during an episode of transient global amnesia. The patients are unable to learn during this time, and most have a retrograde amnesia covering hours, days, or even years before the accident.

In cases in which the blow does not render the recipient unconscious, he appears dazed and may go through the motions of purposeful activity but is actually both confused and disoriented. This latter situation is best exemplified in sports injuries where a player may continue the game or boxing match even though he may have no memory of it the following day. Dazed boxers have been known to complete a fight without anyone realizing that they were concussed (probably because boxing is an overlearned, almost automatic, activity). With the football player (North American football) who must remember plays and signals called at the beginning of each play, the extent of the head injury is soon realized when he commits an obvious error.

The confusional period fades to the point of normal functioning in most cases, but at times the patients seem to suddenly "snap out of it" and say, "Hey, what am I doing here, and what's going on?" The concussive period is considered over when the patient becomes fully oriented and full consciousness has been achieved. Full consciousness refers to the ability to remember all ongoing events and to maintain orientation.[104] At this point, the patient can be questioned concerning his memory of the preceding events, and post-traumatic amnesia can be established. The retrograde amnesia is usually short, almost always less than 30 min, and usually only a few seconds in duration.[95] The anterograde amnesia is usually much longer but, in most cases of minor injury, lasts less than 24 hours.

Several interesting features of these amnesic periods are of both practical and theoretical importance. The first is the period of retrograde amnesia. In most cases, this period of amnesia shortens as the patient recovers.[9] Events before the injury are at first unknown or indistinct, but with the passage of time, the patient is able to retrieve details that are closer to the time of impact. In the typical case, it is only the few seconds immediately before the accident that are lost forever. Some cases have been reported, however, in which the retrograde amnesia actually lengthens. This has been described in both severe injuries[100] and in the minor concussions without loss of consciousness seen in football players.[115] In several football players, the memory of the play that resulted in injury was present on initial examination immediately after their head injury but was lost on subsequent examination after conclusion of the game.[115] In these latter cases, the memories of the play were most probably retained in short-term or immediate memory but, as a result of trauma to the limbic system, could not be consolidated, stored, and retrieved from long-term or permanent memory. In cases of more severe injuries, this explanation would not hold, because the time for recovery of consciousness is longer than the period for which information can be held in short-term memory. The patient's account of an automobile accident or blow to the head by an assailant is often of critical legal importance—if initial questioning soon after injury does not reveal the pertinent information, the facts may be retrievable at a later time in those cases in which the amnesic period shrinks.

The period of anterograde amnesia is not always absolute. The patient's memory for events occurring during the confusional period is usually permanently lost, but the confusional behavior characteristically fluctuates so dramatically, the lucid periods may leave islands of memory in the sea of amnesia.[95] Even after the confusion has cleared and the patient appears to be remembering normally during examination, memories may still not be fully consolidated, and events of one day may be forgotten on the next. In such cases, the total post-traumatic amnesia can actually lengthen after consciousness has been regained.

After return to full consciousness and assurance by the physician that the results of the neurologic examination are normal, the patient with a concussion of mild or moderate degree is usually discharged from the emergency room or hospital. He is encouraged to remain at home for several days and then to slowly return to a normal working routine. During this post-traumatic period, subtle organic behavioral defects may be unappreciated for what they are and blamed on the patient's emotional reaction or his desire for compensation. Careful studies of postconcussive patients within days of injury, however, suggest clear evidence of cognitive and emotional changes directly attributable to disrupted brain physiology.[10] The problems experienced by mildly brain-injured patients tend to be similar in quality to those experienced by more seriously injured patients, differing only in degree because of differences in degree of brain damage.[4] It is extremely important for the physician to discuss these symptoms with the patient before discharge. By being understanding and sympathetically supportive, many of the problems can be easily handled without undue anxiety.

One of the more common problems that we encounter clinically is the patient with complaints of continuing memory and concentration difficulties. The patient feels well enough to return to work but finds that he cannot keep his mind on the job and forgets details that were easily retained previously. Because the medical release mentions no neurologic abnormalities, employers often interpret the patient's complaints as a deliberate attempt to avoid work or get a greater amount of compensation. The patient is caught between his very real problems and the normal neurologic examination. Gronwall and co-workers[40,41] and others have studied this problem extensively and have convincingly demonstrated the difficulty that the postconcussive patient has in processing incoming information. The deficit, which has been demonstrated in a paced serial addition test and selective reminding tasks, correlated positively with the length of post-traumatic amnesia. Performance gradually returned to normal levels 35 days after injury in all patients with amnesia of less than 1 hour and 54 days after injury in those with amnesia of 1 to 24 hours. The difficulty experienced by the patients during the recovery period was attributed to fatigue, inattention, and defects in rapid information processing. As with many sequelae of head trauma, older patients and patients with previous head trauma fared poorly in contrast to those who were younger.

Persistent memory difficulty is also a major complaint and shows a relationship to post-traumatic amnesia and age. In one series, 59 percent of patients with mild head injury and 90 percent of moderately injured patients reported memory problems.[89,90] In patients with no amnesia, no symptoms of memory difficulty are found. With amnesia of less than 5 minutes duration, approximately 1 patient in 20 will complain; with 5 to 15 minutes of amnesia, 1 in 10 will complain; and with 1 to 4 hours of amnesia, 40 percent will have both memory and concentration problems.[46] Again, these complaints in the patient with mild or moderate concussion are usually transient, with full recovery over time. Residual lingering deficits are not uncommon, however, occurring in up to 15 percent of patients studied 1 year postinjury.[98]

In conjunction with memory and concentration problems, many patients experience one or more other psychologic symptoms. Anxiety, fear, insomnia, restlessness, fatigue, and nervousness have been described in as high as 80 percent of patients with recent head injury.[28] These symptoms tend to be more prominent during the second week after the injury[67] and subside in most patients, as do the other symptoms, during the first month to 6 weeks after the injury.

Other than problems with information processing and memory difficulty, disturbances of higher cognitive function are rare with minor head trauma unless a subsequent subdural hematoma develops. Aphasia, for example, was seen in only 13 of 750 patients with closed head injury admitted to a large neurosurgical service.[44] The aphasia was usually not severe and was primarily anomic. Constructional apraxia is very rarely reported in patients with mild head injury.[10] Such cognitive deficits are much more frequent in cases of penetrating brain wounds or severe closed head injury with or without concomitant hematoma formation or brain laceration.

Two other nonbehavioral symptoms that very commonly occur after closed head injury should be mentioned to complete the description of the post-traumatic syndrome. These are headache and dizziness. These symptoms usually appear during the first 24 hours after injury but may be delayed in their onset for days or even weeks. Headache is a very prominent symptom and is reported in 60 to 95 percent of all such patients.[25,28,46] Dizziness, although relatively less common, is seen in over half of the patients during the initial post-traumatic period.

Concentration difficulties, memory problems, emotional changes, insomnia, headache, and dizziness in the weeks after closed head trauma are sufficiently common that these symptoms, in various combinations, have been labeled the "post-traumatic" or "post-concussive" syndrome. The syndrome varies in intensity and complexity, and no specific cluster of symptoms appears to be more common than any other.[10,25,26,28,46,77] In general, half of these patients will be symptom-free in 6 weeks; conversely there are patients whose complaints persist for over a year.[97] Many patients report persistent subjective complaints that cannot be documented by currently available assessment techniques.[77] This disparity does not minimize the reality of the patients' complaints; rather it points to the need for more refined and systemic studies of these problems. Many factors influence the prognosis and speed of recovery and must be appreciated when treating the individual patient. As is well known, physical exercise, mental aggravation, and use of alcohol can all exacerbate or cause a resurgence of problems. At least two thirds of the patients will have additional trouble in the first few days after discharge from the hospital.[67] This difficulty may be due to physical and/or mental stress but also is partly due to the patients' and their families' perception that they are "supposed" to be well, whereas actually they do not feel completely normal. This unfortunate situation arises primarily because of the physician's failure to adequately advise the patient regarding the possible resurgence of post-traumatic symptoms.

The definition of this post-traumatic syndrome and the determination of its cause have been and remain very problematic. Findings on the neurologic examination and CT scan are usually normal, as are the EEG and other neurodiagnostic tests. For this reason, some physicians consider any patient who has symptoms lasting longer than a few weeks or a month after injury to have emotional or other reasons (e.g., a desire for compensation) for the perpetuation of symptoms.[78,87] Conversely, other investigators have found no correlation between the preinjury personality or litigation and the development of a post-traumatic syndrome and have concluded that the syndrome is not a neurosis but is, in fact, organic.[76,105]

We tend to agree with Symonds,[104] Peterson,[86] and Binder,[10] who concur that a combination of organic, emotional, and social factors is responsible for the subacute and chronic symptoms after head trauma. Supporting this position is the finding of transient and permanent pathologic changes in both experimental animals and human patients dying of other causes after mild head injury.[84] In addition, there is evidence of neurophysiologic dysfunction as assessed by standard neurodiagnostic tests in patients with mild head trauma (e.g., EEG,[71] electronystagmogram,[109] and brain stem auditory-evoked potential[93]). Increasingly sophisticated procedures such as brain mapping, magnetic resonance imaging,[48] and positron emission tomography may well provide important data to confirm the presence of physiologic or structural disruption of the brain in cases with no clinically apparent structural lesions.

Pre-existing head trauma must always be considered in dealing with postconcussional patients; it is frequently an exacerbating factor when present.[89] This topic will be discussed later in this chapter.

Age also appears to be significant. Symptoms are definitely increased in older patients, a finding that may be of multifactorial cause but certainly suggests that the older, less plastic, brain cannot adjust to trauma as well as the younger one can. These observations, combined with the fact that the syndrome occurs in many patients without pre-existing emotional problems and no hope of compensation or other pending legal matters, provide a strong suspicion that an organic brain disturbance is at the seat of many of these symptoms.

Although pretraumatic neurosis does not generally seem to be a significant factor in development of the post-traumatic syndrome, it is definitely the case in some.[43] Other personality factors, however, may be important, (e.g., a history of parental rejection or overprotection, chronic maladjustment, depression, alcohol abuse, and proneness to accidents[85]). It seems reasonable that presence of premorbid psychiatric problems may contribute to the development of a postconcussive syndrome.

The context in which the injury occurs also seems to influence the prognosis of the post-traumatic symptoms. Work-related injuries and automobile accidents in which compensation and legal awards are predicated on such abstract consideration as "pain and suffering" may lead some patients either consciously or unconsciously to prolong symptoms in order to receive the maximum financial settlement. Some physicians are convinced that most cases of extended post-traumatic symptoms are frank malingering to increase financial reward. Miller[78] reported that 90 percent of his patients completely improved after settlement had been rendered. Other evidence in support of Miller's view is provided by the incidence of post-traumatic symptoms in persons concussed on the job or in their cars compared with the incidence in those receiving equally severe injuries during sports contests. Although the initial post-traumatic symptoms are similar in both groups, sports injuries have been found to produce far fewer prolonged complaints,[25,114] the theory being that in sports injuries, the participant expects an occasional bump on the head and cannot seek any compensation for it. Others, however, have found no objective neurobehavioral differences between patients involved in litigation and those who are not.[76,89] Present evidence suggests that the number of subjective complaints among litigants is greater,[76] but that compensation claims do not affect the degree of objective deficits or symptoms.[10] The post-traumatic syndrome has been reported to be more common in patients after minor head injuries than in those sustaining severe injuries, a finding that has been used by some as support for the importance of psychogenic factors.[35,78]

Other factors that have been noted to have a high incidence in patients with lengthy post-traumatic symptoms are those related to the social problems that existed in these persons' lives before the accident. A combination of job difficulty, difficulty in marriage, and declining economic status was found to be present in more than 90 percent of the symptomatic patients in one study and in only 35 percent of the patients with no prolongation of symptoms after minor head trauma.[85]

Socioeconomic status seemingly is related to the duration of disability but not to the severity of symptoms. Professional and managerial patients tend to fare better than unskilled or semiskilled workers.[57] This difference is probably because of the greater control that higher-level personnel can exert over their own vocational destinies and because they do not have to perform heavy physical labor.

In essence, the post-traumatic syndrome must be viewed as the sequela of a complex interaction of organic, emotional, and social factors. The initial symptoms of concentration and memory difficulty, headache, and dizziness are very likely organic. The insomnia, fatigue, nervousness, and other psychologic symptoms may very well be primarily organic, although emotional and social overtones are certainly present. The worsening or perpetuation of these symptoms after several months seems less likely to be purely organic than to be a combination of the patient's personality, fears about the accident, effects on social, emotional, and vocational functioning, compensation and legal claims, other intangible social factors, and some persistent organic dysfunction.

The incidence of frank malingering and the deliberate overexaggeration of symptoms is now considered to compose a small proportion of closed head trauma cases, regardless of litigation or other circumstances.[4,11] Regardless of the exact cause or blend of causes in each patient, post-traumatic symptoms are major economic, medical, and legal problems in our society. The accurate prediction of prognosis is complicated and must be based on all of the factors discussed above. The primary lingering effects of mild closed head injury are subtle neuropsychologic deficits and subjective complaints. Such problems persist in a minority of patients for up to 3 years.[76] Patients with a mild head injury (post-traumatic amnesia of less than 24 hours), however, are usually back to full work in 3 months. Russell's study[95] showed that 93 percent of patients under the age of 40 and 78 percent of those over 40 were working 2 months after injury. Lidvall and associates[67] found that less than 25 percent of their patients had any symptoms after 3 months. One must never forget, however, that minor head trauma does occasionally lead to serious complications such as subdural hematoma. In one series of 275 cases of "trivial" head injury, 1 percent died and 1.7 percent had hematomas.[87] In the same series, 93 percent had no residual signs and symptoms. Accordingly, in most cases, the minor head injury is an aggravating yet relatively benign event.

The American Psychiatric Association has established a specific diagnostic category, the post-traumatic stress disorder, that is applicable to many of the emotional changes seen after head injury.[6] This disorder is characterized by the development of a specific cluster of symptoms following a traumatic event, physically and/or psychologically, that is outside the usual range of human experience. Head trauma sustained as the result of a motor vehicle or industrial accident, an assault, or an unexpected blow falls within the criteria necessary for this diagnosis. See Chapter 15 for a more complete description of this syndrome.

Repeated Minor Head Trauma

If a person is sufficiently unlucky to sustain several or even many blows to the head over time, the effect of each succeeding injury becomes more significant, recovery is slower, and eventually permanent brain damage can result. Gronwall and Wrightson[42] studied a group of persons who had sustained two concussions, an average of 4 1/2 years apart. Although both injuries were mild, the concentration and information-processing deficit experienced by the patients after the second concussion was as great as that seen in patients after a severe first concussion. Even though all of Gronwall and Wrightson's patients did ultimately recover to normal levels on the tests used, their recovery was significantly slower than that of patients who had sustained only one concussion.

Professional sportsmen have provided the best opportunity for study of the cumulative effects of multiple closed head trauma. Boxing subjects its participants to by far the most gruesome display of continuing head trauma, but football players, steeplechase riders, wrestlers, and others have also been reported to have suffered the lasting ill effects of repeated head trauma.[32] The plight of these athletes is typified by the following case:

A 41-year-old boxer was first seen some 12 years after retirement from his professional boxing career. He complained that he was having difficulty walking and had noticed that his memory was not as sharp as it previously was. He worked as a dealer in a Las Vegas casino and was having trouble keeping track of the players' cards. His boxing career had started at a young age. In fact, he had stretched the truth a bit and began fighting professionally at the age of 16. He was very successful and won the world title in his weight class at the height of his career. He fought steadily for 13 years. He did not remember exactly how many fights he had had, but he claimed never to have been knocked out (he was knocked down 10 times and lost three fights on technical knockouts).

He retired at age 29 and functioned adequately until age 36, when he was hospitalized for "paranoid behavior." When we first saw him at age 41, he was employed and doing well except for problems with his gait and minor memory problems. On examination he had rather pronounced slurring and scanning of speech, which he reported was normal for him and "not like those punch-drunk guys who hang around the gym." In fact, throughout the examination, although admitting that he had some trouble that he attributed to his boxing, he vehemently denied that he was like "those other punchy guys."

His gait was slightly ataxic, and on finger-to-nose testing he displayed mild clumsiness and dysmetria (left worse than right). Rapid alternating movements were carried out poorly, tone was slightly increased in the legs, the right biceps reflex was increased, and there was a questionable extensor toe sign on the left. Results of sensation and cranial nerve examinations were within normal limits. Memory was poor: He did not remember the name of the doctor who had sent him to our office 1 hour before, he knew the name of the present President but not the previous one, and he had great difficulty learning any new material. He was not aphasic, calculations, drawings, and proverb interpretation were good.

This clinical syndrome, often called dementia pugilistica or the punch drunk syndrome, consists of both motor and behavioral signs. Motorically, patients develop a scanning dysarthric speech, striatal tremor, mixed pyramidal and extrapyramidal signs, cerebellar trunkal and limb signs, seizures, and sometimes a parkinsonism syndrome.[91] The behavioral change is often equally dramatic, with slowness of thought processes, fatuousness, euphoria, emotional lability, dementia, paranoia, swings of mood that can often lead to violence, temper outbursts, and a generally disinterested attitude towards the environment and those in it.[29,110] We saw one 51-year-old retired veteran of 163 fights who told us with glee how he "punched out" the bellman in his building because our patient did not think that the man was being sufficiently helpful to a lady guest at the hotel. The degree of behavioral disinhibition seen in such patients suggests the probability of a frontal-lobe syndrome secondary to multiple concussions and contusions of the frontal poles bilaterally. Such dysfunction in patients with apparent good physical recovery from head injury can produce significant obstacles to functional ability.[74] In conjunction with their erratic behavior, patients with dementia pugilistica usually have memory and concentration problems and are very sensitive to the effects of alcohol.[27] Trauma to the temporal lobes and hippocampus is a likely cause.

This syndrome is unfortunately extremely common in professional fighters who have fought for at least 3 years. Both CT scan and EEG indications of brain pathology are directly related to the number of bouts.[21,92] Roberts[91] found 28 percent of over 200 British pugilists examined to be suffering from central nervous system damage. The condition is regrettably nonreversible and in a surprising number is actually slowly progressive after the fighter retires. For example, Roberts found evidence of encephalopathy in 47 percent of all retired fighters over the age of 50 who had fought for at least 10 years during their lifetime, but in only 25 percent of younger fighters with the same number of fights. Even young active boxers, however, have been reported to display a pattern of neuropsychologic deficits that are consistent with the "punch drunk syndrome" found in older boxers.[31] This study found that 79 percent of a sample of boxers under the age of 25 performed within the brain-damaged range on the Halstead-Reitan impairment index, with a significant relationship between degree of dysfunction and the numbers of losses and draws. This finding again suggests a cumulative progressive process.

The chance of becoming demented from an athletic career correlates highly with the severity and frequency of head trauma. Again the best statistics are obtained from the study of boxers, who show a marked increase in encephalopathy in instances of long careers that encompassed many fights.[22] A 10-year career with 150 fights results in a 50 percent chance of dementia developing, whereas a shorter fighting career with fewer than 50 fights results in only a 5 to 10 percent risk.[91]

Although the boxer may be the extreme example of the recipient of repeated minor head trauma, the effects of previous head trauma have been documented in other situations as well.[114] One wonders how truly benign any trivial head trauma is over time.

Severe Closed Head Trauma

The definition of a *severe closed head injury* varies somewhat from investigator to investigator, but the patient must have a post-traumatic amnesic period of at least 24 hours. In most studies of patients with severe head injuries, the average period of amnesia has been greater than 7 days[15,16,50] and in some centers a minimum of 7 days is used as the criterion for severe concussion.[50] Length of coma is another factor often included in the definition, yet again there is a discrepancy in the duration of coma required to define an injury as severe; a coma of 1 hour is used by some[17] and of 6 hours by others.[50] Because of the difference in opinion concerning this measurement, it is difficult to compare the results of various investigators and to arrive at any firm consensus regarding prognosis (both for the degree of expected disability and the projected length of the recovery period). Nevertheless, we will attempt to summarize the available data, so that when faced with a specific case, the clinician will be able to provide the patients and his family with some sensible expectations regarding recovery and rehabilitation.

Many aspects of the severe injury are similar to those of minor head injury but are extended over time. The initial coma is longer, and the period of post-traumatic amnesia is much longer, as is the period of confusional behavior during the return to full consciousness. Unfortunately, with the lengthy recovery process come significant neurologic and behavioral deficits that are often irreversible. Some of these are obvious, such as hemiparesis or aphasia, whereas others of equal significance are more difficult to recognize and may go unnoticed by the inexperienced examiner. These are the unsuspected factors that can interfere with full rehabilitation, particularly with vocational and social readjustment. The following case exemplifies some of the problems that are frequently encountered.

A 20-year-old man, who had sustained a severe closed head injury complicated by neurosurgical debridement of frontal lobe tissue (coma of 3 weeks and postcoma confusional state of 4 weeks), was referred for evaluation 3 months postinjury because of disinhibited aggressive behav-

ior, disorientation, and hyperphagia. He was reported to be disinterested and uncooperative in all rehabilitation therapies, frequently spending the therapy time talking incessantly and grandiosely about plans to develop an elaborate electronics business (he had been a delivery truck driver for a stereo store at the time of his motor vehicle accident). When questioned specifically, the therapists found the patient to be overly active, inattentive to directions, irritable, demanding, and totally unable to remember the nature of instructions and structure necessary for day-to-day rehabilitation. Therapists had become actively hostile toward the patient because they perceived his behavior as being manipulative and resistant to offers of help. One therapist discontinued all contact with him because of his tendency to expel gas during therapy sessions.

A far different impression was obtained on examination. The patient was obviously hyperactive and inattentive but was friendly and cooperative with the examiner. He displayed an almost total lack of insight regarding his situation, a notable deficit in vigilance (18 errors on the Strub-Black mental status vigilance test), an inability to process new information, significantly impaired learning and short-term memory, and an absence of abstract reasoning. Neuropsychologic testing revealed significant deficits in virtually all areas assessed, including intelligence (WAIS-R Full Scale IQ = 75), memory (Randt Memory Index = 63), language, and constructional ability. The patient was unable to complete the Wisconsin Card Sorting Test or the Categories Test, and was significantly impaired on all other tests of abstraction and higher cognitive processes. An interview with family members indicated that the current behavioral, emotional and cognitive status reflected a total change from the patient's premorbid functioning. The patient's "difficult" behavior and inability to comply with the demands of rehabilitation were obviously organic in nature, not intentional, and were caused by frontoparietal, temporal, and subcortical damage.

The patient was again evaluated 1 year after transfer to a long-term rehabilitation facility. Unfortunately, he had made less than optimal recovery and continued to demonstrate most of the early problems, albeit at a somewhat reduced level. It is most unfortunate that the emotional and behavior problems, especially a lack of insight and social control, have proved most resistant to improvement. The persistence of these problems has continued to interfere with multiple comprehensive attempts at rehabilitation. Despite low-average intelligence and normal language and motor ability, the patient is now waiting for placement in a chronic care facility.

PERSONALITY CHANGE

This young man experienced many of the behavioral changes commonly seen in severe head injury, memory difficulty[17] and a personality change characteristic of frontal lobe damage being the most prominent. Because these changes are not as readily apparent as motor weakness or aphasia, they must be specifically sought in examination. The personality change can be particularly difficult to recognize because the main features of apathy, euphoria, irritability, and inappropriate behavior often appear to be or are misinterpreted as being intentional. The identification of the behavioral change as organic makes it much easier for the staff to work with the patient but, unfortunately, means that the prognosis is often less favorable.

Levin and Grossman,[63] in a well-studied sample of patients with closed head injury, found a rather distinct profile of behavioral disturbance in their moderately to severely injured patients (coma of less than 24 hours with or without concomitant neurologic deficit). The outstanding features were cognitive disorganization manifested by disconnected thought processes, disorientation and conceptual disorganization, emotional withdrawal, various affective disturbances including excitement and blunting of affect, and motor retardation. The degree of behavioral disturbance was directly related to the severity of neurologic disturbance and the length of coma. A number of studies of victims of severe head trauma and their relatives further document the persistence of minor physical deficits, but significant cognitive, psychologic, and behavioral problems for periods in excess of 5 years after injury.[19,33,70,83,103,111] After improvement of major cognitive deficits, the lasting psychologic and social problems in combination with memory and conceptual deficits cause major obstacles to successful readjustment.

COGNITIVE DISTURBANCES

Other cognitive disturbances are also seen as sequelae of severe head injury, although these are less common unless an associated hematoma or brain laceration is present. Frank phasic disturbances are reported in a third of patients having very severe closed head injury (mean post-traumatic amnesia period of 43 days);[16,61] Sarno,[99] however, reported that no patient admitted for rehabilitation of the sequelae of head trauma was spared some degree of verbal impairment. A decline in overall intellectual functioning is also expected in this group.[13] Early in the recovery period, the performance (nonverbal) IQ suffers the greatest drop. The Performance IQ improves during recovery, and by 6 months after the injury, both verbal and performance scores have generally stabilized at about equal levels.[72] The Verbal IQ improved to that of the control group after 1 year, whereas recovery of the Performance IQ continued over about 3 years. This pattern is true only for uncomplicated closed head trauma; if the patient sustains a depressed skull fracture or an associated focal lesion, the cognitive disturbance has the additional features secondary to the focal lesion.

Emotional and behavioral sequelae of severe closed head injury are more frequent than physical symptoms, especially after the period of rapid spontaneous recovery. Long-term follow-up studies have amply documented these significant organically based obstacles to normal adjustment.[18,62] Lingering cognitive deficits, impaired social judgment, deficient planning ability, and a lack of full insight frequently coexist with normal general intelligence and good physical recovery.[19,81,111] Unfortunately, the overt improvements in motor functioning and ability to communicate in a previously deeply comatose patient allow families, and at times professionals, to overlook or minimize the very real organic residual problems suffered by most of these patients. Patients with recurrent psychiatric hospitalization, numerous encounters with legal authorities, and even prolonged jail terms point to the necessity of carefully examining the organic basis of personality and behavior changes in patients with a medical history of head injury.[113]

The relatives of brain-injured patients frequently develop significant psychiatric and social dysfunction because of disrupted family relationships and the frustrations implicit in coping with the stresses of a seriously injured patient who seemingly improves but is left with persistent cognitive and behavioral problems.[19,20,70] In this way, the social impact of a single injury is multiplied considerably by the number of family members involved in the patient's care. There is obviously a great need for family member support as an integral part of rehabilitation programs.

During the period of recovery from a severe closed head injury, some patients go through a very bizarre stage in which their behavior is very much akin to that described by Drs. Klüver and Bucy in monkeys after bilateral temporal lobectomy.[58,59] We saw one young man 5 months after injury who had to be tied to his bed or chair because of violent behavioral outbursts and sexual advances to the female staff members. He also displayed marked hyperorality. Although this clinical picture is uncommon, elements of the syndrome are seen in some patients as they recover from significant head trauma. On occasion, these behaviors have been reported to persist and appear to be related to bilateral temporal lobe seizure activity.[45]

NEUROPATHOLOGY

In severe head trauma, considerable torsional and shearing forces are directed at the deep white matter of the cerebral hemisphere and the structures in the upper brain stem, principally the midbrain.[24,55,60,101] The resultant injuries can produce several syndromes that have direct behavioral manifestations. Bilateral damage to the corticobulbar tracts, particularly in the region of the striatum, frequently results in a pseudobulbar syndrome with a marked lability of emotional expression. The patients cry or laugh with the least provocation, frequently in neutral or inappropriate situations. These outward expressions of emotion are involuntary and usually do not represent an expression of true emotion. It is important for the personnel working with patients with pseudobulbar syndrome to recognize the involuntary nature of these emotional outbursts and also to help the family realize that they do not reflect depression. Family members often feel very guilty if their every remark makes the patient cry; accordingly it is important to discuss these pseudobulbar features frankly with them.

Damage to the midbrain secondary to significant head injury is common. During the actual injury, as the head is moved violently, the brain twists and turns within the cranial vault, causing tremendous distortion to the midbrain structures. It is damage to the brain stem reticular substance that results in the prolonged coma in these cases, but many other structures in this area are concomitantly damaged. The resultant syndrome is fairly stereotyped; the patients have marked dysarthria, imbalance, ataxia, limb tremor with dysmetria, occasionally signs of oculomotor nerve damage, and pyramidal tract signs, particularly early in the recovery period.[15,55,60,106] In those patients having severe dysarthria as well as other neurologic abnormalities, it is very easy to assume that the patients are also demented. Frequently, however, this is not the case. Often the brain stem has borne the brunt of the damage, and the higher cortical functions are relatively spared. The dysarthria makes the patients appear demented, but with continued questioning and use of a nonverbal response modality such as nodding the head, it is frequently possible to help them demonstrate their cognitive capacities. Because these patients have sustained significant trauma, they often have some memory and other specific cognitive deficits, as well as frontal lobe behavioral changes, but their basic intellectual processes are often remarkably intact.

DEPRESSION

Emotional disturbance of a functional nature can also be present in the patient with severe head injury. This seems to be somewhat related to the patient's insight as to the extent and implication of his disability. Genuine depression (as opposed to apathy) with anxiety can be organic or a reactive emotional response to the injury.[68] Younger patients who experience cognitive and/or behavioral deficits and those whose deficits persist for a longer time postinjury are most likely to develop depression.[8,22] Such patients require psychiatric care as a component of their general rehabilitation. In many cases, depression is seen in patients with a premorbid predisposition towards depression or personality imbalance,[14] although this is not universally true.[68] Depression is the most common emotional reaction to head injury. Psychotic reactions are known to occur, although they are distinctly uncommon.[3,68] Functional emotional changes after head injury represent the result of a complex interplay among premorbid traits, the nature and severity of the injury, any cognitive or physical deficits, the patient's insight, and the family and social environment surrounding the patient during recovery.

POST-TRAUMATIC SYNDROME

A curious feature in patients with severe injuries is the paucity of headaches, dizziness, and the other features of the post-traumatic syndrome.[35,79] This phenomenon may be merely a selection artifact, but it has been reported frequently enough that we believe there may well be a decreased incidence of these findings in such patients. The mechanism resulting in the post-traumatic syndrome in cases of mild head injury is so unclear that to venture an explanation for its absence in severe injury would be sheer speculation.

PROGNOSIS

The question of prognosis, both of survival per se and of the quality of survival of those who do survive a severe head injury, is an important one. Various investigators have used different methods of reporting their case material; accordingly, it is impossible to fully summarize all the available information in a simple table. We can provide a number of statistics, however, that will give an overall impression of prognosis in terms of time lost from work, percentage of patients able to work, and some of the factors determining quality of survival and eventual social and vocational readjustment. A severity scale established by Jennett and associates[51,55] is useful in categorizing patients after injury. The most severe level on the scale is, of course, death. Next is *the persistent vegetative state,*[34] in which the patients recover from coma to the point that their eyes open and appear to search the room, but they remain in a state that has been described as "unresponsive, speechless wakefulness with only primitive postural motor activity."[49] The next level is *severe disability;* the patients are conscious but are totally dependent on others. With a *moderate disability,* the patients are sufficiently independent to ride public transportation and to work in a sheltered work situation but have prominent neurologic abnormalities. In the category of *recovery* (good outcome), the patients are completely independent and able to return to their regular employment, although there may be some minor neurologic signs.

Favorable outcome has a consistent inverse relationship to age, duration of coma, and length of post-traumatic amnesia.[13,49,55] This relationship is true for quality of survival as well as basic survival. In general, the cognitive and behavioral handicap is the limiting factor both in vocational readjustment and in the successful re-establishment of social and family relationships. Mental problems including personality change, intellectual deficit, and memory problems improve rapidly in the initial 6 months after the injury but tend to improve less dramatically or to stabilize after that point.[13,17] This observation is not to imply that recovery does not occur after this time in individual cases; there are now ample examples of unexpected late recovery many months and even years after head injury. For practical purposes, it is important to develop a recovery curve to determine at what time most of the recovery will have taken place.[55] The physical handicap has a much more gradual recovery course and can show continued improvement over a number of years.[79] Estimates of overall functional recovery can be given accurately at 6 months, whereas a prognosis after 3 months or less is often unnecessarily pessimistic. One study reported that one third of the patients rated severely or moderately disabled at 3 months after injury had improved to the moderate and good categories respectively when tested after 1 year.[51] None of the patients, however, who were originally rated "severely disabled" had been reclassified to the "good" category. Only a small percentage of patients followed up for more than 18 months showed sufficient improvement after 12 months for their category of outcome to be changed.[55]

Although the prognosis can be accurately given in many cases 6 months after injury, some persons will continue to improve over a number of years.[69,79] The exact mechanism of this long-term recovery is not known, but much of it must represent compensatory mechanisms and strategies used by the patient rather than actual neurologic recovery.

In general, the overall outcome from severe head injury is as follows: death occurs in 50 to 52 percent of patients before they leave the hospital, another 19 percent die during the initial 5 years after the accident, 3 percent remain in a persistent vegetative state and usually die within 1 year, 10 percent are severely disabled, 20 percent are moderately disabled, and 17 percent have a good recovery.[56,79] Age plays an important part in mortality, as can be seen in the statistics reported by Russell[95] from a series of patients with less severe injuries: death rate under 40 years of age was 3 to 4 percent; between 40 and 50 years of age, 12 percent; and over 50 years of age, 27 percent. A similar age-related trend is seen for all levels of severity in those patients who survive the initial injury.

Studies relating prognosis to coma and amnesia demonstrate that for patients with coma of over 2 months' duration, the full recovery rate is only 6 percent, whereas it is 57 percent in cases of coma of less than 2 months.[56] Patients with an amnesia of over 3 to 4 weeks generally have been reported to have significant mental problems and persistent memory deficits.[13,51]

A final group of statistics important in the assessment of prognosis in head-injured patients is the time lost from work and the ultimate job level after severe injury. Guttman[43] reported means of 4.5 weeks lost time with injuries causing 24 hours of amnesia, 8.8 weeks lost with 1 to 7 days amnesia, and 13.7 weeks work lost in patients with over a 1-week period of post-traumatic amnesia. Miller and Stern[79] found that their patients averaged 13 months away from work. In Brooks'[16] series of patients with an average amnesia of 43 days, 65 percent had returned to work after 1 year. Russell[95] reported that two thirds of his patients with an amnesia of greater than 3 days did not return to work for 6 months and that only 14 percent were back at work within 2 months. About half of the patients suffered no earning loss when returning to work, but 25 to 35 percent were required to take a less responsible job because of their disability.[35,79] More recent reviews of vocational outcome after head trauma report similar findings when all variables are considered.[61] It is obvious from these statistics that severe head injuries are not always hopeless when a full rehabilitative effort is put forth.

SECONDARY COMPLICATIONS

Some secondary complications of closed head and general trauma must be mentioned because they frequently are heralded by behavioral changes in a patient who has apparently recovered from the initial concussive incident. One is raised intracranial pressure and the development of a post-traumatic communicating hydrocephalus. Intracranial hypertension secondary to brain edema is common after closed head injury, being present in two thirds of patients admitted in coma, and it remains a management problem in one third of patients with diffused head trauma.[73] The primary features are gait difficulty, frontal lobe behavior changes, incontinence, and in the acutely developing case, a progressive decrease in the level of consciousness. The symptoms of this condition have been discussed at length in Chapter 7, Other Dementias. Hydrocephalus is always an important differential consideration in any victim of head injury who begins to regress during the recovery period. A second complication that should always be considered is subdural hematoma. We have seen several patients in whom a fluctuating mild aphasia was the only clue that their recovery was atypical. Whenever a patient is recovering normally and then takes a downward turn, an epidural and subdural clot must be assiduously sought.[38] A third post-traumatic problem, one that is associated with bone fracture with or without head trauma, is fat embolism. The patient with fat embolism typically experiences an uneventful recovery for the first 24 to 72 hours and then rapidly develops a classic acute confusional state. Fat droplets are dispersed throughout the body and are seen on microscopic examination of the urine. Fortunately, a rapid recovery is experienced by most patients with this complication. Other problems of a systemic nature, including shock, hypoxia, and anemia, may occur soon after injury, resulting in both mortality and morbidity.

The development of post-traumatic epilepsy is a well-recognized possible consequence of head injury that has implications for the patient's physical and neurobehavioral state.[14] Typical grand mal or tonic-clonic seizures are usually easily detected. The development of abnormal episodic psychologic behaviors, however, should alert the clinician to the possibility of temporal lobe or limbic seizures. Unexplained behavior after seemingly good recovery in head-injury patients must be evaluated by a careful epilepsy work-up.

A final, less common, consequence of mild and severe head trauma is the development of a form of progressive dementia. This insidious condition is decidedly rare but has been reported,[66] and we have seen such cases in our clinical practice. Head trauma has been hypothesized to increase the risk of Alzheimer's disease in later life[94]; however, the condition is also seen in younger persons and may be similar to the neuropathic process seen in dementia pugilistica. The nature of this condition in all clinical cases remains unknown to date.

NEUROBEHAVIORAL EVALUATION

If a patient is seen shortly after awakening from any head injury, he will generally show signs of confusional behavior. During this confusional period, the patient will be unable to establish new memories and will be able to give only sketchy details about the events leading up to his trauma. With the passage of time, his mind will clear and, at some point, he will be fully conscious and remember all ongoing events. At this point, the post-traumatic amnesia has ended, and the length of time elapsed since the trauma can be used as a gauge of the severity of the injury. It is not always easy to determine the exact time of return to full consciousness; confusional behavior fluctuates and what would appear to be a total clearing of mentation at 8:00 AM might not remain constant throughout the day and night. Multiple determinations must be made, and the true length of the amnesia may be extremely difficult to establish. The use of a formal charting method is useful in objectifying the patient's status (see Chapter 3). As we pointed out in the clinical section of this chapter, there will often be subtle memory and concentration problems for a month, even in patients with minor head injury. These problems, however, should not be taken into account in calculating the amnesic period. The post-traumatic amnesia must represent a period of rather significant memory loss.

During the initial confusional period, it is important to watch for any significant, sustained decrease in level of alertness because it may be the only clinical sign of a developing hematoma or hydrocephalus. Periodic mental status screening is useful. Although patients are expected to have many mild cognitive deficits, the appearance of a significant specific defect or a sudden worsening of one function (e.g., language or drawing) may suggest the development of a focal lesion.

When the patient with a minor head injury has recovered from the initial traumatic period and is ready for discharge, it is advisable for the clinician to be prepared and to prepare the patient for the appearance of post-traumatic symptoms and problems. We take a brief history to assess most of the factors that influence the appearance and prolongation of a post-traumatic syndrome: (1) Is a lawsuit likely to ensue? (2) Does the patient hold someone else responsible for the accident? (3) Was the patient experiencing financial or personal problems before the accident? (4) Is there any indication of a pretraumatic personality or character problem? It is also important to inquire about previous trauma, because multiple trauma often significantly extends the period of recovery.

Before discharge, a complete mental status examination should be done, and specific attention must be given to eliciting any behavioral change, anxiety, and concentration or memory problems. Frequently the entire management plan for a given patient will be predicated on the results of this examination.

For patients who have survived a severe head injury, a more complete neurobehavioral evaluation is required. To gain an initial estimate of prognosis, the examiner must know the patient's age, the length of coma, length of amnesia, and whether any surgery was done or an associated focal lesion identified. The mental status examination that follows should be comprehensive because the examiner is attempting to document areas of cognitive and emotional deficits as well as residual strengths. Again, the specific search for frontal lobe personality change is very important. It is essential that the clinician contact someone who knew the patient well before the accident to verify any personality change. We recently saw a teenage boy who had been involved in a motorcycle accident. We thought that he was acting unusually silly, disinhibited, and immature after his injury. We were interested to hear his mother rather disgustedly report, "He was always like that!" Had we not checked with the mother, we could easily have reported that the boy had suffered significant frontal lobe damage with a subsequent behavioral change.

A careful evaluation of memory, language, praxis, and abstract reasoning is also an important aid in planning the comprehensive rehabilitation program. Signs of depression should be carefully sought; the success or failure of a patient's rehabilitation and readjustment is often directly related to the presence of significant emotional/behavioral factors.

MEDICAL AND LABORATORY EVALUATION

The question of when to obtain a skull x-ray or brain scan of a patient with a head injury is a difficult one; certainly any patient who is unconscious for more than a few seconds should have a skull x-ray. With the increasing amount of litigation in cases of head injury, it is more and more important to obtain appropriate diagnostic tests to ensure that no possibility is overlooked. The skull x-ray is a good screening test for subdural hematomas. In one series, only 5 percent of the patients with hematomas secondary to head injury had neither positive neurologic signs nor a skull fracture.[38]

The use of the electroencephalogram (EEG) is more equivocal, particularly in cases of minor head injury. Many studies have demonstrated that the incidence of abnormal EEGs in patients with minor concussion is similar to that of the normal population.[67] Repeating the EEG in those patients with abnormalities frequently shows no improvement, because the abnormality was actually related to a premorbid variation and not to the head trauma. These "false-positive" cases can lead to the erroneous conclusion that such patients had really sustained lasting brain damage. In cases of more severe trauma, the EEG is abnormal in proportion to the severity of the injury. In such cases, the EEG can be used to follow the patient's improvement and can at times detect subdural hematomas. Again, the legal aspects of head trauma have caused physicians to order far more EEGs than are realistically necessary. This situation has resulted in the label of "post-traumatic brain damage" being applied to many patients who do not actually have it.

The computerized tomography scan (CT) and magnetic resonance image (MRI) are extremely useful in cases of head trauma. These scans can differentiate hematoma, edema, and contusion, as well as demonstrate communicating hydrocephalus or post-traumatic atrophy.[5,80] Because of their expense, the CT and MRI scans should probably not be routinely used in cases of minor head trauma unless the skull x-ray shows a fracture, the patient is unduly slow to recover, or neurologic signs are present or develop in the post-traumatic period. The development of these neuro-diagnostic tools has practically eliminated the need for arteriography in cases of trauma. In one recent series, the CT scan clearly identified 57 of 60 hematomas and implied their presence in the remaining 3 (which were isodense), by virtue of ventricular distortion.[53] In this series, there were no false-positive or false-negative scans. Magnetic resonance imaging is becoming an even more sensitive tool for identifying brain lesions after head trauma and in the future may replace most other diagnostic imaging procedures.[39,64] Cerebral arteriography is still used in evaluating some cases of acute head trauma, but this procedure should always be either completed by or supervised by a neurosurgeon.

Some investigators have measured serum-myelin-basic-protein levels in patients with severe head injuries and have reported some encouraging initial results.[107] In patients with a poor prognosis, the levels of the myelin protein were higher during the first week and stayed higher for a longer period (over 2 weeks) than in the patients who had a good outcome.

Although experimental at present, this type of test could become extremely useful for the early evaluation of the degree of brain damage.

CONSULTATIONS

On many occasions in the evaluation and management of head trauma cases, consultation with specific colleagues is strongly indicated. After the acute injury, particularly if it is severe, a neurosurgeon should be asked to see the patient and should share the responsibility for early patient care. The neurosurgeon is the best person to decide when and what neurodiagnostic laboratory tests are indicated and whether immediate hospitalization is necessary. The neurosurgeon, of course, is the only one qualified to provide surgical management when necessary.

During the management of the patient with a post-traumatic syndrome from minor head trauma, it is sometimes comforting to the patient to see a neurologist or to revisit the neurosurgeon. Usually, however, any competent physician can help the patient cope with the headache, dizziness, insomnia, and nervousness that are part of the syndrome. If the patient complains of concentration and memory problems, it is frequently advisable to refer the patient to a neuropsychologist for evaluation and assistance in management. Serious or persistent minor cognitive problems must be documented and honestly discussed with the patient in regard to their social and vocational implications.

In case of severe head trauma, full rehabilitation resources are necessary. Physical therapy is generally the mainstay, but a number of other services are often required. Every patient with severe head injury requires a full neuropsychologic evaluation. Information gained from that evaluation can be essential in helping the patient during the therapeutic process as well as during the period of adjustment following hospitalization. A neurologist should probably see all patients with severe brain injury because he can often make useful suggestions, particularly by assessing the extent of the injury and localizing its greatest areas of damage. We find that the bilateral brain damage present in many patients is not always fully appreciated by the therapists working with them; a good neurologic examination can usually highlight these deficits and thereby provide crucial information.

MANAGEMENT

Because management of the patient with a head injury depends to a major degree on the severity of the trauma, we will discuss first the management of the patient with minor trauma and then that of the patient with severe injury, realizing that there is a continuum between them. We will concentrate our discussion on the elements in the management plan that directly relate to the behavioral aspects of the trauma and not concentrate on the specific medical or surgical management of such conditions as subdural hematomas or depressed skull fractures. This material is adequately handled in other basic texts.

With cases of minor head trauma, the basic plan is bed rest, symptomatic medication, and supportive sympathy with gentle encouragement to resume regular activities. The general principles are straightforward, but the specifics as to when to admit the patient to the hospital, how long he should remain in bed, and when he should be encouraged to resume work are impossible to standardize.

As a rule, the first question is when to hospitalize a patient for observation. Although some physicians advocate admitting all patients for 1 week,[87] we consider this unnecessary. Patients who have been dazed for only a few seconds to minutes and who are neurologically and cognitively clear on arrival at the hospital can usually go home safely after the initial examination. Those patients who have a documented period of unconsciousness or who are still lethargic or confusional on arrival at the hospital are best admitted for at least one night. Patients who live alone or at a great distance from the hospital should be admitted. The adult who is vomiting or has a skull fracture should also be admitted in all cases.

In general, there is a tendency to overadmit. Several recent reports bear this out and firmly state that precautionary admission in minor head injury is unnecessary.[52,108] When the patient is fully conscious and has negative results of neurologic examination and skull x-ray, he may safely go home. Admitting such patients does not seem to increase the early detection of hematoma formation.[52]

During the first few days after an injury, other than checking the patient for any developing signs of intracranial hematoma, bed rest is the most efficacious treatment. Two to four days of rest is generally necessary for most patients, but depending on the age of the patient (older patients require additional rest) and the severity of the trauma, some patients require several weeks of supervised rest. If a patient is kept in bed overly long, he will begin to develop additional post-traumatic symptoms, so in most cases it is best to err on the side of less treatment rather than to be overly cautious.[112] We usually spend some time during the first few days reassuring the patient and also preparing him for the possible post-traumatic symptoms that he may experience. They are told that headache, dizziness, insomnia, fatigue, nervousness, and concentration difficulties are common and that they will be understood and treated if they do occur. The patients are encouraged to sit up when they feel able and also to ambulate at will. Because exercise and any effort, either mental or physical, can exacerbate symptoms, the patient is warned about this possibility, told to take it easy for a bit longer if symptoms become troublesome, and told to report such symptoms to the physician.

When the patient leaves the hospital or is preparing to return to work, it is important to warn both the patient and his employer that he should start with part-time or light work for an initial period. In the young patient with an uncomplicated course, 2 weeks should be sufficient to have him back to a full work schedule, but again this prognosis is related to many factors. Patients should also be warned that alcohol will have the same tendency to reactivate post-traumatic symptoms as will heavy work.

The most common mistake that we see in the management of cases of minor head trauma is that which Courville[28] warned against a quarter of a century ago—the quick "brush off." In such cases, the x-ray evidence is negative, and the result of the neurologic examination is negative, and so the patient is declared to have no sequelae from the head injury and told to go back to work. The patient tries to do so, does not function adequately, and is sent back to the doctor, who then reaffirms his earlier opinion. Neither the doctor nor the employer believe that the patient is still symptomatic, and the patient is frequently told either to work or to take off from work at his own expense. Understandably this situation breeds tremendous anger, and such patients develop many additional tension-related symptoms. They then become hostile and aggressively seek medical or financial compensation. At this point, what could have been a minor accident resulting in a 2-week loss of work becomes a complicated situation that drags on for many months. It is much easier and more efficacious to warn patients and employers of possible sequelae, put the patients on a graduated work schedule, and treat them with analgesics, mild tranquilizers if necessary, and sympathy for their plight. Thus, the emotional agony and time lost from work can be minimized. Unfortunately this simple plan does not always work because of the long, drawn-out legal proceedings involved in many such cases. In these cases, one can only do the best one can and hope that an early settlement is made.

The management of the severely brain-damaged patient requires more intensive and comprehensive efforts. After survival has been assured and the patient is conscious and able to begin a comprehensive rehabilitation program, it is important to undertake a complete neurologic and neuropsychologic evaluation. With an accurate conception of the patient's disabilities and residual strengths, it is then possible to outline a realistic program. Evidence of frontal lobe damage, memory problems, and specific cognitive disturbances are all very important to note; these defects are so often the limiting factors in the patient's rehabilitation. As previously mentioned, the mental symptoms improve rapidly during the first 6 months after trauma. Accordingly, it is best not to attempt to predict the patient's eventual level of recovery too early in the post-traumatic period. Unfortunately, there is currently no effective therapy for most of these mental deficits, and one must await spontaneous recovery while working diligently on the physical impairments. During this initial recovery period, emotional reactions such as depression or anxiety should be treated as they would in any setting. Psychiatric consultation can frequently be of major importance and should be requested at the first signs of a significant mood disturbance.

When the patient's mental status begins to stabilize, the next major step in the comprehensive rehabilitation program is to devise a logical vocational plan. This is often the most difficult and least satisfying part of the entire rehabilitation process. These patients have both physical and mental disabilities, and career plans are very difficult to formulate and then even more difficult to realize. The ultimate impediment to successful rehabilitation is often the presence of frontal lobe damage. Thus afflicted, the patient loses his basic drive, and the resultant apathy makes a productive career impossible even when the cognitive and physical problems have been overcome.

Because of his multiple handicaps, the patient with a severe head trauma must rely very heavily on family resources, both personal and financial, and family counseling is a critical part of the patient's total rehabilitation program. The family must understand the patient's deficits and capabilities if they are to work effectively with the patient after discharge. Without the family's support, the patient will flounder. Social workers are of inestimable value in preparing the family for the patient's return home, in arranging community resources and financial aid, and in providing continuing support.

Since publication of the first edition of this book, the growth of specialized rehabilitation centers, both as components of general hospitals and as free-standing facilities, has been tremendous. Such programs attempt to facilitate recovery through a comprehensive multidisciplinary therapeutic milieu and provide a transitional level between medical hospitalization and independent living. In addition, there are now long-term rehabilitation centers that focus on patients who no longer require hospitalization, but who are incapable of living independently or with their families. The availability of such programs offers an extremely useful, albeit expensive, alternative for many victims of closed head injury. In addition to traditional physical, occupational, and language therapy, such programs frequently concentrate on efforts to remediate the cognitive and behavioral deficits seen in many head-injured patients. Although cognitive remediation seems theoretically promising, the literature to date suggests that this field is still in its infancy and its methods and results are not yet well established.

NEUROPATHOLOGY

The brain is damaged both directly and indirectly by several mechanisms in trauma. There is cortical contusion both at the point of impact and, in contrecoup fashion, on the opposite side of the head. Subcortical white matter is also extensively injured from the rotational and torsional forces in effect while the head is recoiling from the blow.

These torsional forces that are generated by a freely movable head lead to the actual concussion.[30] The midbrain is one of the points of maximum rotation, and accordingly this structure suffers an initial and often prolonged injury. The ascending activating system at this level is thereby paralyzed, and loss of consciousness ensues. If significant damage is done at this level, a prolonged coma is seen. In mild injuries, where consciousness is quickly regained, dysfunction of these ascending fibers may very possibly be responsible for the attention and concentration problems experienced by some patients.

Secondary damage can occur when the injury is complicated by hematoma formation, vasospasm, massive cerebral edema, and penetrating fragments.[1] Here we will consider these factors in a very general fashion and not attempt an exhaustive discussion of the pathophysiology or experimental models.

With mild head injury, the consensus in the literature has been that the condition is relatively benign pathologically. Recent studies, however, have shown that there is considerable pathologic change even in patients with post-traumatic amnesia of 10 to 15 min or less.[1,84,96] Tiny capillary hemorrhages, severed nerve fibers, surface shearing, and contusion are all seen in these minor injuries. Some axons are torn, and there is considerable distortion of synaptic connections. Although clinical recovery usually occurs, Russell[96] seriously questions whether complete recovery is ever achieved in such patients.

In persons with repeated minor trauma, the pathologic effects are clearly documented. The demented pugilist, for example, has evidence of multiple cortical contusions, petechial hemorrhages that have scarred, a marked decrease in white matter resulting in enlargement of the lateral ventricles, and rupture of the septum pellucidum.[10,27,75] Alzheimer's tangles are seen diffusely throughout the brain stem and substantia nigra as well as in the cortex. Nerve fiber degeneration is also significant.[102] The prominent changes in the substantia nigra, which are responsible for the parkinsonlike syndrome, are due to cell loss and neurofibrillary degeneration. The neurofibrillary changes seen in the brain are concentrated in the medial temporal gray matter, although they are seen throughout the brain. Unlike Alzheimer's disease, the trauma patient does not develop the characteristic senile plaques of Marinesco.[27] Once initiated, the dementia often progresses even without further trauma; therefore, the trauma itself must trigger some aberrant physiologic process that can then become self-perpetuating.

In cases of severe head injury, patients have multifocal lesions. Contusions are seen in almost all patients, many (40 to 60 percent) have evidence of intracranial hemorrhage, and white matter degeneration is extensive.[47] In patients with prolonged coma, the deeper structures are more prominently involved. In patients with persistent vegetative states, the white matter destruction is the primary feature, with lesions in the posterior walls of the third ventricle also present in some cases.[47,101] In those patients with better levels of recovery, the deep lesions are less frequent. It is in these more serious injuries that secondary pathologic processes occur and greatly add to the morbidity and mortality.

The recovery process in these severe cases is slow. The pathophysiologic nature of the recovery process is uncertain, but recent work gives some hope that actual regeneration within the central nervous system does occur.[88] If such regeneration can be stimulated and guided, it is possible that the outlook for the patient with severe head injury will be more encouraging in the future than it is today.

REFERENCES

1. Adams, JH, Graham, DI, and Gennarelli, TA: Contemporary neuropathological considerations regarding brain damage in head injury. In Becker, DP and Poulishock, JT (eds): Central Nervous System Trauma Status Report—1985. National Institute of Neurological and Communicative Disorders and Stroke, Washington, 1985, pp 65–77.
2. Ad Hoc Committee of the Congress of Neurological Surgeons: Head injury nomenclature: A glossary of head injury. Clin Neurosurg 12:386, 1966.
3. Aita, JA and Reitan, RM: Psychotic reactions in the late recovery period following brain injury. Am J Psychiatry 105:161, 1948.
4. Alves, WM and Jane, JA: Mild brain injury: Damage and outcome. In Becker, DP and Poulishock, JT (eds): Central Nervous System Trauma: Status Report—1985. National Institute of Neurological and Communicative Disorders and Stroke, Washington, 1985, pp 255–270.
5. Ambrose, J, Gooding, MR, and Uttley, D: E.M.I. scan in the management of head injuries. Lancet 1:847, 1976.
6. American Psychiatric Association Task Force: Diagnostic and Statistical Manual: III. American Psychiatric Association, Washington, 1980.
7. American Psychiatric Association Task Force: Diagnostic and Statistical Manual: IV. American Psychiatric Association, Washington, 1987.
8. Atteberry-Bennett, J et al: The relationship between behavioral and cognitive deficits, demographics and depression in patients with minor head injuries. Int J Clin Neuropsychol 8:114, 1986.
9. Benson, DF and Geschwind, N: Shrinking retrograde amnesia. J Neurol Neurosurg Psychiatry 30:539, 1967.

10. Binder, LM: Persisting symptoms after mild head injury: A review of the postconcussive syndrome. J Clin Exp Neuropsychol 8:323, 1986.
11. Boll, TJ: Behavioral sequelae of head injury. In Cooper, PR (ed): Head Injury. Williams & Wilkins, Baltimore, pp 363–375.
12. Boller, FC et al: Enlargement of the sylvian aqueduct, a sequel of head injury. J Neurol Neurosurg Psychiatry 35:463, 1972.
13. Bond, M: Assessment of the psychosocial outcome after severe head injury. In Outcome of Damage to the Central Nervous System. Ciba Foundation Symposium 34 (new series), Elsevier, New York, 1975, pp 141–155.
14. Bond, M: The psychiatry of closed head injury. In Brooks, DN (ed): Closed Head Injury. Oxford University Press, New York, 1984, pp 148–178.
15. Brooks, DN: Memory and head injury. J Nerv Ment Dis 155:350, 1972.
16. Brooks, DN: Recognition memory and head injury. J Neurol Neurosurg Psychiatry 37:794, 1974.
17. Brooks, DN: Weschler Memory Scale performance and its relationship to brain damage after severe closed head injury. J Neurol Neurosurg Psychiatry 39:593, 1976.
18. Brooks, DN: Closed Head Injury. Oxford University Press, New York, 1984.
19. Brooks, DN et al: The five year outcome of severe blunt head injury: A relative's view. J Neurol Neurosurg Psychiatry, 49:764, 1986.
20. Brooks, DN and McKinlay, W: Personality and behavioral change after severe blunt head injury—a relative's view. J Neurol Neurosurg Psychiatry 46:336, 1983.
21. Casson, IR et al: Neurological and CT evaluation of knocked out boxers. J Neurol Neurosurg Psychiatry 45:170, 1982.
22. Casson, IR et al: Brain damage in modern boxers. JAMA 251:2663, 1984.
23. Clifton, GL: Head-injury incidence and organization of pre-hospital care. In Appel, SH (ed): Head Injury: Principles of Modern Management. Geigy Pharmaceuticals, Princeton, NJ, 1982, pp 3–5.
24. Compton, MR: Brain stem lesions due to closed head injury. Lancet 1:669, 1971.
25. Cook, JB: The effects of minor head injuries sustained in sport and the postconcussion syndrome. In Walker, AE, Caveness, WF, and Critchley, M (eds): The Late Effects of Head Injury. Charles C Thomas, Springfield, IL, 1967, pp 408–413.
26. Coonley-Hoganson, R et al: Sequelae associated with head injuries in patients who were not hospitalized: A follow-up survey. Neurosurgery 14:315, 1984.
27. Corsellis, JAN, Bruton, CJ, and Freeman-Browne, D: The aftermath of boxing. Psychol Med 3:370, 1973.
28. Courville, CB: Commotio Cerebri. San Lucas Press, Los Angeles, 1953.
29. Critchley, M: Medical aspects of boxing, particularly from a neurological standpoint. Br Med J 1:357, 1957.
30. Denny-Brown, D and Russell, WR: Experimental cerebral concussion. Brain 64:93, 1941.
31. Drew, RH et al: Neuropsychological deficits in active licensed professional boxers. J Clin Psychol 42:520, 1986.
32. Editorial: Brain damage in sport. Lancet 1:401, 1976.

33. Ellis, DW and Zahn, BS: Psychological functioning after severe closed head injury. J Pers Assess 49:125, 1985.

34. Evans, CD: Discussion of scale, scope and philosophy of the clinical problem. In Outcome of Severe Damage to the Central Nervous System. Ciba Foundation Symposium 34 (new series), Elsevier, New York, 1975, pp 12–18.

35. Fahy, JT, Irving, MH, and Millac, P: Severe head injuries: A six year follow-up. Lancet 2:475, 1967.

36. Fisher, CM: Concussion amnesia. Neurology 16:826, 1966.

37. Frankowski, RF, Anngers, JF, and Whitman, S: Epidemological and descriptive studies. Part I: The descriptive epidemology of head trauma in the United States. In Becker, DP and Poulishock, JT (eds): Central Nervous System Trauma Status Report — 1985. National Institute of Neurological and Communicative Disorders and Stroke, Washington, 1985, pp 23–43.

38. Galbraith, S and Smith, J: Acute traumatic intracranial hematoma without skull fracture. Lancet 1:501, 1976.

39. Gandy, SE et al: Cranial nuclear magnetic resonance imaging in head trauma. Ann Neurol 16:254, 1984.

40. Gronwall, DMA and Sampson, H: The Psychological Effects of Concussion. Auckland/Oxford Press, New Zealand, 1974.

41. Gronwall, DMA and Wrightson, P: Delayed recovery of intellectual function after minor head injury. Lancet 2:605, 1974.

42. Gronwall, DMA and Wrightson, P: Cumulative effect of concussion. Lancet 2:995, 1975.

43. Guttman, E: The prognosis in civilian head injuries. Br Med J 1:94, 1943.

44. Heilman, KM, Safran, A, and Geschwind, N: Closed head trauma and aphasia. J Neurol Neurosurg Psychiatry 34:265, 1971.

45. Hooshmand, H, Sepdham, T, and Uries, JK: Klüver-Bucy syndrome, successful treatment with carbamazepine. JAMA 229:1782, 1974.

46. Jacobson, SA: Mechanisms of the sequelae on minor craniocervial trauma. In Walker, AE, Caveness, WF, and Critchley, M (eds): Late Effects of Head Injury. Charles C Thomas, Springfield, IL, 1969, pp 35–45.

47. Jellinger, K and Seitelberger, F: Protracted post-traumatic encephalopathy: Pathology and clinical implications. In Walker, AE, Caveness, WF, and Critchley, M (eds): The Late Effects of Head Injury. Charles C Thomas, Springfield, IL, 1969, pp 168–181.

48. Jenkins, A et al: Brain lesions detected by magnetic resonance imagining in mild and severe head injuries. Lancet 2:445, 1986.

49. Jennett, B: Scale, scope and philosophy of the clinical problem. In Outcome of Severe Damage to the Central Nervous System. Ciba Foundation Symposium 34 (new series), Elsevier, New York, 1975, p 7.

50. Jennett, B: Assessment of severity of head injury. J Neurol Neurosurg Psychiatry 39:647, 1976.

51. Jennett, B and Bond, M: Assessment of outcome after severe brain damage. Lancet 1:480, 1975.

52. Jennett, B and Galbraith, SL: Head injury and admission policy. Lancet 1:552, 1979.

53. Jennett, B et al: EMI scan and head injuries. Lancet 1:1026, 1976.
54. Jennett, B and Plum, F: Persistent vegetative state after brain damage. Lancet 1:734, 1972.
55. Jennett, B and Teasdale, G: Management of head injuries. FA Davis, Philadelphia, 1981.
56. Jennett, B et al: Predicting outcome in individual patients after severe head injury. Lancet 1:1031, 1976.
57. Kelly, R: The post-traumatic syndrome: An iatogenic disease. Forensic Science 6:17, 1975.
58. Klüver, H and Bucy, PC: 'Psychic blindness' and other symptoms following bilateral temporal lobectomy in rhesus monkeys. Am J Physiol 119:352, 1937.
59. Klüver, H and Bucy, PC: Preliminary analysis of functions of the temporal lobes in monkeys. Arch Neurol Psychiatry 42:979, 1939.
60. Kremer, M, Russell, WR, and Smyth, GE: A mid-brain syndrome following head injury. J Neurol Neurosurg Psychiatry 10:49, 1947.
61. Levin, HS: Neurobehavioral recovery. In Becker, DP and Poulishock, JT (eds): Central Nervous System Trauma: Status Report—1985. National Institute of Neurological and Communicative Disorders and Stroke, Washington, 1985, pp 281–289.
62. Levin, HS, Benton, AL, and Grossman, RG: Neurobehavioral consequences of closed head injury. Oxford University Press, New York, 1982.
63. Levin, HS and Grossman, RG: Behavioral sequelae of closed head injury. Arch Neurol 35:720, 1978.
64. Levin, HS et al: Magnetic resonance imaging after 'diffuse' nonmissile head injury: A neurobehavioral study. Arch Neurol 42:963, 1985.
65. Levin, HS, O'Donnell, VM, and Grossman, RG: Galveston Orientation and Amnesia Test (GOAT). J Neurol Neurosurg Psychiatry 107:675, 1979.
66. Lewin, W, Marshall, TF, and Roberts, AH: Long-term outcome after severe head injury. Br Med J 2:1533, 1979.
67. Lidvall, HF, Linderoth, B, and Norlin, B: Causes of the postconcussional syndrome. Acta Neurol Scand (Supp) 56:3, 1974.
68. Lishman, WA: The psychiatric sequelae of head injury: A review. Psychol Med 3:304, 1973.
69. Lishman, WA: Organic Psychiatry. Blackwell Scientific Publications, Oxford, 1978, pp 191–261.
70. Livingston, MG, Brooks, DN, and Bond, MR: Patient outcome in the year following severe head injury and relatives' psychiatric and social functioning. J Neurol Neurosurg Psychiatry 48:876, 1985.
71. MacFlynn, G et al: Measurement of reaction time following minor head injury. J Neurol Neurosurg Psychiatry 47:1326, 1984.
72. Mandleberg, LA and Brooks, DN: Cognitive recovery after severe head injury. J Neurol Neurosurg Psychiatry 38:1121, 1975.
73. Marshall, LF, Smith, RW, and Shapiro, HM: The outcome with aggressive treatment in severe head injuries. I. The significance of intracranial pressure monitoring. J Neurosurg 50:20, 1979.
74. Massy, EW and Coffey, CE: Frontal lobe personality syndromes. Postgrad Med 73:99, 1983.

75. Mawdsley, C and Ferguson, FR: Neurological disease in boxers. Lancet 2:795, 1963.
76. McKinlay, WW, Brooks, DN, and Bond, MR: Post-concussional symptoms, financial compensation and outcome of severe blunt head injury. J Neurol Neurosurg Psychiatry 46:1084, 1983.
77. McLean, A et al: The behavioral sequelae of head injury. J Clin Neuropsychol 5:361, 1983.
78. Miller, H: Mental after-effects of head injury. Proc R Soc Med 59:257, 1966.
79. Miller, H and Stern, G: The long-term prognosis of severe head injury. Lancet 1:225, 1965.
80. New, PFJ and Scott, WR: Computed Tomography of the Brain and Orbit. Williams & Wilkins, Baltimore, 1975, pp 426–439.
81. Newton, A and Johnson, DA: Social adjustment and interaction after severe head injury. Br J Clin Psychol 24:225, 1985.
82. Novack, TA, Daniel, MS, and Long, CJ: Factors relating to emotional adjustment following head injury. Int J Clin Neuropsychol 6:139, 1984.
83. Oddy, M et al: Social adjustment after closed head injury: A further follow-up seven years after injury. J Neurol Neurosurg Psychiatry 48:564, 1985.
84. Oppenheimer, DR: Microscopic lesions in the brain following head injury. J Neurol Neurosurg Psychiatry 31:299, 1968.
85. Ota, Y: Psychiatric studies on civilian head injuries. In Walker, AE, Caveness, WF, and Critchley, M (eds): Late Effects of Head Injury. Charles C Thomas, Springfield, IL, 1969, pp 110–118.
86. Peterson, GC: Organic brain syndromes associated with brain trauma. In Freedman, AM, Kaplan, HI, and Sadock, BJ (eds): Comprehensive Textbook of Psychiatry. Williams & Wilkins, Baltimore, 1975, pp 1093–1108.
87. Plaut, MR and Gifford, RRM: Trivial head trauma and its consequences in a perspective of regional health care. Milit Med 141:244, 1976.
88. Raisman, A: What hope for repair of the brain? Ann Neurol 3:101, 1978.
89. Rimel, RW et al: Disability caused by minor head injury. Neurosurgery 9:221, 1981.
90. Rimel, RW et al: Moderate head injury: Completing the clinical spectrum of brain trauma. Neurosurgery 11:344, 1982.
91. Roberts, AH: Brain Damage in Boxers. Pitman, London, 1969.
92. Ross, RJ et al: Boxers—computed tomography, EEG, and neurological evaluation. JAMA 252:538, 1982.
93. Rowe, MJ and Carlson, C: brain stem auditory evoked potentials in postconcussion dizziness. Arch Neurol 37:670, 1980.
94. Rudelli, R et al: Post-traumatic premature Alzheimer's disease. Arch Neurol 39:570, 1982.
95. Russell, WR: The Traumatic Amnesias. Oxford Press, London, 1971.
96. Russell, WR: Recovery after minor head injury. Lancet 2:1315, 1974.
97. Rutherford, WH, Merret, JD, and McDonald, JR: Sequelae of concussion caused by minor head injuries. Lancet 1:1, 1977.
98. Rutherford, WH, Merrett, JD, and McDonald, JR: Symptoms at one year following concussion from minor head injuries. Injury 10:225, 1979.

99. Sarno, MT: The nature of verbal impairment after closed head injury. J Nerv Ment Dis 168:685, 1980.
100. Sisler, G and Penner, H: Amnesia following severe head injury. Can Psychiatr Assoc J 20:333, 1975.
101. Strich, SJ: Shearing of nerve fibers as a cause of brain damage due to head injury. Lancet 2:443, 1961.
102. Strich, SJ: Cerebral trauma. In Blackwood, W and Corsellis, JAN (eds): Greenfield's Neuropathology. Arnold, London, 1976, p 329.
103. Sunderland, A, Harris, JE, and Gleave, J: Memory failure in everyday life following severe head injury. Int J Clin Neuropsychol 6:127, 1984.
104. Symonds, C: Concussion and its sequelae. Lancet 1:1, 1962.
105. Taylor, AR: Post-concussional sequelae. Br Med J 3:67, 1967.
106. Teasdale, G and Mendelow, D: Pathophysiology of head injuries. In Brooks, N (ed): Closed Head Injury. Oxford University Press, New York, pp 4–36.
107. Thomas, DGT, Palfreyman, JW, and Ratcliff, JA: Serum-myelin-basic protein assay in diagnosis and prognosis of patients with head injury. Lancet 1:113, 1978.
108. Totten, J and Buxton, R: Were you knocked out? Lancet 1:369, 1979.
109. Tuohimaa, P: Vertibular disturbances after acute mild head injury. Acta Oto-Laryngologica Suppl 359, 1978.
110. Unterhornscheidt, FJ: Injuries due to boxing and other sports. In Vinken, PJ and Bruyn, GW (eds): Handbook of Clinical Neurology, Vol 23. Elsevier, New York, 1975, pp 527–593.
111. Van Zomeren, AH and Van Den Berg, W: Residual complaints of patients two years after severe head injury. J Neurol Neurosurg Psychiatry 48:21, 1985.
112. Verjaal, A and Van T Hooff, F: Commotio and contusio cerebri (cerebral concussion). In Vinken, PJ and Bruyn, GW (eds): Handbook of Clinical Neurology, Vol 23. Elsevier, New York, 1975, pp 417–444.
113. Weinstein, GS and Wells, CE: Case studies in neuropsychiatry: Post-traumatic psychiatric dysfunction — Diagnosis and treatment. J Clin Psychiatry 42:120, 1981.
114. Wrightson, P and Gronwell, P: Time off work and symptoms after minor head injury. Injury 12:445, 1981.
115. Yarnell, PR and Lynch, S: The "ding": Amnesic states in football trauma. Neurology 23:196, 1973.

Chapter 10

Toxic Substances

DESCRIPTION OF THE CLINICAL SYNDROMES
 Organic Solvent and Other Industrial Chemicals
 Carbon Monoxide
 Heavy Metals
 Alcohol
  Acute Intoxication
  Withdrawal
  Wernicke-Korsakoff Syndrome
  Effects of Chronic Abuse
 Drugs
  Prescription and Over-the-Counter Drugs
  Cocaine
  Marijuana
  Hallucinogens
  Amphetamines
  PCP
  "Designer Drugs"
  Permanent Brain Damage
EVALUATION
MANAGEMENT
PATHOLOGY

A 35-year-old artist was cleaning brushes in her low-ceilinged, closed studio when she began to feel very light-headed and to see double. She sat down to rest and was found in that spot shortly thereafter by a friend. The friend reported that the patient was quite confusional and could not express herself at all clearly. He opened the windows, and within several minutes the patient felt much better, had clearing of the double vision, and was more coherent.

Although subjectively and clinically much improved, the patient continued to have difficulty in thinking clearly and felt that her memory was faulty. The next day in her job as an art teacher she attempted to write a simple report but found that her writing ability had deteriorated remarkably. Her friend described her mental function during this period as being "very fuzzy." These symptoms generally improved over the course of 5 to 6 weeks. She still complained of mild memory problems, however, when we saw her 6 months later. Her friends also thought that she still did not think clearly and stated that she was extremely forgetful and anxious.

Our findings in the patient's routine neurologic examination were completely normal. Neuropsychologic testing, however, showed distinct abnormalities. She was anxious and highly apprehensive throughout the evaluation and had difficulty concentrating on tasks for sustained periods. Her affect was generally appropriate, although, on occasion, emotionality in the form of nervous laughter was exhibited in what appeared to be inappropriate situations. She had mild difficulty in naming objects to confrontation and also had noticeable word-finding difficulty in free conversation. She often resorted to circumlocution when unable to retrieve a specific word. Articulation and comprehension were normal.

Intelligence testing revealed a WAIS Full Scale IQ of 103 (Verbal IQ, 98; Performance IQ, 110). The subtest scores were considerably scattered, with the lowest scores achieved on tests of attention and concentration. Her memory, as objectively tested by the Wechsler Memory Scale Form II, showed a significantly disproportionate impairment in performance compared with her general level of intelligence. The Memory Quotient was 69. Visual memory was excellent, with most of her memory difficulties being with verbal material. Verbal abstract reasoning as tested by the Shipley-Hartford Test was grossly impaired (Conceptual Quotient = 50), but visual reasoning was shown to be within normal limits by performance on the Raven's Coloured Progressive Matrices. An MMPI was normal. Both an EEG and brain scan were normal. Unfortunately the patient was lost to follow-up.

The above case represents some of the behavioral sequelae of exposure to toxic materials. In today's society, there are many similar potential risks: the accidental or inadvertent risk of a single overwhelming exposure as was true in this case, the insidious repeated exposure experienced by workers who habitually use hydrocarbon solvents or organic insect sprays, the tragic mass poisonings with heavy metals (in particular, mercury) when such metals are mistakenly introduced into the food chain, and finally the intentional, repeated insults of alcohol and all manner of other noxious chemicals abused by some members of our culture to cope with the stress of day-to-day living. An additional distressing problem is the ever-increasing presence of industrial toxic waste—in the air, in the water, and in "toxic waste dumps."

In this chapter, we cannot and do not intend to make a general review of toxicology, nor do we wish to discuss at length the many acute intoxication syndromes and their clinical management; rather we limit this presentation to some of the lasting behavioral side effects that can occur with both a single heavy exposure and with repeated exposure, whether intentional or accidental. In many such cases, the effects on memory, intellectual performance, and emotionality can be devastating, while the effect on basic motor and sensory systems can be nil. Diagnostic tests such as the EEG, CT scan, and MRI are often normal; therefore, many cases of mild to moderate encephalopathy have been considered to be hysterical or malingering. We believe that with careful mental-status testing and neuropsychologic evaluation, this error can be avoided and adequate precautions can be provided for those persons coming into contact with these compounds.

DESCRIPTION OF THE CLINICAL SYNDROMES

Organic Solvent and Other Industrial Chemicals

Numerous volatile hydrocarbon substances have been produced since the beginning of the industrial revolution, and all of us are exposed to them in one form or another almost every day.[49]

Aluminum from a variety of sources has now been tentatively implicated in Alzheimer's disease, and a variety of trace metals, hydrocarbons, and other noxious materials are appearing in increasing amounts in our air and water, transported for vast distances by acid rain. Gasoline, cleaning fluids, insecticides, and paint solvents are commonly found in the home. In industry, a vast array of similar chemicals is used to process synthetic materials, to clean machines, and as solvents in many products. If properly used in adequately ventilated spaces, their toxicity to workers is minimal. With carelessness or disregard for safety precautions, however, acute intoxication or subtle insidious behavioral changes can develop.

We recently evaluated three women who complained of lassitude, depression with irritability, inattention, and memory problems. All had been initially seen by their family physicians, who were unable to document objective physiologic findings and concluded (with their employer) that the three women had psychiatric problems. Neurobehavioral examinations did reveal the presence of genuine deficits in memory, learning, and higher cognitive functioning, as well as the more obvious emotional changes. A careful drug-and-toxic-exposure history indicated that the women had been employed in a building undergoing interior renovation and that before the development of symptoms new carpeting had been installed by use of a toluene-based adhesive. Unfortunately, because of the season, the workers' cubicles had not been well ventilated during the 2-week installation period. Although two of the patients seemingly recovered full function over time, the cognitive problems of the remaining patient persisted until her death of unrelated causes several years after exposure.

With little thought for their deleterious effects, scores of young people have embraced the toxic side effects of many substances as being enjoyable and have repeatedly exposed themselves to highly concentrated noxious fumes. Sniffing glue, in which toluene is the major solvent, and inhaling the fumes of gasoline have been the most popular, although nitrous oxide, amyl nitrate, and other potentially noxious substances also have their adherents. Although such abuse is a negative and dangerous practice, by studying the abuser one can gain valuable information concerning the potential toxicity of chronic exposure to these substances.

The clinical picture of acute intoxication is similar for most of these agents: general inebriation, giddiness, confusion, dizziness, nausea, and vomiting if the exposure is extreme. With overwhelming exposure, stupor, coma, and even death can occur. The general consensus in the literature is that, barring significant anoxia, complete recovery from an acute episode is usually expected. However, given the fact that these substances are fat-soluble, they tend to concentrate in the highly lipid dense white matter of the central nervous system. Therefore, it seems logical to assume that these substances can accumulate in brain and damage nervous tissue. Our experience, an example of which was presented at the beginning of the chapter, confirms this assumption and suggests that such exposures are not nearly as benign as was previously believed. Patients with mild memory or behavioral changes after a single exposure have been considered in much the same way that post-traumatic patients have been evaluated: as malingering, seeking compensation, or emotionally unstable. We have examined several patients with rather significant neuropsychologic deficits after toxic exposure and believe that the true toxicity of these substances has not been fully appreciated.

In persons who suffer repeated subacute intoxicating levels of exposure (e.g., the spray painter or auto mechanic who works in a poorly ventilated, enclosed space), a chronic syndrome develops that is related to the cumulative total exposure. Such persons become progressively depressed, weak, anorexic, increasingly sensitive to the effects of alcohol, and experience difficulty in concentrating.[59] They also become easily fatigued, frequently experience headache,[27] and often exhibit the signs and symptoms of peripheral neuropathy (axonal neuropathy). Psychomotor agility is decreased both in terms of basic dexterity and speed of performance,[61] and verbal reasoning and memory also show significant decrements in performance.[32,43] Workers who are suspected of having an overt problem of toxic exposure demonstrate the most significant abnormalities, but asymptomatic workers tested at random at the same facilities also show significant cognitive difficulties.[43] These changes, although being statistically significant, are not pronounced enough to be noted by the casual observer, and because of their nature (i.e., cognitive and behavioral) are usually not detected in routine medical examinations. Nonetheless, the risk is present, and the full effects of a working lifetime of 30 years' exposure to these solvent fumes have not yet been fully documented. In one study of 50 factory workers exposed to trichloroethylene for an average of 4 years, 66 percent had overt complaints. Careful psychiatric and psychologic evaluation of the 50 patients demonstrated a slight to moderate "psycho-organic syndrome" in 34 percent.[27] Although these symptoms are often reversible when the person is withdrawn from the toxic environment, cases have been reported in which significant symptoms were still present after 14 months.[59]

More recent studies of postacute, solvent-exposed patients also show a high incidence of cognitive, pyramidal, cerebellar, brain stem, and psychiatric symptoms.[35,40,62,63] Standard neurodiagnostic procedures including the CT scan, EEG, and brain stem auditory-evoked responses confirm the presence of residual brain dysfunction in such patients. As the industrial use of aromatic hydrocarbons increases, the possibility of chronic, organically based cognitive and personality changes in exposed workers is a mounting problem.[6] A careful chemical exposure history has become a necessary part of the medical evaluation of any patient who has an unexplained cognitive or behavioral change.

The population with the most extensive toxic exposure is that of the intentional "sniffers" who use glue, gasoline, or paint to induce repeated intoxication. Although toluene is the most frequently reported neurotoxic solvent, a number of other aromatic hydrocarbons have been implicated as well. Permanent moderate to severe encephalopathy has been frequently reported in this population.[21,35-37] Most studies have found evidence of diffuse, widespread deficiencies in many areas of cognitive functioning and suggest that inhalant abusers tend to perform less adequately on cognitive testing than do other drug users.[36] The results are difficult to interpret in many instances because the patient population is typically drawn from a low socioeconomic group of people with poor cognitive and educational backgrounds. Some of these persons have significant personality problems, have previously experienced serious head trauma, and also use a variety of other drugs. It has therefore been difficult to use this population to extrapolate the possible effects of repeated industrial exposure in the normal worker. Many investigators in this field are convinced, however, that irreversible central nervous system damage does occur in people who chronically misuse these solvents.[51] More refined studies using sophisticated neurodiagnostic and neuropsychologic techniques have confirmed these impressions.[35,40]

Carbon Monoxide

Acute carbon monoxide poisoning produces a biphasic neurologic syndrome, initially characterized by a reduced level of consciousness, disorientation, seizures, and focal neurologic abnormalities.[56] This condition represents an anoxic encephalopathy. Patients surviving this initial hypoxic episode recover variably and can remain with neurologic deficits that reflect the severity of the CNS injury. Some patients are overtly normal (although undoubtedly with neuropsychologic deficits), whereas others show more obvious signs of cognitive and motor disabilities. The second phase of acute carbon monoxide exposure is a syndrome of delayed neurologic deterioration. This condition is rare, occurring in less than 1 percent of affected persons, and begins 2 to 4 weeks after hospital discharge.[56] The syndrome apparently represents a progressive multifocal cortical and white matter disease that may either improve over time or progress to a state of confusion, excitement, and motor deficits, which ultimately can result in a full, persistent vegetative state. Neuropathologically, it is believed to represent a combination CNS tissue hypoxia and selective impairment of cerebral perfusion akin to other hypoxic encephalopathies.[25]

Heavy Metals

Mental symptoms either preceding or accompanying other neurologic symptoms are commonly seen in many of the heavy metal intoxications. By far the most frequent and important offenders traditionally have been lead and mercury. In most cases of chronic exposure, the patients display irritability, apathy, headache, dizziness, weakness, and fine tremor. In lead toxicity, peripheral neuritis is common, particularly of the radial nerve resulting in wrist drop. In mercury poisoning, ataxia, stomatitis, dermatitis, and blue gum lines assist in making the clinical diagnosis.[24]

Two rather different syndromes result from mercury poisoning, with the presentation being determined by the chemical form of mercury to which the patient has been exposed. When the toxicant is methylmercury (i.e., organic mercury) such as that which polluted Minamata Bay in Japan and was used as a fungicide on the grain consumed in Iraq in 1972, the syndrome consists primarily of motor and sensory abnormalities: cerebellar ataxia, slurred speech, paresthesia, visual field constriction, tremor, pyramidal signs, and often complete cortical destruction.[24,38,45,54] Although depression and dementia are common, these are not the outstanding features of the clinical manifestation of organic mercury poisoning. Chelating agents can reduce the blood levels of methylmercury, although the efficacy of such treatment in ameliorating the cognitive symptoms is unknown.

Inorganic mercury, conversely, is well known for its ability to cause a primary psychiatric condition immortalized in the character of the "mad hatter" in Lewis Carroll's *Alice's Adventures in Wonderland.* The main symptoms include irritability, excitability, a tendency to lose control in public, which causes a withdrawal from society, memory difficulty, and often a full-blown psychosis.[45,52] Headaches, fine tremor, and weakness, although frequently present, are minor compared with the behavioral aspects. Symptoms do improve with treatment.

Because manganese is a constituent of modern steel, exposure has increased in recent years, causing an uncommon, but real, problem. Mood disturbances including depression, irritability, and sleep disorders are the first indications of manganese intoxication. Parkinsonian features are a less common secondary development.

Exposure to heavy metals is a constant threat in an industrial society, and it is only through careful adherence to safety precautions and alertness on the part of industrial medicine personnel that such horrors as those that occurred in Minamata and Iraq can be avoided.

Alcohol

Alcohol abuse and its frequent companion, malnutrition, are the cause of a wide variety of neurobehavioral syndromes. Because alcoholism is such a major problem in the world, all physicians should become familiar with its various toxic manifestations and their management.

ACUTE INTOXICATION

The acute stage of alcoholic intoxication is all too familiar to most of us, whether from personal experience or from working in a hospital emergency ward. Little elaboration of its symptoms seems necessary other than to mention that it can frequently appear as an acute confusional state and must be considered in the differential diagnosis of that syndrome.

Not all persons, however, follow the usual course of inebriation. A number undergo a rather remarkable personality and behavioral transformation after only a few drinks. This so-called alcoholic idiosyncratic intoxication[3] or pathologic intoxication[7] is a very dramatic event, one that has been viewed with a jaundiced eye by some clinicians.[34] The typical history is that of a young to middle-aged man who may or may not be a habitual drinker and who, usually after only a few drinks, becomes suddenly disoriented, paranoid, anxious, and violent. Such persons frequently state that they feel extraordinarily strong and often are physically very violent. In many reported cases, these people have actually severely injured or killed people unfortunate enough to be in their immediate environment.[7] After the sudden explosive outburst, the person is usually fatigued and falls easily to sleep. On awakening he typically has little or no memory of the episode. Many of these individuals basically have rather pathologic personalities, and it is difficult to totally excuse the behavior as occurring as a completely unconscious and uncontrolled act. The exact pathophysiology of these reactions, however, is not known. They may represent a type of alcohol-induced dissociative episode. An organic cause, however, cannot be totally excluded.

WITHDRAWAL

The habituated alcohol user runs the risk of developing one or a variety of more serious organic brain disorders. Once addicted, the person may suffer the acute symptoms of withdrawal should he abruptly stop drinking, or more significantly, he can develop irreversible amnesia (Korsakoff's syndrome) or dementia. The most familiar syndrome secondary to alcohol withdrawal is delirium tremens. Already discussed in Chapter 5, this state is a syndrome of tremulousness and agitated confusion that develops during the first few days of abstinence and can last from a few days to a week. Visual and tactile hallucinations, paranoia, and wild agitation are present in severe cases. Generalized seizures occur in a few cases, with status epilepticus being one of the most serious problems encountered in management. As with any confusional state, the course will fluctuate during the day, with nocturnal exacerbations being characteristic. Treatment regimens vary, but vitamins, adequate nutrition, sedation (chlordiazepoxide up to 400 mg per day), anticonvulsants (diphenylhydantoin 300 mg per day), and physical restraint when absolutely necessary have been the most satisfactory for us.

A fascinating, rare withdrawal syndrome is seen in a very small number of alcoholics — chronic alcoholic hallucinosis.[64] The hallucinations are usually auditory, unlike the vivid visual and tactile hallucinations of delirium, and are present in a person with an otherwise completely clear sensorium. The syndrome most frequently occurs after a delirium, and although usually lasting only a few weeks, it can persist for years. Whether this syndrome is totally an effect of alcohol or is really a schizophrenic syndrome in an alcoholic is not known.

WERNICKE-KORSAKOFF SYNDROME

The central nervous system of the alcoholic is subjected to various insults: the very probable toxic effects of alcohol itself; repeated head trauma; the secondary effects from liver disease; and, in many alcoholics, severe nutritional deficiency. In those persons with inadequate nutrition, the vitamin thiamine often becomes grossly deficient. Thiamine deficiency results in one of the most devastating syndromes associated with the abuse of alcohol, the Wernicke-Korsakoff syndrome.[50,67] The condition appears in a small percentage of the alcoholic population. Recent experimental evidence strongly suggests that those affected have an inborn predisposition.[6] Some of those affected have been shown to have a genetic defect in the enzyme transketolase that prevents thiamine binding. This leaves them particularly vulnerable to thiamine deficiency. This syndrome is seen in chronically malnourished alcoholics and usually develops over a period of a few days to a few weeks.

The acute phase of the condition, the Wernicke's encephalopathy or hemorrhagic polioencephalitis, is heralded in two thirds of the cases by a state of mental confusion, often called a global confusional state.[67] Unlike the patient in active delirium tremens, the patient with a confusional state secondary to Wernicke's encephalopathy is most often quiet or lethargic. The condition has all of the features of a confusional state described at length in Chapter 5, except that the alcoholic more frequently shows the physical appearance of dereliction and is somewhat less likely to have hallucinations. In association with the mental changes, the patients demonstrate nystagmus (85%), various ocular rotation abnormalities (lateral rectus palsy [54%]), conjugate gaze difficulty (44%), and complete ophthalmoplegia (rare), ataxia (87%), and polyneuropathy (82%).[22,67] Unlike Wernicke's solely caused by malnutrition, alcoholics with this syndrome do not develop beriberi cardiac disease. The diagnosis is not difficult to make clinically if suspected, and treatment of the acute episode is relatively simple. Significantly, Wernicke's encephalopathy is the only ethanol-related disorder that can be corrected.

Once diagnosed, the specific treatment is intramuscular or intravenous thiamine, 50 to 100 mg per day for several days, then oral thiamine 50 mg per day for 1 month or until such time as the patient resumes a normal diet. Avoid using concentrated glucose solutions *particularly before* administering thiamine because the metabolism of the glucose further depletes the patient's thiamine stores, thus causing an acute deterioration of the patient's status. Seizures are not a usual problem nor is severe agitation; accordingly sedatives and anticonvulsants should be used only when necessary.

Recovery from the neurologic deficits and the mental confusion is usually rapid, and the mortality during the acute stage is less than 20 percent.[67] Lateral gaze problems may regress in a matter of hours and are almost always clear within a week's time.[67] The gaze palsy clears more slowly, with restitution of function being complete in 95 percent of the patients within 4 weeks. Nystagmus and ataxia may linger in 31 and 52 percent of patients respectively[67] after 1 month's treatment. Confusional behavior is present in 33 percent of the patients after 1 month, but this problem has usually cleared after 2 months. A residual cerebellar disorder may persist despite proper treatment and resolution of other neurologic symptoms. As the confusional behavior and neurologic abnormalities clear, a high percentage of patients with Wernicke's encephalopathy are found to have a significant residual memory deficit — 84 percent according to Victor and associates.[67] This memory defect is a typical organic amnesia with recent memory (ability to learn new material) significantly affected, whereas immediate recall and remote memory are unimpaired.[14] Other cognitive functions including intelligence, language, and constructional ability are often remarkably preserved. At this stage, such patients are diagnosed as having a Korsakoff's syndrome. It is often very difficult to ascertain when the patient passes from the acute Wernicke's encephalopathy into the chronic amnesic Korsakoff stage. Although this is the natural progression, the amnesic patient often appears confusional because of his memory troubles. Similarly, the patient in the last throes of a confusional state often has difficulty with memory whether he eventually develops a Korsakoff's syndrome or not. There is no specific laboratory test to help with the differential diagnosis; accordingly the examiner must rely on clinical acumen to make the distinction.

The Korsakoff syndrome when fully developed is a profound amnesic state. The patients are literally suspended in time. No new experiences can be recorded for more than a few moments, and patients are hopelessly incapable of maintaining an independent existence.

Under specific experimental conditions, such patients have some limited capability to learn and to retrieve some memories; however, there is almost no generalization of these abilities. Korsakoff patients are generally totally unaware and unconcerned about their memory limitations. During the first weeks or months of his amnesia, the patient with Korsakoff's syndrome has a strong tendency to confabulate whenever specific information is asked of him. This phase passes in time, and the patient with the chronic condition is generally apathetic, somewhat withdrawn, and as a salubrious side effect, no longer addicted to alcohol. This spontaneous cure of the alcoholism may be a direct effect of hypothalamic lesions or possibly a behavioral effect relating to a general lack of concern. As was pointed out in Chapter 8, the patient's general intelligence does not suffer significantly during the course of the disease, with the most outstanding cognitive defect being recent memory.

The prognosis for the patient with Korsakoff's syndrome is not hopeless; at least 20 to 50 percent ultimately recover completely. An additional 20 to 30 percent show significant improvement in memory function. Unfortunately the remainder demonstrate either no or only slight improvement in memory processing. Those who do recover usually do so over a period of months, although occasionally the period of recovery can be as short as a few weeks or as long as 2 years. There is no known treatment.[22]

The pathology of Korsakoff's syndrome is primarily in the midline structures in the diencephalon, most frequently the mamillary bodies and the dorsomedial nucleus of the thalamus. Lesions are also found with regularity throughout the brain stem and cerebellum as well as in the cerebral cortex. A complete discussion of the neuropathology in such cases can be obtained from the work of Victor and colleagues[67] or Diamond and Charness.[22]

Although the Wernicke-Korsakoff syndrome is most often seen in the malnourished alcoholic, it has been reported in other starvation syndromes (e.g., concentration camp survivors, anorexia nervosa, and patients after gastrointestinal surgery to control obesity), in systemic disease, and in patients with persistent vomiting.

EFFECTS OF CHRONIC ABUSE

The Wernicke-Korsakoff syndrome is a dramatic, acute condition that frequently leaves the patient with an equally dramatic chronic neurobehavioral change. The question of a gradual deterioration of mental and neurologic function in the alcoholic has been less adequately documented. In Chapter 7, we discussed much of the evidence to support the hypothesis that an alcoholic dementia does exist, and we will not reiterate the arguments here. As with most dementias, deterioration is slow, and in the case of chronic alcoholism, can be arrested but not reversed at any time if permanent abstinence is achieved.

An extensive series of neuropsychologic studies of alcoholics has amply demonstrated that the chronic alcoholic without overt dementia does in fact demonstrate multiple deficits in a number of areas.[11,19,26,44,47,48] With abstinence, test performance tends to improve over a period of a few weeks.[8,47] After this initial period of improvement, however, the alcoholic continues to have significantly lower scores than do matched controls on tests of nonverbal functioning, memory, and abstract reasoning.[8,11,47] The degree of residual permanent mental deficit seems to be directly related to the amount of alcohol consumed and the cumulative years of alcohol abuse, although not all studies agree.[29,41,47] Most investigations were done on older men (mid 40s and older), which favored the hypothesis that many years of heavy drinking were necessary to produce mental change. Other reports concerning alcoholics in their mid 30s gave differing results.[12,29,41]

One study showed significant intellectual impairment in 59 percent of those studied and cerebral atrophy (maximal frontally) on CT scanning in 49 percent,[41] whereas another study, equally carefully done, failed to demonstrate any significant neuropsychologic deficit in these young alcoholics.[29] Regardless of the actual number of years of alcoholism necessary to cause mental impairment, the fact remains that heavy, chronic alcohol intake is not uniformly well tolerated by the brain.

An excellent review series summarizing recent research methodologies and findings in this area has been published by the American Psychological Association.[4] These reviews continue to report previously noted cognitive deficits in chronic alcoholics, while offering the cautious optimism that such deficits are most frequent and severe in specific groups, especially older alcoholics, and that recovery is related to the duration of total abstinence. Normal social drinkers seem to be immune to these effects—at least we hope so.

Drugs

The literature covering the untoward effects of prescription and illicit drugs is voluminous and virtually impossible to summarize briefly. Therefore, in this section we will review only some of the recent opinions concerning the possible long-term behavioral side effects of chronic drug abuse. Comprehensive reviews of the acute effects, pharmacology, management, and social aspects of drug abuse are readily available for the interested reader. We have discussed in Chapter 5 the fact that many drugs, licit or illicit, can produce an acute confusional state as a symptom of intoxication. This intoxication syndrome varies somewhat (e.g., the strange mute state or aggressive agitated delirium with phencyclidine [PCP][20] and the active paranoiac hallucinatory states with LSD), but it basically can be characterized by an altered sensorium, clouded consciousness, inattention, and a fluctuating course.

PRESCRIPTION AND OVER-THE-COUNTER DRUGS

The chronic overuse or abuse of prescribed hypnotics, analgesics or sedatives,[9] and over-the-counter drugs can produce acute psychiatric symptoms and long-term signs of cognitive impairment. Discontinuation of drug use usually reverses the symptomatology, although demonstrable intellectual deficits have been noted for as long as 3 months after drug withdrawal. Because many such drugs are taken surreptitiously by unlikely drug-abuse candidates or are not even considered to be true "drugs" by many patients, the need for a careful drug history is apparent in the patient presenting with an unexplained behavioral change.

COCAINE

Use of the alcaloid cocaine has increased substantially since publication of the first edition of this book. It is now the drug of choice of many abusers and is reaching a much wider spectrum of the population than more traditionally used illicit drugs. Cocaine can be used in isolation (intranasally, smoked, or intravenously) or in combination with a variety of other drugs including heroin, marijuana, hashish, or PCP. A cocaine psychosis characterized by paranoia, agitation, hypervigilance, and hallucinations can occur with high doses or chronic use.[39] More chronic conditions resembling mania, paranoid schizophrenia, or generalized fatigue and lassitude are now coming to attention.[57] Subarachnoid hemorrhage and intracranial bleeding may result from abrupt increases in blood pressure, causing obvious neurologic deficits and even death.

MARIJUANA

A review of the literature reveals that, in general, chronic marijuana use does not result in any significant change in intellectual or emotional behavior.[18,39,55,58,66] The most impressive and well-controlled study was done in Costa Rica, a country that does not have the strong legal and social sanctions against marijuana present in the United States. This study evaluated a group of men who had smoked a mean of nine marijuana cigarettes daily for an average of 17 years. No significant impairment was demonstrated on an extensive neuropsychologic battery.[55] The use of other drugs by the population was not extensive; thus, the results seem to give a reasonable estimate of the long-term effects of heavy cannabis use. The possibility of longlasting, adverse effects of one-time usage of cannabis in highly susceptible persons, especially those with pre-existing psychopathology, has been reported.[23] This possibility suggests that the use of any psychoactive drug may have the potential to precipitate decompensation and exacerbate symptoms in persons having underlying psychiatric symptomatology.

HALLUCINOGENS

The problems involved in the study of the chronic use of hallucinogens are also complex. Seldom used in isolation, their specific long-term effects are difficult to judge accurately. Some high-level cognitive loss seems to be associated with heavy use,[31] but these data have not been satisfactorily corroborated.[30] Review studies suggest that documented deficits tend to improve with abstinence and time.[16] One of the long-term residua that has been well described is the recurrent hallucinatory experience (flashbacks) noted in both chronic and short-term abusers of hallucinogens. Such episodes may occur in excess of 5 years after cessation of drug use and tend to be visual in nature. The hallucinatory experiences are exacerbated by phenothiazines and can be effectively treated by benzodiazapines.[1] In addition to LSD, phencyclidine has also been reported to produce abrupt lapses into bizarre confusional and "schizophrenia-like" states weeks to months after acute intoxication.[39] Because hallucinogenic drugs have been shown to affect virtually every neurotransmitter studied, a disruption of CNS chemistry seems the probable cause of such states.

The psychiatric effects of hallucinogens are also poorly documented and much of the research in the field has not been scientifically rigorous. Some investigators hypothesize that the lasting psychiatric side effects are seen only in previously emotionally disturbed persons who took the drugs in crisis situations or in unstable environments.[46] Others have observed serious psychiatric sequelae in perfectly normal persons after minimal exposure to LSD or other such drugs.[2,23] No genetic predisposition toward schizophrenia has been reported in those who develop a psychosis secondary to hallucinogen use,[33] but some premorbid personality problems or constitutional factors such as childhood hyperactivity may be possible contributing factors.[60]

AMPHETAMINES

Several drugs seem to be particularly hazardous, with more consistent and objective demonstration of their deleterious side effects having been made. Drugs within the amphetamine class are one group. Both behavioral and physical effects can be catastrophic. With acute toxicity a full-blown paranoid psychosis is often seen, and in some patients who consistently use high doses of these drugs, a marked disruption in the brain's normal microvasculature can occur. Venules as well as arterioles are involved, and the resultant diffuse small-vessel occlusions and petechial hemorrhage can lead to a profound encephalopathy.[53] Pharmacologically, the amphetamines significantly disrupt the catecholaminergic system in the CNS, causing serious neurochemical dysfunction.

PCP

Another devasting drug is phencyclidine (PCP or "angel dust"). During the acute intoxication stage, the patients are often extremely psychotic and violent. With large doses, excited or stuporous catatonia, mutism, and seizures can develop. Acute schizophrenic reactions lasting for several months have been reported.[16,20] Chronic abuse tends to result in organic cognitive problems, with memory and speech difficulties predominating.[20] There does seem to be a clearing of cognitive deficits in 6 to 12 months, although intermittent psychiatric flashbacks are not uncommon.[39]

"DESIGNER DRUGS"

Designer drugs (e.g., MPTP) are an increasing problem to modern society. In part, the problem is related to the popularity and rapid development of these uncontrolled substances. In addition, the active components and all-too-frequent contaminants of the drugs are unknown to the consumer or to the physician attempting to deal with the patient's problem. Most illicit designer drugs known to date have selective neurotoxic properties that cause a wide range of neurologic symptoms varying from visual blurring, tremors, rigidity, bradykinesia, and a parkinson-like syndrome to psychosis and possible premature aging of selective brain cells.[39] Because illicit chemistry is apparently moving more rapidly (and dangerously) than medical research in this area, the use of newer and potentially more damaging substances will continue to present very real problems to the physician.

PERMANENT BRAIN DAMAGE

Chronic overuse of any psychoactive substance can produce toxic behavioral symptoms that superficially appear like dementia because of their chronicity; actually the clinical picture is more akin to a chronic confusional state. This condition usually reverses promptly with cessation of use of the drug. The contention that chronic misuse of either prescribed psychotropics or illicit street drugs results in permanent brain damage has not yet been firmly substantiated. Death and permanent brain damage are common with use of many street drugs. In the vast majority of cases, however, the causes of this serious central nervous system morbidity and mortality are inadvertent massive overdose, adulterants that are used to dilute the drug (particularly strychnine), vasospasm, or vasculitis or sepsis from contaminated syringes and needles. Overdose can lead to serious brain anoxia or, in the case of amphetamine and cocaine, severe vascular changes and hypertension that can lead to micro-infarcts (primarily cardiac) and cerebral hemorrhage.

Most heavy drug users use a variety of drugs and the toxic effects of a single drug are difficult if not impossible to define accurately. Accordingly, many studies group patients and discuss the resultant findings as the effect of polydrug abuse. The last, and one of the most difficult problems, is that of obtaining research subjects who have chronically used drugs but have subsequently stopped. Many studies have been carried out in which subjects have been studied after all signs of intoxication or withdrawal have subsided. The subjects, however, have been totally free from drug use for no more than several days or, at the most, 1 or 2 months. Because many of the studies do show areas of impaired cognitive performance, it is important to determine whether those performance deficits are temporary and would clear with an extended period of abstinence. The absolute answer to the question of permanent brain damage from drug abuse remains uncertain, although it is now obvious that residual neuropsychologic and neurologic deficits are seen in a percentage of patients using a wide variety of illicit drugs.[39]

Polydrug users, particularly those abusing heroin, sedatives, minor tranquilizers, and hallucinogens, are not as fortunate as the marijuana smoker in escaping lasting toxic effects from their drug abuse. Significant impairment on neuropsychologic testing is shown by 35 to 65 percent of chronic polydrug users.[5,9,16,17,28,30,31,39] The cognitive functions that are affected most noticeably are those of high-level reasoning, tasks involving conceptual shifting (e.g., Halstead category test), and overall intellectual functioning. These findings seem true by consensus, but are not supported by all investigators. One group of 87 prisoners, who had been heavy multiple drug users, had no significant deficits when tested on a comprehensive psychologic test battery.[13] One of the reasons for the disparate results may have been that the prisoners had been drug-free for a much longer time than the typical subjects, and some of the effects seen in the nonincarcerated drug users may have been only temporary. Some support for this latter hypothesis is provided by a study of 66 heavy drug users who initially had a 46 percent incidence of cognitive impairment but on retest 5 months later had only a 27 percent incidence.[28] These results suggest an intermediate stage of encephalopathy much like that seen in the alcoholic. Whether improvement continues over a longer period is not yet known. Whatever the usual outcome, patients with lasting deficits have been reported, indicating that abstinence does not always result in a remission of symptoms.

EVALUATION

The neurobehavioral side effects of toxic substances are evaluated in the same manner as for those of brain damage of any cause. Careful history taking, however, is extremely important in these cases. A complete occupational, environmental, and alcohol/drug history is necessary. In evaluating the drug or alcohol abuser, the accurate history often has to be obtained from a relative or friend rather than the patient. Therefore, it is prudent to interview the patient and family separately. After the history, a complete neurologic examination including mental status testing must be carried out. In any patient in whom there is any suggestion of cognitive or emotional change, a complete neuropsychologic battery should be administered. The objective data obtained from a test battery can be especially valuable in documenting the patient's recovery, establishing the nature and degree of deficit for insurance and legal purposes, and planning the treatment and rehabilitation program.

The particular laboratory studies chosen—drug screening, heavy-metal analysis of urine and serum, or alcohol levels—will depend on the suspected toxin. For purposes of assessing the degree of encephalopathy in chronic cases, the CT scan or MRI are useful, and the EEG is also occasionally of some help. In general, we find that the clinical data from mental status testing and neuropsychologic testing are the most helpful.

MANAGEMENT

Two basic aspects of the management of the patient with toxic exposure are important: (1) management of the toxic symptoms or residual effects in the person and (2) identification and management of the toxic source itself. With industrial pollution or exposure, the problem is often a complex epidemiologic and environmental one. In some instances, simple safety precautions at a particular factory or shop will eliminate the problem; however, in other cases (e.g., the possible toxic effects of trace metals in drinking water in cities along the lower Mississippi), the solution is less obvious. One problem regarding toxic exposure that has not been dealt with sufficiently is the potential effect of combined exposure to toxic substances. Animal research evidence indicates that there is a synergic effect among some neurotoxins and that the combined effect is greater than the sum of the toxicity of the individual toxins. The U.S. Department of Labor requires all companies producing volatile substances to file a "Material Safety Data Sheet" discussing the hazard potential and safe levels of exposure for each chemical. This information is vital to the safety officer in an individual plant where the substance is used. What is not known is the total toxic effect of multiple substances, all used at their individual safe levels. Another problem that has not received adequate attention is the effect of toxic substances in the social drinker, diabetic, or hypertensive. These factors may make the hazard of exposure to a given substance greater and place certain persons at greater risk of toxicity than is currently recognized.

The problem of medically managing the drug addict or the alcoholic is vastly different. The toxin is usually known, and prevention of side effects and sequelae is simple—abstinence and symptomatic treatment with appropriate medications. That is a simple solution, but unfortunately it is very difficult either to impose or to enforce. The general emotional and social rehabilitation problems involved in alcoholism and drug addiction are great and beyond the scope of this book.

The actual medical management of the patient suffering from exposure to toxins is somewhat easier. First, the patient must be immediately removed from contact with the toxic agent, and the acute symptoms must be treated. This acute treatment depends on the specific toxin, and the correct information is best obtained from standard medical and toxicology texts. After the acute effects have passed, the patient should be thoroughly examined by a physician and, if there has been any suggestion of encephalopathy, a neurologist; in many cases, a psychologist should also evaluate the patient. It is usually better to wait several weeks before undertaking extensive neuropsychologic testing because of the rather gradual recovery of full mental capacity in some of these patients. If significant cognitive impairment is present, the patient may require vocational assessment and retraining. As with patients with head injury with mild or moderate encephalopathy, family counseling and environmental manipulation may be necessary to help the patients cope with their limitations.

PATHOLOGY

Very little is known concerning the pathology of the mild encephalopathies seen with solvent exposure, alcohol, or drugs. There are reports of cortical atrophy in alcoholics, the degree of atrophy being in direct proportion to the alcoholic's performance on psychologic tests. Therefore, it is fairly certain that brain damage is a gradual cytotoxic process in the alcoholic. Alcoholic dementia and Wernicke-Korsakoff syndrome have been discussed previously, and the pathology of these states is well known. These syndromes are more completely discussed in Chapters 7 and 8.

In drug abuse (excluding the serious effects of anoxia from overdose and the vasculitis in amphetamine abuse), there is little information about pathologic changes, although the disruption of neurotransmitters by illicit drugs has now been well documented.[39] An early report of cerebral atrophy secondary to chronic cannabis use has been much criticized in the literature and probably suffered from a sampling error.[15]

In general, toxic substances attack the metabolic processes of the neurons. With low levels of exposure, the neuron can withstand this challenge, whereas high doses or chronic medium-sized doses cause the cells to shrink and eventually to die. With sufficiently extensive cell death, irreversible mental changes and atrophy occur.

REFERENCES

1. Abrahams, HD: Visual phenomenology of the LSD flashback. Arch Gen Psychiatry 40:884, 1983.
2. Abruzzi, W: Drug-induced psychoses . . . or schizophrenia? Am J Psychoanal 35:329, 1975.
3. American Psychiatric Association: Diagnostic and Statistic Manual III of Mental Disorders. American Psychiatric Society, Washington, DC, 1980.
4. American Psychological Association: Alcoholism series. Am Psychologist 41:1045, 1986.

5. Aniline, O and Pitts, FNI: A review and perspectives. CRC Crit Rev Toxicol 10:145, 1982.

6. Arlien-Soborg, P et al: Chronic painters' syndrome. Acta Neurol Scand 60:149, 1979.

7. Banay, RS: Pathologic reaction to alcohol. Quart J Stud Alcohol 4:580, 1944.

8. Bennett, AE: Diagnosis of intermediate state of alcoholic brain disease. JAMA 172:1143, 1960.

9. Bergman, H, Borg, S, and Holm, L: Neuropsychological impairment and exclusive abuse of sedatives or hypnotics. Am J Psychiat 137:215, 1980.

10. Blass, JP and Gibson, GE: Abnormality of a thiamine-requiring enzyme in patients with Wernicke-Korsakoff syndrome. N Engl J Med 297:1367, 1977.

11. Blusewicz, MJ et al: Neuropsychological correlates of chronic alcoholism and aging. J Nerv Ment Dis 165:348, 1977.

12. Brandt, J et al: Cognitive loss and recovery in long-term alcohol abuses. Arch Gen Psychiatry 40:435, 1983.

13. Bruhn, P and Maage, N: Intellectual and neuropsychological functions in young men with heavy and long-term pattern of drug abuse. Am J Psychiatry 132:397, 1975.

14. Butters, N and Cermak, LS: Alcoholic Korsakoff's Syndrome: An Information-processing Approach to Amnesia. Academic Press, New York, 1980.

15. Campbell, A, Evans, M, and Thompson, J: Cerebral atrophy in young cannabis smokers. Lancet 1:1219, 1971.

16. Carlin, AS: Neuropsychological consequences of drug abuse. In Grant, I and Adams, KM (eds): Neuropsychological Assessment of Neuropsychiatric Disorders. Oxford University Press, New York, 1986, pp 478–497.

17. Carlin, AS et al: Drug abuse style, drug use type, and neuropsychological deficit in polydrug uses. Addict Behav 5:229, 1980.

18. Carlin, AS and Trupin, EW: The effect of long-term chronic marijuana use on neuropsychological functioning. Int J Addict 12:617, 1977.

19. Clarke, J and Haughton, H: A study of intellectual impairment and recovery rates in heavy drinkers in Ireland. Br J Psychiatry 126:178, 1975.

20. Cohen, S: Angel dust. JAMA 238:515, 1977.

21. Comstock, BS: A review of psychological measures relevant to central nervous system toxicity, with specific reference to solvent inhalation. Clin Toxicol 11:317, 1977.

22. Diamond, I and Charness, MC: Alcohol neurotoxicity. In Asbury, AK, McKhann, GM, and McDonald, WI (eds): Diseases of the Nervous System. WB Saunders, Philadelphia, 1986, pp 1324–1332.

23. Gersten, SP: Long-term adverse effects of brief marijuana use. J Clin Psychiat 41:60, 1980.

24. Gerstenbrand, F et al: Apallic syndrome in chronic mercury poisoning. Eur Neurol 15:249, 1977.

25. Ginsberg, M: Carbon monoxide. In Spencer, PS and Schaumburg, HH (eds): Clinical Neurotoxicology. Williams & Wilkins, Baltimore, 1980.

26. Goodwin, DW and Hill, SY: Chronic effects of alcohol and other psychoactive drugs on intellect, learning and memory. In Rankin, JA (ed): Alcohol, Drugs and Brain Damage: Alcoholism and Drug Addiction. Research Foundation of Ontario, Toronto, 1975, pp 55–69.

27. Grandjean, E et al: Investigations into the effects of exposure to trichlorethylene in mechanical engineering. Br J Ind Med 12:131, 1955.

28. Grant, I and Judd, LL: Neuropsychological and EEG disturbances in polydrug users. Am J Psychiatry 133:1039, 1976.

29. Grant, I, Adams, K, and Reed, R: Normal neuropsychological abilities of alcoholic men in their late thirties. Am J Psychiatry 136:1263, 1979.

30. Grant, I et al: Neuropsychological deficit in polydrug users. Drug Alcohol Depend 2:91, 1977.

31. Grant, I et al: A neuropsychological study of polydrug users. Arch Gen Psychiatry 33:973, 1976.

32. Hanniner, H et al: Behavioral effects of long-term exposure to a mixture of organic solvents. Scand J Work Environ Health 4:240, 1976.

33. Hays, P and Tilley, JR: The difference between LSD psychosis and schizophrenia. Can Psychiatr Assoc J 8:331, 1973.

34. Hollender, M: Pathological intoxication — Is there such an entity? J Clin Psychiatry 40:424, 1979.

35. Hormes, JT, Filley, CM, and Rosenberg, NL: Neurologic sequelae of chronic solvent vapor abuse. Neurology 36:698, 1986.

36. Korman, M, Matthews, RW, and Lovitt, R: Neuropsychological effects of abuse of inhalants. Percept Mot Skills 53:547, 1981.

37. Knox, JW and Nelson, JR: Permanent encephalopathy from toluene inhalation. N Engl J Med 275:1494, 1966.

38. Kurland, LT, Faro, SN, and Siedler, H: Minamata disease: The outbreak of a neurologic disorder in Minamata, Japan, and its relationship to the ingestion of seafood contaminated by mercuric compounds. World Neurology 1:370, 1960.

39. Langston, JW and Langston, EB: Neurological consequences of drug abuse. In Asbury, AK, McKhann, GM, and McDonald, WI (eds): Diseases of the Nervous System. WB Saunders, Philadelphia, 1986, pp 1333–1340.

40. Lazar, RB et al: Multifocal central nervous system damage caused by toluene abuse. Neurology 33:1337, 1983.

41. Lee, K et al: Alcohol-induced brain damage and liver damage in young males. Lancet 2:759, 1979.

42. LeQuesne, PM: Metal toxicity. In Asbury, AK, McKhann, SM, and McDonald, WI (eds): Diseases of the Nervous System. WB Saunders, Philadelphia, 1986, pp 1315–1323.

43. Lindstrom, K: Psychological performances of workers exposed to various solvents. Scand J Work Environ Health 10:151, 1973.

44. Long, AJ and McLachlan, JFC: Abstract reasoning and perceptual-motor efficiency in alcoholics. Quart J Stud Alcohol 35:1220, 1974.

45. Maghazaji, HI: Psychiatric aspects of methyl mercury poisoning. J Neurol Neurosurg Psychiatry 37:954, 1974.

46. McWilliams, SA and Tuttle, RJ: Long-term psychological effects of LSD. Psychol Bull 79:341, 1973.

47. Page, RD and Linden, JD: "Reversible" organic brain syndrome in alcoholics. Quart J Stud Alcohol 35:98, 1974.

48. Page, RD and Schaub, LH: Intellectual functioning in alcoholics during six months abstinence. J Stud Alcohol 38:1240, 1977.

49. Prockop, L: Neurotoxic volatile substances. Neurology 29:862, 1979.

50. Reuler, JB, Girard, DE, and Cooney, TG: Wernicke's encephalopathy. N Engl J Med 312:1035, 1985.

51. Riding, A: Derelict Mexican boys sniff toxic chemicals. The New York Times, April 9, 1978, p 21.

52. Ross, WD et al: Need for alertness to neuropsychiatric manifestations of inorganic mercury poisoning. Compr Psychiatry 18:595, 1977.

53. Rumbaugh, CL: Small vessel cerebral vascular changes following chronic amphetamine intoxication. In Ellinwood, EH, Jr and Kilbey, MM (eds): Cocaine and Other Stimulants. Plenum Press, New York, 1977, pp 241–251.

54. Rustam, H and Hamdi, T: Methyl mercury poisoning in Iraq. Brain 97:499, 1974.

55. Satz, P, Fletcher, JM, and Sutker, LS: Neuropsychologic, intellectual and personality correlates of chronic marijuana use in native Costa Ricans. Ann NY Acad Sci 282:266, 1976.

56. Schaumburg, HH and Spencer, PS: Chemical toxicity. In Asbury, AK, McKhann, GM, and McDonald, WI (eds): Diseases of the Nervous System. WB Saunders, Philadelphia, 1980, pp 1303–1314.

57. Siegel, RK: Changing patterns of cocaine use: Longitudinal observations, consequences, and treatment. In National Institute on Drug Abuse: Cocaine Pharmacology, Effects, and Treatment of Abuse. US Department of Health and Human Services, Washington, 1984, pp 92–110.

58. Stefanis, C et al: Chronic hashish use and mental disorder. Am J Psychiatry 133:225, 1976.

59. Sterner, JH: Study of hazards in spray painting with gasoline as a diluent. J Indust Hyg Toxic 23:437, 1941.

60. Stone, MH: Drug-related schizophrenic syndrome. Int J Psychiatry 11:391, 1973.

61. Stopps, GJ and McLaughlin, M: Psychophysiological testing of human subjects exposed to solvent vapors. Am Ind Hyg Assoc J 28:43, 1967.

62. Struwe, G, Knave, B, and Mindus, P: Neuropsychiatric symptoms in workers occupationally exposed to jet fuel—a combined epidemiological and casuistic study. Acta Psychiatr Scand 67 (Suppl 303):55, 1983.

63. Struwe, G and Wennberg, A: Psychiatric and neurological symptoms in workers occupationally exposed to organic solvents—results of a differential epidemiological study. Acta Psychiatr Scand 67 (Suppl 303):68, 1983.

64. Surawicz, FG: Alcoholic hallucinosis: A missed diagnosis. Can J Psychiatry 25:57, 1980.

65. Trites, R: Neuropsychological deficits in 'primary' and 'secondary' nonmedical drug users. Can Psychiatr Assoc J 20:351, 1975.

66. Tunving, K: Psychiatric effects of cannabis use. Acta Psychiatr Scand 72:209, 1985.

67. Victor, M, Adams, RD, and Collins, GH: The Wernicke-Korsakoff Syndrome. FA Davis, Philadelphia, 1971.

Chapter 11

Infections of the Central Nervous System

A 52-year-old accountant began to experience generalized headaches while at work. The patient lived alone and called a relative to tell her that he was not feeling well, had a fever, and would remain home from work the following day. On the next day, the relative telephoned the patient but received no answer. On the third day, she again tried to reach him by phone but he did not answer. Concerned, she went to his house, broke in, and found him in bed, virtually moribund. He was unresponsive, rigid, and covered with a petechial rash. He was immediately taken to a nearby hospital.

On initial examination in the emergency room, he was stuporous, with grimacing and decorticate posturing in response to painful stimulation. His neck was extremely rigid; he was febrile (39.2°C), had an extensive petechial and purpuric rash, and appeared to have a left hemiparesis. A spinal puncture was done; the fluid was grossly purulent with an opening pressure of 300 mm H_2O. It contained 27,200 leukocytes (all polymorphonuclear cells). The protein was 185 mg per 100 ml. Gram stains of the spinal fluid and peripheral blood demonstrated intracellular gram-negative diplococci; the diagnosis of meningococcal meningitis with meningococcemia was confirmed. He was immediately placed on therapy of high doses of intravenous penicillin (20 million units daily).

Within 48 hours, he began to show distinct improvement and by the third hospital day was awake and alert, yet mental status examination showed general confusional behavior. A moderate left hemiparesis was still present. At this time, we first appreciated his left-sided neglect. He would never turn to his left when spoken to from that side, and any examiner who approached him from the left was totally ignored. As his general medical condition improved, the neglect persisted, and he developed evidence of implicit denial. From his conversation, it was apparent that he thought he was in another hospital that was next door to his house and reported that he was only in the hospital "to see about a painful left knee" (he had developed joint pain during the acute stage of his illness and had an effusion of the left knee). This denial persisted for only several days and gradually disappeared as his general orientation improved and his mental state cleared.

Twenty-five days after admission, the patient was ambulating well and was conversing normally, although there was a continued weakness of the left side. He was discharged from the hospital and went to stay with a relative. A CT scan done on the day of discharge was normal.

Re-evaluation 1 month later showed no motor deficit. The patient reported that he was again playing the piano and typing as proficiently as before his illness. It was his opinion that he was ready to return to work on a part-time basis. To enable us to advise him concerning any possible organic mental deficits secondary to the meningitis, we administered a full neuropsychologic battery. The evaluation demonstrated several clinically interesting problems. Throughout the testing, he was moderately anxious. He also had a substantial degree of denial, which was judged to be a combined neurologic and psychologic origin.

On specific cognitive testing, performance varied considerably. On the

Wechsler Adult Intelligence Scale, he performed well on the Information and Comprehension subtests but significantly less adequately on verbal abstract reasoning as tested by the Similarities subtest. He had great difficulty with all performance subtests, in particular the Digit Symbol Test and Block Designs. His Bender Gestalt protocol showed mild constructional difficulties, and the Raven's Standard Progressive Matrices (a test of spatial analysis and nonverbal reasoning) was very severely impaired (less than the 5th percentile). The Trail Making Test showed impairment on form B (less than the 15th percentile with two errors) in which conceptual shifting is required. His Wechsler Memory quotient was significantly depressed (MQ = 83) compared with his Full Scale IQ (105). Memory for paragraphs showed the least adequate performance, but visual memory was also significantly impaired.

In general, the testing showed well-retained verbal skills, with relative impairment of verbal and nonverbal memory, abstract reasoning, constructional ability, and the ability to make conceptual shifts. We were unsure about his ability to return to his demanding accounting job, but he, reinforced by a healthy amount of denial, stated that he "could do the job half asleep." Subsequent reports indicate that he was right, because 3 months after discharge he was back to work full time and living alone in his own house. A discussion with his employer raised no reservations concerning his performance. Accordingly, despite his residual cognitive deficits, either this patient has been able to make the necessary adjustments to his disabilities or, more likely, he was fortunate in that his illness did not affect those cognitive skills necessary for his particular job. At follow-up, 10 years after this initial illness, he has continued to work at his usual job without difficulty. He continues to play the piano for recreation, and, according to his physician brother-in-law, the patient seems exactly as he was before his illness.

The above case demonstrates one of the ways in which infection of the brain can produce behavioral sequelae in patients with no or only minor residual motor or sensory deficits. In this patient, the deficits fortunately did not interfere with his social and vocational reintegration. Had he been an architect, engineer, or surgeon, however, his impaired perceptual motor skills could have significantly affected his work, or if he had been an independent business executive or lawyer, his memory, verbal reasoning, and conceptual deficits could have produced a substantial vocational disability.

In this chapter, we do not intend to extensively review infectious diseases and their treatments but rather will discuss in general those infectious entities that either present primarily with behavioral symptoms or, as in the case above, have behavioral sequelae that can be a significant factor in the patient's readjustment after illness.

Infectious disease has various modes of presentation in the brain. Abscess, for instance, produces the picture of a focal lesion, whereas encephalitis is frequently manifested as a more generalized behavioral disturbance. Meningitis, conversely, may start with very innocuous generalized symptoms and subsequently develop into a severe encephalopathy with focal vascular lesions or hydrocephalus. In general, the behavioral abnormalities are determined more by the mode of presentation than by the specific agent responsible for the infection. For instance, a brain abscess caused by anaerobic *Streptococcus, Nocardia,* or *Echinococcus* may all produce the same focal behavioral changes although one infectious agent was bacterial, one fungal, and one parasitic. Despite the lack of specific correlation of the clinical syndrome with an individual infectious agent, classes of agents tend to act in a somewhat similar fashion: Viruses usually produce encephalitis or meningitis and not an abscess, whereas bacteria, fungi, and parasites more frequently cause meningitis or abscess and rarely a diffuse encephalitis.

In recent years several unusual mechanisms of infections of the brain have been recognized that have relevance to neurobehavior. The first is the discovery, by Dr. Gajdusek and his coworkers, of unconventional viruses and their ability to produce a transmissible dementia (e.g., kuru and Creutzfeldt-Jakob disease).[23-26] The second is a special sensitivity to generally nonpathogenic agents in patients who have suppression of their normal immune mechanisms. In these patients (e.g., those with myeloproliferative disease, immunosuppression for transplantation, acquired immunodeficiency syndrome, and other treatment with high-dose steroids), either a variety of diseases becomes reactivated, such as toxoplasmosis, or normally nonpathogenic agents, such as *Cryptococcus*, become opportunistic. These infections frequently present with new behavioral abnormalities in an already ill patient. Unfortunately, these new behavioral abnormalities are all too frequently ascribed to the primary disease and are not recognized as being a suprainfection by one of the uncommon agents. The third mechanism is the specific clinical problem of acquired immunodeficiency syndrome (AIDS). These cases have a possibility of both superinfection by opportunistic agents and the invasion of brain cells by the AIDS virus itself.[48,49] A fourth interesting type of condition is that in which a dormant infection becomes virulently reactivated for no apparent reason. This is the case with measles virus in subacute sclerosing panencephalitis, a tragic disease of childhood that is classically heralded by a gradual change in the child's behavior.

In any field of medicine, an early diagnosis with early treatment affords the patient the most favorable prognosis. This is particularly true for infectious disease. Bacterial and fungal diseases respond well to medication, and we are now seeing encouraging responses to medication with some viral illnesses, in particular herpes simplex encephalitis. Accordingly, early clinical recognition of these conditions is becoming increasingly important.

BRAIN ABSCESS

By its nature, the brain abscess presents as a focal mass lesion and produces symptoms relative both to its location and to the general effects of cerebral edema and increased intracranial pressure. Confusional behavior, headache, papilledema, and seizures are the most prominent features, with focal neurologic and behavioral signs being less common. The source of the infection in brain abscess is usually the middle ear or paranasal sinuses (predominantly the frontal sinuses[34]), but in some reported series metastatic abscesses from congenital heart disease and pulmonary infection form the majority of cases.[54] Dental abscess is an uncommon yet important source to consider, particularly with frontal lobe abscess.[31]

Because the infection often enters the brain by direct extension from a purulent infection in the frontal sinuses or the middle ear and the mastoid processes, the incidence of both frontal lobe and inferior temporal lobe abscesses is much higher than expected. Patients with frontal abscesses have an increased tendency to present with confusional behavior, whereas a frontal lobe syndrome is not common unless both frontal lobes are involved. With an inferior temporal lobe abscess in the language-dominant hemisphere, a dramatic anomic aphasia or a fluent aphasia with poor comprehension is frequently the presenting sign. In patients with systemic infection, most commonly originating in the lung, the abscesses are randomly distributed, with approximately half of such patients having multiple lesions.

The evaluation and treatment of brain abscess have improved dramatically since the introduction of the CT scan.[54] With this procedure, it is now much easier to diagnose, localize, and follow the course of an abscess, particularly when multiple or loculated abscesses are present.

Treatment usually involves a combined approach of aggressive antibiotic treatment and surgical extirpation or aspiration[11]; however, with the use of repeated CT or MRI scans, some patients can be treated with antibiotics alone. Antibiotic treatment should be tailored to the specific organism grown on culture.[16] Although culture of peripheral tissues is often negative, cultures of material aspirated from the abscess itself and immediately placed on culture medium are almost always positive.[17]

Prompt and aggressive medical plus surgical treatment has helped to greatly reduce the mortality from brain abscess to about 20 percent,[17,58] a vast improvement from the mortality figure of 60 percent reported in 1950 for untreated abscess.[64] Use of the CT scan has resulted in even more favorable statistics, with a recent report of no mortality in 20 consecutive cases diagnosed with the aid of CT scanning.[54]

MENINGITIS

Virus, bacteria, mycobacteria, fungus, and some parasites can all produce an inflammatory disease of the meninges and, except for the more insidious onset of the fungal diseases, the behavioral symptoms are remarkably similar. An alteration in level of consciousness with or without confusion is the primary behavioral symptom. In viral meningitis, lethargy, headache and fever are the features of the acute illness. Neurologic and behavioral features are rare, as are sequelae. As discussed in Chapter 7, the chronic meningitides caused by fungus, tuberculosis, or *Cryptococcus* can sometimes manifest as a rather rapid (several weeks) dementing illness but rarely, if ever, without the associated signs of fever, headache, and stiff neck.

Early diagnosis is very important because many of the diseases can be very destructive if not rapidly arrested. Some agents are more pathogenic than others, but all nonviral meningitis results in very high mortality and morbidity if not treated. Probably the agent most infamous for producing extensive brain damage, seizures, and cranial nerve (especially the auditory nerve) damage is *Hemophilus influenzae*. Seen primarily in children, this infection can leave its host with mental retardation, seizures, deafness, hemiplegia, blindness, or a variety of lesser physical and mental symptoms. Of the purulent meningitides, pneumococcus is most likely to leave the adult patient with significant mental sequelae. Overall sequelae rate is over 50 percent, with memory complaints present in 20 percent. The probability of neurologic sequelae is inversely related to the level of consciousness during the acute phase of the illness.[5] *Meningococcus*, by contrast, is relatively benign once the initial infection is controlled. Tuberculosis and fungal meningitis often cause focal brain and cranial nerve damage but in general are less devastating than the *Hemophilus* bacteria.

There are two main types of sequelae in nonviral meningitis: (1) communicating hydrocephalus from scar-tissue formation around the base of the brain and over the convexities and (2) focal lesions of the cortex. Hydrocephalus must always be considered when a patient's infection is apparently responding to medication, yet his mental status and neurologic examination either fails to improve or worsens. The clinical features of the hydrocephalus are similar to those discussed in Chapter 7—gait disturbance, urinary incontinence, and signs of mental change.

Meningitis can cause focal lesions through many mechanisms; often more than one mechanism may be operating in any individual case. Local invasion of brain parenchyma by toxic products or the agents themselves will cause an area of cerebritis (cortical infection). These areas are often unstable electrically and serve as a nidus for seizures. Eventually these areas will show actual cell loss and focal damage. The other principal problem in meningitis is invasion of the walls of both veins and arteries by the infection, with subsequent venous and arterial occlusion. When major arteries or the venous sinuses are occluded in this way, a stroke-like picture evolves, and the patient suffers a substantial brain infarction. Unfortunately, in many patients, particularly those infected with *Hemophilus*, pneumococcus, or tuberculosis, multiple infarction frequently occurs. In these cases, a severe encephalopathy and attendant cognitive loss result. Meningitis is further complicated by the effects of massive cerebral edema and congestion. This then compromises the cerebral circulation and metabolism and produces brain herniation in many cases.

SYPHILIS

Syphilis has various manifestations at different stages of the illness. In the earlier stages, the neurologic symptoms result from meningeal and vascular inflammation, whereas in the later stages, parenchymatous involvement is the most prevalent. It is impossible to classify all cases, since features of meningeal, vascular, and parenchymatous disease can all exist in a single patient.[45] The meningitis seen with syphilis is similar to any subacute meningitis. We saw one man in his 50s who came to the emergency room with a history of having suffered a seizure while at work. On examination, he was quite confusional, was febrile, and had early papilledema. A spinal fluid examination demonstrated 250 cells (50 percent polymorphonuclear, 50 percent lymphocytes) and a strongly positive Kolmer reaction. With prompt treatment, his meningitis cleared, and he escaped without any vascular or cranial nerve lesions.

On occasion, a focal meningeal granulomatous lesion (gumma) will occur and produce a picture of a slowly progressive mass lesion. The more common focal lesion is of vascular origin and is due to a specific endarteritis. These lesions have an acute onset and resemble a typical stroke.

In the chronic stage of syphilis (tertiary syphilis), parenchymatous degeneration occurs, with the classic behavioral syndrome being that of general paresis. This condition had been more fully discussed in Chapter 7 as one of the progressive dementias.

ENCEPHALITIS

Encephalitis is a generalized infection of the brain that is usually caused by the viral invasion of neuronal or glial cell bodies. In some instances, other infectious agents can present as encephalitis because of their widespread involvement of brain tissue; *Toxoplasma gondii* is one such agent. Although often producing a generalized infection with diffuse mental symptoms, some forms of encephalitis manifest as focal or multifocal disease; herpes simplex encephalitis, progressive multifocal leukoencephalopathy, and toxoplasmosis are three such conditions. Many of the clinical and behavioral characteristics of these diseases allow early diagnosis.

Toxoplasmosis

The protozoa *Toxoplasma gondii* produces several different clinical syndromes of the central nervous system: (1) a focal or multifocal infection, (2) a widespread inflammatory disease that can be rightfully called an encephalitis, and (3) a meningoencephalitis.[62] Seventy percent of the cases present with a picture of focal or multifocal lesions, but in 20 percent, the general signs of confusion and lethargy are all that are evident on examination.[62] The disease is progressive and, depending on its mode of presentation, is indistinguishable clinically from expanding mass lesions, progressive multifocal leukoencephalopathy, cryptococcal or other chronic meningitis, or viral encephalitis. As with many of the conditions mentioned above, toxoplasmosis of the central nervous system in adults is seen much more frequently in patients who have been treated by immunosuppressive drugs or have immunodeficiency syndromes. The largest single group of patients acquiring toxoplasmosis is that of patients treated for myeloproliferative illness or AIDS. In a review of 315 AIDS patients with central nervous system complications, 103 had infections caused by *Toxoplasma*.[39] Given this fact, when treating the immunosuppressed patient in whom focal or general cerebral symptoms develop, it is critical to consider the possibility of a treatable infectious agent rather than to assume that the CNS symptoms are secondary to the spread of the primary disease.

Viral Encephalitis

Many conventional viruses produce encephalitis, a condition that can have a variety of clinical manifestations. Certain viruses, such as mumps, often produce a mild encephalitis with lethargy, headache, and irritability as the principal features. In these cases, behavioral and neurologic sequelae are rare, and the entire disease is usually highly benign. Other agents, cat-scratch virus for instance, may produce a rapidly evolving, devastating, yet completely reversible encephalopathy as the following case reveals.[61]

A young psychiatric house officer was neurologically intact on morning rounds but by afternoon was grossly confusional and paranoid. By

early evening he was mute, suspicious, combative, and increasingly diffi-
cult to arouse. Within hours he became comatose and decerebrate. He was
sustained on a respirator for 2 days and thereafter recovered rapidly. A
diagnosis of cat-scratch encephalitis was made immunologically. Two
months after onset he had returned to work with no residual problems
noted on an extensive neuropsychologic battery. He subsequently com-
pleted his psychiatry residency and then a full neurology residency. He is
currently in practice and has no residual effects from his illness.

Other viral agents, however, not only cause severe behavioral and neurologic symptoms during the acute phase of infection but are also known to produce very serious long-term residual behavioral deficits. Among the most frequent are arbor viruses and the herpes simplex virus. Because herpes simplex encephalitis is such an interesting condition from a behavioral standpoint and also because early diagnosis holds promise for treatment and prevention of sequelae, we will discuss its clinical picture more fully.

HERPES SIMPLEX ENCEPHALITIS

The most common of the serious viral encephalitides, herpes simplex has a rather short prodromal phase (3 to 5 days) of fever and headache.[6] Rapidly thereafter, a fulminant encephalitis develops with either acute delirium or focal, usually temporal lobe, signs[68] (i.e., aphasia, apraxia, agnosia, memory disturbance, and emotional change). Some patients display fragments of the Klüver-Bucy syndrome—excessive mouthing of objects, poor memory, mood changes, and aggressive behavior.[28] Such patients are typically bereft of normal facial and emotional expression. A decreased level of consciousness, seizures, memory problems, and focal neurologic and behavioral signs are common.[50] The signs are often asymmetric and can be misinterpreted as being secondary to a mass lesion rather than to encephalitis.

The diagnosis can usually be strongly suspected from the history and clinical presentation; however, certain laboratory tests can be useful, and at times, diagnostic of the condition. A CT or MRT scan should be the first such test done. The finding of wedge-shaped translucent areas of edema in the temporal lobes greatly strengthens the diagnosis, and treatment should be started. If the results of the scan are negative, the EEG can be helpful because it often shows rather characteristic temporal sharp and slow-wave activity, a finding not usually seen in other encephalitides.[10,20] Spinal fluid examination is normal in 25 percent of cases but shows some blood and lymphocytes (<500) in the remaining 75 percent.[50] It is virtually impossible to retrieve the virus from the spinal fluid, but specific immunofluorescent antibody studies on the cerebrospinal fluid leukocytes are positive in many cases, even when culture results are negative.[59] In the past, the medications used to treat the disease were so toxic that brain biopsy was recommended in all cases before initiating treatment. With the introduction of acyclovir, toxic problems are minimal and "routine brain biopsy is obsolete."[19]

Treatment is now greatly improved compared with that available 5 years ago. Three factors are critical: (1) treatment must be initiated before the patient becomes comatose if there is to be any chance for a decent quality of survival,[66,67] (2) cerebral edema can be controlled by high doses of steroids, mannitol, or decompression, as brain swelling and herniation are the primary causes of death,[40] and (3) treatment with acyclovir should be started immediately when the diagnosis is suspected. This drug has dropped the mortality to 19 to 28 percent, with 38 to 56 percent of the patients able to return to normal work routines.[57,67]

Pathologically, herpes simplex infection has a predilection for the limbic structures in the medial temporal lobes and the orbital surface of the frontal lobes.[14] This unusual distribution suggests that the infection spreads to the brain from structures in or around the base of the brain rather than via the blood stream, unless there is a specific selective cell vulnerability in these brain regions. Microscopic examination shows that all cell types (neurons and glia) are involved in the inflammatory process. This observation adds support to the theory that the infection spreads from and through contiguous tissues rather than in specific vulnerable cell populations. Why the virus affects limbic mesocortex and not overlying isocortex is not known. For some time it was believed that the infection reached the brain through the nose and olfactory system, but recent evidence strongly suggests that the virus either spreads from the trigeminal ganglion or is activated from latency in the brain itself.[15] Because many persons harbor herpes virus in a latent state in their trigeminal ganglion, this is an appealing hypothesis. This theory leaves only the question as to why some persons contract encephalitis yet most do not.

SUBACUTE SCLEROSING PANENCEPHALITIS (SSPE)

Of the various encephalitides that are caused by the recrudescence of a latent central nervous system virus, subacute sclerosing panencephalitis is a very important one. The condition, caused by the reactivation of latent measles virus, is seen primarily in older children (ages 4 to 10) or in young adolescents (90 percent of cases occur between ages 4 and 16).[29] In the first stage of the illness, almost all of the symptoms are those of behavioral change. The following case demonstrates the typical early behavior changes:

The patient, a 16-year-old boy, had been a well-liked, social young man who was not a superior student but was a good musician and had his own rock band. About a year before we saw him, his family began to notice that he would occasionally have difficulty expressing himself and tended to use words out of context. Concurrently, he became withdrawn, depressed, and lost both skill and interest in his guitar playing. He did not display any inappropriate social behavior but often became lost in the school halls and could not find his room. In the 3 months before our seeing him, he developed a distinct stutter, had progressive memory loss, and began to display facial grimaces and a stumbling gait.

On initial examination, the patient was neat, well behaved, and seemed quite concerned about his problem. His speech was fluent yet slurred and contained grammatical errors and frequent word-finding pauses. Comprehension, naming, reading, and writing were all impaired. There was evidence of ideomotor apraxia, dyscalculia, and constructional difficulty. The patient had occasional subtle choreiform and myoclonic movements of the face, arms, and legs and also had a mild snout reflex and prominent palmomental reflexes.

Cerebral dysfunction with behavioral abnormalities such as decreased school performance, withdrawal, aggressiveness, inappropriate nonchalance, and a variety of intellectual and emotional changes characterize the first stage of the disease.[32,35] In this initial phase, there is little, if any, motor or sensory abnormality. In the second stage, motor findings begin to appear, including choreiform movements, myoclonus, ataxia, and various early extrapyramidal signs. The motor findings are initially subtle, as in the case above, but can progress to be disabling. We saw one 10-year-old boy who had significant myoclonic movements in his legs as a presenting symptom. The patient had such massive lower-extremity myoclonus that he would actually be thrown to the floor whenever the contractions occurred.

The third and fourth stages of SSPE involve progressive intellectual deterioration and ultimate mutism. Neurologically, seizures develop as do spasticity, brain stem dysfunction, and hypothalamic dysfunction. In the fourth stage, the myoclonus decreases, and the patients become comatose and often opisthotonic.

The diagnosis is usually easy to make clinically by the time myoclonus is present, but two laboratory examinations are especially useful in establishing a firm diagnosis: the EEG and the immunoglobulin levels in serum and spinal fluid. The EEG shows periodic diphasic or triphasic delta bursts that occur every 5 to 7 sec (Fig. 11–1)[41] and frequently persist into the sleeping state.[33,65] This characteristic pattern is not always present in the

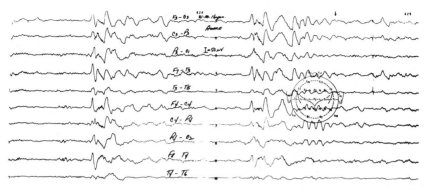

Figure 11-1. Electrocardiogram of patient with subacute sclerosing panencephalitis.

first stage of the illness[56] but inevitably appears as the disease progresses.

The second, and by far the most specific, test is the IgG level in cerebrospinal fluid. In SSPE, the level of spinal fluid IgG is extremely high, and 25 to 75 percent of the IgG is measles-specific antibody.[44] A comparison of IgG in serum to IgG in cerebrospinal fluid shows that the cerebrospinal fluid level is considerably elevated, giving strong evidence that the antibodies are being produced in the central nervous system and are not transferred from serum.[37,52]

Once the diagnosis has been made, the treatment of choice is adenine arabinoside, an anti-DNA substance that has been shown to arrest the condition and improve survival rate but tends to stabilize rather than reverse the condition.[63] The prognosis in untreated SSPE is grim: 50 percent die in the first year; the range of survival is from 6 weeks to 8 years.[29] Many survivors have severe encephalopathies, and only 1 in 100 is normal mentally. Early detection and early treatment may alter these statistics.

The pathogenesis of these slow or latent viruses is not yet known. In SSPE, the dormant virus has been proved to be measles virus. Children in whom SSPE develops usually have had a rather severe primary measles infection early in life (less than 2 years of age).[35] In some fashion, the measles virus remains dormant until years later. It has been hypothesized that the later panencephalitis is caused by a transformation of the RNA measles virus to a DNA form by a concomitant second viral infection. This new DNA virus is believed to become the pathogenic agent in SSPE.[1]

The virus attacks the deep layers of cortex and adjacent white matter, causing a subacute inflammatory reaction. All brain areas except the cerebellum are affected. Demyelination, necrosis, and gliosis occur, with the eventual pathologic picture being one of diffuse severe destruction.

PROGRESSIVE MULTIFOCAL LEUKOENCEPHALOPATHY (PML)

Progressive multifocal leukoencephalopathy is another central nervous system inflammatory disease caused by the activation or reactivation of a latent virus. Like toxoplasmosis, PML most commonly afflicts those persons with compromised cellular immunity. Patients with AIDS, myeloproliferative and lymphoproliferative diseases, sarcoid, tuberculosis, polycythemia, cancer, and artificially induced immunosuppression from cytotoxic drugs and steroids are all at risk for the development of this type of leukoencephalopathy. Because of the availability of drugs to treat this condition, it is important for physicians to become acquainted with PML and consider it in their differential diagnosis in immunosuppressed patients in whom central nervous system symptoms develop.

The clinical picture is one of a somewhat rapidly progressive encephalopathy (2 to 4 months from first symptoms to death) that frequently begins with confusional behavior, alterations in language function, and other neurologic signs and symptoms, particularly visual field defects, seizures, and pyramidal findings.[22,53] Frequently, the initial signs are focal and, in the case of the cancer patient, simulate those of a metastasis. Most lesions occur in the cerebral hemispheres and have a distinct predilection for the posterior quadrants. Brain stem and cerebellum are sometimes involved.

The diagnosis can certainly be suspected clinically from history and examination, but the CT or MRI scan can be especially helpful in differentiating PML from a variety of other diseases, especially metastatic tumor. The lesions in PML, as visualized on the CT scan, are low density, found in the central and convolutional white matter, and have scalloped lateral borders. They produce no mass effect, do not enhance with the infusion of contrast, and are more commonly seen posteriorly.[8,13] Most routine laboratory studies are much less diagnostic: the EEG may be slow and the arteriogram abnormal, but none of these is as specific as the CT scan.[38,53]

Treatment with cytosine arabinoside has been encouraging in some individual cases, but a substantial treatment experience has not yet been obtained.[2,7,12,42]

The cause and pathology of this condition are interesting. The basic pathogens causing this syndrome of progressive, multifocal, white-matter degeneration are a small group of viruses, mostly papovaviruses (principally the CJ virus).[47,51,53] These viruses are usually not pathogenic unless a patient has a defect in immunologic competence. Under such conditions of immunosuppression, the host is then either vulnerable to attack by these opportunistic viruses from the environment or is unable to continue to suppress the activity of the virus, which may have lain dormant for years in the host tissue.[23,30] Irrespective of the mechanism, these viruses attack the oligodendroglial cells (the myelin-producing cells of the central nervous system), causing them first to swell and then to degenerate.[53] Subsequent to the damage of the oligodendrocytes, the myelin dies, and patches of demyelination appear. Inflammatory changes are scarce except for some perivascular infiltrate of lymphocytes, plasma cells, and macrophages. Astrocytes are also affected, becoming extremely large and developing bizarre form. On electron microscopic study, the cell nuclei, particularly the oligodendroglia, are packed with viral particles.

ACQUIRED IMMUNE DEFICIENCY SYNDROME

Acquired immune deficiency syndrome (AIDS) is now a public health problem of major significance. It has been defined by the Centers for Disease Control as a "reliably diagnosed disease that is at least moderately indicative of an underlying cellular immunodeficiency in a person who has no known underlying cause of cellular immunodeficiency nor any other cause of reduced resistance."[9] In addition to a wide range of systemic and end organ complications, disorders of the central nervous system frequently develop in AIDS patients. Neurological signs and symptoms reportedly occur in a high percentage of all AIDS cases, varying from motor weakness and parasthesias to progressive dementia, seizures, focal deficits, and psychosis.[21]

The most common causes of the cerebral disorders are (1) obstructive hydrocephalus; (2) primary or metastatic CNS lymphoma; (3) Kaposi's sarcoma; (4) a variety of opportunistic infections, including toxoplasmosis, progressive multifocal leukokencephalopathy, cryptococcal meningitis, herpes simplex viral encephalitis; and (5) a number of less frequent viral, bacterial, and fungal infections.[39,49] Such conditions account for about 30 percent of the neurologic complications affecting AIDS patients. Some infections are generalized and clinically resemble the encephalitis or meningitis expected from the infectious agent. Other conditions, especially lymphoma, progressive multifocal leukencephalopathy, and *Toxoplasma gondii* infection present as mass intracranial lesions, with more focal clinical manifestations.

The development of a progressive dementia is a more frequent clinical presentation, occurring in about 70 percent of reported cases.[48,49] The dementia typically has an insidious onset, with a steady rapidly progressive course (1 to 9 months), with intellectual impairment, behavioral change, and motor disturbance being the initial symptoms. The characteristic full-blown picture consists of generalized cognitive impairment, accompanied by slowed verbal and motor responses. As with any dementia, the final stage is characterized by mutism, paraplegia, incontinence, and little or no response to the environment.[49] Pathologic studies of the brains of patients having the AIDS dementia complex have demonstrated abnormalities in more than 90 percent, with the abnormalities primarily involving the white matter and subcortical structures, with relative sparing of the cortex.[48]

Studies have strongly suggested that this relatively distinct dementia is due to direct LAV/HTLV-III infection of CNS tissue.[48,55] Primary tissue cultures from brain biopsy specimens reveal the presence of the virus in 90 percent of the studied cases.[27]

The evaluation and treatment of the AIDS patient with central nervous system complications is a complicated process. The primary focus of such an evaluation is to detect a treatable neuropathic condition. Potentially treatable AIDS-related conditions include obstructive hydrocephalus, toxoplasmosis, cryptococcal infections, and other bacterial and fungal meningitides. The basic diagnostic procedures are the CT or MRI scan to look for mass lesions or hydrocephalus. After the scan, a spinal tap should be done to detect treatable CNS infections. If no treatable condition is diagnosed, the most probable disorder is AIDS encephalitis, which unfortunately is not responsive to the treatments that are currently available. Statistically, this is also the most probable CNS complication in AIDS patients. See Levy and associates[39] for an excellent systematic approach to the clinical evaluation and treatment of the AIDS patient with neurologic dysfunction.

TRANSMISSIBLE VIRAL DEMENTIA

In the past two decades, largely as a result of the investigative efforts of Dr. D. Carleton Gajdusek, a completely different type of slow or latent infection of the brain has been discovered.[24] The infectious agent has not been absolutely identified. Amyloid fibrils have been found in the brains of diseased patients, and it is thought that one of the proteins associated with the amyloid may be the infectious agent.[46] The term *prion* (proteinaceous infectious particle) has been coined and adopted by some investigators[4] to describe this agent. Called the *subacute spongiform virus encephalopathies*, conditions caused by this unconventional virus are transmitted by the direct inoculation of infected tissue in the recipient host. This mode of transmission and the nature of these diseases were first understood through the study of kuru in the cannibalistic Fore tribe in New Guinea.[24] In that group, the eating of fresh human brain caused contamination by infected tissue through either the conjunctiva or open cuts. The resultant encephalopathy was a slowly progressive disease that did not respond to any treatment effort.

It was soon recognized that the familiar presenile dementia, Creutzfeldt-Jakob disease, was a similar type of encephalopathy; its transmission to monkeys was experimentally achieved via direct tissue inoculation. The clinical picture of Creutzfeldt-Jakob disease is described in Chapter 7; in brief, it is a progressive encephalopathy that has a variety of neurologic signs, the most prominent being confusion, dementia, pyramidal and extrapyramidal motor signs, and myoclonus. The mode of transmission of this disease in humans is still not known, but the reports of transmission to patients undergoing corneal transplantation,[18] to neurosurgeons via direct inoculation from contaminated brain during surgery or autopsy of infected specimen,[26] and to patients undergoing surgery for epilepsy via depth electrodes[3] suggest that many of those affected may have actually been inoculated in some way by infected tissues. In addition to these reports, it has been observed that a large percentage of Creutzfeldt-Jakob patients had undergone previous brain surgery.[25] This again suggests the possibility of some direct contamination of the host tissues.

It is known that simple person-to-person contact is not involved in transmission, so isolation of patients is not necessary. Because of the possibility of tissue contamination, however, great care must be exercised in handling both the tissues of patients with Creutzfeldt-Jakob disease and any instruments that have been used to cut or probe their tissues. Unfortunately, the unconventional virus that causes this disease is resistant to the usual methods of sterilization by heat and formalin. A review of the recommendations for contact with patients and their tissues has been published.[43]

The pathophysiology of these slow viruses, particularly the unconventional transmissible viruses, is much different than that of normal viral infection. Incubation periods are very long, there are none of the usual inflammatory changes seen in conventional viral disease, resistance to chemical and physical agents vastly differs and these viral agents act in a very different fashion biologically.[24]

REFERENCES

1. Adams, DH and Bell, TM: The relationship between measles virus infection and subacute sclerosing panencephalitis (SSPE). Med Hypotheses 2:55, 1976.
2. Baver, WR, Turel, AP, and Johnson, KP: Progressive multifocal leukoencephalopathy and cytarabine. JAMA 226:174, 1973.
3. Bernoulli, C et al: Danger of accidental person-to-person transmission of Creutzfeldt-Jakob disease by surgery. Lancet 1:478, 1977.
4. Bockman, JM et al: Creutzfeldt-Jakob disease prion proteins in human brains. N Engl J Med 312:73, 1985.
5. Bohr, V, Paulson, OB, and Rasmussen, N: Pneumococcal meningitis: Late neurologic sequelae and features of prognostic import. Arch Neurol 41:1045, 1984.
6. Boyle, RS and Landy, PJ: Herpes simplex encephalitis. Aust NZ J Med 7:408, 1977.
7. Buckman, R and Wiltshaw, E: Progressive multifocal leukoencephalopathy successfully treated with cytosine arabinoside. Br J Haematol 34:153, 1976.

8. Carroll, BA et al: Diagnosis of progressive multifocal leukoencephalopathy by computed tomography. Radiology 122:137, 1977.
9. Centers for Disease Control: Prevention of acquired immune deficiency syndrome (AIDS): Report of interagency recommendations. MMWR 32:101, 1983.
10. Chien, LT et al: Characteristic early electroencephalographic changes in herpes simplex encephalitis. Arch Neurol 34:361, 1977.
11. Choudhury, AR, Taylor, JC, and Whitaker, R: Primary excision of brain abscess. Br Med J 2:1119, 1977.
12. Conomy, JP et al: Cytarabine treatment of progressive multifocal leukoencephalopathy. JAMA 229:1313, 1974.
13. Conomy, JP et al: Computed tomography in progressive multifocal leukoencephalopathy. Radiology 127:663, 1976.
14. Damasio, AR and Van Hoesen, GW: The limbic system and the localisation of herpes simplex encephalitis. J Neurol Neurosurg Psychiatry 48:297, 1985.
15. Davis, LE and Johnson, RT: An explanation for the localization of herpes simplex encephalitis? Ann Neurol 5:2, 1979.
16. DeLouvois, J: The bacteriology and chemotherapy of brain abscess. J Antimicrob Chemother 4:395, 1978.
17. DeLouvois, J, Gortvai, P, and Hurley, R: Bacteriology of abscesses of the central nervous systems: A multicentre prospective study. Br Med J 2:981, 1977.
18. Duffy, P et al: Possible person-to-person transmission of Creutzfeldt-Jakob disease. N Engl J Med 299:693, 1974.
19. Editorial: Herpes simplex encephalitis. Lancet 1:535, 1986.
20. Elian, M: Herpes simplex encephalitis. Arch Neurol 32:39, 1975.
21. Elkin, GM et al: Intracranial lesions in the acquired immunodeficiency syndrome: Radiological (computed tomographic) features. JAMA 253:393 1985.
22. Fermaglich, J, Hardman, JM, and Earl, KM: Spontaneous progressive multifocal leukoencephalopathy. Neurology 20:479, 1970.
23. Gajdusek, DC: Slow virus disease of the central nervous system. Am J Clin Pathol 56:320, 1971.
24. Gajdusek, DC: Unconventional viruses and the origin and disappearance of kuru. Science 197:943, 1977.
25. Gajdusek, DC et al: Precautions in medical care of, and handling materials from patients with transmissible virus dementia (Creutzfeldt-Jakob disease). N Engl J Med 297:1253, 1977.
26. Gajdusek, DC et al: Transmission of subacute spongiform encephalopathy to the chimpanzee and squirrel monkey from a patient with papulosis atrophicans maligna of Kohnmeier-Doegs. In Neurology, Proceedings of the Tenth International Congress of Neurology, Barcelona, September 8–15, 1973.
27. Gartner, S et al: Virus isolation from and identification of HTLV-III/LAV-producing cells in brain tissue from a patient with AIDS. JAMA 256:2365, 1986.
28. Greenwood, R et al: Behaviour disturbance during recovery from herpes simplex encephalitis. J Neurol Neurosurg Psychiatry 46:809, 1983.

29. Haddad, FS, Risk, WS, and Jabbour, JT: Subacute sclerosing panencephalitis in the Middle East: Report of 99 cases. Ann Neurol 1:211, 1977.
30. Ho, M: Virus infections after transplantation in man. Arch Virol 55:1, 1977.
31. Inghman, HR et al: Abscesses of the frontal lobe of the brain secondary to covert dental sepsis. Lancet 2:497, 1978.
32. Jabbour, JT, Duenan, DA, and Modlin, J: SSPE: Clinical staging, course and frequency. Arch Neurol 32:493, 1975.
33. Jabbour, JT et al: Subacute sclerosing panencephalitis. JAMA 207:2248, 1969.
34. Jefferson, AA and Keogh, AJ: Intracranial abscesses: A review of treated patients over 20 years. Quart J Med 46:389, 1977.
35. Johnson, KP, Byington, DP, and Goddis, L: Subacute sclerosing panencephalitis. Adv Neurol 6:77, 1974.
36. Kaufman, DM, Zimmerman, RD, and Leeds, NE: Computed tomography in herpes simplex encephalitis. Neurology 29:1392, 1979.
37. Kiessling, WR et al: Measles–virus-specific immunoglobulin-M response in subacute sclerosing panencephalitis. Lancet 1:324, 1977.
38. Kirsh, J et al: Progressive multifocal leukoencephalopathy. Radiology 119:399, 1976.
39. Levy, RM, Bredensen, DE, and Rosenblum, ML: Neurological manifestations of the acquired immunodeficiency syndrome (AIDS): Experience at UCSF and review of the literature. J Neurosurg 62:475, 1985.
40. Longson, M: The treatment of herpes encephalitis. J Antimicrob Chemother 3(Suppl A):115, 1977.
41. Markand, ON and Panszl, JG: The electroencephalogram in subacute sclerosing panencephalitis. Arch Neurol 32:719, 1975.
42. Marriott, PJ et al: Progressive multifocal leukoencephalopathy: Remission with cytarabine. J Neurol Neurosurg Psychiatry 38:205, 1975.
43. McIntegart, V: A cause for concern. Nursing Times 78:1283, 1982.
44. Mehta, PD, Kane, A, and Thormar, H: Quantitation of measles virus—specific immunoglobulins in serum, CSF and brain extract from patients with subacute sclerosing panencephalitis. J Immunol 118:2254, 1977.
45. Merritt, HH, Adams, RD, and Solomon, HC: Neurosyphilis. Oxford University Press, New York, 1946.
46. Merz, PA et al: Infection-specific particle from the unconventional slow virus diseases. Science 225:437, 1984.
47. Narayan, O et al: Etiology of progressive multifocal leukoencephalopathy. N Engl J Med 289:1278, 1973.
48. Navia, B et al: The AIDS dementia complex: II. Neuropathology. Ann Neurol 19:525–535, 1986.
49. Navia, BA, Jordan, BO, and Price, RW: The AIDS dementia complex: I. clinical features. Ann Neurol 19:517, 1986.
50. Oxbury, JM and MacCallum, FO: Herpes simplex encephalitis: clinical features and residual damage. Postgrad Med J 49:387, 1973.
51. Padgett, BL et al: JC papovavirus in progressive multifocal leukoencephalopathy. J Infect Dis 133:686, 1976.
52. Polna, I and Cendrowski, W: Serological studies on the etiological role of measles-like virus in subacute sclerosing panencephalitis. J Neurol 216:301, 1977.

53. Richardson, EP: Our evolving understanding of progressive multifocal leuko-encephalopathy. Ann NY Acad Sci 230:358, 1974.
54. Rosenblum, ML et al: Decreased mortality from brain abscesses since advent of computerized tomography. J Neurosurg 49:658, 1978.
55. Shaw, GM et al: HTLV-III infection in brains of children and adults with AIDS encephalopathy. Science 227:177, 1985.
56. Sisk, M and Griffith, JF: Normal electroencephalograms in subacute sclerosing panencephalitis. Arch Neurol 32:575, 1975.
57. Skoldenberg, B et al: Acyclovir versus vidarabine in herpes simplex encephalitis. Lancet 2:707, 1984.
58. Snell, GE: Sinogenic and otogenic brain abscesses—a review of 63 cases occurring at Toronto General Hospital, 1956–75. J Otolaryngol 7:289, 1978.
59. Taber, LH et al: Diagnosis of herpes simplex virus infection by immunofluorescence. J Clin Microbiol 3:309, 1976.
60. Thomson, JLC: The computed axial tomography in acute herpes simplex encephalitis. Br J Radiol 49:86, 1976.
61. Torres, JR et al: Cat-scratch disease causing reversible encephalopathy. JAMA 240:1628, 1978.
62. Townsend, JJ et al: Acquired toxoplasmosis: A neglected cause of treatable nervous system disease. Arch Neurol 32:335, 1975.
63. Webb, HE, Kelly, RE, and Adams, DH: Intravenous and intrathecal adenine arabinoside phosphate in a child with subacute sclerosing panencephalitis. Lancet 2:978, 1977.
64. Webster, JE and Gurdijian, ES: The surgical management of intracranial suppuration. Int Abst Surg 90:209, 1950.
65. Westmoreland, BF, Gomez, MR, and Blume, WT: Activation of periodic complexes of subacute sclerosing panencephalitis by sleep. Ann Neurol 1:185, 1977.
66. Whitley, RJ et al: Adenine arabinoside therapy of biopsy-proved herpes simplex encephalitis. N Engl J Med 297:289, 1977.
67. Whitley, RJ et al: Vidarabine versus acyclovir therapy in herpes simplex encephalitis. N Engl J Med 314:144, 1986.
68. Wilson, LG: Viral encephalitis mimicking functional psychosis. Am J Psychiatry 133:165, 1976.

Chapter 12

Epilepsy

A 65-year-old woman came to medical attention because of an initial, generalized seizure of tonic-clonic type (grand mal) at age 61. The family described a 2-month period preceding the seizure during which the patient had begun to exhibit progressively bizarre behavior. After seizure, the patient was treated with phenobarbital. The seizures ceased as did the abnormal behavior. After 6 months, she became noncompliant and discontinued her medication.

A year later she became very "foggy" in conversation and would frequently stop talking in the middle of a conversation. Occasionally during these arrests of conversation, she would display restless automatic movements of her hands and mouth, but no adversive movements. She was often drowsy and could not remember common personal details. The patient had always led a rather structured and compulsive existence, but at this time she began to show very ritualized behavior such as very rigid dieting, sleeping on the floor with exactly 14 Reader's Digest magazines under her head, and constantly expressing dissatisfaction about how the house looked and with her personal appearance.

The patient was again brought to the hospital. On examination, she appeared very dazed and responded laconically, answering only a few questions and staring into space most of the time. Findings on the neurologic examination were completely normal. An EEG showed bursts of irregular, sharp waves in the frontal region. She was again treated with phenobarbital with a resulting improvement in mental functioning. As she became more communicative and natural in her behavior, the EEG also became normal. She still displayed some abnormal behavior, however, and demonstrated a significant thought disorder. The patient was then hospitalized in the psychiatric unit for further treatment of what was diagnosed as paranoid schizophrenia. Result of complete mental status examination for organic disease was normal except for concreteness in proverb interpretation. This was attributed to the thought disorder and not to brain dysfunction. Findings on CT scan of the brain were normal.

For several years the patient was maintained on both phenobarbital and phenothiazines. She had no further seizures or "foggy spells" but continued to show evidence of an intermittent thought disorder. She recently died secondary to a myocardial infarction.

This case demonstrates some of the puzzling behavioral changes that can occur in patients with epilepsy. This person always had a "strange personality" according to her family but compensated well until the onset of the seizures. Her first symptoms were reminiscent of the type of chronic confusional behavior seen in absence status, but her EEG showed only episodic trains of frontal sharp activity. We assume, because her behavior ameliorated considerably after the control of the abnormal discharges, that this subclinical seizure activity was responsible for both producing the confusional behavior and unmasking or exacerbating an underlying psychiatric disorder. Her behavior before the onset of seizures had been obsessive and somewhat paranoid, but with the onset of the seizures she became clinically schizophrenic. It is possible that her EEG had been abnormal for many years and that her odd lifelong behavior reflected this physiologic disturbance; however, this can only be a speculation.

It is not our intent to provide a comprehensive overview of the very complex problem of epilepsy; however, the importance of these syndromes to the practicing clinician cannot be overestimated. Epilepsy is a common disease, and one that is frequently associated with significant behavioral change. The social, vocational, and emotional impact of epilepsy on the patient, his family, and society in general is considerable. In this chapter we provide a relatively brief description of the various types of epilepsy and their incidence. The behavioral changes that are seen either in association with the seizures themselves or as chronic interictal phenomena are emphasized. More comprehensive reviews of both the medical and social/rehabilitative aspects are readily available to the interested reader.[3,9,98,99,120,123,139]

Epilepsy is among the most common of the chronic neurologic disorders. Although the incidence varies with the particular study and the sample studied, between 20 to 120 cases per 100,000 is the generally reported annual incidence for newly diagnosed cases.[77,78,116,120] In addition, an unknown but substantial number of cases go undiagnosed and untreated. About 1 to 3 percent of the general population have recurrent seizures,[118] suggesting that more than 2.5 million persons in the United States alone suffer from this problem.

The term "epilepsy," as used by most physicians, implies a recurrent paroxysmal uncontrolled discharge of cerebral neurons resulting in clinical signs and symptoms that interfere with normal functioning.[120] In most cases there is impaired thinking, awareness of and/or observable convulsive movements or repetitive behaviors (automatisms).[37] During attacks in which the seizure discharge remains well localized without spread, there may be no loss of consciousness. In other cases with a deeper locus or bilateral spread, lapses in consciousness can be a very prominent feature of the disorder. One of the most striking clinical features of epilepsy is the intermittent nature of the disorder and the almost total lack of overt symptoms between the actual seizures in most patients. Some patients may experience multiple seizures daily, whereas the majority have intervals of many months or years between attacks.

Because of the complex nature of epilepsy and the wide spectrum of its clinical manifestations, a simple definition and a universal concise clinical description are impossible. Nor is it possible to provide an all-encompassing discussion of the treatment of this complicated medical problem. Therefore, this chapter provides only a framework for the clinical classification of epilepsy and definitions of basic relevant terms.

The most commonly used classification system is that proposed by Gastaut,[50] who groups patients by symptomatology. This system has been adopted by the International League Against Epilepsy and the World Federation of Neurology. This classification (Table 12–1) provides a stan-

Table 12–1. International Classification of Epileptic Seizures

I. Partial Seizures (seizures beginning locally)
  A. Partial seizures with elementary symptomatology (generally without impairment of consciousness)
    1. With motor symptoms
      a. Focal motor
      b. Jacksonian
      c. Versive (generally contraversive)
      d. Postural
      e. Somatic inhibitory (?)
      f. Aphasic
      g. Phonatory (vocalization and arrest of speech)
    2. With special sensory or somatosensory symptoms
      a. Somatosensory
      b. Visual
      c. Auditory
      d. Olfactory
      e. Gustatory
      f. Vertiginous
    3. With autonomic symptoms
    4. Compound forms
  B. Partial seizures with complex symptomatology (generally with impairment of consciousness)
    1. With impaired consciousness only
    2. With cognitive symptomatology
      a. With dysmnesic disturbances
      b. With ideational disturbances
    3. With affective symptomatology
    4. With "psychosensory" symptomatology
      a. Illusions
      b. Hallucinations
    5. With "psychomotor" symptomatology (automatisms)
    6. Compound forms
  C. Partial seizures secondarily generalized

Table 12-1. International Classification of
Epileptic Seizures *(continued)*

II. Generalized Seizures (bilaterally symmetrical and without local onset)
   A. Absences (petit mal)
      1. Simple absences with impairment of consciousness only
      2. Complex absences with other associated phenomena
         a. With mild clonic components (myoclonic)
         b. With increase of postural tone (retropulsive)
         c. With diminution or abolition of postural tone (atonic)
         d. With automatisms
         e. With automatic phenomena (e.g., enuresis)
         f. Mixed forms
   B. Bilateral massive epileptic myoclonus (myoclonic jerks)
   C. Infantile spasms
   D. Clonic seizures
   E. Tonic seizures
   F. Tonic-clonic seizures ("grand mal" seizures)
   G. Atonic seizures
      1. Of very brief duration (drop attacks)
      2. Of longer duration (including atonic absences)
III. Unilateral or Predominantly Unilateral Seizures
IV. Unclassified Epileptic Seizures (includes all seizures that cannot be classified because of inadequate or incomplete data)

---

dardized and uniform system that is internationally recognized and has greatly aided communication among epileptologists.

It may be of value to briefly review several of the terms most frequently used in describing epilepsy. Generalized seizure-tonic-clonic type *(grand mal)* is a generalized convulsion with accompanying loss of consciousness and a sequence of tonic-clonic motor movements. Absence *(petit mal)* refers to a seizure characterized by brief absences, occurring predominantly in children, and with an EEG pattern of paroxysmal 3 per second spike-and-wave bursts. The seizure may be accompanied by a rhythmic blinking of the eyes, automatisms, and at times by a myoclonic jerking of the extremities. Previously, the term was used to refer to any minor seizure attack. *Temporal lobe seizures* or *psychomotor attacks* are partial seizures with complex symptomatology.

The *prodrome* is a behavioral or mood change that may precede the actual onset of a seizure by hours or even days. Such symptoms are difficult to directly relate to the seizure itself and may reflect either alterations in basic physiologic processes such as premenstrual water retention or the gradual accentuation of unstable electrochemical activity that interferes with normal central nervous system functioning.[114]

Aura is the consciously recalled experience (often sensory) that heralds the actual onset of the seizure and is recognized as a component of the seizure itself.[114,120] This behavioral component is clinically relevant, as the nature of its manifestation can be useful in localizing the seizure focus.

The *ictus* is the overt seizure itself. The *postictal* period immediately follows the seizure and is typically characterized by changes in behavior, which may include drowsiness, confusion, poorly directed activity, and at times abnormal motor movement. *Interictal* denotes the interval between actual seizures, in which the patient is not experiencing any direct seizure effects. Interictal changes in behavior and personality in epileptic patients have been reported for centuries and are one of the most interesting aspects of the interaction between epilepsy and behavior. There is little doubt that the behavioral and emotional concomitants or sequelae of epilepsy are as diverse as the manifestations of the seizures themselves. On the other hand, the cause and precise nature of these behavioral disorders have been the source of considerable, often conflicting, speculations.[87,102] Tizard's[128] review of the world's literature regarding the emotional consequences of epilepsy and the conclusions of most workers in this field provide little support for the long-held theory that a characteristic "epileptic personality" exists. The data do, however, suggest (1) that the incidence of personality disturbances may be higher than expected in the epileptics and (2) that different types of personality disorders may be associated with different types of epilepsy.[34,114,128]

Accurate statistics concerning the actual incidence of clinically significant behavioral changes associated with epilepsy are difficult to obtain because of problems in the comparability of the various studies in this area and the quality of many such reports (e.g., case studies, anecdotal reports, studies of a particular problem associated with a discrete form of epilepsy). The consensus of these investigations, however, is that a far higher than expected incidence of problems in intellectual, emotional, and social functioning does exist within the epileptic population, with estimates of the frequency of such problems ranging from 10 to 70 percent in the various samples under study.[40,102] Such disorders in all probability result from a complex interaction of personality structure, environment, brain pathophysiology, and the effects of anticonvulsant medication.[32,35,82]

The frequency and variety of emotional and behavioral changes seen in epileptic patients are sufficiently high, and the psychologic and social impact of such disorders can be so great that the clinician should be thoroughly prepared to recognize their presence, make the appropriate neurobehavioral diagnosis, and provide treatment and/or referral. The remainder of this chapter provides one conceptual framework for classifying these behavioral changes and descriptions of the most frequently encountered clinical syndromes.

To help in the categorization and understanding of the wide range of behavioral changes seen in patients with epilepsy, we propose the use of the following outline adapted from Pond.[102] This system has the advantage of attempting to relate a particular behavioral disturbance to an underlying neurophysiologic dysfunction rather than being merely a tedious compilation of every clinical symptom. Although no such system is universally accepted, we have found this outline to be logical and clinically useful.

Behavior Change and Epilepsy
  I. Behavior changes directly related to clinical seizures
    A. Preictal: Events preceding or leading to overt seizures
      1. Prodromal states
      2. Psychophysiologic precursors
    B. Ictal: Disorders directly related to ongoing epileptic discharges.
      1. Aura
      2. Disturbances in consciousness
      3. Psychomotor expressions of discharge
    C. Postictal: Disturbances following overt seizures
      1. Alterations in consciousness
        a. Focal paralyses
        b. Automatism with amnesia
      2. Violent behavior
      3. Confusional behavior
    D. Emotional reactions to ictal experiences
  II. Interictal behavior changes
    A. Cognitive dysfunction
    B. Emotional changes
      1. Neuroticlike disorders
      2. Psychoticlike disorders
      3. Characterologic disorders
      4. Special problems of temporal lobe epilepsy

DESCRIPTION OF THE CLINICAL SYNDROMES

As the reader may assume from the classification schema, a wide variety of emotional, behavioral, and cognitive changes has been reported to be associated with epilepsy. These changes range from increased anxiety and irritability levels to episodic violent behavior, characterologic-like disorders, and the schizophreniform psychosis. Those that have been most frequently reported are described in some detail, whereas certain more uncommon behavioral changes are briefly reviewed.

Behavior Change Directly Related
to Clinical Seizures

PREICTAL BEHAVIORAL CHANGES

Prodromal States/Psychophysiologic Precursors

Premonitory or prodromal symptoms are primarily psychologic in manifestation (including depression, mental dullness, irritability, social withdrawal, and hypomania). Theoretically, auras may be differentiated from the prodromal states. The former have clear neuropathophysiologic bases (i.e., a focal epileptic discharge that may be documented by electroencephalogram [EEG] before the onset of an overt seizure). In contrast, the prodromal states are not associated with a worsening of the EEG during the days or hours preceding a seizure[102] and may be related to a variety of physiologic states (e.g., premenstrual hormonal changes or water retention). Certain patients or their close associates are able to accurately predict an impending seizure before its onset on the basis of these changes in behavior.

The cause of these generalized emotional changes is as yet uncertain, but probably they are physiologically related to the seizure disorder (i.e., a build-up of epileptic interference with brain function) and represent a type of premonitory emotional response by the patient to the imminent seizure. The patient's conscious perception of an emotional response to the prodrome constitutes one additional common type of epilepsy-associated behavioral change.

In some cases, the patient's actual behavior precipitates an overt seizure. Categorized as self-induced reflex epilepsy, this subject has been well covered in the literature.[7,13,66,92] Environmental stress, photic stimulation (either environmentally or personally induced), reading, listening to music (in some cases, even specific types of music), repetitive motoric activity, acute startle, and other similar stimuli have been known to precipitate a seizure in the electrophysiologically susceptible individual.

One theory of the physiologic origin of an epileptic focus is the concept of kindling, a situation in which there is a progressive development of cerebral electrical abnormalities and spontaneous, sustained seizures as the result of brief intermittent subclinical electrical stimulation of the brain. Experimentally, the limbic areas of the brain are most susceptible to this process. It has been considered likely that the kindling phenomenon may explain the development of active seizures, mirror and daughter epileptic foci, and gradual progression of behavioral changes in patients with chronic temporal-limbic epilepsy.[122] Systemic use of drugs having local anesthetic properties, such as cocaine and alcohol, has also been shown to result in limbic epilepsy.[136]

ICTAL BEHAVIORAL CHANGES

Aura

Often patients will remember and repeat the initial subjective experience of a seizure—the aura. This is particularly true of temporolimbic seizures, although some patients with focal or generalized tonic-clonic epilepsy do describe brief autonomic or other sensations before onset of the overt seizure. In the late 1880s, Hughlings Jackson[70] described a man with a glioma of the frontotemporal area whose overt seizures were preceded by an aura consisting of a "dreadful disagreeable smell" that was then followed by "chewing movements of the jaws and spitting of saliva." Although this particular manifestation is certainly not common,[64] the combination of a psychic aura and unprovoked automatic behavior is representative of this category of ictal behavioral. Many classic aura manifestations have been repeated, including the sensory alterations of pain, discomfort, numbness, vertigo, illusions or hallucinations in any sensory modality, emotional changes including fear, erotic feelings, and deja vu. Autonomic manifestations including flushing, shortness of breath, apnea, and tachycardia may also occur.[57,122]

Other focal seizures, not confined to the medial aspect of the temporal lobe, can produce a subjective aura. The most frequently reported include sensory phenomena secondary to stimulation of the postcentral gyrus, vertiginous feelings with posterior temporal seizures, and visual hallucinations, usually but not exclusively of poorly formed images, associated with occipital and occipital-temporal foci.

A standard neurologic examination during such episodes often fails to document objective sensory findings in these patients even during an actual seizure.[141] It is the patient's subjective experience at the central nervous system level that constitutes these sensory auras.[122]

Disturbances in Consciousness

The significant self-sustained electrical discharge that characterizes the overt ictal phase of an epileptic seizure can result in a wide variety of both physiologic and psychologic changes. The most obvious and most physiologically based behavioral changes involve varying degrees of disturbed levels of consciousness. The alterations range from the deep comalike state of the generalized-tonic-clonic seizure to the transitory lapse of awareness in the absence (petit mal) seizure or the complex dreamlike states that are typical of some seizures originating deep within the temporal lobes. Accordingly, the patient with a history of intermittent lapses in awareness or consciousness should be fully evaluated to assess the possibility of epilepsy.

Mental and behavioral changes have been reported as manifestations of absence seizures since the first description of this disorder.[80] Such manifestations have received a variety of labels including "prolonged twilight state," "prolonged behavioral disturbance," "ictal psychosis" and "acute prolonged confusion."[39,42,112,138] Clinical manifestations include: (1) normal or subjective impairment of awareness, (2) deep stupor, (3) impaired motivation and initiative, (4) deficits in planning, (5) aphasiclike language disorders including paraphasia and perseveration, (6) confusion and disorientation, (7) infantile behavior (primarily in children), (8) incontinence, (9) amnesic periods, (10) fuguelike states, (11) hallucinations, paranoia, (12) delusional ideation, (13) manic-depressive affectual changes, and (14) apraxia.[6,39] Although absence status has primarily been reported in children, the onset in middle-age has been described.[53] Ellis and Lee[39] reported on six patients between the ages of 42 and 69 with no past history of seizures who initially presented with an acute behavioral change characterized by the abrupt, unprovoked onset of fluctuating confusion, memory dysfunction, and psychoticlike symptomatology; this was associated with continuous, generalized 1- to 1½-Hz multiple spike and wave EEG activity.

Transient psychotic-like episodes that may mimic depressive, hysterical, and schizophrenic reactions unaccompanied by clinically observable seizures are relatively uncommon among patients with epilepsy but have been reported.[103,138] Such states may so dominate the clinical picture that the patient may be repeatedly admitted to a psychiatric unit before the true nature of the patient's condition is accurately diagnosed.[1] Any patient who presents with a behavioral change and (1) a history of previous seizures, (2) intellectual deterioration, or (3) intermittent periods of confusion, mental dullness, or schizophreniform behavior, with periods of complete (or almost complete) resolution should strongly alert the clinician to suspect seizure activity.[115]

Psychomotor Expressions of Seizure Discharge

The behavioral changes associated with temporal lobe seizure foci have been among the most widely reported and certainly the most readily noticed behavioral changes in the field of epilepsy. The term "psychomotor attacks" was traditionally used to categorize and describe this form of seizure.[55] In the current nomenclature, this form of seizure is included in the category of partial seizures with complex symptomatology. Classically, the *ictal automatism* is defined as a seizure resulting in a period of altered behavior for which the patient is amnesic and during which he responds to the environment in a limited, often stereotyped, fashion as if only partially conscious.[114] In most patients, the seizure begins with a recognizable aura and progresses to motor symptoms often associated with emotional and behavioral changes. The most characteristic feature of the partial seizure with complex symptomatology is the actual ictal automatism. This typically includes stereotyped nonpurposeful motor movements (e.g., lip smacking, leg kicking, picking at clothing, chewing movements) that may be repeated in similar form from attack to attack.[120] At times, partial seizures may be so brief and discrete that they are not noticed by the casual observer, whereas in other cases it is difficult, if not impossible, to fail to recognize the prolonged and bizarre repetitious behavior of the seemingly dazed or "wide-eyed" patient (e.g., the stereotyped "sniffing" of the air followed by shouting of "hallelujah" observed by one of us [F.W.B.] in a patient with a significant penetrating missile wound of the right temporal lobe).

In addition to sensory aura and psychomotor automatisms experienced by the patient with temporal lobe involvement, higher cognitive and emotional functions are often altered. Such alterations in behavior may include illusory and hallucinatory experiences, sexual arousal, feelings of prescience or familiarity (the deja vu phenomenon previously mentioned), feelings of strangeness or unreality, ictal pleasure, violence, fear, depression, and cognitive dysfunction.[21,48,109,132] Subsequent to the active seizure, the patient is typically amnesic for the episode and is often confused and drowsy. Although rare, it is usually during this latter stage of the seizure that ictal rage reactions and aggressive behavior occur (particularly if attempts are made to restrain the patient).[109,130] The actual reported incidence of violent or aggressive behavior in patients with temporal lobe dysfunction, including epilepsy, is decidedly low despite the popularization of this aspect of psychomotor epilepsy in the lay and even some professional literature.[130] Violence as an expression of ictal behavior is a special situation that is discussed later in this chapter.

From theoretic, physiologic, and clinical viewpoints, the basis of the ictal emotional and behavioral phenomena is important. It is generally conceded that such focal abnormalities are related to dysfunction of the limbic portions of the frontal and temporal lobes. Temporolimbic and frontolimbic structures are of considerable importance in the development and expression of emotions and emotional behavior. Obviously, however, the precise association between emotions and behavior and these structures is yet to be fully elucidated.

For a more comprehensive review of this complex area, refer to the many reviews dealing with the behavioral manifestations of temporal lobe epilepsy.[12,14,118]

POSTICTAL BEHAVIORAL CHANGE

The postictal period is that time immediately following an active seizure. It is characterized by behavioral changes including drowsiness, confusion, abnormal motor movement, and semipurposeful activity.

There is a gradual transition from the ictal to the postictal phase of the seizure and some overlap in the behavioral manifestations during each stage. Hypothetical causes for postictal behavioral changes include a metabolic derangement of cells secondary to the hypoxia associated with the active seizure,[93] an active inhibitory state,[38] and cellular metabolic exhaustion.[41]

Disturbances in Consciousness

The most frequent of the postictal behavioral disturbances are those associated with an alteration of both level and content of consciousness. Those behavioral changes that are of primary psychiatric importance occur when the electrical discharge involves the area of cortex that serves as a substrate for consciousness (particularly the deep temporal areas).[102] Some investigators[71] believe that automatisms with amnesia for the event result only when the previous seizure has involved at least all of one hemisphere and the contralateral lobe (i.e., relatively bilateral generalized epileptic activity). During the postictal phase, the patient is typically confused initially (although this may be imperceptible in some patients) and then gradually interacts with the environment in an increasingly more organized fashion. Conversation becomes possible, and behavior appears reasonably coherent, although the patient is often unable later to recall the events that transpire during this latter stage of the postictal phase.[17] The duration of this postictus is variable, but typically lasts from 2 to 10 minutes, with an outside range of a few seconds to several hours. Prolonged confusional or delirious states lasting from hours to days may follow generalized seizures. If there has been a series of seizures, the altered state of consciousness may persist for as long as several weeks.[17] The severity of the disorder as well as its clinical manifestations may fluctuate both during a given day and over the course of several days. In this regard, the postictal confusional state is analogous to confusion from any cause, as discussed in Chapter 5. Acts committed during this confusional state vary widely in the degree to which they are coherently organized and overtly or inadvertently directed towards people or objects in the environment. Psychogenic factors including basic personality make-up, pre-existing modes of reacting in given situations, and particular environmental stress play a major role in the manifestation of acts committed during the confusional state. Theoretically, during the state of clouded consciousness, there is a diminution of the highest levels of emotional and behavioral control, allowing expression of more basic, highly emotionally charged impulses.[2] On a more pragmatic level, the behavior during this postictal state and its underlying dynamics are akin to a state of alcoholic or drug intoxication in which behavior that is usually under relatively adequate control (e.g., aggression, sexuality, dysinhibition, or even psychosis) may be expressed with minimal provocation, much to the detriment of the person and the environment.

The behavioral changes associated with altered levels of consciousness have sometimes been termed "psychotic" and both a classification system and descriptions of the various states are widely disseminated in the literature.[17] Although some of the behaviors exhibited by patients during the postictal stage do meet the American Psychiatric Association's[4] (American Psychiatric Association, 1987) criteria for psychosis (i.e., gross impairment in reality testing), we believe it to be more in keeping with the total clinical picture of these patients to classify such behavioral changes as components or associates of the altered level of consciousness rather than to categorize the behavior on the basis of one psychiatric clinical feature.

Violence

Increased irritability and overtly violent behavior, although infrequent in most patients, is a sufficiently common feature of the ictal and postictal stages to deserve special mention here. Aggression, irritability, and at times outbursts of extreme violence have been reported in patients during seizures and the confusional amnesic postictal stage.[17,72,102] Such behaviors are usually nondirected and unexpected. They occur most frequently when attempts are made to physically restrain the patient. This has been termed "resistive violence."[130] Criminal attacks including homicide are not unknown but are extremely rare during such states. Accordingly, this aspect of epileptic behavioral change may have medicolegal significance.[60,75] There is no evidence that violent behavior is more common among epileptics than nonepileptics nor more common in patients with temporal lobe epilepsy than in those with other types of epilepsy.[130] The three primary points that the clinician should keep in mind are (1) such dramatic behavioral changes do occur and must be recognized; (2) genuine ictal and postictal violent behavior takes place during a confusional period, and the patient's amnesia for the event is genuine, not feigned; and (3) seizure-related violence is very rare, is stereotyped, and almost never consists of a series of purposeful behaviors. The complex medicolegal ramifications implicit in such cases are beyond the scope of this text. The interested reader is referred to Juul-Jensen[72] for more thorough reviews of this subject.

EMOTIONAL REACTIONS TO ICTAL EXPERIENCES

Both the ictal and postictal direct effects of an epileptic discharge are, by their electrophysiologic nature, paroxysmal and transitory. How patients respond to their perception and experience of the ictal phenomena, however, are of major significance in the development of longstanding behavioral changes. The perception of an ictal sensation, emotion, or motor behavior is basically a passive experience and generally thought to be something alien to the individual.[102] The intermittent and unexpected imposition of any ictal phenomenon (e.g., feeling of fear) without appropriate environmental stimuli is usually disquieting at the very least (although some patients actually enjoy and self-induce their seizures). In most patients, the repeated occurrence of unpredictable events such as prodromes, auras, and seizures understandably leads to the development of anxiety, paranoia, anger, and other emotional reactions. Compounding this basic process of ictal stimulus and emotional response are the reactions of others to the overt manifestations of the patient's seizures.[98] The seizure produces behavioral changes that are often strange, frankly bizarre, and frightening to the patient's family as well as the naive observer. It represents a total lack of control to the patient and, usually, to those around him.[59] The long history of negative social reaction to epilepsy and its sufferers has been well documented and needs no reiteration here. Many of the emotional and social problems experienced by the epileptic patient are not directly related to preictal, ictal, or postictal phenomena but are associated with a complex interplay among (1) the ictal experience, (2) the patient's emotional and behavioral response, and (3) emotional and social responses by persons within the patient's environment to his epilepsy per se and to its overt (or covert) manifestations.

Interictal Behavior Changes Not Clearly Related to Clinical Seizures

The behavioral changes in this category are those psychologic changes that occur in patients with documented epilepsy but that are not directly related to the physiologically induced preictal, ictal, or postictal phenomena. Included are changes in cognitive functioning, the controversial "epileptic personality," and the wide range of psychologic disorders that have been reported in proven epileptics. Literature on this topic strongly suggests that most of the psychologic disturbances noted in epileptic patients cannot be directly related to the actual seizure discharge. Much of the early work in this area involved an attempt to delineate an "epileptic personality" characteristic of all or most epileptics. This included rather specific psychopathologic changes that were considered an integral part of the epileptic syndrome. In contrast has been the contention of recent writers that the basic personality of the epileptic is normal and that the only observable emotional differences between the epileptic and others are secondary to the unusual anxieties generated by recurrent unpredictable seizures and exclusion from the opportunities of a normal life by public attitude.[8] Probably the best reviews of this controversy are those of Tizard.[128] The concept of a universal characteristic epileptic personality has been largely discounted in the current literature. There appears to be a greater incidence of cognitive, emotional, and social disturbances interictally in patients with epilepsy than would be expected in the general population.[102] It has anecdotally been reported that this is particularly true for patients with temporal lobe seizures,[11,17,99,114] although a recent review of the relevant literatures suggests that no substantive evidence supports the theory of increased behavioral abnormality in temporal lobe epilepsy.[34] Such disturbances are reported to be equally distributed in epileptics and other patients with similar brain dysfunction.

COGNITIVE DYSFUNCTION

The incidence of mental retardation among epileptic patients is higher than among the normal population. Most noninstitutionalized epileptics do have intelligence quotients within the normal range, although their scores tend to cluster at the lower end of this range.[108] The prevalence of seizures among mentally retarded persons increases proportionately with the degree of retardation. Tredgold and Soddy[129] found that more than 50 percent of institutionalized persons with IQs within the most severe category of retardation had epilepsy, whereas only a small proportion of epileptics in the community are of significantly subnormal intelligence.[102] The correlation between epilepsy and increasing degrees of mental retardation undoubtedly had cultural, environmental, and pharmacologic associations as well as neuropathologic factors. Institutionalized patients with severe mental retardation have brain abnormalities or damage of some type,[113] thereby increasing the chance of epilepsy. The age of onset of major motor seizures[30] and the frequency of such seizures[31] have been demonstrated to be associated with greater psychologic impairment in adults as assessed by both IQ functioning and a broad range of tests of adaptive abilities. This association does, of course, depend to a great extent on the type of seizure (e.g., a patient having dozens of petit mal seizures daily may have very adequate cognitive functioning in contrast to a patient with chronic, poorly controlled, generalized seizures who does have impaired intelligence).

Three factors concerning cognitive functioning deserve special attention: (1) the specific effects of focal epileptogenic activity, particularly within the temporal lobe, (2) the question of intellectual deterioration in patients with chronic, inadequately controlled epilepsy, and (3) the effects of anticonvulsant medication on cognition. Dennerll,[28] after reviewing the literature pertaining to the effects of lateralized epileptic foci, reported significant differences in specific test performances relating to laterality. Patients with left-hemisphere lesions, particularly temporal, demonstrated deficits on tests of verbal abilities, whereas those with right-hemisphere lesions showed the expected deficits in perceptual motor and visual spatial skills. Relatively poorer performance on tests of short-term memory has been reported in unilateral temporal lobe epileptics compared with a similar group of patients with generalized seizure disorders[58,98] although the study was unable to demonstrate any consistent effects of laterality. Glowinski[58] explained his findings by postulating an impairment in encoding that interferes with the consolidation stage of the memory process and produces the chronic interictal memory deficit. Other studies also provide evidence that the diffuse or focal nature of the epileptic process will cause different types of cognitive dysfunction. For example, attention and more generalized cognitive performance may be depressed in diffuse or absence seizures,[95,124] whereas specific cognitive functions are impaired in patients with focal epileptic activity.[94]

No definitive studies have been done to support the generally held contention that intellectual deterioration is seen in chronic epileptics. However, data on neonates suggest that both generalized and focal seizures result in brain damage that may worsen over time.[135] A similar process in children and adults could well account for changes in cognitive functioning. Satisfactory delineation of this factor will require long-term longitudinal studies with adequate control of the complicating variables of age, seizure onset, duration of epilepsy, forms of the seizure disorder (to include etiology and presence or absence of frank brain damage), patient's socioeconomic status and intellectual level before the onset of seizures, anticonvulsant medication used and both its dosage and serum levels, seizure frequency, and elapsed time between the last seizure and examination.[99]

The most significant factor appears to be the severity of the seizure disorder rather than the mere presence of epilepsy. In those cases with documented intellectual deterioration, the basic problem is likely the underlying neuropathologic process, which can be progressive when inadequately treated. For most epileptic patients, the disease is relatively benign in terms of cognitive functioning.[82] Although there has been some evidence of intellectual deterioration with poorly controlled seizures,[108] the consensus is that deterioration is by no means universal and, if present, may well not be permanent in all cases, but rather reflects drug effects or the state of the patient at the time of testing. By their demonstration of the positive effect of carbamazepine on the neuropsychologic performance of epileptics compared with that of phenytoin, Dodrill and Troupin[35] showed the importance of drugs as a factor.

Anticonvulsant medication at toxic levels can result in mental deterioration in some patients. With proper usage, however, toxicity is a significant problem in only a minority of patients. The advantages of medication generally outweigh the potential drawbacks.[82]

In summary, the research on the cognitive performance of epileptics generally has found that (1) epileptics as a group have slightly lower average IQ scores than nonepileptic controls,[90] (2) the lower IQ scores may be related to age of seizure onset,[30] (3) poorer cognitive performance appears to be associated with the frequency of seizures,[31] (4) patients in whom the cause of the seizures is known perform less adequately than those in whom the cause is not apparent,[73] (5) institutionalized patients routinely have lower test scores than do epileptics being treated at public clinics, who in turn have lower IQ scores than patients in private care,[114] (6) specific cognitive deficits (as opposed to full scale IQ scores) may correlate to a degree with the laterality or localization of the epileptic focus,[24] and (7) anticonvulsant medication has the potential to cause cognitive deterioration when used at levels toxic for the individual, but usually does not when appropriately used. For a more complete review of the effects of epilepsy on psychologic test performance and adaptive abilities, see Dodrill,[33] Lesser and associates,[82] and Reitan.[104]

EMOTIONAL CHANGE

There is general agreement that the frequency of clinically recognizable, relatively stable chronic personality disorders is higher in the population of epileptics than in that of normal persons. The personality change referred to here is not the transient emotional and behavioral change directly related to ictal discharges, but rather a more generalized change in personality that is interictal and unrelated to the actual seizure. Discounting the now outdated "epileptic personality," these conditions can be broadly grouped as follows: (1) disturbances resembling neuroses, (2) disorders resembling psychoses or schizophreniform disorders, and (3) those conditions including aggressive and/or violent behavior, hypersexuality or hyposexuality, and the wide range of symptoms seen with temporal lobe or psychomotor seizures.

Disorders Resembling Neuroses

A wide variety of personality changes resembling neuroses has been reported in epileptic patients. These changes occur with far higher incidence than would be expected within the general population.[88,101] A number of conditions resembling neuroses manifesting as interictal phenomena probably result from a combination of the effects of (1) chronic intermittent stimulation of autonomic centers and catecholaminergic areas in the brain by the epileptic focus, (2) long-term exposure to the abnormal behavioral and emotional experiences (e.g., fear, disagreeable sensory perceptions, confusion) that are related to physiologic factors (i.e., active spike discharges without seizure), (3) environmental response to the patient's seizure disorder (e.g., misunderstanding, anxiety, overprotection), and (4) the patient's emotional response to the seizure disorder itself and its social and environmental consequences.

The association between the functional syndrome of neurotic hysteria and epilepsy has been the focus of centuries of philosophizing and research.[56] The problem is of clinical importance because (1) some epileptic patients have hysteriform personality traits, (2) hysterical or psychogenic seizures (pseudoseizures) must be differentiated from actual epileptic attacks, and (3) some epileptics have a complex combination of both syndromes. Differentiating pseudoseizures from genuine epileptic seizures is not always easy, particularly if one relies on only the patient's report of the event. The situation is somewhat improved if the episode has been observed, but this too can be discouragingly inadequate in many instances. The most useful approach is to ask the patient or observer to describe the attack in detail and see whether there are any inconsistencies between the report and what is expected in a real seizure. Pseudoseizure patients often report a significant degree of awareness during their seizure, a feature uncommon in epilepsy except for certain focal seizures. The functional patient also may evidence uncharacteristic movements such as arching of the back, flailing from side to side, or, on occasion, purposeful movements such as striking at people around him. The pseudoseizure frequently encompasses a wide and varying repertoire of movements, whereas the movements of a true epileptic seizure are rather stereotyped. Urinary incontinence and tongue biting are usually not seen other than in genuine seizures, but, of course, their absence does not rule out epilepsy, particularly of temporal lobe origin. The postictal period in true epilepsy is usually one of confusion, depression, and lethargy, features not often seen in the functional patient.

The diagnosis is made much easier with use of the EEG because (1) in true seizures epileptic features may be present, (2) if used shortly after the seizure, postictal slowing may be seen in genuine seizures, (3) hysterical patients are often suggestible, and a "seizure" can sometimes be precipitated by careful encouragement while the EEG is being performed. In most instances, a skilled electroencephalographer can separate true seizure discharges from muscle artifact and correctly diagnose a pseudoseizure. Of importance is the fact that many patients will have both true and psychogenic seizures; in such cases, full control is difficult, and the physician often finds himself very unsure about the patient's actual seizure frequency. A recent objective study of patients with only pseudoseizures failed to demonstrate any single consistent personality factor but did show a high incidence of cognitive dysfunction, suggesting that the cause of pseudoseizures is multifactorial and involves a variety of psychopathologic processes and sometimes brain dysfunction.[134]

Disorders Resembling Psychoses

A schizophreniform psychosis (organic delusional disorders) has been reported in epileptic patients, most frequently in patients with temporal lobe seizures.[21,22,24,127] It is most common in patients whose seizures are poorly controlled for an extended period[56]; psychosis may also develop, however, as the overt seizures are decreasing in frequency.[100,106] The psychosis seen with psychomotor seizures is discussed in greater detail in the section regarding temporal lobe personality changes.

Dongier,[36] in a study of psychotic episodes occurring in 516 epileptic patients, reported that a high proportion of the episodes in patients with nontemporal lobe epilepsy tended to be relatively brief and characterized primarily by ictal and/or postictal confusional behavior or delirium. In contrast, the psychotic periods occurring in temporal lobe epileptics tend to last longer and are associated with disorders of affect and fluctuating mood, but without confusion or alterations in the level of consciousness.[23]

Psychotic-like episodes manifesting as dysphoric states (i.e., transient changes in mood that occur and then gradually diminish in intensity),[79,84] hypomanic states,[36] and depressive states[27,137] have been reported in patients with both generalized and temporal lobe seizures. Other conditions of psychotic proportions described in epileptics include prolonged or even chronic psychosis, paranoid syndromes, marked regressive psychosis, and manic-depressive psychosis.[23] A syndrome characterized by episodic affective disturbances, intermittent cognitive dysfunction, and "spells" (e.g., absences, dreamlike episodes, or staring spells) with normal functioning between episodes has been described in a series of patients with documented temporal lobe epilepsy.[132]

Any consideration of the general topic of psychosis and epilepsy must at least briefly touch on the many etiologic theories. The reader is cautioned that, although a variety of hypotheses have been advanced, none has yet received definitive support. The major theories that have been adapted from Bruens[23] are as follows:

I. Epilepsy and psychosis are not directly related because there is a statistical chance occurrence of two relatively common diseases. This chance combination theory has been largely discounted on the basis of epidemiologic data that suggest a higher than chance incidence of psychosis among epileptics.[22,107]

II. There is a direct causal relationship between epilepsy and psychosis that can be further subdivided into the following categories:

A. Psychosis is precipitated by seizures (usually chronic) in patients who are genetically predisposed to the development of a particular psychotic state (e.g., schizophrenia). As with the chance combination theory, epidemiologic studies do not provide strong support for this hypothesis because there tends to be very little evidence of hereditary predisposition in most cases of epilepsy-related psychosis.[22,107]

B. The psychosis can be directly related to the epilepsy, in which case the following possibilities must be considered: (1) The psychosis results from an organic brain lesion that was caused by long-term, poorly controlled seizures (i.e., overt seizures cause brain damage that in turn can result in psychosis). (2) The psychosis is a nonspecific organic condition that results from the underlying organic disorder, which also underlies the epilepsy. (3) The psychosis is a behavioral manifestation of subclinical seizures that are not overtly apparent or demonstrated on the routine surface electrode EEG. (4) The psychosis is an emotional reaction to the seizure disorder and to its social ramifications.

A number of researchers have reported an inverse relationship between seizure frequency and degree of psychosis. Flor-Henry,[47] Standage and Fenton,[123] and Taylor[126] found that epileptic patients with destructive lesions had a higher incidence of psychosis than did a similar group with mesial sclerotic lesions (scars resulting from anoxia). These data do not provide strong support for theories one and two and, in fact, suggest that severity of epilepsy, at least as expressed by the frequency of seizures, is not related to psychosis. A recent objective survey of 833 epileptics in the University of Washington Regional Epilepsy Center found evidence of a slight relationship between abnormal or maladaptive behavior and underlying brain disorder.[34] Some authors have suggested that the psychosis manifested by some epileptics, especially those with discharges in the deep temporal structures, is a reflection of subclinical seizures that are not overt and cannot be demonstrated with standard scalp EEG electrodes.[47] Because the association between limbic structures and behavior and emotion has been well documented, it seems highly possible that the development of a schizophreniform psychosis does result from chronic subictal electrical discharges within the limbic system occurring over years. With our current lack of knowledge regarding the electrical status of deep brain structures both with psychosis and during a seizure, the theory that psychosis is a manifestation of undetected seizures remains speculative and in need of further investigation.

The early literature regarding the association of psychosis and epilepsy considered the psychiatric syndrome to be a functional emotional reaction to the physical and social stresses engendered by the seizures.[24] Functional or psychogenic factors cannot be discounted in the explanation of any psychoticlike state in epileptics, but they do not appear to be the sole causative variable in all cases.

III. The psychosis results from anticonvulsant medication. Two main theories regarding this hypothesis are (1) the theory that psychosis becomes more frequent and apparent on "forced normalization" of the EEG with medication and (2) the theory that chronic anticonvulsant therapy itself may cause psychosis through either metabolic interference or a toxic effect on mental functioning. The results of those studies that have concentrated on the "forced normalization" hypothesis[43,106,123] are in considerable disagreement and cannot be considered strong support for this theory. Reynolds[105,106] suggested that anticonvulsant medication itself may lead to psychosis. His research indicated a diminution of folic acid levels in the serum, red blood cells, and spinal fluid in treated epileptic patients, and he then suggested that the behavioral changes seen in epileptic psychosis might result from a similar depression of folate and B_{12} in brain tissue. Other researchers have been unable to replicate Reynolds' observations.[25,96]

It seems unlikely that actual drug toxicity is a significant factor in producing psychosis in most patients because of the lack of association between medication dosage and the incidence or severity of the psychosis[99] (although the potential toxicity of anticonvulsant drugs has been well documented, and occasional toxic psychosis undoubtedly occurs). Psychoses also develop in untreated epileptics at least as frequently as in treated patients.[10] Interestingly, some limited evidence from the work of Reynolds and Travers indicate that those patients treated with diphenylhydantoin and/or phenobarbital who had extreme behavioral abnormalities tended to have higher serum phenytoin levels than did those without such symptoms.[107]

The cause of the psychosis in epileptic patients is a complex, multifaceted series of variables of both organic and psychogenic origin. The complicated interplay of physiologic, social, and psychologic factors undoubtedly varies from patient to patient and helps to explain both why some epileptics become psychotic and others do not and the disparate manifestations of the behavioral disturbance among patients with similar seizure and treatment histories.

Characterologic Disorders

In the past, the traits commonly ascribed to the so-called "epileptic personality" were perseveration, excessive religiosity, paranoia, egocentric selfishness, impulsivity, mental slowness, emotional viscosity, circumstantiality, irritability, and mood fluctuations. There may be some agreement that such traits have a higher than expected incidence among epileptics, especially in patients with temporal lobe epilepsy. There are also indications, however, that these behavioral features are as common in other brain-damaged persons as in epileptic patients.[34] The consensus now is that these and similar traits do not constitute a symptom cluster deserving of the label "epileptic personality".[128] In fact, there is no single characterologic disorder that either is typically found only among epileptics or is characteristic of epileptics as a group. The range of personality change observed in epileptic patients appears to be as wide (and in many cases as variable) as that seen either in other neurologically or psychiatrically impaired populations or among those with no discernible central nervous system disease.

Violence and/or impulsive behavior as well as sexual deviations, both often considered characterologic disorders, are discussed in the section dealing with temporal lobe disorders because these changes are seen most commonly in those patients with temporal lobe or psychomotor seizure disorders.

Behavior Changes Associated with Temporal Lobe Epilepsy

The nature and incidence of the behavioral changes associated with seizures localized within the temporal lobe and its limbic projection areas are sufficiently interesting and frequent that this topic deserves special mention. On both theoretic and clinical grounds, the importance of the investigation of temporal lobe behavioral changes has been succinctly pointed out by Geschwind,[52] who refers to the use of temporal lobe epilepsy as a probe for research of the neurophysiology of human emotion. Accordingly, in this section we briefly review three behavioral changes commonly reported to occur in patients with temporal lobe epilepsy: (1) an increased incidence and severity of all emotional and behavioral changes, (2) violent behavior, and (3) alterations in sexuality.

General Behavioral and Personality Changes. It has been traditionally reported that the incidence of virtually all behavioral and personality changes is higher among those patients with temporal lobe seizures than any other seizure group. Historically, researchers and clinicians have noted a relatively high incidence of a wide variety of psychiatric disorders among psychomotor epileptics, ranging from schizophreniclike psychosis to characterologic and neurosislike changes.[12,48,54,125] There are also, however, statistical comparisons of psychomotor and nonpsychomotor epileptics that have failed to find significant behavioral differences between the two groups.[34,91,119] Bear[12,13] and Rodin[110] suggest that these apparent contradictions may be accounted for by the high incidence of behavioral change seen in temporal lobe patients who have more than one type of seizure. There are few significant differences when only one seizure type is present. Prominent among the behavioral changes noted both clinically and statistically are (1) increased emotionality, (2) elation or euphoria, (3) depression, (4) anger and irritability, (5) hostility and aggressive behavior, (6) compulsive behavior, (7) circumstantiality, (8) viscosity (i.e., stickiness in general mode of behavior), (9) hypergraphia, (10) religiosity, (11) overconcern with philosophy, (12) dependence and passivity, (13) lack of humor, and (14) paranoia.[12] Bear,[11,12] in studies of patients with unilateral temporal lobe epilepsy, found a lateralized distinction in behavior, with right-temporal lobe patients being more overtly or externally emotional (e.g., aggressive, depressed, and labile), whereas patients with left-temporal foci had a characteristic ideational pattern of behavioral traits including religiosity, philosophical interest, belief in personal destiny, and hypergraphia. These findings support the suggestion of previous studies[15,49] that distinctive emotional changes are associated with focal right-hemisphere lesions, whereas language-related functions are affected by left-hemisphere lesions.

Perhaps the most interesting and certainly the most clinically noteworthy behavioral change associated with temporal lobe epilepsy is the development in some patients of chronic paranoid hallucinatory states resembling schizophrenia, which have been termed "schizophreniform psychosis."[14,65,100,127] Although this disorder is relatively rare and the term itself is somewhat controversial, there is little doubt that it does occur.[17,102] The symptoms tend to resemble those of simple or paranoid schizophrenia. A careful history almost always reveals the onset of epileptic attacks many years before the appearance of the psychotic symptoms. The clinical examination demonstrates a relatively warm and basically appropriate affect in such patients, in contrast to "true" schizophrenia.[14] In addition, the hallucinations noted in patients with temporal lobe epilepsy tend to be visual or auditory in the form of noises or music, contrary to the voices and verbal comments on personal behavior more common in schizophrenics.[127] Accordingly, although the temporal lobe schizophreniform psychosis may overtly mimic true schizophrenia, the two conditions can usually be differentiated on the basis of the history and the nature of the symptoms elicited during examination. The American Psychiatric Association classifies these disorders as organic delusional syndromes.

Violence. The possible relationship between epilepsy and violent behavior has been a controversial area of study. Numerous anecdotal case reports of increased violence, particularly in patients with temporolimbic epilepsy, seemingly conflict with literature reviews[130] that suggest that violence is no more common among epileptics than nonepileptics, and that violence is not more frequent in patients with temporal lobe epilepsy than in those with other types of epilepsy. The issue is not unequivocally resolved, however, and remains important because of the increasing use of the "epilepsy defense" in criminal cases.[130] Increased irritability, aggressiveness, and occasional violent outbursts are among the most common of the behavioral changes reported in patients with temporal lobe epilepsy.[61] "Pathological aggressiveness" was noted in 38 percent of the psychomotor epileptics studied by Falconer and Taylor,[43] whereas others have reported somewhat lower but still high incidence rates.[89] As previously described, this tendency has been found to be particularly characteristic of patients with seizure foci in the right hemisphere[11] and is also reported in other patients with right-hemisphere lesions.[63] Like other epilepsy-related behavioral changes, impulsive-irritable behavior, whether manifested as generalized irritability or as outbursts of abusive or even physically aggressive behavior, develops gradually over a period of years.[17,29] Such episodes are characteristically noted during the confusional ictal and postictal phases, particularly in the patient who is restrained. Aggressive-irritable behavior, although observed, is distinctly less common during the later phase of the postictal stage.[75] In general, the typical episodic impulsive-aggressiveness tends to occur on provocation, is directed towards the environment, is not associated with overt seizure phenomena, and tends to be recalled by the patient.[17] The relationship of this behavior and epilepsy remains controversial.

Two primary lines of research have been followed in attempts to investigate this complicated sociomedical problem: One has been the study of increased frequency and levels of violence among temporal lobe epileptics; the second involves a review of the frequency of EEG abnormalities (especially of the temporal lobe) among persons known to be violent. Despite numerous controversies that have been well described by Pincus and Tucker,[99] most researchers conclude that when social factors and the operational definition of "violence" are held relatively constant, there is an increase in aggressive and violent behavior among temporal lobe epileptics. The study of temporal lobe EEG abnormalities in violent persons has been fraught with problems of patient selection and definition and the difficulty in establishing the diagnosis of temporal lobe seizures by using routine scalp EEG. A high incidence of epilepsy in general has been reported in prison populations, although literature reviews do not show a greater prevalence of epilepsy in persons convicted of violent crimes compared with matched nonviolent prisoners.[131]

Other researchers, however, have noted an increased incidence of either temporal lobe epilepsy or evidence of cerebral dysfunction in known violent or aggressive persons.[83,86,89] Such studies are limited by methodological problems but do tend to support the hypothesis that some, but certainly not all, violent behavior may well have basic neurophysiologic determinants. The limbic structures are most readily implicated because of their known association with emotions and behavior. This is also consistent with the experimental evidence provided by neurologic and electroencephalographic studies. The reader must be cautioned that, as with all other behavioral changes associated with epilepsy, a unitary physiologic theory is untenable and careful attention must be given to the roles played by social and psychogenic factors.[62,109] Personality development, family dynamics, and socioeconomic factors undoubtedly exert a strong predisposing or suppressing influence on the exhibition of aggressive and violent behavior, whatever its basic cause. Another example of abnormal aggressiveness, often termed the "episodic dyscontrol syndrome," will be discussed in detail in Chapter 14. For more comprehensive reviews of aggressive and violent behavior in epileptics see Mark and Erwin,[89] Valenstein,[133] Fields and Sweet,[46] and Treiman.[130]

Alterations in Sexual Behavior. Disturbances in sexual function have been described in epileptic patients, especially those with temporal lobe seizure foci. Both hyposexuality and hypersexuality have been described as well as a variety of odd, if not bizarre, sexual manifestations of ictal discharge. Global hyposexuality, at times to the point of total sexual disinterest and even impotence, has been considered as the most frequent sexual behavioral change associated with temporal lobe seizures.[20,51,67] The most significant feature of this problem is a lack of development of normal sexual arousal and drive (hyposexuality), despite normal development of appropriate secondary sexual characteristics, and is not usually a true impotence.[21] Both genders appear to be equally affected. The onset of the sexual dysfunction seems to parallel the onset of the overt seizures; intervention, either with the use of medication or neurosurgery, may result in normal sexual interest and performance.

Although relatively less common, frank impotence (in contrast to a lack of sexual interest) has been described in temporal lobe epileptics.[67,68] Hierons[67] postulated a reflex arc between the temporal lobe and the septum and hypothalamic structures that are known to be related to penile erection as a mechanism to explain this phenomenon physiologically. Results of experimental animal studies relating the amygdala to sexual arousal[74] and limbic structures to erection[85] support this theory.

Other research has suggested a higher than expected incidence of a variety of sexual deviations among temporal lobe epileptics.[16,76] Among the disorders reported have been homosexuality, hypersexuality, transvestism, exhibitionism, and fetishism. In addition to these more stable interictal changes, sexual auras, ictal sexual arousal (at times to the point of overt behavior including transvestism), and postictal sexuality have been reported. Sexual automatisms in both male and female patients are among the more common of the ictal sexual behaviors.[121] Blumer and colleagues[19,21] provide a thorough overview of the neural bases of sexual behavior and further description of the range of behaviors seen.

EVALUATION

The medical evaluation of the patient with suspected or known epilepsy is very similar to the evaluation of any patient with brain dysfunction. A careful family and medical history is necessary to obtain information regarding the seizure or behaviors suggestive of seizure activity (e.g., lapses in awareness, periods of eye blinking) both from the patient himself and from members of his family. Specific attention should be given to objective and subjective events occurring before (i.e., aura and prodrome), during (i.e., ictal phenomenon), and after (e.g., postictal confusion) the seizure. Seizure type, frequency, and possible precipitating events or stresses should be investigated. Similarly, the possible association between the seizures and drug ingestion (including alcohol) must be thoroughly evaluated. The patient and his family should be asked about any changes in behavior that occur between seizure episodes (i.e., interictal behavior).

The neurologic evaluation of the epileptic is relatively routine. Owing to the recent advances in medical treatment,[45] however, neurologic consultation may be very valuable. The neurologist can be of great assistance in the initial evaluation, differential diagnosis, and institution of the appropriate medication regimen.

The electroencephalogram is, of course, the neurodiagnostic test of choice in evaluating the epileptic patient. The routine EEG should include recording periods during which the patient is awake but calm, drowsy, asleep, hyperventilating, and photically stimulated. These latter activation procedures may precipitate abnormalities in the EEG when the patient is resting or sleeping that are absent in the record when the patient is awake. The sleep EEG is very important in evaluating temporal lobe epilepsy because a significantly higher incidence of abnormalities is seen during sleep. If abnormal activity is strongly suspected, specialized EEG procedures such as the use of sphenoid or nasopharygeal leads, computer averaging, or brain mapping may be useful. Repeat EEG or 24-hour continuous monitoring is also of value when an abnormality cannot be demonstrated on the initial recording by any of the above procedures.

In addition to the EEG, MRI scan (of particular use in temporal lobe epilepsy),[69] CT scan of the brain, and serum electrolyte determinations including calcium level and complete blood count should be obtained. Many new sophisticated investigational tools that are available at large medical centers can give valuable data but are not widely used in routine clinical practice: BEAM (brain electrical activity mapping), PET scan (positron emission tomography), and SPET scan (single-positron emission tomography) are additional neurodiagnostic procedures that can provide information about the metabolism of the brain.

As we have repeated throughout this chapter, behavioral factors are critically important in epilepsy, because they may (1) serve as precipitants of seizures, (2) mimic a "true" seizure disorder (i.e., hysterical seizures), (3) be a partial or even the sole manifestation of a seizure, or (4) serve as significant obstacles to successful emotional, social, and vocational adjustment. Accordingly, the neurobehavioral evaluation is advised in all patients with epilepsy. The minimal evaluation should consist of the mental status examination. In more complex cases or in situations in which psychogenic variables are obvious factors, consultation for a more thorough neuropsychologic and psychiatric evaluation is valuable.

MANAGEMENT

As with most of the neurologic conditions discussed in this volume, the two components of the management of the epileptic patient are (1) medical control of the actual seizure disorder and (2) psychosocial management of the psychologic, social, and vocational problems experienced by many such patients. All too often, the sole emphasis in treatment is on the first category of management, much to the detriment of the patient's overall adjustment. The complex, often multifaceted nature of the problems experienced by the epileptic patient must be carefully considered in the organization of the total management program, and all necessary specialists and treatment modalities should be consulted and instituted as early as is feasible.

It is not our intent to provide a discussion of the specifics of medical and psychosocial treatment of the epilepsies. Complete information is readily available in all medical school curricula and in numerous standard texts.[45,98,110,111,120,139]

The psychosocial management of the epileptic patient has been directed toward: (1) attempts to reduce seizure frequency through behavior modification and alleviating possible precipitant stress factors by environmental manipulation (or eliminating seizures entirely as in the case of "hysterical seizures"); (2) helping the patient to deal with the psychogenic associations and ramifications of the seizure disorder by the use of various modes of psychotherapy; and (3) planning comprehensive social, educational, vocational and rehabilitation programs for patients in need of such services. The adjunctive use of behavior modification has shown some early encouraging results in reducing the frequency of stress-induced and reflex epilepsy. An excellent current review of this approach has been provided by Feldman and Ricks.[44] The methods of ancillary psychotherapy and rehabilitation programs are very similar to those described in previous sections of this volume; comprehensive resource material covering this essential component of the total management of the epileptic patient is readily available.[12]

REFERENCES

1. Adebimpe, VR: Complex partial seizures simulating schizophrenia. JAMA 237:1339, 1977.
2. Aggernaes, M: The differential diagnosis between hysterical and epileptic disturbances of consciousness or twilight states. Acta Psychiatr Scand (Suppl) 185:9, 1965.
3. Aird, RB et al: Epilepsies: A critical review. New York, Raven Press 1984.
4. American Psychiatric Association: Diagnostic and Statistical Manual of Mental Disorders (DSM III). American Psychiatric Association, Washington, 1980.
5. American Psychiatric Association: Diagnostic and Statistical Manual of Mental Disorders (DSM IV). American Psychiatric Association, Washington, 1987.
6. Andermann, F and Robb, MP: Absence status. Epilepsia 13:177, 1971.
7. Anderson, NE and Wallis, WE: Activation of epileptiform activity by mental arithmetic. Arch Neurol 43:624, 1986.
8. Angers, WP: Patterns of abilities and capacities in the epileptic. J Genet Psychol 103:59, 1963.
9. Asbury, AK, McKhann, GM, and McDonald, WJ (eds): Diseases of the Nervous System. WB Saunders, Philadelphia, 1986.

10. Asuni, T and Pillutla, US: Schizophrenia-like psychosis in Nigerian epileptics. Br J Psychiatry 113:1375, 1967.

11. Bear, D: The significance of behavior change in temporal lobe epilepsy. McLean Hospital Journal (Special Issue), 1977, pp 9–21.

12. Bear, DM: Temporal lobe epilepsy: A syndrome of sensory-limbic hyperconnection. Cortex 15:357, 1979.

13. Bear, D, Schenk, L, and Benson, H: Increased autonomia response to neutral and emotional stimuli in patients with temporal lobe epilepsy. Am J Psych 138:843, 1981.

14. Beard, AW and Slater, E: The schizophrenic-like psychosis of epilepsy. Proc R Soc Med 55:311, 1962.

15. Black, FW: Unilateral brain lesions and MMPI performances: A preliminary study. Percept Mot Skills 40:87, 1975.

16. Blumer, D: Transsexualism, and sexual dysfunction, and temporal lobe disorder. In Green, R and Money, J (eds): Transexualism and Sexual Reassignment. Johns Hopkins Press, Baltimore, 1969.

17. Blumer, D: Temporal lobe epilepsy and its psychiatric significance. In Benson, DF and Blumer, D (eds): Psychiatric Aspects of Neurologic Disease. Grune & Stratton, New York, 1975, pp 171–198.

18. Blumer, D: Treatment of patients with seizure disorder referred because of psychiatric complication. McLean Hospital Journal (Special Issue) 1977, pp 53–73.

19. Blumer, D and Benson, DP: Psychiatric manifestations of epilepsy. In Benson, DF and Blumer, D (eds): Psychiatric Aspects of Neurologic Disease, Vol 2. Grune & Stratton, New York, 1982, pp 25–48.

20. Blumer, D and Levin, K: Psychiatric complications in the epilepsies: Current research and treatment. McLean Hospital Journal (Special Issue) 1977, pp 4–103.

21. Blumer, D and Walker, AE: The neural basis of sexual behavior. In Benson, DF and Blumer, D (eds): Psychiatric Aspects of Neurologic Disease. Grune & Stratton, New York, 1975, pp 199–217.

22. Bruens, JH: Psychosis in epilepsy. Psychiatr Neurol Neurosurg 74:175, 1971.

23. Bruens, JH: Psychosis in epilepsy. In Vinken, PJ and Bruyn, GW: Handbook of Clinical Neurology, Vol 15, The Epilepsies. Elsevier, New York, 1974, pp 593–610.

24. Clark, RA and Lesko, JM: Psychoses associated with epilepsy. Am J Psychiatry 96:595, 1939.

25. Cramer, JA, Mattson, RH, and Brillman, J: Folinic acid therapy in epilepsy. Fed Proc 35:582, 1976.

26. Daly, DD: Ictal clinical manifestations of complex partial seizures. In Penry, JK and Daly, DD (eds): Advances in Neurology, Vol 11, Complex Partial Seizures and Their Treatment. Raven Press, New York, 1975.

27. Delay, J, Deniker, P, and Baraude, R: Lesuicide des epileptiques. Encephale 46:401, 1957.

28. Dennerll, RD: Cognitive deficits and lateral brain dysfunction in temporal lobe epilepsy. Epilepsia 5:177, 1964.

29. Devinsky, O and Bear, D: Varieties of aggressive behavior in temporal lobe epilepsy. Am J Psychiatry 141:651, 1984.

30. Dikmen, S and Matthews, CG: Effect of major motor seizure frequency upon cognitive-intellectual functions in adults. Epilepsia 18:21, 1977.
31. Dikmen, S, Matthews, CG, and Harley, JP: The effect of early versus late onset of major motor epilepsy upon cognitive-intellectual performances. Epilepsia 16:73, 1975.
32. Dodrill, CB: Diphenylhydantoin serum levels, toxicity and neuropsychological performance in patients with epilepsy. Epilepsia 16:593, 1975.
33. Dodrill, CB: Psychosocial consequences of epilepsy. In Filskev, SB and Boll, TF (eds): Handbook of Clinical Neuropsychology. Wiley-Interscience, New York, 1986, pp 338–363.
34. Dodrill, CB and Batzel, LW: Interictal behavioral features of patients with epilepsy. Epilepsia (Suppl 2)27:64, 1986.
35. Dodrill, CB and Troupin, AS: Psychotropic effects of carbamazepine in epilepsy: A double-blind comparison with phenytoin. Neurology 27:1023, 197.
36. Dongier, S: Statistical study of clinical and electroencephalographic manifestations of 536 psychiatric episodes occurring in 516 epileptics between clinical seizures. Epilepsia 1:117, 1959.
37. Dreifuss, FE: The nature of epilepsy. In Wright, GN (ed): Epilepsy Rehabilitation. Little, Brown & Co, Boston, 1975, pp 8–27.
38. Efron, R: Post-epileptic paralysis: Theoretical critique and report of a case. Brain 84:381, 1961.
39. Ellis, JM and Lee, SI: Acute prolonged confusion in later life as an ictal state. Epilepsia 19:119, 1977.
40. Epilepsy Foundation of America: Basic Statistics on the Epilepsies. FA Davis, Philadelphia, 1975.
41. Epstein, MH and O'Conner, JS: Destructive effects of prolonged status epilepticus. J Neurol Neurosurg Psychiatry 29:251, 1966.
42. Escueta, AV et al: Prolonged twilight state and automatisms: A case report. Neurology 24:331, 1974.
43. Falconer, MA and Taylor, DC: Surgical treatment of drug resistant epilepsy due to mesial temporal sclerosis. Arch Neurol 18:353, 1968.
44. Feldman, RG and Ricks, NL: Neuropharmacologic and behavioral methods. In Ferris, GW (ed): The Treatment of Epilepsy Today. Medical Economics, Oradell, NJ, 1978, pp 89–111.
45. Feffis, GW: Treatment of epilepsy today. Medical Economics, Oradell, NJ, 1978.
46. Fields, WS and Sweet, WH: The neural basis for violence and aggression. Warren H Green, St Louis, 1975.
47. Flor-Henry, P: Psychosis and temporal lobe epilepsy. Epilepsia 10:363, 1969.
48. Flor-Henry, P: Ictal and interictal psychiatric manifestations in epilepsy: Specific or non-specific? Epilepsia 13:773, 1972.
49. Gainotti, G: Emotional behavior and hemispheric side of the lesion. Cortex 8:41, 1972.
50. Gastaut, H: Clinical and electroencephalographical classification of epileptic seizures. Epilepsia 11:102, 1970.
51. Gastaut, H and Colomb, H: Etude due comportement sexual chez les epileptiques psychomoteurs. Ann Med Psychol (Paris) 112:657, 1954.

52. Geschwind, N: Current research: Introduction. McLean Hospital Journal (Special Issue) 1977, pp 6–8.

53. Gibberd, FB: Petit mal status presenting in middle age. Lancet 1:269, 1972.

54. Gibbs, FA: Ictal and nonictal psychiatric disorders in temporal lobe epilepsy. J Nerv Ment Dis 113:522, 1951.

55. Gibbs, FA, Gibbs, EL, and Lennox, WG: Likeness of cortical dysrhythmias of schizophrenia and psychomotor epilepsy. Am J Psychiatry 95:255, 1938.

56. Glasser, GH: Epilepsy, hysteria and possession. J Nerv Ment Dis 166:268, 1978.

57. Gloor, P et al: The role of the limbic system in experiential phenomena of temporal lobe epilepsy. Ann Neurol 12:129, 1982.

58. Glowinski, H: Cognitive deficits in temporal lobe epilepsy. J Nerv Ment Dis 153:129, 1973.

59. Goldin, GJ and Margolin, RJ: The psychosocial aspects of epilepsy. In Wright, GN (ed): Epilepsy Rehabilitation. Little, Brown & Co, Boston, 1975, pp 66–80.

60. Gunn, J: Epileptic homicide: A case report. Br J Psychiatry 132:510, 1978.

61. Gunn, J: Evaluation of violence. Proc R Soc Med 66:1133, 1973.

62. Harbin, HT: Episodic dyscontrol and family dynamics. Am J Psychiatry 134:1113, 1977.

63. Hecaen, H: Clinical symtomatology in right and left hemisphere lesions. In Mountcastle, V (ed): Interhemispheric Relations and Cerebral Dominance. Johns Hopkins Press, Baltimore, 1962, pp 215–243.

64. Hecker, A, Andermann, F, and Rodin, EA: Spitting automatism in temporal lobe seizures. Epilepsia 13:767, 1972.

65. Herrington, RN (ed): Schizophrenia, epilepsy, the temporal lobe. Current problems in neuropsychiatry. Br J Psychiatry Special Publication No 4, 1969.

66. Herskowitz, J, Rosman, P, and Geschwind, N: Seizures induced by singing and recitation, a unique form of reflex epilepsy in childhood. Arch Neurol 41:1102, 1984.

67. Hierons, R: Impotence in temporal lobe lesions. J Neuro-Visceral Relations (Suppl 10):447–481, 1971.

68. Hierons, R and Saunders, M: Impotence in patients with temporal lobe lesions. Lancet 2:761, 1966.

69. Jabbari, B et al: Magnetic resonance imaging in partial complex epilepsy. Arch Neurol 43, 869, 1986.

70. Jackson, JH: In Taylor, J (ed): Selected writings of John Hughlings Jackson, Vol 1. Basic Books, New York, 1958, p 500.

71. Jasper, HH: Some physiological mechanisms involved in epileptic automatisms. Epilepsia 5:1, 1964.

72. Juul-Jensen, P: Social prognosis. In Vinken, PJ and Bruyn, GW (eds): Handbook of Clinical Neurology, Vol 15, The Epilepsies. Elsevier, New York, 1974, pp 800–814.

73. Klove, H and Matthews, CG: Psychometric and adaptive abilities in epilepsy with differential etiology. Epilepsia 7:330, 1966.

74. Klüver, H and Bucy, PC: Preliminary analysis of functions of the temporal lobes in monkeys. Arch Neurol Psychiatry 42:979, 1939.

75. Know, SJ: Epileptic automatism and violence. Med Sci Law 8:96, 1968.
76. Kolorsky, A et al: Male sexual deviation. Arch Gen Psychiatry 17:735, 1967.
77. Kurland, LT: The incidence and prevalence of convulsive disorders in a small urban community. Epilepsia 1:143, 1959.
78. Kurtzke, JF et al: Convulsive disorders. In Kurland, LT, Kurtzke, JF, and Goldberg, ID (eds): Epidemiology of Neurologic and Sense Organ Disorders (American Public Health Association Monograph). Harvard University Press, Cambridge, MA, 1973.
79. Landolt, H: Serial-EEG investigation during psychotic episodes in epileptic patients and during schizophrenic attacks. In Lorentz de Haas, AM (ed): Lectures on Epilepsy. Elsevier, New York, 1958, pp 91–133.
80. Lennox, WG: The treatment of epilepsy. Med Clin North Am 29:1114, 1945.
81. Lennox, WG: Epilepsy and Related Disorders, Vol 2. Little, Brown & Co, Boston, 1960.
82. Lesser, RP et al: Mental deterioration in epilepsy. Epilepsia (Suppl 2) 27:105, 1986.
83. Lewis, DO: Delinquency, psychomotor epileptic symptomatology and paranoid symptomatology: A triad. Am J Psychiatry 133:1395, 1976.
84. Lorentz de Haas, AM and Magnus, O: Clinical and electro-encephalographic findings in epileptic patients with episodic mental disorders. In Lorentz de Haas, AM (ed): Lectures on Epilepsy. Elsevier, New York, 1958, pp 134–167.
85. MacLean, PD and Ploog, DW: Cerebral representation of penile erection. J Neurophysiol 25:29, 1962.
86. Maletzky, BM: The episodic dyscontrol syndrome. Dis Nerv Sys 34:178, 1973.
87. Marchand, L and DeAjuriaguerra, J: Epilepsies, leurs formes cliniques ex leurs traitements. Desclee de Brouwer et Cie, Paris, 1948.
88. Master, DR, Toone, B, and Scott, DF: Interictal behaviour in temporal lobe epilepsy. In Porter, RJ et al (eds): Advances in Epileptology: 15th Epilepsy International Symposium. Raven Press, New York, 1984, pp 557–565.
89. Mark, VH and Ervin, FR: Violence and the Brain. Harper & Row, New York, 1970.
90. Matthews, CG and Klove, H: Differential psychological performances in major motor, psychomotor, and mixed seizure classifications of known and unknown etiology. Epilepsia 8:117, 1967.
91. Matthews, CG and Klove, H: MMPI performances in major motor, psychomotor and mixed seizure classifications of known and unknown etiology. Epilepsia 9:43, 1968.
92. Merlis, JK: Reflex epilepsy. In Vinken, PJ and Bruyn, GW (eds): Handbook of Clinical Neurology, Vol 15, The Epilepsies. Elsevier, New York, 1974, pp 440–456.
93. Meyer, JS and Portnoy, HD: Post-epileptic paralysis. Brain 82:162, 1959.
94. Milner, B: Psychological defect produced by temporal lobe excision. Res Publ Assoc Res Nerv Ment Dis 36:244, 1956.
95. Mirsky, AF et al: A comparison of the psychological test performances of patients with focal and nonfocal epilepsy. Exp Neurol 2:75, 1960.

96. Norris, JW and Pratt, RF: A controlled study of folic acid in epilepsy. Neurology 21:659, 1971.

97. Pedley, TA (ed): Epilepsy and behavior. Epilepsia 26 (Suppl 2), 1986.

98. Penry, JK and Daly, DD (eds): Complex partial seizures and their treatment. Adv Neurol 11:1, 1975.

99. Pincus, JH and Tucker, GJ: Behavioral Neurology. Oxford University Press, New York, 1985.

100. Pond, DA: Psychiatric aspects of epilepsy. J Indian Med Prof 3:1401, 1957.

101. Pond, DA: The influence of psychophysiological factors on epilepsy. J Psychosom Res 9:15, 1965.

102. Pond, DA: Epilepsy and personality disorders. In Vinken, PJ and Bruyn, GW (eds): Handbook of Clinical Neurology, Vol 15, The Epilepsies. Elsevier, New York, 1974, pp 559–575.

103. Ramani, V and Gumnit, RJ: Intensive monitoring of interictal psychosis. Ann Neurol 11:613, 1982.

104. Reitan, RM: Psychological testing of epileptic patients. In Vinken PJ and Bruyn, GW (eds): Handbook of Clinical Neurology, Vol 15, The Epilepsies. Elsevier, New York, 1974, pp 559–575.

105. Reynolds, EH: Schizophrenia-like psychoses of epilepsy and disturbances of folate and vitamin B12 metabolism induced by anticonvulsant medication. Br J Psychiatry 113:911, 1967.

106. Reynolds, EH: Anticonvulsant drugs, folic acid metabolism, fit frequency and psychiatric illness. Psychit Neurol Neurochir 76:167, 1971.

107. Reynolds, EH and Travers, RD: Serum anticonvulsant concentrations in epileptic patients with mental symptoms. Br J Psychiatry 124:440, 1974.

108. Rodin, EA: The Prognosis of Patients with Epilepsy. Charles C Thomas, Springfield, IL, 1968.

109. Rodin, EA: Psychomotor epilepsy and aggressive behavior. Arch Gen Psychiatry 28:210, 1973.

110. Rodin, EA: Psychosocial management of patients with complex partial seizures. Adv Neurol 11:383, 1975.

111. Rodin, EA: Psychosocial management of patients with seizure disorders. McLean Hospital Journal (Special Issue), 1977, pp 74–84.

112. Roger, J, Lob, H, and Tassinari, CA: Generalized status epilepticus expressed as a confusional state (petit mal status or absence status epilepticus). In Vinken, PJ and Bruyn, GW (eds): Handbook of Clinical Neurology, Vol 15, The Epilepsies. Elsevier, New York, 1974, pp 167–175.

113. Sarason, SB and Doris, J: Psychological Problems in Mental Deficiency. Harper & Row, New York, 1969.

114. Schmidt, RP and Wilder, BJ: Epilepsy. FA Davis, Philadelphia, 1968.

115. Shev, EE: Syndrome of petit mal status in adult. Electroencephalogr Clin Neurophysiol 17:466, 1964.

116. Shorvon, SD: The temporal aspects of prognosis in epilepsy. J Neurol Neurosurg Psychiatr 47:1157, 1984.

117. Shorvon, SD: Classification of epilepsy. In Asbury, AK, McKhann, GM and McDonald, WI (eds): Diseases of the Nervous System. WB Saunders, Philadelphia, 1986, pp 970–981.

118. Slater, E, Beard, A, and Glithero, E: The schizophrenia-like psychoses in epilepsy. Br J Psychiatry 109:95, 1963.

119. Small, JG, Small, LF, and Hayden, MP: Further psychiatric investigations of patients with temporal and nontemporal lobe epilepsy. Am J Psychiatry 123:303, 1966.

120. Solomon, GE and Plum, F: Clinical Management of Seizures. WB Saunders, Philadelphia, 1976.

121. Spencer, SS et al: Sexual automatisms in complex partial seizures. Neurology 33:527, 1983.

122. Spiers, PA et al: Temporolimbic epilepsy and behavior. In Mesulum, M-M: Principles of Behavioral Neurology. FA Davis, Philadelphia, 1985, pp 289–326.

123. Standage, KF and Fenton, GW: Psychiatric symptoms profiles of patients with epilepsy. Psychol Med 5:152, 1975.

124. Stores, G, Hart, JH, and Piran, N: Inattentiveness in school children with epilepsy. Epilepsia 19:169, 1978.

125. Taylor, DC: Mental state and temporal lobe epilepsy. Epilepsia 13:727, 1972.

126. Taylor, DC: Facts influencing the occurrence of schizophrenia-like psychosis in patients with temporal lobe epilepsy. Psychol Med 5:249, 1975.

127. Taylor, DC: Epileptic experience, schizophrenia and the temporal lobe. McLean Hospital Journal (Special Issue), 1977, pp 22–39.

128. Tizard, B: The personality of epileptics. A discussion of the evidence. Psychol Bull 59:196, 1962.

129. Tredgold, AF and Soddy, K (eds): Textbook of Mental Deficiency. Bailliere, Tindall and Cox, London, 1963.

130. Treiman, DM: Epilepsy and violence: Medical and legal issues. Epilepsia (Suppl 2) 27:77, 1986.

131. Treiman, DM and Delgado-Escuerta, AV: Violence and epilepsy: A critical review. In Pedley, TA and Meldrum, BS (eds): Recent Advances in Epilepsy, Vol 1. Churchill, Livingstone, London, 1983, pp 179–209.

132. Tucker, GJ et al: Phenomenology of temporal lobe dysfunction: A link to atypical psychosis. J Nerv Ment Dis 174:348, 1986.

133. Valenstein, ES: Brain Control. John Wiley & Sons, New York, 1973.

134. Vanderzant, CW et al: Personality of patients with pseudoseizures. Neurology 36:664, 1986.

135. Wasterlain, CG and Dwyer, BE: Brain metabolism during prolonged seizures in neonates. In Delgado-Escuelta, AV et al (eds): Status Epilepticus. Raven Press, New York, 1983, pp 241–260.

136. Wasterlain, CG, Masouka, D and Janet, V: Chemical kindling: A study of synaptic pharmacology. In Wada, J (ed): Raven Press, New York, 1981, pp 315.

137. Weil, A: Ictal depression and anxiety in temporal lobe disorders. Am J Psychiatry 113:149, 1956.

138. Wells, CE: Transient ictal psychosis. Arch Gen Psychiatry 32:1201, 1975.

139. Wright, GN (ed): Epilepsy Rehabilitation. Little, Brown & Co, Boston, 1975.

140. Wright, GN: Rehabilitation and the problem of epilepsy. In Wright, GN (ed): Epilepsy Rehabilitation. Little, Brown & Co, Boston, 1975, pp 1–7.

141. Young, EB and Blume, WT: Painful epileptic seizures. Brain 106:537, 1983.

Chapter 13

Cerebrovascular Disease

DESCRIPTION OF THE CLINICAL SYNDROMES
    Transient Ischemic Attacks
    Cardiac Surgery
    Behavioral Changes with Cerebral Lupus Erythematosus
    Subarachnoid Hemorrhage
    Akinetic Mutism
EVALUATION
MANAGEMENT

    A 63-year-old hypertensive woman was admitted to the Charity Hospital in New Orleans because of the sudden onset of paranoid and abusive behavior. Her husband reported that they often argued but that on the day of admission she was totally irrational and believed that he was trying to kill her. In response to this false belief, she attacked her husband with a knife. The police were called, and she was admitted to the hospital in a most agitated state.
    On initial examination, she was raving incoherently yet was also intermittently lethargic. Her paranoid delusions persisted for some time, and on

occasion she claimed she saw her husband lurking in the hall outside her ward despite numerous assurances that he had returned home. The initial diagnostic impression of the admitting psychiatrist was a confusional state caused either by a metabolic imbalance or by a toxic effect from medication. Results of subsequent laboratory and toxicology screenings proved negative, and accordingly we were consulted.

When we first saw her, she had calmed considerably. She was still lethargic but was more attentive than she had been on admission. Her speech was fluent and had lost much of its paranoid content, but she had definite word-finding difficulty and produced several paraphasic errors. Comprehension was intact for general conversational questions. However, she did not understand more exacting questions such as "Is a fork good for eating soup?" or "Is a hammer good for chopping wood?" She also could not point accurately on command to objects in the room. Repetition was marked by hesitation and paraphasias, particularly when the sentence contained many nouns and transitive verbs. Confrontation naming was grossly paraphasic. Visual memory was good, drawings were impaired, and most other cortical testing was invalid because of the patient's disturbed language.

Because of the aphasia, we strongly suspected that the patient had an infarction or hemorrhage in the left temporoparietal area. A brain scan showed a wedge-shaped infarct in the appropriate area. The confusional state and paranoia cleared quickly during the following few days, and the patient was left with only a mild anomic aphasia.

The above case demonstrates a type of organic behavioral change that can be seen in occlusive cerebrovascular disease. The stroke patient may be confusional at the onset and can easily be misdiagnosed as having a primary psychiatric condition or a metabolic or toxic encephalopathy unless outstanding neurologic findings such as hemiplegia are present. Frequently, a careful mental status examination of the confusional patient will reveal focal behavioral findings (e.g., aphasia, neglect, or denial) that are out of proportion to the changes usually seen with confusional behavior alone. The elucidation of such focal symptoms changes the entire diagnostic approach. This case demonstrates one of the myriad ways in which cerebrovascular disease can produce behavioral symptoms. For comprehensive discussions of the behavioral changes seen in cerebrovascular disease, see Benton[5] and Brown, Baird, and Shatz.[11]

Many of the clinical syndromes seen with cerebral vascular disease have been discussed in the sections on dementia and focal brain lesions; however, there are some aspects of the broad topic that deserve special mention. The primary purpose of this brief chapter is to emphasize the fact that such behavioral changes *are* a common presenting symptom in vascular disease and must be appreciated for their importance in both diagnosis and patient management. Because cerebrovascular disease ranks third among the most frequent causes of death from medical disease in America, every physician will encounter its effects regularly. The possibility of a cerebrovascular accident or transient ischemic attack is high in any patient as he ages but particularly in patients with hypertension, heart disease, diabetes, gout, and peripheral vascular disease. As seen in the case above, the symptoms of a stroke may be manifested solely as a radical change in the patient's behavior, without the usual "hard" neurologic findings.

Each year in the United States, more than 150,000 people die of various types of stroke, and a significant number of new cases are reported.[26] There are many types of stroke: 65 to 80 percent are caused by thromboembolic disease, 10 to 15 percent by intracerebral hemorrhage, 5 to 10 percent by subarachnoid hemorrhage, and 5 to 10 percent by other less common disorders.[26,47]

A very important aspect of cerebrovascular disease is the tremendous social impact it has on its victims and their families. The patient is frequently left mentally as well as physically compromised.[1] Employment may no longer be possible. The patient's family and the community at large (as taxpayers) are required to share in the major financial burden of rehabilitation and maintenance. As the percentage of elderly persons in our society increases, the problem of stroke will grow accordingly. It should be the goal of every physician to learn to recognize the warning signals and risk factors in cerebrovascular disease and to identify and treat these conditions before irreversible brain damage occurs.

DESCRIPTION OF THE CLINICAL SYNDROMES

There are many types of cerebrovascular disease, but by far the most common are thromboembolic disease secondary to atherosclerosis and hypertensive cerebrovascular disease with intracerebral hemorrhage. With increased age, fatty deposits collect on the endothelium of major blood vessels throughout the vascular system. These deposits occur at any point along the major vessels but are particularly likely to occur at points of bifurcation. Atheromatous plaques are commonly found in the carotid and vertebral vessels, and these are important locations of narrowing, thrombosis, and subsequent stroke. In the region of the bifurcation of the common carotid in the neck, large plaques often form and become ulcerated. Within the cavities of these ulcers, platelets commonly aggregate and often embolize to the brain, causing transient ischemia or acute cerebral infarction. A second source of cerebral embolism is the heart. Patients with recent myocardial infarction often form mural thrombi over the area of infarction; pieces of these clots frequently embolize to the brain. By the above mechanisms, most of the focal cortical stroke syndromes occur.

Hypertensive vascular disease with cerebral hemorrhage is somewhat different because the hemorrhages usually occur deep in the brain, most commonly in the corpus striatum, thalamus, cerebellum, or pons. The syndrome resulting from these lesions is usually more devastating neurologically than it is behaviorally because the cortex is relatively spared. The major behavioral feature of deep cerebral hemorrhage is a decrease in the level of alertness of the patient, with an associated confusion.

Vascular disease can present as any of the primary clinical behavioral syndromes and must always be considered in the differential diagnosis in any patient presenting with confusional behavior, dementia, or focal symptomatology. In previous chapters, we have discussed some of the behavioral aspects of many of the vascular diseases commonly seen in clinical practice, and we will not reiterate them here other than to identify them in tabular form (Table 13–1).

Table 13–1 Behavioral Syndromes and Symptoms
Seen with Cerebrovascular Disease

Symptoms	Causes
Confusional states and/or delirium	1. Acute vascular occlusion 2. Transient ischemia: focal, particularly limbic, or whole brain secondary to bilateral carotid stenosis 3. Subarachnoid hemorrhage 4. Acute systemic lupus erythematosus 5. Subdural hematoma 6. Intracerebral hemorrhage 7. Hypoxia during surgery or arteriography
Dementia	1. Multiple infarcts 2. Borderzone atrophy (granular atrophy) 3. Rare cases of bilateral severe extracranial vessel stenosis 4. Binswanger's disease 5. Systemic lupus erythematosus 6. Subdural hematoma
Focal symptomatology	1. Infarct: extracranial or intracranial occlusion, embolus, vasculitis 2. Intracerebral hemorrhage 3. Subdural or epidural hemorrhage 4. Hemorrhage from aneurysm or arteriovenous malformation

Transient Ischemic Attacks

Two very important specific clinical features of vascular diseases are (1) its frequent sudden onset and (2) the common occurrence of warning symptoms (transient ischemic attacks) that precede the ictus and mimic the actual attack. Transient ischemic attacks (TIAs) are often the harbinger of a major cerebrovascular accident, and frequently the TIA is characterized by behavioral symptoms alone. Transient aphasia, agraphia, amnesia, geographic disorientation, and confusion are all well described in the literature and frequently seen clinically.[18,27] Such symptoms should always be taken seriously and the patient investigated fully. By definition, the neurologic signs and symptoms of a TIA must clear within 24 hours. The presence of symptoms beyond this time is suggestive of a more completed stroke-like syndrome. If careful neuropsychologic testing is conducted during the first week after a carotid TIA, however, many subtle deficits in higher cortical function may be demonstrated.[9,14] It is likely that the cumulative accretion of these subtle deficits over time may eventually lead to the development of multi-infarct dementia.

Transient focal cerebral ischemia is often caused by either severe carotid stenosis or embolism from ulcerated plaques in the carotid arteries. The recognition of this process has led to the widespread use of surgical procedures for removal of the atheromatous material from the extracranial portion of the cartoid artery, a procedure called carotid endarterectomy.[29]

From a neurobehavioral point of view, two questions have been asked with reference to this surgical procedure: (1) Is there a neuropsychologic risk involved in the surgery? (2) Does this surgery improve long-term cognitive functioning? As with much of the research on cerebrovascular disease, no definitive answer can yet be given to either question, although a number of studies have addressed the issues directly. Some of these results bear mention. As to the question of the safety of the surgery, a small number of patients will experience strokes during the procedure itself and develop obvious significant residual effects; this is uncommon. One study of postoperative patients without obvious neurologic residuals demonstrated a decrease in neuropsychologic function during the first week post-surgery only in those patients who experienced significant intraoperative ischemia.[10] This effect was reported to be transient. Other follow-up studies of such patients have not shown any deterioration in cognitive function that could be attributed to the surgery.[8,25,31,35]

Regarding the question of the efficacy of carotid endarterectomy in improving cognitive function, the evidence currently available remains inconclusive.[8,31,35] When the variables of test-retest practice effect, time between surgery and testing, and characteristics of the study sample are carefully controlled, there is no consensus that such surgery actually improves either the mental status or the psychosocial functioning of patients undergoing these procedures.

A second surgical procedure that had been popular was the extracranial/intracranial arterial bypass operation (temporal artery to middle cerebral artery anastomosis). This was used in an effort to increase the blood flow to a cerebral hemisphere that was ischemic by virtue of stenosis of the internal carotid or middle cerebral artery within the head. The procedure did not prove to be effective in preventing stroke.[16] Although some early reports noted subtle improvement in cognitive performance after the surgery,[32,54] others did not.[15] Because of the generally negative results from this type of surgery, it is doubtful that further studies to assess its effect on behavior will be conducted.

Although TIAs are most common in older patients with atheromatous disease of their major cerebral vessels, identical symptoms can be seen in younger patients with arteriovenous malformations, aneurysms that have leaked causing vascular spasm, collagen vascular disease, and migraine. We saw one 18-year-old girl with a migraine attack who presented with a clinical picture similar to that of the case described at the beginning of this chapter. She became acutely confusional and could only scream, hold her head, and mumble incoherently. Within several hours, her confusion begin to clear, although her speech was decidedly paraphasic and her comprehension was poor. Ten hours after the onset, she had recovered, and the findings on her mental status examination were completely normal.

Cardiac Surgery

Cardiac surgery, either for valve replacement or for coronary artery bypass surgery, can produce cerebral vascular insufficiency, from either microemboli or hypoperfusion states. Cerebral blood flow studies have shown significant decreases in blood flow during the first 8 to 10 days after surgery in such patients.[20] Neuropsychologic function is also significantly affected in more than half of the patients during this early postoperative period.[45] Steady cognitive improvement is experienced over the months after surgery. At 2 months, only 30 percent of patients showed neuropsychologic abnormalities,[45] and, by 6 to 12 months, most patients had regained premorbid blood flow and cognitive function.[20,22,46] There were some patients who demonstrated chronic residual deficits; the most prominent were deterioration in some of the nondominant hemisphere functions (visual-perceptual speed or visual-spatial perception),[24] short-term memory, attention,[46] and psychopathology, especially depression.[52]

Behavioral Changes with Cerebral Lupus Erythematosus

Another vascular condition that can result in either transient or permanent vascular symptoms is systemic lupus erythematosus (SLE), an autoimmune disorder that frequently causes vasculitis. The most common mental symptom associated with SLE is a confusional state or delirium.[17,23,40] This can appear concurrently with other symptoms of SLE or may be the sole initial manifestation in a small percentage of the cases. As mentioned in Chapter 7, some patients with longstanding disease will develop dementia. One aspect of SLE not covered previously in this text is the spectrum of psychiatric manifestations that can mimic functional psychiatric disease and constitute as much as 50 percent of all the mental changes reported in some series of patients.[23,33,40] The most common clinical syndrome encountered is depression, but anxiety reactions, asocial behavior, paranoid behavior, and manic behavior have all been described. In one large series (140 patients), 15 percent of the patients were considered to have definable psychiatric symptoms; the authors, however, deduced that all but 1 percent showed clear evidence of organicity on careful mental status examination.[17] There are cases in which the onset of psychiatric problems preceded the neurologic or systemic features of the illness by as many as 10 years. In other cases, the psychiatric features sufficiently overshadowed the medical problems so that the diagnosis was delayed.

A 20-year-old woman was first seen at Charity Hospital in 1966 with a clinical picture of catatonic schizophrenia. On the review of systems at admission, she had given a history of joint pain; this was not pursued, however, because of the pressing matter of her severe catatonia. She subsequently developed a low-grade fever that was then felt to be secondary to hypostatic pneumonia. She was discharged after remission of the overt psychosis. In 1969, she was again admitted because of exacerbation of the schizophrenic reaction. A fever was again noted, but at that time, she had a perirectal abscess that was considered to be the cause of the fever. An RA factor was positive but again was not pursued. In 1973, she was again admitted with schizophrenia and a fever of undetermined origin; on this admission, she also had wrist drop on the right. During this hospitalization, a full medical evaluation was carried out and a positive diagnosis of SLE was made. On a later admission (January 1976) she still showed evidence of schizophrenia, yet showed no signs of organic mental change on a full mental status examination. She has since been lost to follow-up.

One could question whether the patient had schizophrenia plus SLE or had lupus alone as the origin of her psychosis. We suspect the latter is the case, because the patient had had some symptoms of SLE (although they went unrecognized) during her initial and all subsequent psychotic episodes.

The exact pathophysiology of both the transient and permanent behavioral changes has become elusive. It was long thought that the vasculitis per se, with its associated vascular occlusions and ischemia, resulted in the mental symptoms.[23] This is certainly true in many cases of SLE-related dementia, but it has since been demonstrated that a different mechanism may be responsible for producing the acute psychotic episodes. One hypothesis is that the psychiatric symptoms are caused by a generalized membrane failure in the endothelial cells of the cerebral capillaries. This membrane failure or lysis is caused by active biogenic amines that are produced during the complement cascade seen during the acute exacerbation of the disease.[36] IgG levels are low in the cerebrospinal fluid, and it has been shown that antibodies are attached to capillary membranes; it is this immune complex that then sets off the complement cascade.[4] A second hypothesis, the most recent in this field, proposes that the cryoprecipitates from the serum of SLE patients actually contain a lymphotoxic antibody that also attacks neurons.[7] If true, the central nervous system forms of SLE may not represent just a collagen vascular process but also a direct effect of antibodies on the nerve cells themselves. Whatever the mechanism, it is readily apparent why the anti-immune effects of steroids can so quickly reverse the mental symptoms when treatment is begun promptly.

Subarachnoid Hemorrhage

A 63-year-old woman was examined 14 years after she was operated on for the rupture of an anterior communicating artery aneurysm. She was living with a niece at the time. She had tried to live alone, but was unable to take care of her personal needs. On several occasions she required hospitalization for malnutrition. After these hospitalizations, she returned to the care of her family. Her niece reported that the patient had had a complete personality change since her surgery; previously a neatly dressed, decorous woman, she had become sloppy, unclean, impatient, and "silly." Her memory was so poor that the family had to be with her almost constantly.

On examination, the woman was jocular, almost flirtatious at times, yet was alert, attentive, and cooperative. Verbal fluency was slightly reduced (14 animals in 60 seconds), but other language functions were intact. Recent memory for historical facts and new learning ability were poor. She could recall only one of four words at 5, 10, and 30 min; but, typical of Korsakoff patients, she could recognize the correct words when they were presented from a list of similar items. Her drawings were good, calculations excellent, fund of information excellent, and proverb interpretations also excellent. She showed no evidence of apraxia, agnosia, right-left disorientation, or problems with alternating sequences. No frontal lobe release signs were present. In summary, this patient demonstrated the syndrome of recent memory loss and frontal-lobe personality change frequently seen as a residual behavioral effect of anterior communicating artery aneurysm rupture.

Subarachnoid hemorrhage, usually secondary to rupture of a saccular aneurysm, is a devastating neurologic condition. It is associated with a high mortality and a high morbidity in those who survive. Many survivors have significant neurologic as well as behavioral sequelae. However, in some patients, such as the woman in the case presented above, cognitive and psychosocial deficits are the sole long-term residua. Ljunggren and associates[28] evaluated 40 such patients and found that, despite full neurologic recovery, 53 percent had severe cognitive deficits, and 30 percent had moderate cognitive deficits. Ropper and Zervas[38] reported equally discouraging results: Of the 46 percent of their patients who fully recovered medically from their aneurysm ruptures, only 44 percent were able to return to their previous jobs, and 25 percent reported psychologic and emotional problems that interfered substantially with their daily lives. Säveland and associates[41] reported that no patient suffering a subarachnoid hemorrhage escapes without some psychosocial or cognitive problems. The picture is not positive in general, but certainly is not totally bleak, as many patients are able to return to productive and satisfying lives. It is important for physicians, particularly neurosurgeons, and rehabilitation personnel to realize that it is the behavioral sequelae, not overt neurologic dysfunction, that frequently interfere with full social and vocational reintegration.

The reason for the high incidence of behavioral deficits is clear when one examines the pathologic anatomy of aneurysm rupture and subarachnoid hemorrhage. The aneurysms develop at the base of the brain, most frequently around the circle of Willis. When the aneurysm ruptures, it damages tissue locally, causing the formation of hematomas and ischemia secondary to vasospasm. With anterior communicating aneurysms, damage is primarily to the orbital frontal lobe, anterior cingulate gyrus, anterior hypothalamus, septum, and many limbic pathways entering the frontal lobe. Severe vasospasm may also occur; this may produce bilateral medial frontal lobe infarction, thus resulting in a dramatic frontal lobe syndrome.[48] The middle cerebral aneurysm may bleed into temporal lobe limbic structures or into parasylvian tissue (temporal and parietal lobes and inferior/lateral frontal lobe). Other than local damage and the multifocal areas of ischemia secondary to spasm, some patients will also develop a communicating hydrocephalus with its characteristic behavioral features. Because of the frequent damage to limbic system tissue, it is easy to understand why behavior is so frequently affected.

There are several behavioral syndromes or symptoms that are commonly seen in aneurysm cases. In acute cases, changes in level of consciousness and confusional behavior are the most frequent findings. Among the chronic residua, the most common are organic amnesia, frontal lobe personality change, neurasthenia (chronic fatigue and lassitude), and mood change.[3,28,30,34,50] A Korsakoff-type memory loss is most commonly associated with anterior communicating aneurysms, seemingly produced by occlusion or ischemia of the anterior perforating arteries that ascend from the anterior communicating artery into the septal area and surrounding tissue. Surgery in which this vessel is clamped at both ends in an effort to trap the aneurysm rather than clip it results in an extremely high incidence of amnesia; in Gade's series[19] there were 9 per 11 entrapment cases (82 percent) versus 6 per 37 cases (16 percent) in which a clip was placed at the aneurysm neck. The exact pathologic anatomy underlying the amnesia in these cases is not known. Damasio and associates,[13] from data accumulated through careful radiologic examination and surgical observation, postulated that the tissue damage extends posteriorly from orbital frontal cortex to include septal nuclei, the nuclei of the diagonal band of Broca and into the substantia innominata. Also partially damaged is the nucleus basalis of Meynert, the principal subcortical nucleus of origin for the acetylcholine pathways to the hippocampus.

Frontal lobe personality change is more common with anterior communicating aneurysms, whereas organic mood changes are more often seen in middle cerebral aneurysms. Interestingly, one study reported that the change after aneurysm rupture actually improved the personality of some patients.[49] In a study of 50 patients, depression lifted, and some previously violent, sarcastic patients became docile after what amounted to an unplanned frontal lobotomy. In addition to the primary deficit (e.g., amnesia, frontal lobe syndrome), many patients will have additional scattered but less dramatic cognitive disturbances. Such disturbances occur more frequently with middle cerebral aneurysms than anterior communicating ones, but can occur in either.

Other behavioral residua of subarachnoid hemorrhage include general cognitive loss, inattention, anxiety,[51] akinetic mutism[21] (discussed below), catatonia, and rarely, an anterior corpus callosum syndrome.[6]

Akinetic Mutism

An interesting type of behavioral syndrome that can be seen in cases of cerebrovascular disease is that of akinetic mutism. The clinical picture is fascinating, as the following case demonstrates.

A 35-year-old hypertensive woman entered the hospital with a 6-hour history of rapidly progressive headache and leg weakness. Within several hours after admission, she had a stiff neck and was stuporous. A spinal puncture revealed grossly bloody spinal fluid, and a subsequent CT scan and arteriogram demonstrated an anterior communicating artery aneurysm with an interhemispheric clot between the frontal lobes. As her level of consciousness improved, she lay on the bed and regarded her surroundings with sentient intensity. She offered no speech or spontaneous movement yet would eat when fed and seemed to be observing the activity around her. When spoken to, she would turn and look at the examiner and, with great encouragement, she would follow complicated commands such as "Wiggle one finger on your right hand and two on the left." She never spoke but occasionally would cough audibly to command. She had good arm movement control but a flaccid paraparesis. Repeat CT scan showed resolution of her clot and no evidence of hydrocephalus. Unfortunately, the patient remained mute and akinetic and eventually required transfer to a chronic nursing facility.

This type of akinetic mutism, often called a "coma vigil," is caused by a destruction of the deep structures in the frontal lobe: septal nuclei, anterior cingulate gyrus, and many reticulocortical fibers in their course to the frontal lobes. The condition can be caused by destruction of tissue, as in the case above, or the effects of hydrocephalus developing secondary to subarachnoid hemorrhage. Such patients seem intellectually intact, yet are totally unable to muster adequate reticular or limbic energy stimulate the cortex to action. The sensory receiving system is passive and does not require extensive effort for merely observing the environment; therefore, the patients seem to be cognizant of the activity around them. The alert appearance is uncanny at times, and we have had families come to us distraught because they believed the patient was consciously refusing to speak to them for some psychologic reason because they did not appreciate the organic cause.[43] Some of these patients can be successfully treated with dopamine agonists. The response to treatment depends on the locus of the lesion. If the damage is confined to the anterior hypothalamus and surrounding tissue yet spares the cingulate gyrus, the dopamine agonist is postulated to stimulate the dopamine receptor targets in the cingulate.[39]

Another state, clinically almost indistinguishable from the above, can be seen when an occlusion of the small perforating vessels at the distal end of the basilar artery causes an infarct in the subthalamic region.[42] These patients have the same picture of akinetic mutism described above with the frontal lesion, but they tend to be more apathetic. They also can have a variety of signs of midbrain dysfunction (convergence difficulty, oculomotor nerve dysfunction, up-gaze paralysis, reflex changes, and occasionally Babinski's toe signs) from damage to contiguous structures. The basic lesion causing the syndrome is a butterfly-shaped infarct that disconnects the mesencephalic reticular formation from the midline reticular structures.[42] The effect is the same as that in the frontal lesion; reticular innervation to higher structures is impaired, and the patients cannot adequately stimulate the motor cortex to initiate action. Additional mechanisms are also impaired, and the patients cannot sustain attention for more than short intervals.

These mute states, although not common, are clinically interesting examples of the correlation of basic behavioral phenomena and neuroanatomic structure. Mutism, as a symptom, can be seen in a variety of diseases, and not only in vascular disease. The original description of the clinical state was of a patient with an epidermoid cyst of the third ventricle.[12] Subsequent reviews have described akinetic mutism in hydrocephalus, basal ganglion tumors and diseases, viral encephalitis, central pontine myelinolysis, and basilar artery occlusion.[44] Psychiatric disease, particularly catatonic schizophrenia, psychotic depression,[2] and hysterical coma or psychiatric unresponsiveness[37] must also be considered in the differential diagnosis. Psychiatric states are usually easily differentiated from organic conditions because of the dearth of concomitant positive medical or neurologic signs.

EVALUATION

The extensive topic of evaluating the medical and neurologic aspects of vascular disease is far beyond the scope or intention of this chapter. We wish only to point out some specific factors of significance with respect to behavioral change and to mention the general principles involved in evaluation.

The first important point is that vascular disease should be suspected whenever a patient presents with a history of a sudden behavioral change. As a corollary to this point, the patient with known vascular disease must be watched or questioned concerning the onset of any acute behavioral change, because such changes are common in these patients.

A second point is the frequent history of similar, but transient, episodes of behavioral change occurring in the past. The transient ischemic attack is well known to cause behavioral symptoms; therefore, the history of such events must be assiduously pursued. A history of TIAs makes the diagnosis of a thrombotic or embolic vascular accident more certain.

Of the neurobehavioral symptoms of vascular disease, focal symptoms are by far the most common. Because of this, a full mental status exam should be performed to ensure that specific symptoms will be elucidated. In addition, however, there are frequently other general medical and neurologic symptoms and signs (e.g., headache [particularly in hemorrhagic disease], dizziness, weakness, visual sensory change).

To evaluate fully the patient with a vascular insult to the brain, one must obtain history and physical examination information concerning the following areas.

1. Age
2. Handedness
3. Blood pressure
4. Heart disease
5. Diabetes
6. Smoking
7. Use of medications, particularly birth control pills
8. Peripheral vascular disease
9. Carotid artery examination—palpation (internal and extracranial vessels) and auscultation

Laboratory examinations should include a hematocrit, lipid screen, blood sugar, uric acid, blood urea nitrogen, EEG, and cardiac rhythm monitoring for the first several days after a thromboembolic stroke. The CT scan has become indispensable in differentiating hypertensive hemorrhage, infarct, tumor, and hemorrhage infarct. The MRI scan is particularly good for identifying the changes in early infarct. Arteriography is often necessary, particularly in younger patients, but should only be ordered after a consulting internist, vascular surgeon, neurologist, or neurosurgeon has evaluated the case.

MANAGEMENT

As with the evaluation of vascular disease, a comprehensive review of the medical and surgical treatment of all vascular disease would be out of place in this volume. The general treatment modalities are summarized in Table 13–2.

After the patient's medical condition has stabilized, and the acute phase of the vascular event is over, it is important to conduct a comprehensive neuropsychologic and rehabilitation evaluation and start a management program. This process is similar to that outlined in preceding chapters and must take into full account the patient's strengths and weaknesses in the formulation of a final plan. Because patients sustaining vascular accidents are generally in the older age range, the plan is often directed toward activities of daily living rather than vocational rehabilitation. These activities are important to the patient, his family, and society, because achieving independence for a stroke patient can be the difference between a meaningful social life and custodial care.

Table 13-2 Treatment Modalities in
Cerebrovascular Disease

Disease Process	Treatment Available
Systemic lupus erythematosus	1. Steroids
Hypertensive and arteriosclerotic vascular disease (general)	1. Blood pressure control 2. Control of blood lipids 3. Control of diabetes mellitus 4. Control of hyperuricemia 5. Termination of smoking 6. Correction of cardiac arrhythmias 7. Possibly control of hematocrit (to below 42)
Transient ischemic attacks	1. Carotid artery surgery if an ulcerated or significantly stenotic plaque is found 2. Anticoagulants 3. Aspirin

REFERENCES

1. Adams, GF and Hurwitz, LJ: Mental barriers to recovery from strokes. Lancet 2:533, 1963.
2. Akhtar, S and Buckman, J: The differential diagnosis of mutism: A review and a report of three unusual cases. Dis Nerv Syst 38:558, 1977.
3. Alexander, M and Freedman, M: Amnesia after anterior communicating artery aneurysm rupture. Neurology 34:752, 1984.
4. Bennahum, DA and Messner, RP: Recent observations on central nervous system lupus erythematosus. Semin Arthritis Rheum 4:253, 1975.
5. Benton, AL (ed): Behavioral Change in Cerebrovascular Disease. Harper & Row, New York, 1970.
6. Beukelman, DR, Flowers, CR, and Swanson, PD: Cerebral disconnection associated with anterior communicating artery aneurysm: Implications for evaluation of symptoms. Arch Phys Med Rehabil 61:18, 1980.
7. Bluestein, HG: Heterogeneous neurocytotoxic antibodies in systemic lupus erythematosus. Clin Exp Immunol 35:210, 1979.
8. Bornstein, RA, Benott, B, and Tites, R: neuropsychologic changes following carotid endarterectomy. Can J Neurol Sci 8:127, 1981.
9. Bornstein, RA: Relationship of age and education to neuropsychological performance in patients with symptomatic carotid artery disease. J Clin Psychol 39:470, 1983.
10. Brinkman, SD et al: Neuropsychological performance one week after carotid endarterectomy reflects intraoperative ischemia. Stroke 15:497, 1984.

11. Brown, GG, Baird, AD, and Shatz, MW: The effects of cerebral vascular disease and its treatment on higher cortical functioning. In Grant, I and Adams, KM: Neuropsychologic assessment of neuropsychiatric disorders. Oxford University Press, New York, 1986, pp 384–414.

12. Cairns, H et al: Akinetic mutism with an epidermoid cyst of the 3rd ventricle. Brain 64:273, 1941.

13. Damasio, AR et al: Amnesia following basal forebrain lesions. Arch Neurol 42:263, 1985.

14. Delaney, RC, Wallace, JD, and Egelko, S: Transient cerebral ischemic attacks and neuropsychologic deficit. J Clin Neuropsychology 2:107–114, 1980.

15. Drinkwater, JE, Thompson, SK, and Lumley, JSP: Cerebral function before and after extra-intracranial carotid bypass. J Neurol Neurosurg Psychiatry 147:1041, 1984.

16. The EC/IC Bypass Study Group: Failure of extracranial-intracranial arterial bypass to reduce the risk of ischemic stroke: Results of an international randomized trial. N Engl J Med 313:1191, 1985.

17. Feinglass, EJ et al: Neuropsychiatric manifestation of systemic lupus erythematosus: Diagnosis, clinical spectrum, and relationship to other features of the disease. Medicine 55:323, 1976.

18. Futty, DE et al: Cooperative study of hospital frequency and character of transient ischemic attacks. V. Symptom analysis. JAMA 238:2386, 1977.

19. Gade, A: Amnesia after operation on aneurysms of the anterior communicating artery. Surg Neurol 18:46, 1982.

20. Henriksen, L: Evidence suggestive of diffuse brain damage following cardiac operations. Lancet 1:816, 1984.

21. Hijdra, A et al: Delayed cerebral ischemia after aneurysmal subarachnoid hemorrhage: Clinicoanatomic correlations. Neurology 36:329, 1986.

22. Jenkins, CD et al: Coronary artery bypass surgery: Physical, psychological, social and economic outcomes six months later. JAMA 250:782, 1983.

23. Johnson, RT and Richardson, EP: The neurologic manifestations of systemic lupus erythematosus. Medicine 47:337, 1968.

24. Juolasmaa, A et al: Effect of open heart surgery on intellectual performance. J Clin Neuropsychol 3:181, 1981.

25. Kelly, MP, Carron, DC, and Javid, H: Carotid artery disease, carotid endarterectomy, and behavior. Arch Neurol 37:743, 1986.

26. Kurtzke, JF: An introduction to the epidemiology of cerebrovascular disease. In Scheinberg, P (ed): Cerebrovascular Disease. Tenth Princeton Conference. Raven Press, New York, 1976, pp 239–254.

27. Lishman, WA: Organic Psychiatry. Blackwell Scientific Publications, London, 1978, pp 450–526.

28. Ljunggren, B et al: Cognitive impairment and adjustment in patients without neurologic deficits after aneurysmal SAH and early operation. J Neurosurg 62:673, 1985.

29. Loftus, CM and Quest, DO: Current status of carotid endarterectomy for atheromatous disease. Neurosurgery 13:718, 1983.

30. Logue, V et al: The quality of survival after rupture of an anterior cerebral aneurysm. Br J Psychiatry 114:137, 1968.

31. Matarazzo, RG et al: IQ and neuropsychologic changes following carotid endarterectomy. J Clin Neuropsychology 1:97, 1979.
32. Nielsen, H et al: A neuropsychologic study of 12 patients with transient ischemic attacks before and after EC/IC bypass surgery. Acta Neurol Scand 71:317, 1985.
33. O'Conner, JF: Psychosis associated with systemic lupus erythematosus. Ann Intern Med 51:526, 1959.
34. Okawa, M et al: Psychiatric symptoms in ruptured anterior communicating aneurysms: Social prognosis. Acta Psychiat Scand 61:306, 1980.
35. Parker, JC et al: Mental status outcomes following carotid endarterectomy: A six-month analysis. J Clin Neuropsychology 5:345, 1983.
36. Petz, LD et al: Serum and CSF complement. Medicine 50:259, 1971.
37. Plum, F and Posner, J: Diagnosis of Stupor and Coma. FA Davis Co, Philadelphia, 1972.
38. Ropper, AH and Zervas, NT: Outcome one year after SAH from cerebral aneurysm: Management morbidity, mortality, and functional status in 112 consecutive good-risk patients. J Neurosurg 60:909, 1984.
39. Ross, ED and Stewart, RM: Akinetic mutism from hypothalamic damage: Successful treatment with dopamine agonists. Neurology 31:1435, 1981.
40. Sargent, JS et al: Central nervous system disease in systemic lupus erythematosus. Am J Med 58:644, 1975.
41. Säveland, H et al: Outcome evaluation following subarachnoid hemorrhage. J Neurosurg 64:191, 1986.
42. Segarra, J and Angelo, J: Anatomical determinants of behavior change. In Benton, A (ed): Behavioral Change in Cerebrovascular Disease. Harper & Row, New York, 1970, pp 3–14.
43. Shraberg, D and D'Souza, T: Coma vigil masquerading as psychiatric illness. J Clin Psychiatry 43:375, 1982.
44. Skultety, FM: Clinical and experimental aspects of akinetic mutism. Arch Neurol 19:1, 1968.
45. Smith, PLC et al: Cerebral consequences of cardiopulmonary bypass. Lancet 1:823, 1986.
46. Sotaniemi, KA: Brain damage and neurologic outcome after open-heart surgery. J Neurol Neurosurg Psychiatry 43:127, 1980.
47. Stallones, RA et al: Epidemiology for stroke facilities planning. In Sahs, AL and Hartman, EC: Fundamentals of Stroke Care. US Department of Health, Education, and Welfare Publication, No (HRA) 76–14016, 1976, pp 5–13.
48. Steinman, DR and Bigler, E: neuropsychologic sequelae of ruptured anterior communicating artery aneurysm. Int J Clin Neuropsychol 8:135, 1986.
49. Storey, PB: Brain damage and personality change after subarachnoid hemorrhage. Br J Psychiatry 117:129, 1970.
50. Teissier du Cros, J and Lhermitte, F: neuropsychologic analysis of ruptured saccular aneurysms of the anterior communicating artery after radical therapy (32 cases). Surg Neurol 22:353, 1984.
51. Walton, JN: The late prognosis of subarachnoid haemorrhage. Br Med J 2:802, 1952.

52. Willner, AE and Rabiner, CJ: Psychopathology and cognitive dysfunction five years after open-heart surgery. Comp Psychiatry 20:409, 1979.
53. Wylie, CM: Epidemiology of cerebrovascular disease. In Vinken, PJ and Bruyn, GW (eds): Vascular Diseases of the Nervous System, Vol 11, Handbook of Clinical Neurology. Elsevier, New York, 1972, pp 183–207.
54. Younkin, D et al: Superficial temporal-middle cerebral artery anastomosis: Effects on vascular, neurologic, and neuropsychologic function. Neurology 35:462, 1985.

Chapter 14

Brain Tumor

EVALUATION
DIFFERENTIAL DIAGNOSIS
LABORATORY INVESTIGATION
MANAGEMENT AND PATHOLOGY

A 73-year-old retired dock worker had enjoyed good health until 3 weeks before his hospital admission. At that time, he began to have difficulty finding words in spontaneous speech, and his family thought that he was easily confused. During the 3 weeks preceding his admission, his symptoms gradually became more prominent, and he also developed chronic, dull, early morning headaches.

On admission, the patient was alert and attentive to the examiner, but this mental state tended to fluctuate throughout the day. His spontaneous speech was fluent, and he could carry on a relatively adequate superficial conversation, but word searching and paraphasic errors marred his language production. Comprehension was relatively intact for general conversation, but he was able to point accurately to only two items in succession. Repetition was normal, but naming to confrontation was very poor. Naming was characterized by perseveration, paraphasia, and total inability to name some items. He was fully oriented, and his memory for recent events was *good. His drawings showed only minimal organic features (loss of three-dimensionality). Proverb interpretation, however, was concrete. Results of his motor, sensory, and cranial nerve examinations were all normal. The CT scan showed a left frontal mass that at surgery proved to be a glioblastoma.*

This case demonstrates some of the many behavioral symptoms that can be produced by a tumor of the cerebral hemispheres. Tumors, because they are focal expanding lesions, can produce one or a combination of several general types of behavioral symptoms: focal symptoms such as the aphasia seen in the case above, confusional behavior from the increased intracranial pressure, dementia, and purely psychiatric symptoms primarily with tumors of the frontal or temporal lobe. Even though the focal behavioral features of tumors are not unique, we believe that a short chapter discussing some of the subtle general features seen in patients with brain tumor is useful. The whole clinical picture of the patient with an expanding intracranial mass is distinctly different from the picture seen in acute vascular lesions. Because tumors are focally destructive lesions, motor, sensory, and other general neurologic features will also frequently accompany or even dominate the clinical picture. Seizures are common and have been described in as many as 20 to 30 percent of all tumor cases.[9,12] They can be generalized in type but more typically are focal; this is particularly true when the tumor is located in the temporal lobe. It is not uncommon for a seizure to be the initial neurologic symptom. Headaches and dizziness are variably present, with headache alone being reported in over 85 percent of the cases in one series.[12] Papilledema is also especially common (45 to 65 percent) and must always be sought if brain tumor is suspected.[9,12] Incontinence, although uncommon during the early stages of tumor growth, is, when present, a very strong indicator of organic disease.

Although these general neurologic features are extremely important, we will concentrate our discussion on the behavioral aspects of the clinical picture; these aspects of the problem should be highlighted because behavioral symptoms are very common with cerebral neoplasm and are frequently the initial symptom of the disease. In a large series of brain tumors reported from the Ochsner Clinic, over 50 percent of the patients had mental symptoms when first admitted to the hospital.[14] The mode of presentation and clinical course vary considerably but, in general, the symptoms evolve slowly over a period of several months. Because of the general nature of tumors, the symptoms may fluctuate over time, and anything causing the tumor or surrounding tissue to accumulate or lose edema fluid will produce a change in clinical symptoms. An acute stroke-like presentation is uncommon, however, unless a hemorrhage has occurred into the substance of the tumor or there is an acute increase in intracranial pressure, such as that accompanying a sneeze, cough, or when cerebral spinal fluid flow is blocked.

Various features of the tumor, such as type, growth characteristics, and location, are important in determining the nature of the particular behavioral symptoms displayed. With slowly growing hemispheric masses, gradual focal deficits usually develop. In tumors located in the limbic structures of the frontal or temporal lobes, psychiatric rather than cognitive behavioral change is more likely to occur.[10] Occasionally, a slowly growing tumor can produce a clinical picture that resembles simple dementia; however, this is not common.

In contrast, tumors that are very large, rapidly growing, or associated with considerable edema (primarily metastatic) produce a rapid rise in intracranial pressure and an attendant acute confusional state. In these patients, one of the earliest signs is a general decrease in level of alertness and a slowing of mental processes. We saw one woman with a large meningioma who came into the emergency room complaining only of general fatigue, but it took her at least 5 minutes to laboriously tell us of this chief complaint.

Another factor influencing the nature of the symptoms produced is the type of tumor. Meningiomas, for example, are extrinsic to the brain, slow growing, and produce pressure on a specific area of cortex. Such tumors most frequently cause focal symptoms until they become very large, at which point they more significantly impair neuropsychologic functions. Gliomas are intrinsic, grow through the white matter of the brain, and frequently present with significant specific neuropsychologic deficits. In time, extensive growth of the tumor results in a picture of generalized mental deterioration.[1]

Most patients with tumors have a combination of behavioral features, although one clinical symptom may predominate. The most remarkable aspect is the brain's phenomenal ability to adapt to the encroachment of the mass lesion without producing any neurologic or neurobehavioral symptoms or signs. We are always impressed by the paucity of findings demonstrated in some patients with large tumors, irrespective of their type, growth pattern, or location. Because of this, it is often impossible to clinically diagnose these lesions when they are small and easily resectable.

In the 1870s, John Hughlings Jackson wrote that the effects of all brain tumors started with both an almost imperceptible decline in delicate intellectual processes and a loss of finer emotions.[5] He thought that such patients suffered a "limitation in intellectual field" that was not sufficient to attract the notice of the casual observer and was certainly not apparent in their day-to-day routine. As the tumor grew, Jackson stated that these subtle changes became accentuated, memory failed, and a general dementia developed. In 18 to 50 percent of all patients with brain tumors, the initial diagnosis is a psychiatric disorder.[3,8,12,16] The mode of presentation varies considerably, and no single behavioral syndrome caused by brain tumor exists. A gradual dementia develops in some patients, as described by Jackson, but far more patients have other behavioral symptoms, both cognitive and emotional.

Owing to the focal nature of most tumors, specific behavioral symptoms are commonly seen: aphasia; geographic disorientation; reading, writing, and calculating difficulties; and frontal lobe symptoms. Because the focal syndromes have been discussed in Chapter 8, only several specific points referable to brain tumors need to be made here. The first is that the relationship between lesion size and the magnitude of symptoms is usually far slighter with tumor than with destructive lesions such as cerebral infarction.[1] Tumors push and infiltrate brain tissue rather than devastate it, and the resultant lesions are often surprisingly large compared with their neurobehavioral effects. Second, focal symptoms tend to be slowly progressive, a very important point in differentiating tumor from stroke. Third, as stated in the last section, with rapidly growing lesions, the focal symptoms are soon accompanied by signs of confusional behavior, particularly decreased alertness and clouding of all mental processes.[4]

Acute confusion with or without the symptoms of focal disease is a very important organic behavioral change to recognize because it is seen in 50 to 67 percent of those brain-tumor patients who have mental symptoms.[9,16] The patient's behavior is clinically the same as that seen in any acute confusional state and differs only if outstanding focal symptoms such as aphasia are found concurrently. Confusional behavior is usually seen when the brain substance can no longer accommodate to the expanding mass and increases in intracranial pressure occur. This is most frequently found in rapidly growing tumors, very large lesions, or tumors in which massive edema is present (a common finding in metastatic lesions). Although organic mental changes are very common in tumor patients, some patients have clinical symptoms that are preponderantly emotional. It is common for textbooks and newspaper articles to point out the number of patients who, dying in mental institutions, at autopsy are found to harbor an undiagnosed brain tumor. The actual percentage of such cases, however, is small and is growing smaller with the increasing awareness that organic disease can mimic psychiatric states. Yet the salient fact remains that the slowly growing cerebral neoplasm is capable of producing mental states that resemble functional psychiatric diseases in almost every way. As we have previously said, many of these cases will have evidence of organic features if they are carefully evaluated (some authors claim figures as high as 80 to 95 percent)[2,9] but, unfortunately, in the patient hospitalized with a psychiatric diagnosis, many subtle organic features are unappreciated.

About 50 percent of all patients with brain tumors will have some psychiatric symptoms,[14] but only about 15 percent are actually hospitalized with a primary psychiatric diagnosis.[12] Those patients with preponderantly psychiatric features are usually those with tumors involving the limbic portions of the frontal and temporal lobes.[7,10,12] In fact, it has been reported that as many as 88 percent of patients whose psychiatric syndromes were associated with a tumor had lesions in those areas.[12] The actual psychiatric features are varied.[7,10,11,13] Depression, for example, is found in half of the reported cases; schizophreniform psychosis in 10 to 40 percent (greater in temporal than frontal loci); anxiety in 5 to 15 percent. Paranoia, mania,[6] and personality change are less frequently reported. Some patients may have had overt or incipient psychiatric illness before the onset of their tumors, and still others may, in some way, develop psychiatric symptoms as a reaction to other symptoms caused by the tumors, but it appears to us that many of these major behavioral changes are a direct effect of the mass lesion localized within limbic structures.

Frontal lobe tumors are probably the tumors most likely to produce psychiatric symptoms. Depression, apathy, euphoria, social impropriety, and marked changes in basic personality are all well-known symptoms of frontal lobe damage. Hallucinations (olfactory, gustatory, auditory, and visual) and delusions may also be present, albeit less frequently. Problems of bladder and bowel incontinence are common in cases of frontal tumor (35 percent) and are certainly major clues to the organicity in an individual case.[15]

Temporal lobe tumors are clinically somewhat different, because epileptic phenomena play an important part in the overall presentation. Temporal lobe ictal and interictal behavioral phenomena are seen in almost all patients with temporal lobe tumors and, therefore, can serve as important diagnostic features.[10] Hallucinations, which are probably frequently epileptic phenomena, are somewhat more common in patients with temporal lobe tumors; however, the only specific and localizing type are those in which a half-field–formed visual hallucination is experienced.[8] In such instances, the hallucination is pathognomonic of a lesion within the contralateral, posterior temporal region.

No specific psychiatric syndrome is seen exclusively with temporal lobe tumors. Depression is as frequent in this group as in patients with frontal tumors. A rather high incidence (45 percent) of schizophreniform psychosis has been reported;[10] however, clinically this does not include any specific features that differentiate it from the schizophrenic syndrome seen with tumors in other locations. Subtle personality change is also common (50 percent) and has been noted to be the earliest symptom in over 20 percent of patients with temporal lobe tumor presenting with behavioral change.[8] Because of the memory circuits and language centers in the temporal lobe, it is frequently possible to elicit evidence of memory difficulty and aphasia in these patients. Basically it is the associated focal behavioral features of aphasia, amnesia, hemihallucinations, and temporal lobe epileptic manifestations and not the specific character of the psychiatric symptoms alone that help the clinician to localize a tumor to the temporal lobe.

EVALUATION

The clinical evaluation of a patient with a brain tumor is similar to that of any patient undergoing a progressive behavioral change. The history and physical examination must include specific elements that will help identify those patients with tumor. One abiding principle is that a tumor must be suspected in any person of middle age or older in whom any slowly progressive behavioral change, whether cognitive or emotional, develops. This is particularly true when the change arises in a patient who has never had any such symptoms in the past. The elements of the history that must be carefully assessed are as follows:

Elements in History	*Abnormality in Presence of Tumor*
1. Speed of onset	Gradual, unless associated with hemorrhage into the tumor
2. Character of course	Usually steady progression, but can show an intermittent course
3. Seizures	Quite frequent, particularly with temporal lobe tumors
4. Headache	Common (85 percent), usually mild, sometimes localized, often worse at night and in morning
5. Visual complaints	Visual blurring or diplopia, as intracranial pressure increases
6. Hallucinations	All varieties, but a relatively uncommon manifestation
7. Specific neurobehavior and psychiatric symptoms	Changes in memory, language, affect, personality, and a host of other similar areas of symptomatology
8. History of carcinoma or symptoms of active cancer	Metastic cancer to the brain very frequent with such common cancers as lung, breast, and melanoma

9. Neurologic symptoms   Specific motor, sensory, or cranial nerve abnormalities often present, although usually preceded by the behavioral change

The examination should, as in all behavioral cases, include a complete neurologic and mental status examination. Funduscopic examination is of critical importance because papilledema is a very common finding with cerebral neoplasm.

DIFFERENTIAL DIAGNOSIS

The differential diagnosis depends on the mode of presentation of the tumor; if focal, then brain abscess or vascular lesions are considered. Usually the slowness of onset clearly distinguishes an expanding mass from a vascular event, but within the spectrum of mass lesions the features are similar. Patients with tumors who present with confusional behavior or dementia must be identified and differentiated from those having other causes of those conditions.

If the patient has the symptoms of a psychiatric syndrome, it behooves the physician and the psychiatrist to exhaustively seek any organic or neurologic signs before beginning extensive and expensive psychiatric treatment. The dire consequences of an incorrect diagnosis in these often confusing cases are obvious.

LABORATORY INVESTIGATION

The CT and MRI scans of the brain have made recognition of brain tumors considerably easier. These are certainly the examinations of choice if a tumor is suspected. If the patient presents with confusional behavior or dementia, the appropriate laboratory studies for that diagnosis should be done. One of the major questions is always how much screening laboratory work is necessary in cases of routine psychiatric disease? Is it financially justifiable to order an EEG and a CT scan on all psychiatric cases? The answer to this question is not easy. Obviously a 35-year-old man who has had a diagnosis of simple schizophrenia since age 19 is not very likely to have a brain tumor; neither is the 50-year-old woman with a 20-year history of bipolar manic-depressive illness. Middle-aged or older patients with no previous history of psychiatric illness, however, probably deserve a neurologic examination and at least an EEG but preferably a CT scan before the institution of lengthy psychotherapy. The cost, both financial and emotional, of long-term psychiatric therapy or hospitalization is far greater than that involved in a brief, yet thorough, evaluation for organic disease during the diagnostic phase of the psychiatric consultation.

MANAGEMENT AND PATHOLOGY

The surgical management and neuropathology of brain tumors are topics that are not germane to the central theme of this book and the reader is referred to the standard texts of neurosurgery and neuropathology. Management of the neurobehavioral sequelae of neurosurgical excision, chemotherapy, and radiation therapy is a matter of significance and is similar to the rehabilitation of other patients with focal brain lesions. Prognosis varies depending upon the malignancy and location of the lesion.

REFERENCES

1. Farr, SP, Greene, RL, and Fisher-White, SP: Diseases process, onset, and course and their relationship to neuropsychologic performance. In Filskov, SB and Boll, TJ (eds): Handbook of Clinical Neuropsychology, Vol 2. Wiley-Interscience, New York, 1986, pp 213–253.
2. Fisher, RG: The psychiatric symptoms of patients having neurosurgical lesions. J Med Soc NJ 11:963, 1976.
3. Hobbs, GE: Brain tumors simulating psychiatric disease. Can Med Assoc J 88:186, 1963.
4. Hom, J and Reitan, RM: Neuropsychological correlates of rapidly vs slowly growing intrinsic cerebral neoplasm. J Clin Neuropsychol 6:309, 1984.
5. Jackson, JH: Lectures on the diagnosis of tumors of the brain. In Taylor, J (ed): Selected Writings of John Hughlings Jackson, Vol 2. Basic Books, New York, 1958, pp 270–286.
6. Jamieson, RC and Wells, CE: Case studies in neuropsychiatry: Manic psychosis in a patient with multiple metastatic brain tumors. J Clin Psychiatry 40:280, 1979.
7. Kanakaratnam, G and Direkze, M: Aspects of primary tumors of the frontal lobe. Br J Clin Pract 30:220, 1976.
8. Keschner, M, Bender, MB, and Strauss, I: Mental symptoms in cases of tumor of the temporal lobe. Arch Neurol Psychiatry 35:572, 1936.
9. Levin, S: Brain tumors in mental hospital patients. Am J Psychiatry 105:897, 1949.
10. Malmud, N: Psychiatric disorders with intracranial tumors of the limbic system. Arch Neurol 17:113, 1967.
11. Pool, JL and Correll, JW: Psychiatric symptoms masking brain tumor. J Med Soc NJ 55:4, 1958.

12. Redlich, FC, Dunsmore, RH, and Brody, EB: Delays and errors in the diagnosis of brain tumor. N Engl J Med 339:945, 1948.
13. Remington, FB and Rubert, SL: Why patients with brain tumors come to the psychiatric hospital: A thirty-year survey. Am J Psychol 119:256, 1962.
14. Soniat, TLL: Psychiatric symptoms associated with intracranial neoplasm. Am J Psychiatry 108:19, 1951.
15. Strauss, I and Keschner, M: Mental symptoms in cases of tumor of the frontal lobe. Arch Neurol Psychiatry 33:986, 1935.
16. Williams, SE, Bell, DS, and Gye, RS: Neurosurgical disease encountered in a psychiatric service. J Neurol Neurosurg Psychiatry 37:112, 1974.

BORDERLINE NEUROBEHAVIORAL DISORDERS

Chapter 15

Other Neurobehavioral Syndromes and Neurologic Aspects of Psychiatric Disease

The border between neurology and psychiatry becomes less distinct when the discussion doesn't concern the classic neurobehavioral disorders of delirium, dementia, and the focal syndromes. Conditions such as schizophrenia, sleep disorders, and Gilles de la Tourette's syndrome currently are placed within a borderland category of psychiatric diseases that probably have organic substrates of etiology. In this chapter we briefly enumerate and review some of the diseases in this borderland category to complete our overview of the field of neurobehavior as currently defined.

SLEEP DISORDERS

During the past decade there has been a growing interest in a wide range of sleep disorders, which include insomnia, narcolepsy, somnambulism, and sleep apnea. Sleep laboratories have been established in major medical centers, and the pathophysiology of these disorders is slowly being elucidated. With the understanding of the basic mechanisms of these disorders, patient management has become more satisfactory. Although all sleep disorders are clinically relevant, the conditions with the most interesting neurobehavioral symptoms are the narcoleptic syndrome and the syndrome of periodic hypersomnia and bulimia (Kleine-Levin syndrome).

Narcolepsy

Narcolepsy is a reasonably common and extremely curious syndrome. Patients with this disease have a variety of very interesting symptoms in different combinations. The principal symptom is the sleep attack or narcoleptic spell itself. This attack is characterized by a sudden inopportune dropping off to sleep. This sudden sleep can occur at most inappropriate times; we have one patient who is a professional roofer and has been known to fall asleep while sitting on the edge of a roof. Another worked as a tour-bus driver and would sleep at very brief tour stops as he was describing historic sights. Although these episodes are sensitive to environmental ennui and such stress as a high-carbohydrate meal, they can occur at any time. They tend to have incidences ranging from several to many times per day and last about 15 min. Electroencephalographically, they are associated with the almost immediate onset of rapid eye movement (REM) sleep.

The second cardinal feature of narcolepsy and the one that separates this syndrome from mere hypersomnia is the cataplectic attack. In cataplexy, the patient experiences a sudden loss of voluntary muscle control and falls precipitously to the ground. Such episodes are routinely brought on by a sudden expression of emotion such as laughter, fear, or excitement. They are short-lived and do not involve a loss of consciousness. Seventy percent of all true narcoleptics have a combination of sleep attacks and cataplexy.[87] For this reason, it is very important to inquire carefully about episodes of sudden emotion-induced hypotonia when examining the patient with a complaint of hypersomnia.

The third symptom is sleep paralysis, an inability to move and sometimes breathe when first falling asleep or, less frequently, on awakening. This symptom is experienced by 50 percent of all narcoleptic patients but is present as the sole manifestation of the syndrome in only 5 percent of the cases.[87] The fourth clinical feature is hypnagogic hallucinations. These may be auditory or visual, are often vivid and frightening, and by definition, occur at the onset or termination of sleep.

A final, and very fascinating, behavioral feature of this syndrome is what has been called automatic behavior.[59,89] Clinically, this behavior is similar to the episodes experienced with transient global amnesia. The patient becomes absentminded and is totally unable to appreciate the passage of time but is able to carry out routine, yet not demanding, tasks and on occasion will have involuntary outbursts of meaningless words. These episodes may last from a few minutes to several hours, and the patients are usually at least partially, if not completely, amnesic for the duration of the episode.

The onset of narcolepsy has been reported to range in age from 4 to 72 years, but these age extremes are rare.[59] Its usual onset is before the age of 30 (most frequently in adolescence or shortly thereafter), and it may continue throughout the patient's life.[47] In some families, the condition is dominantly inherited, but most cases are genetically sporadic.

Treatment of narcolepsy and hypersomnia has been highly successful, with methylphenidate being the drug of choice for most patients.[88] Dosage varies with patient response, but daily doses of more than 100 mg may be needed. The drug is best given 45 minutes before meals to ensure adequate absorption and should not be given after 5 PM to preclude interference with the patient's sleep. Methylphenidate, unfortunately, will not usually help the cataplectic component of the problem, so the cautious addition of imipramine (25 mg tid) is usually necessary in those cases in which both symptoms are present. Other sympathomines have also been used effectively in the long-term treatment of this disorder.

The pathophysiology of narcolepsy is not yet fully understood, but sleep research and neuropharmacologic studies suggest a basic imbalance in the biogenic amines in the brain stem. Because serotonin augments REM sleep and noradrenalin inhibits it, the assumption that a defect in these neurotransmitters is the basis of the syndrome seems quite feasible. There are now suggestions of a genetic marker in a neurotransmitter or receptor factor in at least some cases.[51]

Kleine-Levin Syndrome

Another clinically interesting episodic sleep disorder is the Kleine-Levin syndrome, a rare condition in which patients experience symptoms of periodic hibernation. This condition is predominately seen in the male and is first manifested in adolescence. The clinical course follows a fairly regular sequence. From their usual level of functioning, such patients enter an initial phase of personality change. They become irritable, giddy, hostile, and sometimes confusional; this phase may last from a few hours to 2 weeks. The patients then become more hostile, withdrawn, and frequently nauseated. Other autonomic signs such as cold extremities can occur, and hallucinations have been reported.[59] This phase is also of variable length, usually lasting days to 2 weeks.[32] The third phase is a period of hibernation, during which the patient sleeps and eats excessively (bulimia or megaphagia). This final phase also lasts for a few days to 2 weeks but can last for months; the patients often gain considerable weight (e.g., 20 to 30 pounds) in a very short time and sexual interest may increase and irritability may be present.[14] After the attack ceases, the patient returns to his normal mode and level of functioning. The episodes recur on an average of once every 5 months[17] but occur monthly in some patients.

The laboratory evaluation of these cases has not revealed any consistent medical, endocrine, or neurologic dysfunction. During the hibernation phase, the EEG is often slow and disorganized, with some patients demonstrating sleep onset REM sleep, but these findings are far from uniform.[64] From the clinical features of abnormal sleep patterns, disturbed eating habits, and other autonomic symptoms, it is logical to assume that some form of hypothalamic or brain stem dysfunction is present, but it has been difficult to clinically or pathologically identify it. One autopsy study of a Kleine-Levin syndrome patient revealed mild depigmentation of the locus ceruleus and substantia nigra, with elevated CSF levels of 5-hydroxytroptamine and 5-hydroxyindoleacetic acid, giving further evidence that neurotransmitter imbalance may be the cause of many of the symptoms of this disorder.[49] Another autopsy case showed lesions in the medial thalamus, considered to be compatible with a viral cause for Kleine-Levin syndrome.[11]

Treatment has been attempted with various psychotropics, but little success has been achieved. The hypersomnic phase has been helped by the use of methylphenidate in some cases,[14] but in other patients this medication has exacerbated some of the negative behavioral effects.[86] Fortunately, the disorder is usually self-limited, and the symptoms typically remit permanently by age 30.

Sleep Apnea

Sleep apnea or, more appropriately, the sleep apnea syndromes are characterized by an involuntary cessation of airflow at the nostrils and mouth lasting for at least 10 seconds.[37,38,50] These are a group of relatively uncommon, yet very real, disorders, that may often produce behavioral abnormalities. The disorder is clinically important to psychiatrists and neurobehaviorists because it frequently presents initially with psychiatric symptoms. Although sleep apnea has traditionally been reported in association with rare otolaryngologic and neurologic disorders (e.g., Shy-Drager syndrome, muscular dystrophy, or Ondine's curse), it has received increasing attention during the past decade as a problem that may present without other complications to the general practitioner or psychiatrist. The uncomplicated disorder has been differentiated into those syndromes caused by an obstruction of the upper airway and those syndromes of central apnea with transient discontinuation of all respiratory motor activity.[25] Medically, these disorders are important, because identification and appropriate therapeutic approaches in many cases may prevent acute hypoxia, chronic cardiorespiratory failure, or sudden death.[24,50] The sleep apnea syndromes do produce a wide range of behavioral changes including daytime hypersomnia, altered states of awareness, periods of automatic behavior, hallucinations, increased irritability, depression, impotence, and a deterioration in the general quality of daily performance.[37] The social impact of these behavioral factors on the patient's day-to-day life is obvious. The evaluation of such patients has become increasingly accurate with polygraphic recording of EEG, airflow and respiratory movement, and monitoring of arterial Po_2 and PCo_2. Because most adult cases of sleep apnea have proved to be of obstructive cause, surgical intervention is the most frequently used treatment. Demand ventilation, diaphragm pacing, and respiratory stimulants may, perhaps, be useful with those patients with central nonobstructive apnea.[33,50]

PERIODIC PSYCHOSIS

Other episodic pathologic behavioral disorders have been reported. One such syndrome is a periodic psychosis that has been seen in association with the menstrual cycle.[28] The patients begin to experience the episodes at the age of puberty. Many have had some minor emotional problems before the onset of the disorder but nothing to compare with the symptoms experienced during these attacks. The episodes have a typical pattern: in the 5- to 10-day period before menstruation, the patients acutely display symptoms that are not merely those of exaggerated premenstrual tension but are characterized by delusions, illusions, and actual hallucinations. Autonomic disturbances are also present, including nausea, flushing, and anorexia.[28] With the onset of the menstrual period, the symptoms quickly recede, and behavior returns to the patient's baseline functioning. This cycle has been reported to repeat as many as 3 to 14 times and then to cease permanently. Electroencephalographic abnormalities are often seen during the attacks, and there are some alterations in the rhythmic excretion of hormones; however, no major endocrinologic disease has ever been found. This condition is probably related to, but should be distinguished from, the so-called premenstrual syndrome, which is currently the subject of considerable controversy in the professional literature. Periodic psychosis seemingly is a true organically based personality change, whereas PMS remains an uncertain entity requiring further study. Periodic psychosis appears to represent one type of organic disease in which a temporary imbalance of endocrine and transmitter function is present in the early menstrual years. Why this occurs and the exact mechanism of the symptom production are not yet known.

EPISODIC DYSCONTROL

Episodic violence is yet another paroxysmal behavioral disorder that includes both neurologic and psychiatric features. In Chapter 12, we touched briefly on the organically induced violence seen with temporal lobe epilepsy, but that is only one aspect of this problem. The spectrum of violent behavior is wide-ranging, from psychopathic violence of wholly environmental etiology to the strictly organic violence occurring with the Klüver-Bucy syndrome, hypothalamic tumors, or temporal lobe epilepsy. Between these extremes is a syndrome that has been called the "episodic dyscontrol syndrome." Patients thus afflicted are given to sudden, destructive outbursts that are in stark contrast to their normal personalities and emotional functioning.

This disorder was first officially recognized by the American Psychiatric Association in the DSM III[1] as an "intermittent explosive disorder" and includes the following diagnostic criteria:

1. At least three discrete paroxysmal episodes of significant loss of control of aggressive impulses resulting in serious assault or property destruction.
2. The magnitude of the behavior during an episode is grossly out of proportion to any psychosocial stressors that may have played a role in precipitating the episode.
3. After each episode, there is genuine regret or self-reproach at the consequences of the action and the inability to control the aggressive impulse.
4. Between the episodes, there are no signs of generalized impulsivity or aggressiveness.
5. The syndrome does not meet the criteria for any other diagnostic condition.

The attacks themselves are usually provoked by a very minimal environmental stress and on many occasions are totally unprovoked. The first symptoms take the form of an aura, with rising anxiety, drowsiness, headache, visual illusions, hyperacusis, extremity numbness, and in many patients, staring.[4,53] Some clinicians have noted that many persons with this disorder sense an increasing feeling of tension before the overt behavioral outburst and may attempt to abort the episode by avoiding interpersonal contact and isolating themselves either in a room or by walks or driving.[5] The attack itself lasts from 15 min to 2 hours and is very violent. Aggression is directed against objects or family members, and in one series of patients actually led to homicide by 5 of the 22 reported patients.[53] After termination of the attack many patients claim amnesia for the attacks and remorse for the havoc wreaked. In the immediate postviolent period, they frequently feel very fatigued and often sleep heavily.

Physical assaultiveness is not the only component of this syndrome; many patients also have (1) a great sensitivity to alcohol with associated pathologic intoxication, (2) multiple inexplicable traffic accidents and moving violations, and (3) a history of sexual impulsiveness that is occasionally violent.[54,65] Neurologic examination often reveals minor neurologic signs, and the EEG can be abnormal. In one large series of patients with episodic violent behavior, however, the incidence of EEG abnormalities did not differ from that of the normal population.[67]

Although the etiology of this condition is probably varied, there are many predisposing factors in the past histories of these patients. Sixty percent were known to have been hyperactive children,[4,53] a large number have had significant birth injury or early central nervous system disease, mental subnormality is common, previous psychiatric problems are found in 50 percent,[53] and, last, there is often a history of disrupted present and past households with violence being present in many. As is true with the general problem of violence, this group of persons seems to represent a mosaic of social and organic factors. Many cases probably are the result of early damage to the temporal limbic structures; some are associated with actual temporal lobe epilepsy; some are associated with irritative areas in the temporal lobes that are electrophysiologically demonstrable yet do not cause overt seizures; and in others the episodic abnormal electrical phenomena are only discovered by the use of depth electrodes and extensive study.

Some cases may represent an extreme on the normal spectrum of constitutional temperament. Such cases include those persons who are not consistently seriously violent yet are overwhelmed by impulses of anger at the least provocation. We personally have seen one excellent clinical example of this type of patient: her response to medication was sufficiently rewarding to report the details of the case here.

The patient is a 25-year-old woman who was referred because of temporal dysrhythmia on an EEG that was obtained to evaluate the possi-

ble cause of a headache that she had suffered after pelvic surgery. The patient did not report any evidence of overt temporal lobe seizures but did state that she had always been a rebellious girl who had run away from home, gotten into frequent arguments and fights at home, and generally had demonstrated very poor impulse control. Her husband, a very calm physics graduate student, had always resignedly adapted to this behavior although certainly not relishing it. After evaluation, the patient was begun on treatment with diphenylhydantoin 300 mg daily, and has undergone a virtual personality transformation. She no longer allows insignificant problems to upset her, she does not fight with her husband, and she has actually begun to relate well with her family for the first time in 10 years. She feels physically and emotionally well and said symptoms were totally controlled. She subsequently discontinued the medication and has remained symptom-free to date.

We do not mean to intimate by this case that all such temperamental differences and all violent patients have a simple remediable electrical disturbance in the limbic areas of the temporal lobes. The majority, in fact, do not. Some may, however, and it is important to consider this possibility when evaluating the violent patient.

For appropriate patients, treatment is best initiated with diphenylhydantoin, but carbamazepine has also been used efficaciously.[82] In Maletzky's[53] series, 70 percent of the patients were cured by diphenylhydantoin, and an additional 16 percent were reported to be greatly improved. Thioridazine can also be used, but the benzodiazepines can often worsen the symptoms and should be avoided. A wide range of medications including antidepressants, stimulants, lithium, propranolol, diuretics, and hormones have been used to treat patients with episodic dyscontrol, with variable results.[65] Most clinicians concur that psychotherapy is an essential component in the treatment of this condition. Some clinics have devised "crisis lines" for their patients to use when they feel the aura of anxiety developing,[4] and others use family therapy, particularly for their adolescent patients with episodic dyscontrol.[39]

There are no good prognostic statistics yet, because many patients resist and drift out of treatment, but the current contention is that this condition burns itself out by age 50. Few if any cases have been reported in persons over that age.[53] The life history of hyperactivity as a child, episodic violence during adulthood, and gradual diminution during late middle age suggests a basic constitutional, biologic alteration that may well be influenced by hormonal changes or brain damage.[85] Some cases are obviously related to both ictal and interictal seizure phenomena, whereas others probably represent subclinical behavioral seizures.

We realize the difficulties encountered in carrying out research on the violent person, especially that including behavior-controlling neurosurgical operations, but violence is a serious threat to many persons' day-to-day freedom and thereby should not be ignored by the scientific community. The forensic and ethical concerns of episodic dyscontrol are major and must be considered in every case. Many violent persons could and should be helped; accordingly, all clinicians must take this situation seriously and refer these patients for full evaluation and possible help. Although patients do present with a syndrome of seeming episodic dyscontrol and unprovoked aggressive violent behavior, the nosologic validity of this condition as a distinct diagnostic entity is controversial.[19] Thus far there is a lack of consensual findings regarding clinical presentation, etiology, and treatment, suggesting that this is a highly variable clinical disorder that must be dealt with clinically, on an individual basis, but probably has not reached the point of being a well-defined neurobehavioral syndrome.

GENERALIZED TIC

There is a group of conditions, Gilles de la Tourette's syndrome being the most celebrated, in which involuntary motor tics are the primary clinical feature. Some tic disorders are due to well-established organic factors (e.g., high-dose phenothiazine use and after encephalitis), whereas others seem primarily of psychogenic origin, such as the facial tics and grimaces seen in young children.[84] The Gilles de la Tourette's, or Tourette's, syndrome is one in which the etiology is less clear and the behavioral manifestations more dramatic.[76] The syndrome is well illustrated by the following case.

A local physician consulted one of us (R.L.S.) in the hospital corridor one day to discuss some extremely upsetting symptoms that the family had noticed in their eldest daughter, then 23 years of age. The young woman was a school teacher and lived at home with her parents and younger siblings. She did not have difficulty while at school, but in the evenings she would arrive home, park her car in front of the house, and could be heard coming up the walk spontaneously uttering vulgar oaths. The family would retreat to the furthest recesses of the house in the vain hope that it was merely a passerby. At the dinner table, particularly when stressed by her father, the patient would grunt, curse, and make low "barking" noises. The father reported that this behavior had been present to some degree since high school but was steadily worsening. Subsequent neurologic examination was completely normal, and the patient was empirically started on haloperidol therapy 2 mg twice daily. She has clinically done well but has been reluctant to take her medication and appears to resent her father's interference in what she perceives to be her own personal matter. Unfortu-

nately, the patient has failed to maintain appropriate treatment and continues to experience problems from her disorder.

Tourette's syndrome is most likely an organic disorder that is sensitive to environmental stress, rather than one caused primarily by psychogenic factors. The condition typically has onset in childhood, usually by 6 or 7 years of age. It is a progressive disease, with remissions and exacerbation of symptoms being common features.[19] With the exception of an increase in obsessive-compulsive behavior, there does not seem to be any common psychopathology, but there is a well-documented familial, genetic tendency.[27,29,60] The male:female ratio in the incidence of Tourette's syndrome is about 3:1.[21]

Clinically, the initial symptom is usually an involuntary facial twitch or tic. As the condition progresses, the tics become more general, including the arm and then the leg. Respiratory grunting and involuntary utterances that are frequently profane (coprolalia) are eventually manifested in most cases. In some advanced cases, jumping, kicking, gritting of teeth, and bizarre barking are experienced.[26] The symptoms exacerbate during stress and abate during periods of relative emotional calm. Unfortunately some patients progress to the point of a serious mental disorder (occasionally schizophrenia) but do not become demented.[84]

On neurologic examination, there are no gross abnormalities; however, minor motor clumsiness has been demonstrated in 50 percent of the cases carefully studied.[77,81] Thirty-five percent were left-handed,[81] 50 to 70 percent had abnormal EEGs, and 75 percent showed organic signs on neuropsychologic testing.[8,77,81] These data strongly support the hypothesis that this is primarily an organic syndrome with a genetic component and unusual behavioral symptoms that resemble so many of the abnormal involuntary movements seen with basal gangliar disease. Although pathologic studies have demonstrated only suspicious abnormalities in the cell populations in the corpus striatum, pharmacologic evidence has been more encouraging. Dopamine-blocking drugs such as haloperidol have been very effective in treating the clinical symptoms of Tourette's syndrome, whereas the use of levodopa has caused exacerbations. Such observations suggest that there is a basic instability in the dopamine system that is probably a type of hyperactivity or hypersensitivity.[21,56,78] It is hoped that the use of these drugs over longer periods can control the progression of this disease. At present, however, no long-term outcome statistics are available.

DEVELOPMENTAL DISORDERS

A very large and common group of neurobehavioral disorders is the developmental disorders seen in children. This is an especially interesting and important series of conditions because they are both very common and also poorly understood by most physicians. Included within the category of developmental disorders are learning disorders, minimal brain dysfunction, developmental language disorders, and mental retardation. These are very complicated disorders to deal with clinically because they usually appear as a slowness in the developmental process (e.g., slowness in acquisition of language or reading skills). After the appearance of the initial developmental delay, secondary psychologic problems often occur that cloud the general clinical picture. The diagnostic and therapeutic approach to these children is necessarily multidisciplinary, involving the services of psychologists, special education teachers, speech pathologists, social workers, physicians, and neurologic and psychiatric consultants. These pediatric conditions are mentioned here only because we believe there is a strong organic aspect to many of these cases, and they must be approached with this in mind. This area has received an increasing amount of professional attention in the literature. The interested reader is referred to the vast literature concerned with these common disorders.[10,42,72,73,75]

CLASSIC PSYCHIATRIC ILLNESSES THAT MAY HAVE AN ORGANIC BASIS

The major psychoses, schizophrenia, and manic-depressive illness were classically considered to be primarily functional (i.e., environmentally produced) diseases. In recent years, however, genetic, neurologic, and neurochemical research has begun to provide very convincing evidence that these psychoses have not only organic aspects but possibly organic etiology.

Some of the most impressive evidence for the hypothesis of organicity comes from the genetic studies in schizophrenia. (In the discussion to follow, we will be concerned with the slowly developing process schizophrenias rather than reactive schizophrenia.) Studies of twins show a very high concordance rate for schizophrenia (60 percent) in monozygotic twins and a significantly smaller (12 percent) rate in dizygotic twins.[35] Nontwin siblings also showed a 12 percent schizophrenia rate in families with one schizophrenic twin. In these schizophrenic twins, the disease was considered severe in over 75 percent of the cases.[35] The usefulness of these data has been challenged because the twins were reared in the same home environment and therefore had an increased functionally related risk of becoming schizophrenic. In response to this criticism, several studies compared children whose mothers were schizophrenic but who had been adopted by normal families with children of normal background adopted by schizophrenic mothers.[44,48] About 15 percent of the children of schizophrenic parents developed schizophrenia regardless of the environment in which they were raised, whereas children from normal backgrounds (adopted by schizophrenic mothers) developed schizophrenia at the same rate as the general population (0.25 to 0.50 percent). These studies suggest that environment plays a limited role in the production of schizophrenia, whereas heredity appears to be a significant factor.

Genetic predisposition is obviously not the only factor, because concordance rates do not approximate 100 percent. Pollin and Stabenau[62] noted that the twin that became schizophrenic was often the one with the lower birth weight or with other factors providing suspicion of prenatal or perinatal brain damage. Their contention was that both the elements of genetic predisposition and very early brain injury may be necessary to actually produce the full clinical syndrome of schizophrenia.

In pursuit of the concept that brain dysfunction may be an important element in schizophrenia, several investigators have performed careful neurologic examination on groups of schizophrenic patients in search of subtle neurologic abnormalities. In as many as 65 percent of the schizophrenics thus tested, subtle signs of tremor and impaired equilibrium, gait, coordination, and stereognosis were elicited.[62,69] In a matched group of depressed patients, very few such signs were present. Other neurologic examinations of schizophrenic patients have revealed abnormal motor signs and neurologic soft signs in a similarly high percentage of patients.[19] On otoneurologic testing, schizophrenics have also demonstrated abnormal vestibular function, particularly in response to caloric stimulation. Oculomotor pursuit testing in schizophrenics shows a breakdown of smooth following movements into a number of small saccadic steps.[13]

Providing supporting evidence for these observations of brain dysfunction are several studies that have shown that the cerebral ventricles of 60 percent of chronic schizophrenics studied are significantly dilated.[40,46] This finding does not appear related to a concomitant dementing illness, medication use, or trauma.[45] The atrophy in some cases of schizophrenia is also progressive with the progression of the disease; therefore, it does not appear to be secondary to premorbid brain damage alone.[40] Computed tomography reveals abnormalities in 30 percent to 50 percent of schizophrenic patients. Both ventricular dilation and sulcal enlargement have been reported. The abnormalities are seen in young as well as older patients and are correlated with abnormalities found on neuropsychologic testing. There is no relationship between the CT abnormalities and duration of disease, type of treatment, or amount of treatment.[19]

Other CT studies have suggested that CT abnormalities are useful in delineating a subtype of schizophrenia characterized by neuropsychologic impairment, poor premorbid adjustment, monamine disturbance, poor response to neuroleptic treatment, ventricular enlargement, and increased cortical density.[22,34] Recent studies using magnetic resonance scanning indicate that DSM III diagnosed schizophrenics have significantly smaller frontal lobes, as well as smaller cerebrums and craniums.[3] The increased use of sophisticated neuroimaging techniques in the study of schizophrenia seems destined to provide additional evidence for the presence of organic factors in this disorder. Postmortem studies of the brains of schizophrenic patients have revealed (1) neuronal loss and gliotic changes, (2) changes in the concentrations of monamines in various brain regions, and (3) changes in monoamine receptor density or sensitivity.[19] Specific measurements of the basal ganglia and limbic system in schizophrenic patients have demonstrated significantly smaller medial limbic structures of the temporal lobe and the pallidum internum compared with those of normal controls, suggesting degenerative shrinkage of unknown etiology.[7] The reader should be cautioned, however, that such findings are not uniformly verified by autopsies of schizophrenics.

EEG studies of schizophrenic patients have not always been consistent but many have shown a high incidence of basic abnormalities.[19,62,66] Heath and his coworkers,[41] using depth electrodes within the limbic structures of schizophrenic patients, have found very impressive repetitive spiking discharges from the septal area and anterior hippocampus during periods of active psychosis. These discharges were never demonstrable with standard scalp electrodes, only on depth studies. When the patient was treated and with remission of the acute psychotic phase, the abnormal limbic discharge subsided. Although not suggesting that all schizophrenia is an epileptic-related condition, these data demonstrate the degree of organic disturbance that is kindled in the limbic structures of the schizophrenic during those times when he is most actively psychotic.

Another avenue of investigation that has further bolstered the organic hypothesis in relation to the psychoses is the pharmacologic and neurochemical studies of neurotransmitter function in schizophrenia.[30,80] Drugs that restrict dopamine, if used in sufficient quantity, can actually produce a clinical psychosis that resembles a paranoid schizophrenia in many ways. Following the direction suggested by these observations, basic neurochemical research has shown that schizophrenics do not have a primary defect in dopamine production as was originally thought but rather have hypersensitive or excessive numbers of dopamine receptor sites.[18,43] This postsynaptic receptor hypersensitivity is seen most prominently in the nucleus accumbens (septal area), the putamen, and also the caudate nucleus.[58] Whether the dopamine receptor alone represents the essential defect in schizophrenia is not yet known, but such biochemical evidence has been very encouraging thus far.

In reviewing the information currently available, it appears likely that schizophrenia results from a constitutional and often genetic defect in the neurotransmitter systems, particularly that for dopamine, in the subcortical limbic structures. Schizophreniform syndromes have been reported to have been structurally produced by such diseases as temporal lobe epilepsy and focal temporal lobe encephalitis. Chemically, the limbic and basal ganglar structures seem to be those structures in schizophrenics with transmitter abnormalities; accordingly, research has begun to concentrate evidence in favor of this hypothesized limbic-chemical defect in schizophrenia.

The problem of schizophrenia can be studied from another perspective—the observation that certain CNS diseases and structural brain lesions can produce a clinical syndrome that is often virtually indistinguishable from actual schizophrenia. These conditions have been variously labeled as "schizophreniform disorders"[79] or "organic delusional disorders."[1] The incidence of schizophrenialike disorders is far greater in brain-damaged patients than expected in the normal population. A wide range of CNS lesions is known to produce schizophreniform symptoms. See Davidson and Bagley[20] and Strub[80] for a more comprehensive review of the clinicopathologic correlations. Among the more commonly reported lesions responsible for a schizophrenialike clinical presentation are temporal lobe epileptic foci, especially in the left hemisphere, and frontal and deep structure tumors. A review of the pooled data regarding lesion locus indicates that lesions in the deep structures of the brain, left hemisphere more so than right, and especially those involving the limbic areas, are most likely to produce a clinical syndrome resembling schizophrenia.[80]

Catatonia

The catatonic form of schizophrenia should be discussed separately because the outstanding clinical feature, rigidity or waxy flexibility, is also seen as a symptom in a variety of treatable medical illnesses. Therefore, this symptom is not pathognomonic of schizophrenia. The associated autonomic features that are frequently seen in severe cases are also interesting.

Catatonic schizophrenia has an onset in young adulthood and, unlike simple process schizophrenia, can evolve abruptly. Accompanying the schizophrenic withdrawal and thought disorder is a significant disorder of motility: Some patients become hyperkinetic, excited, and often violent, whereas others become mute, immobile, and rigid. Sudden shifts from immobility to excitability are common. In severe cases, the limbs become rigid and remain in unusual postures for extended periods. Many patients refuse food, lie motionless for weeks, and eventually develop a fever of very uncertain origin.[57,63] The disease is often progressive and can produce a dementialike state. During the severe withdrawn state, intravenous amobarbital can often be used to therapeutically mobilize the patient, but frequently electroconvulsive therapy is necessary in an attempt to save the patient's life. The degree of diagnostic consistency, however, is lower in catatonic schizophrenia. More than 50 percent of the diagnosed patients do not consistently present with well-defined catatonic features.[80] On follow-up, previously diagnosed catatonics showed a variety of different conditions including other forms of schizophrenia, depression, substance abuse, hysteria, and organic disease.[36]

Catatonic schizophrenia is an interesting example of the interaction of abnormalities in motor, autonomic, and mental behavior. With the full-blown syndrome, the patients demonstrate basal ganglia, hypothalamic, and arousal dysfunction. It is very tempting to postulate a basic defect in subcortical transmitter systems such as that of dopamine as the explanation of this unusual syndrome.

Catatonic schizophrenia must be differentiated from other conditions that may mimic it.[31] The manic form of manic-depressive illness often has catatonic features yet has a much better prognosis. Hysterical coma or psychiatric unresponsiveness is another psychiatric condition that can produce catatoniclike behavior. Drug overdose with phencyclidine (PCP or "angel dust"), mescaline, amphetamines, and phenothiazines must all be part of the differential diagnosis. Frontal lobe lesions, general paresis, diabetic ketoacidosis, porphyria, hyperparathyroidism, petit mal status, acute systemic lupus erythematosus, viral encephalitis, and Wernicke's encephalopathy can all present with catatonic features. Dementia with associated apathy may also be mistaken for a form of catatonia. Therefore, it is very important to (1) look carefully for true signs of a schizophrenic thought disorder, (2) take a complete history and perform a complete physical examination and laboratory screening, and (3) use the intravenous amobarbital test (the schizophrenic should become more responsive, whereas patients with organic disease will become increasingly lethargic). The organic causes of catatonia are multiple and include virtually every condition compromising the biochemical integrity of the central nervous system. See Strub[80] and Cummings[19] for complete descriptions of this complex interaction of behavior, organic factors, and psychiatric theory.

Affective Disorders

Affective or mood disorders are among the most common of all psychiatric problems. The specific clinical description of these disorders is well handled in most standard psychiatric texts and will not be reiterated here. In general, however, manic-depressive illness is an endogenous, cyclical disease in which the patient exhibits swings of mood that are of psychotic proportion. Some patients have only depressive or only manic episodes (unipolar), whereas others manifest both extremes during the course of a lifetime (bipolar). This illness typically has an onset in adulthood and has a greater than 60 percent recovery rate with treatment.[55] The disease has a strong familial tendency, and the affected members of each family tend to demonstrate the same general type of illness, either monopolar or bipolar.

Many types of depression including neurotic depression, reactive depression, acute psychotic depression, and involutional depression seem to be largely functional diseases brought on by the patient's interaction with the stress of his environment. Both genetic and pharmacologic evidence, however, suggests that manic-depressive illness has basic organic components. The concept that depression was related to a neurochemical process arose serendipitously. The first clue came when depressed tuberculosis patients improved mentally when they were given the monoamine oxidase inhibitor, iproniazid. This drug is known to prevent the breakdown of neurotransmitters (serotonin, dopamine, and norepinephrine); thus, the conclusion was reached that the depression was caused by a deficiency in these biogenic amines or neurotransmitters. A bit of corroborative information came from the observation that hypertensive patients treated with reserpine (a drug that exhausts catecholamines) frequently became depressed. The concept that a deficit in neurotransmitters was the cause of depression was appealing because the hypothesis also explained many of the vegetative signs (e.g., sleep, sexual activity, and eating disturbances). It is known that these functions are controlled by the same biogenic amines in the hypothalamus and brain stem.

Various theories have been postulated as to which transmitter substance is responsible for these conditions, but no firm proof has yet been firmly established for any. It is generally agreed that decreased levels of transmitter substance are responsible for the depressive phase and that increased levels cause the manic phase, but whether these alterations in transmitter levels are the cause or the effect of the disease is still not known. Some investigators believe that serotonin abnormalities alone can cause these conditions,[16] whereas others strongly hold that catecholamines (dopamine or norepinephrine) are the primary transmitters involved.[9] Most of the evidence thus far has been based either on the measurement of metabolites of the various transmitters in the serum or cerebrospinal fluid or on the patient's response to the administration of various transmitter precursors or other pharmacologic agents.

As in schizophrenia, certain structural lesions have been demonstrated to cause a clinical condition that is essentially indistinguishable from a primary affective disorder. In psychiatric terminology this has been classified as an organic affective disorder, manic, depressed, or mixed type.[2] A wide variety of diseases have been implicated in the causation of both depression and mania, with tumor patients providing the best data to date. The literature indicates that brain tumors, especially with frontal and temporal lobe localizations, are the most common in causing depressive symptoms. There is also support for a left lateral predominance.[80] The literature considering the question of mood change and cerebral vascular disease has supported these conclusions, especially the laterality question. A variety of other CNS disorders is also known to cause depression, including multiple sclerosis, systemic lupus erythematosus, and tertiary syphilis. Lastly, certain systemic diseases have a propensity for causing depression, including endocrine and metabolic disease, hypothyroidism, Cushing's disease, Addison's disease, hyperparathyroidism, and pancreatic or gastrointestinal carcinoma. Thus far the clinicopathologic evidence indicates that brain disease can produce depressive symptoms as well as full depressive syndromes, especially with lesions in the limbic system, particularly in the frontal and temporal lobes of the left hemisphere.[80]

Mood elevation or euphoria has been reported as the initial sign of brain disease. Among the CNS conditions causing mood elevation or mania are frontal lobe tumors, multiple sclerosis, general paresis, encephalitis, toxic delirium, steroid use, and right hemispherectomy. The tumor and cerebral vascular studies suggest that right hemisphere lesions are more likely to cause mood elevation. Deep lesions in the brain also appear to have a propensity to produce a manialike syndrome. From a review of the relevant literature, lesions in the frontal and temporal lobes and at the base of the brain, especially those involving the right hemispheres, have the greatest likelihood of producing a clinical picture resembling mania or hypomania.[80] This clinicopathologic evidence is compatible with findings from clinical studies of differential emotional responses after unilateral brain lesions.[68,74] Hemispheric lateralization of depression has now been confirmed by positron emission tomography (PET) studies, which show decreased glucose metabolism in the left hemispheres of depressed patients and the right hemispheres of manic patients.[61]

Seasonal Affective Disorder

Seasonal affective disorder is an uncommon condition characterized by recurrent episodes of depression that occur annually at the same time of year.[70] Although such patients have a high incidence of bipolar affective disorders, it has been hypothesized that seasonal changes in sunlight acting via a photoperiodic mechanism in the secretion of melatonin by the pineal gland mediate the mood changes.[83] Thus, this is primarily a behavioral and emotional condition with organic factors acting as precipitants. Treatment of this "winter depression" is accomplished by extending the length of winter days with bright light in the morning and evening, thus altering the body's basic circadian rhythm.[70]

Organic Anxiety Syndrome

Anxiety frequently accompanies medical, neurologic, and psychiatric disorders. It is also a normal human response to genuine or self-perceived environmental threat and stress. Most cases of anxiety are likely to be purely functional; however, the fact that organic disease can produce a primary, not reactive, anxiety state is unquestioned.[80] Early in the course of generalized brain diseases such as delirium or dementia, anxiety is a frequent initial sign.[52] Focal brain diseases such as tumor are also commonly signaled by symptoms of anxiety. Unfortunately, the observance of obvious emotional symptoms may substantially delay the evaluation and diagnosis of the primary neurologic condition. Because of this potentially serious problem, the physician should be aware of the clinical cues that suggest a medically induced anxiety, rather than a functional neurosis. These include (1) age, with medically induced anxiety being more frequent in middle age or old age, (2) the history, with a relatively short course (less than 6 months) in medical disease, (3) the absence of a premorbid history of anxiety or other neurotic symptoms, and (4) an episodic waxing and waning pattern of anxiety *without* evidence of a precipitating stressor. Recent studies have suggested a neuroendocrine defect within the redox-regulating apparatus of the brain stem as a model for panic attacks and other forms of anxiety.[12] In addition to central nervous system disorders, a wide range of medical conditions classically presents with either sustained or episodic anxiety (see Strub[80] for a review).

Organically Induced Hallucinatory States (Organic Hallucinosis)

Hallucinations are subjective sensory experiences in which there is no realistic environmental source; they may be present in any sensory modality. Auditory hallucinations are most frequently a psychiatric symptom, whereas visual and tactile hallucinations are common in patients with an organic confusional state (delirium) secondary to a wide variety of causes. Olfactory and gustatory hallucinations are the least common hallucinations reported, but can be observed in both organic disease and psychiatric disease. Epilepsy, toxic overdose, and temporal lobe lesions are the most frequent organic cause of this latter symptom.[19]

Organic hallucinosis is a specific condition characterized by the presence of persistent or recurrent hallucinations that occur in a normal state of consciousness and are attributable to a specific organic factor.[1] Certain organic factors tend to produce hallucinations of a particular type. For example, hallucinogens most frequently produce visual hallucinations, whereas alcohol tends to induce auditory and tactile hallucinations. A fascinating neurobehavioral syndrome, Anton's syndrome, occurs in some patients with acquired blindness who subsequently develop visual hallucinations and a denial of their blindness. This condition is generally transient, with a decrease in the hallucinations and denial over time.

A final type of visual hallucination, and one of the most dramatic, is the release hallucination seen with visual loss and lesions affecting the upper brain stem (peduncular hallucinosis). The patients describe well-formed, consistent visual hallucinations, for example, seeing people's faces in flower blossoms or seeing full figures of people in the house. These hallucinations can become chronic and are disturbing to patients but are rarely frightening. When caused by lesions in the anterior visual system, it is assured that the visual association areas are disconnected from visual input yet are actively releasing visual images from stored visual memories. In midbrain or other upper brain stem lesions it is believed that the hallucinations (pedicular hallucinosis) are also released stored images. In these cases, however, the visual system is intact. The lesions can be postulated to activate the panto-geniculo-occipital pathway.

The interplay between emotional states and structural brain disease is far more complex than the overview presented here. A myriad of social, psychologic, and organic factors must be considered in each individual case. The intent of this section is to point out the probable association between organic variables and some affective changes in some patients, a point that is clinically valuable and is theoretically fascinating to the neurobehaviorist.

As in the case of schizophrenia, the answer to this interesting neurobehavioral disorder will undoubtedly be complex. There may be various subtypes of manic-depressive illness that are based on different metabolic defects, or conversely a very complicated interaction among many hormonal, neurochemical, genetic, and environmental factors may be at the root of the disease process. It is a fascinating new area of study and one that demonstrates how firmly many of the psychiatric diseases are established within the borderland between social and physical science.

PSYCHIATRIC DISEASES THAT MIMIC NEUROLOGIC DISEASE

In certain instances, functional psychiatric disease can present in the guise of a neurologic problem. We have previously discussed (Chapter 6) depressive pseudodementia in which the depressed patient demonstrates the apathy, memory dysfunction, and general cognitive impairment so typical of Alzheimer's/senile dementia. The importance of appropriately diagnosing this type of patient cannot be overstressed. Hysterical neurosis with conversion symptoms or dissociative symptoms is another condition that may simulate neurologic disease. Patients with conversion reactions classically demonstrate special sensory or voluntary motor problems such as blindness, hemiparesis, paraparesis, or anesthesia but can have behavioral features as well. An uncommon hysterical conversion behavior seen in hospitalized patients is simulated coma, also known as psychiatric unresponsiveness. This condition is usually fairly easy to distinguish from a true coma by complete physical, neurologic, and laboratory screening. The psychiatric coma patient has completely normal results on examination and overtly looks "too healthy" for his depressed level of consciousness. It is not prudent to make this diagnosis too quickly, however, because the misdiagnosis of an organic coma as hysteric is a considerably more serious error than the reverse.

A dissociative episode (amnesia) is another hysterical syndrome that can at times appear to be of organic cause to the naive examiner. As pointed out in Chapter 8, patients in dissociative episodes or fugue states are able to actively learn during their amnesic periods, whereas organic amnesics cannot. The psychiatric amnesia seen most commonly is that of memory problems associated with anxiety. People under stress can become so preoccupied with their life situation and their anxiety about it that they frequently lose track of day-to-day details. This type of forgetfulness is usually alleviated by (1) demonstrating to the patient that he can and is remembering details about both his personal life and current events (be careful about requesting that patients learn new material because the anxiety will interfere with that type of test), (2) pointing out the emotional stress that the patient is subjected to and reassuring them about the relationship between the anxiety and their perceived memory symptoms, and (3) using tranquilization and/or direct psychotherapy to ameliorate the underlying anxiety.

Another interesting condition that is frequently associated with emotional factors yet simulates a dementia is the Diogenes syndrome.[6,15] Patients with this syndrome are usually elderly and live very peculiarly; they are physically unkempt, their homes are filthy, they are compulsive hoarders (syllogomania), and they neglect their health and nutrition. On initial observation one would assume that they were either demented or chronically schizophrenic, but in fact most are not. Patients with Diogenes syndrome typically have high normal intelligence quotients (an average of 115 in one study),[15] they are not financially destitute, and many were members of responsible professions during their working years. The cause of the syndrome is not known, but it seems in most cases to be a type of emotional reaction to the stress of old age, marginal health, and loneliness. In younger patients, it may reflect more serious psychopathology.[6]

NEUROLOGIC DISEASE THAT RESEMBLES PSYCHIATRIC DISORDERS

These conditions have been previously mentioned; however, we believe that it is important to reemphasize the fact that classic psychiatric disease must always be evaluated very carefully for a possible organic cause. Frontal and temporal lobe tumors, systemic lupus erythematosus, temporal lobe epilepsy, dementia, hydrocephalus, other focal lesions from stroke or abscess, infection, and occasionally a confusional state can all initially demonstrate the clinical features of standard psychiatric disease. In fact, one of the principal purposes of this book has been to acquaint the reader with not only the classic organic syndromes but also the neurobehavioral disorders that simulate psychiatric disease.

COMBINATION SYNDROMES

A single diagnosis that can explain all the patient's symptoms is usually desired, but the reader is cautioned that two conditions do occasionally occur in the same patient. Demented patients suffer strokes, neurotics develop tumors, and the senile frequently develop confusional states. The clinician must be very astute in his diagnostic acumen to appreciate these subtle and complicated neurobehavioral syndromes.

The physician treating patients with neurobehavioral disorders must also be aware of the possibility of emotional reactions superimposed on the basic disease process. These reactions can be treated, and often remarkable restitution of social and integrative function can occur. This is particularly true when the anxiety or depression in an early demented or brain-damaged patient is adequately controlled. The physician working with problems within this borderland between neurology and psychiatry must borrow heavily from both disciplines if he or she is to truly understand these fascinating diseases and offer effective help to patients who are thus afflicted.

REFERENCES

1. American Psychiatric Association: Diagnostic and statistical manual: DSM III. American Psychiatric Association, Washington, 1980.
2. American Psychiatric Association: Diagnostic and statistical manual: DSM III-R. American Psychiatric Association, Washington, 1987.
3. Andreasen, N et al: Structured abnormalities in the frontal system in schizophrenia. Arch Gen Psychiatry 43:136, 1986.
4. Bach-Y-Rita, G et al: Episodic dyscontrol: A study of 130 violent patients. Am J Psychiatry 127:1473, 1971.
5. Benson, DF: Personal communication. October, 1978.
6. Berlyne, N: Diogenes syndrome. Lancet 1:515, 1975.
7. Bogerts, B, Meertz, E, and Schonfeldt-Bausch, R: Basal ganglia and limbic system pathology in schizophrenia. Arch Gen Psychiatry 42:784, 1985.
8. Bornstein, RA, King, G, and Carroll, A: Neuropsychological abnormalities in Gilles de la Tourette's syndrome. J Nerv Ment Disease 171:497, 1983.

9. Brodie, HKH et al: Catecholamines and mania: The effect of alpha-methyl-p-tyrosine on manic behavior and catecholamine metabolism. Clin Pharmacol Ther 12:218, 1971.

10. Buda, FB: The neurology of developmental disabilities. Charles C Thomas, Springfield, IL, 1981.

11. Carpenter, S, Yassa, R, and Ochs, R: A pathologic basis for Kleine-Levin syndrome. Arch Neurol 39:25, 1982.

12. Carr, DB and Sheehan, DV: Panic anxiety: A new biological model. J Clin Psychiatry 45:323, 1984.

13. Cegalis, JA and Sweeney, JA: Eye movements in schizophrenia: A qualitative analysis. Biological Psychiatry 14:13, 1979.

14. Chiles, JA and Wilkus, RJ: Behavioral manifestations of the Kleine-Levin syndrome. Dis Nerv Syst 37:646, 1976.

15. Clark, ANG, Mankikar, GD, and Gray, L: Diogenes syndrome: A clinical study of gross neglect in old age. Lancet 1:366, 1975.

16. Coppen, A et al: Abnormalities of indoleamines in affective disorders. Arch Gen Psychiatry 26:474, 1972.

17. Critchley, M and Hoffman, HL: The syndrome of periodic somnolence and morbid hunger (Kleine-Levin syndrome) Br Med J 1:137, 1942.

18. Crow, TJ et al: Dopamine and schizophrenia. Lancet 2:563, 1976.

19. Cummings, JL: Clinical Neuropsychiatry. Grune & Stratton, New York, 1985.

20. Davidson, K and Bagley, CR: Schizophrenia-like psychoses associated with organic disorders of the central system: A review of the literature. In RN Herrington (ed): Current Problems in Neuropsychiatry. Br J Psychiatry, Special Publication 4. Headly Brothers, Ashford, Kent, 1969, p 113.

21. Devinsky, O: Neuroanatomy of Giles de la Tourette's syndrome. Arch Neurol 40:508, 1983.

22. Dewan, MJ et al: A comprehensive study of chronic schizophrenic patients. Acta Psychiatr Scand 73:152, 1986.

23. Editorial: Narcolepsy and cataplexy. Lancet 1:845, 1975.

24. Editorial: Sleeping and breathing. N Engl J Med 299:1009, 1978.

25. Editorial: Sleep apnea syndromes. Lancet 1:25, 1979.

26. Eisenberg, L, Ascher, E, and Kanner, L: A clinical study of Gilles de la Tourette's disease (maladie des tics) in children. Am J Psychiatry 115:715, 1953.

27. Eldridge, R et al: Gilles de la Tourette's syndrome: Clinical, genetic, psychologic, and biochemical aspects in 21 selected families. Neurology 27:115, 1977.

28. Endo, M et al: Periodic psychosis recurring in association with menstrual cycle. J Clin Psychiatry 39:456, 1978.

29. Fernando, SJM: Six cases of Gilles de la Tourette's syndrome. Br J Psychiatry 128:436, 1976.

30. Fredrickson, P and Richelson, E: Mayo seminars in psychiatry: Dopamine and schizophrenia—a review. J Clin Psychiatry 40:399, 1979.

31. Gelenberg, AJ: The catatonic syndrome. Lancet 1:1339, 1976.

32. Gilbert, GJ: Periodic hypersomnia and bulimia: The Kleine-Levin syndrome. Neurology 14:844, 1964.

33. Glenn, WWL, Phelps, M, and Gersten, LM: Diaphragm pacing in the manage-

ment of central alveolar hyperventilation. In Guilleminault, C and Dement, WC (eds): Sleep Apnea Syndromes. Alan R Liss, New York, 1978, pp 333.

34. Goetz, KL and Van Kammen, DP: Computerized axial tomography scans and subtypes of schizophrenia. J Nerv Ment Dis 174:31, 1986.

35. Gottesman, II and Shields, J: Schizophrenia in twins: 16 years consecutive admissions to a psychiatric clinic. Br J Psychiatry 112:809, 1966.

36. Guggenheim, FG and Babigian, HM: Catatonic schizophrenia: Epidemiology and clinical cause. J Nerv Ment Dis 158:291, 1974.

37. Guilleminault, C et al: Altered states of consciousness in disorders of daytime sleepiness. J Neurol Sci 26:377, 1975.

38. Guilleminault, C and Dement, WC (eds): Sleep Apnea Syndromes. Alan R Liss, New York, 1978.

39. Harbin, HT: Episodic dyscontrol and family dynamics. Am J Psychiatry 134:1113, 1977.

40. Haug, JO: Pneumonoencephalographic investigation of psychiatric patients. Acta Psychiatr Neurol Scand (Suppl) 38:1, 1962.

41. Heath, RG: Studies in Schizophrenia: A multidisciplinary approach to mind-body relationships. Harvard University Press, Cambridge, MA, 1954.

42. Henderson, P: Disability in Childhood and Youth. Oxford University Press, London, 1974.

43. Henn, FA: Dopamine and schizophrenia: A theory revisited and revised. Lancet 2:293, 1978.

44. Heston, LL: Psychiatric disorders in foster home reared children of schizophrenic mothers. Br J Psychiatry 112:819, 1966.

45. Hill, D: Cerebral atrophy and cognitive impairment in chronic schizophrenia. Lancet 2:1132, 1976.

46. Johnstone, EC et al: Cerebral ventricular size and cognitive impairment in chronic schizophrenia. Lancet 2:924, 1976.

47. Kales, A et al: Narcolepsy-cataplexy II. Psychosocial consequences and associated psychopathology. Arch Neurol 39:169, 1982.

48. Kety, S: Genetic aspects of schizophrenia. Psychiatr Ann 6:11, 1976.

49. Koerber, RV et al: Increased cerebrospinal fluid 5-hydroxytryptamine and 5-hydroxyindoleacetic acid in Kleine-Levin syndrome. Neurology 34:1597, 1984.

50. Kwentus, J et al: Sleep apnea: A review. Psychosomatics 26:713–724.

51. Langdon, N et al: Genetic markers in narcolepsy. Lancet 2:1178, 1984.

52. Lipowski, ZJ: Delirium: Acute brain failure in man. Charles C Thomas, Springfield, IL, 1980.

53. Maletzky, BM: The episodic dyscontrol syndrome. Dis Nerv System 34:178, 1973.

54. Mark, VH and Ervin, FR: Violence and the Brain. Harper & Row, New York, 1970, pp 125–135.

55. Morrison, JR et al: The Iowa 500. Arch Gen Psychiatry 29:678, 1973.

56. Munetz, MR, Slawsky, RC, and Neil, JF: Tardive Tourette's syndrome treated with clonidine and mesoridazine. Psychosomatics 26:252–257, 1985.

57. O'Toole, JK and Dyke, G: Report of psychogenic fever in catatonia responding to electroconvulsive therapy. Dis Nerv Syst 38:852, 1977.

58. Owen, F et al: Increased dopamine-receptor sensitivity in schizophrenia. Lancet 2:223, 1978.

59. Parkes, JD: The sleepy patient. Lancet 1:990, 1977.

60. Pauls, DL and Lockman, JF: The inheritance of Gilles de la Tourette's syndrome and associated behaviors. JAMA 315:993, 1986.

61. Phelps, ME et al: Human cerebral glucose metabolism in affective disorders, drug-free states, and pharmacologic effects. In MacKenzie, CT, Seylaz, J, and Bez, A (eds): Neurotransmitters and the Cerebral Circulation. Journal of Cerebral Blood Flow and Metabolism Vol. 3:(Suppl 1)57, 1983.

62. Pollin, W and Stabenau, J: Biological, psychological, and historical differences in a series of monozygotic twins discordant for schizophrenia. In Rosenthal, D and Kety, S (eds): Transmission of Schizophrenia. Pergamon, London, 1968.

63. Powers, P, Douglass, TS, and Waziri, R: Hyperpyrexia in catatonic states. Dis Nerv Syst 37:359, 1976.

64. Reynolds, CF et al: Similarities in EEG sleep findings for Kleine-Levin syndrome and unipolar depression. Am J Psychiatry 137:116, 1980.

65. Rickler, KC: Episodic dyscontrol. In Benson, DF and Blumer, D (eds): Psychiatric Aspects of Neurologic Disease, Vol 2. Grune & Stratton, New York, 1982, pp 49-73.

66. Rieder, R et al: The offspring of schizophrenics. Arch Gen Psychiatry 32:200, 1975.

67. Riley, TL: The electroencephalogram in patients with rage attacks or episodic violent behavior. Milit Med 144:515, 1979.

68. Robinson, RE et al: Mood disorders in stroke patients. Brain 107:81, 1984.

69. Rochford, JM et al: Neuropsychological impairments in functional psychiatric disease. Arch Gen Psychiatry 22:114, 1970.

70. Rosenthal, NE et al: Antidepressant effects of light in seasonal affective disorders. Am J Psychiatry 142:163, 1985.

71. Rosenthal, NE et al: Seasonal affective disorder. Arch Gen Psychiatry 41:72-80.

72. Rourke, BP (ed): Neuropsychology of learning disabilities. Guilford Press, New York, 1985.

73. Rourke, BP et al: Child neuropsychology. Guilford Press, New York, 1983.

74. Ruckdeschel-Hibbard, M, Gordon, WA, and Diller, L: Affective disturbances associated with brain damage. In Filskov, SB and Boll, TJ (eds): Handbook of Clinical Neuropsychology, Vol 2. Wiley Interscience, New York, 1986, pp 305-337.

75. Schain, RJ: Neurology of Childhood Learning Disorders. William & Wilkins, Baltimore, 1977.

76. Shapiro, AK et al: Gilles de la Tourette Syndrome. Raven Press, New York, 1978.

77. Shapiro, AK et al: Organic factors in Gilles de la Tourette's syndrome. Br J Psychiatry 122:659, 1973.

78. Singer, HS et al: Dopaminergic dysfunction in Tourette's syndrome. Ann Neurol 12:361, 1982.

79. Slater, E, Beard, AW, and Glithero, E: The schizophrenic-like psychosis of epilepsy. J Psychosomatic Res 9:9, 1963.

80. Strub, RL: Mental disorders in brain disease. In Vinken, PJ, Bruyn, GW, and Klawans, HL (eds): Handbook of Clinical Neurology, Vol 2(4), Neurobehavioral Disorders. Elsevier, New York, 1985, pp 413–441.

81. Sweet, RD et al: Neurological features of Gilles de la Tourette's syndrome. J Neurol Neurosurg Psychiatry 36:1, 1973.

82. Tunks, ER and Dermer, SW: Carbamazepine in the dyscontrol syndrome associated with limbic system dysfunction. J Nerv Ment Dis 164:56, 1977.

83. Wehr, TA et al: Phototherapy of seasonal effective disorders. Arch Gen Psychiatry 43:870, 1986.

84. Weingarten, K: Tics. In Vinken, PJ and Bruyn, GW, (eds): Diseases of the Basal Ganglia, Vol 6, Handbook of Clinical Neurology. Elsevier, New York, 1968, pp 782–808.

85. Weiss, G and Hechtman, LT: Hyperactive Children Grown-Up. Guilford Press, New York, 1986.

86. Yassa, R and Nair, NPV: The Kleine-Levin: A variant? J Clin Psychiatry 39:254, 1978.

87. Yoss, RE and Daly, DD: Narcolepsy. Arch Intern Med 106:168, 1960.

88. Yoss, RE and Daly, DD: On the treatment of narcolepsy. Med Clin NA 52:781, 1968.

89. Zorick, FJ et al: Narcolepsy and automatic behavior: A case report. J Clin Psychiatry 40:194, 1979.

INDEX

A "t" following a page number indicates a table. A page number in *italics* indicates a figure.